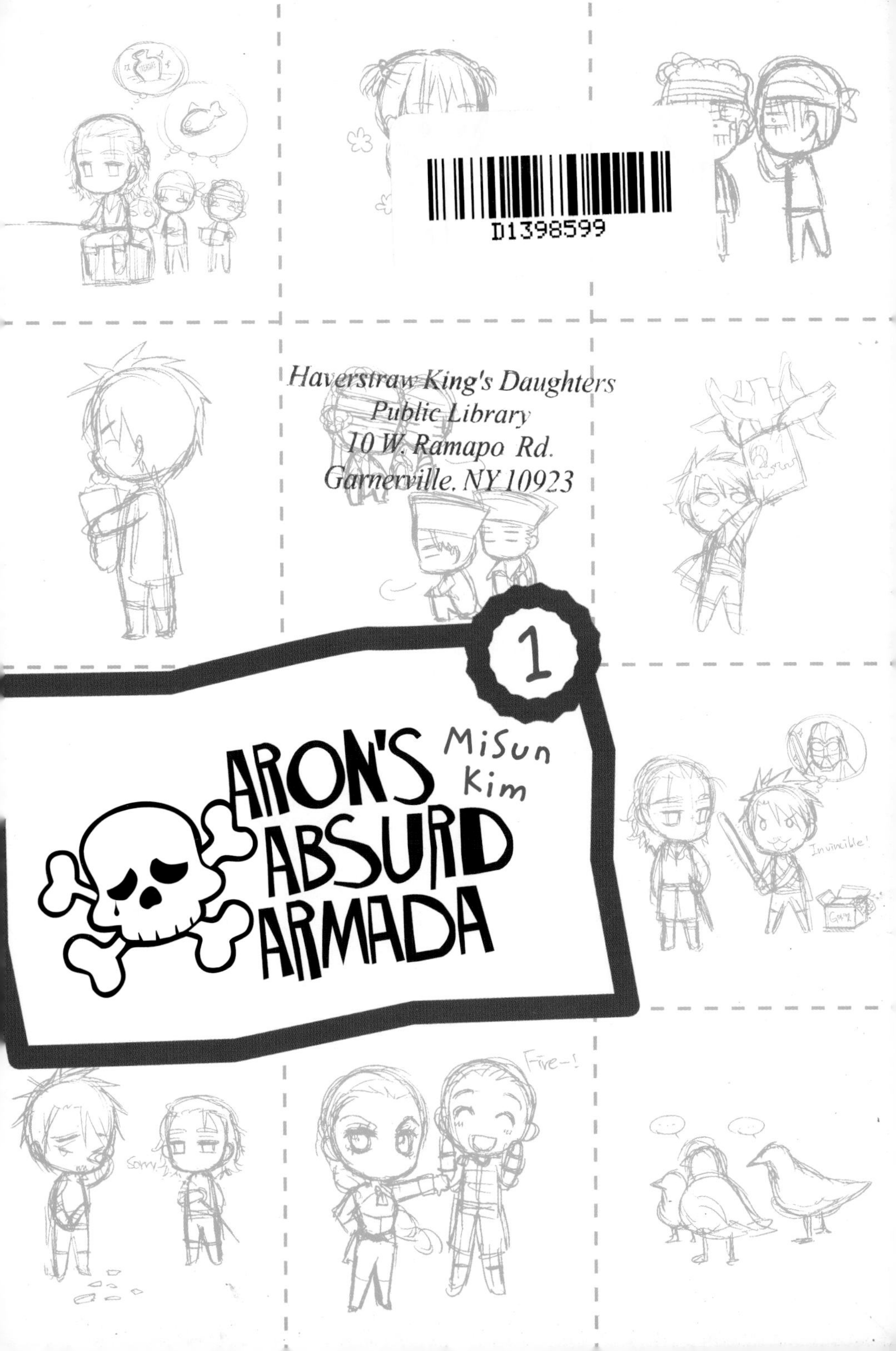
1
ARON'S ABSURD ARMADA
MiSun Kim
Invincible!
Fire--!
Sorry..

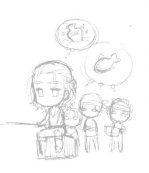

CHARACTER INTRODUCTIONS

ARON

HE WASN'T BORN BAD (ACCORDING
TO HIS MOM).
HE'S BEEN KNOWN TO BE CLEVER
AT TIMES (ACCORDING TO HIS MOM).
HE CAN BE A RESPONSIBLE PERSON IF HE ONLY PUTS FORTH
THE EFFORT (ACCORDING TO HIS MOM).
HE'S AN IMMATURE RASCAL WHO DRIVES PEOPLE UP THE
WALL, AND HE'S A STUPID DUMBASS
(ACCORDING TO EVERYONE ELSE).

RONNIE

LOOKS ARE ALL SHE CARES ABOUT.
(AKA, ROBIN'S THE ONLY ONE SHE LOOKS AT.)
SHE BELIEVES EVERYONE ELSE IS AN
IGNORANT FOOL, EXCEPTING ROBIN
AND HERSELF.
SHE SAYS STUDYING IS THE EASIEST THING
IN THE WORLD. (WTF?!)
AS FOR HER GENDER IDENTITY...AHEM...
(EVERYONE BELIEVES SHE'S A HOMOSEXUAL GUY.)

ROBIN

HE LOVES MONEY. HE'S SUPER-GOOD AT FIGHTING.
HE HAS NO MANNERS.
BUT HE'S LOVED NEVERTHELESS
THANKS TO HIS FACE (BY RONNIE).

WHY ARE WE
GROUPED?!

ANTON & GILBERT

FOR NOW, THEY'RE JUST EXTRAS.
THEY SEEM TO BE FRIENDS,
BUT IT'S REALLY NOT THAT IMPORTANT.
IT DOESN'T MATTER WHICH IS ANTON
AND WHICH IS GILBERT.
BUT IF THEY'RE NOT AROUND...
PEOPLE MISS THEM.

#1. WHAT THEY SEEK

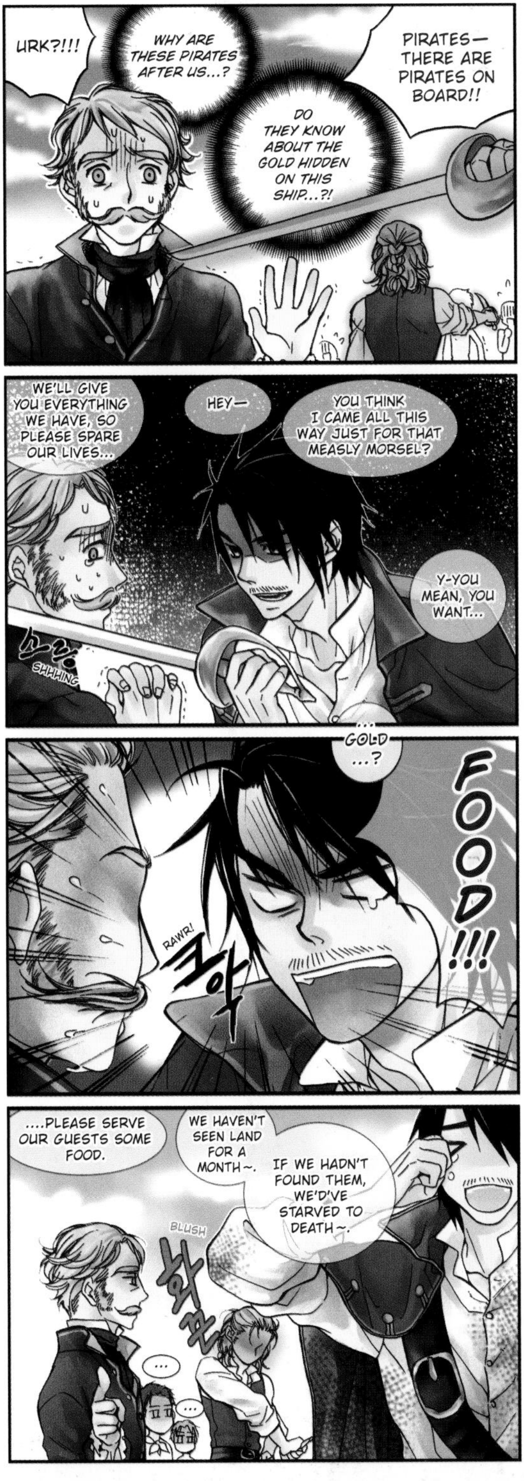
URK?!!!
WHY ARE THESE PIRATES AFTER US...?
PIRATES— THERE ARE PIRATES ON BOARD!!
DO THEY KNOW ABOUT THE GOLD HIDDEN ON THIS SHIP...?!
WE'LL GIVE YOU EVERYTHING WE HAVE, SO PLEASE SPARE OUR LIVES...
HEY—
YOU THINK I CAME ALL THIS WAY JUST FOR THAT MEASLY MORSEL?
Y-YOU MEAN, YOU WANT...
SHHHING
...GOLD...?
FOOD!!!
RAWR!
....PLEASE SERVE OUR GUESTS SOME FOOD.
WE HAVEN'T SEEN LAND FOR A MONTH~.
IF WE HADN'T FOUND THEM, WE'D'VE STARVED TO DEATH~.
BLUSH
...
...

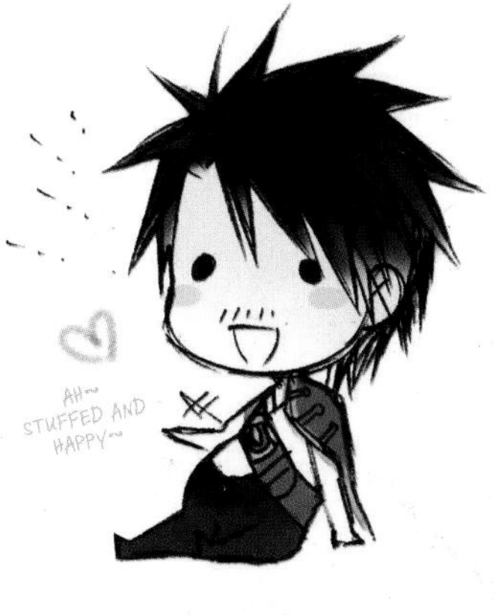
AH~ STUFFED AND HAPPY~

#2. THE FOOLED IS THE FOOL

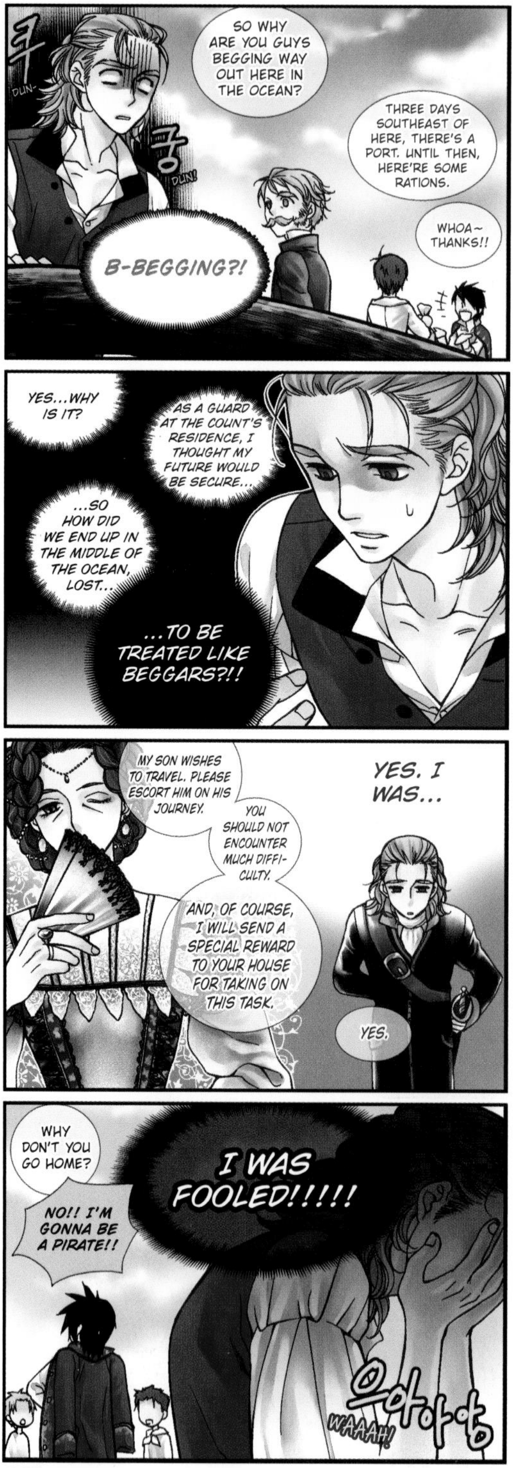
DUN-
DUN!
SO WHY ARE YOU GUYS BEGGING WAY OUT HERE IN THE OCEAN?
B-BEGGING?!
THREE DAYS SOUTHEAST OF HERE, THERE'S A PORT. UNTIL THEN, HERE'RE SOME RATIONS.
WHOA~ THANKS!!
YES...WHY IS IT?
AS A GUARD AT THE COUNT'S RESIDENCE, I THOUGHT MY FUTURE WOULD BE SECURE...
...SO HOW DID WE END UP IN THE MIDDLE OF THE OCEAN, LOST...
...TO BE TREATED LIKE BEGGARS?!!
MY SON WISHES TO TRAVEL. PLEASE ESCORT HIM ON HIS JOURNEY.
YOU SHOULD NOT ENCOUNTER MUCH DIFFI-CULTY.
AND, OF COURSE, I WILL SEND A SPECIAL REWARD TO YOUR HOUSE FOR TAKING ON THIS TASK.
YES.
YES. I WAS...
WHY DON'T YOU GO HOME?
NO!! I'M GONNA BE A PIRATE!!
I WAS FOOLED!!!!!
WAAAH!

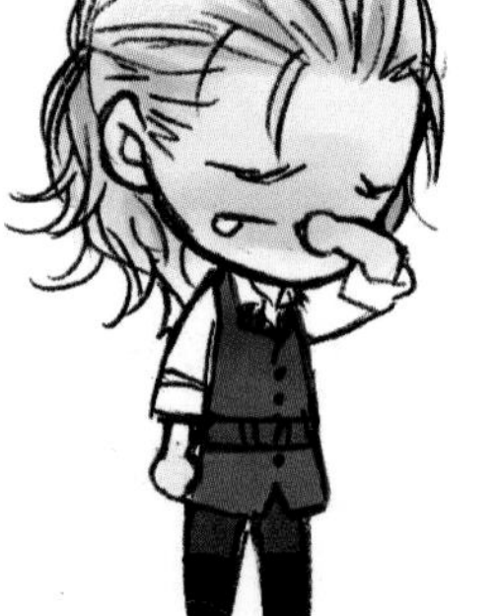

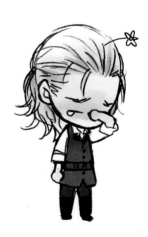

#3. A SHORT-LIVED HOPE

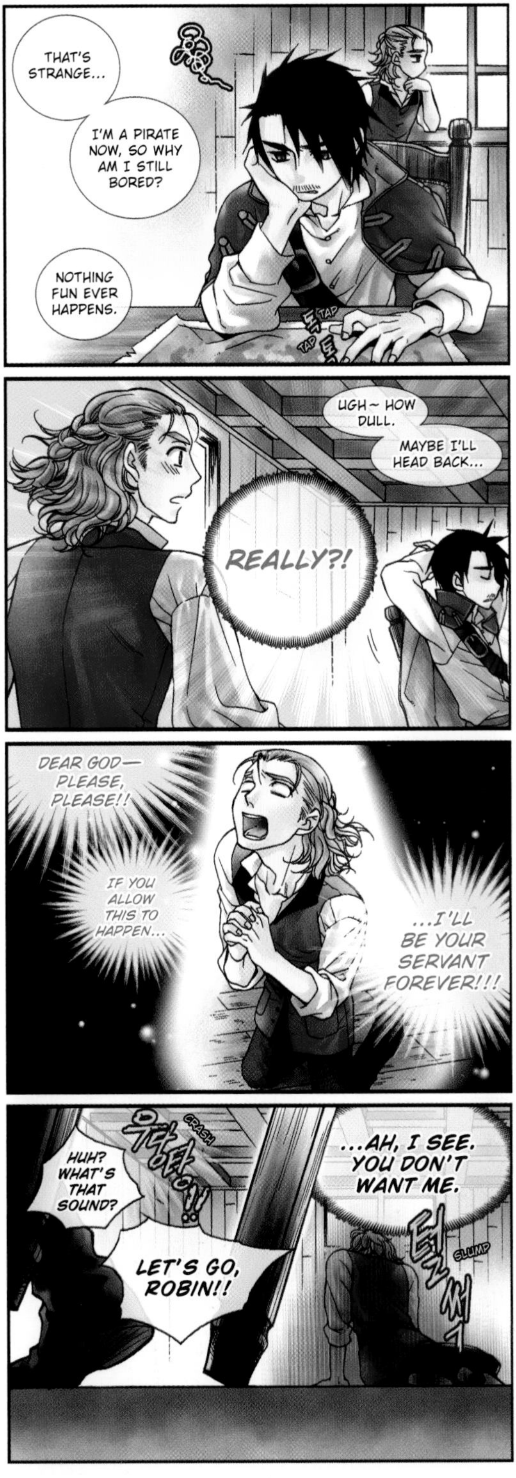
THAT'S STRANGE...
I'M A PIRATE NOW, SO WHY AM I STILL BORED?
NOTHING FUN EVER HAPPENS.
TAP TAP
UGH~ HOW DULL.
MAYBE I'LL HEAD BACK...
REALLY?!
DEAR GOD—PLEASE, PLEASE!!
IF YOU ALLOW THIS TO HAPPEN...
...I'LL BE YOUR SERVANT FOREVER!!!
CRASH
HUH? WHAT'S THAT SOUND?
LET'S GO, ROBIN!!
...AH, I SEE. YOU DON'T WANT ME.
SLUMP

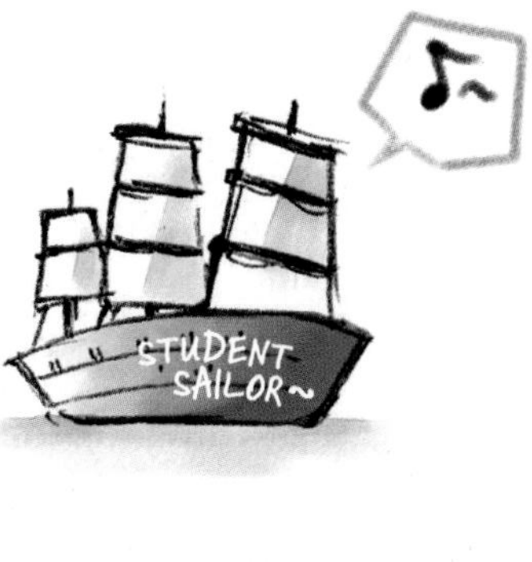
STUDENT SAILOR~

#4. LOSING YOUR TEMPER IS FOLLOWED BY REGRET

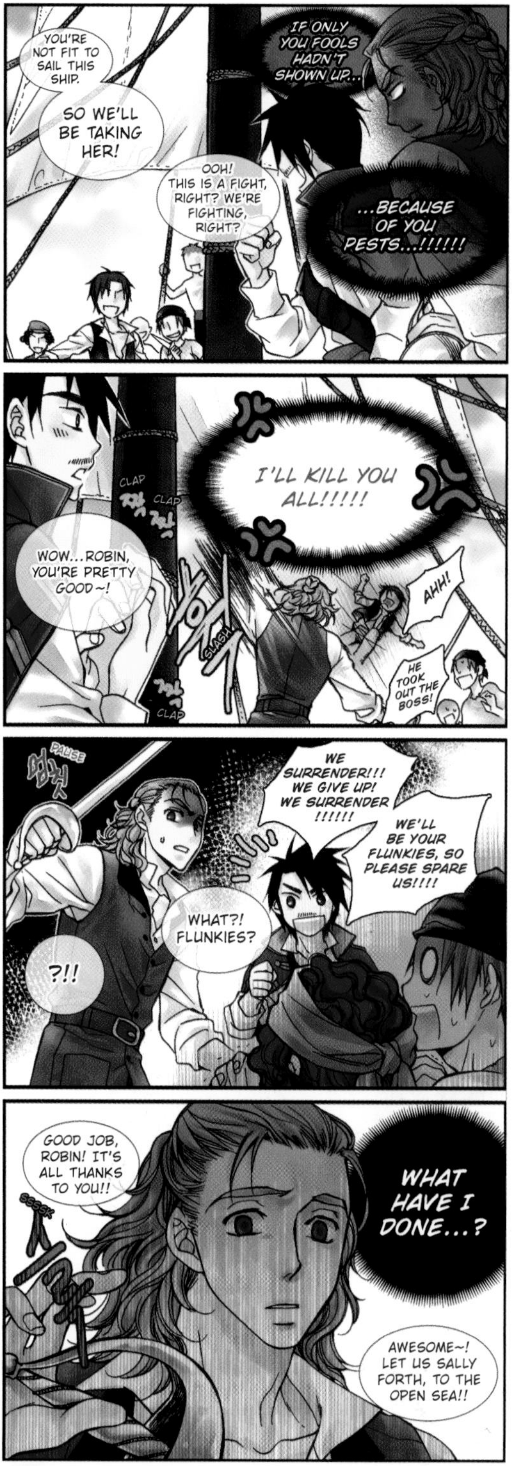

YOU'RE NOT FIT TO SAIL THIS SHIP.
SO WE'LL BE TAKING HER!
IF ONLY YOU FOOLS HADN'T SHOWN UP...
OOH! THIS IS A FIGHT, RIGHT? WE'RE FIGHTING, RIGHT?
...BECAUSE OF YOU PESTS...!!!!!!
I'LL KILL YOU ALL!!!!!
CLAP
CLAP
WOW...ROBIN, YOU'RE PRETTY GOOD~!
SLASH
CLAP
AHH!
HE TOOK OUT THE BOSS!
PAUSE
WE SURRENDER!!! WE GIVE UP! WE SURRENDER!!!!!!
WE'LL BE YOUR FLUNKIES, SO PLEASE SPARE US!!!!
WHAT?! FLUNKIES?
?!!
GOOD JOB, ROBIN! IT'S ALL THANKS TO YOU!!
WHAT HAVE I DONE...?
AWESOME~! LET US SALLY FORTH, TO THE OPEN SEA!!

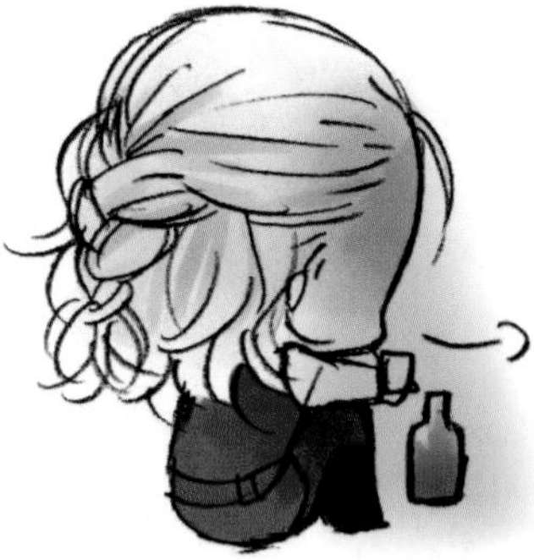

#5. GOLD SOLVES ALL 1

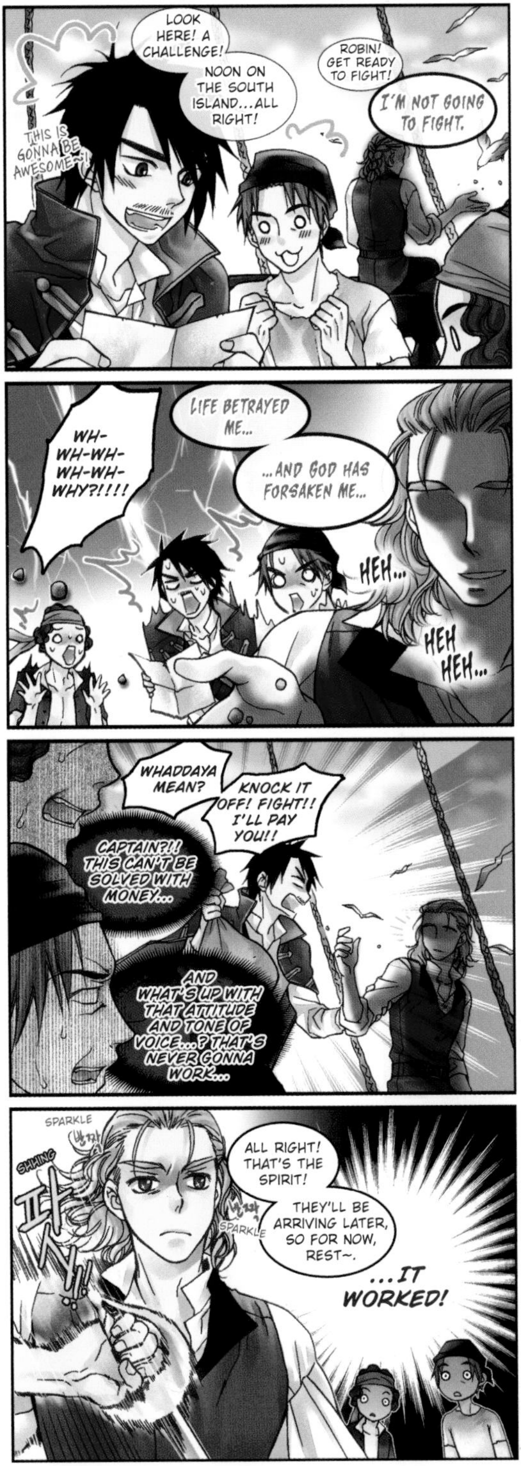
LOOK HERE! A CHALLENGE!
NOON ON THE SOUTH ISLAND...ALL RIGHT!
THIS IS GONNA BE AWESOME~!
ROBIN! GET READY TO FIGHT!
I'M NOT GOING TO FIGHT.
LIFE BETRAYED ME...
...AND GOD HAS FORSAKEN ME...
WH-WH-WH-WH-WH-WHY?!!!!
HEH...
HEH HEH...
WHADDAYA MEAN?
KNOCK IT OFF! FIGHT!! I'LL PAY YOU!!
CAPTAIN?!! THIS CAN'T BE SOLVED WITH MONEY...
AND WHAT'S UP WITH THAT ATTITUDE AND TONE OF VOICE...? THAT'S NEVER GONNA WORK...
SPARKLE
SHHING
ALL RIGHT! THAT'S THE SPIRIT!
SPARKLE
THEY'LL BE ARRIVING LATER, SO FOR NOW, REST~.
...IT WORKED!

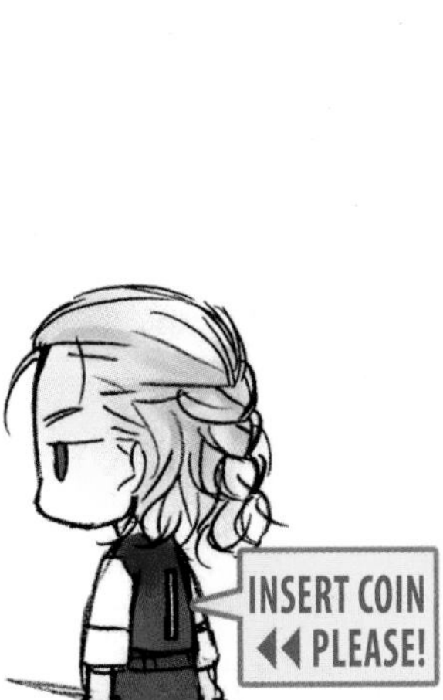
INSERT COIN PLEASE!

#6. GOLD SOLVES ALL 2

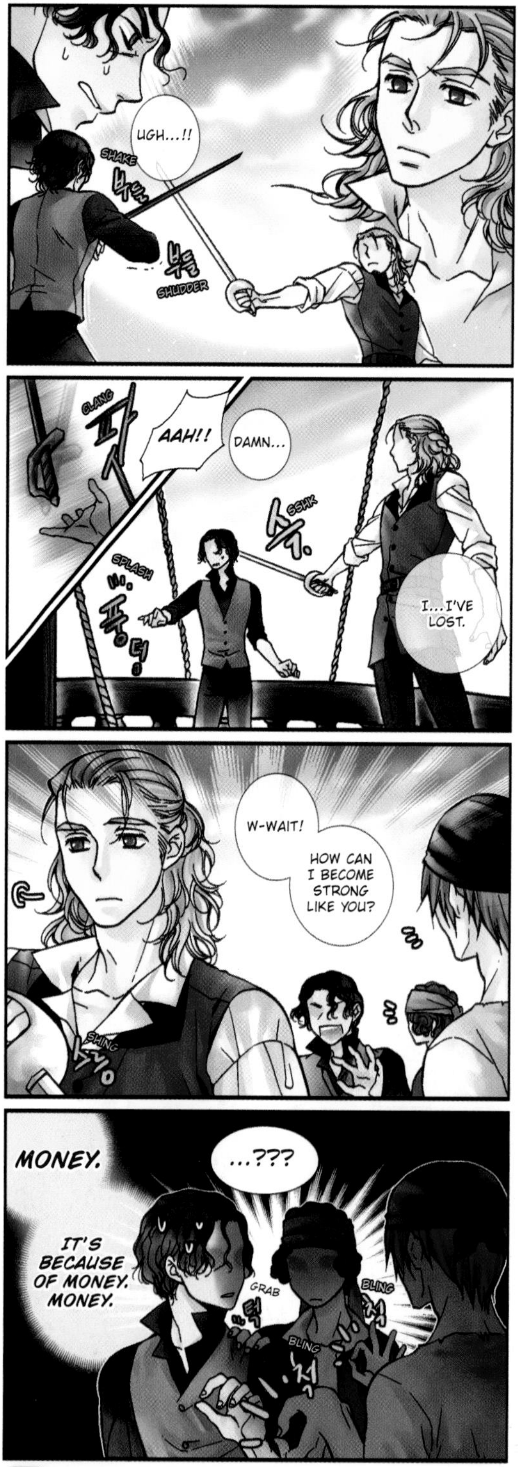
UGH...!!
SHAKE
SHUDDER
CLANG
AAH!!
DAMN...
SSHK
SPLASH
I...I'VE LOST.
W-WAIT!
HOW CAN I BECOME STRONG LIKE YOU?
SHING
MONEY.
...???
IT'S BECAUSE OF MONEY. MONEY.
GRAB
BLING
BLING

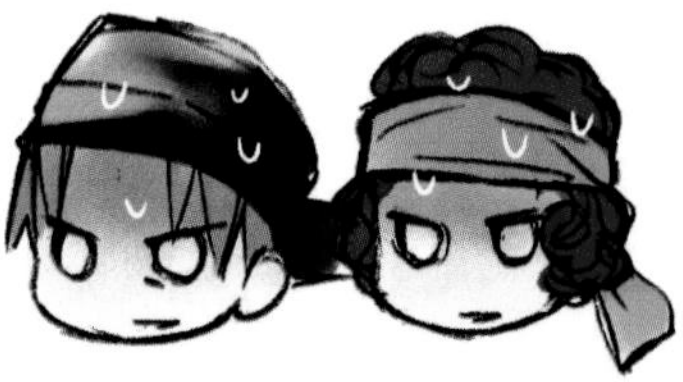

#7. BECAUSE WE'RE PIRATES

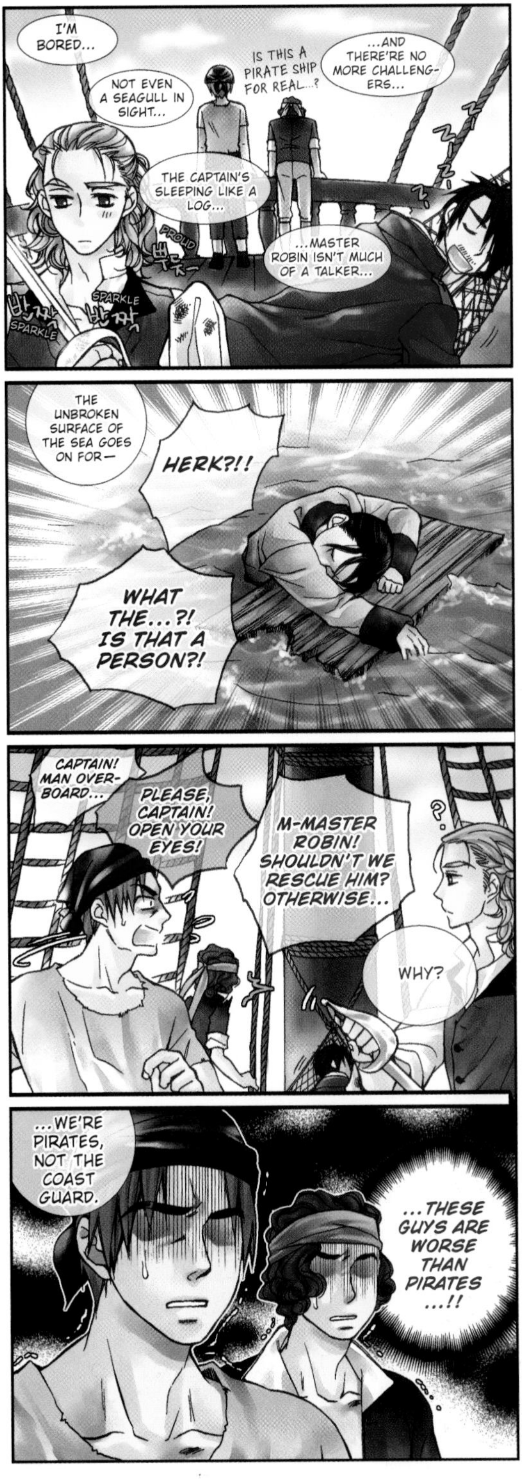

I'M BORED...
NOT EVEN A SEAGULL IN SIGHT...
IS THIS A PIRATE SHIP FOR REAL...?
...AND THERE'RE NO MORE CHALLENG-ERS...
THE CAPTAIN'S SLEEPING LIKE A LOG...
...MASTER ROBIN ISN'T MUCH OF A TALKER...
뿌듯
PROUD
반짝
SPARKLE
반짝
SPARKLE
THE UNBROKEN SURFACE OF THE SEA GOES ON FOR—
HERK?!!
WHAT THE...?! IS THAT A PERSON?!
CAPTAIN! MAN OVER-BOARD...
PLEASE, CAPTAIN! OPEN YOUR EYES!
M-MASTER ROBIN! SHOULDN'T WE RESCUE HIM? OTHERWISE...
?
WHY?
...WE'RE PIRATES, NOT THE COAST GUARD.
...THESE GUYS ARE WORSE THAN PIRATES ...!!

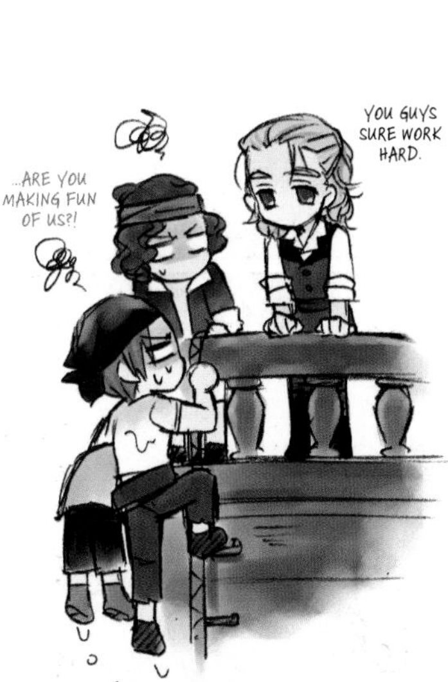

YOU GUYS SURE WORK HARD.
...ARE YOU MAKING FUN OF US?!

#8. MISUNDERSTANDING

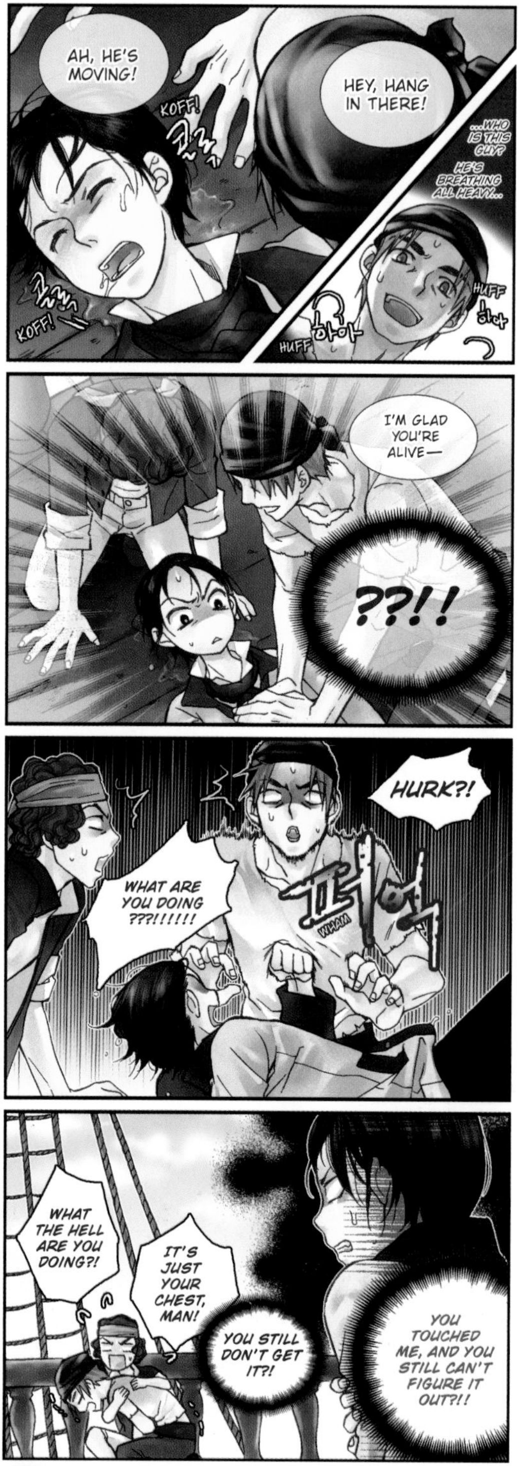
AH, HE'S MOVING!
KOFF!
HEY, HANG IN THERE!
...WHO IS THIS GUY? HE'S BREATHING ALL HEAVY...
KOFF!
HUFF
HUFF
I'M GLAD YOU'RE ALIVE—
??!!
HURK?!
WHAT ARE YOU DOING ???!!!!!!
WHAM
WHAT THE HELL ARE YOU DOING?!
IT'S JUST YOUR CHEST, MAN!
YOU STILL DON'T GET IT?!
YOU TOUCHED ME, AND YOU STILL CAN'T FIGURE IT OUT?!!

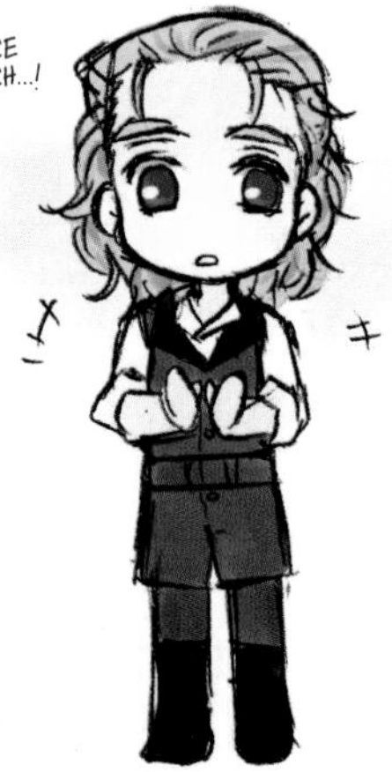
NICE PUNCH...!

#9. MAN'S ROMANCE

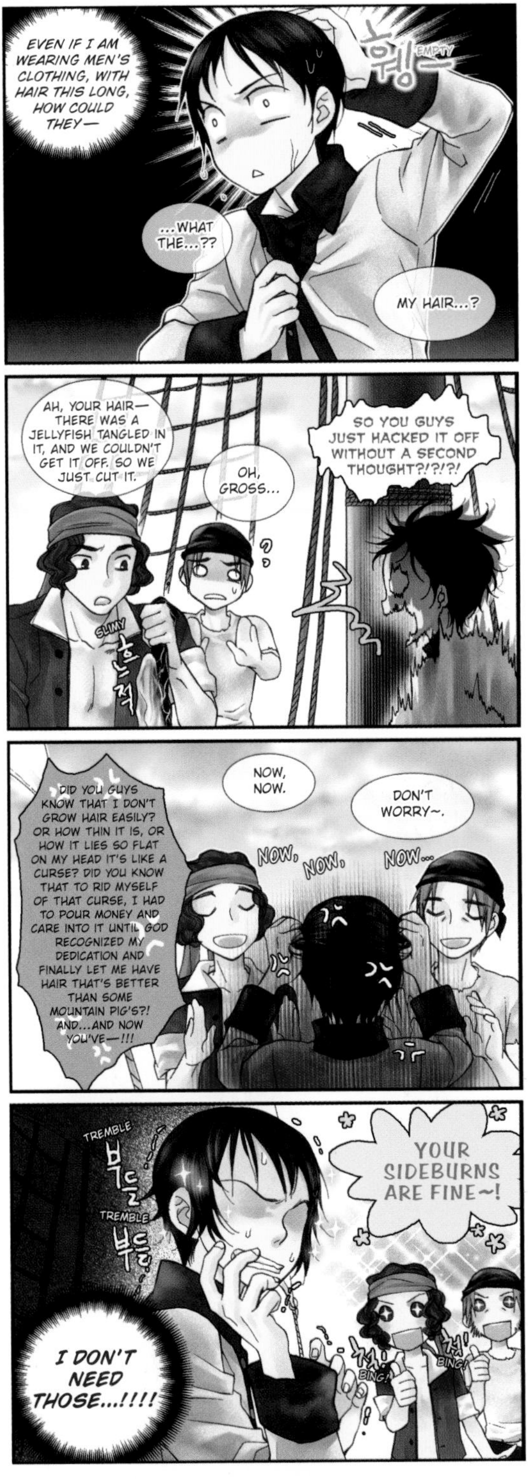

EVEN IF I AM WEARING MEN'S CLOTHING, WITH HAIR THIS LONG, HOW COULD THEY—
EMPTY
...WHAT THE...??
MY HAIR...?
AH, YOUR HAIR— THERE WAS A JELLYFISH TANGLED IN IT, AND WE COULDN'T GET IT OFF. SO WE JUST CUT IT.
OH, GROSS...
SO YOU GUYS JUST HACKED IT OFF WITHOUT A SECOND THOUGHT?!?!?!
SLIMY
흐느적
DID YOU GUYS KNOW THAT I DON'T GROW HAIR EASILY? OR HOW THIN IT IS, OR HOW IT LIES SO FLAT ON MY HEAD IT'S LIKE A CURSE? DID YOU KNOW THAT TO RID MYSELF OF THAT CURSE, I HAD TO POUR MONEY AND CARE INTO IT UNTIL GOD RECOGNIZED MY DEDICATION AND FINALLY LET ME HAVE HAIR THAT'S BETTER THAN SOME MOUNTAIN PIG'S?! AND...AND NOW YOU'VE—!!!
NOW, NOW.
DON'T WORRY~.
NOW, NOW, NOW...
TREMBLE
부들
TREMBLE
부들
YOUR SIDEBURNS ARE FINE~!
I DON'T NEED THOSE...!!!!
척
BING!
척
BING!

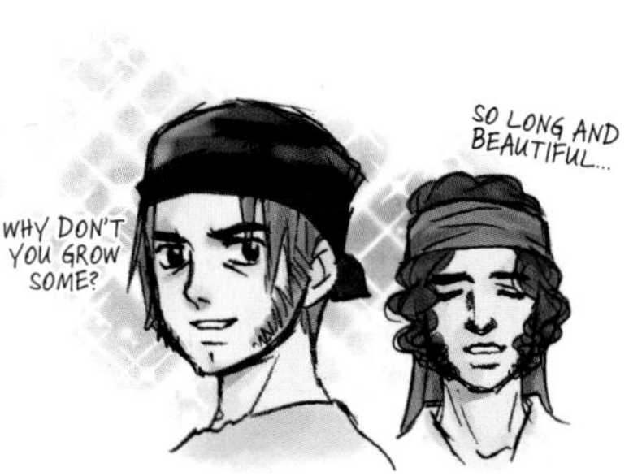

SO LONG AND BEAUTIFUL...
WHY DON'T YOU GROW SOME?

#10. IMPOSSIBLE TO PERSUADE

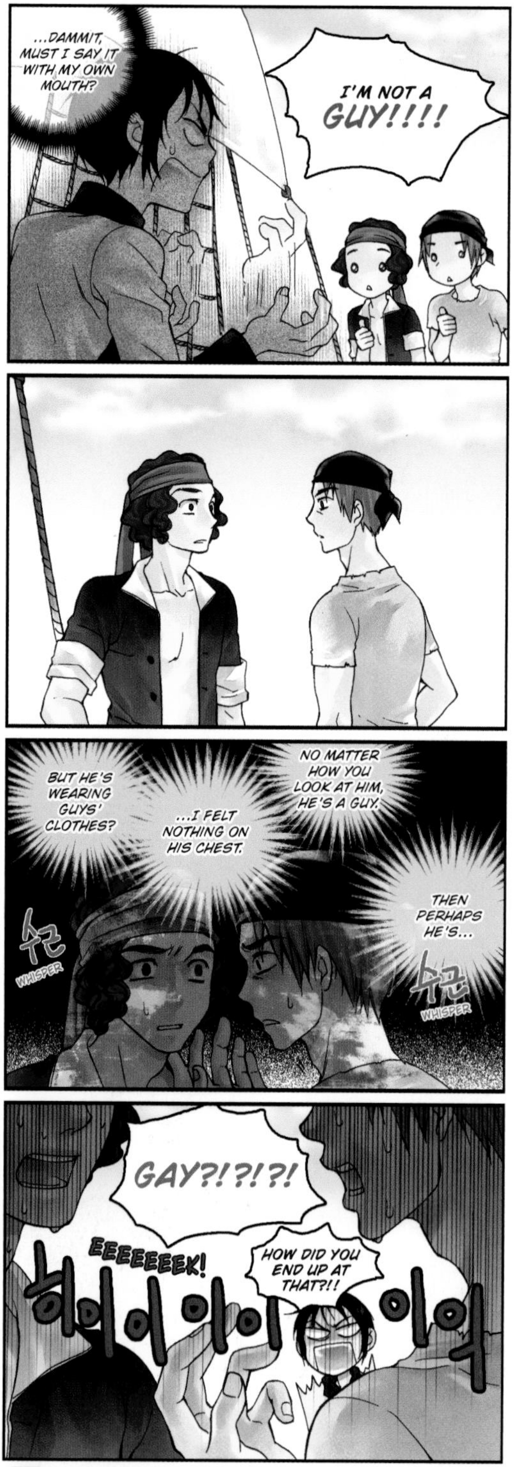
...DAMMIT, MUST I SAY IT WITH MY OWN MOUTH?
I'M NOT A GUY!!!!
BUT HE'S WEARING GUYS' CLOTHES?
...I FELT NOTHING ON HIS CHEST.
NO MATTER HOW YOU LOOK AT HIM, HE'S A GUY.
THEN PERHAPS HE'S...
수군
WHISPER
수군
WHISPER
GAY?!?!?!
EEEEEEEEK!
HOW DID YOU END UP AT THAT?!!

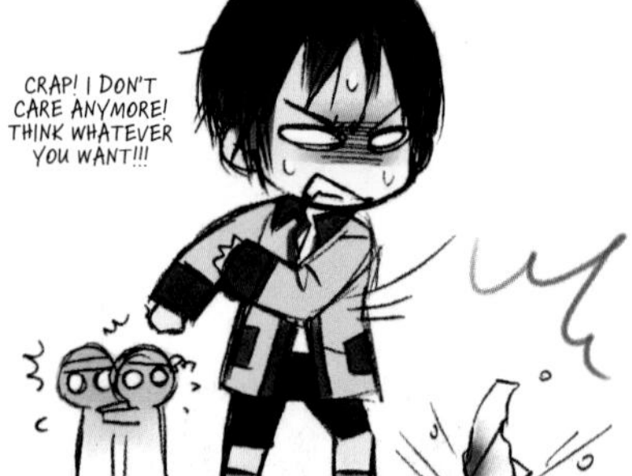
CRAP! I DON'T CARE ANYMORE! THINK WHATEVER YOU WANT!!!

#11. REGRET

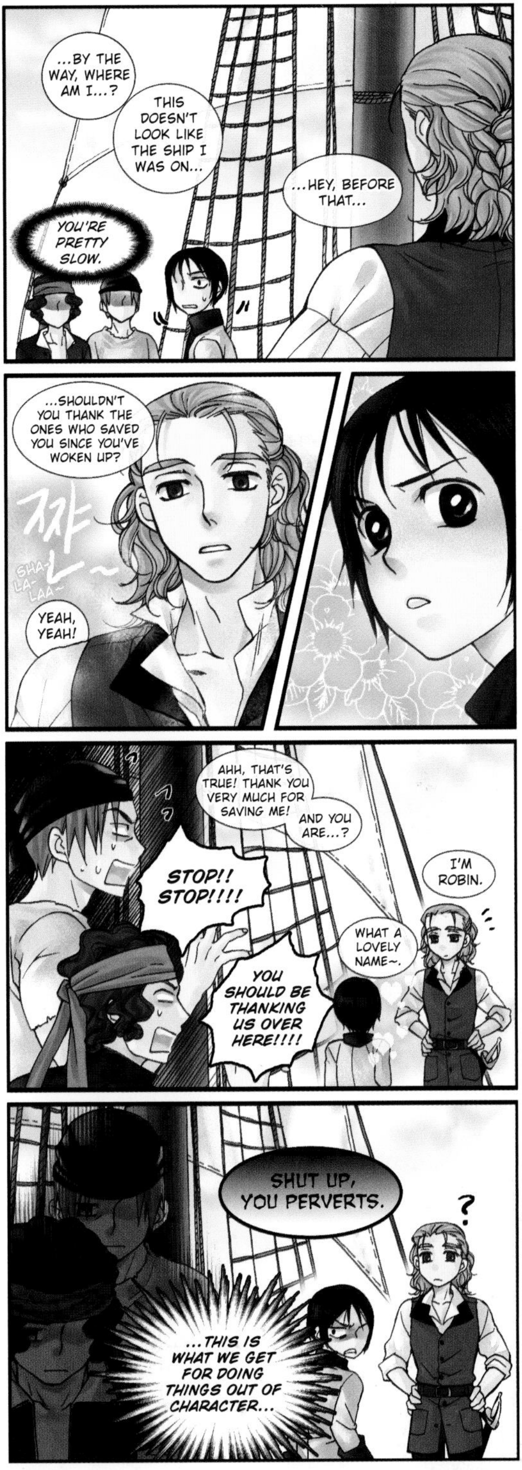
...BY THE WAY, WHERE AM I...?
THIS DOESN'T LOOK LIKE THE SHIP I WAS ON...
...HEY, BEFORE THAT...
YOU'RE PRETTY SLOW.
...SHOULDN'T YOU THANK THE ONES WHO SAVED YOU SINCE YOU'VE WOKEN UP?
SHA-LA-LAA~
YEAH, YEAH!
AHH, THAT'S TRUE! THANK YOU VERY MUCH FOR SAVING ME!
AND YOU ARE...?
I'M ROBIN.
WHAT A LOVELY NAME~.
STOP!! STOP!!!!
YOU SHOULD BE THANKING US OVER HERE!!!!
SHUT UP, YOU PERVERTS.
?
...THIS IS WHAT WE GET FOR DOING THINGS OUT OF CHARACTER...

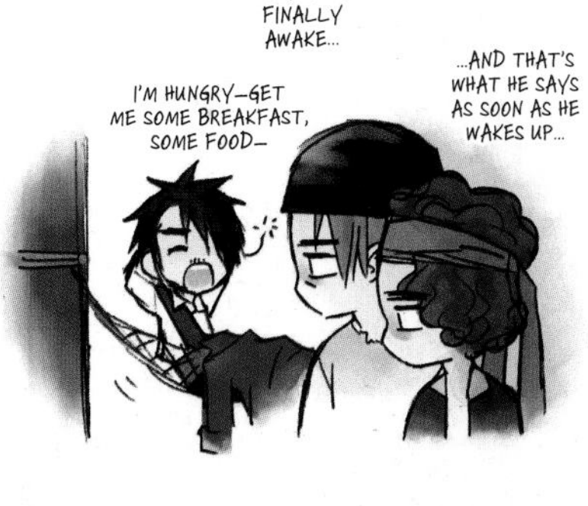
OH, HE'S FINALLY AWAKE...
I'M HUNGRY—GET ME SOME BREAKFAST, SOME FOOD—
...AND THAT'S WHAT HE SAYS AS SOON AS HE WAKES UP...

#12. CONTROL YOUR EXPRESSION

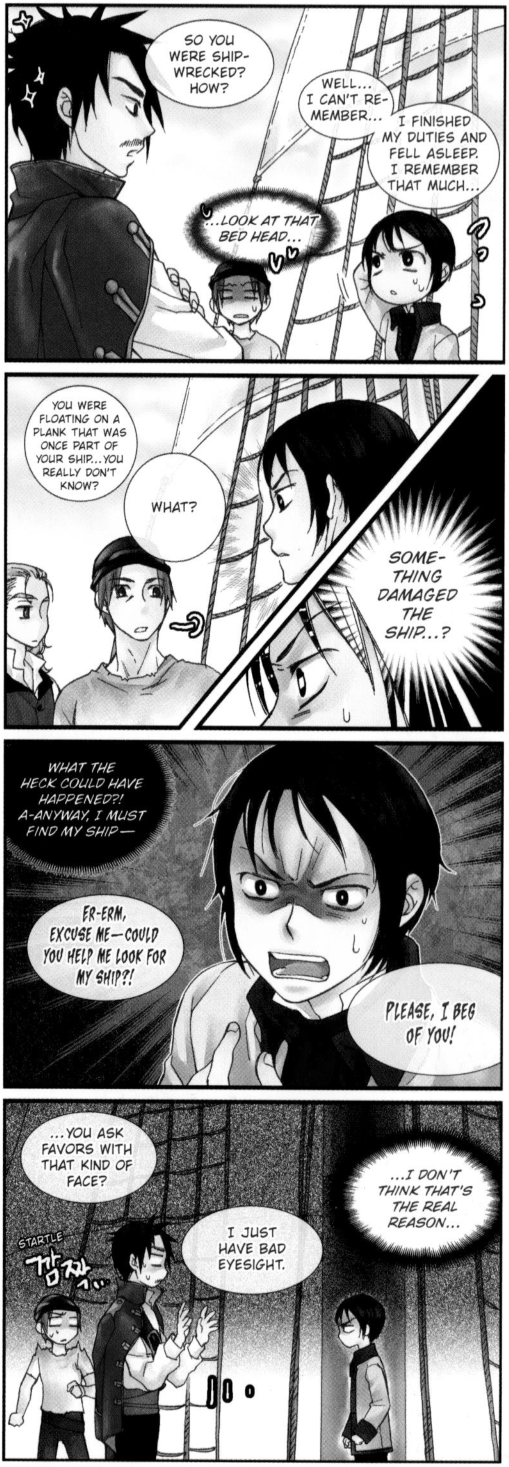
SO YOU WERE SHIP-WRECKED? HOW?
WELL... I CAN'T RE-MEMBER...
I FINISHED MY DUTIES AND FELL ASLEEP. I REMEMBER THAT MUCH...
...LOOK AT THAT BED HEAD...
YOU WERE FLOATING ON A PLANK THAT WAS ONCE PART OF YOUR SHIP...YOU REALLY DON'T KNOW?
WHAT?
SOME-THING DAMAGED THE SHIP...?
WHAT THE HECK COULD HAVE HAPPENED?! A-ANYWAY, I MUST FIND MY SHIP—
ER-ERM, EXCUSE ME—COULD YOU HELP ME LOOK FOR MY SHIP?!
PLEASE, I BEG OF YOU!
...YOU ASK FAVORS WITH THAT KIND OF FACE?
STARTLE
깜짝
I JUST HAVE BAD EYESIGHT.
...I DON'T THINK THAT'S THE REAL REASON...

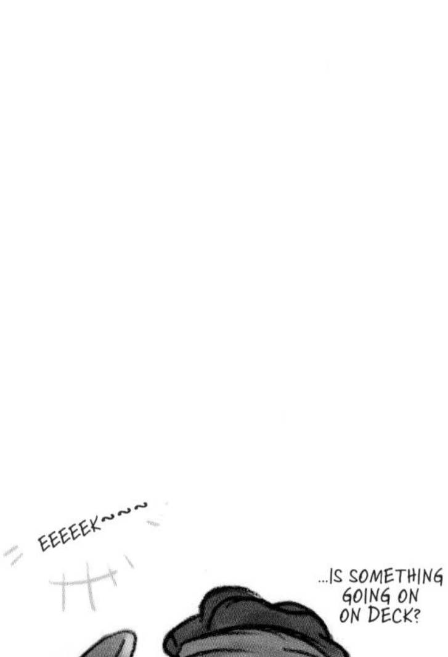
EEEEEK~~~
...IS SOMETHING GOING ON ON DECK?

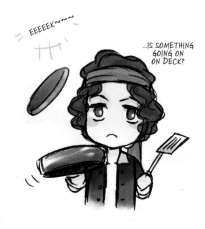

#13. NOT ANYONE CAN BE A PIRATE

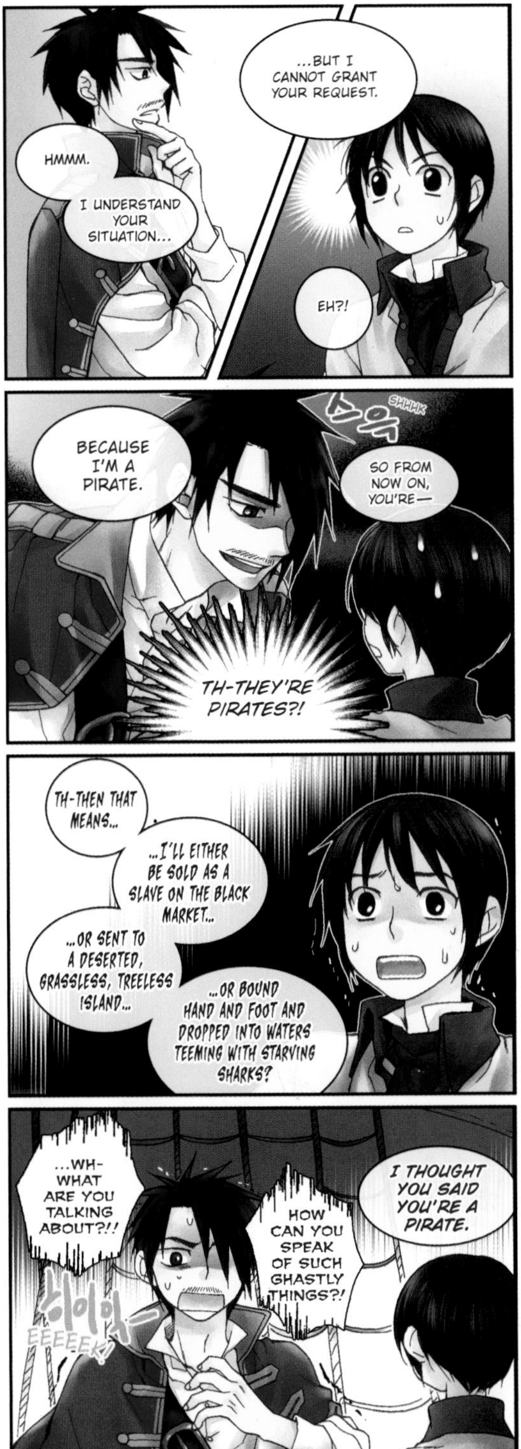
HMMM.
I UNDERSTAND YOUR SITUATION...
...BUT I CANNOT GRANT YOUR REQUEST.
EH?!
BECAUSE I'M A PIRATE.
스윽
SHHHK
SO FROM NOW ON, YOU'RE—
TH-THEY'RE PIRATES?!
TH-THEN THAT MEANS...
...I'LL EITHER BE SOLD AS A SLAVE ON THE BLACK MARKET...
...OR SENT TO A DESERTED, GRASSLESS, TREELESS ISLAND...
...OR BOUND HAND AND FOOT AND DROPPED INTO WATERS TEEMING WITH STARVING SHARKS?
...WH-WHAT ARE YOU TALKING ABOUT?!!
히이익—
EEEEEK!
HOW CAN YOU SPEAK OF SUCH GHASTLY THINGS?!
I THOUGHT YOU SAID YOU'RE A PIRATE.

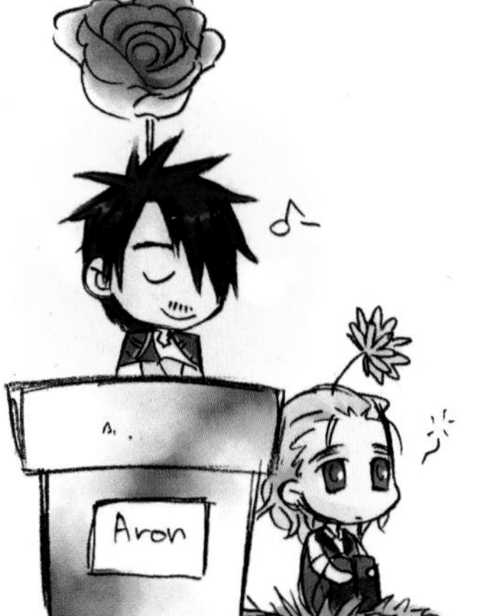
Aron

#14. DEPARTING ANYWAY

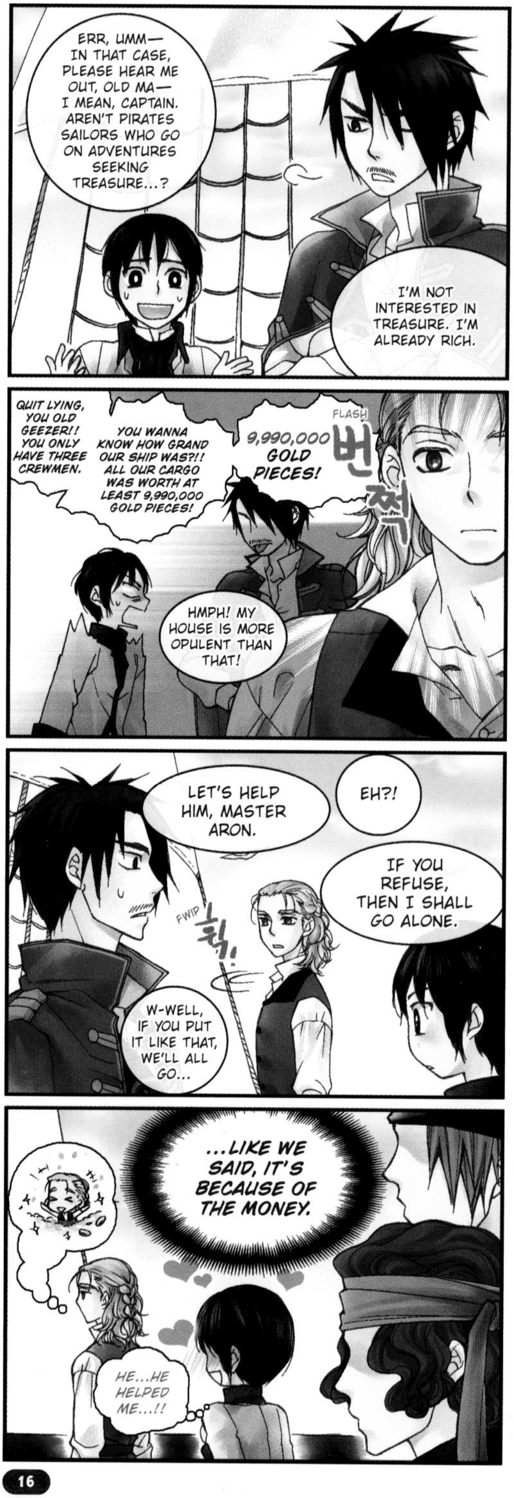
ERR, UMM— IN THAT CASE, PLEASE HEAR ME OUT, OLD MA— I MEAN, CAPTAIN. AREN'T PIRATES SAILORS WHO GO ON ADVENTURES SEEKING TREASURE...?
I'M NOT INTERESTED IN TREASURE. I'M ALREADY RICH.
QUIT LYING, YOU OLD GEEZER!! YOU ONLY HAVE THREE CREWMEN.
YOU WANNA KNOW HOW GRAND OUR SHIP WAS?!! ALL OUR CARGO WAS WORTH AT LEAST 9,990,000 GOLD PIECES!
9,990,000 GOLD PIECES!
FLASH
번쩍
HMPH! MY HOUSE IS MORE OPULENT THAN THAT!
LET'S HELP HIM, MASTER ARON.
EH?!
IF YOU REFUSE, THEN I SHALL GO ALONE.
FWIP
휙
W-WELL, IF YOU PUT IT LIKE THAT, WE'LL ALL GO...
...LIKE WE SAID, IT'S BECAUSE OF THE MONEY.
HE...HE HELPED ME...!!

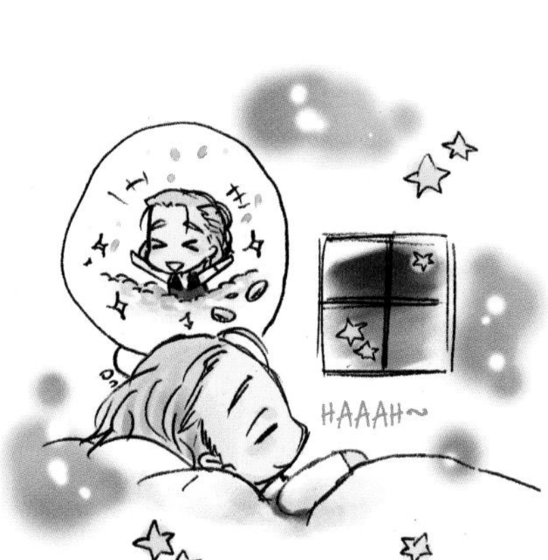
HAAAH~

#15. PRIDE AND PREJUDICE

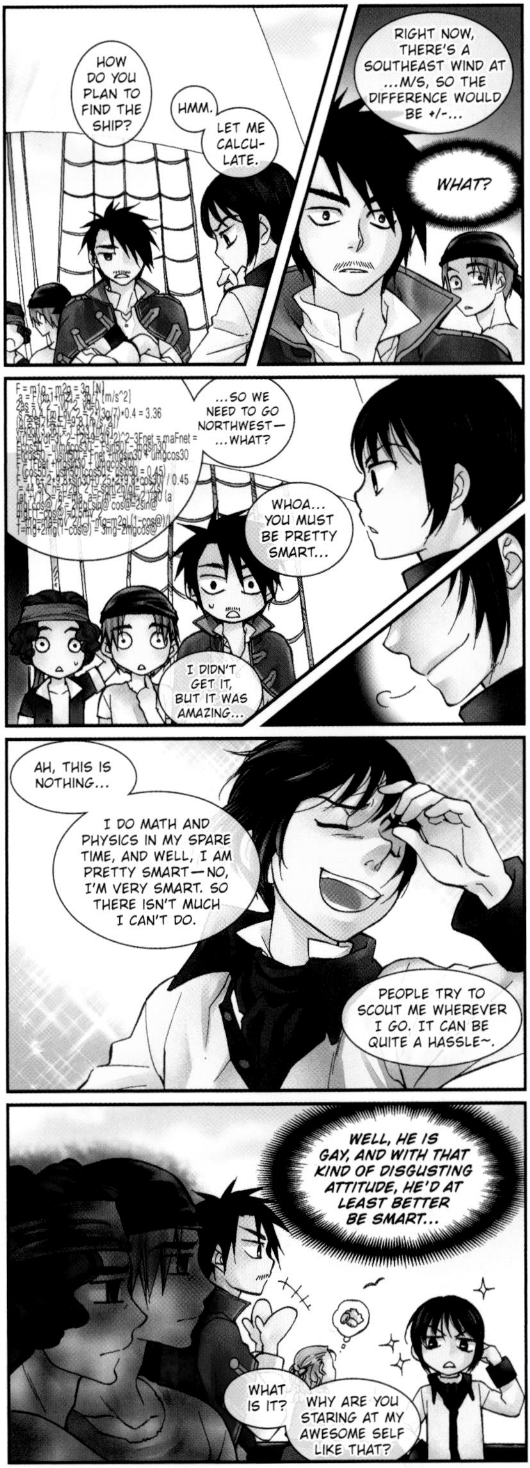

HOW DO YOU PLAN TO FIND THE SHIP?
HMM.
LET ME CALCU-LATE.
RIGHT NOW, THERE'S A SOUTHEAST WIND AT ...M/S, SO THE DIFFERENCE WOULD BE +/-...
WHAT?
...SO WE NEED TO GO NORTHWEST— ...WHAT?
WHOA... YOU MUST BE PRETTY SMART...
I DIDN'T GET IT, BUT IT WAS AMAZING...
AH, THIS IS NOTHING...
I DO MATH AND PHYSICS IN MY SPARE TIME, AND WELL, I AM PRETTY SMART—NO, I'M VERY SMART. SO THERE ISN'T MUCH I CAN'T DO.
PEOPLE TRY TO SCOUT ME WHEREVER I GO. IT CAN BE QUITE A HASSLE~.
WELL, HE IS GAY, AND WITH THAT KIND OF DISGUSTING ATTITUDE, HE'D AT LEAST BETTER BE SMART...
WHAT IS IT?
WHY ARE YOU STARING AT MY AWESOME SELF LIKE THAT?

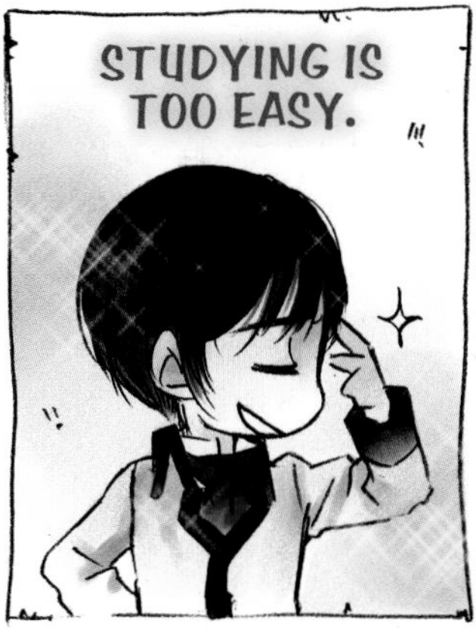

STUDYING IS TOO EASY.

#16. YOU MAY JUMP HIGH, BUT OTHERS FLY

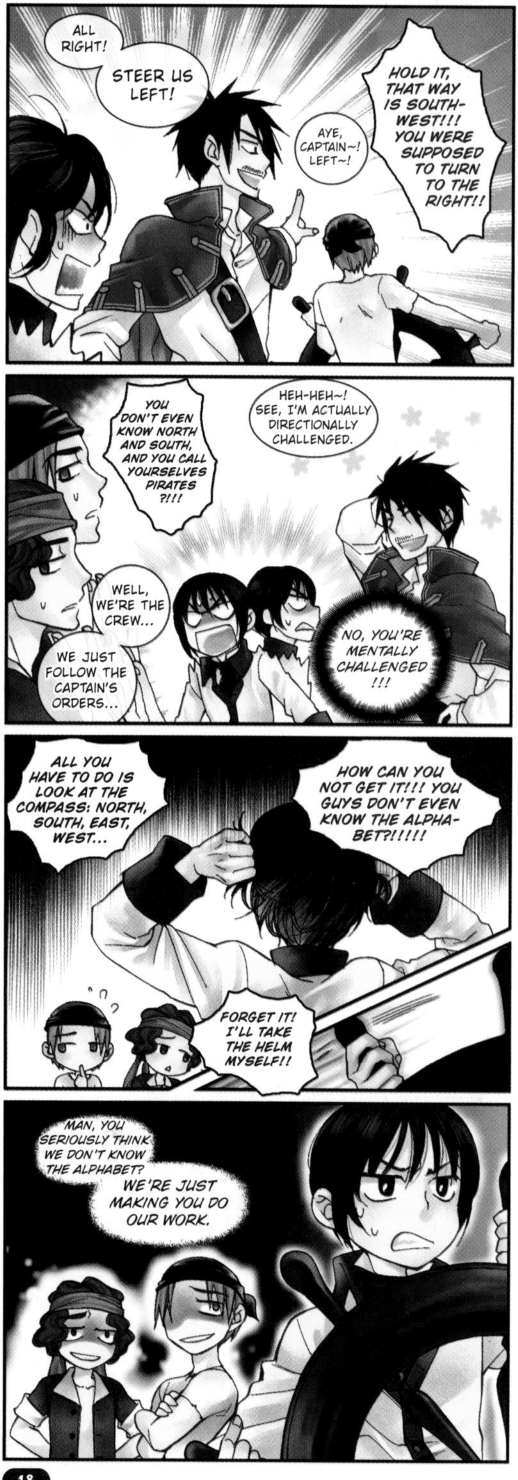
ALL RIGHT!
STEER US LEFT!
AYE, CAPTAIN~! LEFT~!
HOLD IT, THAT WAY IS SOUTH-WEST!!! YOU WERE SUPPOSED TO TURN TO THE RIGHT!!
YOU DON'T EVEN KNOW NORTH AND SOUTH, AND YOU CALL YOURSELVES PIRATES ?!!!
HEH-HEH~! SEE, I'M ACTUALLY DIRECTIONALLY CHALLENGED.
WELL, WE'RE THE CREW...
WE JUST FOLLOW THE CAPTAIN'S ORDERS...
NO, YOU'RE MENTALLY CHALLENGED !!!
ALL YOU HAVE TO DO IS LOOK AT THE COMPASS: NORTH, SOUTH, EAST, WEST...
HOW CAN YOU NOT GET IT!!! YOU GUYS DON'T EVEN KNOW THE ALPHA-BET?!!!!!
FORGET IT! I'LL TAKE THE HELM MYSELF!!
MAN, YOU SERIOUSLY THINK WE DON'T KNOW THE ALPHABET?
WE'RE JUST MAKING YOU DO OUR WORK.

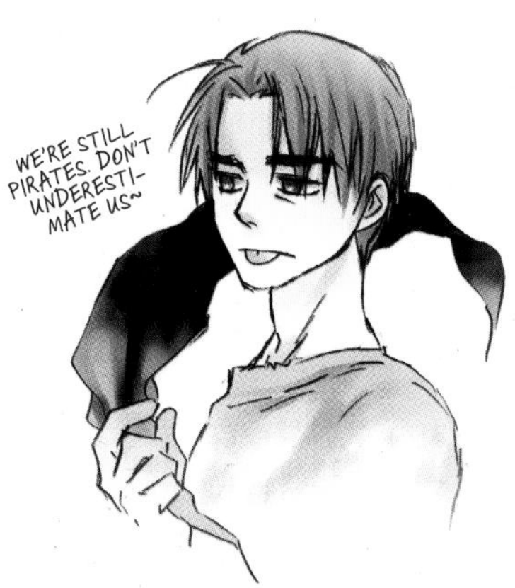
WE'RE STILL PIRATES. DON'T UNDERESTI-MATE US~

#17. THE WALL BETWEEN MEN AND WOMEN

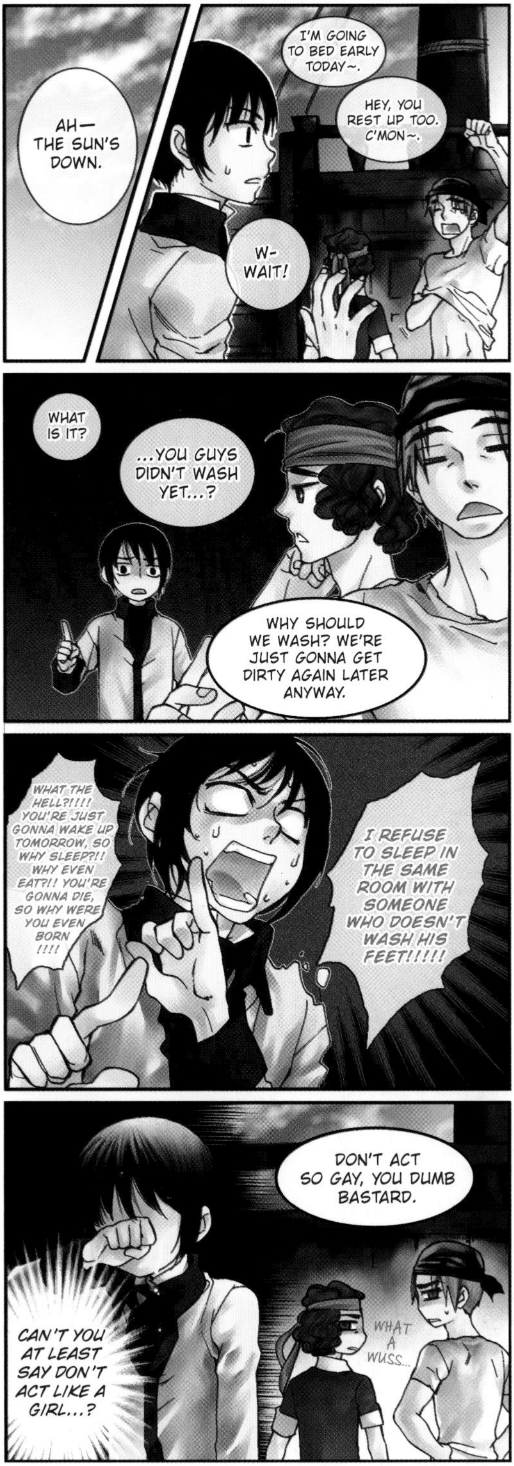

AH— THE SUN'S DOWN.
I'M GOING TO BED EARLY TODAY~.
HEY, YOU REST UP TOO. C'MON~.
W- WAIT!
WHAT IS IT?
...YOU GUYS DIDN'T WASH YET...?
WHY SHOULD WE WASH? WE'RE JUST GONNA GET DIRTY AGAIN LATER ANYWAY.
I REFUSE TO SLEEP IN THE SAME ROOM WITH SOMEONE WHO DOESN'T WASH HIS FEET!!!!!
WHAT THE HELL?!!!! YOU'RE JUST GONNA WAKE UP TOMORROW, SO WHY SLEEP?!! WHY EVEN EAT?!! YOU'RE GONNA DIE, SO WHY WERE YOU EVEN BORN !!!!
DON'T ACT SO GAY, YOU DUMB BASTARD.
CAN'T YOU AT LEAST SAY DON'T ACT LIKE A GIRL...?
WHAT A WUSS...

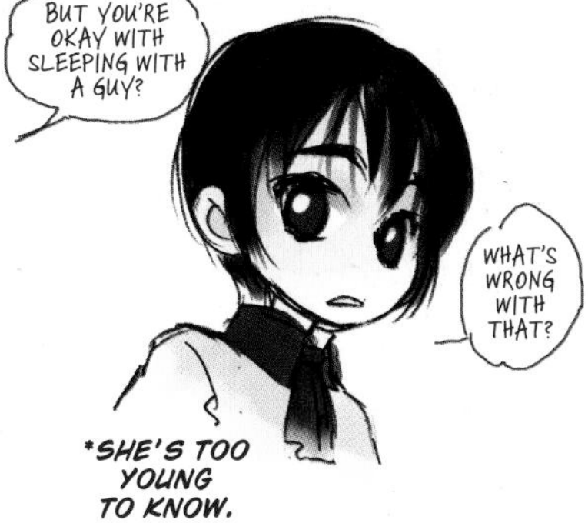

BUT YOU'RE OKAY WITH SLEEPING WITH A GUY?
WHAT'S WRONG WITH THAT?

*SHE'S TOO YOUNG TO KNOW.

#18. SAME BED, DIFFERENT DREAMS

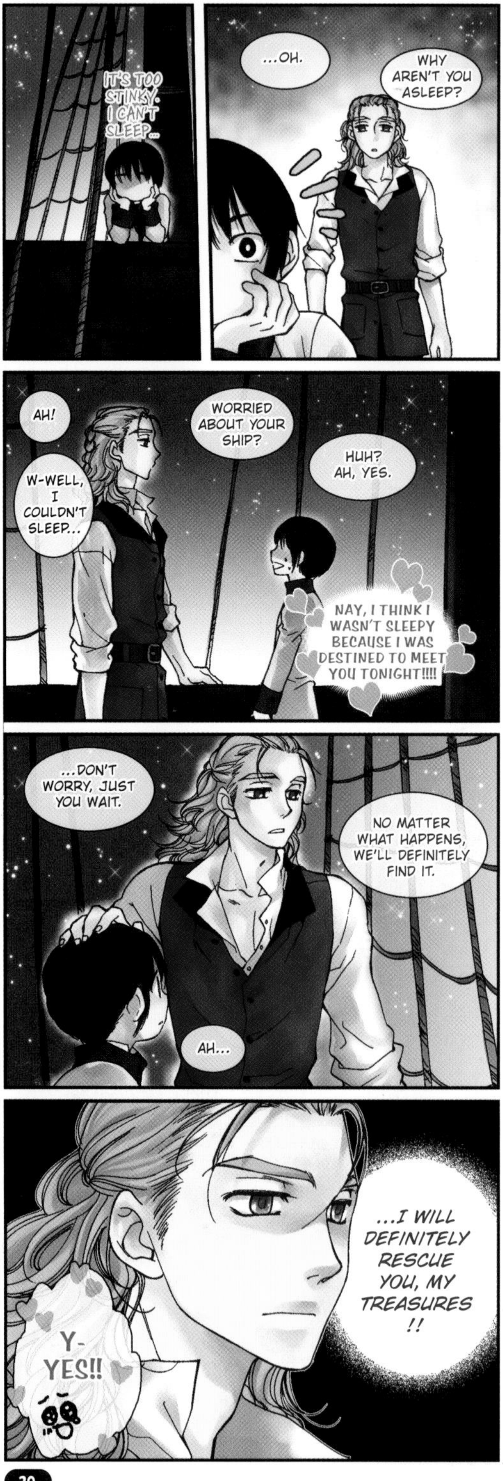
IT'S TOO STINKY. I CAN'T SLEEP...
...OH.
WHY AREN'T YOU ASLEEP?
AH!
WORRIED ABOUT YOUR SHIP?
W-WELL, I COULDN'T SLEEP...
HUH? AH, YES.
NAY, I THINK I WASN'T SLEEPY BECAUSE I WAS DESTINED TO MEET YOU TONIGHT!!!!
...DON'T WORRY, JUST YOU WAIT.
NO MATTER WHAT HAPPENS, WE'LL DEFINITELY FIND IT.
AH...
...I WILL DEFINITELY RESCUE YOU, MY TREASURES !!
Y-YES!!

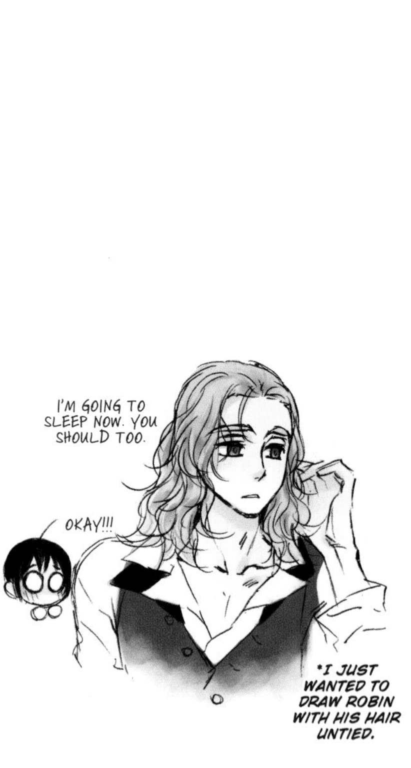
I'M GOING TO SLEEP NOW. YOU SHOULD TOO.
OKAY!!!

*I JUST WANTED TO DRAW ROBIN WITH HIS HAIR UNTIED.

#19. TEACHER'S PET

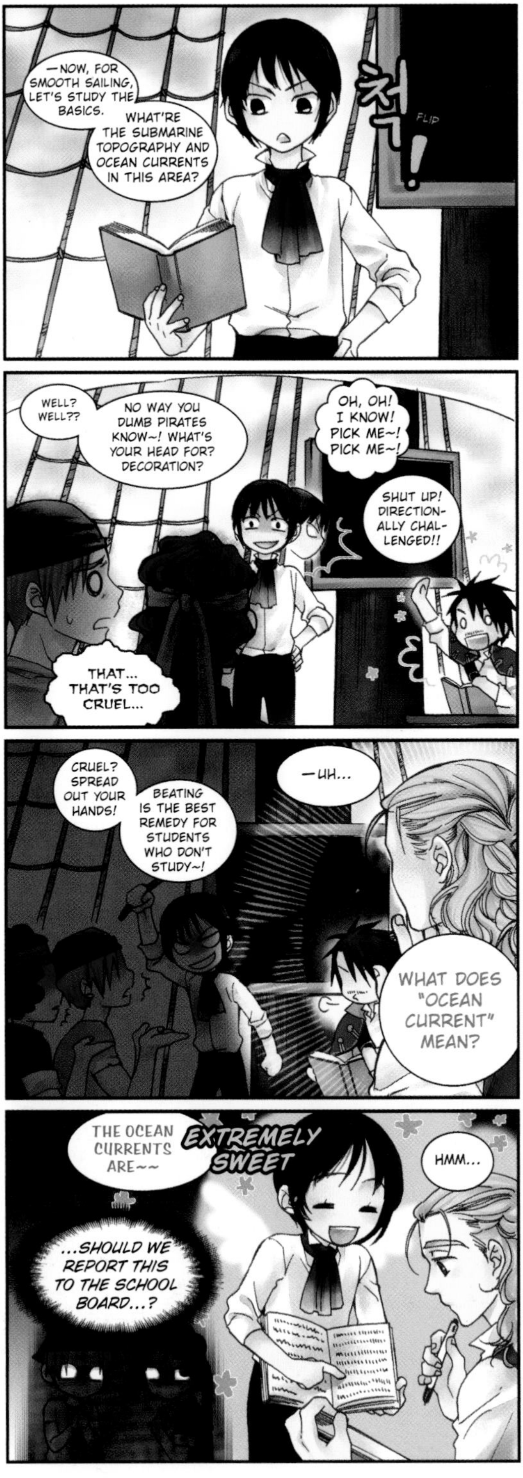
—NOW, FOR SMOOTH SAILING, LET'S STUDY THE BASICS.
WHAT'RE THE SUBMARINE TOPOGRAPHY AND OCEAN CURRENTS IN THIS AREA?
척!
FLIP
WELL? WELL??
NO WAY YOU DUMB PIRATES KNOW~! WHAT'S YOUR HEAD FOR? DECORATION?
OH, OH! I KNOW! PICK ME~! PICK ME~!
SHUT UP! DIRECTION-ALLY CHAL-LENGED!!
THAT... THAT'S TOO CRUEL...
CRUEL? SPREAD OUT YOUR HANDS!
BEATING IS THE BEST REMEDY FOR STUDENTS WHO DON'T STUDY~!
—UH...
WHAT DOES "OCEAN CURRENT" MEAN?
THE OCEAN CURRENTS ARE~~
EXTREMELY SWEET
HMM...
...SHOULD WE REPORT THIS TO THE SCHOOL BOARD...?

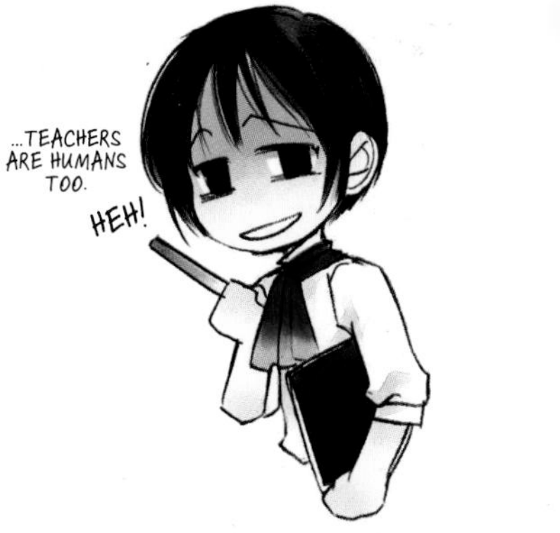
...TEACHERS ARE HUMANS TOO.
HEH!

#20. I GOT IT!

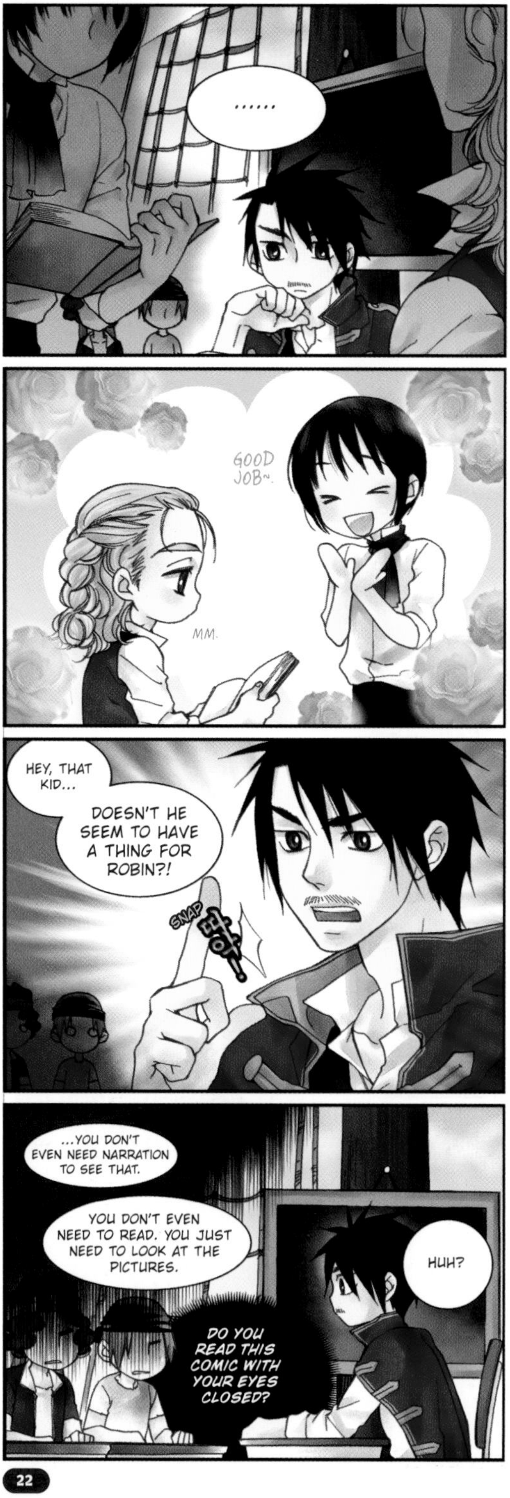
......
GOOD JOB~.
MM.
HEY, THAT KID...
DOESN'T HE SEEM TO HAVE A THING FOR ROBIN?!
SNAP
...YOU DON'T EVEN NEED NARRATION TO SEE THAT.
YOU DON'T EVEN NEED TO READ. YOU JUST NEED TO LOOK AT THE PICTURES.
HUH?
DO YOU READ THIS COMIC WITH YOUR EYES CLOSED?

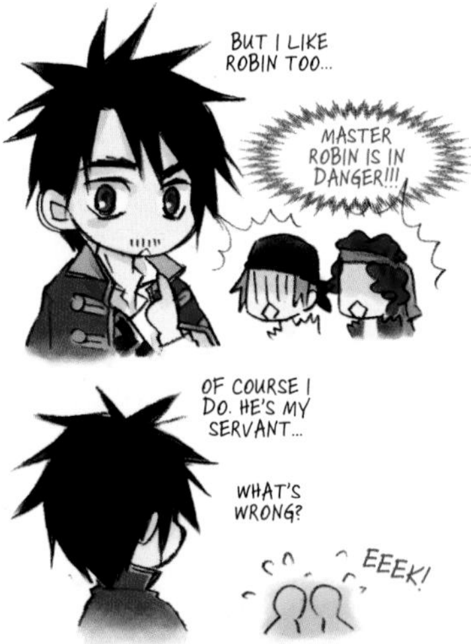
BUT I LIKE ROBIN TOO...
MASTER ROBIN IS IN DANGER!!!
OF COURSE I DO. HE'S MY SERVANT...
WHAT'S WRONG?
EEEK!

#21. DANGEROUS LOVE

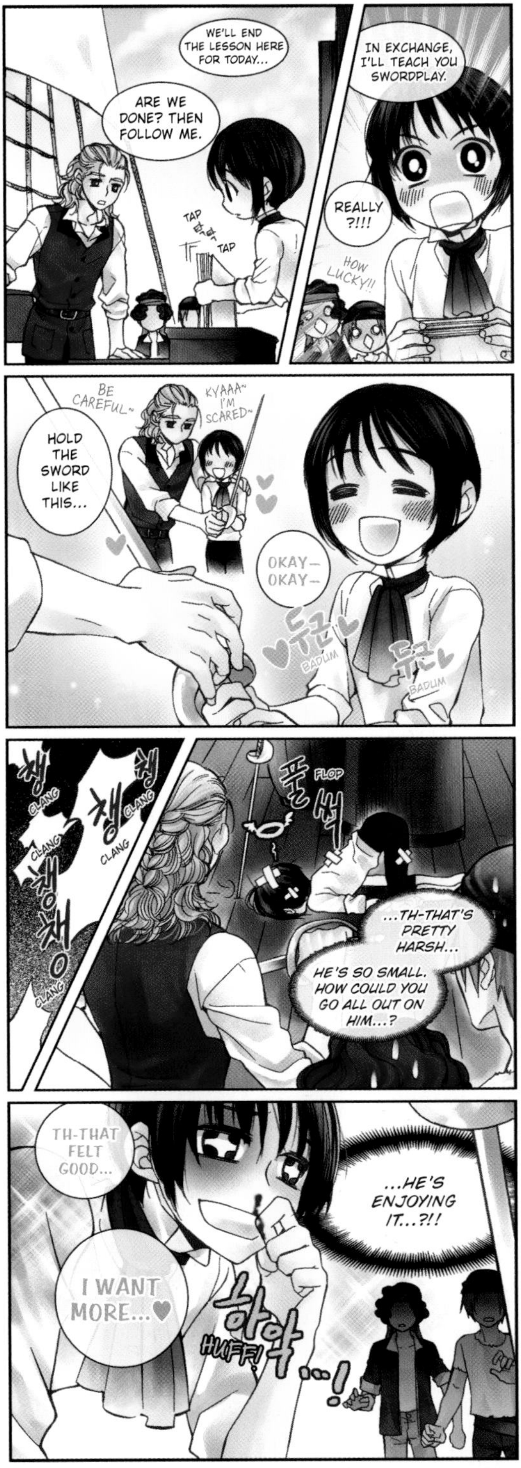

WE'LL END THE LESSON HERE FOR TODAY...
ARE WE DONE? THEN FOLLOW ME.
TAP TAP
IN EXCHANGE, I'LL TEACH YOU SWORDPLAY.
REALLY?!!!
HOW LUCKY!!
BE CAREFUL~
KYAAA~ I'M SCARED~
HOLD THE SWORD LIKE THIS...
OKAY— OKAY—
두근 BADUM
두근 BADUM
CLANG CLANG CLANG CLANG CLANG CLANG
풀썩 FLOP
...TH-THAT'S PRETTY HARSH...
HE'S SO SMALL. HOW COULD YOU GO ALL OUT ON HIM...?
TH-THAT FELT GOOD...
...HE'S ENJOYING IT...?!!
I WANT MORE...♥
하악 HUFF!

CLASS IS OVER = LUNCHTIME

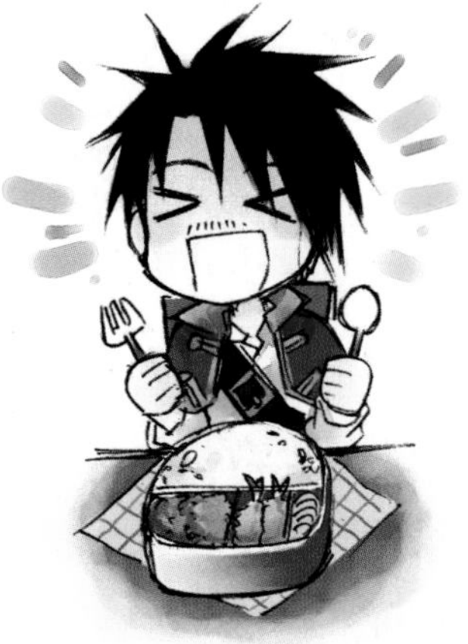

#22. QUICK ON HER FEET

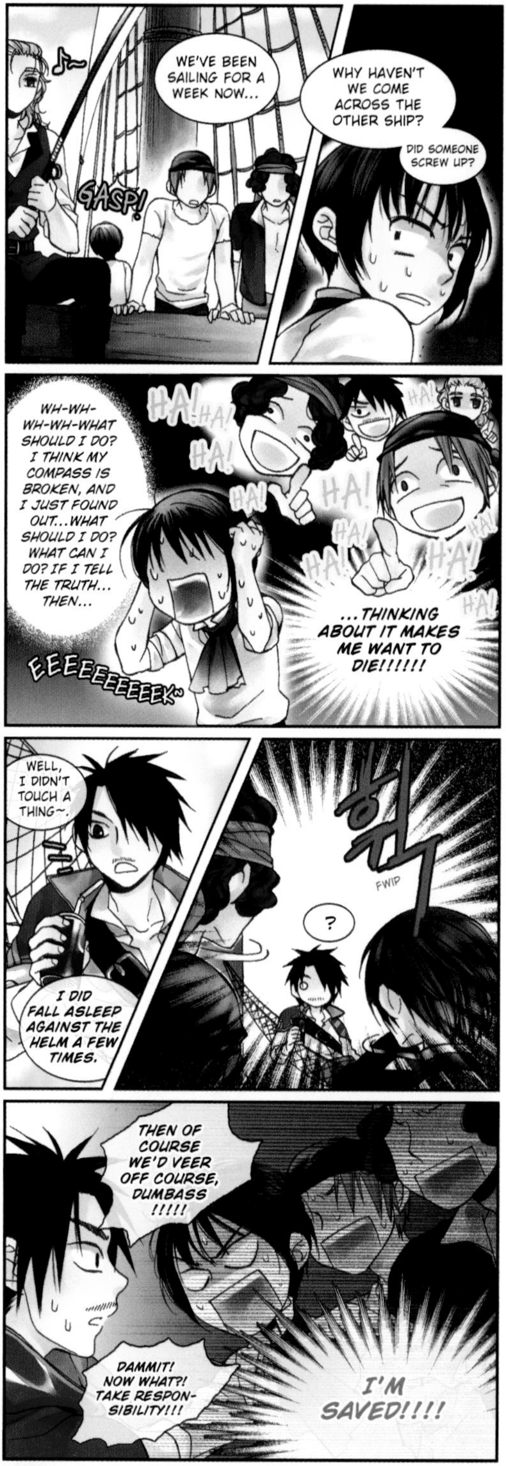
♪~
WE'VE BEEN SAILING FOR A WEEK NOW...
GASP!
WHY HAVEN'T WE COME ACROSS THE OTHER SHIP?
DID SOMEONE SCREW UP?
WH-WH-WH-WH-WHAT SHOULD I DO? I THINK MY COMPASS IS BROKEN, AND I JUST FOUND OUT...WHAT SHOULD I DO? WHAT CAN I DO? IF I TELL THE TRUTH... THEN...
HA! HA! HA! HA! HA! HA! HA! HA! HA! HA! HA!
EEEEEEEEEEEK~
...THINKING ABOUT IT MAKES ME WANT TO DIE!!!!!!
WELL, I DIDN'T TOUCH A THING~.
I DID FALL ASLEEP AGAINST THE HELM A FEW TIMES.
FWIP
?
THEN OF COURSE WE'D VEER OFF COURSE, DUMBASS!!!!!
DAMMIT! NOW WHAT?! TAKE RESPONSIBILITY!!!
I'M SAVED!!!!

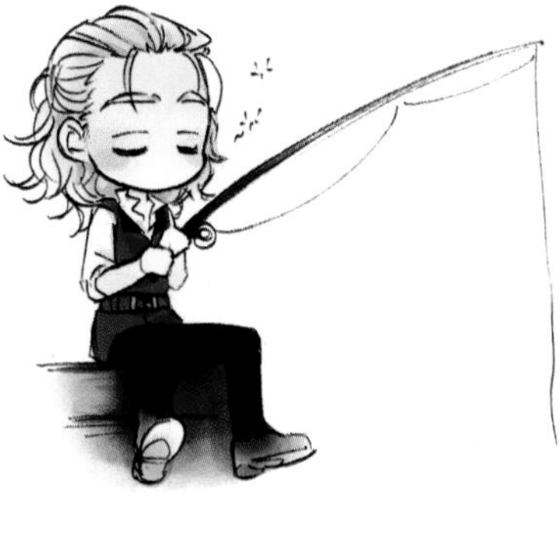

#23. WHATEVER GETS YOU THERE

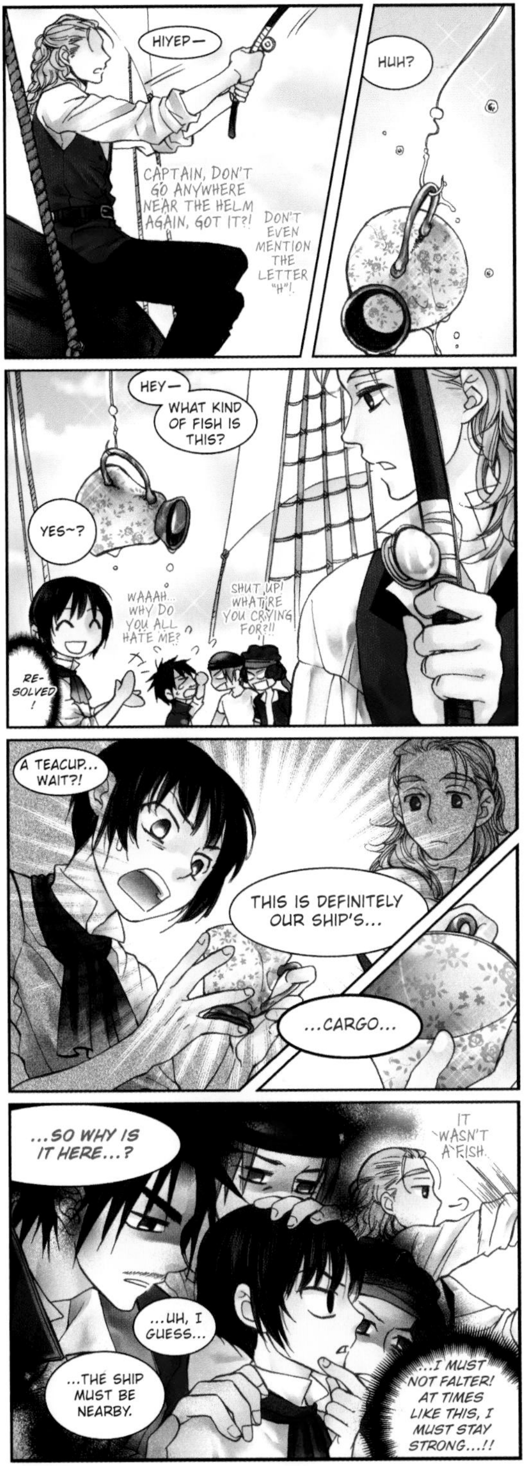
HIYEP—
CAPTAIN, DON'T GO ANYWHERE NEAR THE HELM AGAIN, GOT IT?!
DON'T EVEN MENTION THE LETTER "H"!.
HUH?
HEY— WHAT KIND OF FISH IS THIS?
YES~?
WAAAH... WHY DO YOU ALL HATE ME?
SHUT UP! WHAT'RE YOU CRYING FOR?!!
RE-SOLVED!
A TEACUP... WAIT?!
THIS IS DEFINITELY OUR SHIP'S...
...CARGO...
...SO WHY IS IT HERE...?
IT WASN'T A FISH.
...UH, I GUESS...
...THE SHIP MUST BE NEARBY.
...I MUST NOT FALTER! AT TIMES LIKE THIS, I MUST STAY STRONG...!!

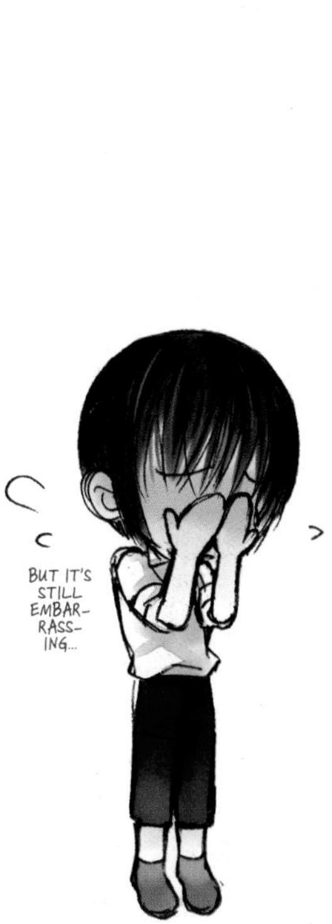
BUT IT'S STILL EMBAR-RASS-ING...

#24. THE REASON SHE WAS SENT ALONE

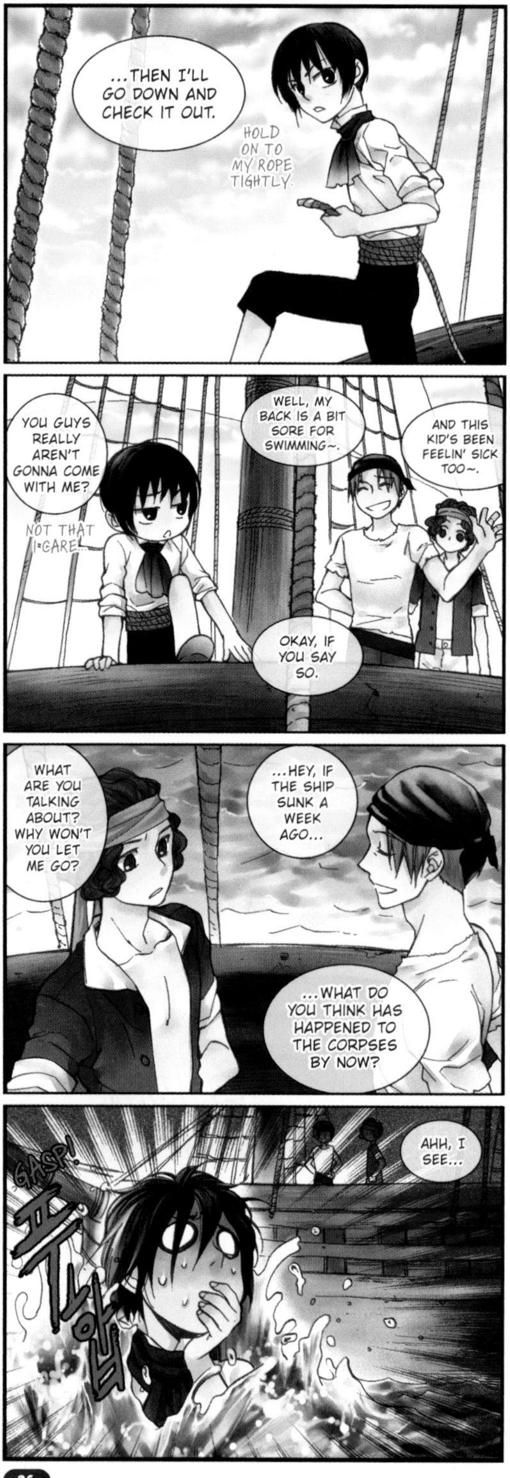
...THEN I'LL GO DOWN AND CHECK IT OUT.
HOLD ON TO MY ROPE TIGHTLY.
YOU GUYS REALLY AREN'T GONNA COME WITH ME?
NOT THAT I CARE...
WELL, MY BACK IS A BIT SORE FOR SWIMMING~.
AND THIS KID'S BEEN FEELIN' SICK TOO~.
OKAY, IF YOU SAY SO.
WHAT ARE YOU TALKING ABOUT? WHY WON'T YOU LET ME GO?
...HEY, IF THE SHIP SUNK A WEEK AGO...
...WHAT DO YOU THINK HAS HAPPENED TO THE CORPSES BY NOW?
AHH, I SEE...
GASP!

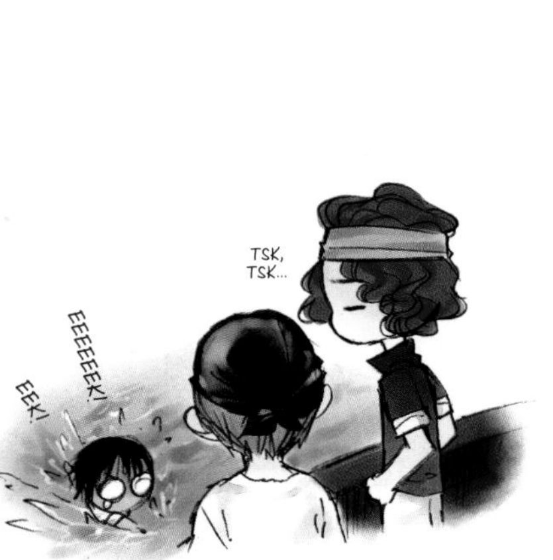
TSK, TSK...
EEEEEEK!
EEK!

#25. THE REASON

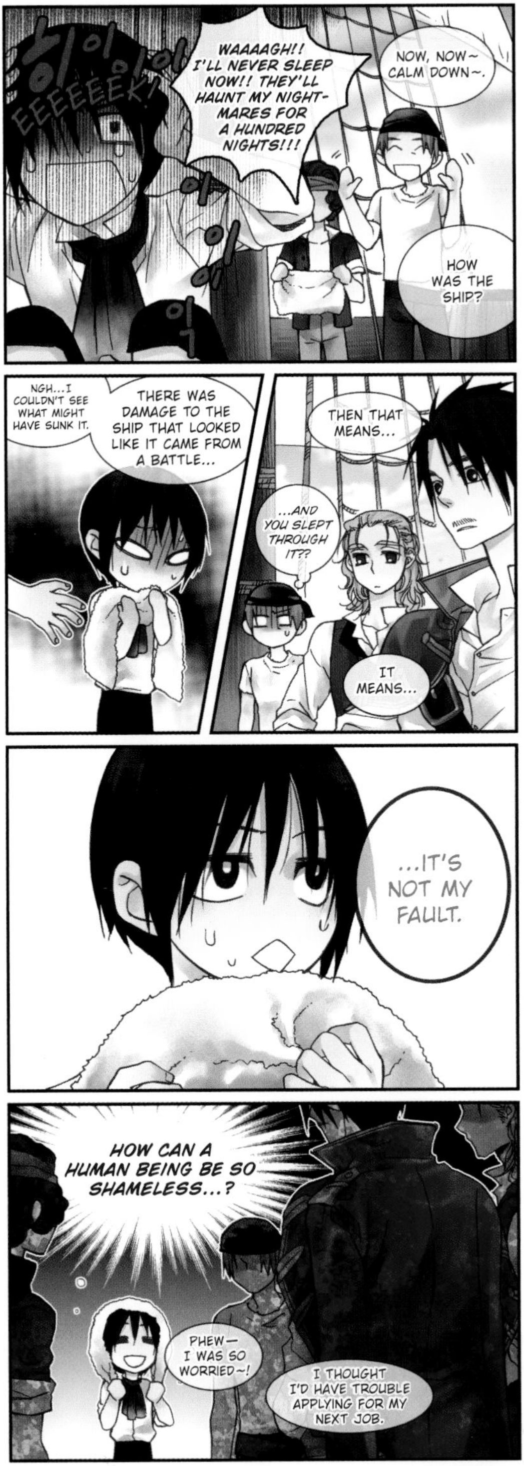
EEEEEEK!
WAAAAGH!! I'LL NEVER SLEEP NOW!! THEY'LL HAUNT MY NIGHT-MARES FOR A HUNDRED NIGHTS!!!
NOW, NOW~ CALM DOWN~.
HOW WAS THE SHIP?
NGH...I COULDN'T SEE WHAT MIGHT HAVE SUNK IT.
THERE WAS DAMAGE TO THE SHIP THAT LOOKED LIKE IT CAME FROM A BATTLE...
THEN THAT MEANS...
...AND YOU SLEPT THROUGH IT??
IT MEANS...
...IT'S NOT MY FAULT.
HOW CAN A HUMAN BEING BE SO SHAMELESS...?
PHEW— I WAS SO WORRIED~!
I THOUGHT I'D HAVE TROUBLE APPLYING FOR MY NEXT JOB.

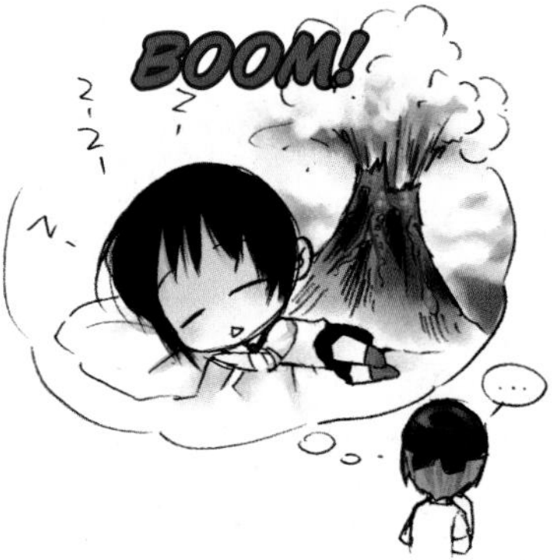
BOOM!
...

#26. FLIRTING WITH MR. ROBIN

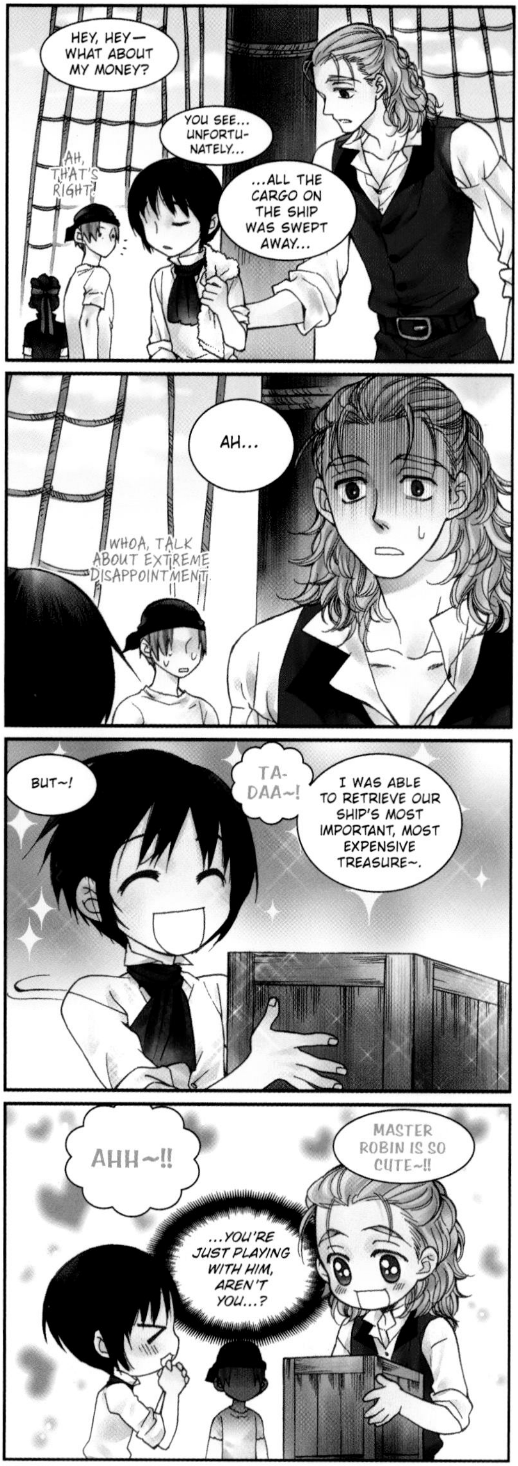
HEY, HEY— WHAT ABOUT MY MONEY?
YOU SEE... UNFORTU-NATELY...
AH, THAT'S RIGHT!
...ALL THE CARGO ON THE SHIP WAS SWEPT AWAY...
AH...
WHOA, TALK ABOUT EXTREME DISAPPOINTMENT.
BUT~!
TA-DAA~!
I WAS ABLE TO RETRIEVE OUR SHIP'S MOST IMPORTANT, MOST EXPENSIVE TREASURE~.
AHH~!!
MASTER ROBIN IS SO CUTE~!!
...YOU'RE JUST PLAYING WITH HIM, AREN'T YOU...?

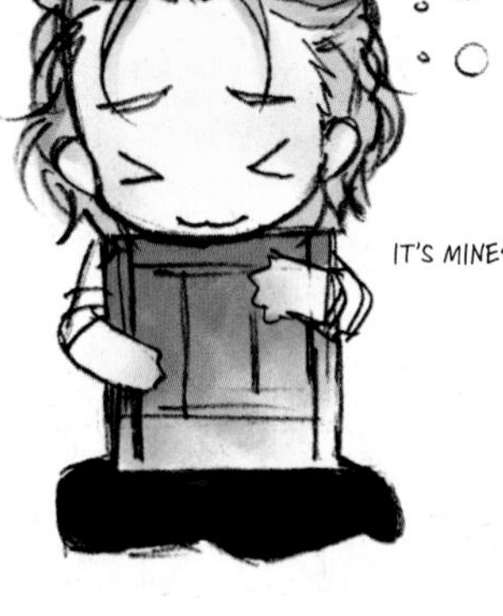
IT'S MINE~.

#27. THE WORD BECOMES THE SEED

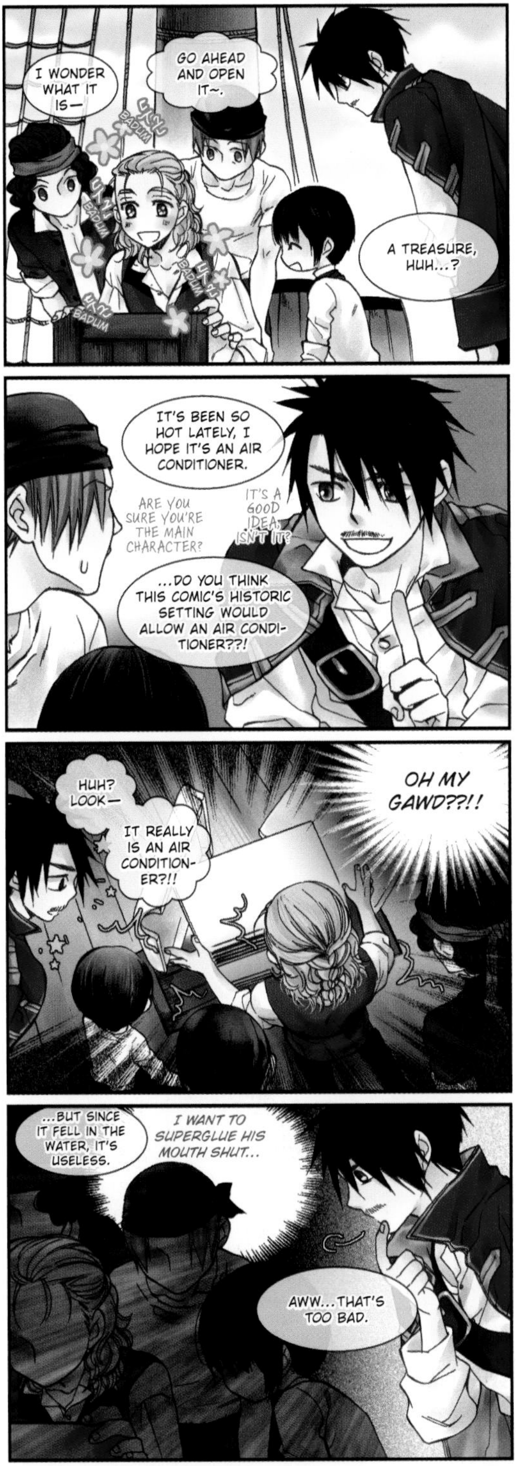
I WONDER WHAT IT IS—
GO AHEAD AND OPEN IT~.
BADUM
BADUM
BADUM
BADUM
A TREASURE, HUH...?
IT'S BEEN SO HOT LATELY, I HOPE IT'S AN AIR CONDITIONER.
ARE YOU SURE YOU'RE THE MAIN CHARACTER?
IT'S A GOOD IDEA, ISN'T IT?
...DO YOU THINK THIS COMIC'S HISTORIC SETTING WOULD ALLOW AN AIR CONDITIONER??!
HUH? LOOK—
IT REALLY IS AN AIR CONDITIONER?!!
OH MY GAWD??!!
...BUT SINCE IT FELL IN THE WATER, IT'S USELESS.
I WANT TO SUPERGLUE HIS MOUTH SHUT...
AWW...THAT'S TOO BAD.

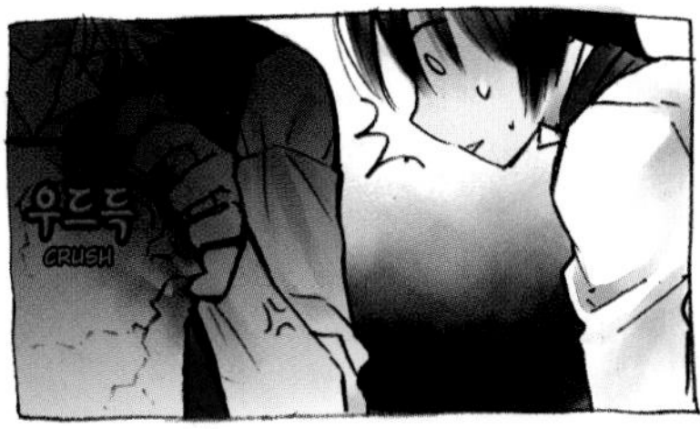
우드득
CRUSH

THANKSGIVING SPECIAL

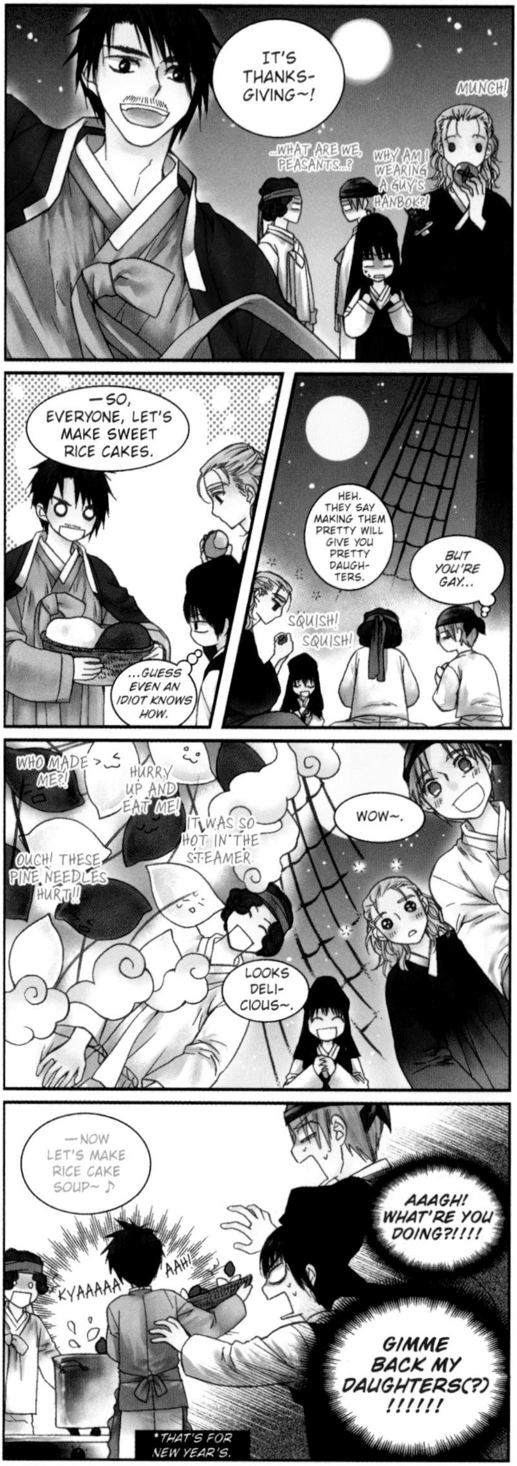

IT'S THANKS-GIVING~!
...WHAT ARE WE, PEASANTS...?
WHY AM I WEARING A GUY'S HANBOK?!
MUNCH!
—SO, EVERYONE, LET'S MAKE SWEET RICE CAKES.
...GUESS EVEN AN IDIOT KNOWS HOW.
HEH. THEY SAY MAKING THEM PRETTY WILL GIVE YOU PRETTY DAUGH-TERS.
BUT YOU'RE GAY...
SQUISH! SQUISH!
WHO MADE ME?!
HURRY UP AND EAT ME!
IT WAS SO HOT IN THE STEAMER.
OUCH! THESE PINE NEEDLES HURT!!
WOW~.
LOOKS DELI-CIOUS~.
—NOW LET'S MAKE RICE CAKE SOUP~ ♪
AAAGH! WHAT'RE YOU DOING?!!!!
KYAAAAA
AAH!
GIMME BACK MY DAUGHTERS(?) !!!!!!
*THAT'S FOR NEW YEAR'S.

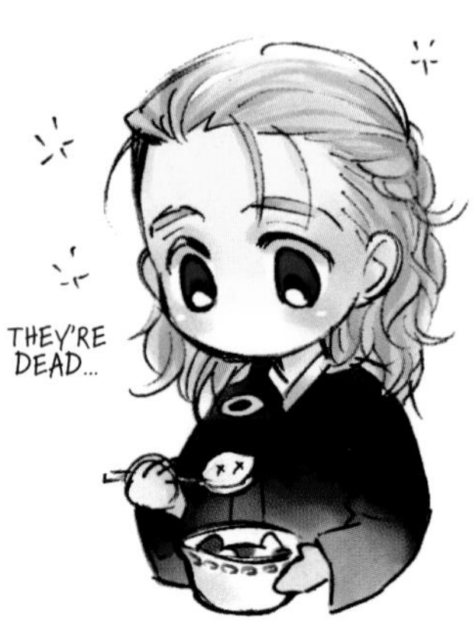

THEY'RE DEAD...

#28. FLIGHT INSTINCT

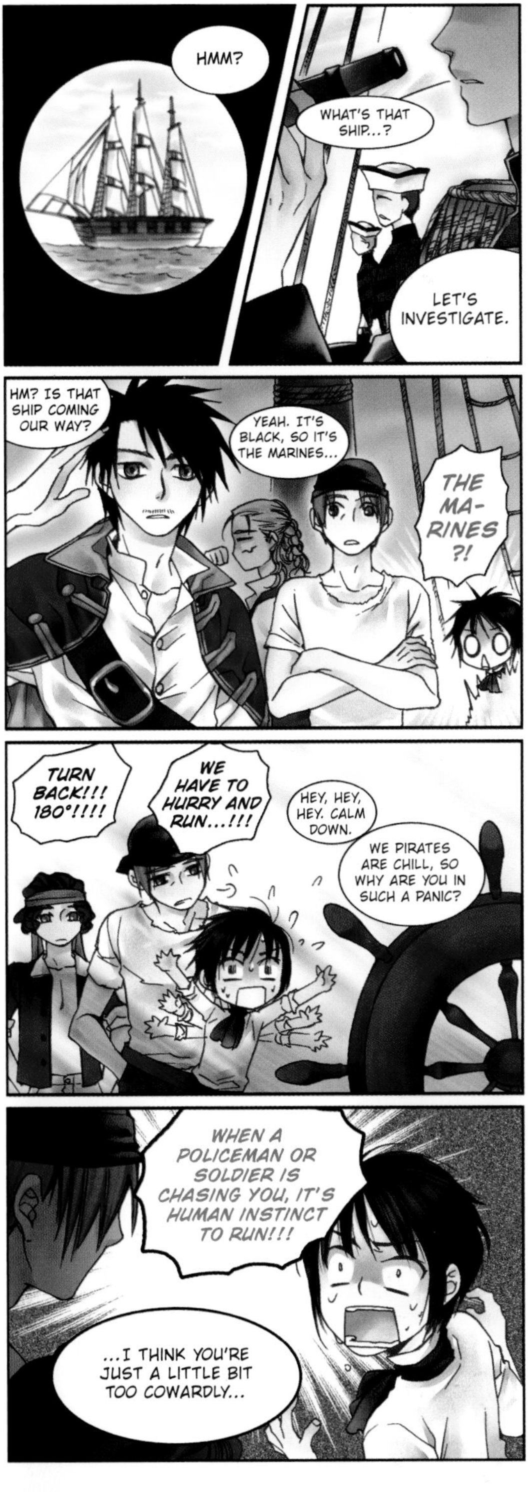

HMM?
WHAT'S THAT SHIP...?
LET'S INVESTIGATE.
HM? IS THAT SHIP COMING OUR WAY?
YEAH. IT'S BLACK, SO IT'S THE MARINES...
THE MA-RINES ?!
TURN BACK!!! 180°!!!!
WE HAVE TO HURRY AND RUN...!!!
HEY, HEY, HEY. CALM DOWN.
WE PIRATES ARE CHILL, SO WHY ARE YOU IN SUCH A PANIC?
WHEN A POLICEMAN OR SOLDIER IS CHASING YOU, IT'S HUMAN INSTINCT TO RUN!!!
...I THINK YOU'RE JUST A LITTLE BIT TOO COWARDLY...

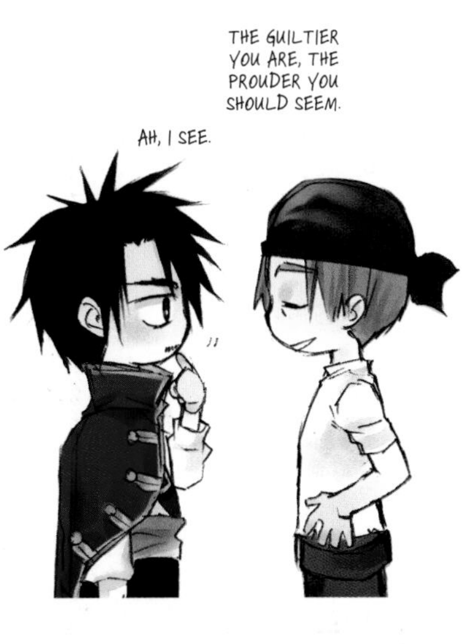

THE GUILTIER YOU ARE, THE PROUDER YOU SHOULD SEEM.
AH, I SEE.

#29. ANYONE CAN BECOME A PIRATE

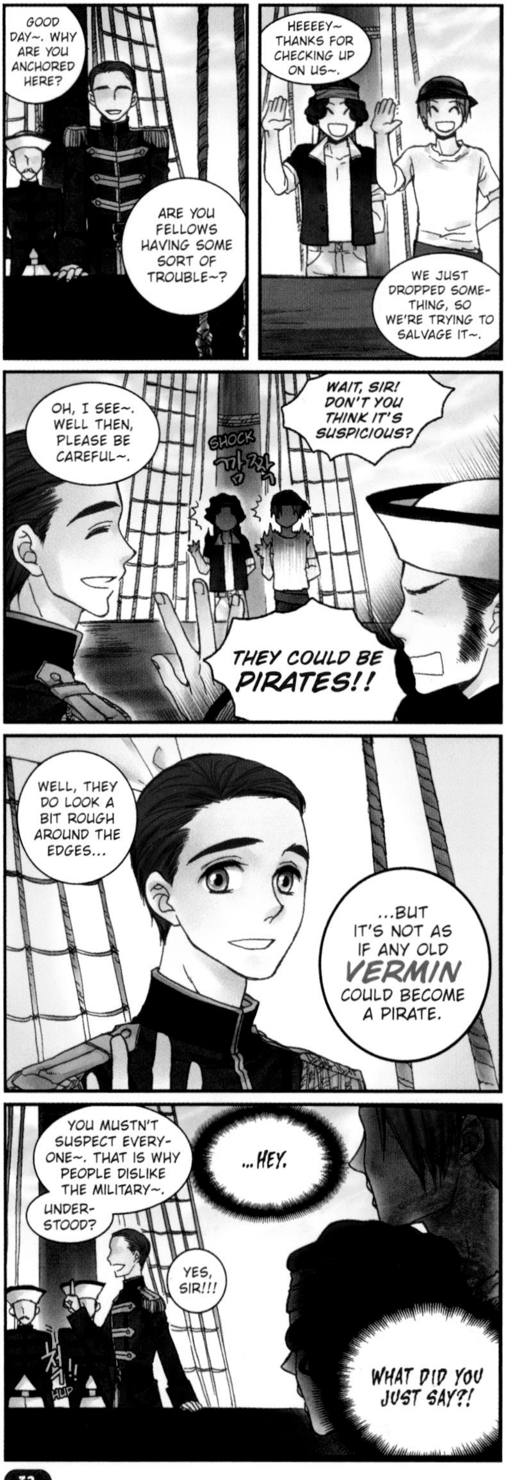
GOOD DAY~. WHY ARE YOU ANCHORED HERE?
ARE YOU FELLOWS HAVING SOME SORT OF TROUBLE~?
HEEEEY~ THANKS FOR CHECKING UP ON US~.
WE JUST DROPPED SOME-THING, SO WE'RE TRYING TO SALVAGE IT~.
OH, I SEE~. WELL THEN, PLEASE BE CAREFUL~.
SHOCK
깜짝
WAIT, SIR! DON'T YOU THINK IT'S SUSPICIOUS?
THEY COULD BE PIRATES!!
WELL, THEY DO LOOK A BIT ROUGH AROUND THE EDGES...
...BUT IT'S NOT AS IF ANY OLD VERMIN COULD BECOME A PIRATE.
YOU MUSTN'T SUSPECT EVERY-ONE~. THAT IS WHY PEOPLE DISLIKE THE MILITARY~.
UNDER-STOOD?
YES, SIR!!!
척!!
HUP
...HEY.
WHAT DID YOU JUST SAY?!

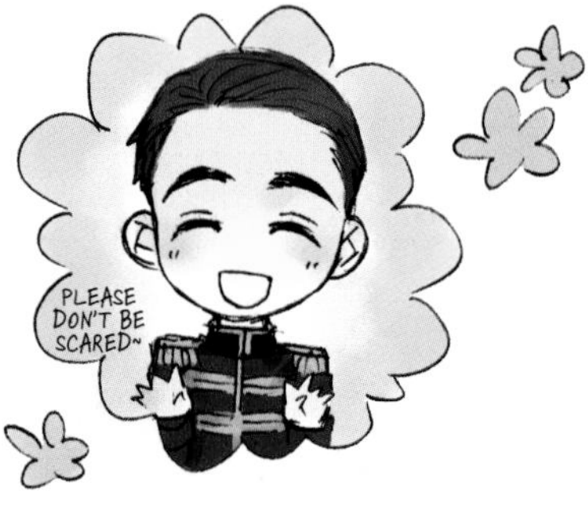
PLEASE DON'T BE SCARED~

#30. NIP IT IN THE BUD

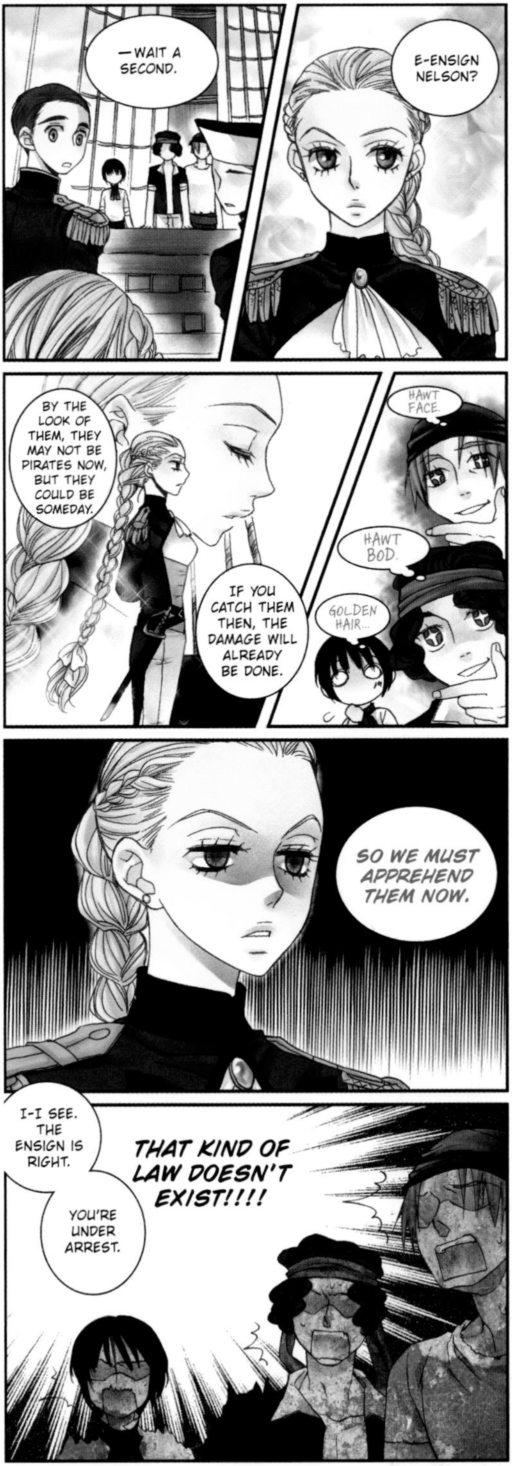
—WAIT A SECOND.
E-ENSIGN NELSON?
BY THE LOOK OF THEM, THEY MAY NOT BE PIRATES NOW, BUT THEY COULD BE SOMEDAY.
IF YOU CATCH THEM THEN, THE DAMAGE WILL ALREADY BE DONE.
HAWT FACE.
HAWT BOD.
GOLDEN HAIR...
SO WE MUST APPREHEND THEM NOW.
I-I SEE. THE ENSIGN IS RIGHT.
YOU'RE UNDER ARREST.
THAT KIND OF LAW DOESN'T EXIST!!!!

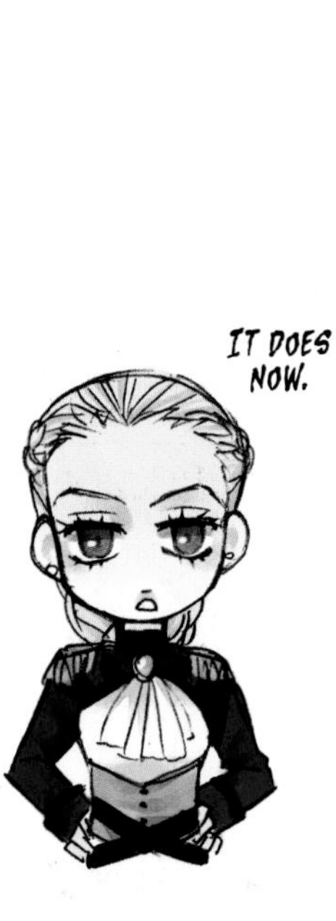
IT DOES NOW.

#31. MOUNTING MINOR MISUNDERSTANDINGS

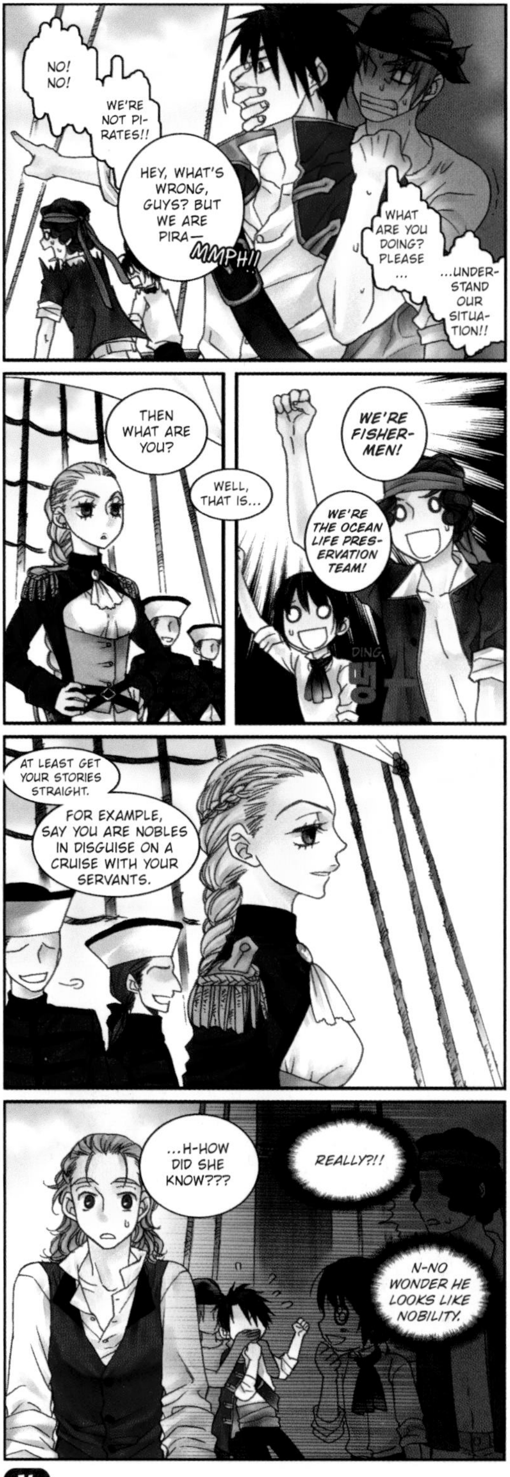
NO! NO!
WE'RE NOT PIRATES!!
HEY, WHAT'S WRONG, GUYS? BUT WE ARE PIRA—
MMPH!!
WHAT ARE YOU DOING? PLEASE ...
...UNDERSTAND OUR SITUATION!!
THEN WHAT ARE YOU?
WELL, THAT IS...
WE'RE FISHERMEN!
WE'RE THE OCEAN LIFE PRESERVATION TEAM!
DING
AT LEAST GET YOUR STORIES STRAIGHT.
FOR EXAMPLE, SAY YOU ARE NOBLES IN DISGUISE ON A CRUISE WITH YOUR SERVANTS.
...H-HOW DID SHE KNOW???
REALLY?!!
N-NO WONDER HE LOOKS LIKE NOBILITY.

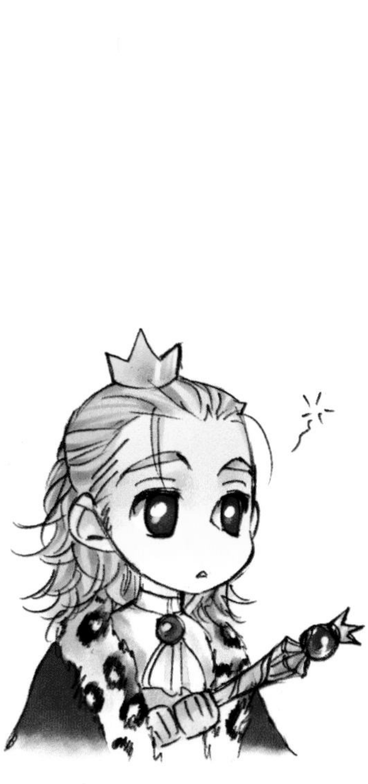

#32. A SUBORDINATE MORE QUALIFIED THAN THE SUPERIOR

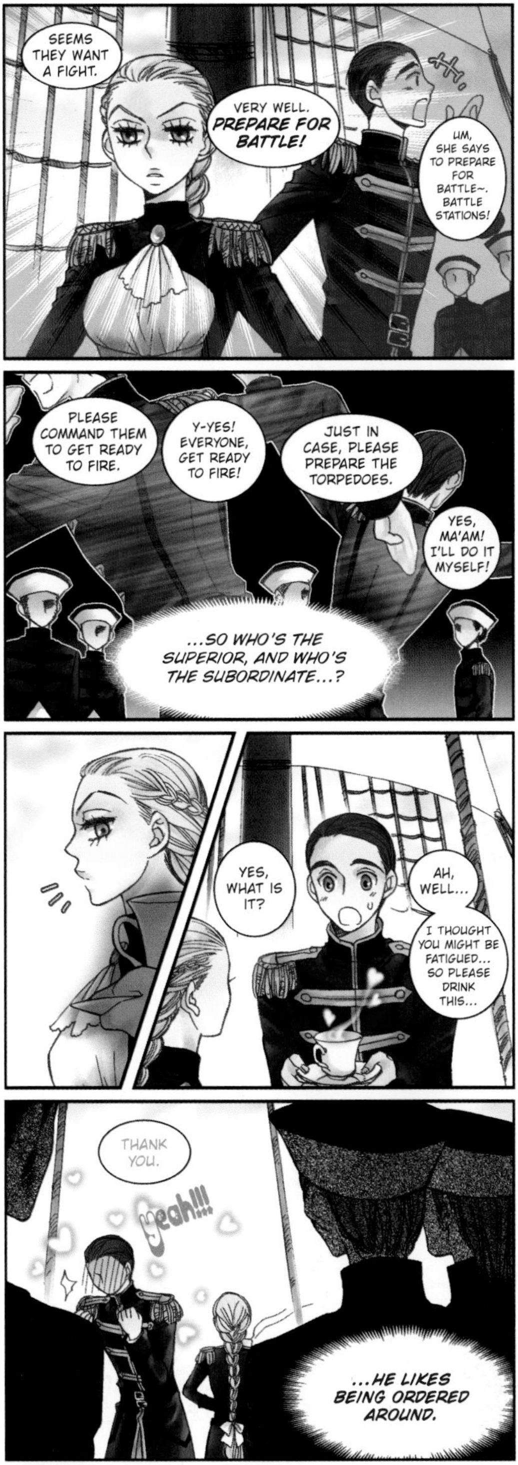
SEEMS THEY WANT A FIGHT.
VERY WELL. PREPARE FOR BATTLE!
UM, SHE SAYS TO PREPARE FOR BATTLE~. BATTLE STATIONS!
PLEASE COMMAND THEM TO GET READY TO FIRE.
Y-YES! EVERYONE, GET READY TO FIRE!
JUST IN CASE, PLEASE PREPARE THE TORPEDOES.
YES, MA'AM! I'LL DO IT MYSELF!
...SO WHO'S THE SUPERIOR, AND WHO'S THE SUBORDINATE...?
YES, WHAT IS IT?
AH, WELL...
I THOUGHT YOU MIGHT BE FATIGUED... SO PLEASE DRINK THIS...
THANK YOU.
Yeah!!!
...HE LIKES BEING ORDERED AROUND.

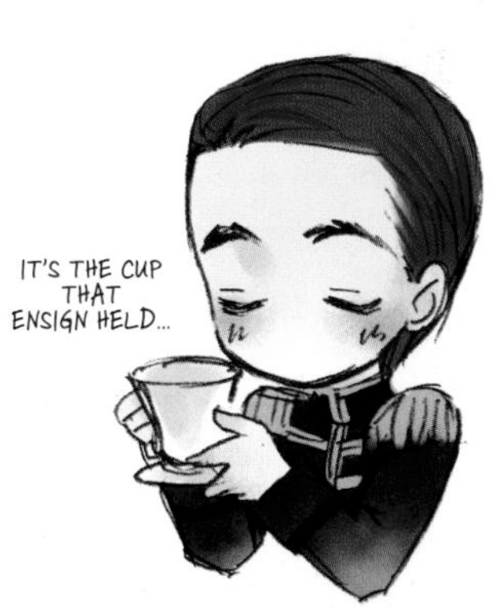
IT'S THE CUP THAT ENSIGN HELD...

*HE'S NOT THINKING DIRTY THOUGHTS.

#33. AN ANGEL JUST FOR YOU

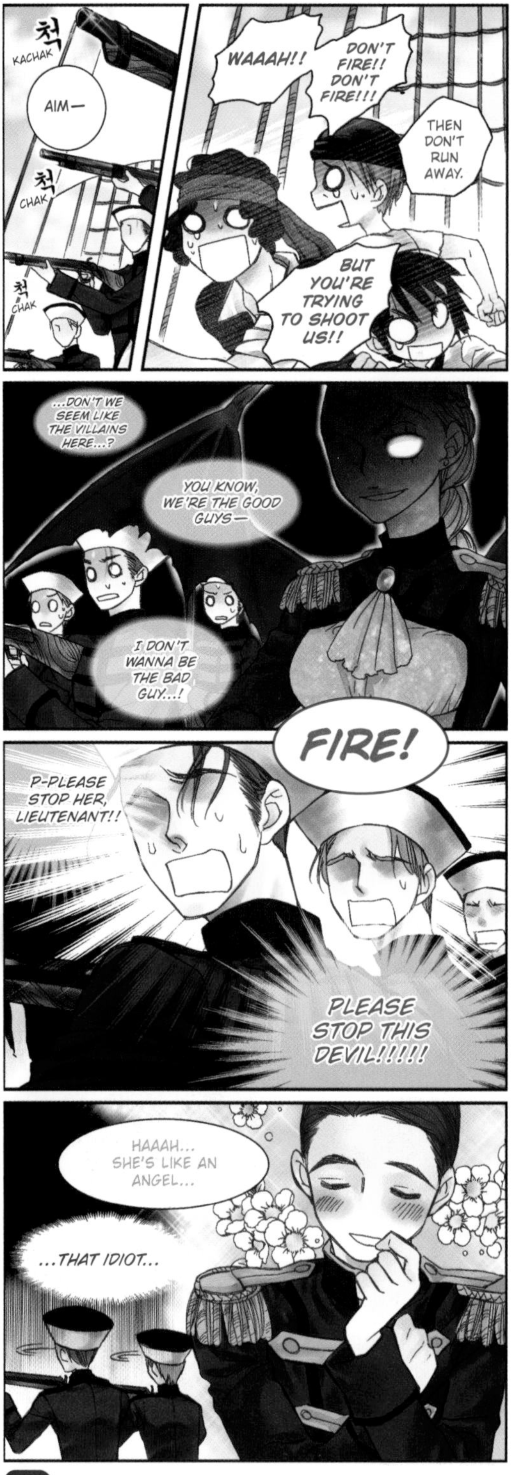
척
KACHAK
AIM—
척
CHAK
척
CHAK
WAAAH!!
DON'T FIRE!! DON'T FIRE!!!
THEN DON'T RUN AWAY.
BUT YOU'RE TRYING TO SHOOT US!!
...DON'T WE SEEM LIKE THE VILLAINS HERE...?
YOU KNOW, WE'RE THE GOOD GUYS—
I DON'T WANNA BE THE BAD GUY...!
FIRE!
P-PLEASE STOP HER, LIEUTENANT!!
PLEASE STOP THIS DEVIL!!!!!
HAAAH... SHE'S LIKE AN ANGEL...
...THAT IDIOT...

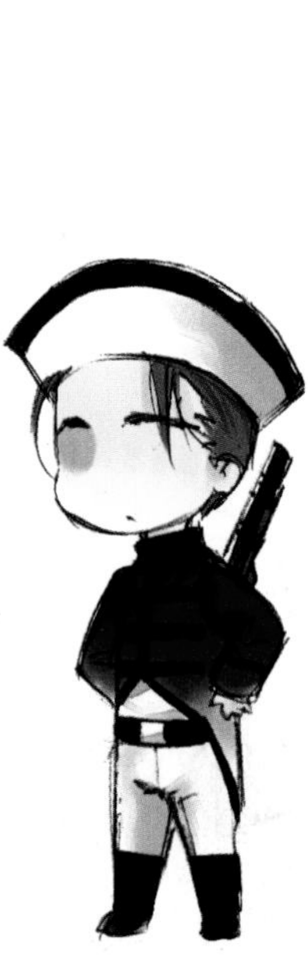

#34. YOU MEET YOUR FRIEND ON A SINGLE-LOG BRIDGE

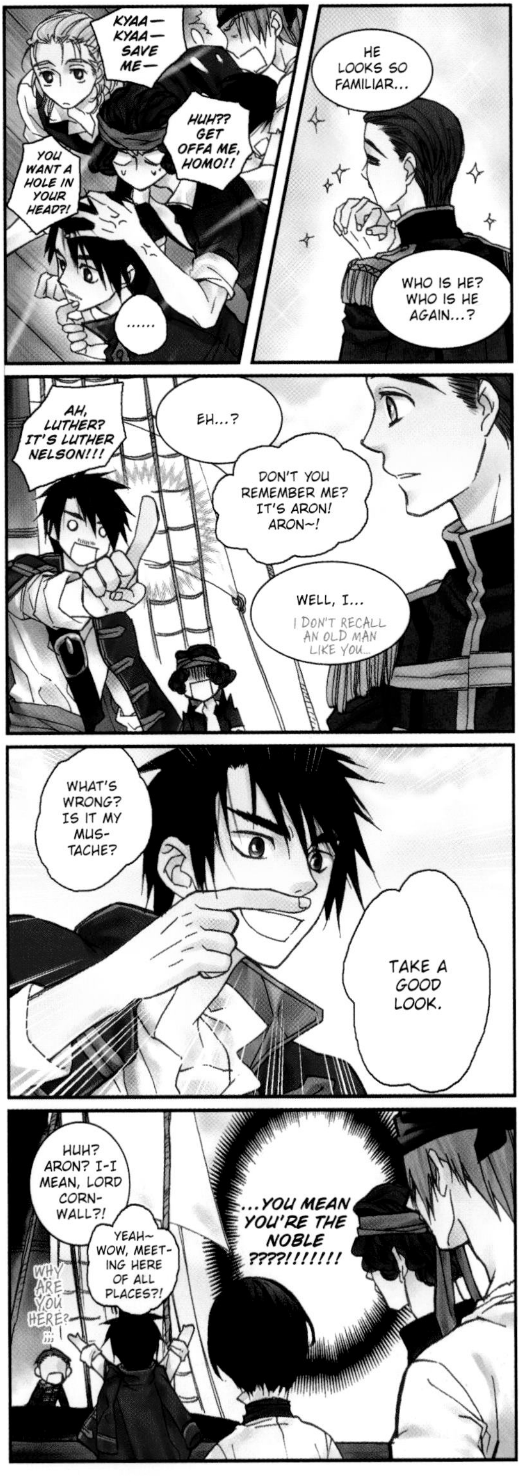
KYAA— KYAA— SAVE ME—
HUH?? GET OFFA ME, HOMO!!
YOU WANT A HOLE IN YOUR HEAD?!
......
HE LOOKS SO FAMILIAR...
WHO IS HE? WHO IS HE AGAIN...?
AH, LUTHER? IT'S LUTHER NELSON!!!
EH...?
DON'T YOU REMEMBER ME? IT'S ARON! ARON~!
WELL, I...
I DON'T RECALL AN OLD MAN LIKE YOU...
WHAT'S WRONG? IS IT MY MUS-TACHE?
TAKE A GOOD LOOK.
HUH? ARON? I-I MEAN, LORD CORN-WALL?!
YEAH~ WOW, MEET-ING HERE OF ALL PLACES?!
WHY ARE YOU HERE? ;;;
...YOU MEAN YOU'RE THE NOBLE ????!!!!!!!

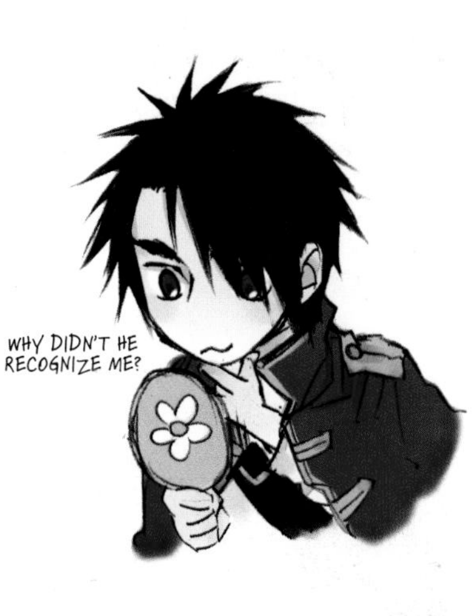
WHY DIDN'T HE RECOGNIZE ME?

#35. THE TRUTH AND THE SHOCK

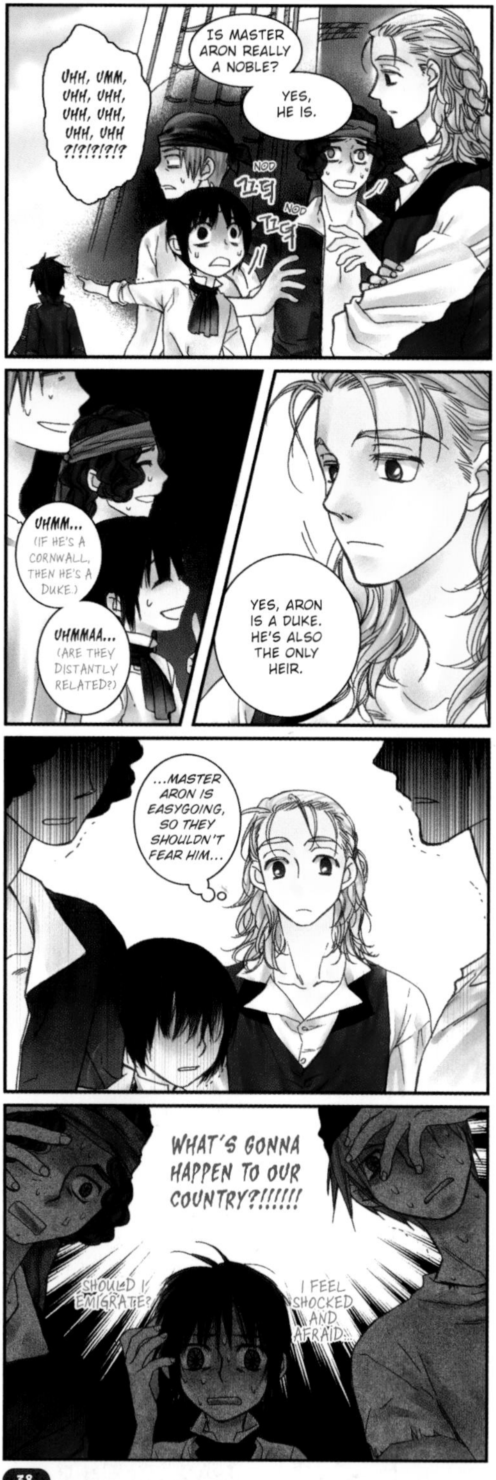
UHH, UMM, UHH, UHH, UHH, UHH, UHH, UHH ?!?!?!?!?
IS MASTER ARON REALLY A NOBLE?
YES, HE IS.
NOD 끄덕
NOD 끄덕
UHMM... (IF HE'S A CORNWALL, THEN HE'S A DUKE.)
UHMMAA... (ARE THEY DISTANTLY RELATED?)
YES, ARON IS A DUKE. HE'S ALSO THE ONLY HEIR.
...MASTER ARON IS EASYGOING, SO THEY SHOULDN'T FEAR HIM...
WHAT'S GONNA HAPPEN TO OUR COUNTRY?!!!!!!
SHOULD I EMIGRATE?
I FEEL SHOCKED AND AFRAID...

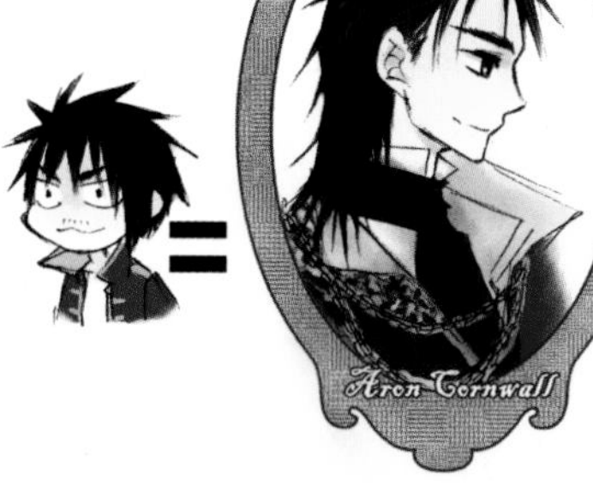
Aron Cornwall

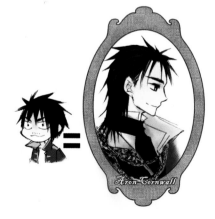

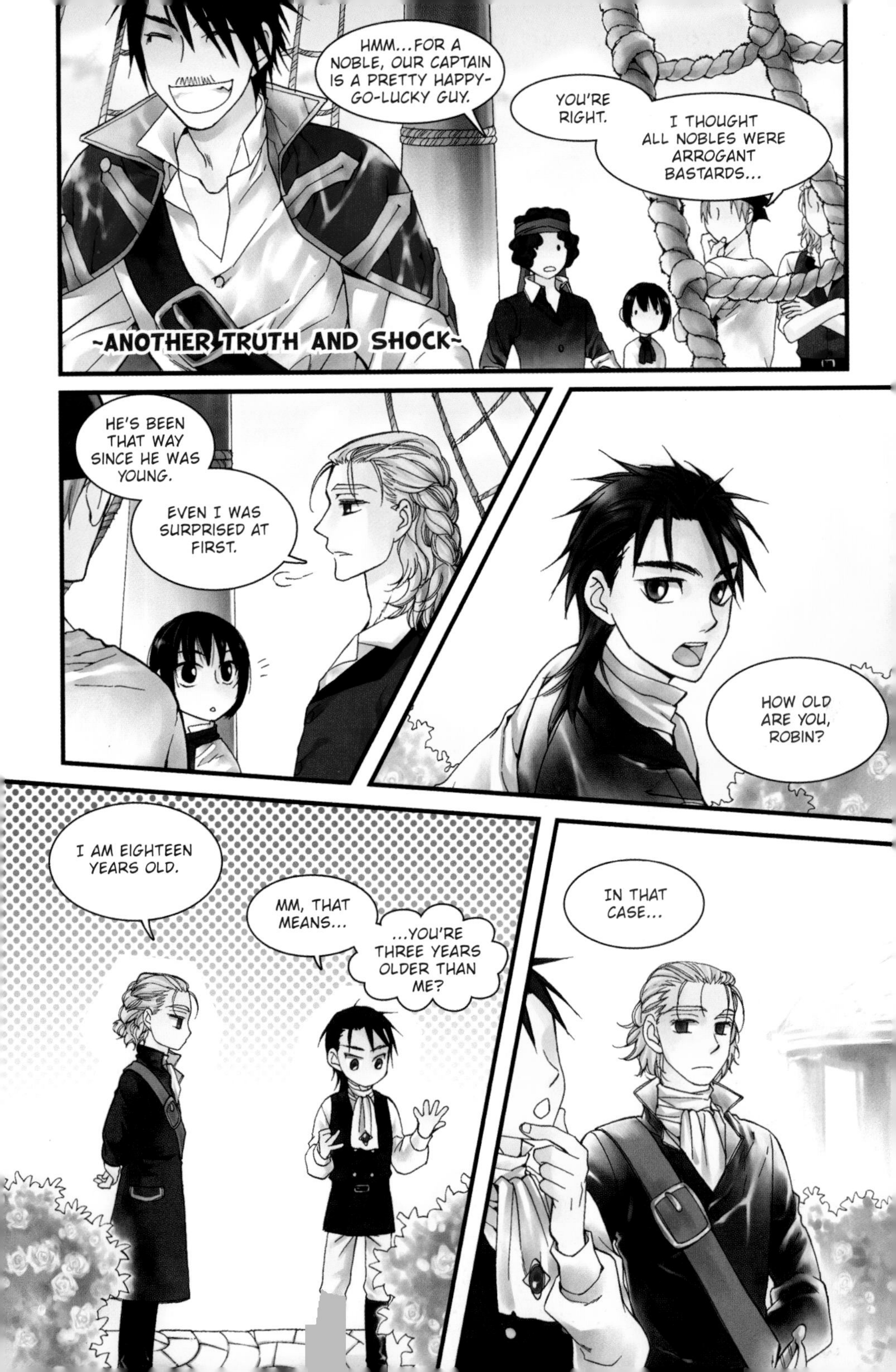
HMM...FOR A NOBLE, OUR CAPTAIN IS A PRETTY HAPPY-GO-LUCKY GUY.
YOU'RE RIGHT.
I THOUGHT ALL NOBLES WERE ARROGANT BASTARDS...
~ANOTHER TRUTH AND SHOCK~
HE'S BEEN THAT WAY SINCE HE WAS YOUNG.
EVEN I WAS SURPRISED AT FIRST.
HOW OLD ARE YOU, ROBIN?
I AM EIGHTEEN YEARS OLD.
MM, THAT MEANS...
...YOU'RE THREE YEARS OLDER THAN ME?
IN THAT CASE...

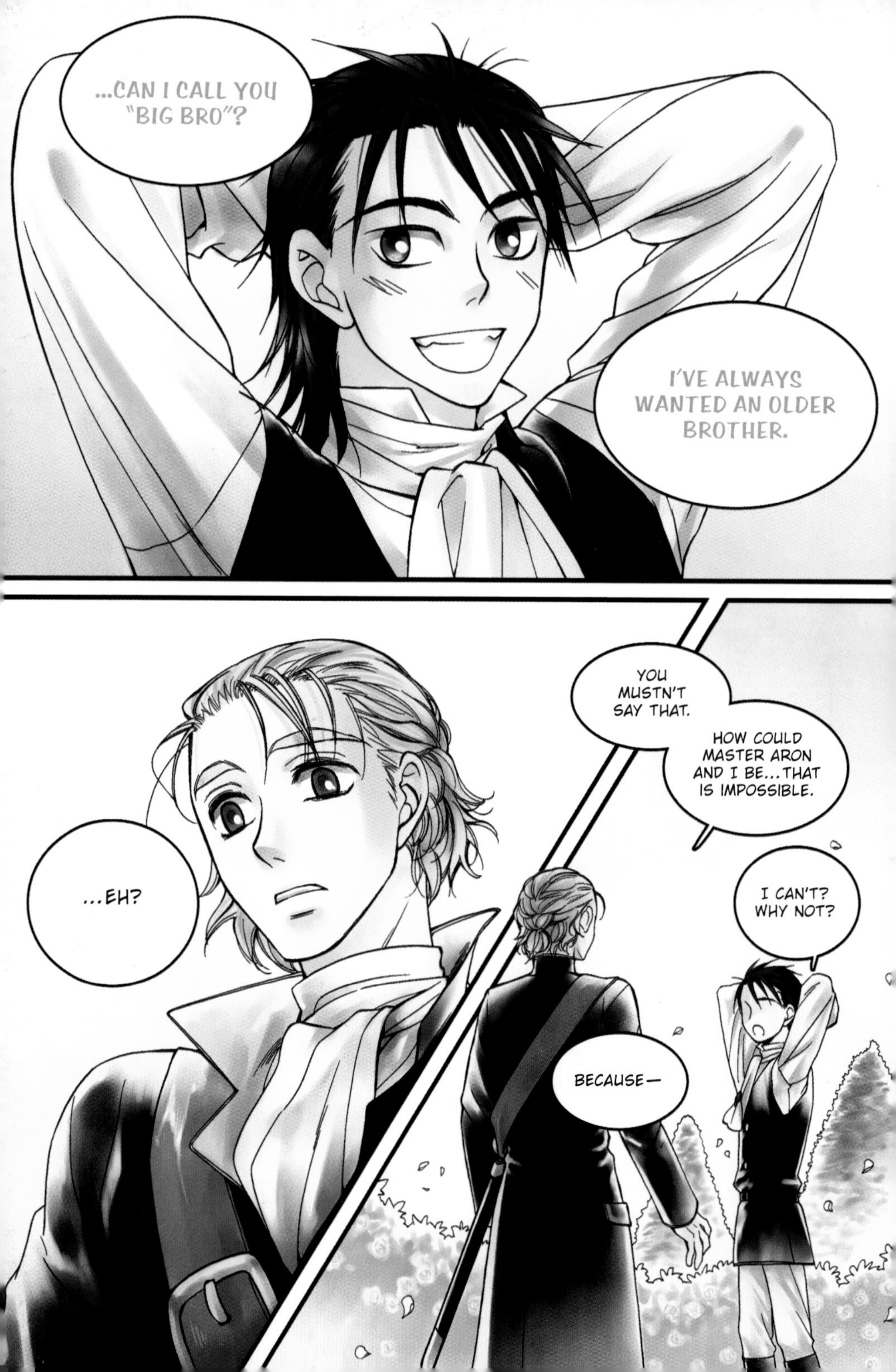
...CAN I CALL YOU "BIG BRO"?
I'VE ALWAYS WANTED AN OLDER BROTHER.
YOU MUSTN'T SAY THAT.
HOW COULD MASTER ARON AND I BE...THAT IS IMPOSSIBLE.
...EH?
I CAN'T? WHY NOT?
BECAUSE—

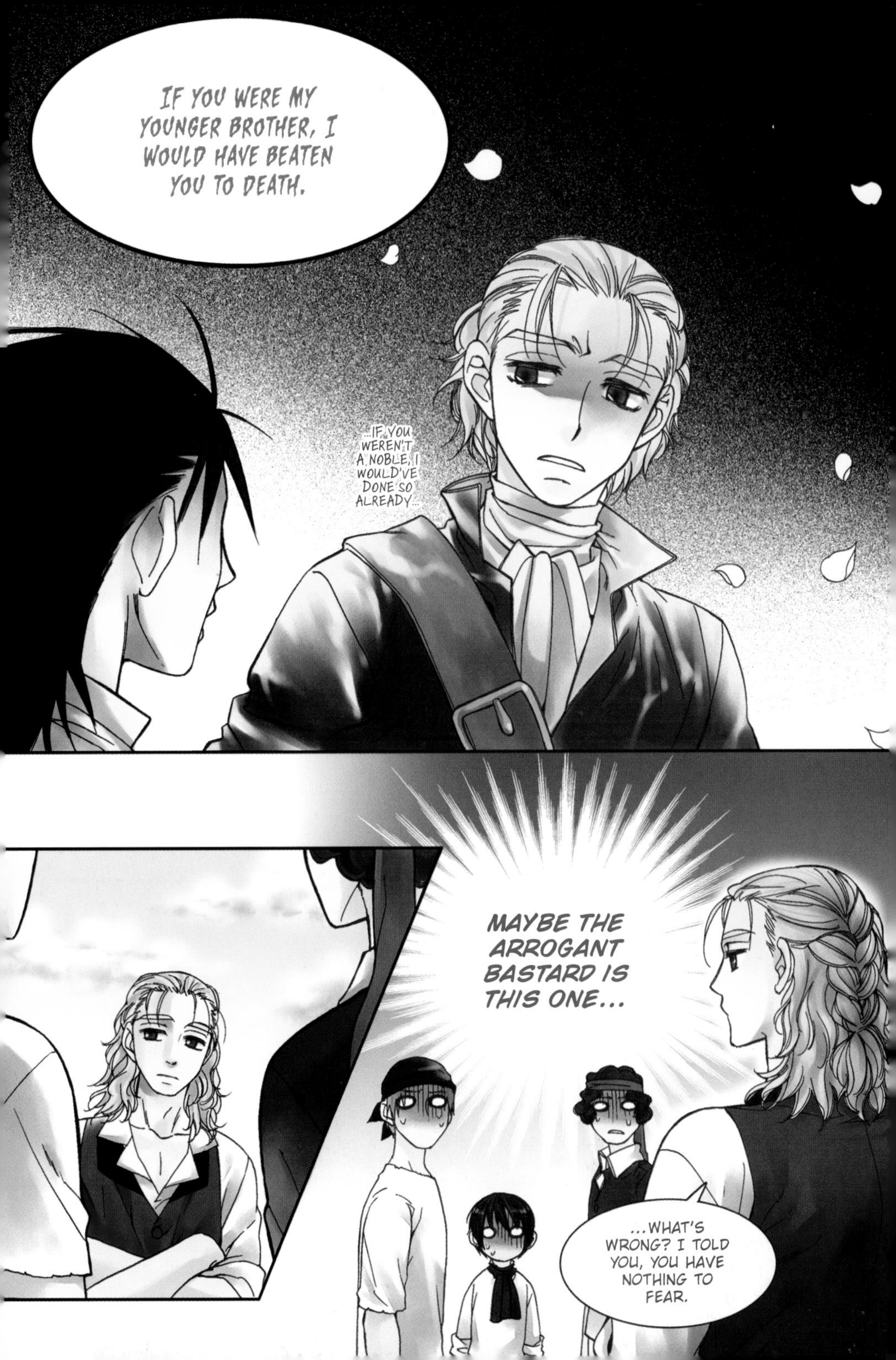
IF YOU WERE MY YOUNGER BROTHER, I WOULD HAVE BEATEN YOU TO DEATH.
...IF YOU WEREN'T A NOBLE, I WOULD'VE DONE SO ALREADY...
MAYBE THE ARROGANT BASTARD IS THIS ONE...
...WHAT'S WRONG? I TOLD YOU, YOU HAVE NOTHING TO FEAR.

#36. NOSTALGIA IS A BEAUTIFUL THING

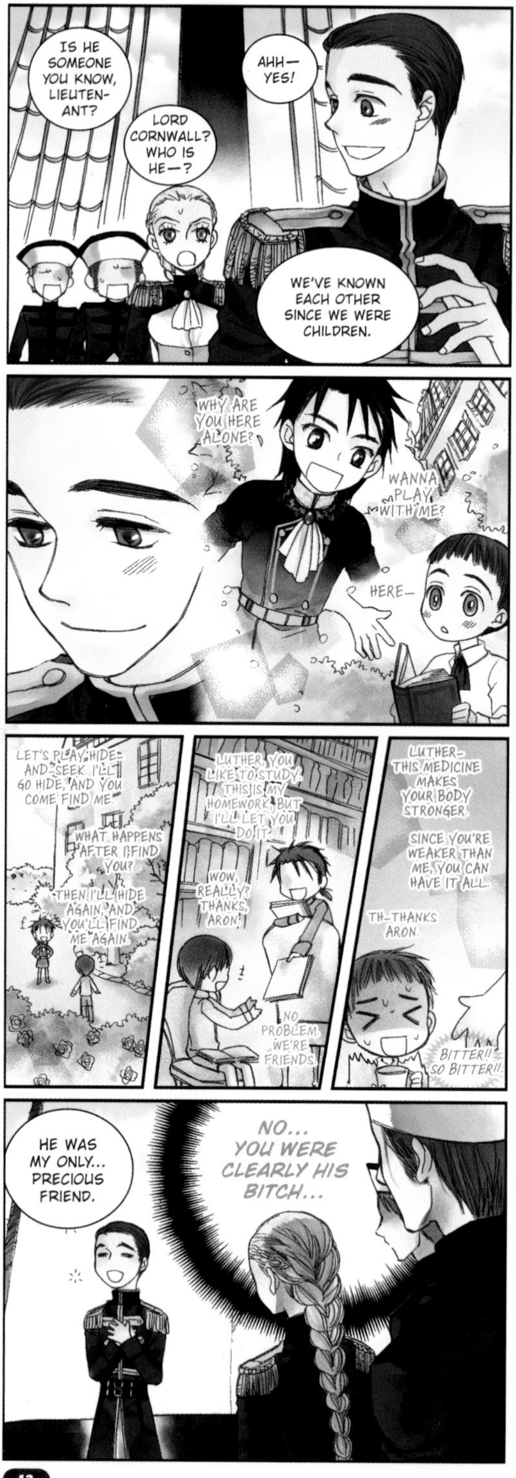

IS HE SOMEONE YOU KNOW, LIEUTEN-ANT?
LORD CORNWALL? WHO IS HE—?
AHH— YES!
WE'VE KNOWN EACH OTHER SINCE WE WERE CHILDREN.
WHY ARE YOU HERE ALONE?
WANNA PLAY WITH ME?
HERE—
LET'S PLAY HIDE-AND-SEEK. I'LL GO HIDE, AND YOU COME FIND ME.
WHAT HAPPENS AFTER I FIND YOU?
THEN I'LL HIDE AGAIN, AND YOU'LL FIND ME AGAIN.
LUTHER, YOU LIKE TO STUDY. THIS IS MY HOMEWORK, BUT I'LL LET YOU DO IT.
WOW, REALLY? THANKS, ARON.
NO PROBLEM. WE'RE FRIENDS.
LUTHER-THIS MEDICINE MAKES YOUR BODY STRONGER.
SINCE YOU'RE WEAKER THAN ME, YOU CAN HAVE IT ALL.
TH-THANKS ARON.
BITTER!! SO BITTER!!
HE WAS MY ONLY... PRECIOUS FRIEND.
NO... YOU WERE CLEARLY HIS BITCH...

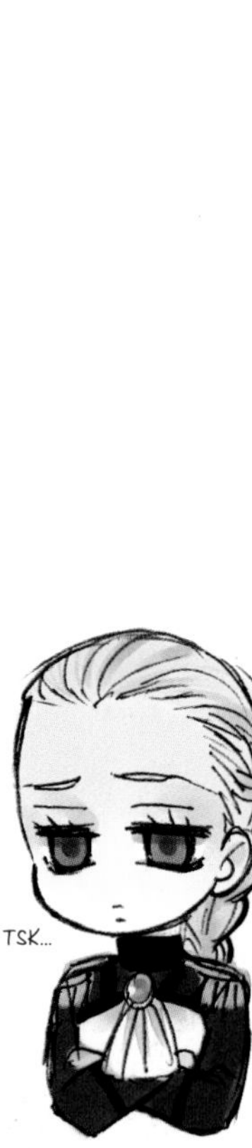

TSK, TSK...

#37. THOUGH IT'S NOT SAID ALOUD, WE KNOW

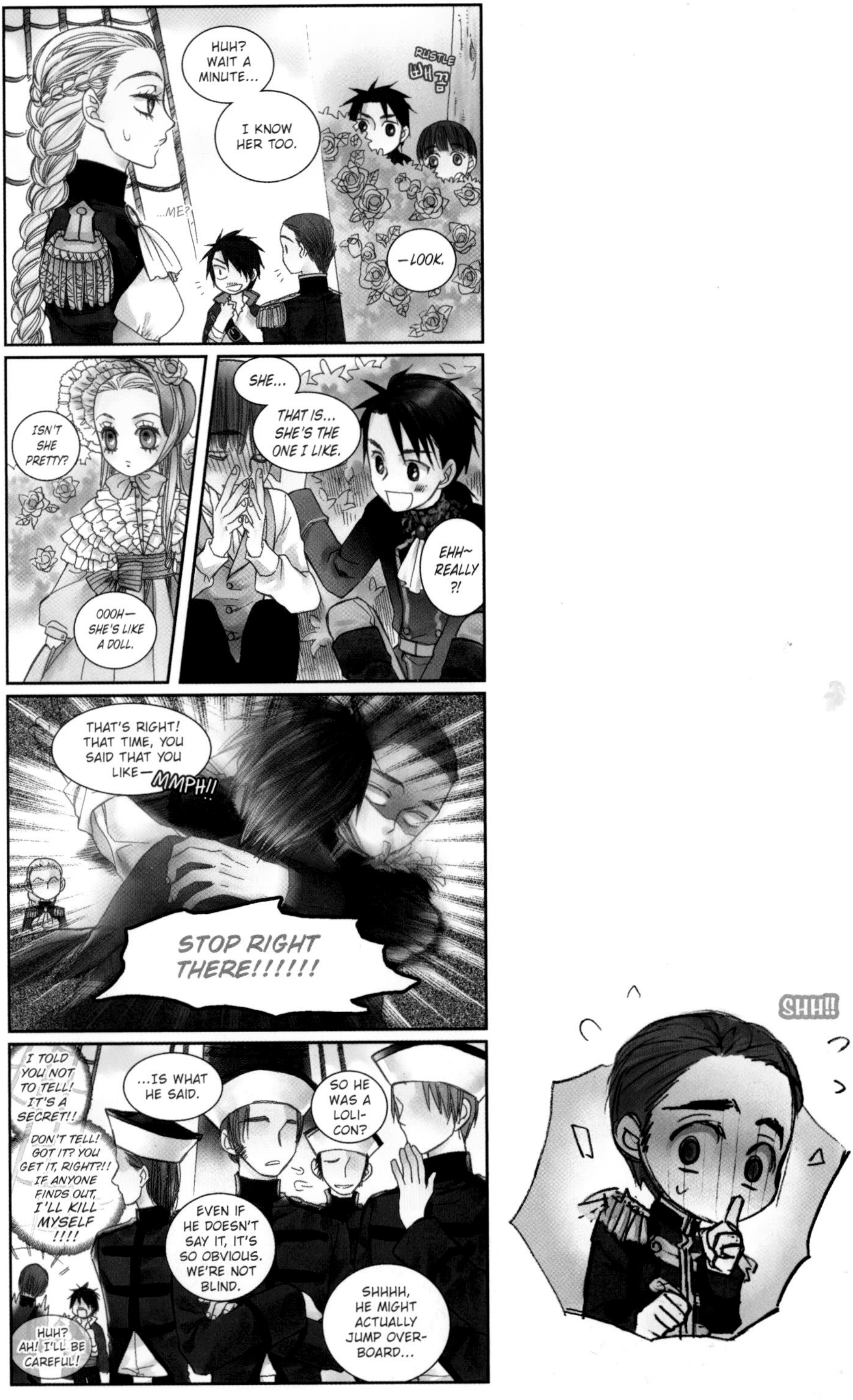
HUH? WAIT A MINUTE...
I KNOW HER TOO.
RUSTLE
빼꼼
...ME?
—LOOK.
ISN'T SHE PRETTY?
OOOH— SHE'S LIKE A DOLL.
SHE...
THAT IS... SHE'S THE ONE I LIKE.
EHH~ REALLY ?!
THAT'S RIGHT! THAT TIME, YOU SAID THAT YOU LIKE—
MMPH!!
STOP RIGHT THERE!!!!!!
I TOLD YOU NOT TO TELL! IT'S A SECRET!!
DON'T TELL! GOT IT? YOU GET IT, RIGHT?!! IF ANYONE FINDS OUT, I'LL KILL MYSELF !!!!
HUH? AH! I'LL BE CAREFUL!
...IS WHAT HE SAID.
SO HE WAS A LOLI-CON?
EVEN IF HE DOESN'T SAY IT, IT'S SO OBVIOUS. WE'RE NOT BLIND.
SHHHH, HE MIGHT ACTUALLY JUMP OVER-BOARD...
SHH!!

#38. NO PROBLEM

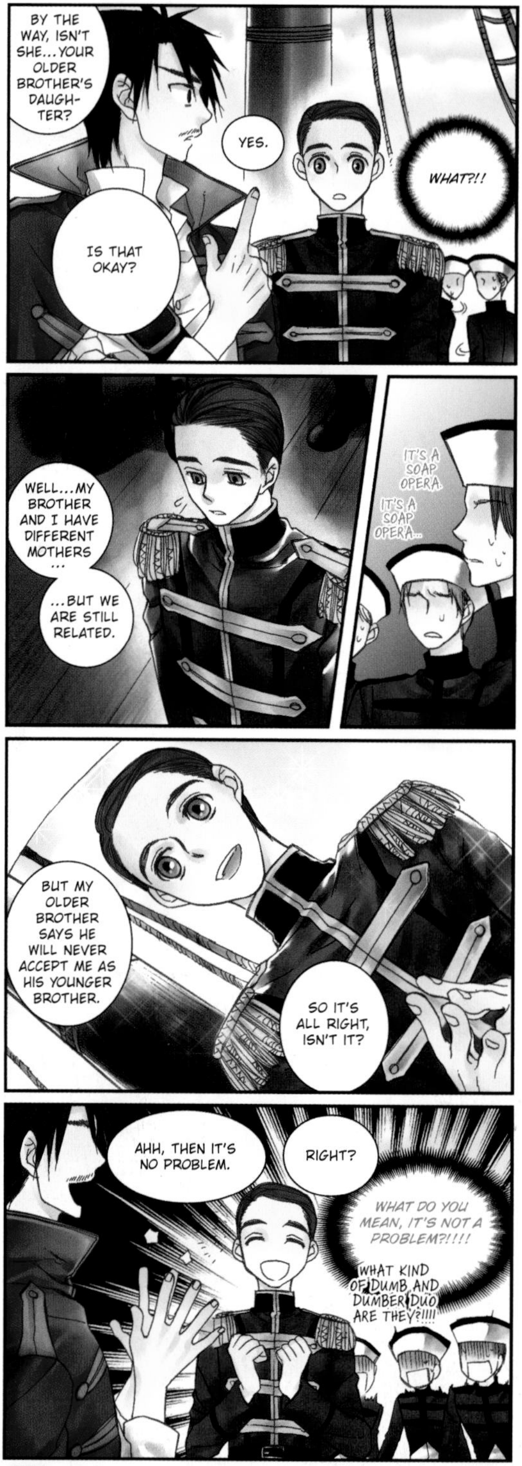
BY THE WAY, ISN'T SHE...YOUR OLDER BROTHER'S DAUGH-TER?
YES.
WHAT?!!
IS THAT OKAY?
WELL...MY BROTHER AND I HAVE DIFFERENT MOTHERS...
...BUT WE ARE STILL RELATED.
IT'S A SOAP OPERA.
IT'S A SOAP OPERA...
BUT MY OLDER BROTHER SAYS HE WILL NEVER ACCEPT ME AS HIS YOUNGER BROTHER.
SO IT'S ALL RIGHT, ISN'T IT?
AHH, THEN IT'S NO PROBLEM.
RIGHT?
WHAT DO YOU MEAN, IT'S NOT A PROBLEM?!!!!
WHAT KIND OF DUMB AND DUMBER DUO ARE THEY?!!!!

NELSON FAMILY

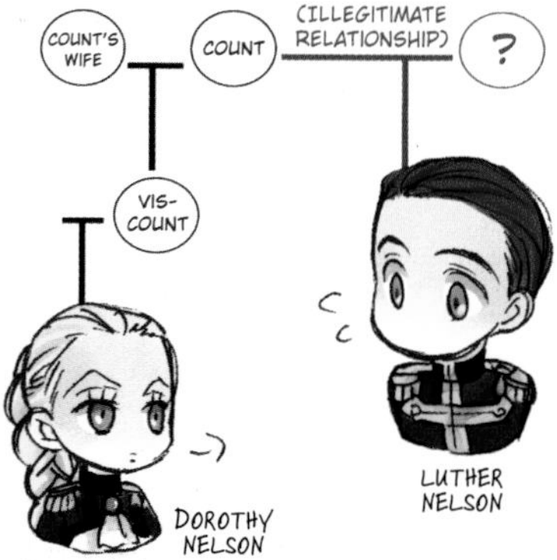
COUNT'S WIFE
COUNT
(ILLEGITIMATE RELATIONSHIP)
?
VIS-COUNT
DOROTHY NELSON
LUTHER NELSON

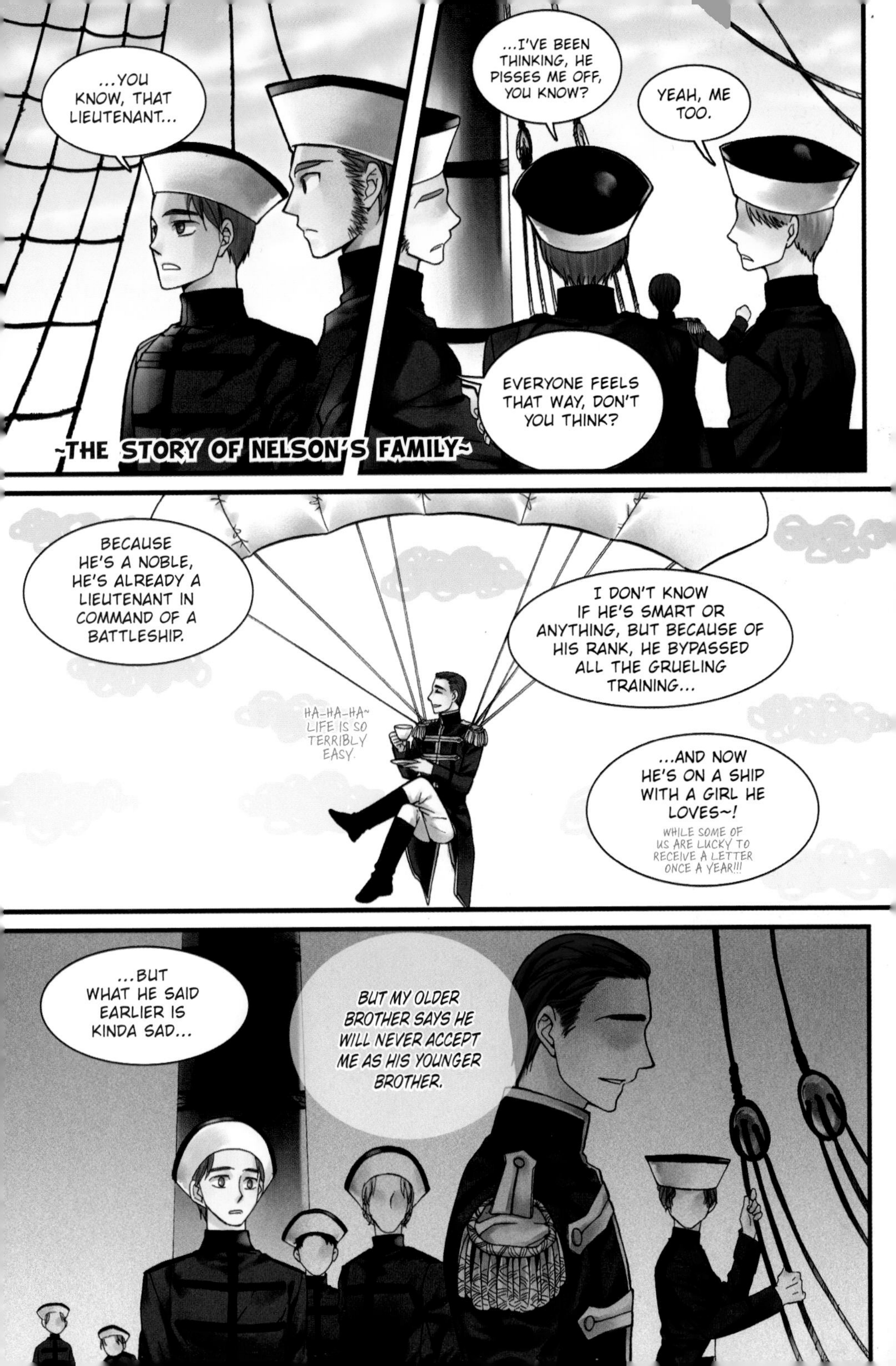
...YOU KNOW, THAT LIEUTENANT...
...I'VE BEEN THINKING, HE PISSES ME OFF, YOU KNOW?
YEAH, ME TOO.
EVERYONE FEELS THAT WAY, DON'T YOU THINK?
~THE STORY OF NELSON'S FAMILY~
BECAUSE HE'S A NOBLE, HE'S ALREADY A LIEUTENANT IN COMMAND OF A BATTLESHIP.
I DON'T KNOW IF HE'S SMART OR ANYTHING, BUT BECAUSE OF HIS RANK, HE BYPASSED ALL THE GRUELING TRAINING...
HA-HA-HA~ LIFE IS SO TERRIBLY EASY.
...AND NOW HE'S ON A SHIP WITH A GIRL HE LOVES~!
WHILE SOME OF US ARE LUCKY TO RECEIVE A LETTER ONCE A YEAR!!!
...BUT WHAT HE SAID EARLIER IS KINDA SAD...
BUT MY OLDER BROTHER SAYS HE WILL NEVER ACCEPT ME AS HIS YOUNGER BROTHER.

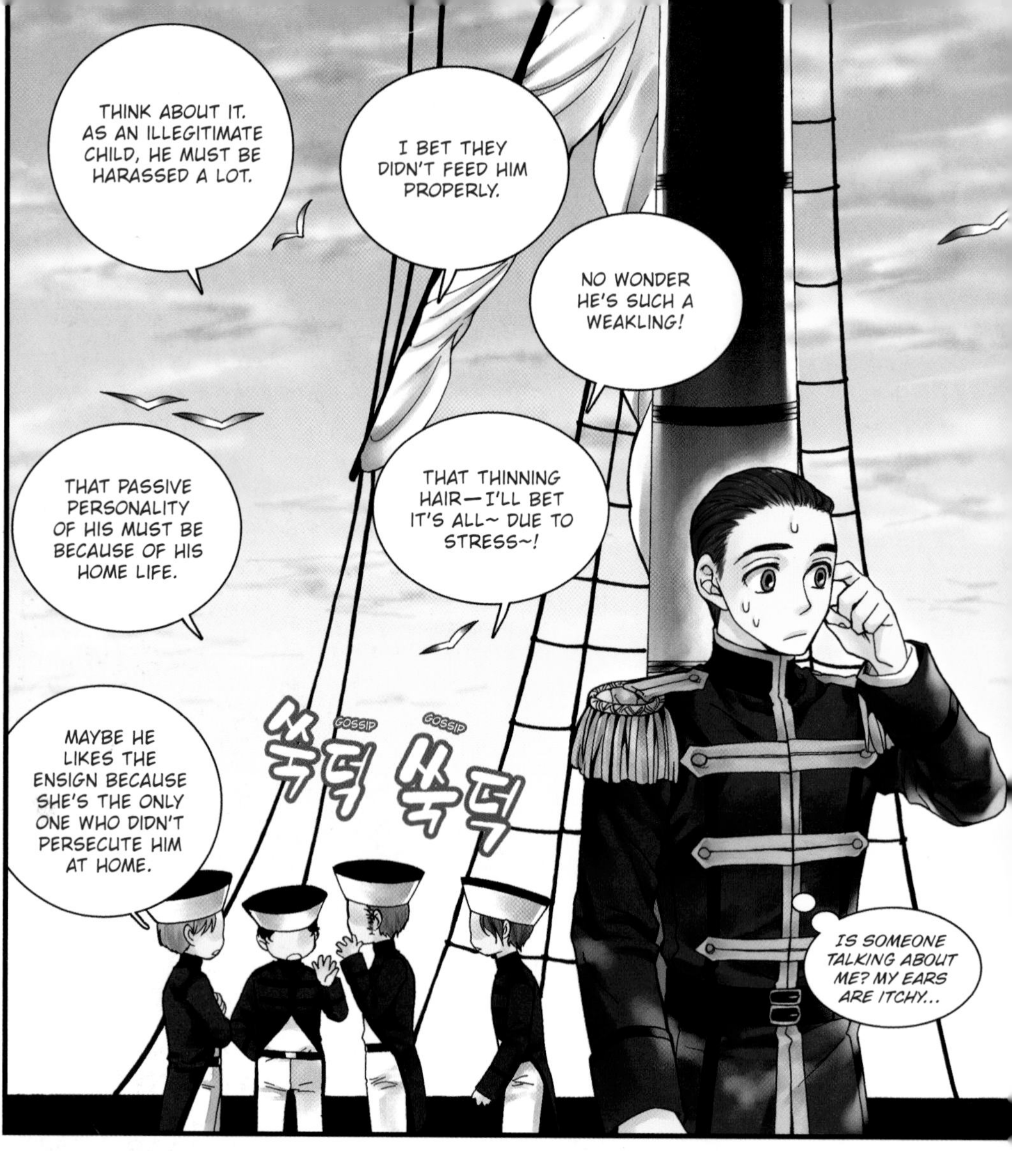
THINK ABOUT IT. AS AN ILLEGITIMATE CHILD, HE MUST BE HARASSED A LOT.
I BET THEY DIDN'T FEED HIM PROPERLY.
NO WONDER HE'S SUCH A WEAKLING!
THAT PASSIVE PERSONALITY OF HIS MUST BE BECAUSE OF HIS HOME LIFE.
THAT THINNING HAIR—I'LL BET IT'S ALL~ DUE TO STRESS~!
MAYBE HE LIKES THE ENSIGN BECAUSE SHE'S THE ONLY ONE WHO DIDN'T PERSECUTE HIM AT HOME.
쑥덕 GOSSIP 쑥덕 GOSSIP
IS SOMEONE TALKING ABOUT ME? MY EARS ARE ITCHY...
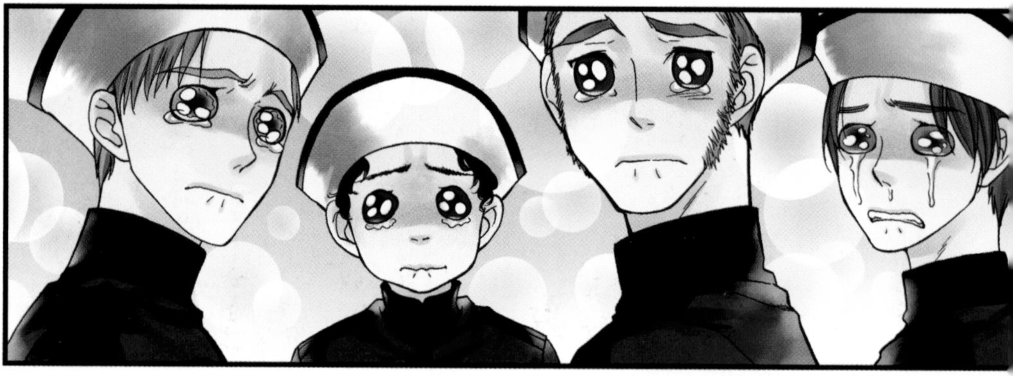

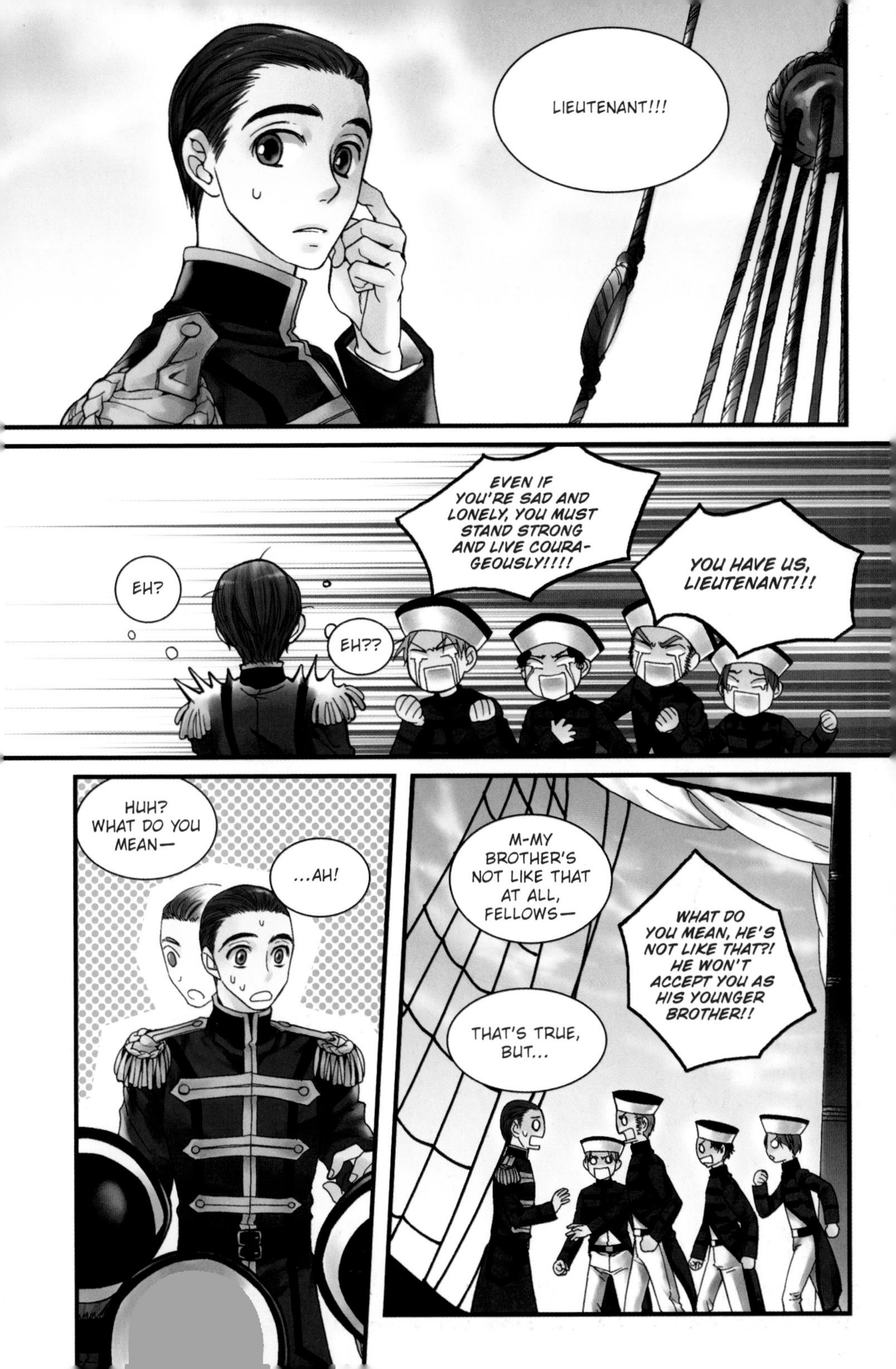
LIEUTENANT!!!
EH?
EH??
EVEN IF YOU'RE SAD AND LONELY, YOU MUST STAND STRONG AND LIVE COURAGEOUSLY!!!!
YOU HAVE US, LIEUTENANT!!!
HUH? WHAT DO YOU MEAN—
...AH!
M-MY BROTHER'S NOT LIKE THAT AT ALL, FELLOWS—
WHAT DO YOU MEAN, HE'S NOT LIKE THAT?! HE WON'T ACCEPT YOU AS HIS YOUNGER BROTHER!!
THAT'S TRUE, BUT...

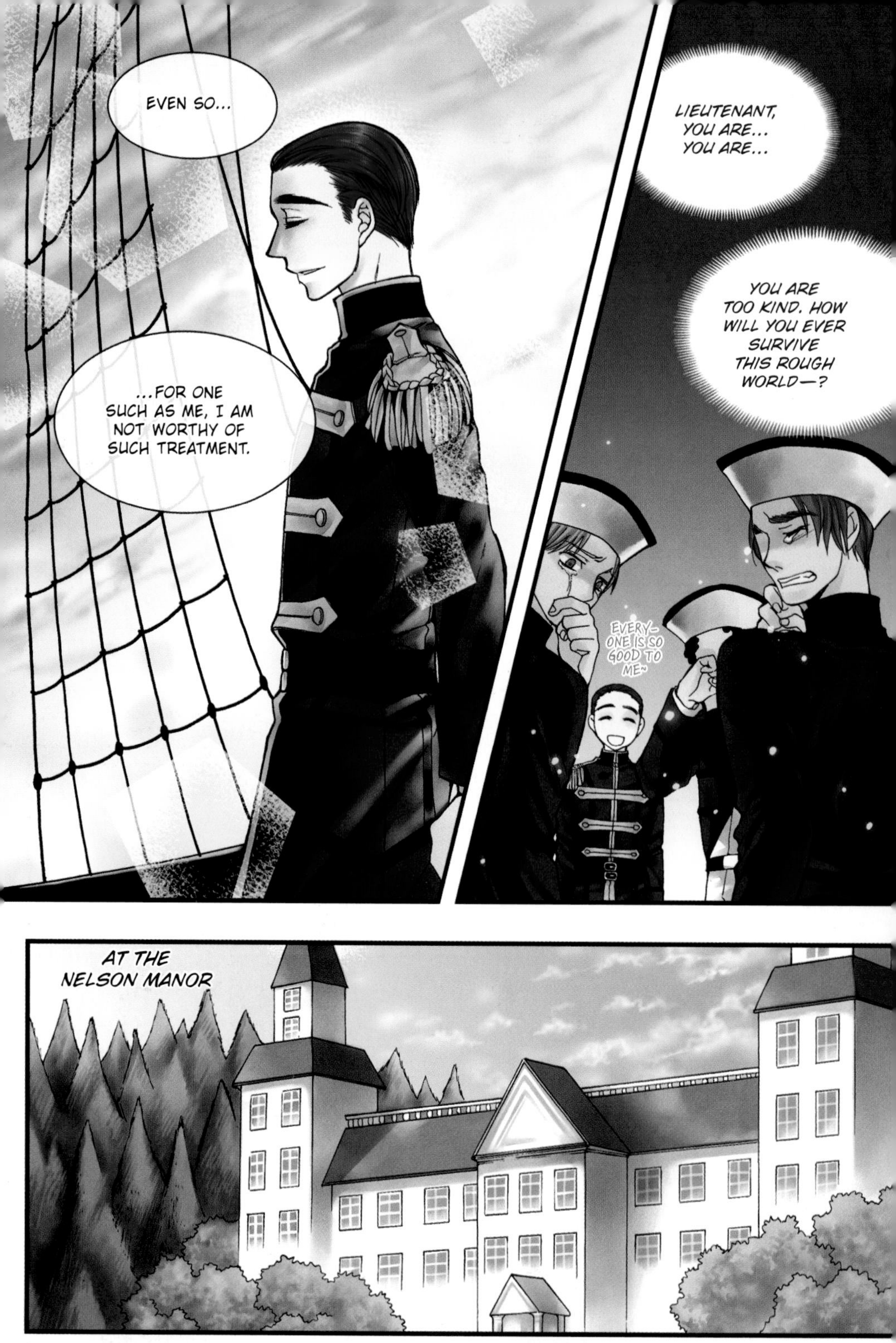
EVEN SO...
...FOR ONE SUCH AS ME, I AM NOT WORTHY OF SUCH TREATMENT.
LIEUTENANT, YOU ARE... YOU ARE...
YOU ARE TOO KIND. HOW WILL YOU EVER SURVIVE THIS ROUGH WORLD—?
EVERY-ONE IS SO GOOD TO ME~
AT THE NELSON MANOR

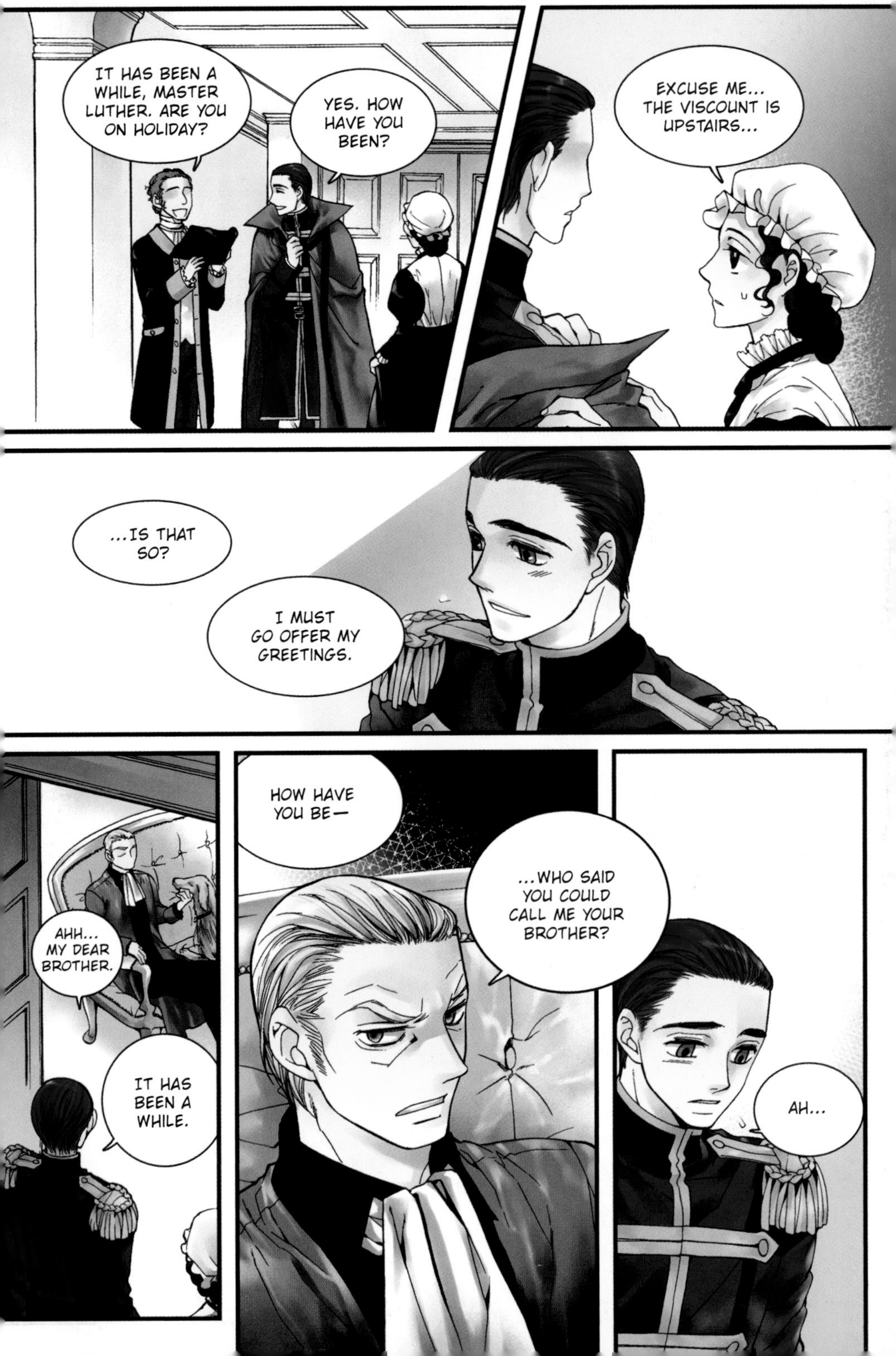
IT HAS BEEN A WHILE, MASTER LUTHER. ARE YOU ON HOLIDAY?
YES. HOW HAVE YOU BEEN?
EXCUSE ME... THE VISCOUNT IS UPSTAIRS...
...IS THAT SO?
I MUST GO OFFER MY GREETINGS.
AHH... MY DEAR BROTHER.
IT HAS BEEN A WHILE.
HOW HAVE YOU BE—
...WHO SAID YOU COULD CALL ME YOUR BROTHER?
AH...

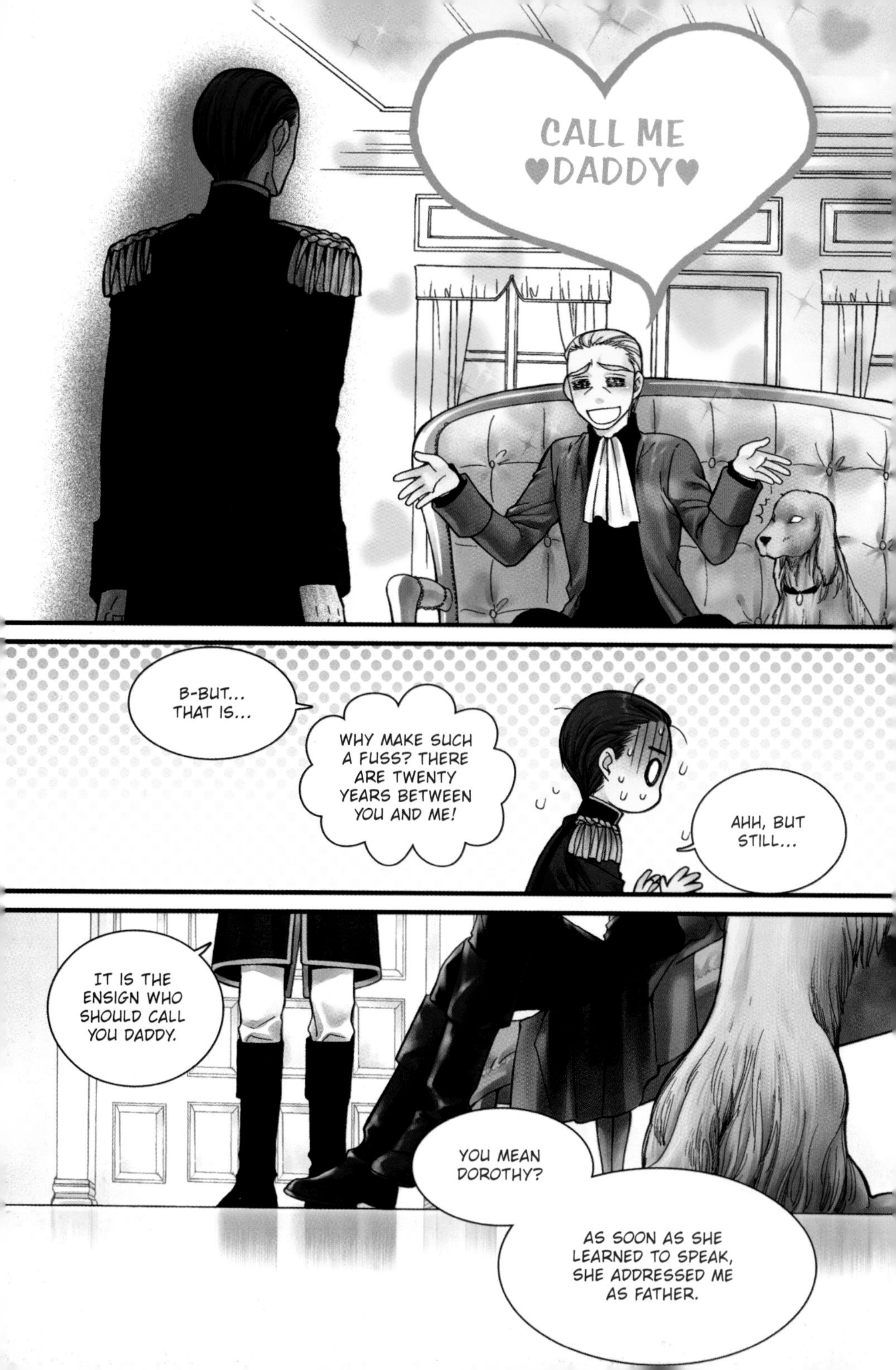
CALL ME ♥DADDY♥
B-BUT... THAT IS...
WHY MAKE SUCH A FUSS? THERE ARE TWENTY YEARS BETWEEN YOU AND ME!
AHH, BUT STILL...
IT IS THE ENSIGN WHO SHOULD CALL YOU DADDY.
YOU MEAN DOROTHY?
AS SOON AS SHE LEARNED TO SPEAK, SHE ADDRESSED ME AS FATHER.

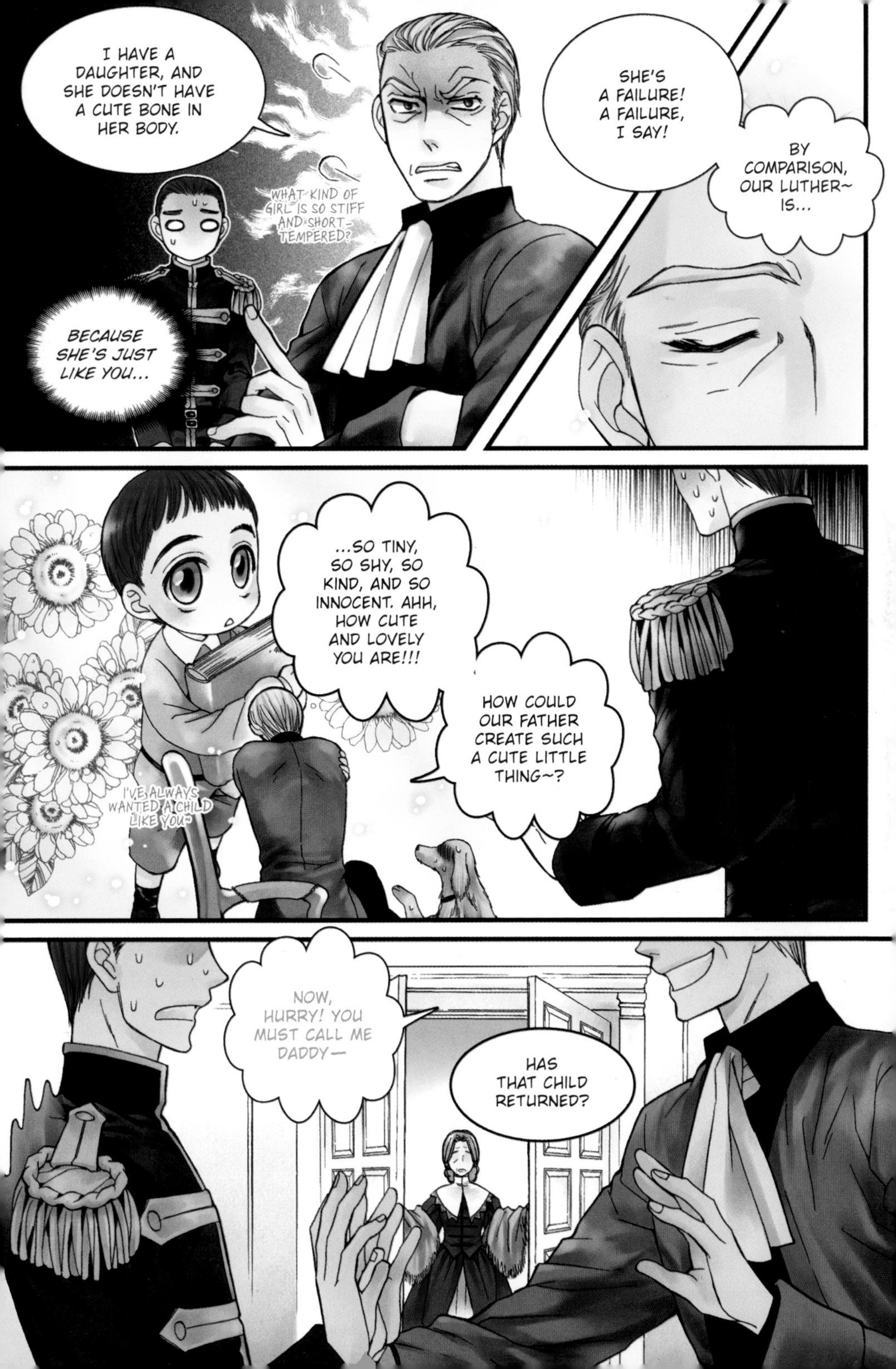
I HAVE A DAUGHTER, AND SHE DOESN'T HAVE A CUTE BONE IN HER BODY.
WHAT KIND OF GIRL IS SO STIFF AND SHORT-TEMPERED?
BECAUSE SHE'S JUST LIKE YOU...
SHE'S A FAILURE! A FAILURE, I SAY!
BY COMPARISON, OUR LUTHER~ IS...
...SO TINY, SO SHY, SO KIND, AND SO INNOCENT. AHH, HOW CUTE AND LOVELY YOU ARE!!!
I'VE ALWAYS WANTED A CHILD LIKE YOU~
HOW COULD OUR FATHER CREATE SUCH A CUTE LITTLE THING~?
NOW, HURRY! YOU MUST CALL ME DADDY—
HAS THAT CHILD RETURNED?

AHH...

...MOTHER...

ARTHUR, NOT YOU AGAIN...!

I TOLD YOU NOT TO BULLY OUR LUTHER—

I'M NOT BULLYING HIM—

HOW COULD YOU?

ARE YOU NOT ASHAMED THAT HE'S ENDURING SUCH HARDSHIP IN THE MILITARY IN YOUR STEAD?

WHAT CAN I DO? I'M ALLERGIC TO SEAWATER.

IT'S YOUR FAULT FOR GIVING BIRTH TO ME THIS WAY.

YOU MUST BE TIRED. YOU LOOK LIKE YOU'VE LOST MORE WEIGHT.

I'M SO SORRY THAT YOU'VE HAD TO GO THROUGH SO MUCH BECAUSE OF HIM...

WHEN I THINK OF MY BROTHER... I MEAN...

...WHEN I THINK OF THE VISCOUNT, I FEEL STRONGER.

AHH, NO, NOT AT ALL—

...I'M SORRY.

NO, REALLY. I AM ALL RI—

...THAT'S NOT IT.

I'M SORRY THAT WE CANNOT REGISTER YOU AS OUR LEGITIMATE SON...

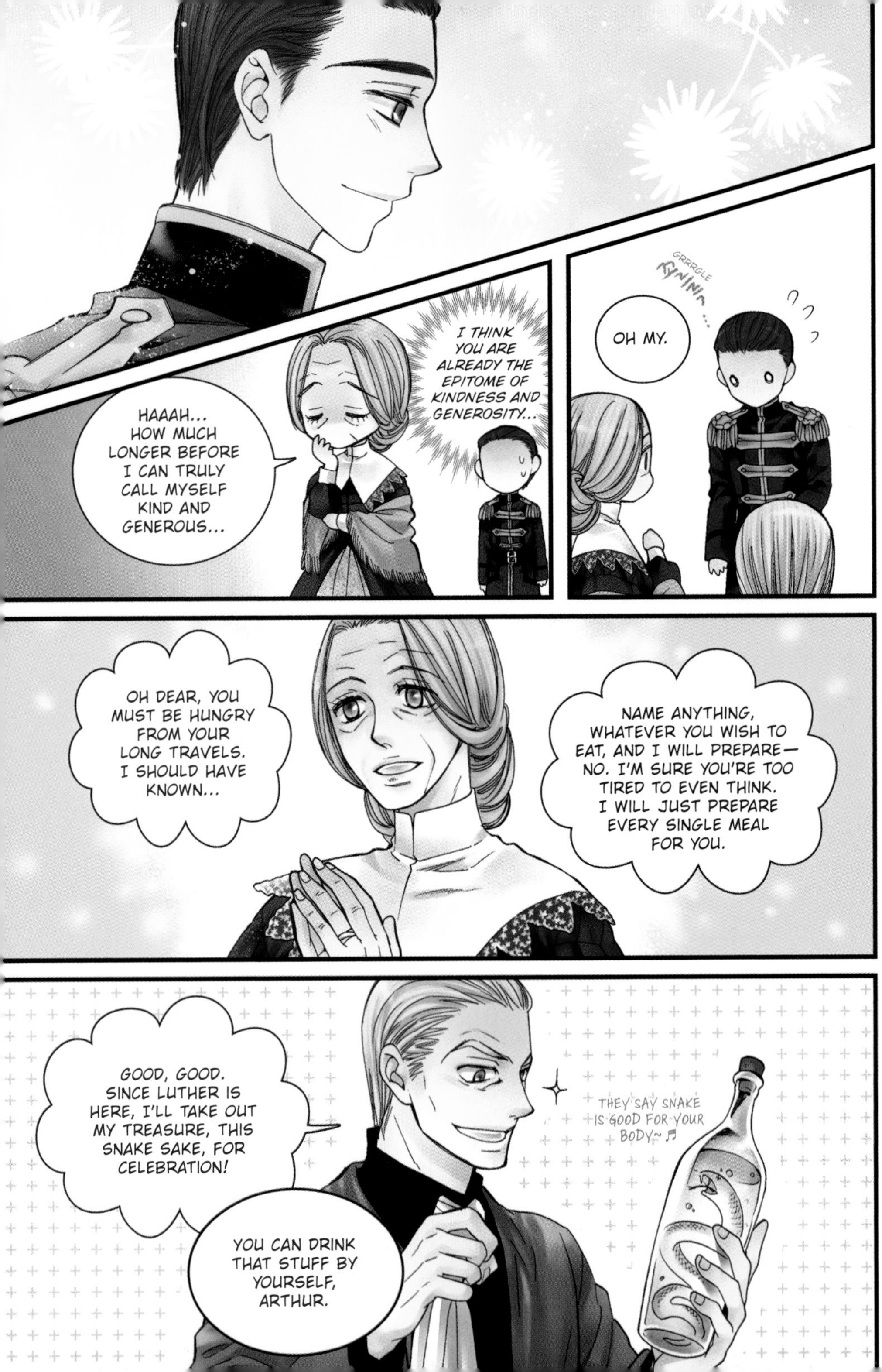

HAAAH... HOW MUCH LONGER BEFORE I CAN TRULY CALL MYSELF KIND AND GENEROUS...
I THINK YOU ARE ALREADY THE EPITOME OF KINDNESS AND GENEROSITY...
GRRRGLE
OH MY.
OH DEAR, YOU MUST BE HUNGRY FROM YOUR LONG TRAVELS. I SHOULD HAVE KNOWN...
NAME ANYTHING, WHATEVER YOU WISH TO EAT, AND I WILL PREPARE— NO. I'M SURE YOU'RE TOO TIRED TO EVEN THINK. I WILL JUST PREPARE EVERY SINGLE MEAL FOR YOU.
GOOD, GOOD. SINCE LUTHER IS HERE, I'LL TAKE OUT MY TREASURE, THIS SNAKE SAKE, FOR CELEBRATION!
THEY SAY SNAKE IS GOOD FOR YOUR BODY~ ♬
YOU CAN DRINK THAT STUFF BY YOURSELF, ARTHUR.

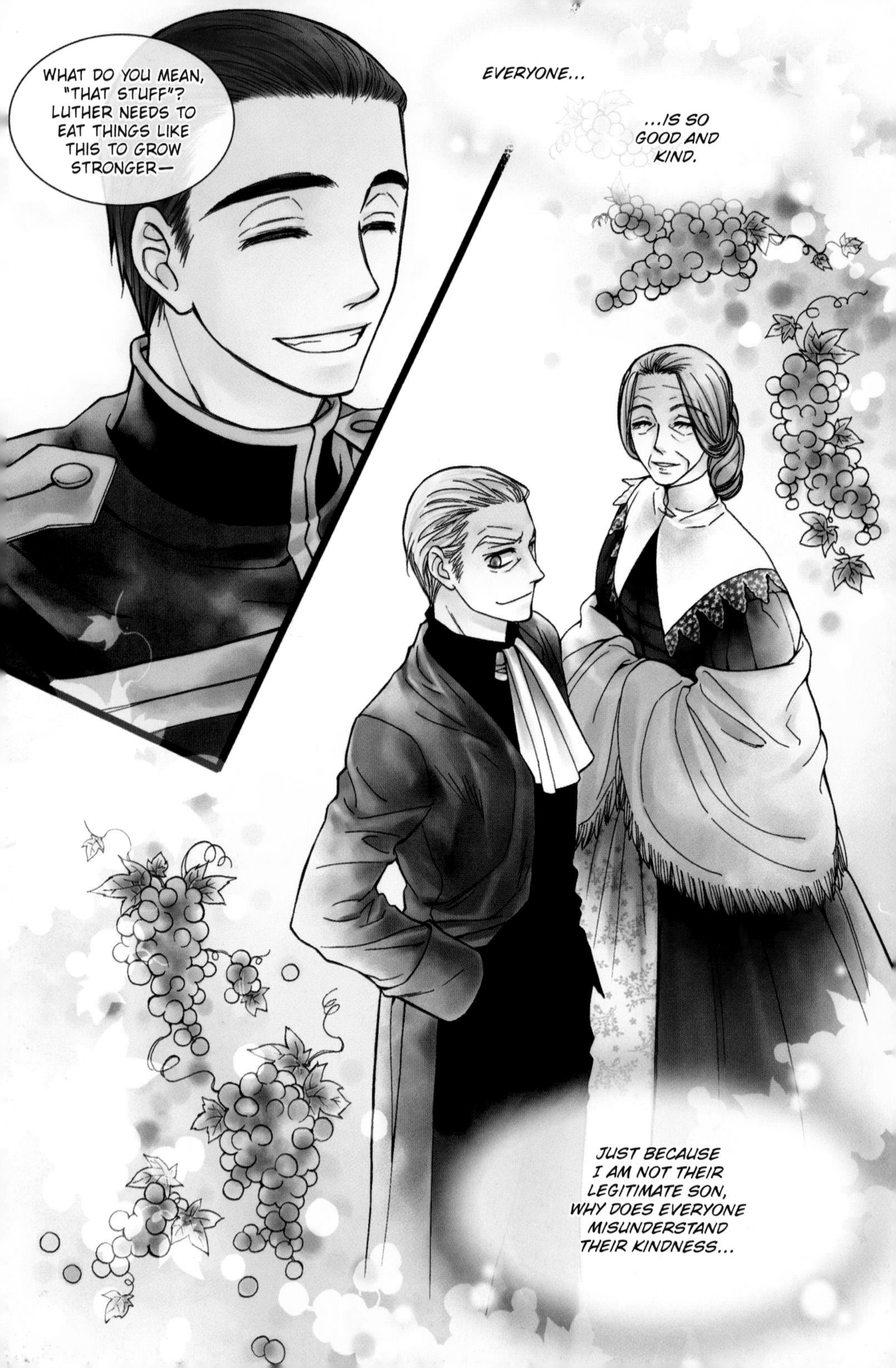
WHAT DO YOU MEAN, "THAT STUFF"? LUTHER NEEDS TO EAT THINGS LIKE THIS TO GROW STRONGER—
EVERYONE...
...IS SO GOOD AND KIND.
JUST BECAUSE I AM NOT THEIR LEGITIMATE SON, WHY DOES EVERYONE MISUNDERSTAND THEIR KINDNESS...

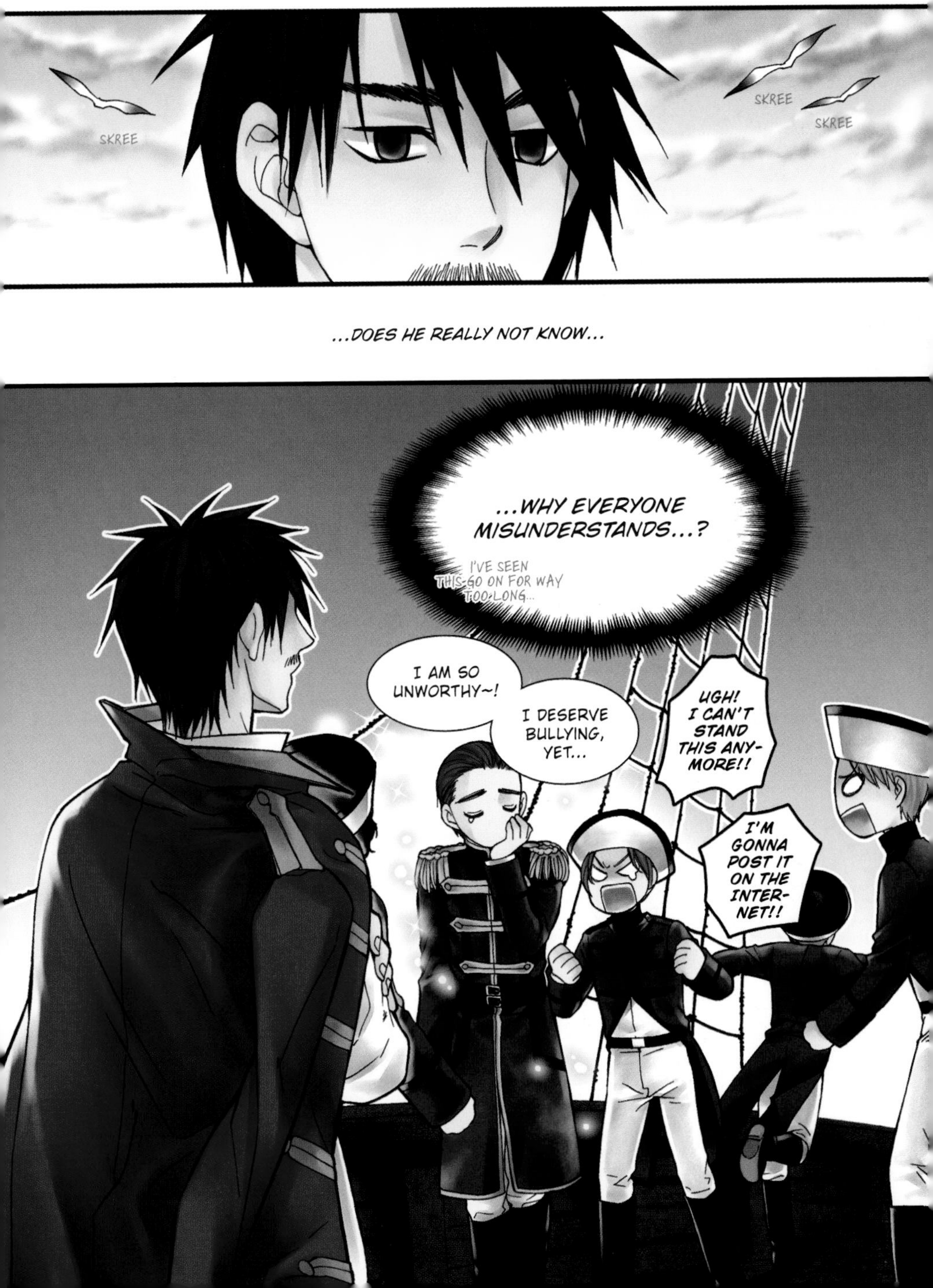
SKREE
SKREE
SKREE
...DOES HE REALLY NOT KNOW...
...WHY EVERYONE MISUNDERSTANDS...?
I'VE SEEN THIS GO ON FOR WAY TOO LONG...
I AM SO UNWORTHY~!
I DESERVE BULLYING, YET...
UGH! I CAN'T STAND THIS ANYMORE!!
I'M GONNA POST IT ON THE INTERNET!!

#39. LEAVE YOUR PERSONAL LIFE AT HOME

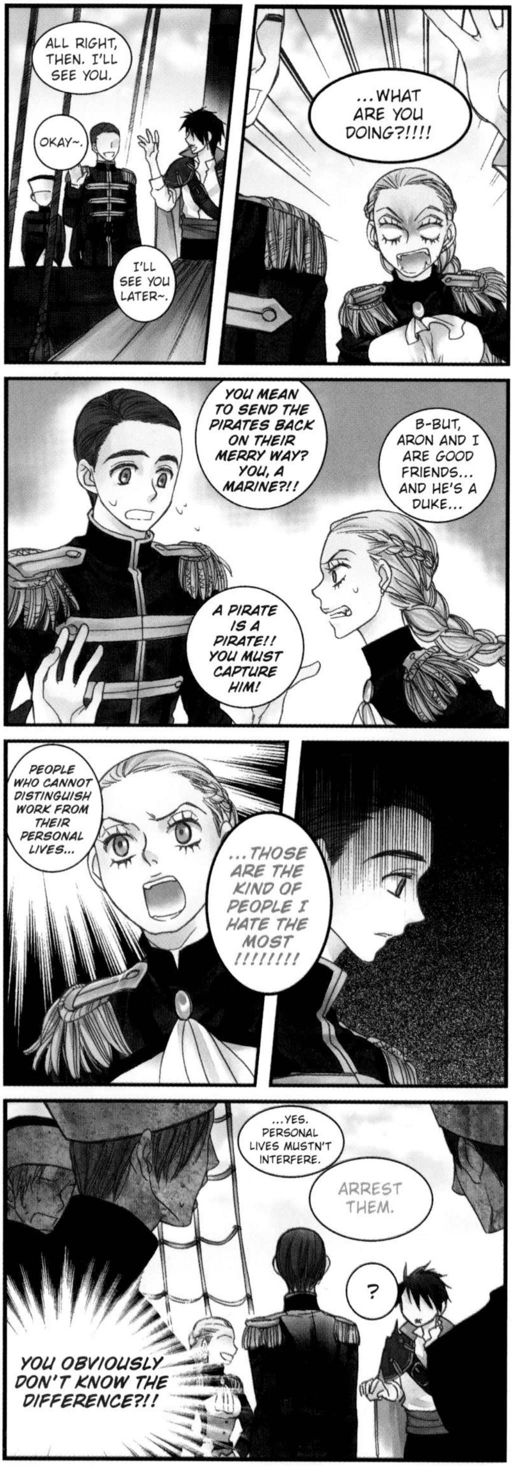
ALL RIGHT, THEN. I'LL SEE YOU.
OKAY~.
I'LL SEE YOU LATER~.
...WHAT ARE YOU DOING?!!!!
YOU MEAN TO SEND THE PIRATES BACK ON THEIR MERRY WAY? YOU, A MARINE?!!
B-BUT, ARON AND I ARE GOOD FRIENDS... AND HE'S A DUKE...
A PIRATE IS A PIRATE!! YOU MUST CAPTURE HIM!
PEOPLE WHO CANNOT DISTINGUISH WORK FROM THEIR PERSONAL LIVES...
...THOSE ARE THE KIND OF PEOPLE I HATE THE MOST !!!!!!!!
...YES. PERSONAL LIVES MUSTN'T INTERFERE.
ARREST THEM.
?
YOU OBVIOUSLY DON'T KNOW THE DIFFERENCE?!!

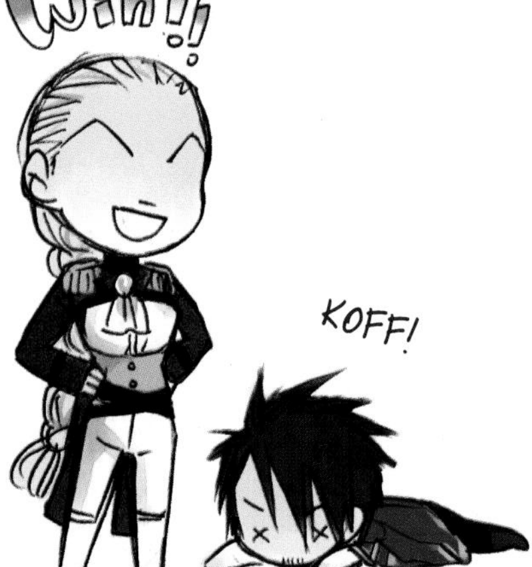
Win!!
KOFF!

#40. THIS IS NOT B.L.

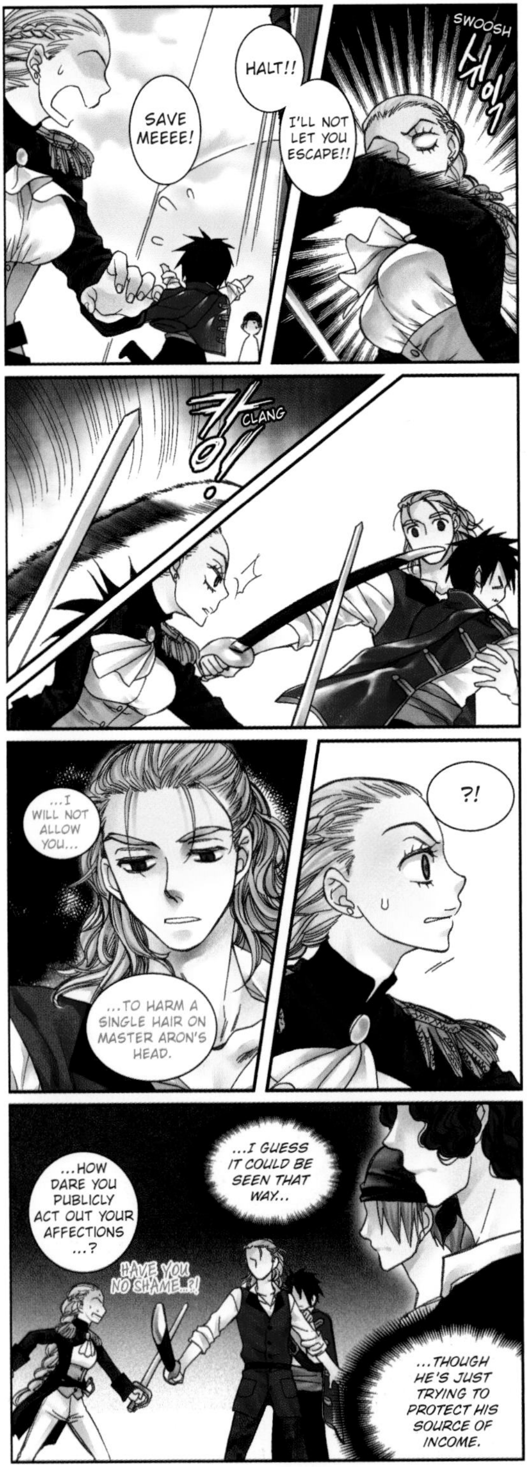
SAVE MEEEE!
HALT!!
I'LL NOT LET YOU ESCAPE!!
SWOOSH
CLANG
...I WILL NOT ALLOW YOU...
...TO HARM A SINGLE HAIR ON MASTER ARON'S HEAD.
?!
...HOW DARE YOU PUBLICLY ACT OUT YOUR AFFECTIONS ...?
HAVE YOU NO SHAME...?!
...I GUESS IT COULD BE SEEN THAT WAY...
...THOUGH HE'S JUST TRYING TO PROTECT HIS SOURCE OF INCOME.

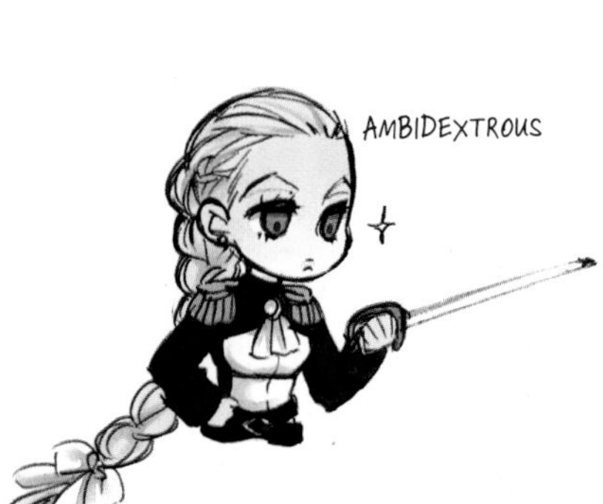
AMBIDEXTROUS

#41. CHIVALROUS

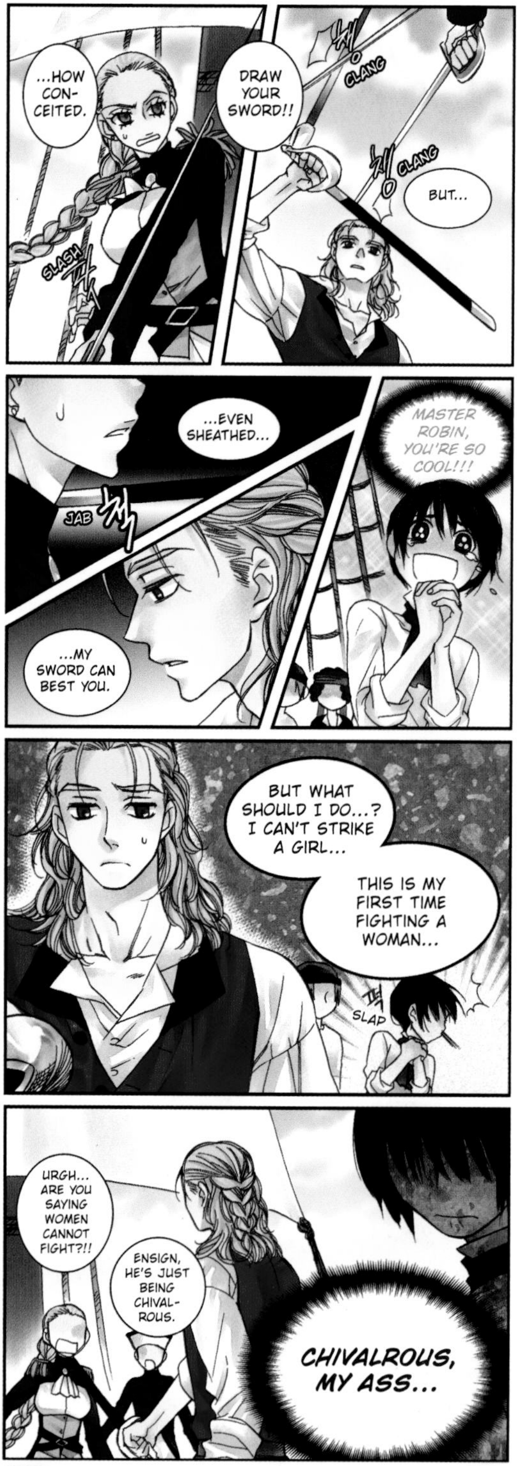

...HOW CON-CEITED.
SLASH
DRAW YOUR SWORD!!
CLANG
CLANG
BUT...
...EVEN SHEATHED...
JAB
...MY SWORD CAN BEST YOU.
MASTER ROBIN, YOU'RE SO COOL!!!
BUT WHAT SHOULD I DO...? I CAN'T STRIKE A GIRL...
THIS IS MY FIRST TIME FIGHTING A WOMAN...
SLAP
URGH... ARE YOU SAYING WOMEN CANNOT FIGHT?!!
ENSIGN, HE'S JUST BEING CHIVAL-ROUS.
CHIVALROUS, MY ASS...

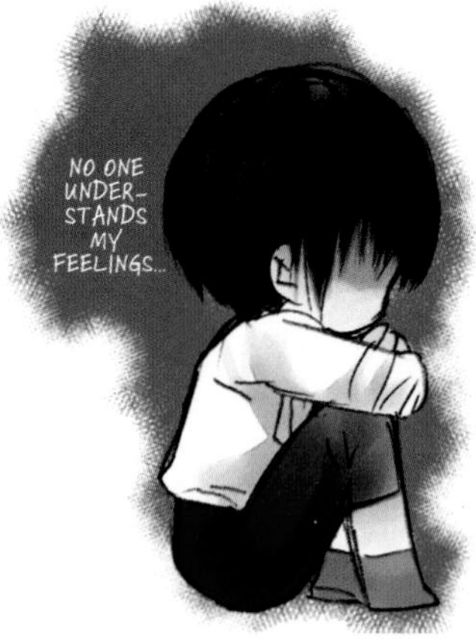

NO ONE UNDER-STANDS MY FEELINGS...

#42. LOVE IS LOOKS

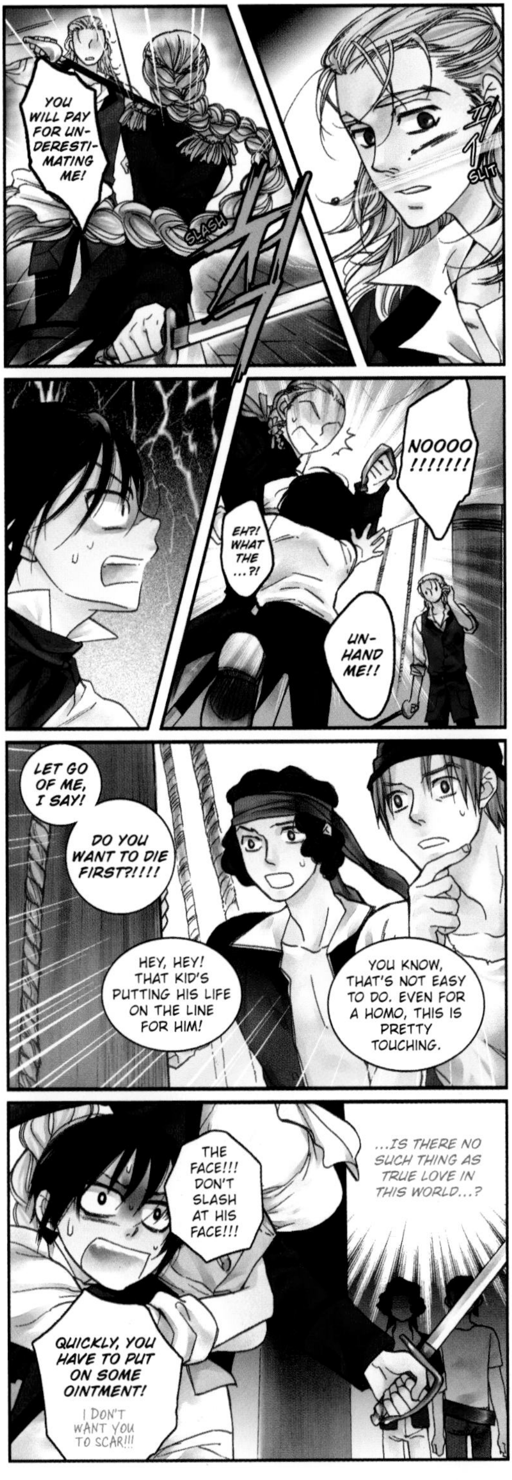
YOU WILL PAY FOR UNDERESTI-MATING ME!
SLASH
SLIT
NOOOO !!!!!!!
EH?! WHAT THE ...?!
UN-HAND ME!!
LET GO OF ME, I SAY!
DO YOU WANT TO DIE FIRST?!!!!
HEY, HEY! THAT KID'S PUTTING HIS LIFE ON THE LINE FOR HIM!
YOU KNOW, THAT'S NOT EASY TO DO. EVEN FOR A HOMO, THIS IS PRETTY TOUCHING.
THE FACE!!! DON'T SLASH AT HIS FACE!!!
QUICKLY, YOU HAVE TO PUT ON SOME OINTMENT!
I DON'T WANT YOU TO SCAR!!!
...IS THERE NO SUCH THING AS TRUE LOVE IN THIS WORLD...?

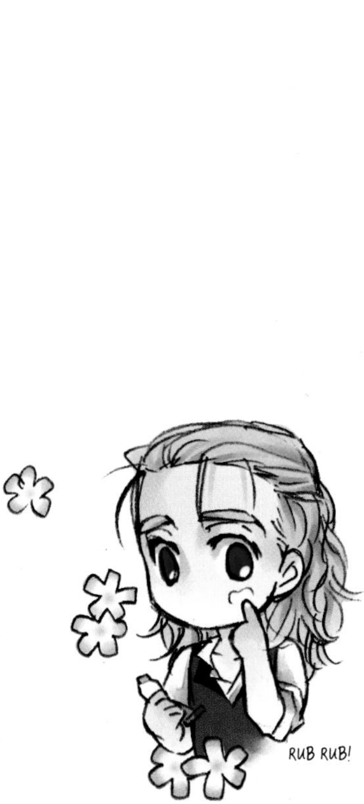
RUB RUB!

#43. THEY ARE REAL

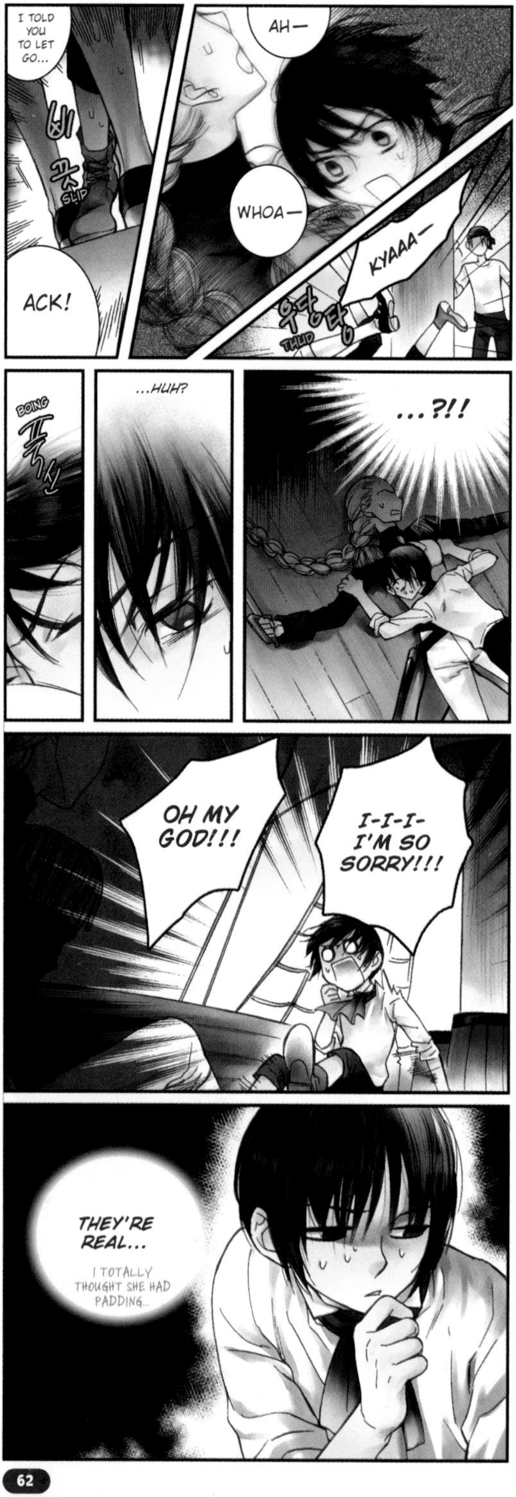

I TOLD YOU TO LET GO...
AH—
SLIP
WHOA—
ACK!
KYAAA—
THUD
BOING
...HUH?
...?!!
OH MY GOD!!!
I-I-I- I'M SO SORRY!!!
THEY'RE REAL...
I TOTALLY THOUGHT SHE HAD PADDING...

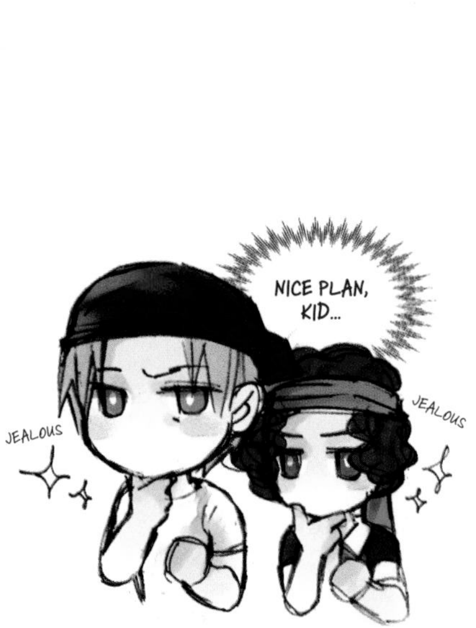

NICE PLAN, KID...
JEALOUS
JEALOUS

#44. A MAN'S JEALOUS HEART

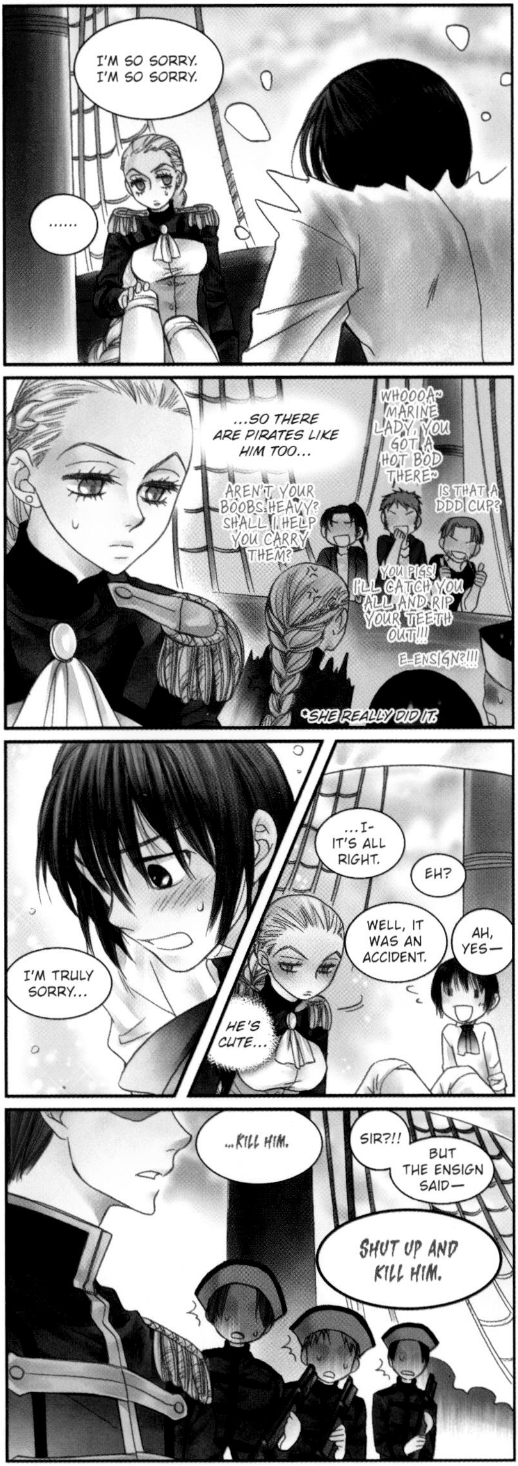
I'M SO SORRY. I'M SO SORRY.
......
...SO THERE ARE PIRATES LIKE HIM TOO...
WHOOOA~ MARINE LADY, YOU GOT A HOT BOD THERE~
AREN'T YOUR BOOBS HEAVY? SHALL I HELP YOU CARRY THEM?
IS THAT A DDD CUP?
YOU PIGS! I'LL CATCH YOU ALL AND RIP YOUR TEETH OUT!!!
E-ENSIGN?!!!
*SHE REALLY DID IT.
I'M TRULY SORRY...
...I- IT'S ALL RIGHT.
EH?
WELL, IT WAS AN ACCIDENT.
AH, YES—
HE'S CUTE...
...KILL HIM.
SIR?!!
BUT THE ENSIGN SAID—
SHUT UP AND KILL HIM.

*THE LIEUTENANT WAS FURIOUS.

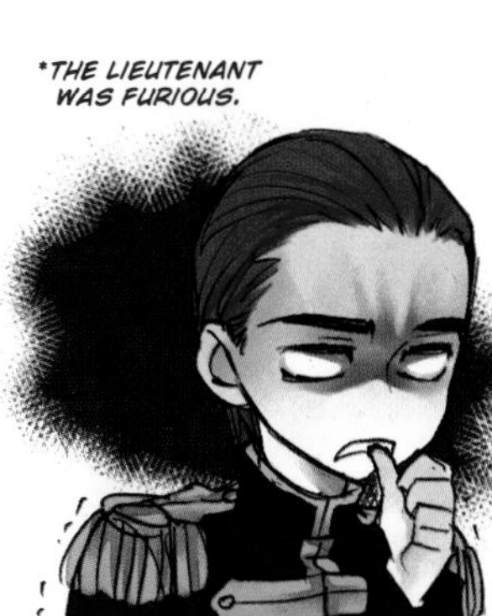

#45. THE SADNESS OF UNREQUITED LOVE

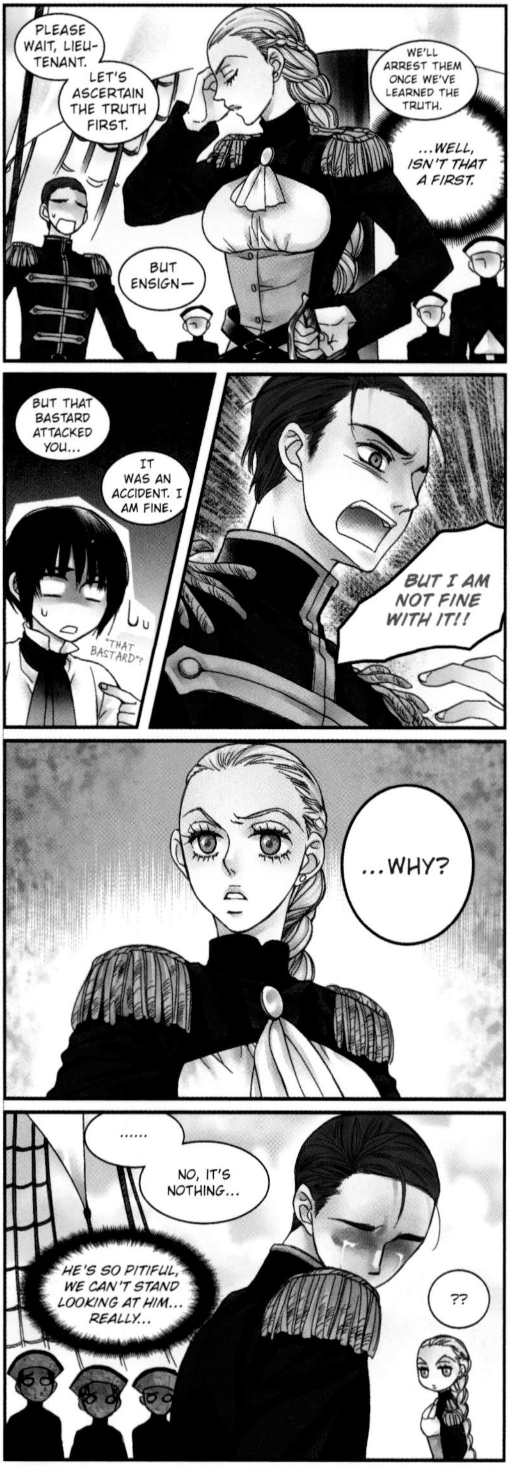
PLEASE WAIT, LIEU-TENANT.
LET'S ASCERTAIN THE TRUTH FIRST.
WE'LL ARREST THEM ONCE WE'VE LEARNED THE TRUTH.
...WELL, ISN'T THAT A FIRST.
BUT ENSIGN—
BUT THAT BASTARD ATTACKED YOU...
IT WAS AN ACCIDENT. I AM FINE.
"THAT BASTARD"?
BUT I AM NOT FINE WITH IT!!
...WHY?
......
NO, IT'S NOTHING...
HE'S SO PITIFUL, WE CAN'T STAND LOOKING AT HIM... REALLY...
??

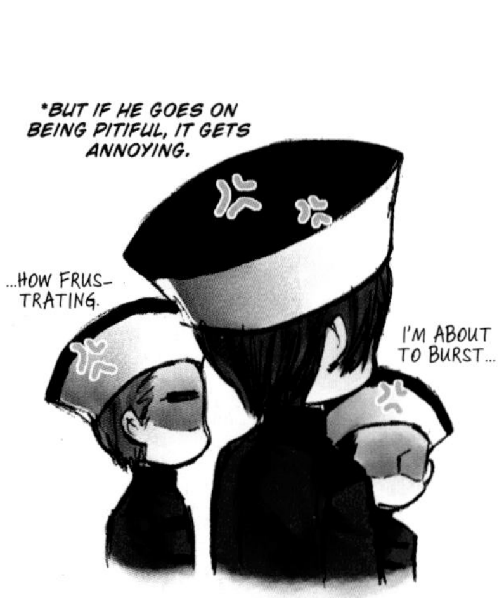
*BUT IF HE GOES ON BEING PITIFUL, IT GETS ANNOYING.
...HOW FRUS-TRATING.
I'M ABOUT TO BURST...

#46. POSTER OF FRIENDSHIP

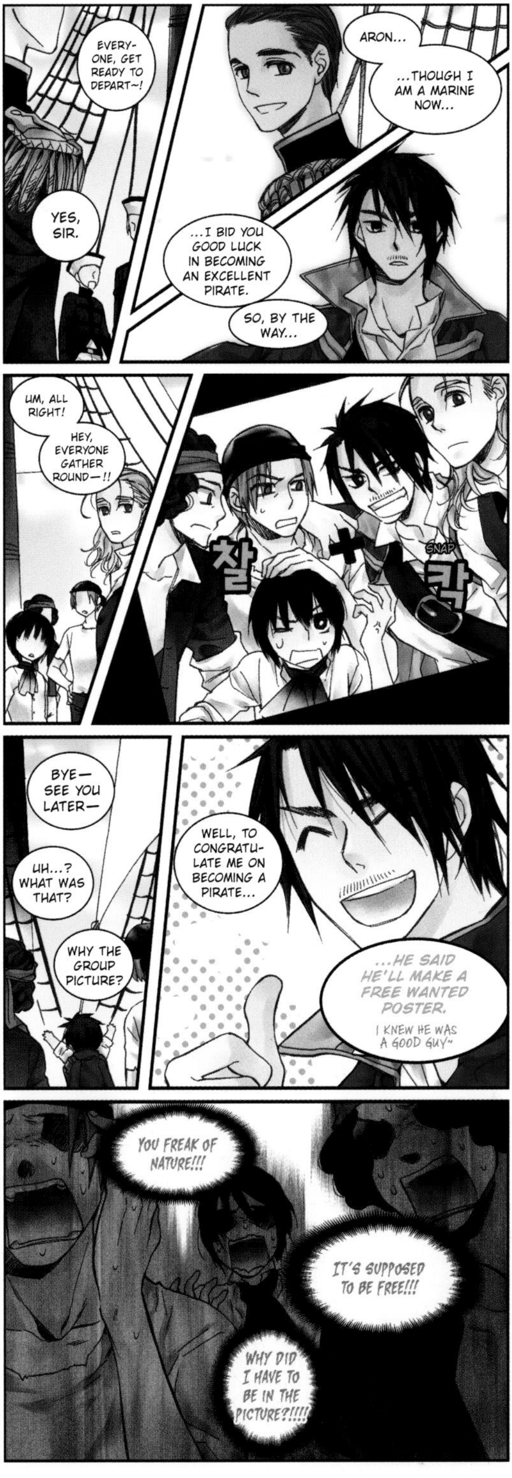
EVERY-ONE, GET READY TO DEPART~!
YES, SIR.
ARON...
...THOUGH I AM A MARINE NOW...
...I BID YOU GOOD LUCK IN BECOMING AN EXCELLENT PIRATE.
SO, BY THE WAY...
UM, ALL RIGHT!
HEY, EVERYONE GATHER ROUND—!!
찰
SNAP
칵
BYE— SEE YOU LATER—
UH...? WHAT WAS THAT?
WHY THE GROUP PICTURE?
WELL, TO CONGRATULATE ME ON BECOMING A PIRATE...
...HE SAID HE'LL MAKE A FREE WANTED POSTER.
I KNEW HE WAS A GOOD GUY~
YOU FREAK OF NATURE!!!
IT'S SUPPOSED TO BE FREE!!!
WHY DID I HAVE TO BE IN THE PICTURE?!!!!

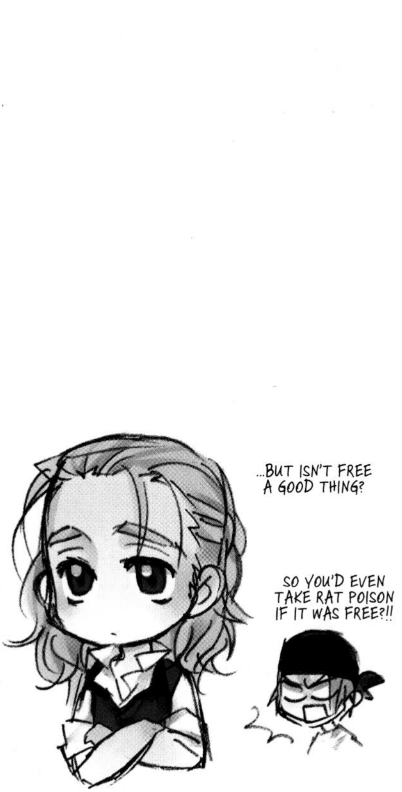
...BUT ISN'T FREE A GOOD THING?
SO YOU'D EVEN TAKE RAT POISON IF IT WAS FREE?!!

#47. LAYING DOWN AND SPITTING ON YOUR OWN FACE

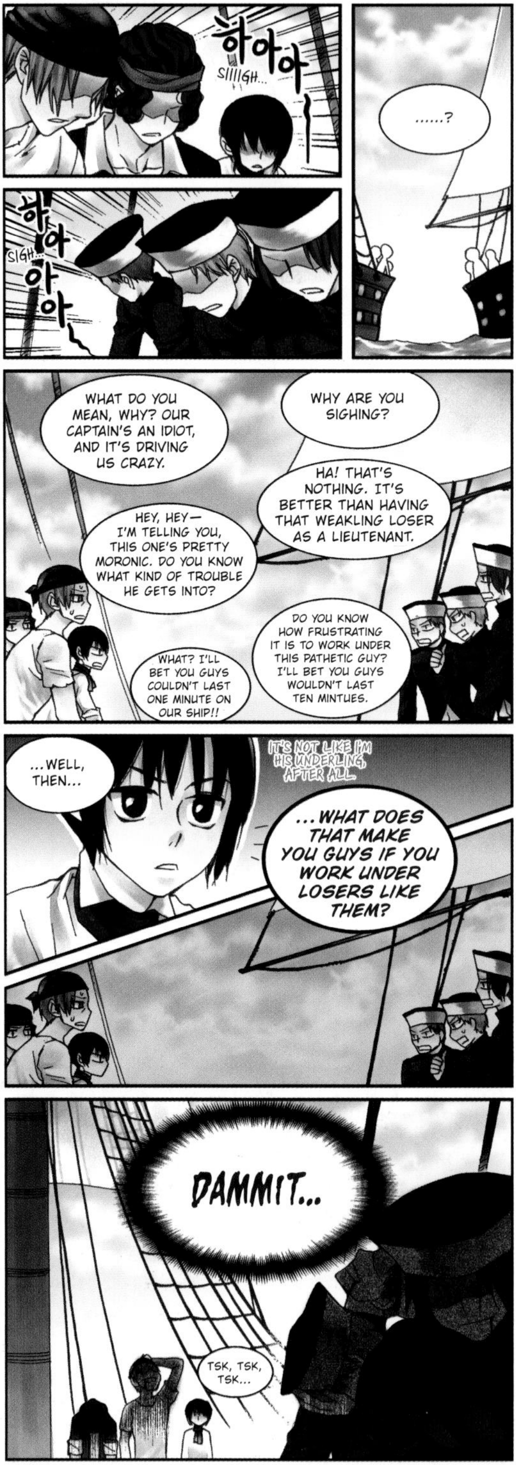
하아아—
SIIIGH...
......?
하아아아
SIGH...
WHY ARE YOU SIGHING?
WHAT DO YOU MEAN, WHY? OUR CAPTAIN'S AN IDIOT, AND IT'S DRIVING US CRAZY.
HA! THAT'S NOTHING. IT'S BETTER THAN HAVING THAT WEAKLING LOSER AS A LIEUTENANT.
HEY, HEY— I'M TELLING YOU, THIS ONE'S PRETTY MORONIC. DO YOU KNOW WHAT KIND OF TROUBLE HE GETS INTO?
DO YOU KNOW HOW FRUSTRATING IT IS TO WORK UNDER THIS PATHETIC GUY? I'LL BET YOU GUYS WOULDN'T LAST TEN MINTUES.
WHAT? I'LL BET YOU GUYS COULDN'T LAST ONE MINUTE ON OUR SHIP!!
...WELL, THEN...
IT'S NOT LIKE I'M HIS UNDERLING, AFTER ALL.
...WHAT DOES THAT MAKE YOU GUYS IF YOU WORK UNDER LOSERS LIKE THEM?
DAMMIT...
TSK, TSK, TSK...

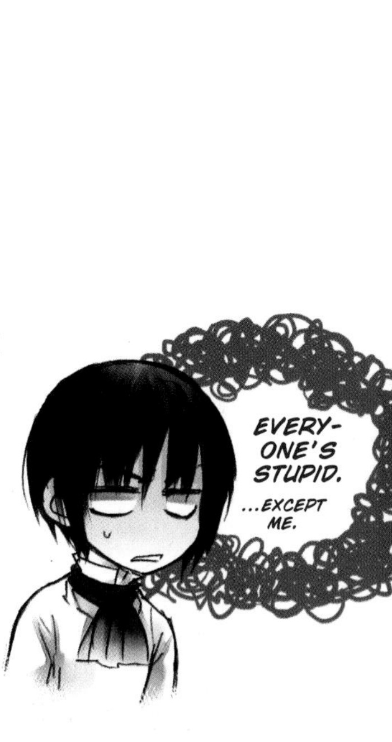
EVERY-ONE'S STUPID.
...EXCEPT ME.

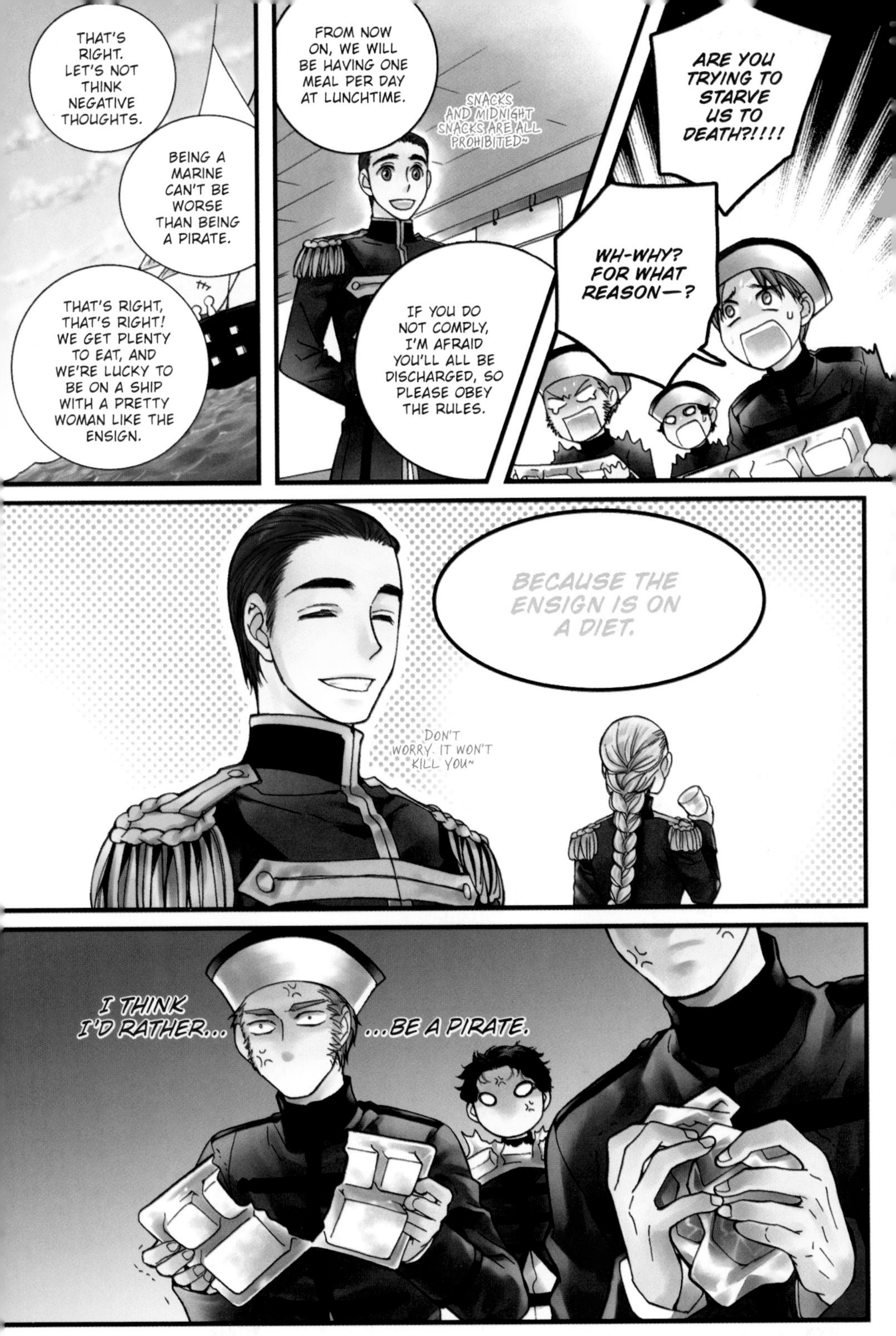
THAT'S RIGHT. LET'S NOT THINK NEGATIVE THOUGHTS.
BEING A MARINE CAN'T BE WORSE THAN BEING A PIRATE.
THAT'S RIGHT, THAT'S RIGHT! WE GET PLENTY TO EAT, AND WE'RE LUCKY TO BE ON A SHIP WITH A PRETTY WOMAN LIKE THE ENSIGN.
FROM NOW ON, WE WILL BE HAVING ONE MEAL PER DAY AT LUNCHTIME.
SNACKS AND MIDNIGHT SNACKS ARE ALL PROHIBITED~
IF YOU DO NOT COMPLY, I'M AFRAID YOU'LL ALL BE DISCHARGED, SO PLEASE OBEY THE RULES.
ARE YOU TRYING TO STARVE US TO DEATH?!!!!
WH-WHY? FOR WHAT REASON—?
BECAUSE THE ENSIGN IS ON A DIET.
DON'T WORRY. IT WON'T KILL YOU~
I THINK I'D RATHER...
...BE A PIRATE.

#48. MY HEART IS BEATING

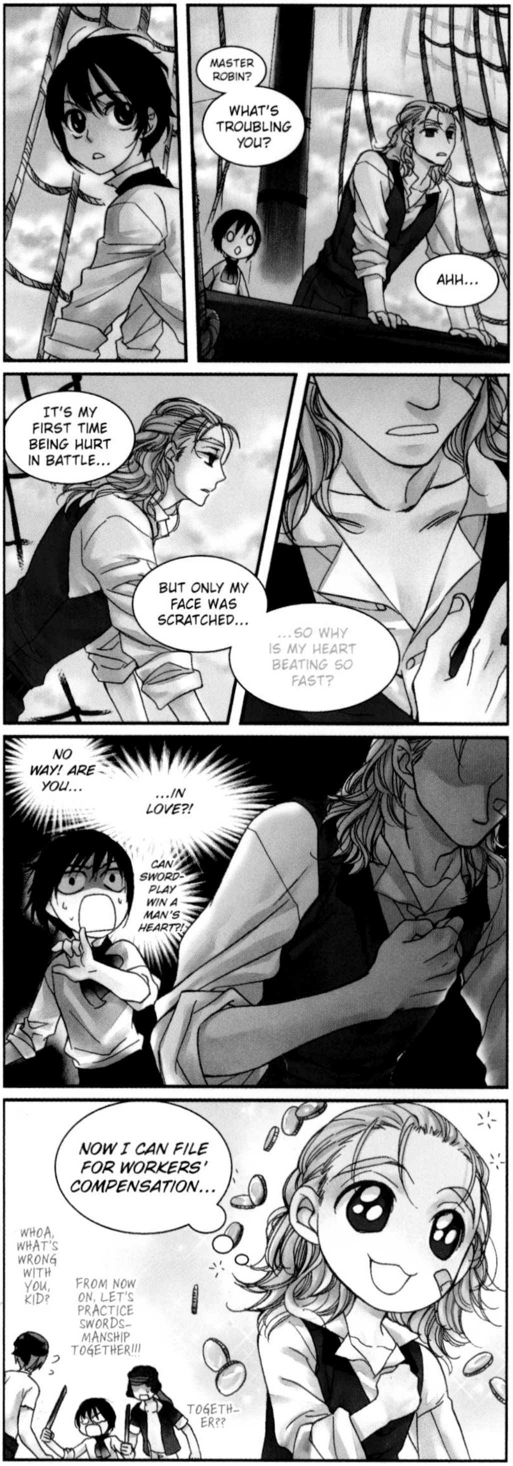
MASTER ROBIN?
WHAT'S TROUBLING YOU?
AHH...
IT'S MY FIRST TIME BEING HURT IN BATTLE...
BUT ONLY MY FACE WAS SCRATCHED...
...SO WHY IS MY HEART BEATING SO FAST?
NO WAY! ARE YOU...
...IN LOVE?!
CAN SWORD-PLAY WIN A MAN'S HEART?!
NOW I CAN FILE FOR WORKERS' COMPENSATION...
WHOA, WHAT'S WRONG WITH YOU, KID?
FROM NOW ON, LET'S PRACTICE SWORDS-MANSHIP TOGETHER!!!
TOGETH-ER??

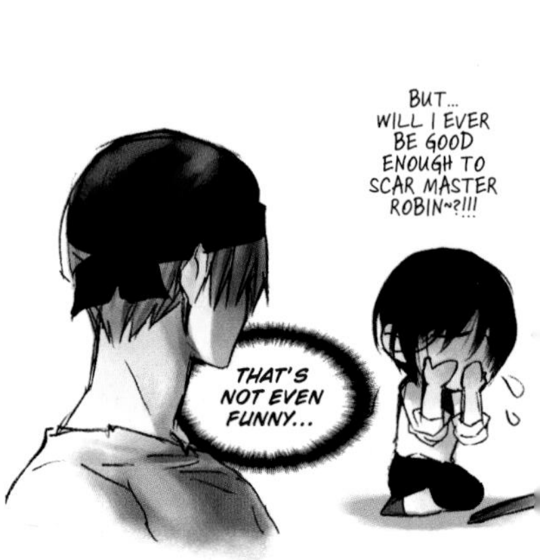
BUT... WILL I EVER BE GOOD ENOUGH TO SCAR MASTER ROBIN~?!!!
THAT'S NOT EVEN FUNNY...

#49. DEFENDING ONE'S TERRITORY

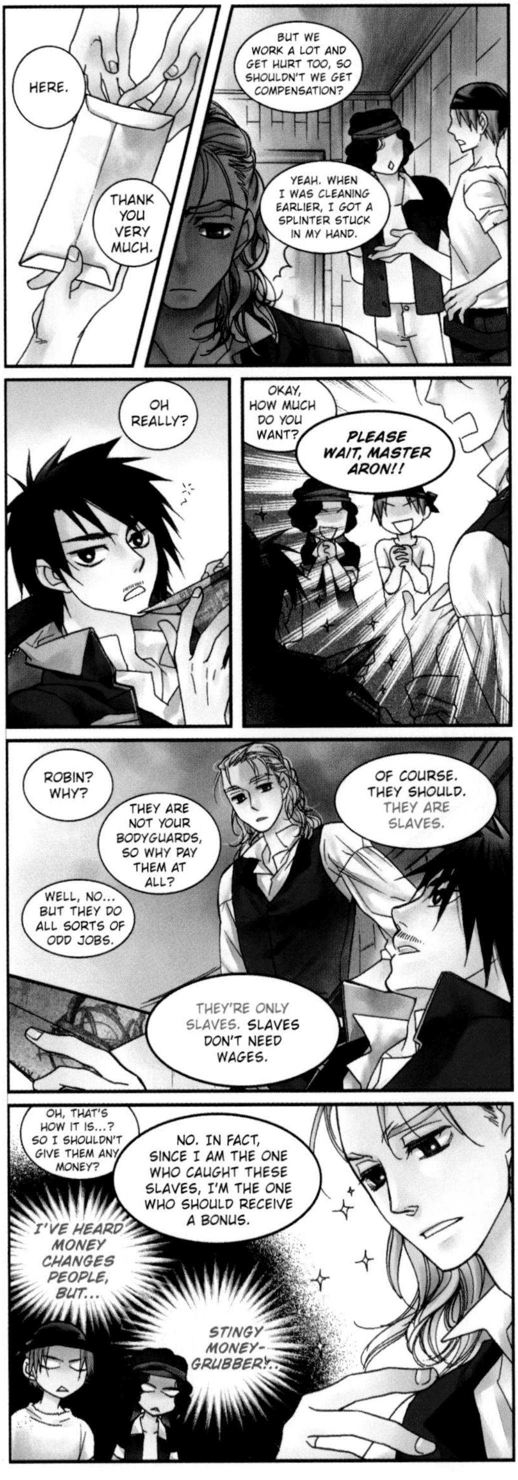
HERE.
THANK YOU VERY MUCH.
BUT WE WORK A LOT AND GET HURT TOO, SO SHOULDN'T WE GET COMPENSATION?
YEAH. WHEN I WAS CLEANING EARLIER, I GOT A SPLINTER STUCK IN MY HAND.
OH REALLY?
OKAY, HOW MUCH DO YOU WANT?
PLEASE WAIT, MASTER ARON!!
ROBIN? WHY?
THEY ARE NOT YOUR BODYGUARDS, SO WHY PAY THEM AT ALL?
WELL, NO... BUT THEY DO ALL SORTS OF ODD JOBS.
OF COURSE. THEY SHOULD. THEY ARE SLAVES.
THEY'RE ONLY SLAVES. SLAVES DON'T NEED WAGES.
OH, THAT'S HOW IT IS...? SO I SHOULDN'T GIVE THEM ANY MONEY?
NO. IN FACT, SINCE I AM THE ONE WHO CAUGHT THESE SLAVES, I'M THE ONE WHO SHOULD RECEIVE A BONUS.
I'VE HEARD MONEY CHANGES PEOPLE, BUT...
STINGY MONEY-GRUBBER!..

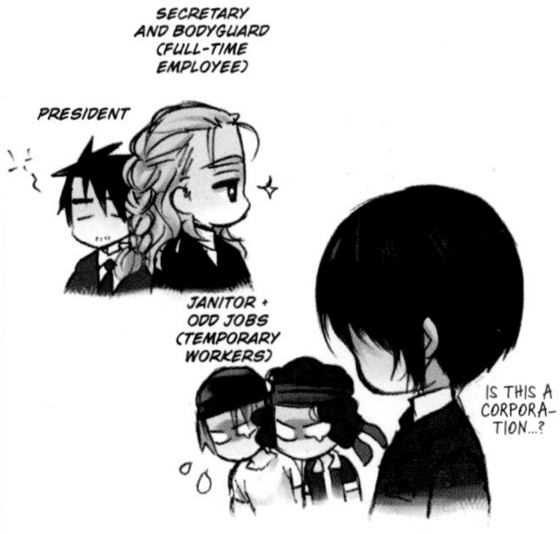
SECRETARY AND BODYGUARD (FULL-TIME EMPLOYEE)
PRESIDENT
JANITOR + ODD JOBS (TEMPORARY WORKERS)
IS THIS A CORPORATION...?

#50. PEOPLE FORGET THE MOST IMPORTANT THINGS

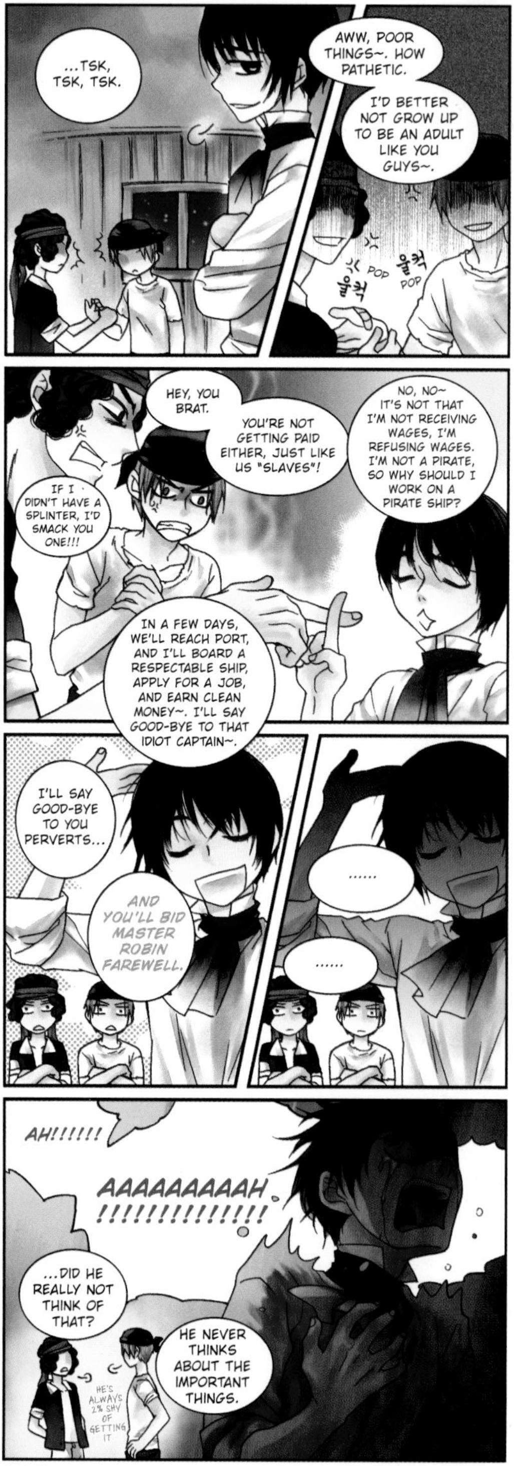
...TSK, TSK, TSK.
AWW, POOR THINGS~. HOW PATHETIC.
I'D BETTER NOT GROW UP TO BE AN ADULT LIKE YOU GUYS~.
울컥 POP
울컥 POP
HEY, YOU BRAT.
YOU'RE NOT GETTING PAID EITHER, JUST LIKE US "SLAVES"!
NO, NO~ IT'S NOT THAT I'M NOT RECEIVING WAGES, I'M REFUSING WAGES. I'M NOT A PIRATE, SO WHY SHOULD I WORK ON A PIRATE SHIP?
IF I DIDN'T HAVE A SPLINTER, I'D SMACK YOU ONE!!!
IN A FEW DAYS, WE'LL REACH PORT, AND I'LL BOARD A RESPECTABLE SHIP, APPLY FOR A JOB, AND EARN CLEAN MONEY~. I'LL SAY GOOD-BYE TO THAT IDIOT CAPTAIN~.
I'LL SAY GOOD-BYE TO YOU PERVERTS...
AND YOU'LL BID MASTER ROBIN FAREWELL.
......
......
AH!!!!!!
AAAAAAAAAH!!!!!!!!!!!!!!
...DID HE REALLY NOT THINK OF THAT?
HE NEVER THINKS ABOUT THE IMPORTANT THINGS.
HE'S ALWAYS 2% SHY OF GETTING IT

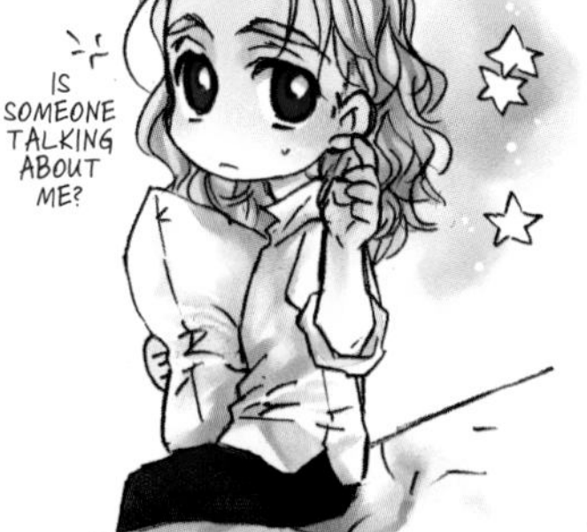
IS SOMEONE TALKING ABOUT ME?

#51. ALL FOR NAUGHT

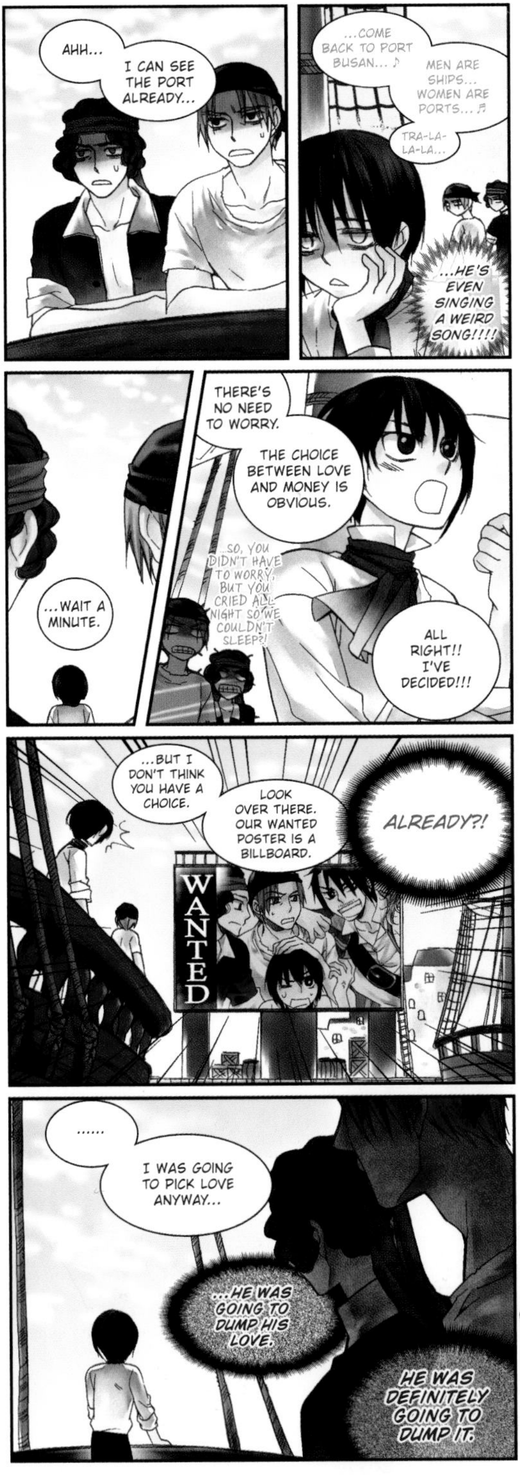
AHH...
I CAN SEE THE PORT ALREADY...
...COME BACK TO PORT BUSAN... ♪
MEN ARE SHIPS... WOMEN ARE PORTS... ♬
TRA-LA-LA-LA...
...HE'S EVEN SINGING A WEIRD SONG!!!!
...WAIT A MINUTE.
THERE'S NO NEED TO WORRY.
THE CHOICE BETWEEN LOVE AND MONEY IS OBVIOUS.
...SO, YOU DIDN'T HAVE TO WORRY, BUT YOU CRIED ALL NIGHT SO WE COULDN'T SLEEP?!
ALL RIGHT!! I'VE DECIDED!!!
...BUT I DON'T THINK YOU HAVE A CHOICE.
LOOK OVER THERE. OUR WANTED POSTER IS A BILLBOARD.
ALREADY?!
WANTED
......
I WAS GOING TO PICK LOVE ANYWAY...
...HE WAS GOING TO DUMP HIS LOVE.
HE WAS DEFINITELY GOING TO DUMP IT.

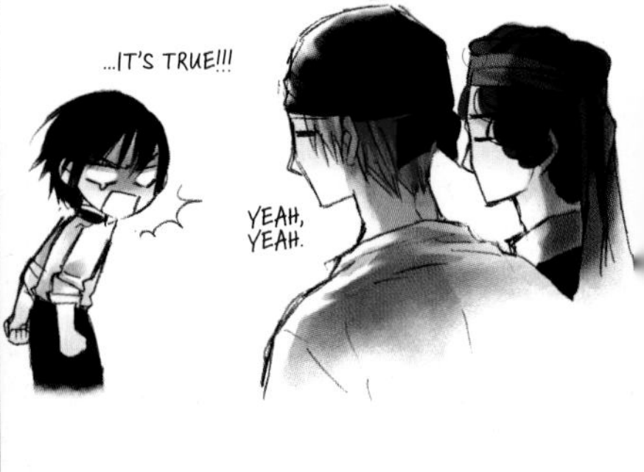
...IT'S TRUE!!!
YEAH, YEAH.

#52. SECRET BEHIND THE WANTED POSTER, PART 1

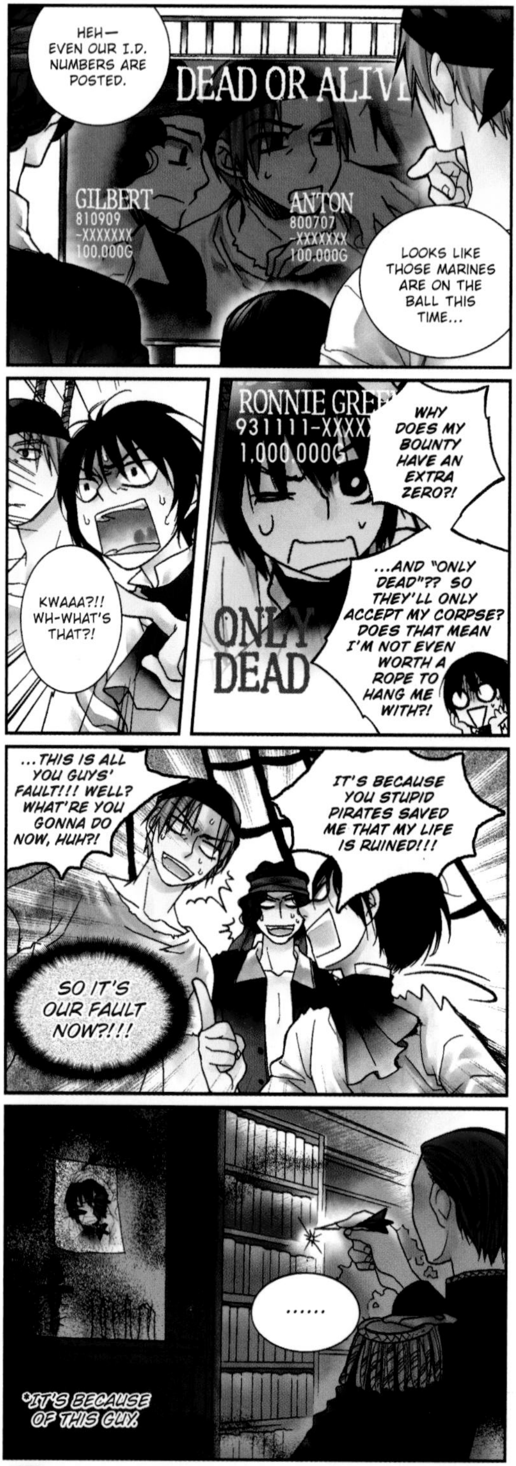
HEH— EVEN OUR I.D. NUMBERS ARE POSTED.
DEAD OR ALIVE
GILBERT
810909
-XXXXXXX
100,000G
ANTON
800707
-XXXXXXX
100,000G
LOOKS LIKE THOSE MARINES ARE ON THE BALL THIS TIME...
RONNIE GREE
931111-XXXX
1,000,000G
KWAAA?!! WH-WHAT'S THAT?!
WHY DOES MY BOUNTY HAVE AN EXTRA ZERO?!
ONLY DEAD
...AND "ONLY DEAD"?? SO THEY'LL ONLY ACCEPT MY CORPSE? DOES THAT MEAN I'M NOT EVEN WORTH A ROPE TO HANG ME WITH?!
...THIS IS ALL YOU GUYS' FAULT!!! WELL? WHAT'RE YOU GONNA DO NOW, HUH?!
IT'S BECAUSE YOU STUPID PIRATES SAVED ME THAT MY LIFE IS RUINED!!!
SO IT'S OUR FAULT NOW?!!!
......
*IT'S BECAUSE OF THIS GUY.

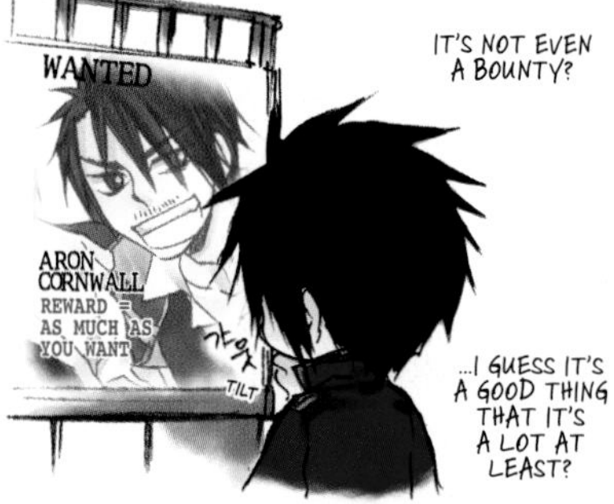
WANTED
ARON CORNWALL
REWARD = AS MUCH AS YOU WANT
TILT
IT'S NOT EVEN A BOUNTY?
...I GUESS IT'S A GOOD THING THAT IT'S A LOT AT LEAST?

#53. SECRET BEHIND THE WANTED POSTER, PART 2

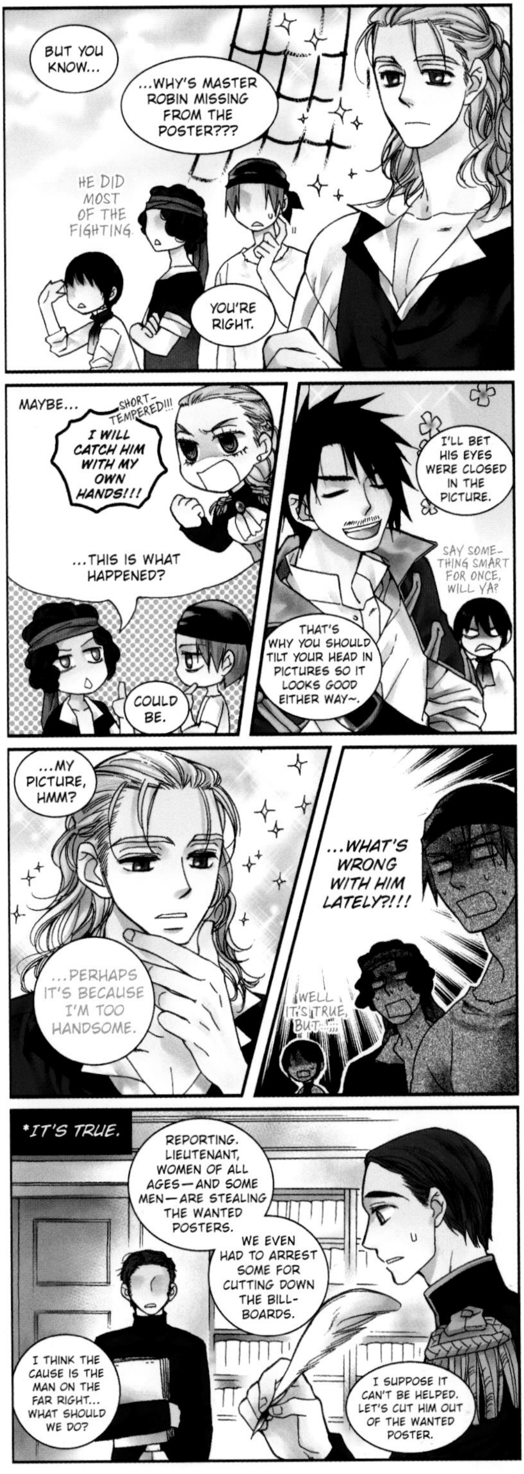

BUT YOU KNOW...
...WHY'S MASTER ROBIN MISSING FROM THE POSTER???
HE DID MOST OF THE FIGHTING.
YOU'RE RIGHT.
MAYBE...
SHORT-TEMPERED!!!
I WILL CATCH HIM WITH MY OWN HANDS!!!
...THIS IS WHAT HAPPENED?
COULD BE.
I'LL BET HIS EYES WERE CLOSED IN THE PICTURE.
SAY SOMETHING SMART FOR ONCE, WILL YA?
THAT'S WHY YOU SHOULD TILT YOUR HEAD IN PICTURES SO IT LOOKS GOOD EITHER WAY~.
...MY PICTURE, HMM?
...PERHAPS IT'S BECAUSE I'M TOO HANDSOME.
...WHAT'S WRONG WITH HIM LATELY?!!!
WELL IT'S TRUE, BUT...
*IT'S TRUE.
REPORTING. LIEUTENANT, WOMEN OF ALL AGES—AND SOME MEN—ARE STEALING THE WANTED POSTERS.
WE EVEN HAD TO ARREST SOME FOR CUTTING DOWN THE BILLBOARDS.
I THINK THE CAUSE IS THE MAN ON THE FAR RIGHT... WHAT SHOULD WE DO?
I SUPPOSE IT CAN'T BE HELPED. LET'S CUT HIM OUT OF THE WANTED POSTER.

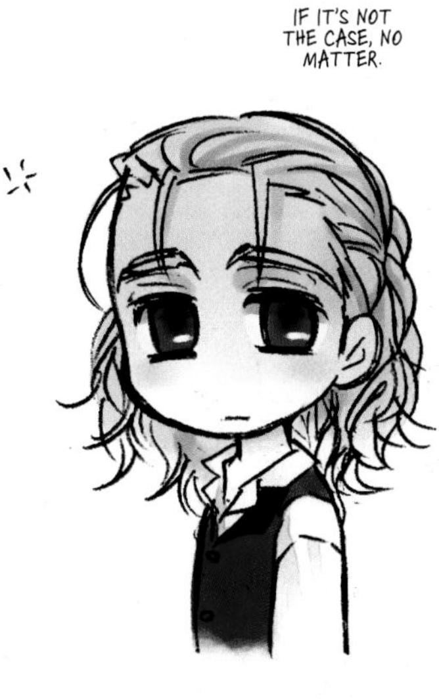

IF IT'S NOT THE CASE, NO MATTER.

#54. SAY MY NAME

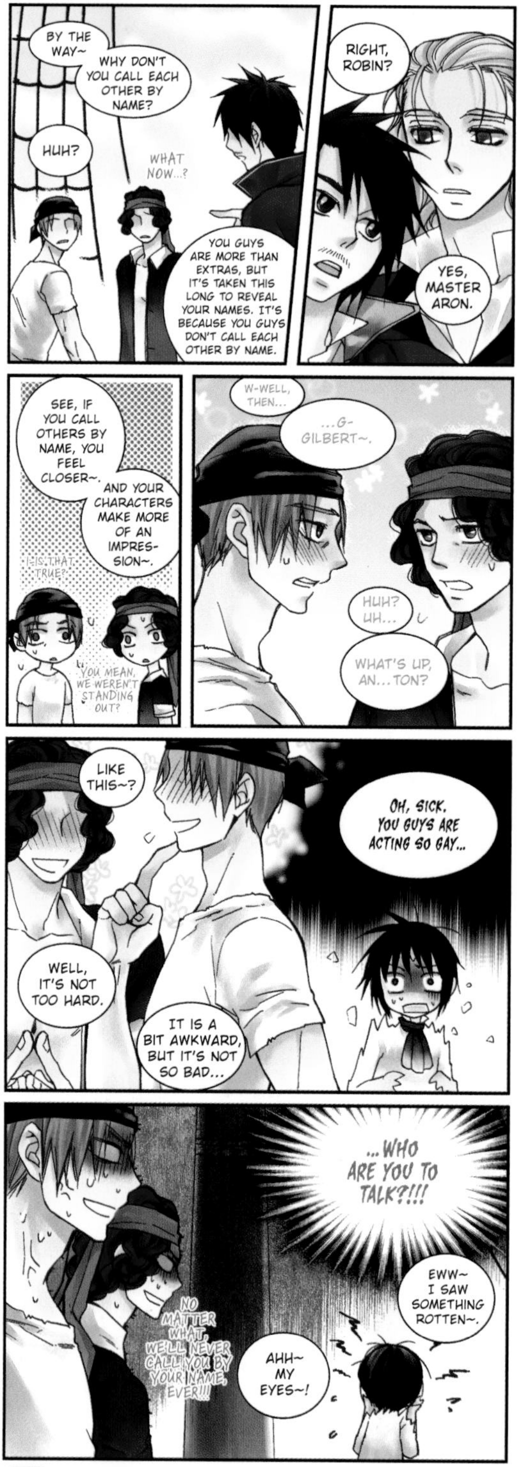
BY THE WAY~
WHY DON'T YOU CALL EACH OTHER BY NAME?
HUH?
WHAT NOW...?
YOU GUYS ARE MORE THAN EXTRAS, BUT IT'S TAKEN THIS LONG TO REVEAL YOUR NAMES. IT'S BECAUSE YOU GUYS DON'T CALL EACH OTHER BY NAME.
RIGHT, ROBIN?
YES, MASTER ARON.
SEE, IF YOU CALL OTHERS BY NAME, YOU FEEL CLOSER~.
AND YOUR CHARACTERS MAKE MORE OF AN IMPRES-SION~.
I-IS THAT TRUE?
YOU MEAN, WE WEREN'T STANDING OUT?
W-WELL, THEN...
...G- GILBERT~.
HUH? UH...
WHAT'S UP, AN...TON?
LIKE THIS~?
WELL, IT'S NOT TOO HARD.
IT IS A BIT AWKWARD, BUT IT'S NOT SO BAD...
OH, SICK. YOU GUYS ARE ACTING SO GAY...
...WHO ARE YOU TO TALK?!!!
NO MATTER WHAT, WE'LL NEVER CALL YOU BY YOUR NAME, EVER!!!
EWW~ I SAW SOMETHING ROTTEN~.
AHH~ MY EYES~!

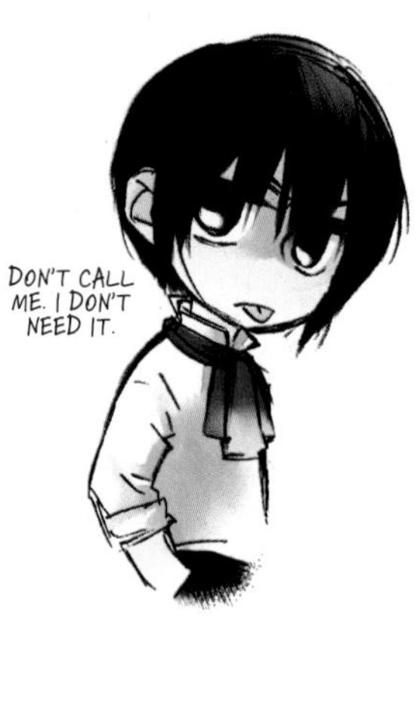
DON'T CALL ME. I DON'T NEED IT.

#55. WHO ARE YOU?

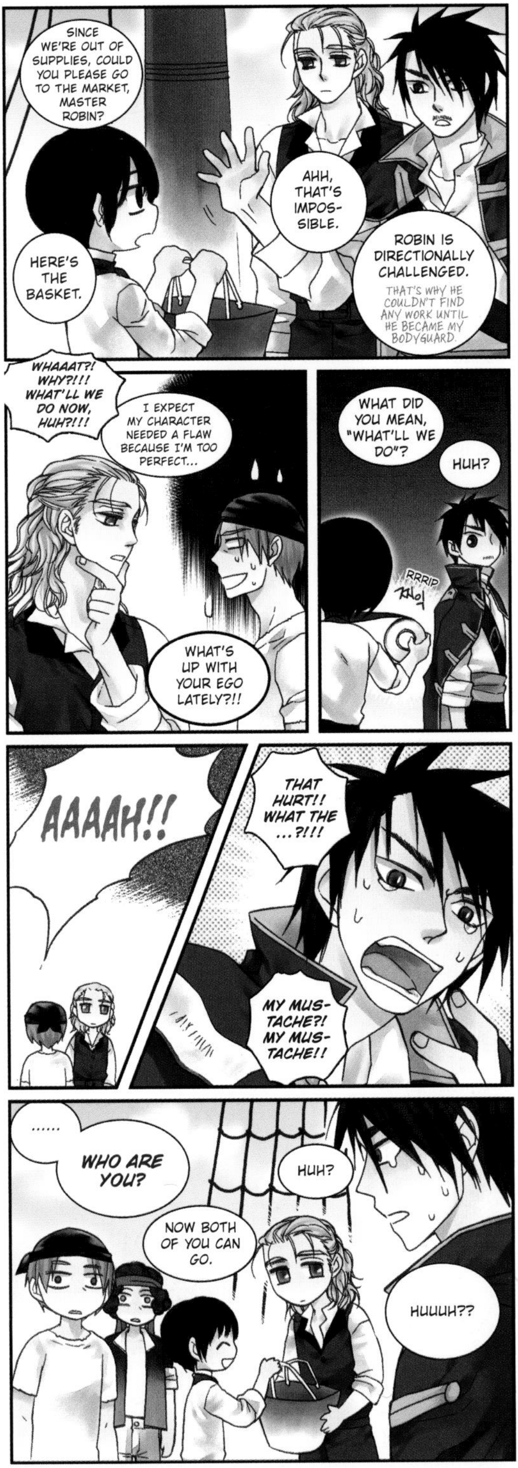

SINCE WE'RE OUT OF SUPPLIES, COULD YOU PLEASE GO TO THE MARKET, MASTER ROBIN?
HERE'S THE BASKET.
AHH, THAT'S IMPOS-SIBLE.
ROBIN IS DIRECTIONALLY CHALLENGED.
THAT'S WHY HE COULDN'T FIND ANY WORK UNTIL HE BECAME MY BODYGUARD.
WHAAAT?! WHY?!!! WHAT'LL WE DO NOW, HUH?!!!
I EXPECT MY CHARACTER NEEDED A FLAW BECAUSE I'M TOO PERFECT...
WHAT'S UP WITH YOUR EGO LATELY?!!
WHAT DID YOU MEAN, "WHAT'LL WE DO"?
HUH?
RRRIP
AAAAH!!
THAT HURT!! WHAT THE ...?!!!
MY MUS-TACHE?! MY MUS-TACHE!!
......
WHO ARE YOU?
HUH?
NOW BOTH OF YOU CAN GO.
HUUUH??

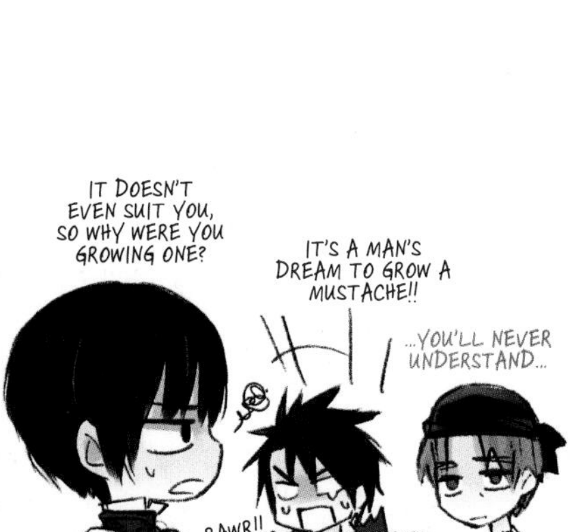

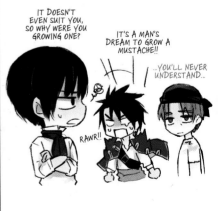

IT DOESN'T EVEN SUIT YOU, SO WHY WERE YOU GROWING ONE?
IT'S A MAN'S DREAM TO GROW A MUSTACHE!!
...YOU'LL NEVER UNDERSTAND...
RAWR!!

#56. KIND MASTER ARON

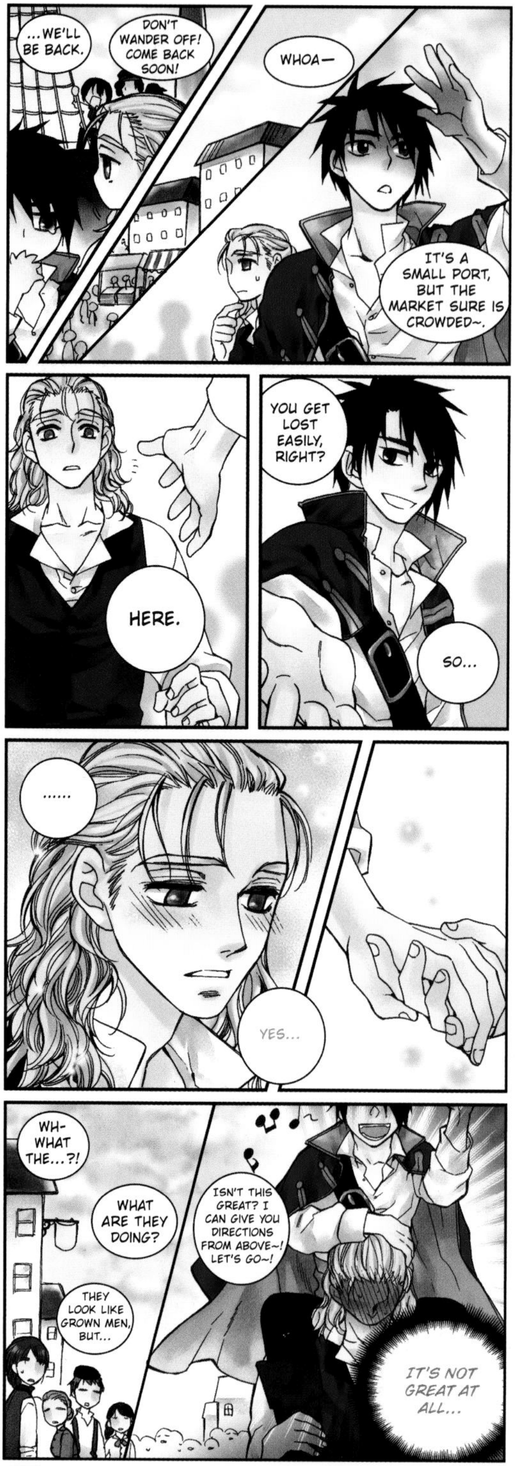
...WE'LL BE BACK.
DON'T WANDER OFF! COME BACK SOON!
WHOA—
IT'S A SMALL PORT, BUT THE MARKET SURE IS CROWDED~.
HERE.
YOU GET LOST EASILY, RIGHT?
SO...
......
YES...
WH- WHAT THE...?!
WHAT ARE THEY DOING?
THEY LOOK LIKE GROWN MEN, BUT...
ISN'T THIS GREAT? I CAN GIVE YOU DIRECTIONS FROM ABOVE~! LET'S GO~!
IT'S NOT GREAT AT ALL...

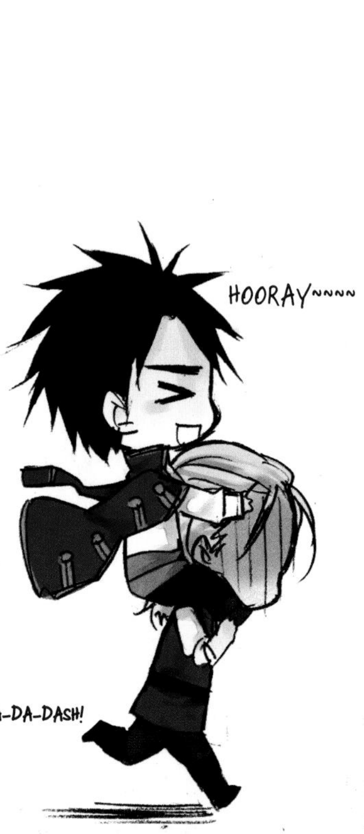
HOORAY~~~~
DA-DA-DASH!

#57. YOU DON'T NEED TO SAY IT

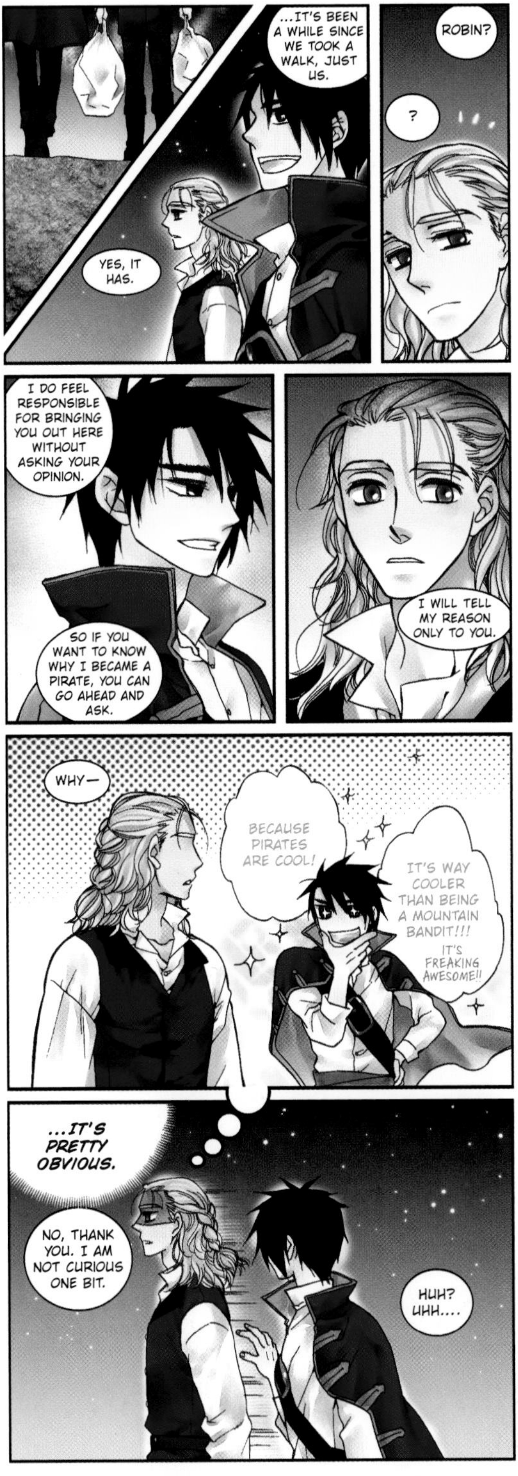
...IT'S BEEN A WHILE SINCE WE TOOK A WALK, JUST US.
YES, IT HAS.
ROBIN?
?
I DO FEEL RESPONSIBLE FOR BRINGING YOU OUT HERE WITHOUT ASKING YOUR OPINION.
SO IF YOU WANT TO KNOW WHY I BECAME A PIRATE, YOU CAN GO AHEAD AND ASK.
I WILL TELL MY REASON ONLY TO YOU.
WHY—
BECAUSE PIRATES ARE COOL!
IT'S WAY COOLER THAN BEING A MOUNTAIN BANDIT!!!
IT'S FREAKING AWESOME!!
...IT'S PRETTY OBVIOUS.
NO, THANK YOU. I AM NOT CURIOUS ONE BIT.
HUH? UHH....

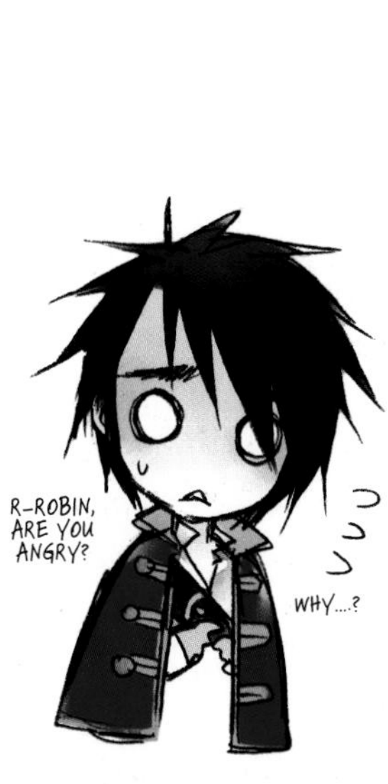
R-ROBIN, ARE YOU ANGRY?
WHY...?

#58. NOT JUST ANYONE SHOULD FETCH THE GROCERIES

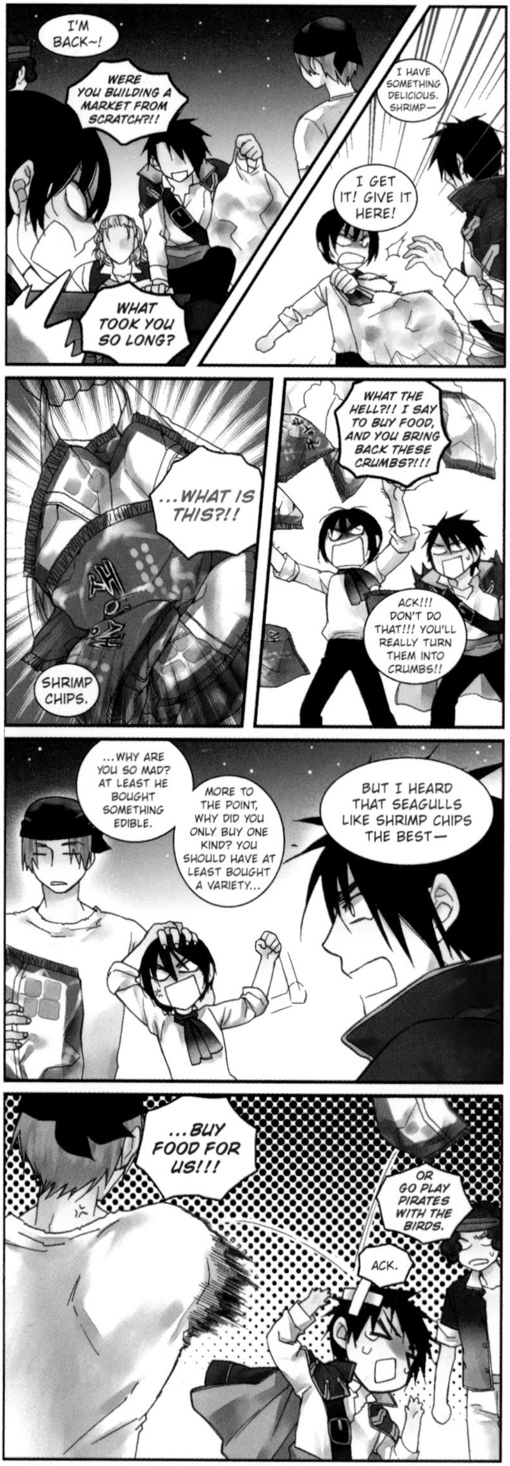
I'M BACK~!
WERE YOU BUILDING A MARKET FROM SCRATCH?!!
WHAT TOOK YOU SO LONG?
I HAVE SOMETHING DELICIOUS. SHRIMP—
I GET IT! GIVE IT HERE!
...WHAT IS THIS?!!
SHRIMP CHIPS.
WHAT THE HELL?!! I SAY TO BUY FOOD, AND YOU BRING BACK THESE CRUMBS?!!!
ACK!!! DON'T DO THAT!!! YOU'LL REALLY TURN THEM INTO CRUMBS!!
...WHY ARE YOU SO MAD? AT LEAST HE BOUGHT SOMETHING EDIBLE.
MORE TO THE POINT, WHY DID YOU ONLY BUY ONE KIND? YOU SHOULD HAVE AT LEAST BOUGHT A VARIETY...
BUT I HEARD THAT SEAGULLS LIKE SHRIMP CHIPS THE BEST—
...BUY FOOD FOR US!!!
OR GO PLAY PIRATES WITH THE BIRDS.
ACK.

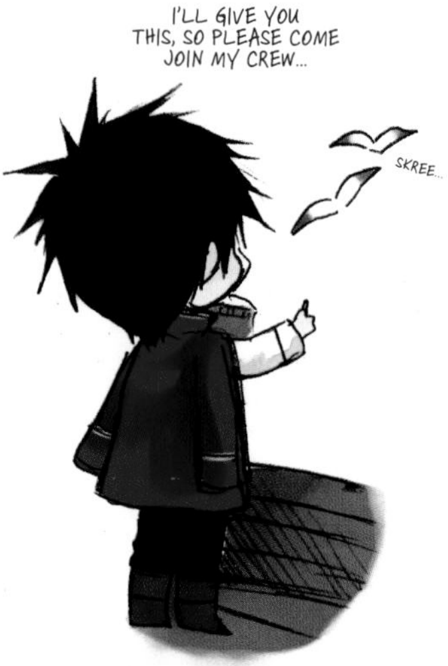
I'LL GIVE YOU THIS, SO PLEASE COME JOIN MY CREW...
SKREE...

#59. WINTER CLOTHES

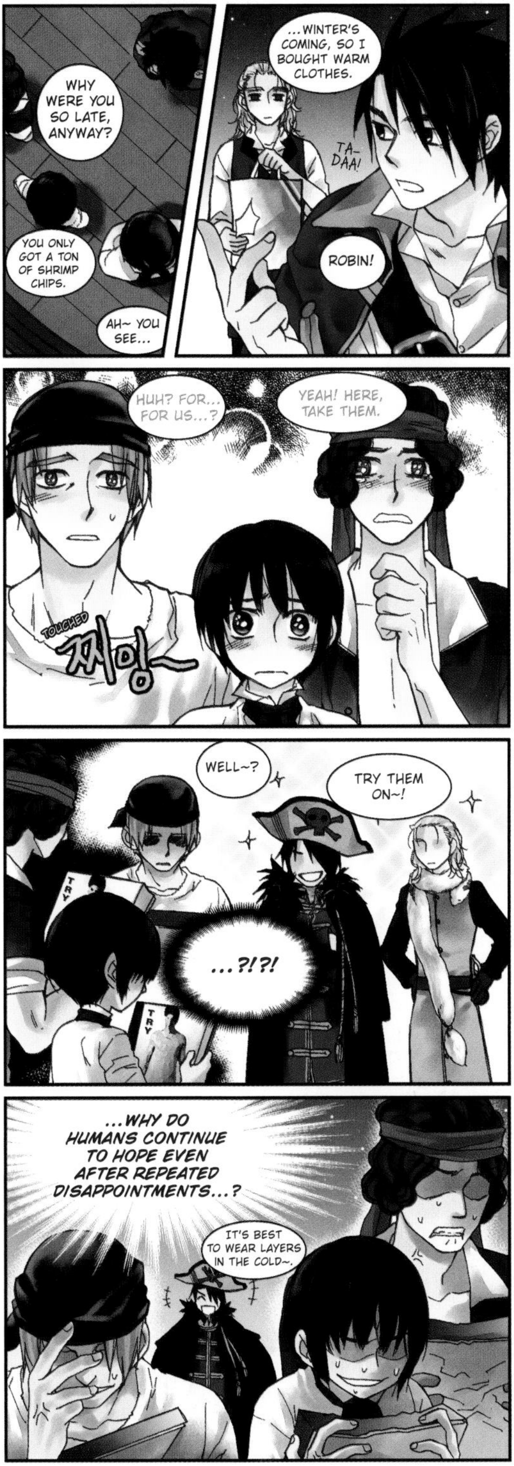
WHY WERE YOU SO LATE, ANYWAY?
YOU ONLY GOT A TON OF SHRIMP CHIPS.
AH~ YOU SEE...
...WINTER'S COMING, SO I BOUGHT WARM CLOTHES.
TA-DAA!
ROBIN!
HUH? FOR... FOR US...?
YEAH! HERE, TAKE THEM.
TOUCHED
찌잉~
WELL~?
TRY THEM ON~!
TRY
TRY
...?!?!
...WHY DO HUMANS CONTINUE TO HOPE EVEN AFTER REPEATED DISAPPOINTMENTS...?
IT'S BEST TO WEAR LAYERS IN THE COLD~.

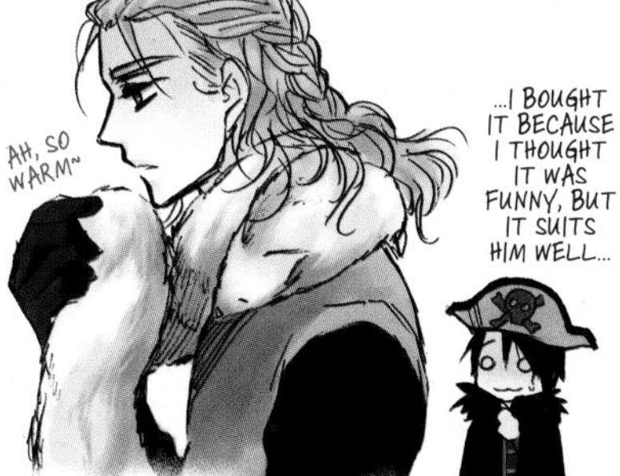
AH, SO WARM~
...I BOUGHT IT BECAUSE I THOUGHT IT WAS FUNNY, BUT IT SUITS HIM WELL...

#60. THE DIFFERENCE OF A SHEET OF PAPER

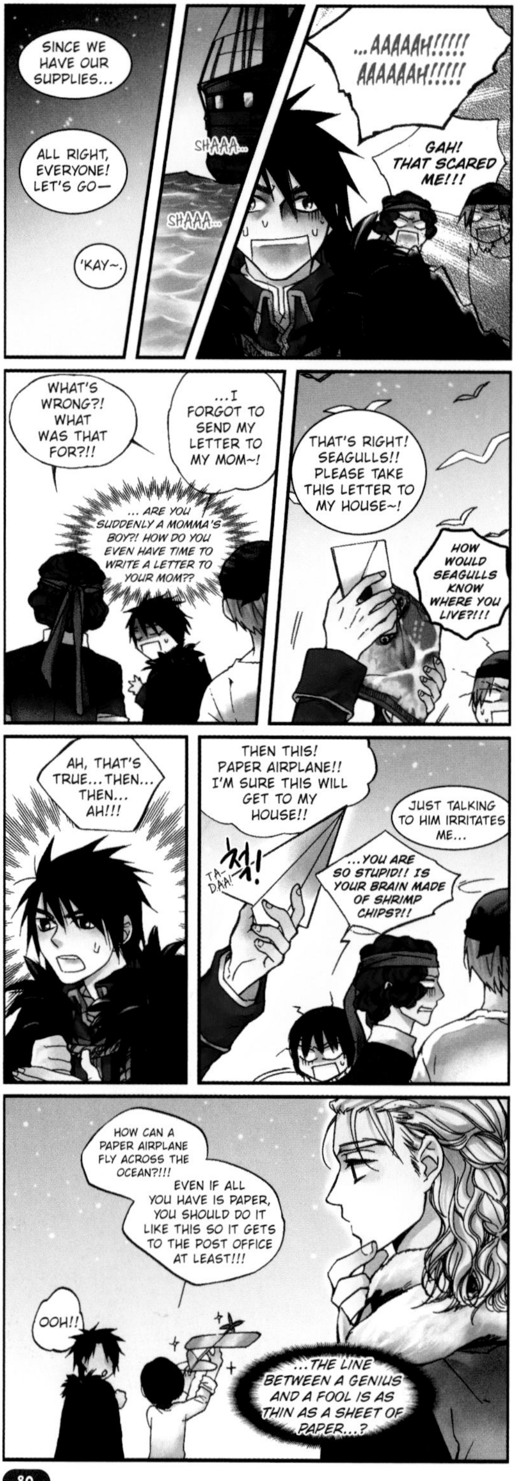

SINCE WE HAVE OUR SUPPLIES...
ALL RIGHT, EVERYONE! LET'S GO—
'KAY~.
SHAAA...
SHAAA...
...AAAAAH!!!!! AAAAAAH!!!!!
GAH! THAT SCARED ME!!!
WHAT'S WRONG?! WHAT WAS THAT FOR?!!
...I FORGOT TO SEND MY LETTER TO MY MOM~!
... ARE YOU SUDDENLY A MOMMA'S BOY?! HOW DO YOU EVEN HAVE TIME TO WRITE A LETTER TO YOUR MOM??
THAT'S RIGHT! SEAGULLS!! PLEASE TAKE THIS LETTER TO MY HOUSE~!
HOW WOULD SEAGULLS KNOW WHERE YOU LIVE?!!!
AH, THAT'S TRUE...THEN... THEN... AH!!!
THEN THIS! PAPER AIRPLANE!! I'M SURE THIS WILL GET TO MY HOUSE!!
TA-DAA!
척!
JUST TALKING TO HIM IRRITATES ME...
...YOU ARE SO STUPID!! IS YOUR BRAIN MADE OF SHRIMP CHIPS?!!
HOW CAN A PAPER AIRPLANE FLY ACROSS THE OCEAN?!!!
EVEN IF ALL YOU HAVE IS PAPER, YOU SHOULD DO IT LIKE THIS SO IT GETS TO THE POST OFFICE AT LEAST!!!
OOH!!
...THE LINE BETWEEN A GENIUS AND A FOOL IS AS THIN AS A SHEET OF PAPER...?

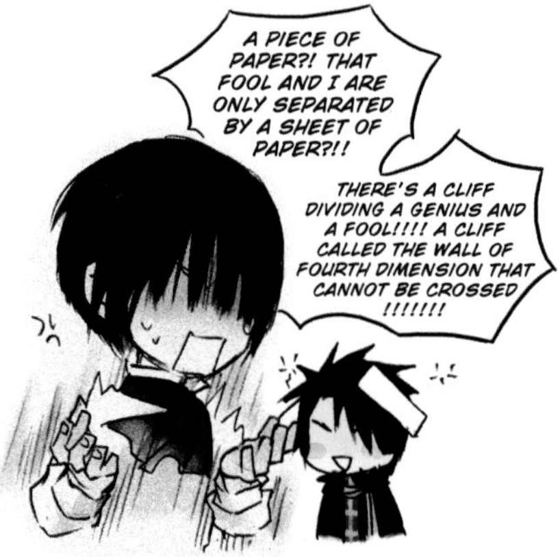

A PIECE OF PAPER?! THAT FOOL AND I ARE ONLY SEPARATED BY A SHEET OF PAPER?!!
THERE'S A CLIFF DIVIDING A GENIUS AND A FOOL!!!! A CLIFF CALLED THE WALL OF FOURTH DIMENSION THAT CANNOT BE CROSSED !!!!!!!

#61. THE LETTER TO THE CORNWALL FAMILY

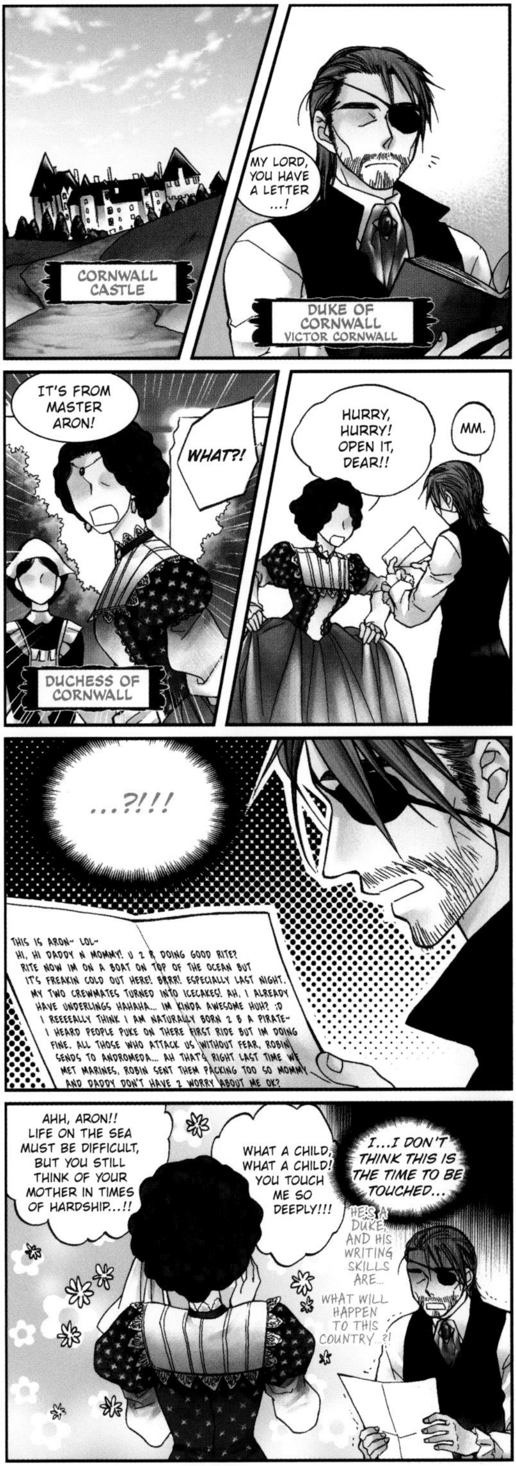
CORNWALL CASTLE
MY LORD, YOU HAVE A LETTER ...!
DUKE OF CORNWALL VICTOR CORNWALL
IT'S FROM MASTER ARON!
WHAT?!
DUCHESS OF CORNWALL
HURRY, HURRY! OPEN IT, DEAR!!
MM.
...?!!!
THIS IS ARON~ LOL~
HI, HI DADDY N MOMMY! U 2 R DOING GOOD RITE?
RITE NOW IM ON A BOAT ON TOP OF THE OCEAN BUT
IT'S FREAKIN COLD OUT HERE! BRRR! ESPECIALLY LAST NIGHT.
MY TWO CREWMATES TURNED INTO ICECAKES! AH, I ALREADY
HAVE UNDERLINGS HAHAHA... IM KINDA AWESOME HUH? ;D
I REEEEALLY THINK I AM NATURALLY BORN 2 B A PIRATE~
I HEARD PEOPLE PUKE ON THERE FIRST RIDE BUT IM DOING
FINE. ALL THOSE WHO ATTACK US WITHOUT FEAR, ROBIN
SENDS TO ANDROMEDA... AH THAT'S RIGHT LAST TIME WE
MET MARINES, ROBIN SENT THEM PACKING TOO SO MOMMY
AND DADDY DON'T HAVE 2 WORRY ABOUT ME OK?
AHH, ARON!! LIFE ON THE SEA MUST BE DIFFICULT, BUT YOU STILL THINK OF YOUR MOTHER IN TIMES OF HARDSHIP...!!
WHAT A CHILD, WHAT A CHILD! YOU TOUCH ME SO DEEPLY!!!
I...I DON'T THINK THIS IS THE TIME TO BE TOUCHED...
HE'S A DUKE, AND HIS WRITING SKILLS ARE...
WHAT WILL HAPPEN TO THIS COUNTRY...?!

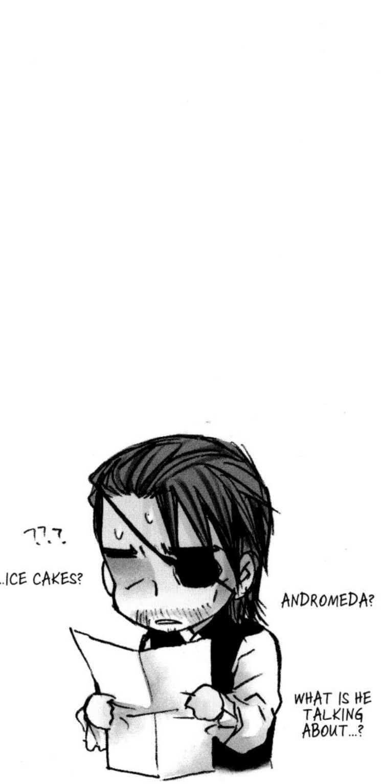
???
...ICE CAKES?
ANDROMEDA?
WHAT IS HE TALKING ABOUT...?

#62. CONVERSATION OF A MARRIED COUPLE, PART 1

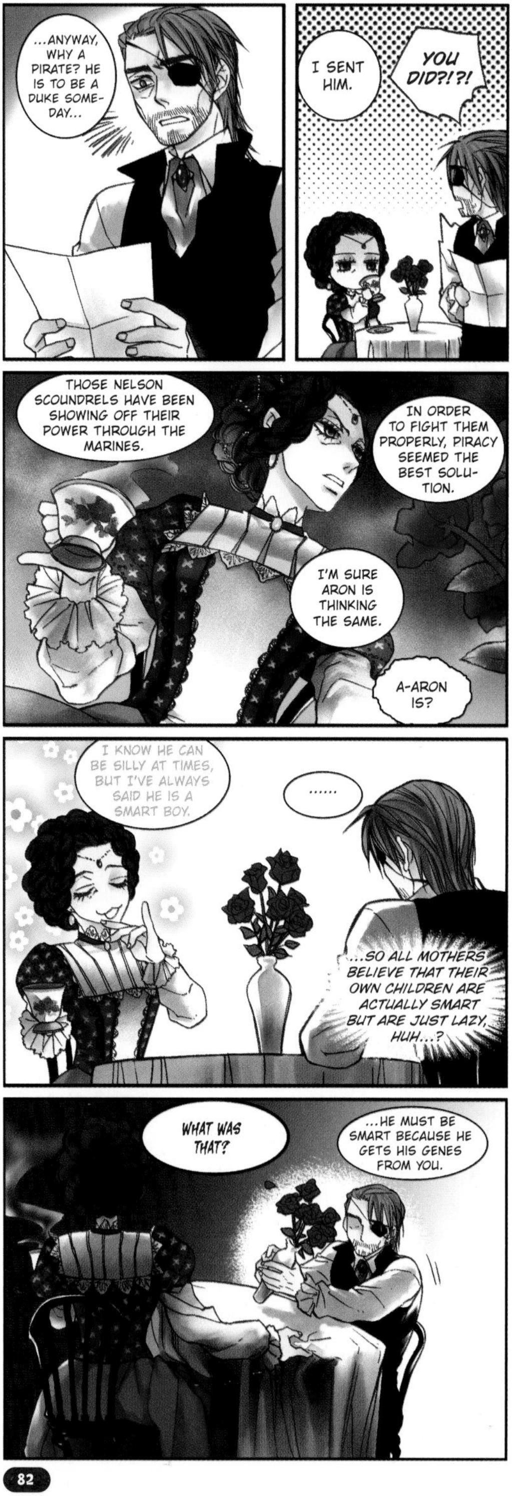
...ANYWAY, WHY A PIRATE? HE IS TO BE A DUKE SOME-DAY...
I SENT HIM.
YOU DID?!?!
THOSE NELSON SCOUNDRELS HAVE BEEN SHOWING OFF THEIR POWER THROUGH THE MARINES.
IN ORDER TO FIGHT THEM PROPERLY, PIRACY SEEMED THE BEST SOLU-TION.
I'M SURE ARON IS THINKING THE SAME.
A-ARON IS?
I KNOW HE CAN BE SILLY AT TIMES, BUT I'VE ALWAYS SAID HE IS A SMART BOY.
......
...SO ALL MOTHERS BELIEVE THAT THEIR OWN CHILDREN ARE ACTUALLY SMART BUT ARE JUST LAZY, HUH...?
WHAT WAS THAT?
...HE MUST BE SMART BECAUSE HE GETS HIS GENES FROM YOU.

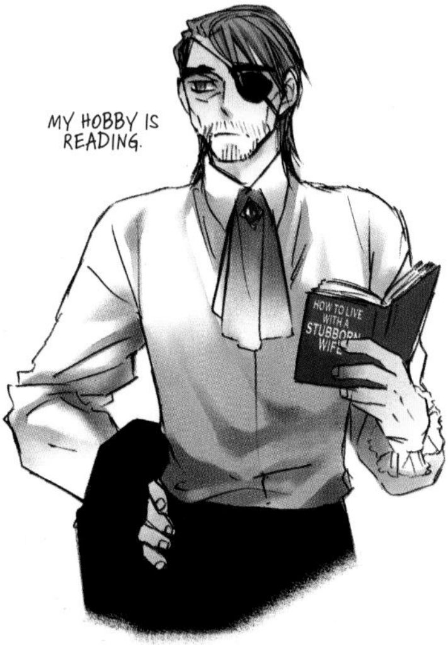
MY HOBBY IS READING.
HOW TO LIVE WITH A STUBBORN WIFE

#63. CONVERSATION OF A MARRIED COUPLE, PART 2

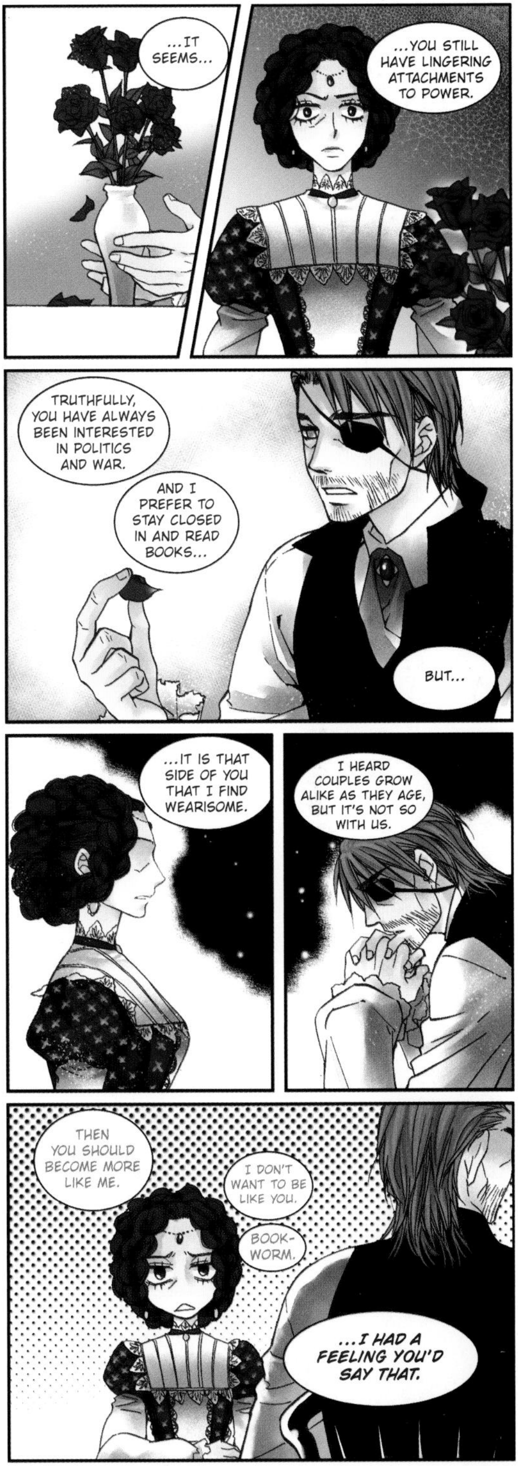
...IT SEEMS...
...YOU STILL HAVE LINGERING ATTACHMENTS TO POWER.
TRUTHFULLY, YOU HAVE ALWAYS BEEN INTERESTED IN POLITICS AND WAR.
AND I PREFER TO STAY CLOSED IN AND READ BOOKS...
BUT...
...IT IS THAT SIDE OF YOU THAT I FIND WEARISOME.
I HEARD COUPLES GROW ALIKE AS THEY AGE, BUT IT'S NOT SO WITH US.
THEN YOU SHOULD BECOME MORE LIKE ME.
I DON'T WANT TO BE LIKE YOU.
BOOK-WORM.
...I HAD A FEELING YOU'D SAY THAT.

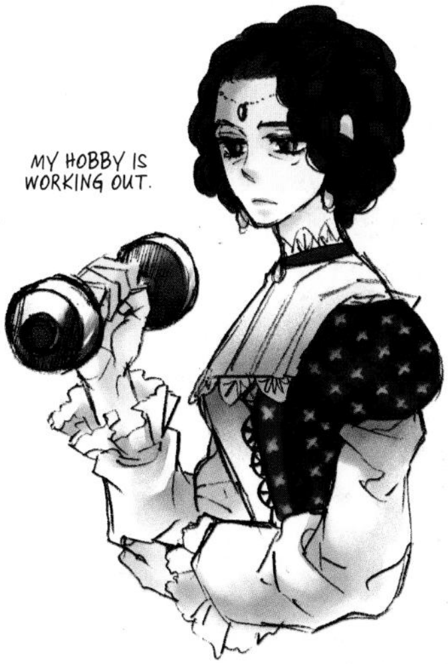
MY HOBBY IS WORKING OUT.

#64. CONVERSATION OF A MARRIED COUPLE, PART 3

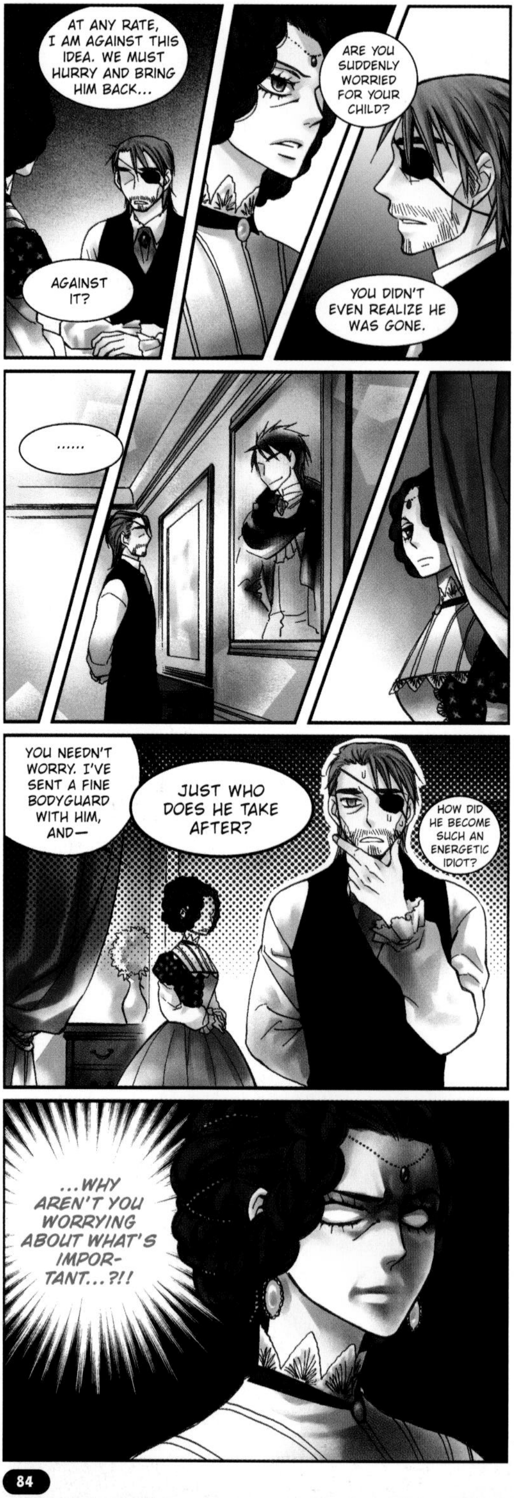

AT ANY RATE, I AM AGAINST THIS IDEA. WE MUST HURRY AND BRING HIM BACK...
AGAINST IT?
ARE YOU SUDDENLY WORRIED FOR YOUR CHILD?
YOU DIDN'T EVEN REALIZE HE WAS GONE.
......
YOU NEEDN'T WORRY. I'VE SENT A FINE BODYGUARD WITH HIM, AND—
JUST WHO DOES HE TAKE AFTER?
HOW DID HE BECOME SUCH AN ENERGETIC IDIOT?
...WHY AREN'T YOU WORRYING ABOUT WHAT'S IMPOR-TANT...?!!

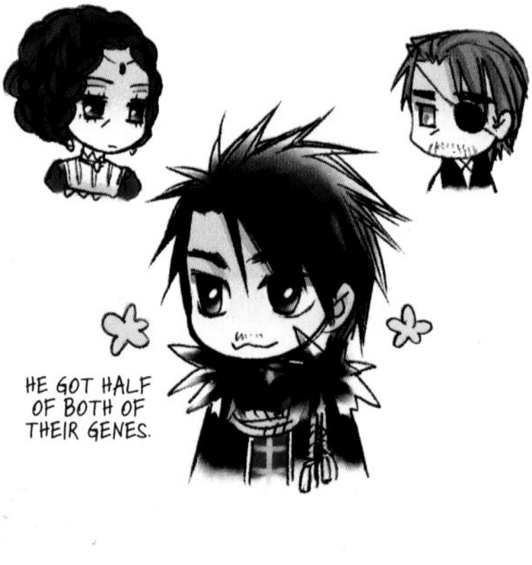

HE GOT HALF OF BOTH OF THEIR GENES.

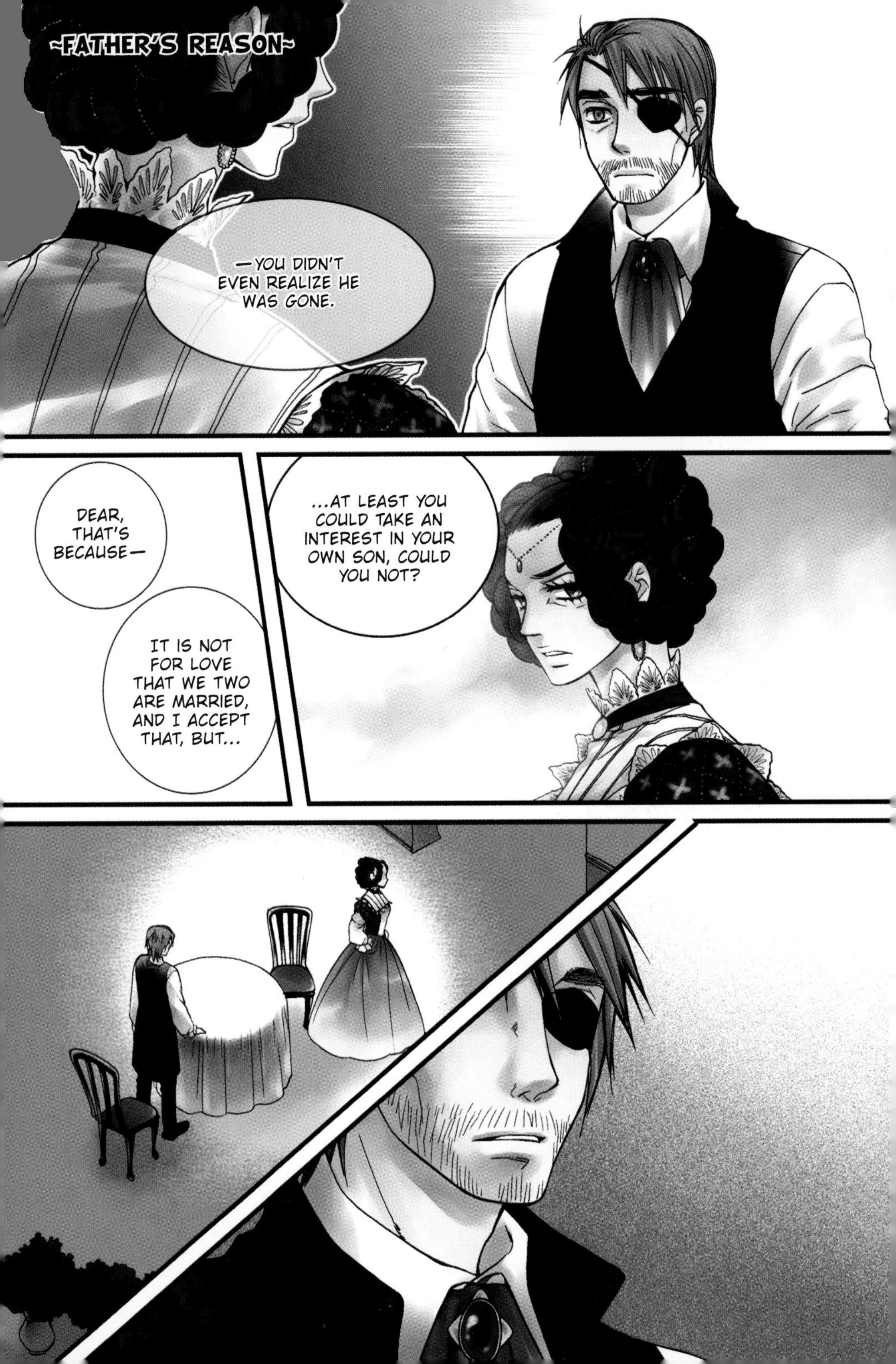
~FATHER'S REASON~
—YOU DIDN'T EVEN REALIZE HE WAS GONE.
...AT LEAST YOU COULD TAKE AN INTEREST IN YOUR OWN SON, COULD YOU NOT?
DEAR, THAT'S BECAUSE—
IT IS NOT FOR LOVE THAT WE TWO ARE MARRIED, AND I ACCEPT THAT, BUT...

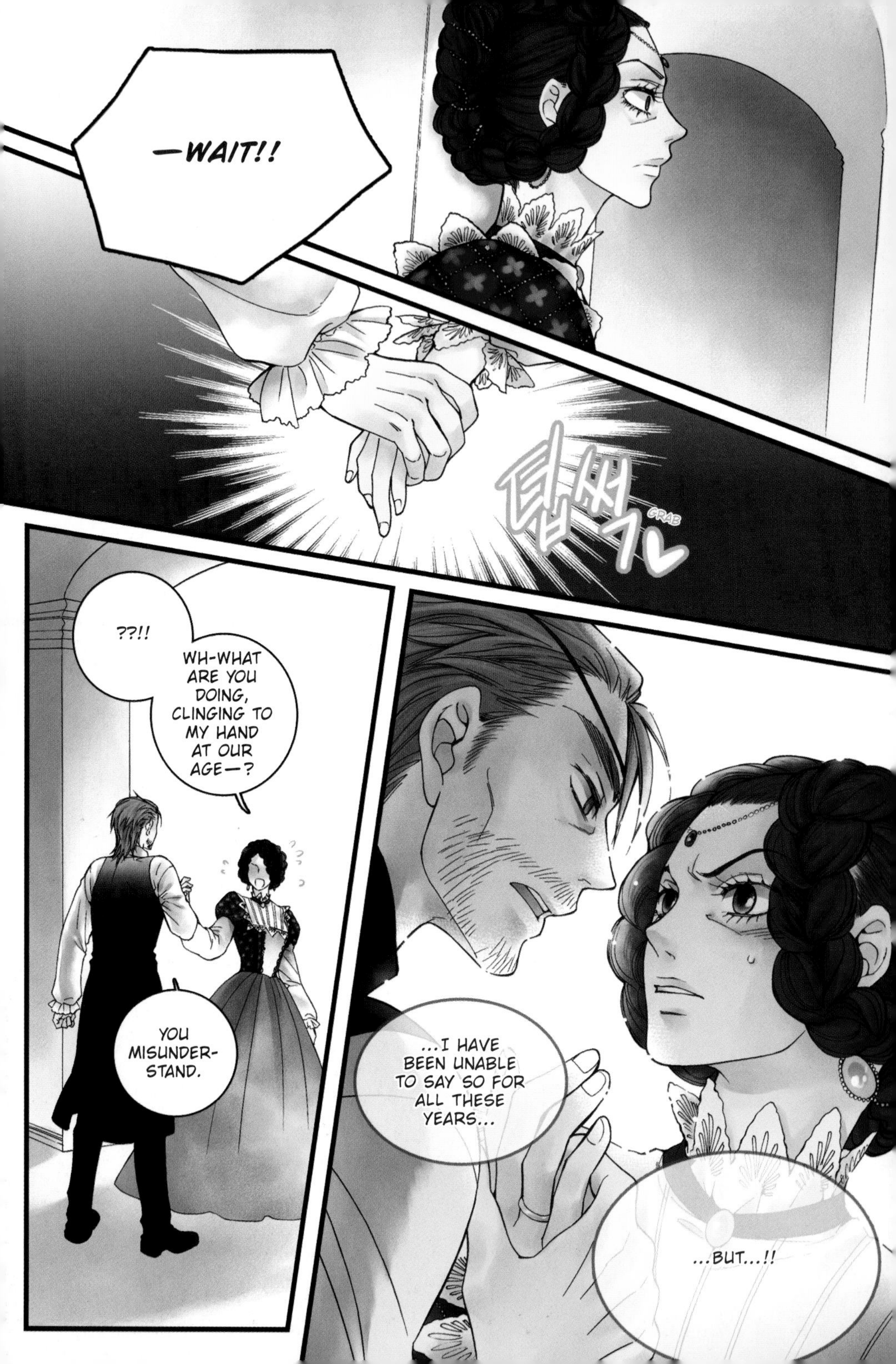
—WAIT!!
탑싹
GRAB
??!!
WH-WHAT ARE YOU DOING, CLINGING TO MY HAND AT OUR AGE—?
YOU MISUNDER-STAND.
...I HAVE BEEN UNABLE TO SAY SO FOR ALL THESE YEARS...
...BUT...!!

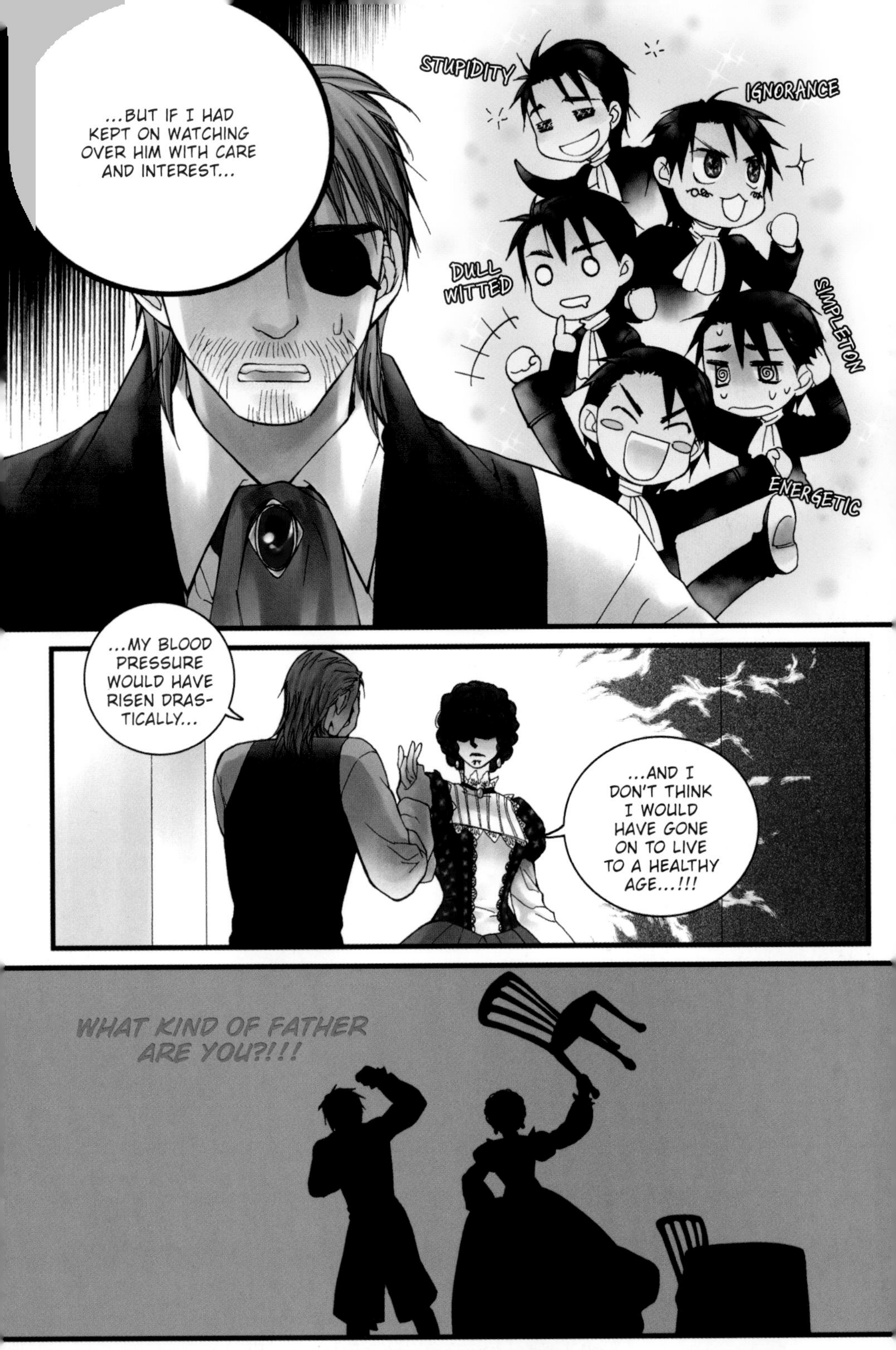
...BUT IF I HAD KEPT ON WATCHING OVER HIM WITH CARE AND INTEREST...
STUPIDITY
IGNORANCE
DULL WITTED
SIMPLETON
ENERGETIC
...MY BLOOD PRESSURE WOULD HAVE RISEN DRASTICALLY...
...AND I DON'T THINK I WOULD HAVE GONE ON TO LIVE TO A HEALTHY AGE...!!!
WHAT KIND OF FATHER ARE YOU?!!!

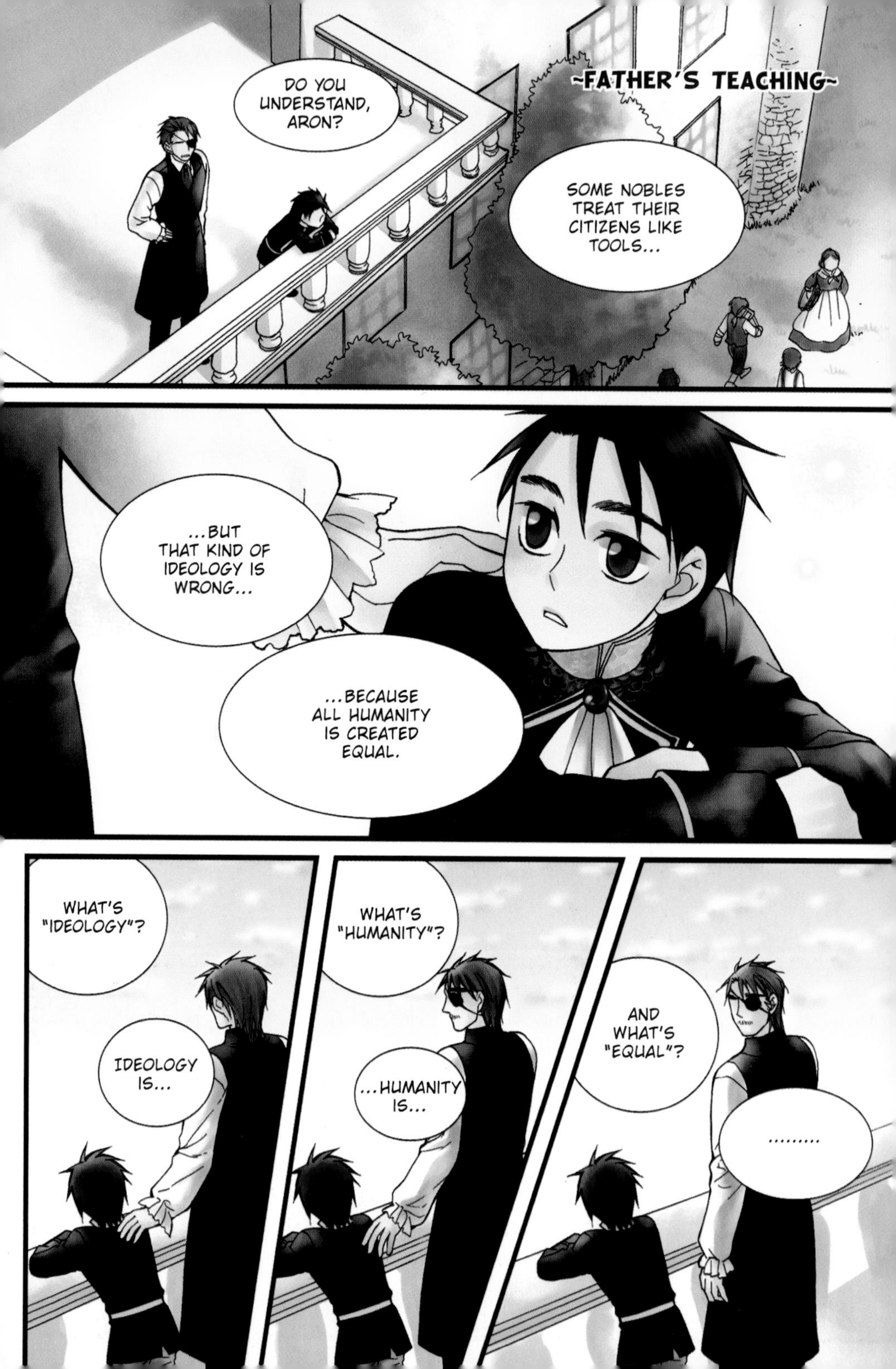
~FATHER'S TEACHING~
DO YOU UNDERSTAND, ARON?
SOME NOBLES TREAT THEIR CITIZENS LIKE TOOLS...
...BUT THAT KIND OF IDEOLOGY IS WRONG...
...BECAUSE ALL HUMANITY IS CREATED EQUAL.
WHAT'S "IDEOLOGY"?
IDEOLOGY IS...
WHAT'S "HUMANITY"?
...HUMANITY IS...
AND WHAT'S "EQUAL"?
....

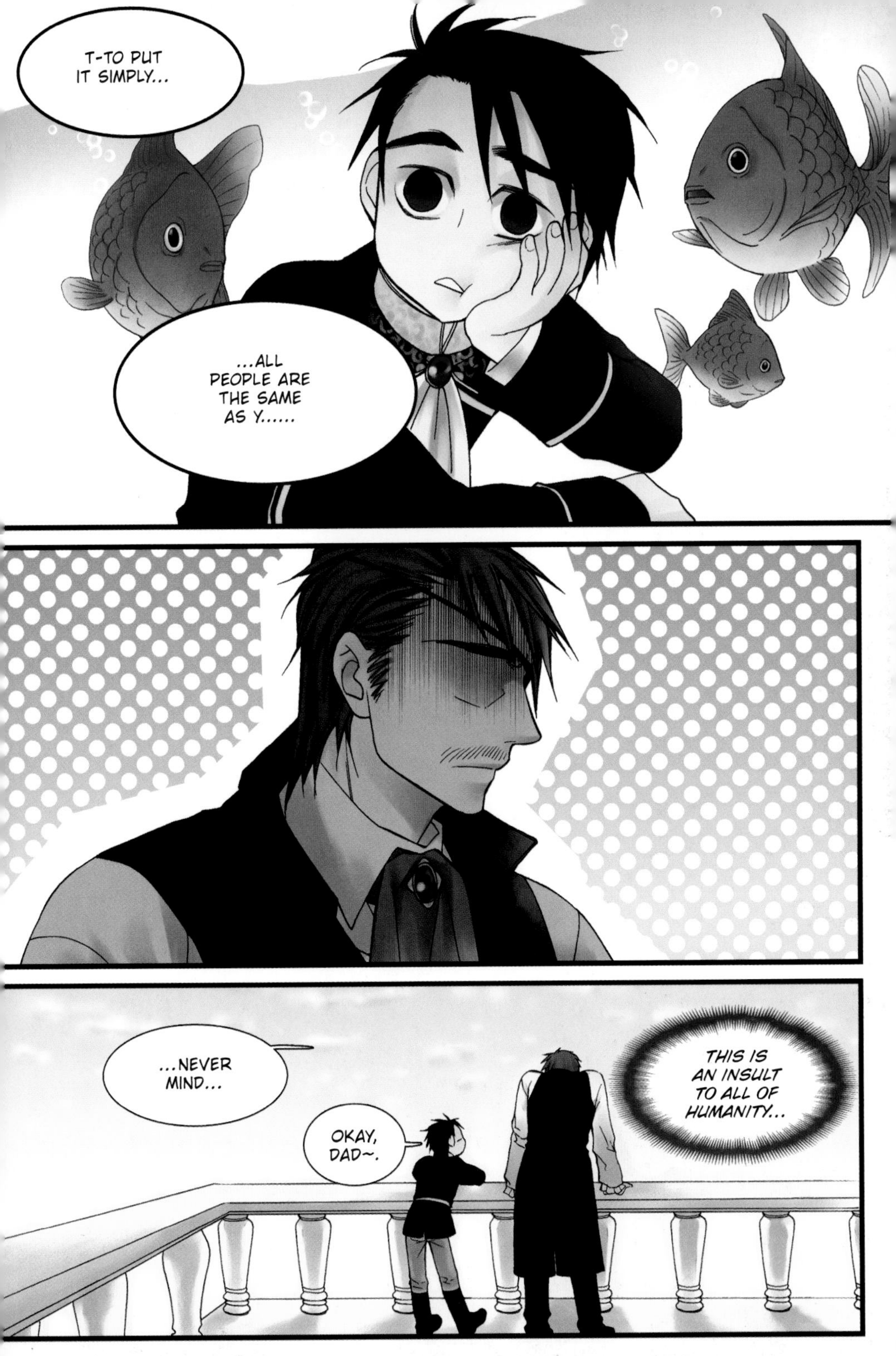
T-TO PUT IT SIMPLY...
...ALL PEOPLE ARE THE SAME AS Y......
...NEVER MIND...
THIS IS AN INSULT TO ALL OF HUMANITY...
OKAY, DAD~.

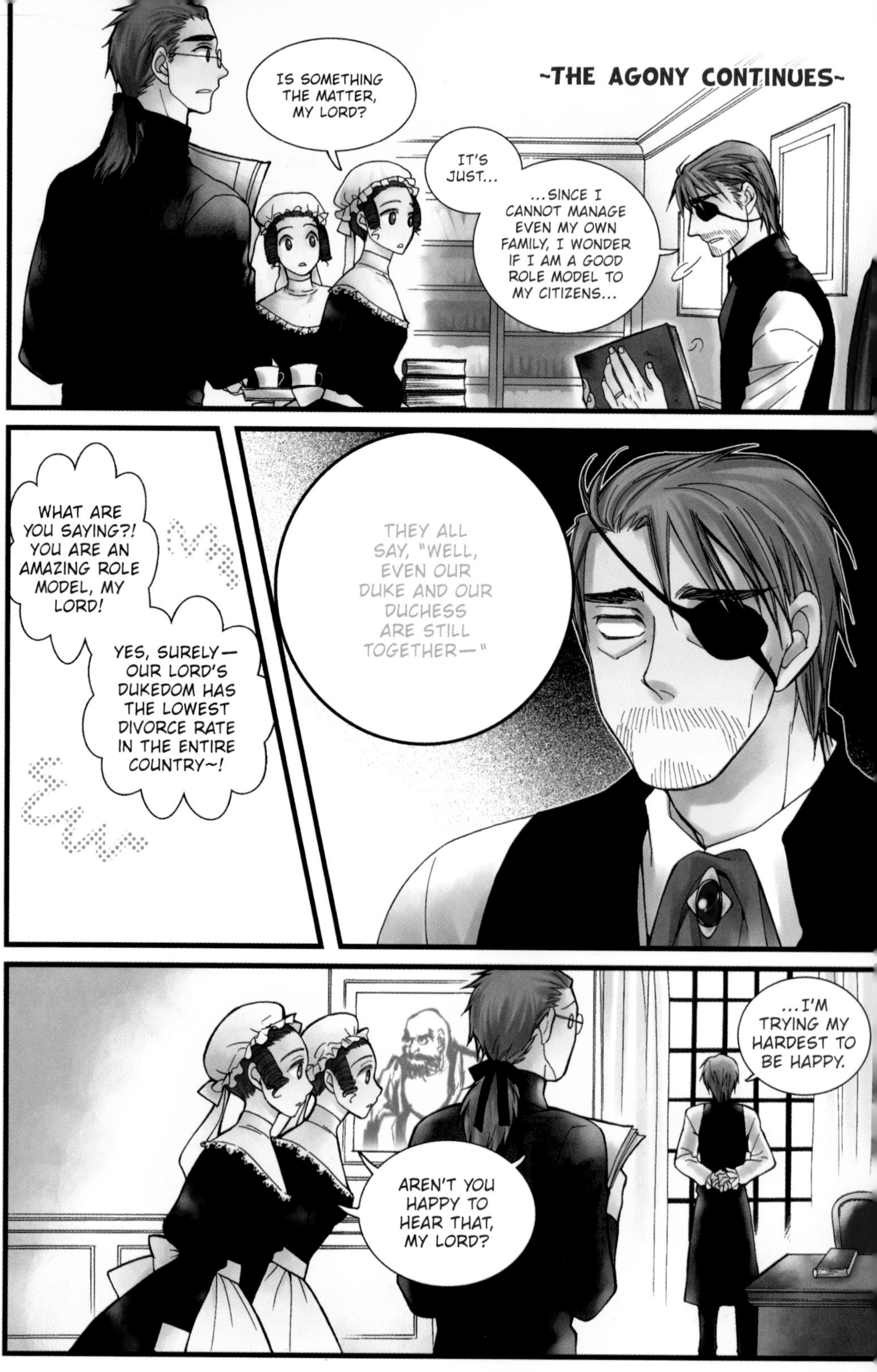
~THE AGONY CONTINUES~
IS SOMETHING THE MATTER, MY LORD?
IT'S JUST...
...SINCE I CANNOT MANAGE EVEN MY OWN FAMILY, I WONDER IF I AM A GOOD ROLE MODEL TO MY CITIZENS...
WHAT ARE YOU SAYING?! YOU ARE AN AMAZING ROLE MODEL, MY LORD!
YES, SURELY— OUR LORD'S DUKEDOM HAS THE LOWEST DIVORCE RATE IN THE ENTIRE COUNTRY~!
THEY ALL SAY, "WELL, EVEN OUR DUKE AND OUR DUCHESS ARE STILL TOGETHER—"
AREN'T YOU HAPPY TO HEAR THAT, MY LORD?
...I'M TRYING MY HARDEST TO BE HAPPY.

#65. THERE'S NO FOOD

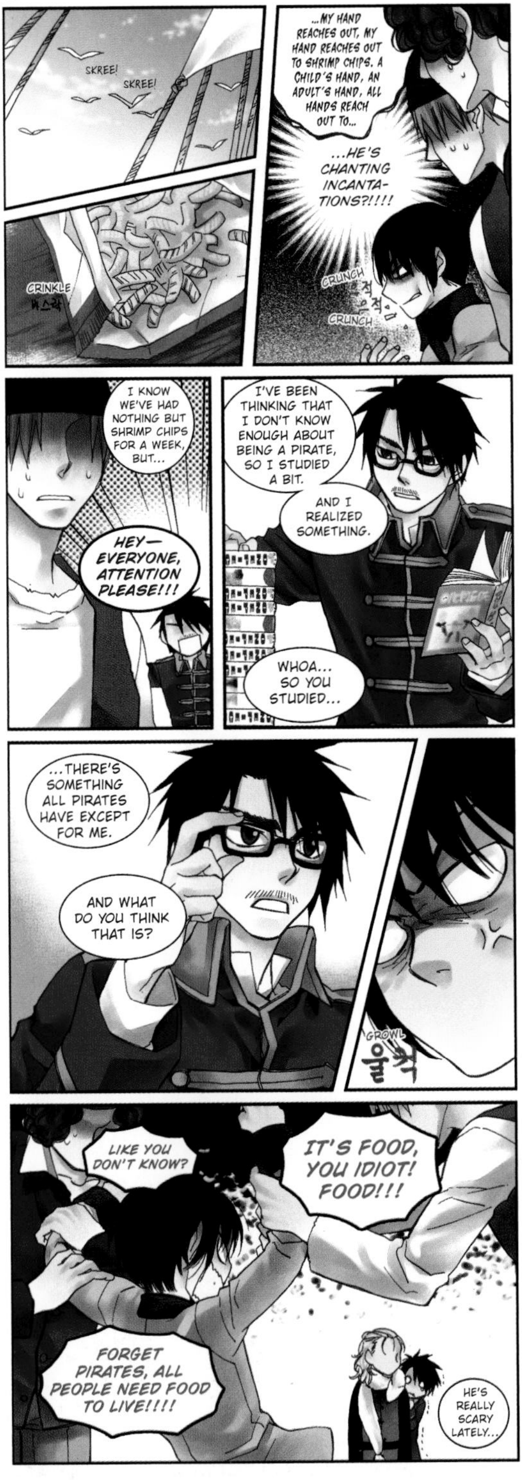
SKREE!
SKREE!
CRINKLE
...MY HAND REACHES OUT, MY HAND REACHES OUT TO SHRIMP CHIPS. A CHILD'S HAND, AN ADULT'S HAND, ALL HANDS REACH OUT TO...
...HE'S CHANTING INCANTATIONS?!!!!
CRUNCH
CRUNCH
I KNOW WE'VE HAD NOTHING BUT SHRIMP CHIPS FOR A WEEK, BUT...
HEY— EVERYONE, ATTENTION PLEASE!!!
I'VE BEEN THINKING THAT I DON'T KNOW ENOUGH ABOUT BEING A PIRATE, SO I STUDIED A BIT.
AND I REALIZED SOMETHING.
WHOA... SO YOU STUDIED...
...THERE'S SOMETHING ALL PIRATES HAVE EXCEPT FOR ME.
AND WHAT DO YOU THINK THAT IS?
GROWL
LIKE YOU DON'T KNOW?
IT'S FOOD, YOU IDIOT! FOOD!!!
FORGET PIRATES, ALL PEOPLE NEED FOOD TO LIVE!!!!
HE'S REALLY SCARY LATELY...

★INSTRUCTION MANUAL: WARNING★
*BECAUSE SHE USES HER HEAD MORE THAN THE OTHERS, SHE MUST BE FED PROPERLY.

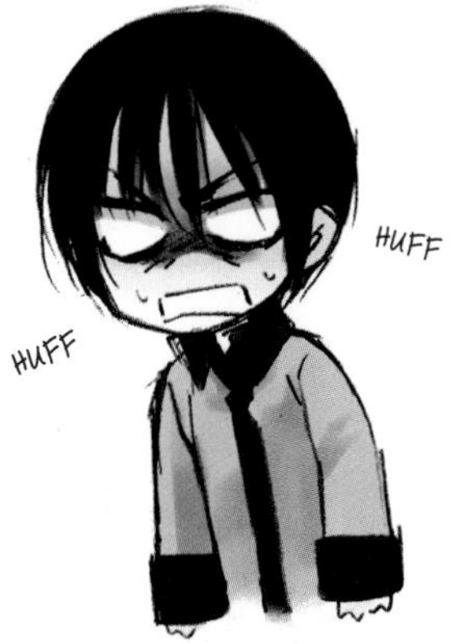
HUFF
HUFF

#66. I HAVE NOTHING BUT MONEY

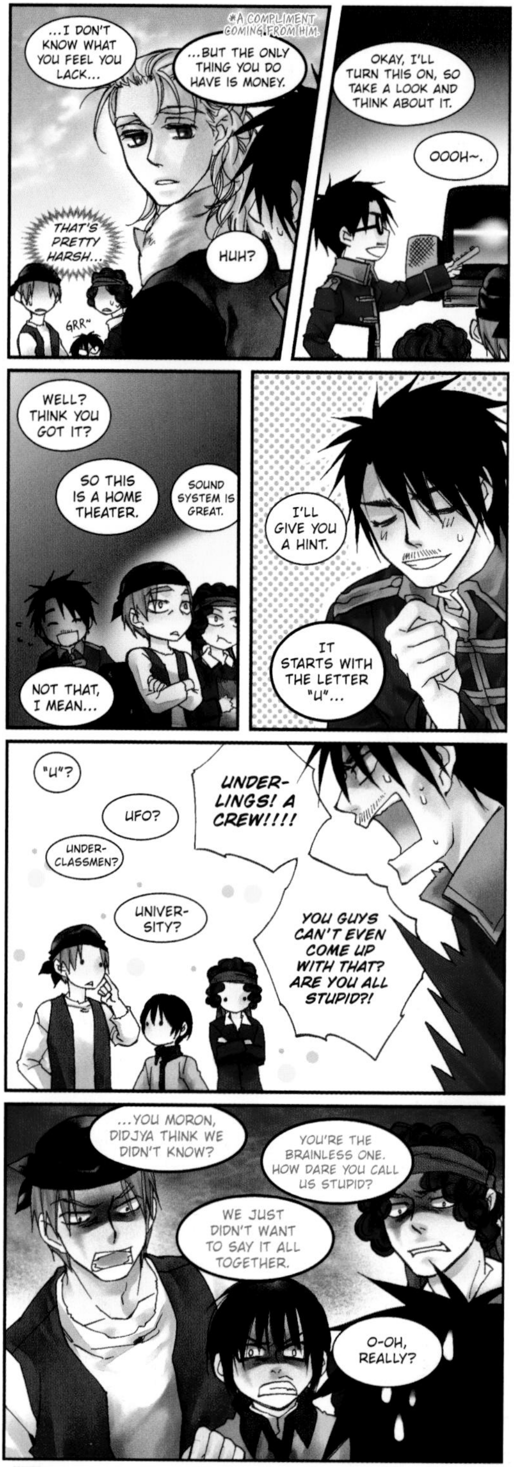
...I DON'T KNOW WHAT YOU FEEL YOU LACK...
...BUT THE ONLY THING YOU DO HAVE IS MONEY.
*A COMPLIMENT COMING FROM HIM.
THAT'S PRETTY HARSH...
HUH?
GRR~
OKAY, I'LL TURN THIS ON, SO TAKE A LOOK AND THINK ABOUT IT.
OOOH~.
WELL? THINK YOU GOT IT?
SO THIS IS A HOME THEATER.
SOUND SYSTEM IS GREAT.
NOT THAT, I MEAN...
I'LL GIVE YOU A HINT.
IT STARTS WITH THE LETTER "U"...
"U"?
UFO?
UNDER-CLASSMEN?
UNIVER-SITY?
UNDER-LINGS! A CREW!!!!
YOU GUYS CAN'T EVEN COME UP WITH THAT? ARE YOU ALL STUPID?!
...YOU MORON, DIDJYA THINK WE DIDN'T KNOW?
YOU'RE THE BRAINLESS ONE. HOW DARE YOU CALL US STUPID?
WE JUST DIDN'T WANT TO SAY IT ALL TOGETHER.
O-OH, REALLY?

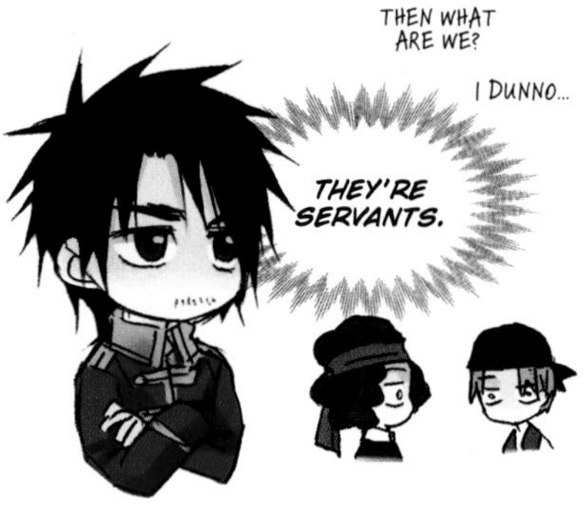
THEN WHAT ARE WE?
I DUNNO...
THEY'RE SERVANTS.

#67. STEADFASTLY ADJUSTING TO THE SITUATION

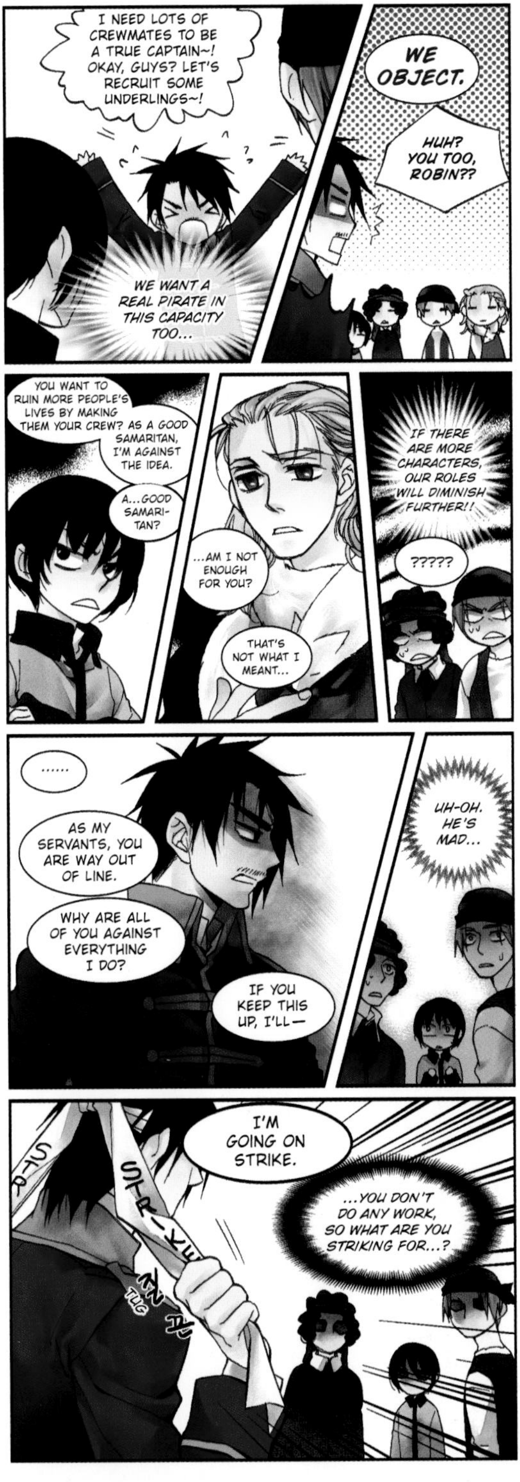

I NEED LOTS OF CREWMATES TO BE A TRUE CAPTAIN~! OKAY, GUYS? LET'S RECRUIT SOME UNDERLINGS~!
WE WANT A REAL PIRATE IN THIS CAPACITY TOO...
WE OBJECT.
HUH? YOU TOO, ROBIN??
YOU WANT TO RUIN MORE PEOPLE'S LIVES BY MAKING THEM YOUR CREW? AS A GOOD SAMARITAN, I'M AGAINST THE IDEA.
A...GOOD SAMARI-TAN?
...AM I NOT ENOUGH FOR YOU?
THAT'S NOT WHAT I MEANT...
IF THERE ARE MORE CHARACTERS, OUR ROLES WILL DIMINISH FURTHER!!
?????
......
AS MY SERVANTS, YOU ARE WAY OUT OF LINE.
WHY ARE ALL OF YOU AGAINST EVERYTHING I DO?
IF YOU KEEP THIS UP, I'LL—
UH-OH. HE'S MAD...
I'M GOING ON STRIKE.
STR
STRIKE
TUG
...YOU DON'T DO ANY WORK, SO WHAT ARE YOU STRIKING FOR...?

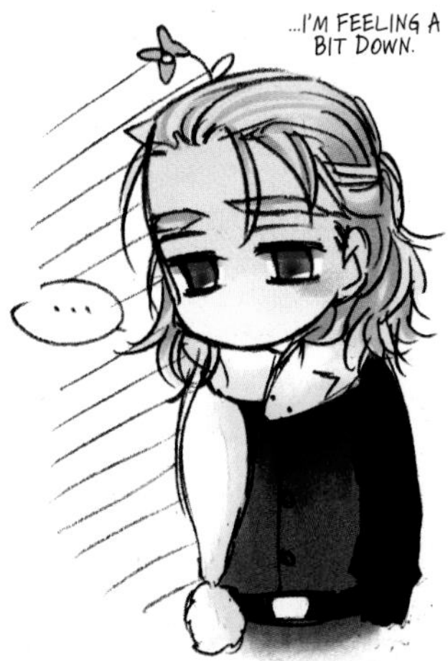

...I'M FEELING A BIT DOWN.
...

#68. CANDLELIGHT VIGIL

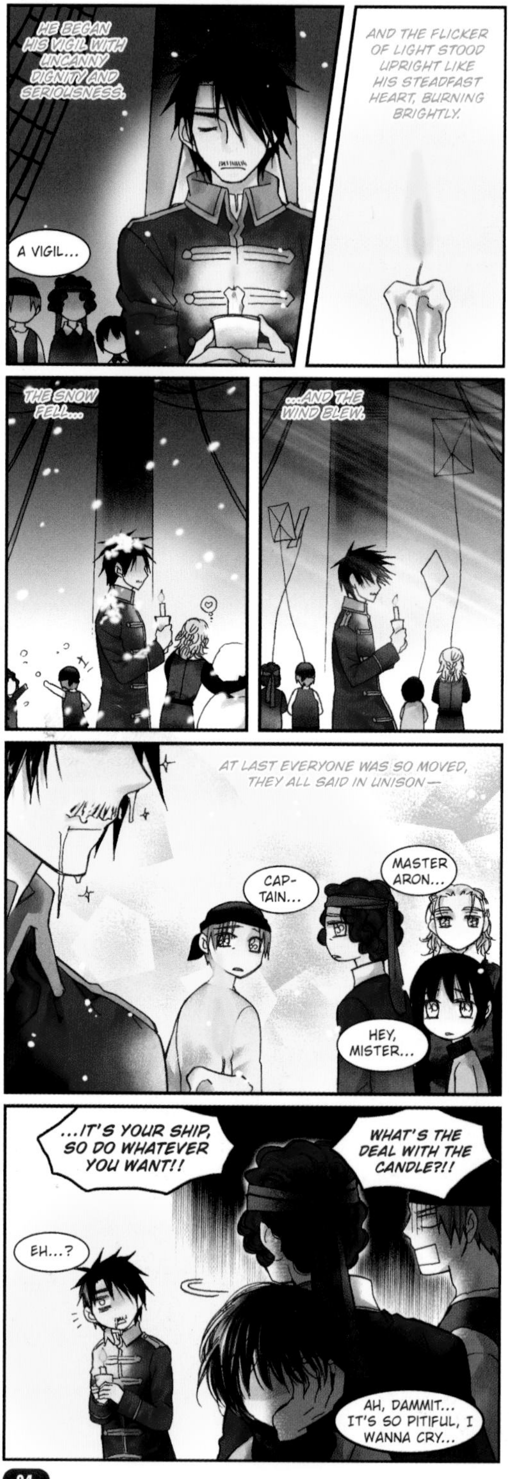
HE BEGAN HIS VIGIL WITH UNCANNY DIGNITY AND SERIOUSNESS.
A VIGIL...
AND THE FLICKER OF LIGHT STOOD UPRIGHT LIKE HIS STEADFAST HEART, BURNING BRIGHTLY.
THE SNOW FELL...
...AND THE WIND BLEW.
AT LAST EVERYONE WAS SO MOVED, THEY ALL SAID IN UNISON—
CAP-TAIN...
MASTER ARON...
HEY, MISTER...
...IT'S YOUR SHIP, SO DO WHATEVER YOU WANT!!
WHAT'S THE DEAL WITH THE CANDLE?!!
EH...?
AH, DAMMIT... IT'S SO PITIFUL, I WANNA CRY...

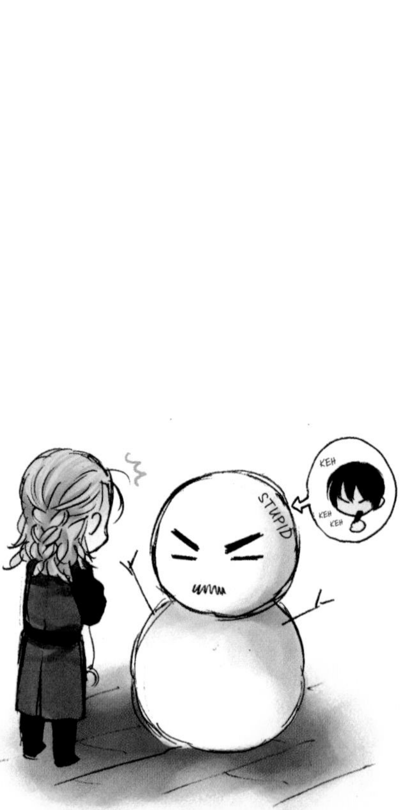
STUPID
KEH
KEH
KEH

#69. I'M NOT AN OUTCAST

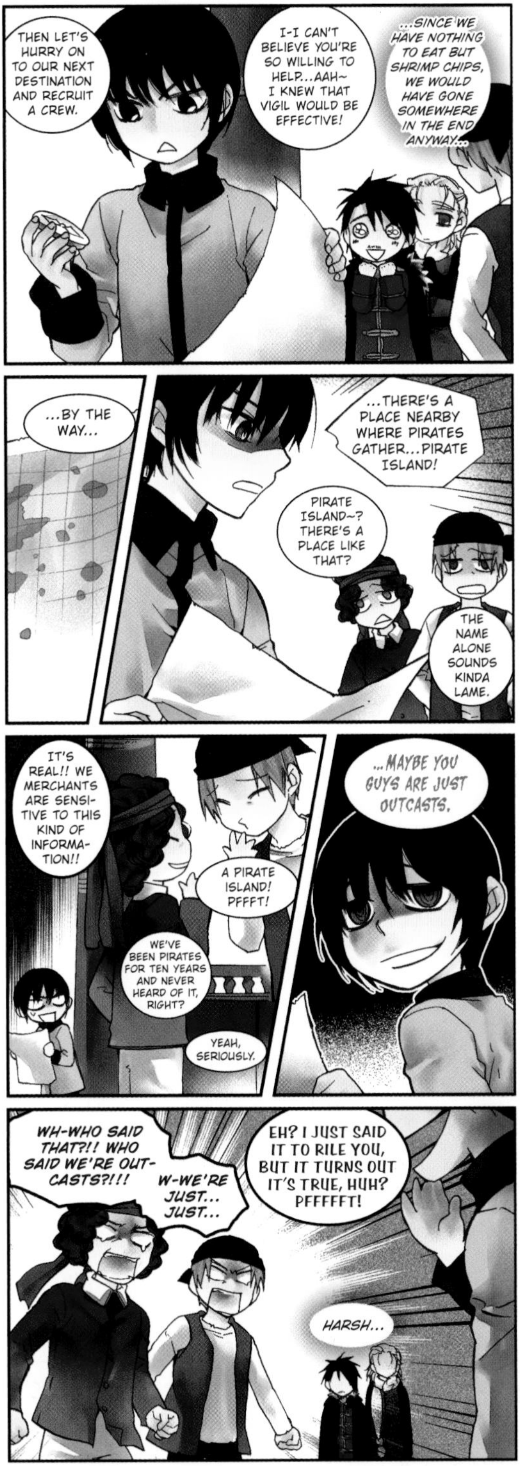

THEN LET'S HURRY ON TO OUR NEXT DESTINATION AND RECRUIT A CREW.
I-I CAN'T BELIEVE YOU'RE SO WILLING TO HELP...AAH~ I KNEW THAT VIGIL WOULD BE EFFECTIVE!
...SINCE WE HAVE NOTHING TO EAT BUT SHRIMP CHIPS, WE WOULD HAVE GONE SOMEWHERE IN THE END ANYWAY...
...BY THE WAY...
...THERE'S A PLACE NEARBY WHERE PIRATES GATHER...PIRATE ISLAND!
PIRATE ISLAND~? THERE'S A PLACE LIKE THAT?
THE NAME ALONE SOUNDS KINDA LAME.
IT'S REAL!! WE MERCHANTS ARE SENSITIVE TO THIS KIND OF INFORMATION!!
A PIRATE ISLAND! PFFFT!
WE'VE BEEN PIRATES FOR TEN YEARS AND NEVER HEARD OF IT, RIGHT?
YEAH, SERIOUSLY.
...MAYBE YOU GUYS ARE JUST OUTCASTS.
WH-WHO SAID THAT?!! WHO SAID WE'RE OUTCASTS?!!!
W-WE'RE JUST... JUST...
EH? I JUST SAID IT TO RILE YOU, BUT IT TURNS OUT IT'S TRUE, HUH? PFFFFFT!
HARSH...

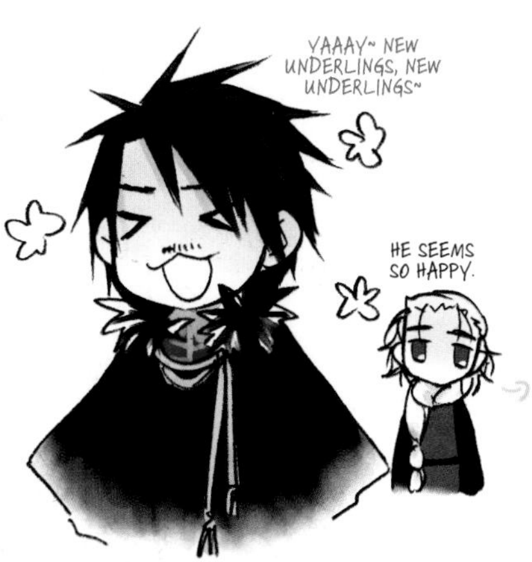

YAAAY~ NEW UNDERLINGS, NEW UNDERLINGS~
HE SEEMS SO HAPPY.

#70. THE TRUTH

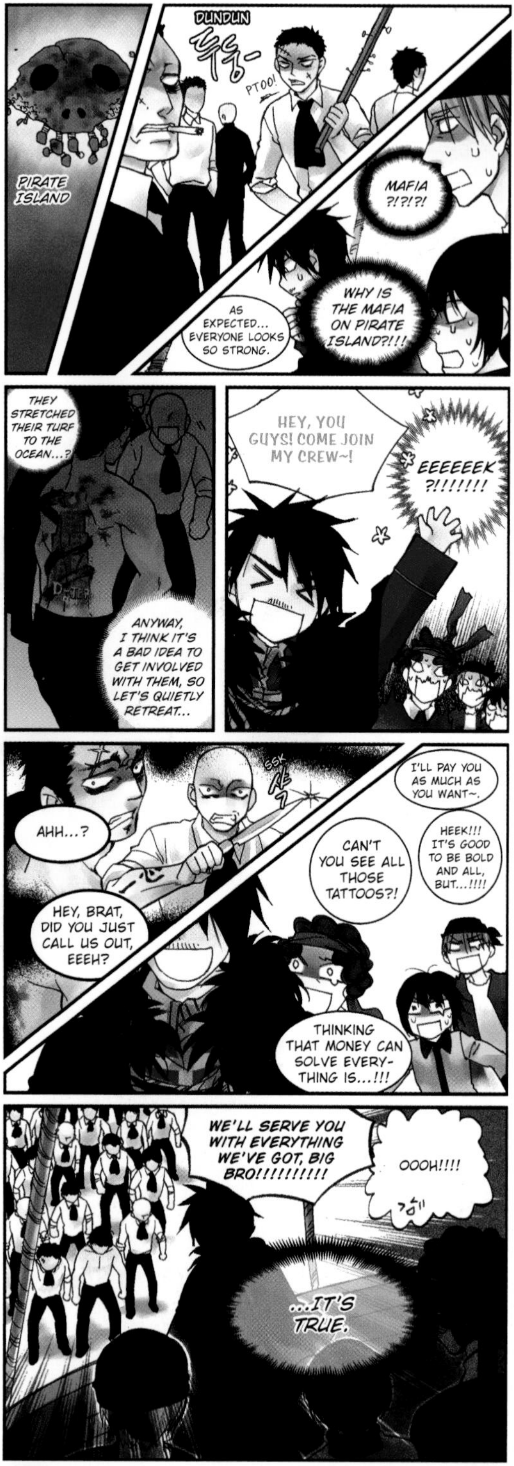
DUNDUN
PIRATE ISLAND
PTOO!
MAFIA ?!?!?!
AS EXPECTED... EVERYONE LOOKS SO STRONG.
WHY IS THE MAFIA ON PIRATE ISLAND?!!!
THEY STRETCHED THEIR TURF TO THE OCEAN...?
ANYWAY, I THINK IT'S A BAD IDEA TO GET INVOLVED WITH THEM, SO LET'S QUIETLY RETREAT...
HEY, YOU GUYS! COME JOIN MY CREW~!
EEEEEEK ?!!!!!!!
SSK
AHH...?
HEY, BRAT, DID YOU JUST CALL US OUT, EEEH?
I'LL PAY YOU AS MUCH AS YOU WANT~.
HEEK!!! IT'S GOOD TO BE BOLD AND ALL, BUT...!!!!
CAN'T YOU SEE ALL THOSE TATTOOS?!
THINKING THAT MONEY CAN SOLVE EVERYTHING IS...!!!
WE'LL SERVE YOU WITH EVERYTHING WE'VE GOT, BIG BRO!!!!!!!!!!
OOOH!!!!
...IT'S TRUE.

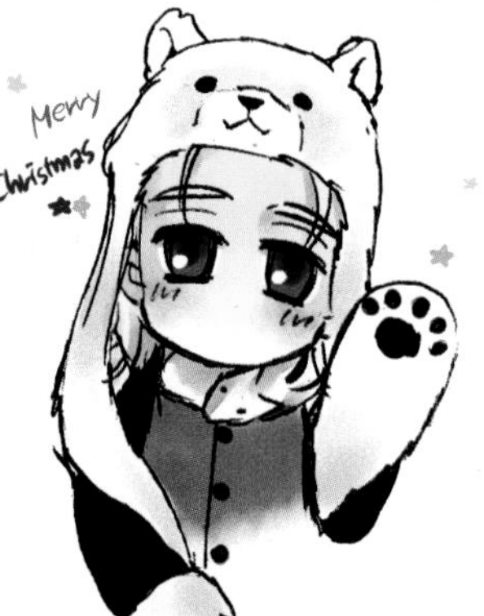
Merry Christmas

#71. IT'S AN AMAZING ABILITY, BUT...

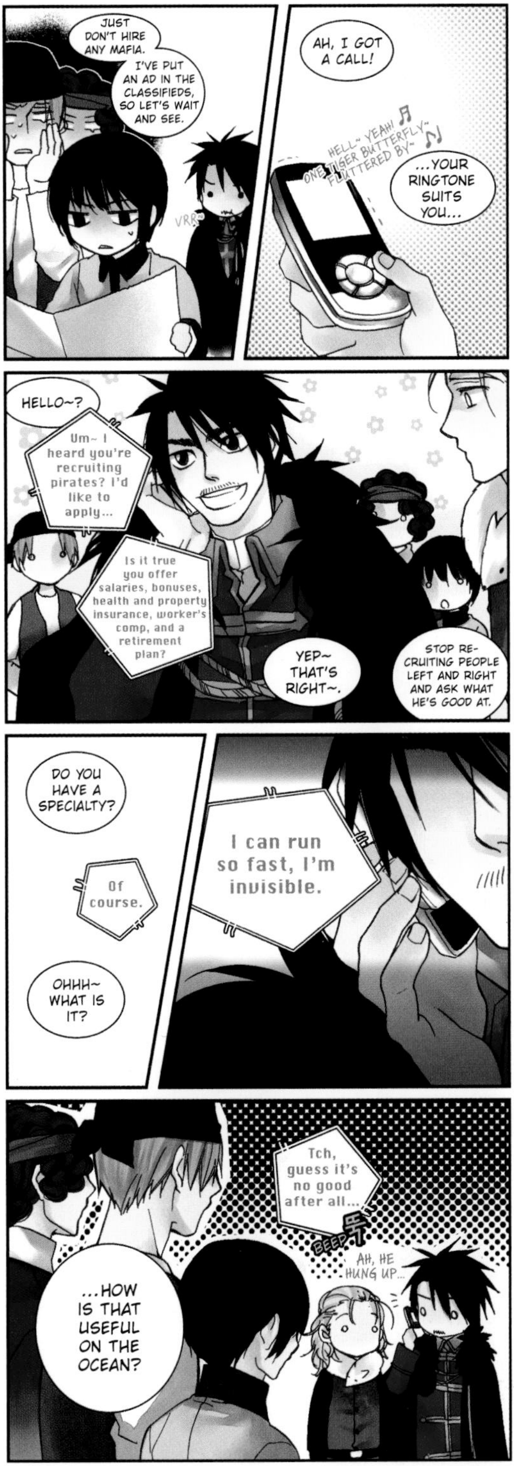
JUST DON'T HIRE ANY MAFIA.
I'VE PUT AN AD IN THE CLASSIFIEDS, SO LET'S WAIT AND SEE.
VRR~
AH, I GOT A CALL!
HELL~ YEAH! ONE TIGER BUTTERFLY FLUTTERED BY~
...YOUR RINGTONE SUITS YOU...
HELLO~?
Um~ I heard you're recruiting pirates? I'd like to apply...
Is it true you offer salaries, bonuses, health and property insurance, worker's comp, and a retirement plan?
YEP~ THAT'S RIGHT~.
STOP RE-CRUITING PEOPLE LEFT AND RIGHT AND ASK WHAT HE'S GOOD AT.
DO YOU HAVE A SPECIALTY?
Of course.
OHHH~ WHAT IS IT?
I can run so fast, I'm invisible.
Tch, guess it's no good after all...
BEEP
AH, HE HUNG UP...
...HOW IS THAT USEFUL ON THE OCEAN?

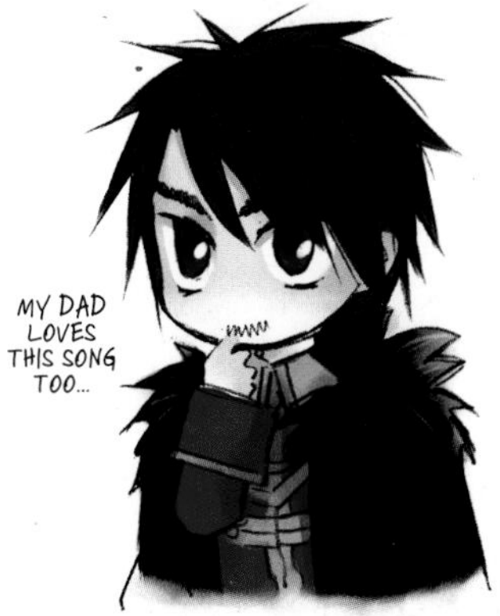
MY DAD LOVES THIS SONG TOO...

#72. NO ONE IS ENTIRELY USELESS

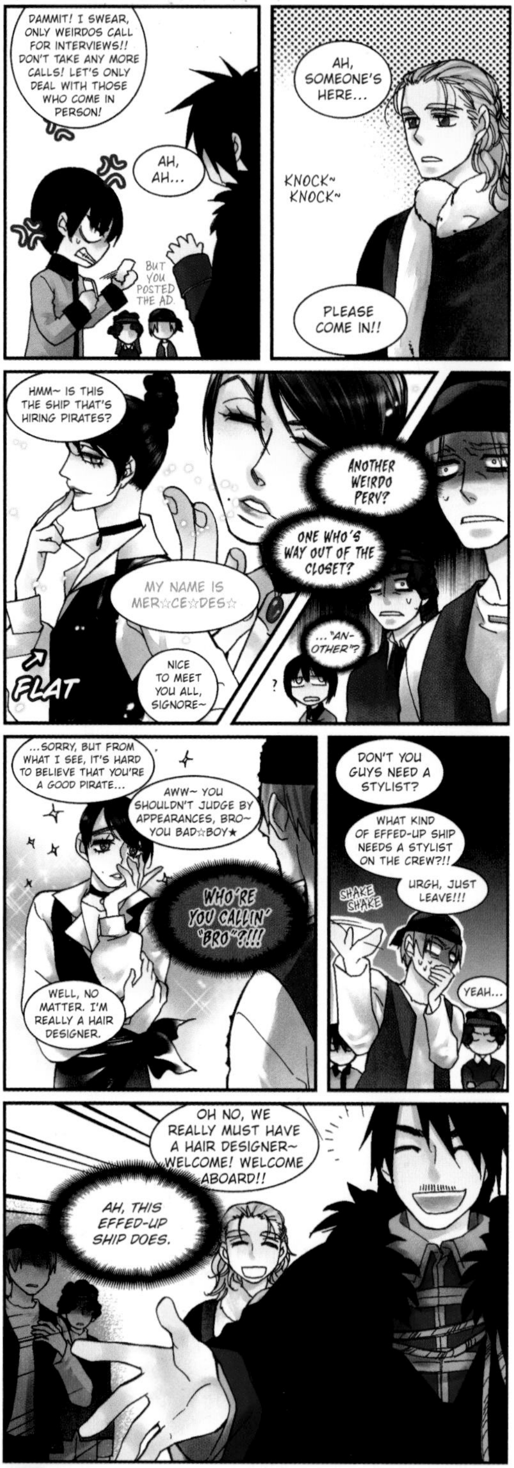
DAMMIT! I SWEAR, ONLY WEIRDOS CALL FOR INTERVIEWS!! DON'T TAKE ANY MORE CALLS! LET'S ONLY DEAL WITH THOSE WHO COME IN PERSON!
AH, AH...
BUT YOU POSTED THE AD.
AH, SOMEONE'S HERE...
KNOCK~ KNOCK~
PLEASE COME IN!!
HMM~ IS THIS THE SHIP THAT'S HIRING PIRATES?
ANOTHER WEIRDO PERV?
ONE WHO'S WAY OUT OF THE CLOSET?
MY NAME IS MER☆CE☆DES☆
..."AN-OTHER"?
FLAT
NICE TO MEET YOU ALL, SIGNORE~
...SORRY, BUT FROM WHAT I SEE, IT'S HARD TO BELIEVE THAT YOU'RE A GOOD PIRATE...
AWW~ YOU SHOULDN'T JUDGE BY APPEARANCES, BRO~ YOU BAD☆BOY★
WHO'RE YOU CALLIN' "BRO"?!!!
WELL, NO MATTER. I'M REALLY A HAIR DESIGNER.
DON'T YOU GUYS NEED A STYLIST?
WHAT KIND OF EFFED-UP SHIP NEEDS A STYLIST ON THE CREW?!!
URGH, JUST LEAVE!!!
SHAKE SHAKE
YEAH...
OH NO, WE REALLY MUST HAVE A HAIR DESIGNER~ WELCOME! WELCOME ABOARD!!
AH, THIS EFFED-UP SHIP DOES.

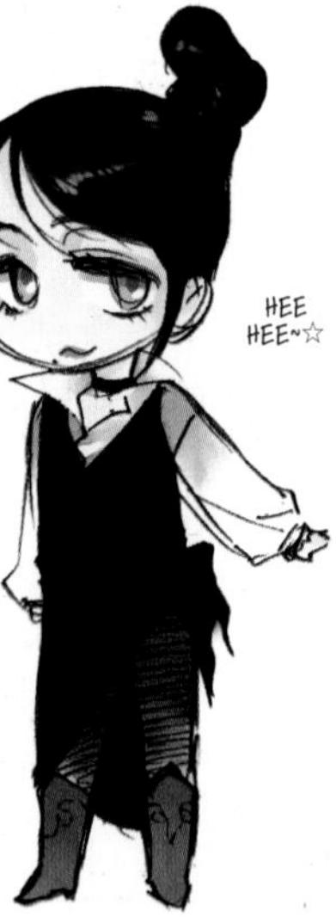
HEE HEE~☆

#73. TURNING THE TABLES

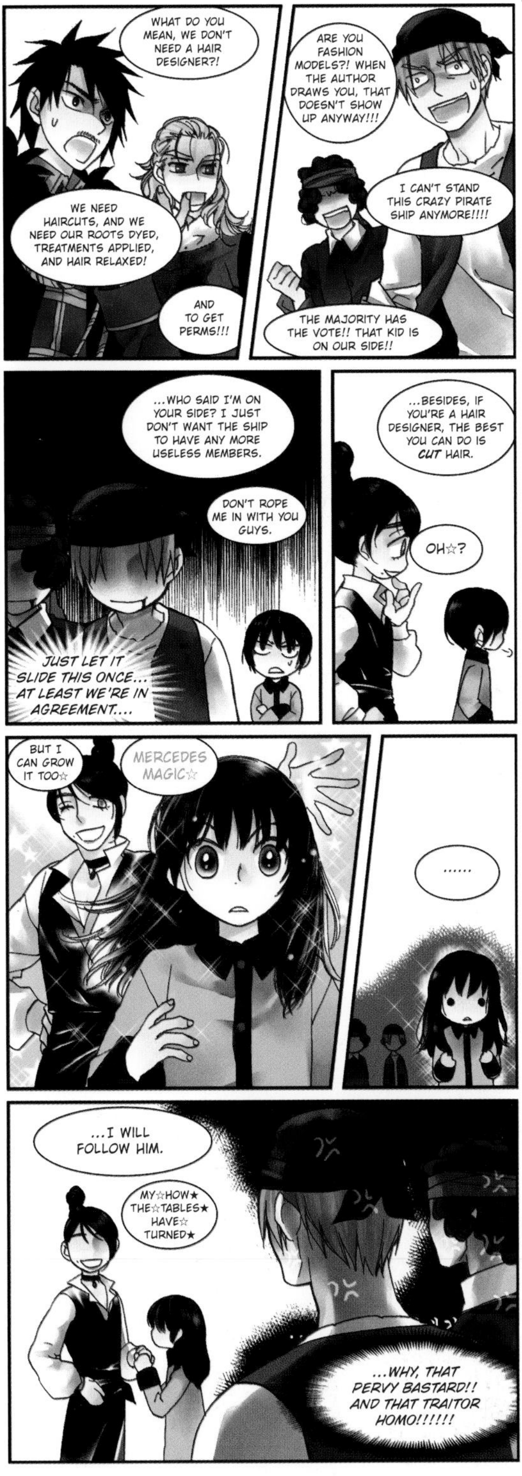
WHAT DO YOU MEAN, WE DON'T NEED A HAIR DESIGNER?!
WE NEED HAIRCUTS, AND WE NEED OUR ROOTS DYED, TREATMENTS APPLIED, AND HAIR RELAXED!
AND TO GET PERMS!!!
ARE YOU FASHION MODELS?! WHEN THE AUTHOR DRAWS YOU, THAT DOESN'T SHOW UP ANYWAY!!!
I CAN'T STAND THIS CRAZY PIRATE SHIP ANYMORE!!!!
THE MAJORITY HAS THE VOTE!! THAT KID IS ON OUR SIDE!!
...WHO SAID I'M ON YOUR SIDE? I JUST DON'T WANT THE SHIP TO HAVE ANY MORE USELESS MEMBERS.
DON'T ROPE ME IN WITH YOU GUYS.
JUST LET IT SLIDE THIS ONCE... AT LEAST WE'RE IN AGREEMENT....
...BESIDES, IF YOU'RE A HAIR DESIGNER, THE BEST YOU CAN DO IS *CUT* HAIR.
OH☆?
BUT I CAN GROW IT TOO☆
MERCEDES MAGIC☆
......
...I WILL FOLLOW HIM.
MY☆HOW★ THE☆TABLES★ HAVE☆ TURNED★
...WHY, THAT PERVY BASTARD!! AND THAT TRAITOR HOMO!!!!!!

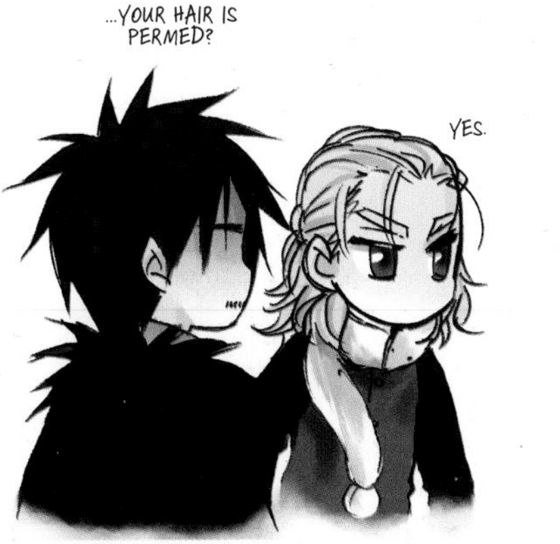
...YOUR HAIR IS PERMED?
YES.

#74. THE KING OF LOSERS IS CROWNED

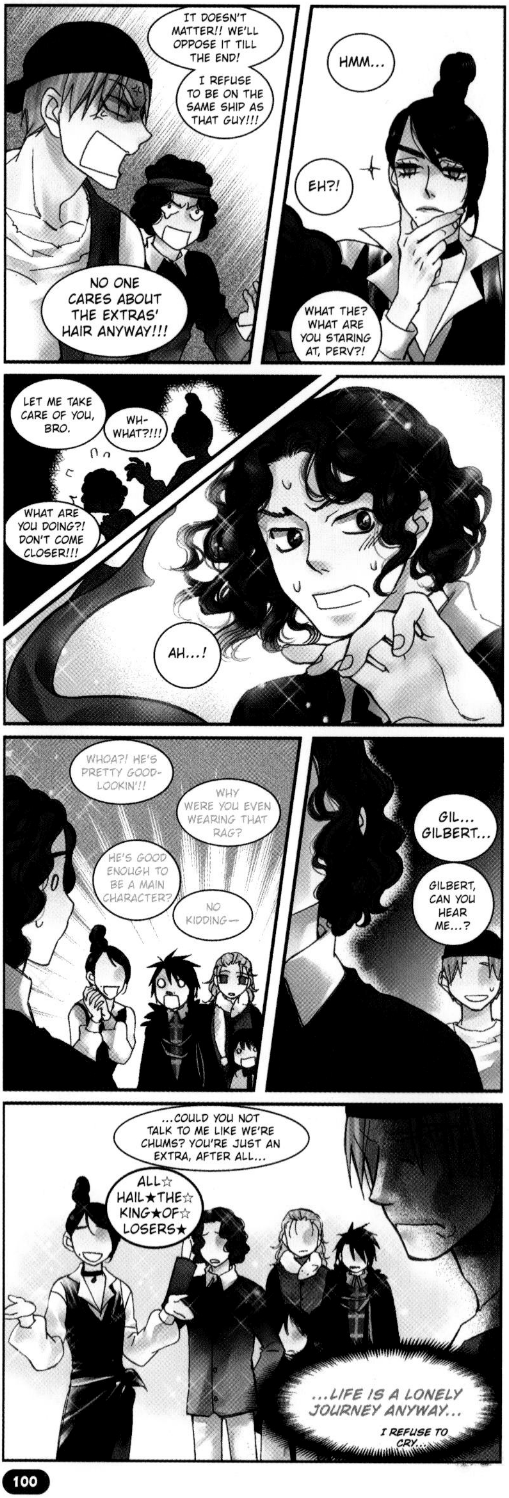

IT DOESN'T MATTER!! WE'LL OPPOSE IT TILL THE END!
I REFUSE TO BE ON THE SAME SHIP AS THAT GUY!!!
NO ONE CARES ABOUT THE EXTRAS' HAIR ANYWAY!!!
HMM...
EH?!
WHAT THE? WHAT ARE YOU STARING AT, PERV?!
LET ME TAKE CARE OF YOU, BRO.
WH-WHAT?!!!
WHAT ARE YOU DOING?! DON'T COME CLOSER!!!
AH...!
WHOA?! HE'S PRETTY GOOD-LOOKIN'!!
WHY WERE YOU EVEN WEARING THAT RAG?
HE'S GOOD ENOUGH TO BE A MAIN CHARACTER?
NO KIDDING—
GIL... GILBERT...
GILBERT, CAN YOU HEAR ME...?
...COULD YOU NOT TALK TO ME LIKE WE'RE CHUMS? YOU'RE JUST AN EXTRA, AFTER ALL...
ALL☆ HAIL★THE☆ KING★OF☆ LOSERS★
...LIFE IS A LONELY JOURNEY ANYWAY...
I REFUSE TO CRY...

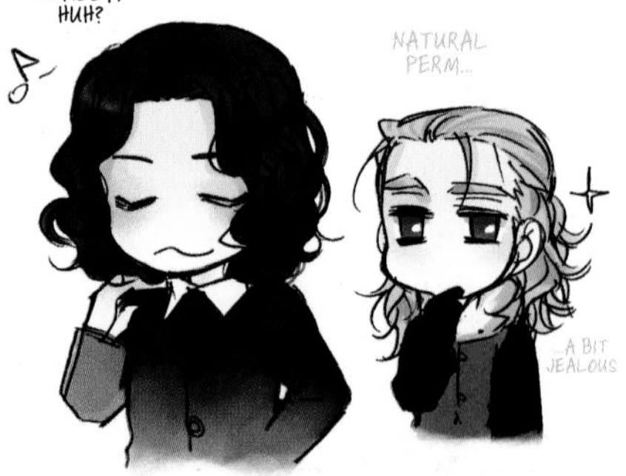

NOT TOO SHABBY, HUH?
NATURAL PERM...
...A BIT JEALOUS

#75. PRECIOUS FRIENDSHIP

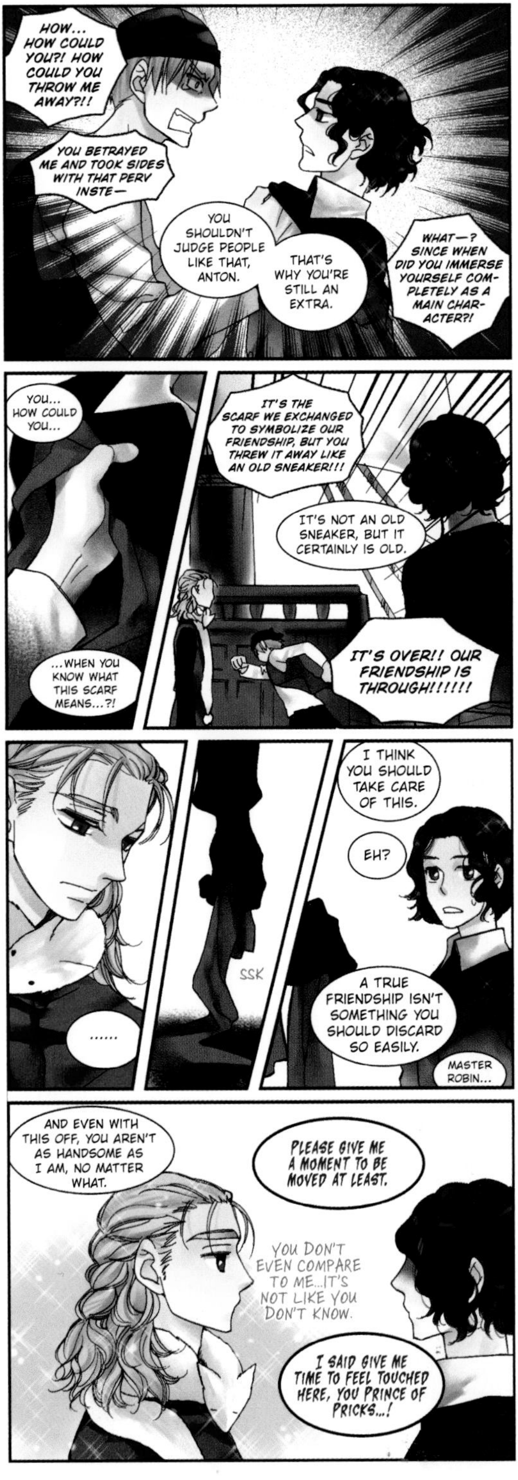
HOW... HOW COULD YOU?! HOW COULD YOU THROW ME AWAY?!!
YOU BETRAYED ME AND TOOK SIDES WITH THAT PERV INSTE—
YOU SHOULDN'T JUDGE PEOPLE LIKE THAT, ANTON.
THAT'S WHY YOU'RE STILL AN EXTRA.
WHAT—? SINCE WHEN DID YOU IMMERSE YOURSELF COMPLETELY AS A MAIN CHARACTER?!
YOU... HOW COULD YOU...
IT'S THE SCARF WE EXCHANGED TO SYMBOLIZE OUR FRIENDSHIP, BUT YOU THREW IT AWAY LIKE AN OLD SNEAKER!!!
IT'S NOT AN OLD SNEAKER, BUT IT CERTAINLY IS OLD.
...WHEN YOU KNOW WHAT THIS SCARF MEANS...?!
IT'S OVER!! OUR FRIENDSHIP IS THROUGH!!!!!!
......
SSK
I THINK YOU SHOULD TAKE CARE OF THIS.
EH?
A TRUE FRIENDSHIP ISN'T SOMETHING YOU SHOULD DISCARD SO EASILY.
MASTER ROBIN...
AND EVEN WITH THIS OFF, YOU AREN'T AS HANDSOME AS I AM, NO MATTER WHAT.
PLEASE GIVE ME A MOMENT TO BE MOVED AT LEAST.
YOU DON'T EVEN COMPARE TO ME...IT'S NOT LIKE YOU DON'T KNOW.
I SAID GIVE ME TIME TO FEEL TOUCHED HERE, YOU PRINCE OF PRICKS...!

THEY MAY HAVE BEEN FRIENDS FOR A LONG TIME. :)

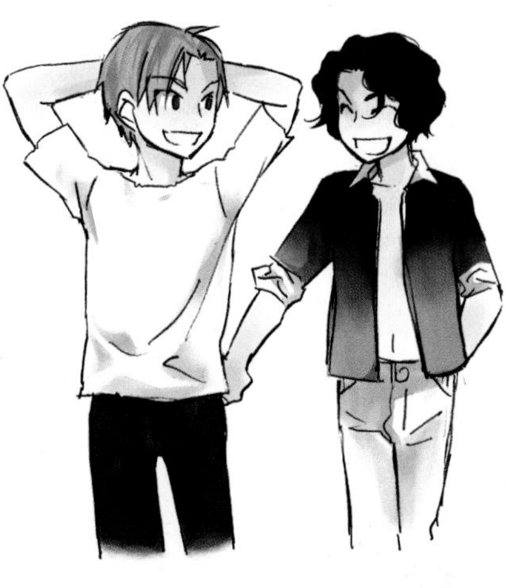

#76. THE RECRUITMENT CONTINUES

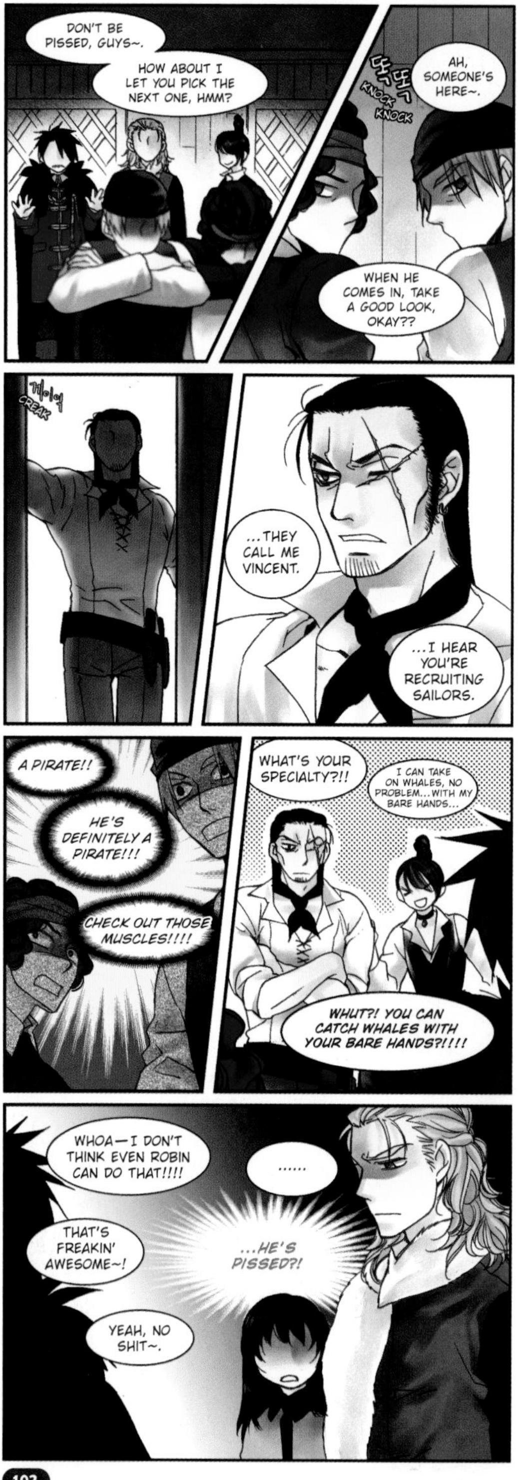
DON'T BE PISSED, GUYS~.
HOW ABOUT I LET YOU PICK THE NEXT ONE, HMM?
똑똑
KNOCK KNOCK
AH, SOMEONE'S HERE~.
WHEN HE COMES IN, TAKE A GOOD LOOK, OKAY??
끼이익
CREAK
...THEY CALL ME VINCENT.
...I HEAR YOU'RE RECRUITING SAILORS.
A PIRATE!!
HE'S DEFINITELY A PIRATE!!!
CHECK OUT THOSE MUSCLES!!!!
WHAT'S YOUR SPECIALTY?!!
I CAN TAKE ON WHALES, NO PROBLEM...WITH MY BARE HANDS...
WHUT?! YOU CAN CATCH WHALES WITH YOUR BARE HANDS?!!!!
WHOA—I DON'T THINK EVEN ROBIN CAN DO THAT!!!!
THAT'S FREAKIN' AWESOME~!
YEAH, NO SHIT~.
......
...HE'S PISSED?!

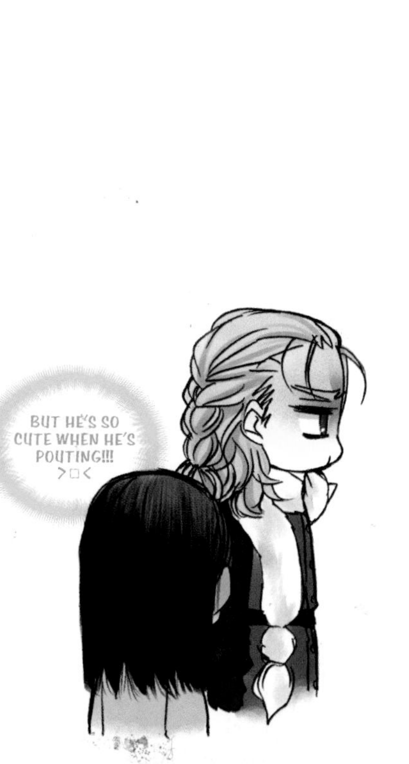
BUT HE'S SO CUTE WHEN HE'S POUTING!!!
>□<

#77. A MAN'S JEALOUSY

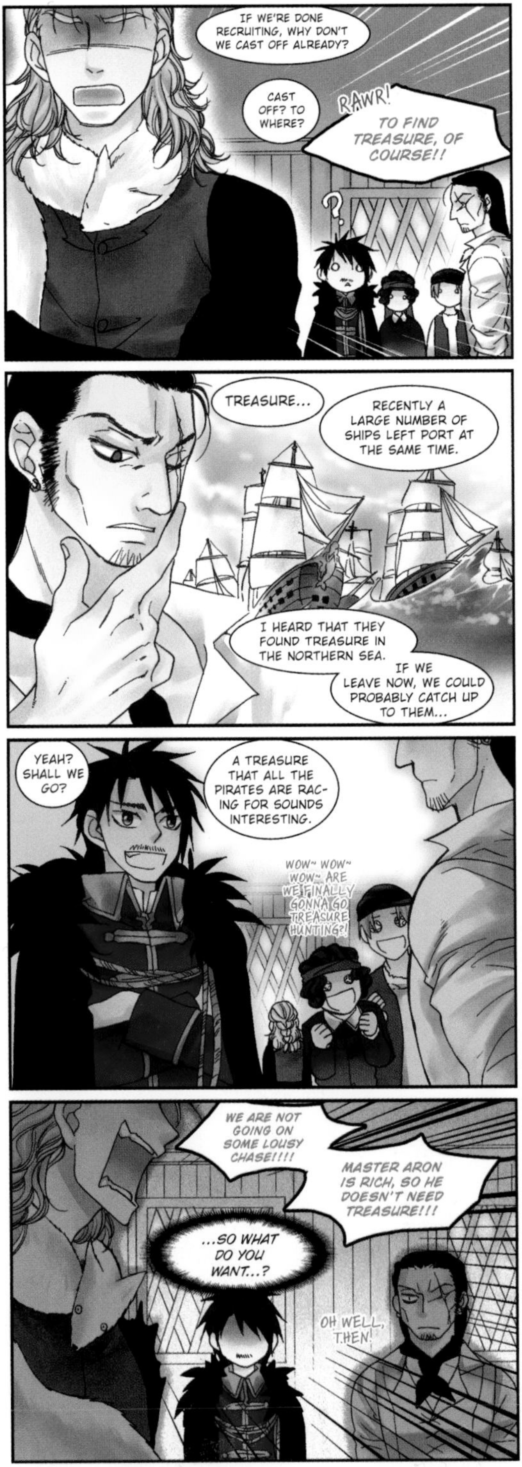

IF WE'RE DONE RECRUITING, WHY DON'T WE CAST OFF ALREADY?
CAST OFF? TO WHERE?
RAWR!
TO FIND TREASURE, OF COURSE!!
?
TREASURE...
RECENTLY A LARGE NUMBER OF SHIPS LEFT PORT AT THE SAME TIME.
I HEARD THAT THEY FOUND TREASURE IN THE NORTHERN SEA.
IF WE LEAVE NOW, WE COULD PROBABLY CATCH UP TO THEM...
YEAH? SHALL WE GO?
A TREASURE THAT ALL THE PIRATES ARE RACING FOR SOUNDS INTERESTING.
WOW~ WOW~ WOW~ ARE WE FINALLY GONNA GO TREASURE HUNTING?!
WE ARE NOT GOING ON SOME LOUSY CHASE!!!!
MASTER ARON IS RICH, SO HE DOESN'T NEED TREASURE!!!
...SO WHAT DO YOU WANT...?
OH WELL, THEN!

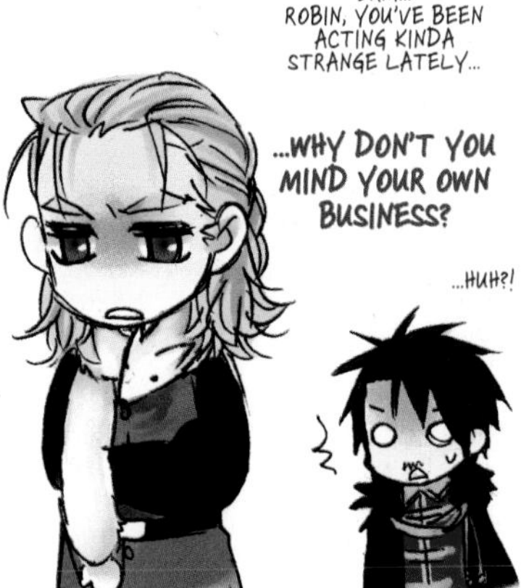

ERM... ROBIN, YOU'VE BEEN ACTING KINDA STRANGE LATELY...
...WHY DON'T YOU MIND YOUR OWN BUSINESS?
...HUH?!

#78. NOT EVEN A MATCH

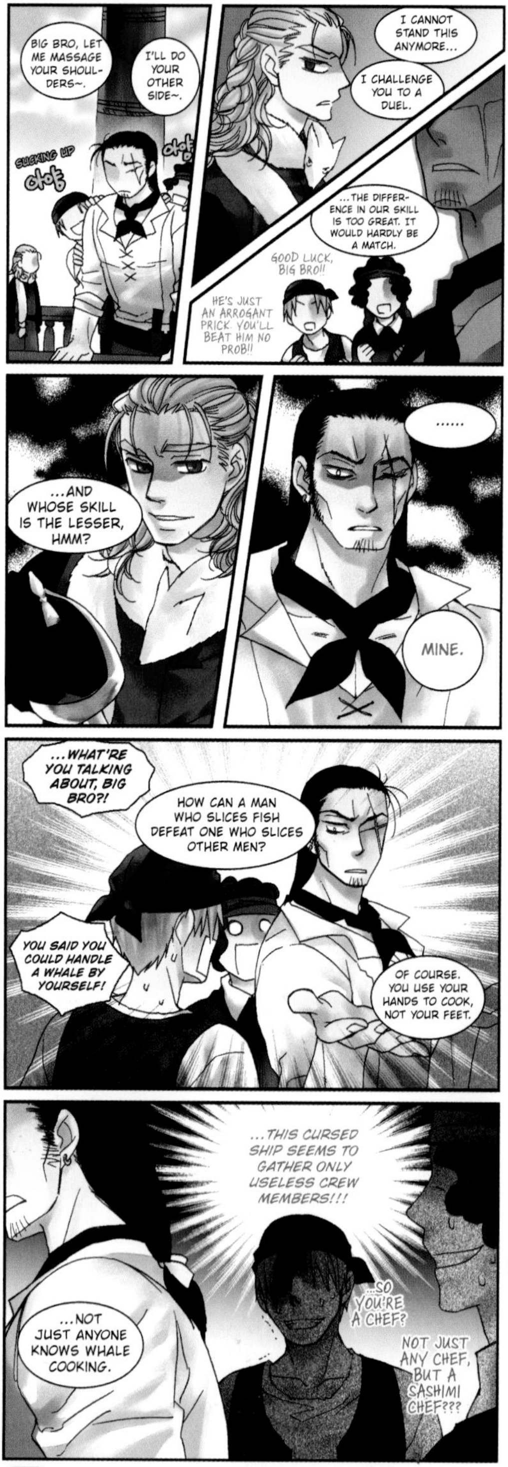

BIG BRO, LET ME MASSAGE YOUR SHOULDERS~.
I'LL DO YOUR OTHER SIDE~.
SUCKING UP
아양
아양
I CANNOT STAND THIS ANYMORE...
I CHALLENGE YOU TO A DUEL.
...THE DIFFERENCE IN OUR SKILL IS TOO GREAT. IT WOULD HARDLY BE A MATCH.
GOOD LUCK, BIG BRO!!
HE'S JUST AN ARROGANT PRICK. YOU'LL BEAT HIM NO PROB!!
...AND WHOSE SKILL IS THE LESSER, HMM?
......
MINE.
...WHAT'RE YOU TALKING ABOUT, BIG BRO?!
HOW CAN A MAN WHO SLICES FISH DEFEAT ONE WHO SLICES OTHER MEN?
YOU SAID YOU COULD HANDLE A WHALE BY YOURSELF!
OF COURSE. YOU USE YOUR HANDS TO COOK, NOT YOUR FEET.
...THIS CURSED SHIP SEEMS TO GATHER ONLY USELESS CREW MEMBERS!!!
...NOT JUST ANYONE KNOWS WHALE COOKING.
...SO YOU'RE A CHEF?
NOT JUST ANY CHEF, BUT A SASHIMI CHEF???

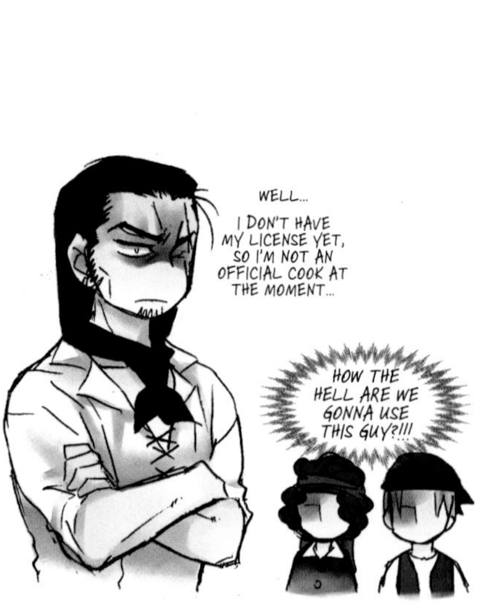

WELL... I DON'T HAVE MY LICENSE YET, SO I'M NOT AN OFFICIAL COOK AT THE MOMENT...
HOW THE HELL ARE WE GONNA USE THIS GUY?!!!

#79. THE CAPTAIN WHO LOVES HIS CREW

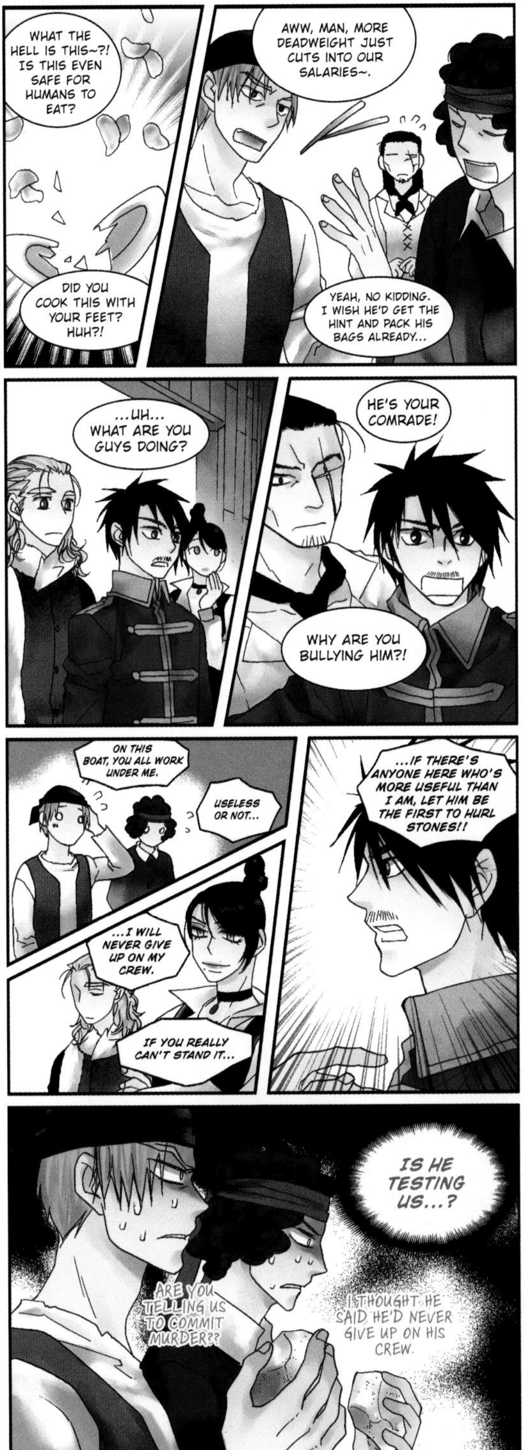

WHAT THE HELL IS THIS~?! IS THIS EVEN SAFE FOR HUMANS TO EAT?
DID YOU COOK THIS WITH YOUR FEET? HUH?!
AWW, MAN, MORE DEADWEIGHT JUST CUTS INTO OUR SALARIES~.
YEAH, NO KIDDING. I WISH HE'D GET THE HINT AND PACK HIS BAGS ALREADY...
...UH... WHAT ARE YOU GUYS DOING?
HE'S YOUR COMRADE!
WHY ARE YOU BULLYING HIM?!
ON THIS BOAT, YOU ALL WORK UNDER ME.
USELESS OR NOT...
...I WILL NEVER GIVE UP ON MY CREW.
IF YOU REALLY CAN'T STAND IT...
...IF THERE'S ANYONE HERE WHO'S MORE USEFUL THAN I AM, LET HIM BE THE FIRST TO HURL STONES!!
IS HE TESTING US...?
ARE YOU TELLING US TO COMMIT MURDER??
I THOUGHT HE SAID HE'D NEVER GIVE UP ON HIS CREW.

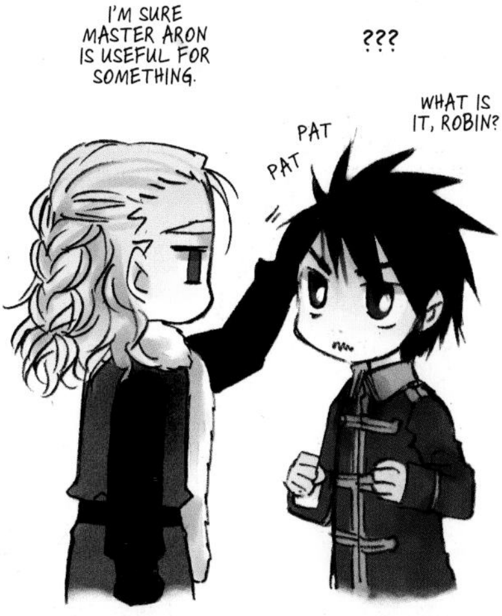

I'M SURE MASTER ARON IS USEFUL FOR SOMETHING.
???
WHAT IS IT, ROBIN?
PAT
PAT

#80. ULTIMATE WEAPON

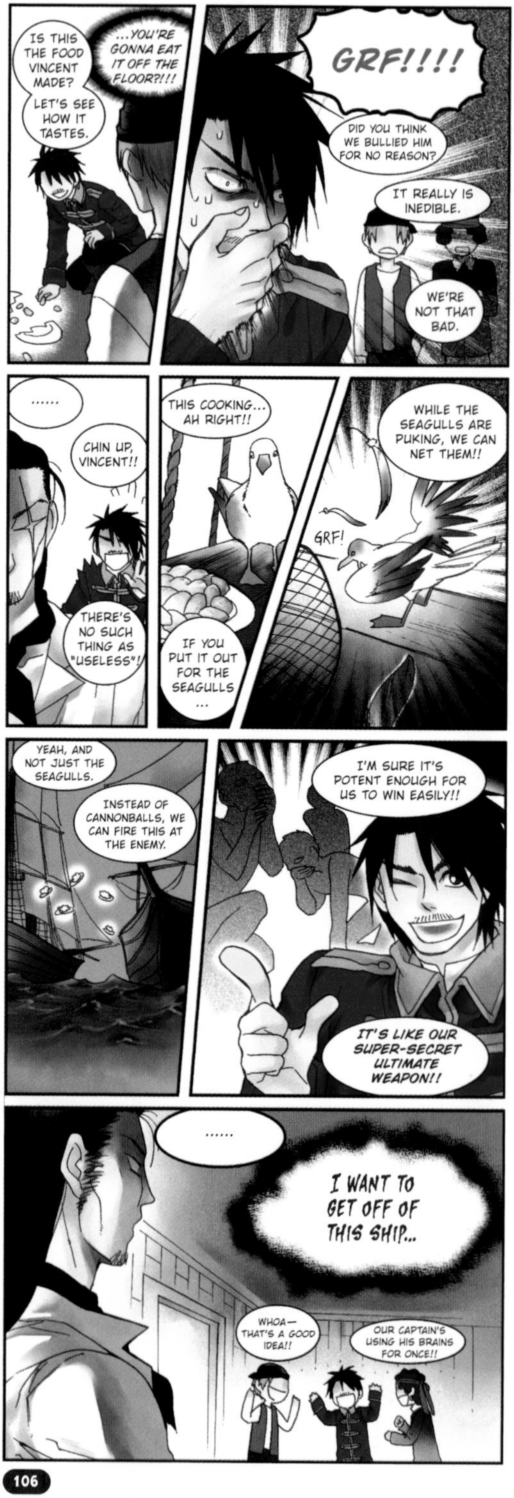
IS THIS THE FOOD VINCENT MADE?
LET'S SEE HOW IT TASTES.
...YOU'RE GONNA EAT IT OFF THE FLOOR?!!!
GRF!!!!
DID YOU THINK WE BULLIED HIM FOR NO REASON?
IT REALLY IS INEDIBLE.
WE'RE NOT THAT BAD.
......
CHIN UP, VINCENT!!
THERE'S NO SUCH THING AS "USELESS"!
THIS COOKING... AH RIGHT!!
IF YOU PUT IT OUT FOR THE SEAGULLS ...
WHILE THE SEAGULLS ARE PUKING, WE CAN NET THEM!!
GRF!
YEAH, AND NOT JUST THE SEAGULLS.
INSTEAD OF CANNONBALLS, WE CAN FIRE THIS AT THE ENEMY.
I'M SURE IT'S POTENT ENOUGH FOR US TO WIN EASILY!!
IT'S LIKE OUR SUPER-SECRET ULTIMATE WEAPON!!
......
I WANT TO GET OFF OF THIS SHIP...
WHOA— THAT'S A GOOD IDEA!!
OUR CAPTAIN'S USING HIS BRAINS FOR ONCE!!

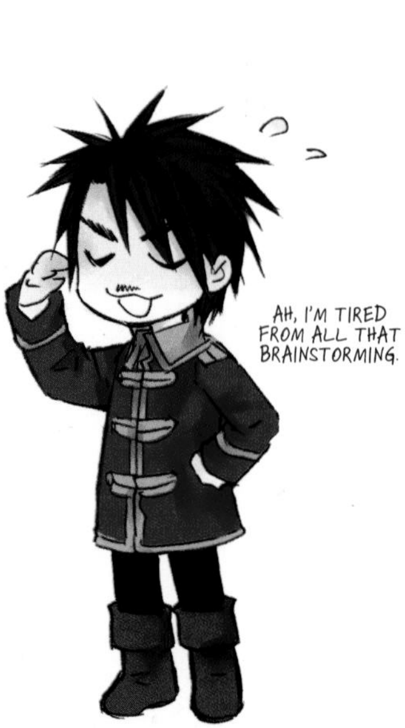
AH, I'M TIRED FROM ALL THAT BRAINSTORMING.

#81. DETECTIVE ARON

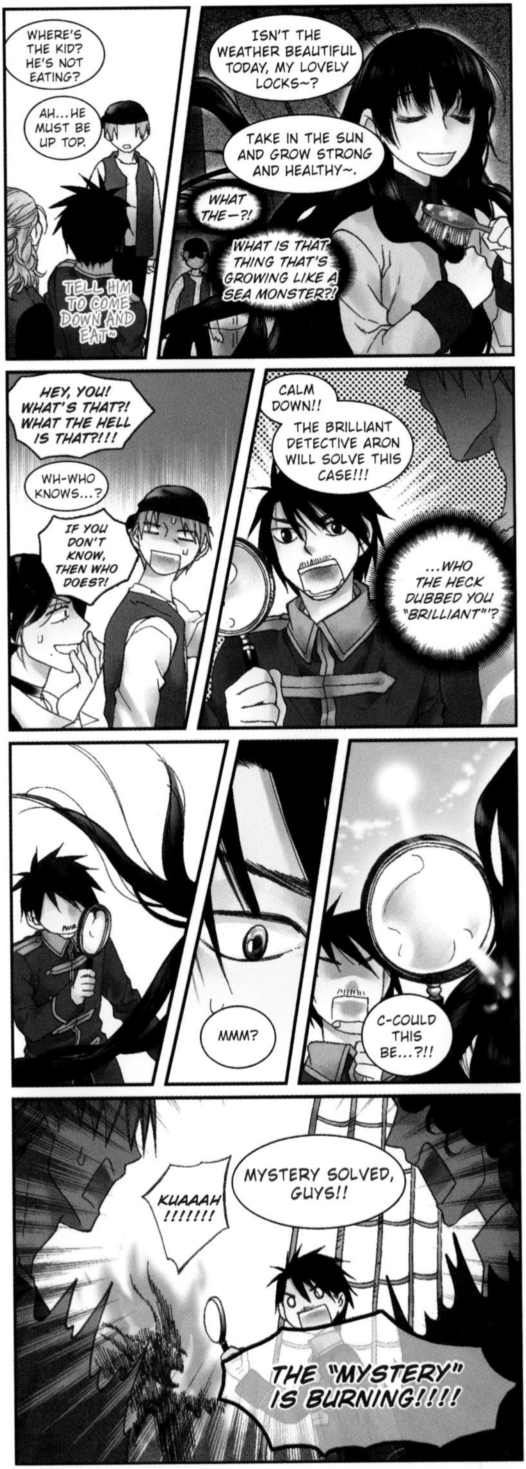
WHERE'S THE KID? HE'S NOT EATING?
AH...HE MUST BE UP TOP.
TELL HIM TO COME DOWN AND EAT~
ISN'T THE WEATHER BEAUTIFUL TODAY, MY LOVELY LOCKS~?
TAKE IN THE SUN AND GROW STRONG AND HEALTHY~.
WHAT THE—?!
WHAT IS THAT THING THAT'S GROWING LIKE A SEA MONSTER?!
HEY, YOU! WHAT'S THAT?! WHAT THE HELL IS THAT?!!!
WH-WHO KNOWS...?
IF YOU DON'T KNOW, THEN WHO DOES?!
CALM DOWN!!
THE BRILLIANT DETECTIVE ARON WILL SOLVE THIS CASE!!!
...WHO THE HECK DUBBED YOU "BRILLIANT"?
MMM?
C-COULD THIS BE...?!!
KUAAAH !!!!!!!
MYSTERY SOLVED, GUYS!!
THE "MYSTERY" IS BURNING!!!!

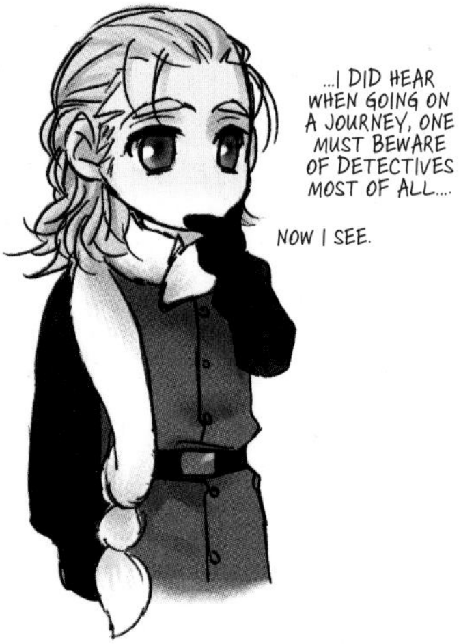
...I DID HEAR WHEN GOING ON A JOURNEY, ONE MUST BEWARE OF DETECTIVES MOST OF ALL....
NOW I SEE.

#82. YOUR BODY COMES FROM YOUR PARENTS

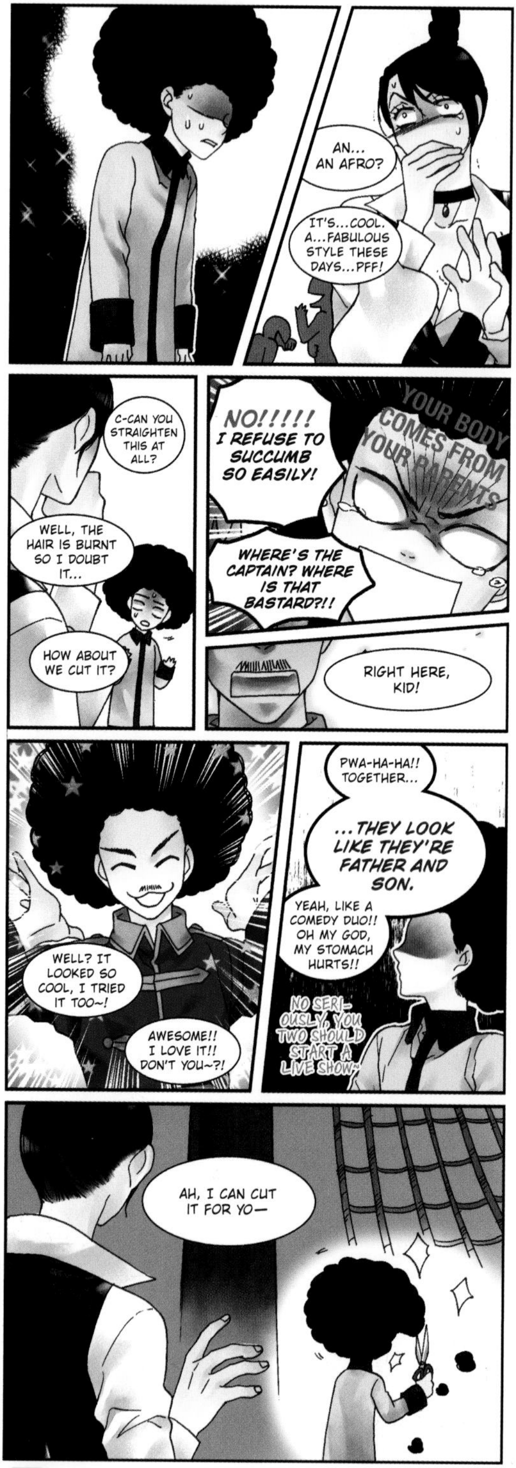
AN... AN AFRO?
IT'S...COOL. A...FABULOUS STYLE THESE DAYS...PFF!
C-CAN YOU STRAIGHTEN THIS AT ALL?
WELL, THE HAIR IS BURNT SO I DOUBT IT...
HOW ABOUT WE CUT IT?
NO!!!!! I REFUSE TO SUCCUMB SO EASILY!
YOUR BODY COMES FROM YOUR PARENTS
WHERE'S THE CAPTAIN? WHERE IS THAT BASTARD?!!
RIGHT HERE, KID!
WELL? IT LOOKED SO COOL, I TRIED IT TOO~!
AWESOME!! I LOVE IT!! DON'T YOU~?!
PWA-HA-HA!! TOGETHER...
...THEY LOOK LIKE THEY'RE FATHER AND SON.
YEAH, LIKE A COMEDY DUO!! OH MY GOD, MY STOMACH HURTS!!
NO SERI-OUSLY, YOU TWO SHOULD START A LIVE SHOW~
AH, I CAN CUT IT FOR YO—

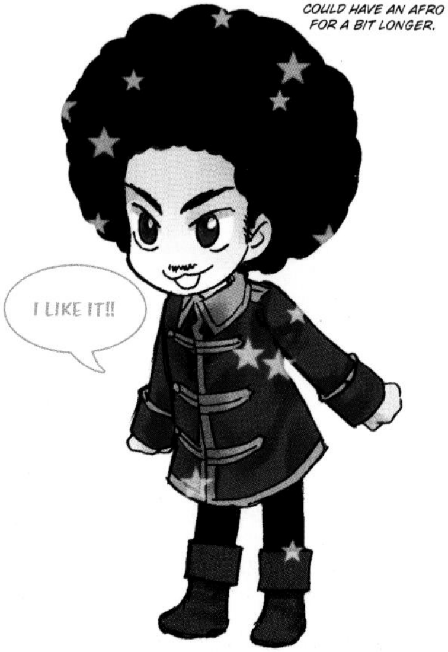
...IT'S SO MUCH EASIER TO COLOR IT THIS WAY. I WISH HE COULD HAVE AN AFRO FOR A BIT LONGER.
I LIKE IT!!

#83. CRUEL CONSOLATION

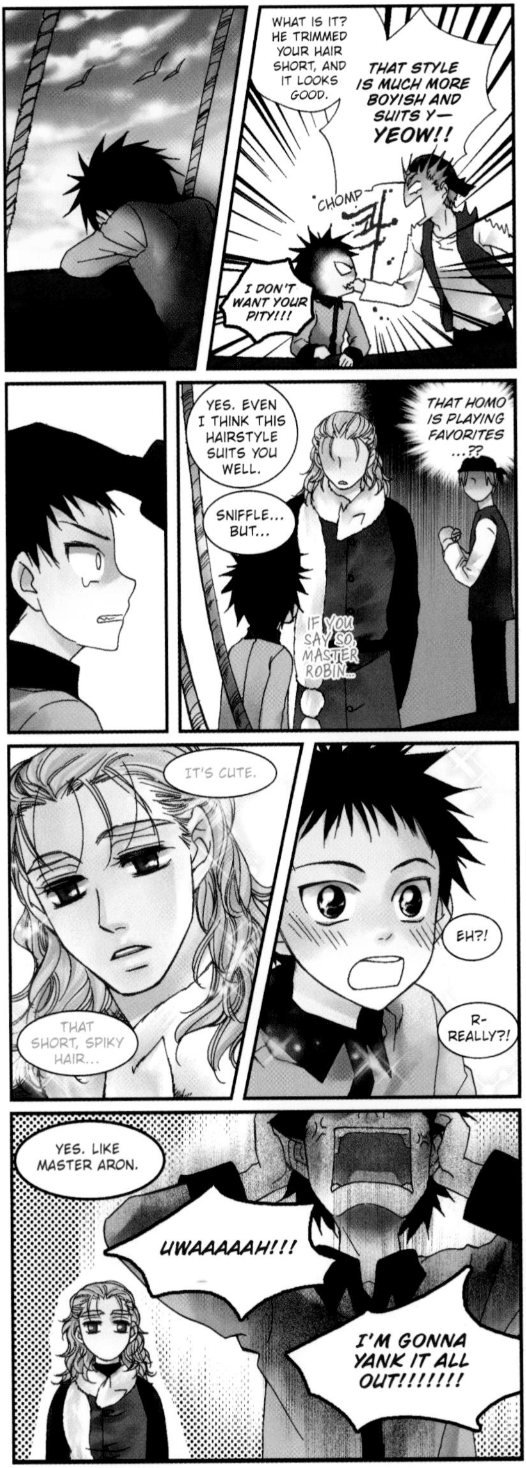
WHAT IS IT? HE TRIMMED YOUR HAIR SHORT, AND IT LOOKS GOOD.
THAT STYLE IS MUCH MORE BOYISH AND SUITS Y— YEOW!!
CHOMP
I DON'T WANT YOUR PITY!!!
YES. EVEN I THINK THIS HAIRSTYLE SUITS YOU WELL.
THAT HOMO IS PLAYING FAVORITES ...??
SNIFFLE... BUT...
IF YOU SAY SO, MASTER ROBIN...
IT'S CUTE.
THAT SHORT, SPIKY HAIR...
EH?!
R- REALLY?!
YES. LIKE MASTER ARON.
UWAAAAAH!!!
I'M GONNA YANK IT ALL OUT!!!!!!!

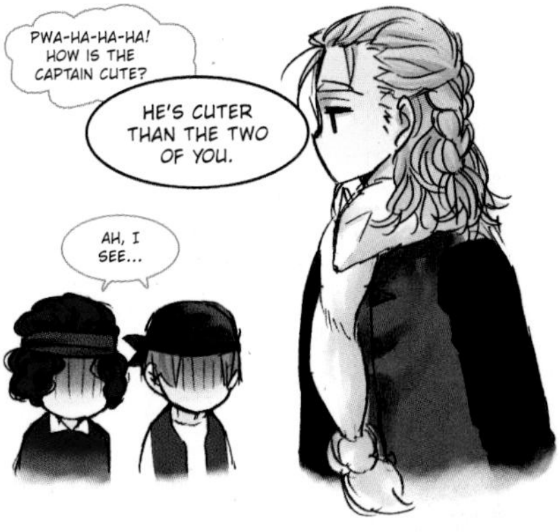
PWA-HA-HA-HA! HOW IS THE CAPTAIN CUTE?
HE'S CUTER THAN THE TWO OF YOU.
AH, I SEE...

#84. WHEN WILL YOU GROW UP?

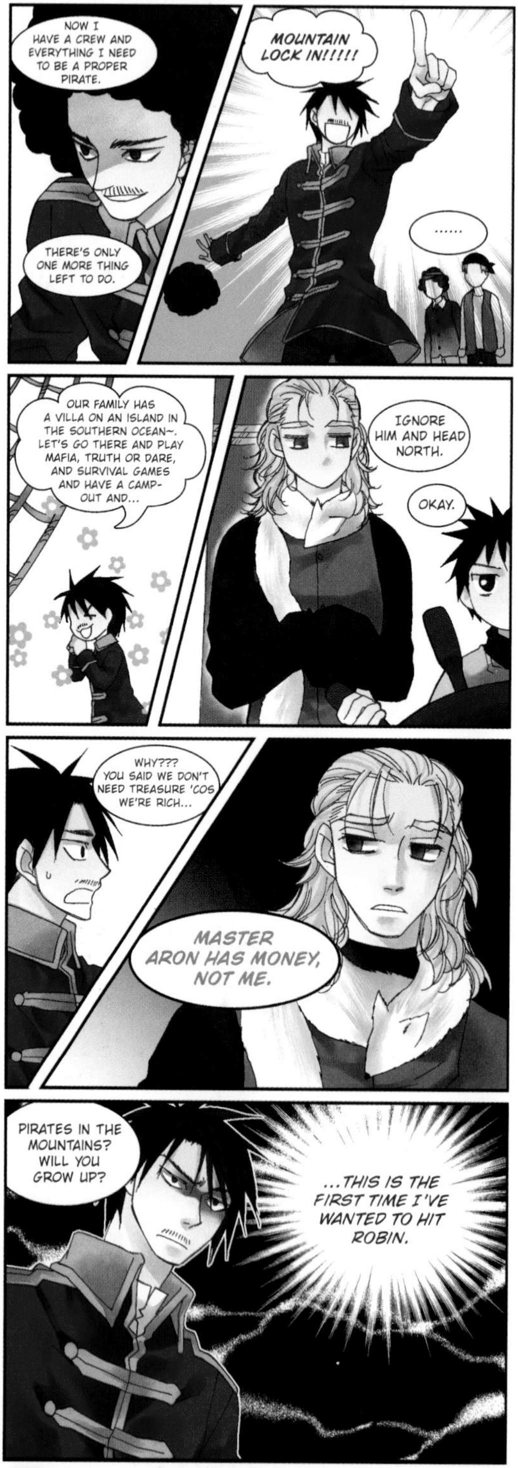
NOW I HAVE A CREW AND EVERYTHING I NEED TO BE A PROPER PIRATE.
THERE'S ONLY ONE MORE THING LEFT TO DO.
MOUNTAIN LOCK IN!!!!!
......
OUR FAMILY HAS A VILLA ON AN ISLAND IN THE SOUTHERN OCEAN~. LET'S GO THERE AND PLAY MAFIA, TRUTH OR DARE, AND SURVIVAL GAMES AND HAVE A CAMP-OUT AND...
IGNORE HIM AND HEAD NORTH.
OKAY.
WHY??? YOU SAID WE DON'T NEED TREASURE 'COS WE'RE RICH...
MASTER ARON HAS MONEY, NOT ME.
PIRATES IN THE MOUNTAINS? WILL YOU GROW UP?
...THIS IS THE FIRST TIME I'VE WANTED TO HIT ROBIN.

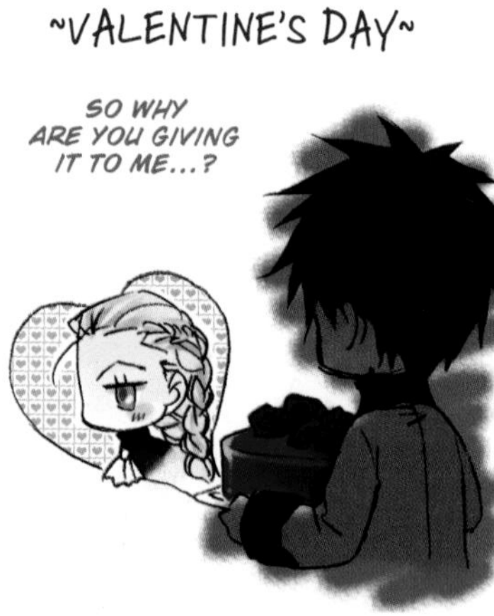
~VALENTINE'S DAY~
SO WHY ARE YOU GIVING IT TO ME...?

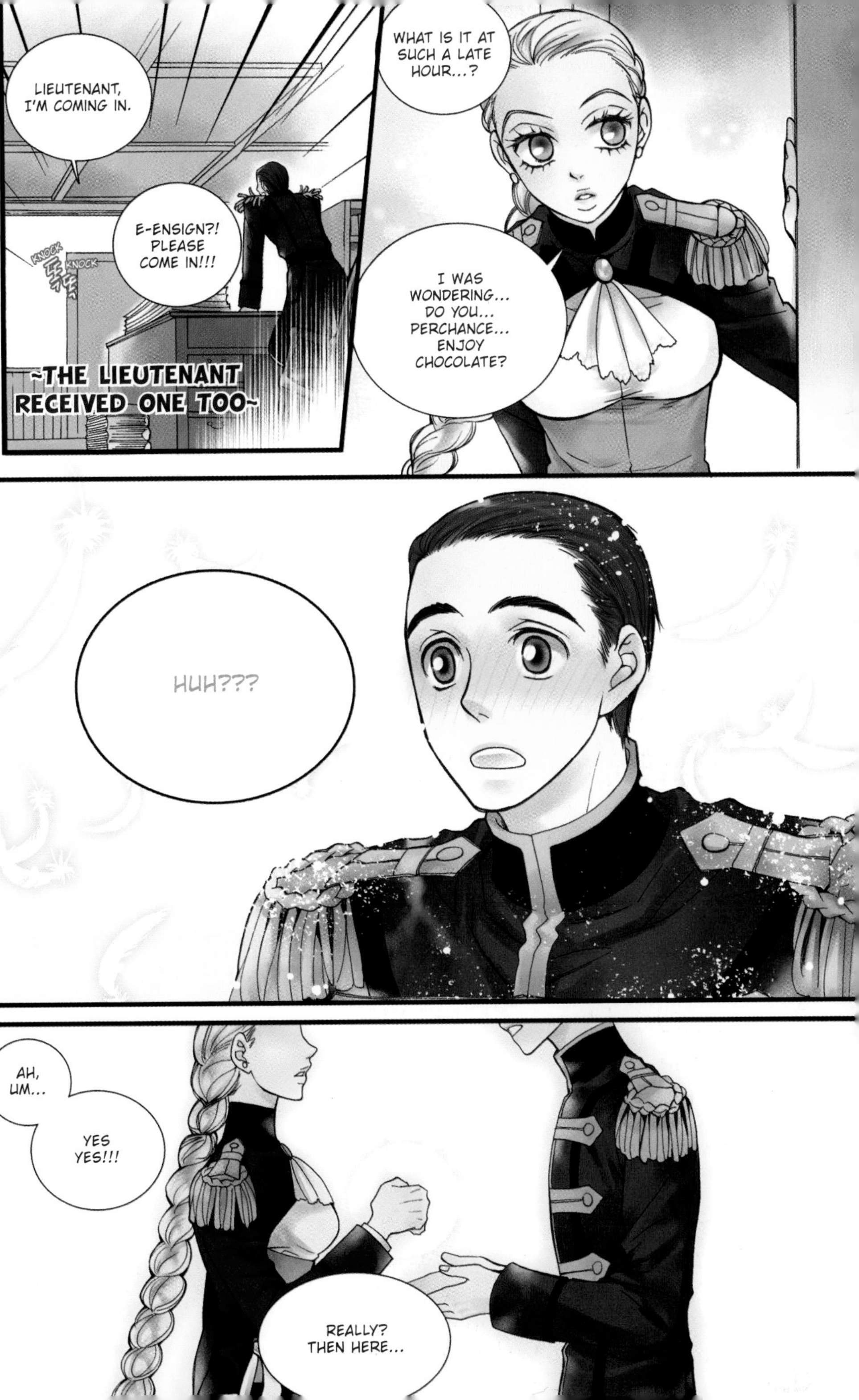
LIEUTENANT, I'M COMING IN.
KNOCK KNOCK
E-ENSIGN?! PLEASE COME IN!!!
~THE LIEUTENANT RECEIVED ONE TOO~
WHAT IS IT AT SUCH A LATE HOUR...?
I WAS WONDERING... DO YOU... PERCHANCE... ENJOY CHOCOLATE?
HUH???
AH, UM...
YES YES!!!
REALLY? THEN HERE...

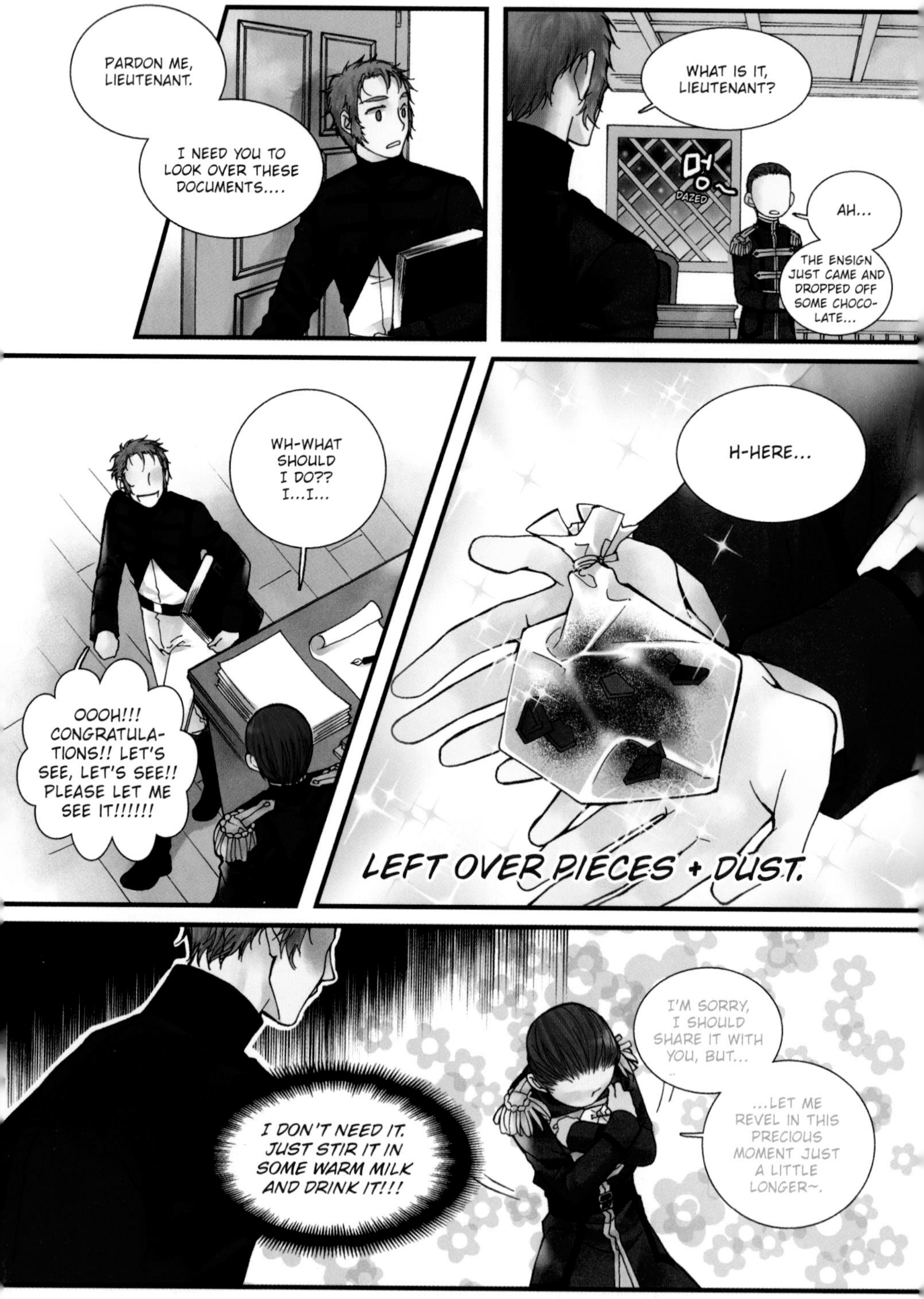

PARDON ME, LIEUTENANT.
I NEED YOU TO LOOK OVER THESE DOCUMENTS....
WHAT IS IT, LIEUTENANT?
멍~
DAZED
AH...
THE ENSIGN JUST CAME AND DROPPED OFF SOME CHOCO-LATE...
WH-WHAT SHOULD I DO?? I...I...
OOOH!!! CONGRATULA-TIONS!! LET'S SEE, LET'S SEE!! PLEASE LET ME SEE IT!!!!!!
H-HERE...
LEFT OVER PIECES + DUST.
I'M SORRY, I SHOULD SHARE IT WITH YOU, BUT...
...LET ME REVEL IN THIS PRECIOUS MOMENT JUST A LITTLE LONGER~.
I DON'T NEED IT. JUST STIR IT IN SOME WARM MILK AND DRINK IT!!!

#85. HE'S GALLANT

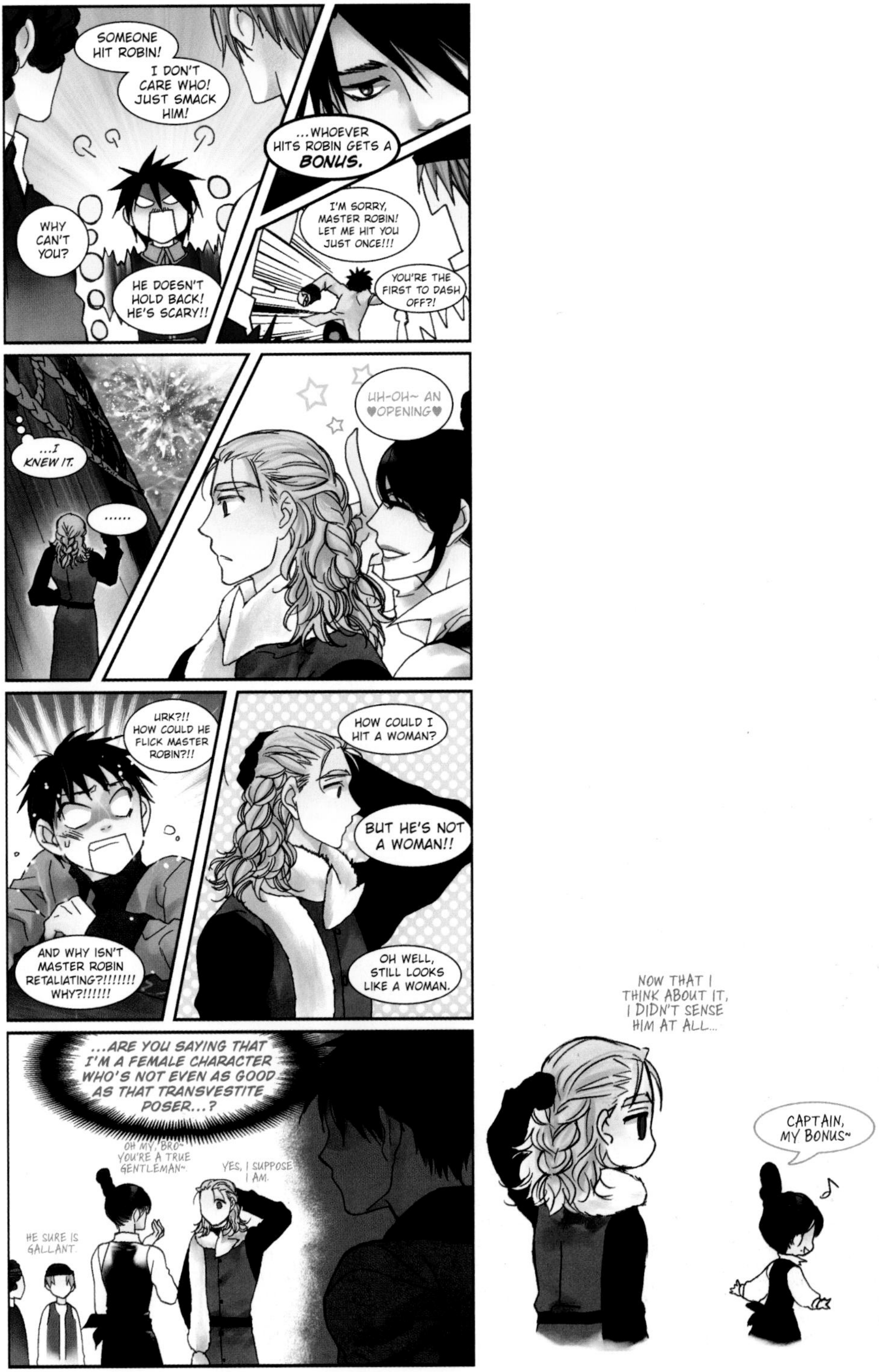
SOMEONE HIT ROBIN!
I DON'T CARE WHO! JUST SMACK HIM!
WHY CAN'T YOU?
HE DOESN'T HOLD BACK! HE'S SCARY!!
...WHOEVER HITS ROBIN GETS A BONUS.
I'M SORRY, MASTER ROBIN! LET ME HIT YOU JUST ONCE!!!
YOU'RE THE FIRST TO DASH OFF?!
...I KNEW IT.
......
UH-OH~ AN ♥OPENING♥
URK?!! HOW COULD HE FLICK MASTER ROBIN?!!
AND WHY ISN'T MASTER ROBIN RETALIATING?!!!!!!! WHY?!!!!!!
HOW COULD I HIT A WOMAN?
BUT HE'S NOT A WOMAN!!
OH WELL, STILL LOOKS LIKE A WOMAN.
...ARE YOU SAYING THAT I'M A FEMALE CHARACTER WHO'S NOT EVEN AS GOOD AS THAT TRANSVESTITE POSER...?
OH MY, BRO~ YOU'RE A TRUE GENTLEMAN~
YES, I SUPPOSE I AM.
HE SURE IS GALLANT.
NOW THAT I THINK ABOUT IT, I DIDN'T SENSE HIM AT ALL...
CAPTAIN, MY BONUS~

#86. ENEMY AND NEIGHBOR

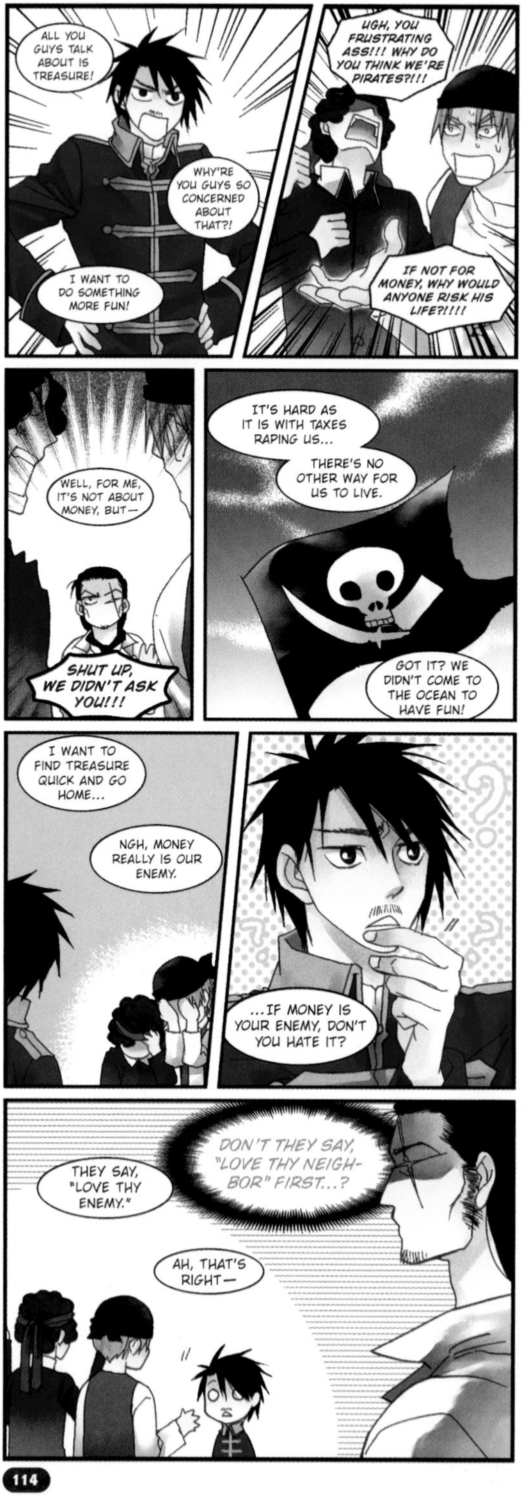
ALL YOU GUYS TALK ABOUT IS TREASURE!
WHY'RE YOU GUYS SO CONCERNED ABOUT THAT?!
I WANT TO DO SOMETHING MORE FUN!
UGH, YOU FRUSTRATING ASS!!! WHY DO YOU THINK WE'RE PIRATES?!!!
IF NOT FOR MONEY, WHY WOULD ANYONE RISK HIS LIFE?!!!!
WELL, FOR ME, IT'S NOT ABOUT MONEY, BUT—
SHUT UP, WE DIDN'T ASK YOU!!!
IT'S HARD AS IT IS WITH TAXES RAPING US...
THERE'S NO OTHER WAY FOR US TO LIVE.
GOT IT? WE DIDN'T COME TO THE OCEAN TO HAVE FUN!
I WANT TO FIND TREASURE QUICK AND GO HOME...
NGH, MONEY REALLY IS OUR ENEMY.
...IF MONEY IS YOUR ENEMY, DON'T YOU HATE IT?
THEY SAY, "LOVE THY ENEMY."
DON'T THEY SAY, "LOVE THY NEIGH-BOR" FIRST...?
AH, THAT'S RIGHT—

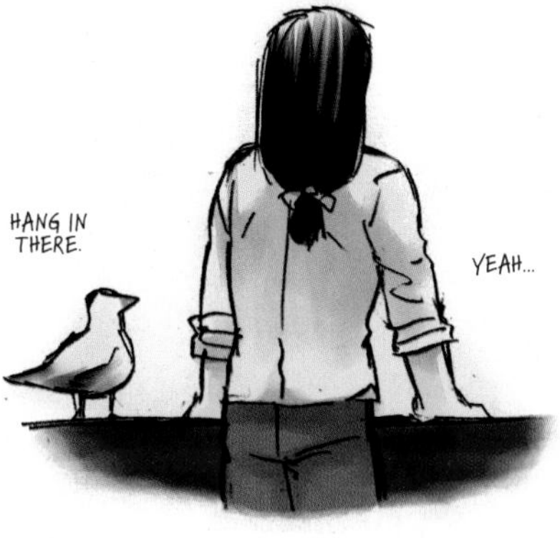
HANG IN THERE.
YEAH...

NEW YEAR'S SPECIAL

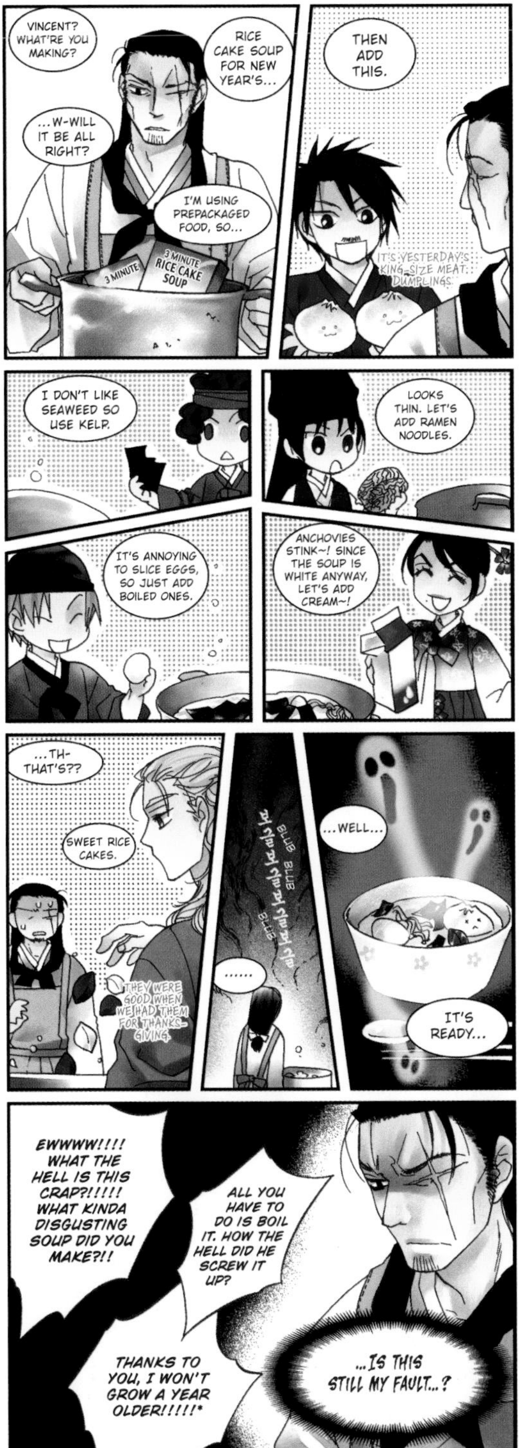
VINCENT? WHAT'RE YOU MAKING?
RICE CAKE SOUP FOR NEW YEAR'S...
...W-WILL IT BE ALL RIGHT?
I'M USING PREPACKAGED FOOD, SO...
3 MINUTE
3 MINUTE RICE CAKE SOUP
THEN ADD THIS.
IT'S YESTERDAY'S KING-SIZE MEAT DUMPLINGS
I DON'T LIKE SEAWEED SO USE KELP.
LOOKS THIN. LET'S ADD RAMEN NOODLES.
IT'S ANNOYING TO SLICE EGGS, SO JUST ADD BOILED ONES.
ANCHOVIES STINK~! SINCE THE SOUP IS WHITE ANYWAY, LET'S ADD CREAM~!
...TH-THAT'S??
SWEET RICE CAKES.
THEY WERE GOOD WHEN WE HAD THEM FOR THANKSGIVING.
BLUB BLUB
......
...WELL...
IT'S READY...
EWWWW!!!! WHAT THE HELL IS THIS CRAP?!!!!! WHAT KINDA DISGUSTING SOUP DID YOU MAKE?!!
ALL YOU HAVE TO DO IS BOIL IT. HOW THE HELL DID HE SCREW IT UP?
THANKS TO YOU, I WON'T GROW A YEAR OLDER!!!!!*
...IS THIS STILL MY FAULT...?

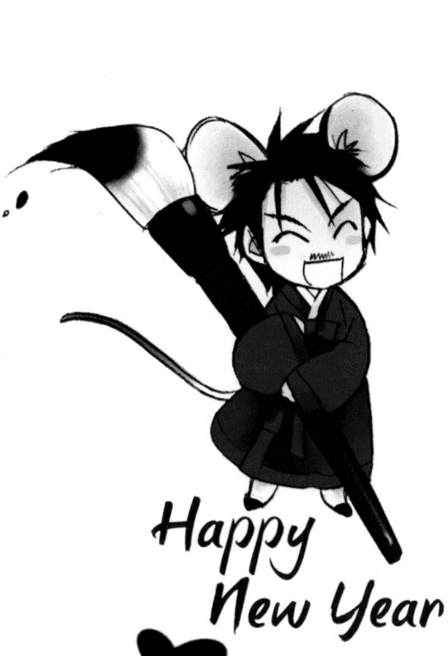
Happy New Year

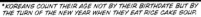

*KOREANS COUNT THEIR AGE NOT BY THEIR BIRTHDATE BUT BY THE TURN OF THE NEW YEAR WHEN THEY EAT RICE CAKE SOUP.

#87. GIVING BOTH THE SICKNESS AND THE CURE

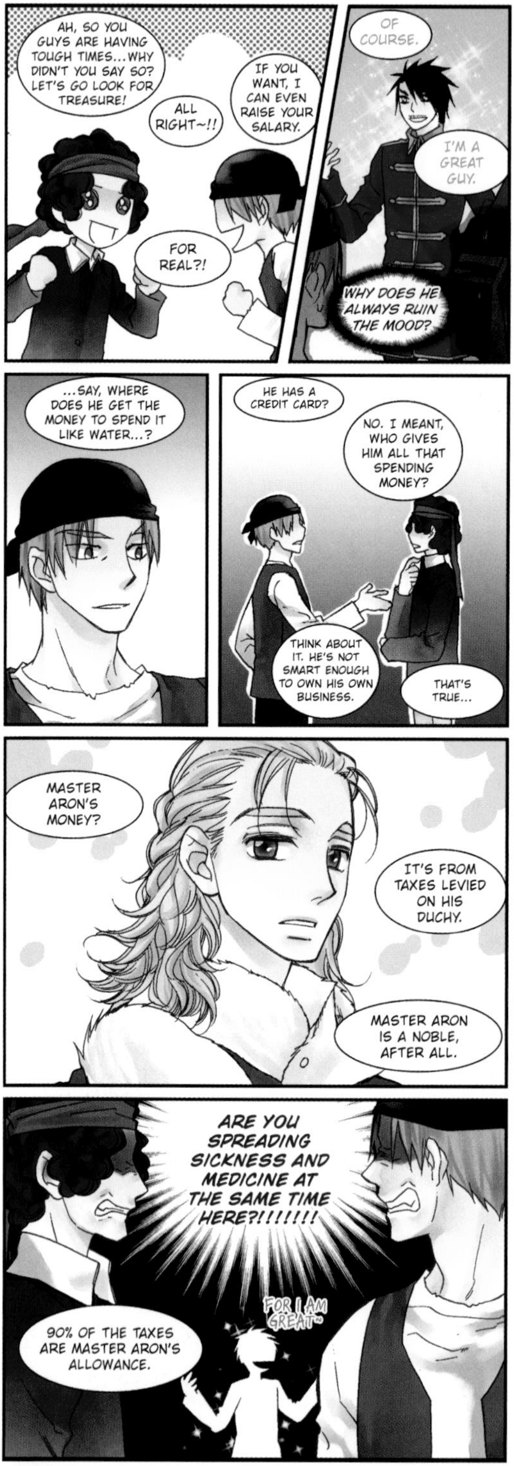
AH, SO YOU GUYS ARE HAVING TOUGH TIMES...WHY DIDN'T YOU SAY SO? LET'S GO LOOK FOR TREASURE!
ALL RIGHT~!!
IF YOU WANT, I CAN EVEN RAISE YOUR SALARY.
FOR REAL?!
OF COURSE.
I'M A GREAT GUY.
WHY DOES HE ALWAYS RUIN THE MOOD?
...SAY, WHERE DOES HE GET THE MONEY TO SPEND IT LIKE WATER...?
HE HAS A CREDIT CARD?
NO. I MEANT, WHO GIVES HIM ALL THAT SPENDING MONEY?
THINK ABOUT IT. HE'S NOT SMART ENOUGH TO OWN HIS OWN BUSINESS.
THAT'S TRUE...
MASTER ARON'S MONEY?
IT'S FROM TAXES LEVIED ON HIS DUCHY.
MASTER ARON IS A NOBLE, AFTER ALL.
ARE YOU SPREADING SICKNESS AND MEDICINE AT THE SAME TIME HERE?!!!!!!!
FOR I AM GREAT~
90% OF THE TAXES ARE MASTER ARON'S ALLOWANCE.

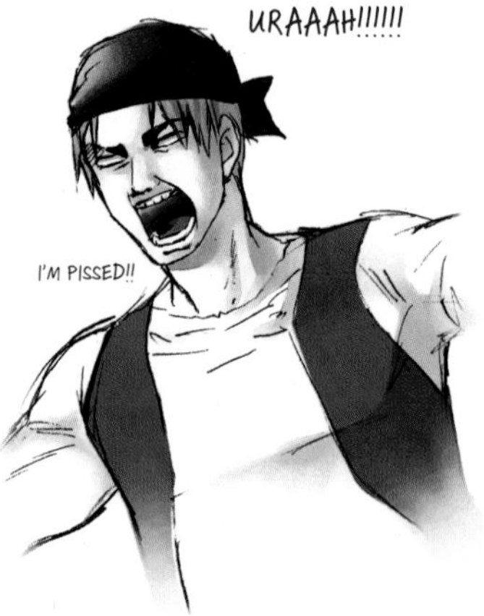
URAAAH!!!!!!
I'M PISSED!!

#88. I DON'T BELIEVE IN FATE

LET'S SEARCH FOR TREA—
EEP!!!
...
WHAT'S THAT?!
KYAA!
IT'S A SWARM OF RAVENS?!
KYAA!
WHY ARE THERE RAVENS IN THE MIDDLE OF THE OCEAN???
KYAA!
I DUNNO, BUT IT'S SCARY AND CREEPY!!!
URK?!!! LOOK, THE RATS ARE ABANDONING SHIP!!!!
WHAT THE...?! THIS IS A BAD OMEN!!
SOMETHING'S ABOUT TO HAPPEN!!
WHAT'S UP WITH THOSE CLOUDS?!
A WARNING FROM THE HEAVENS?!
SOMETHING BAD IS ABOUT TO HAPPEN!!!
...DON'T YOU THINK THE FACT THAT YOU'RE ON THIS SHIP IS A BAD ENOUGH FATE AS IT IS?
AH...TRUE.
CAN'T GET ANY WORSE.
LET'S GO.
LET'S GO.
ROBIN...?

...SNIFFLE.

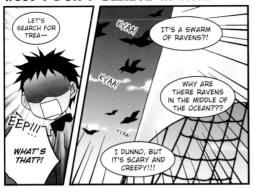

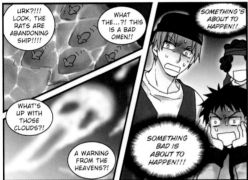

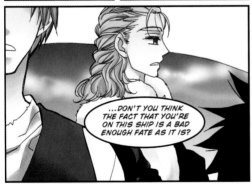

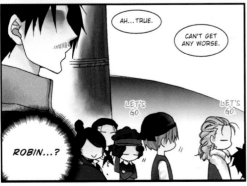

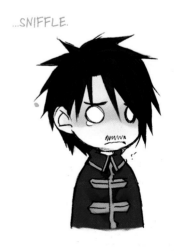

#89. THE CURSE BEGINS

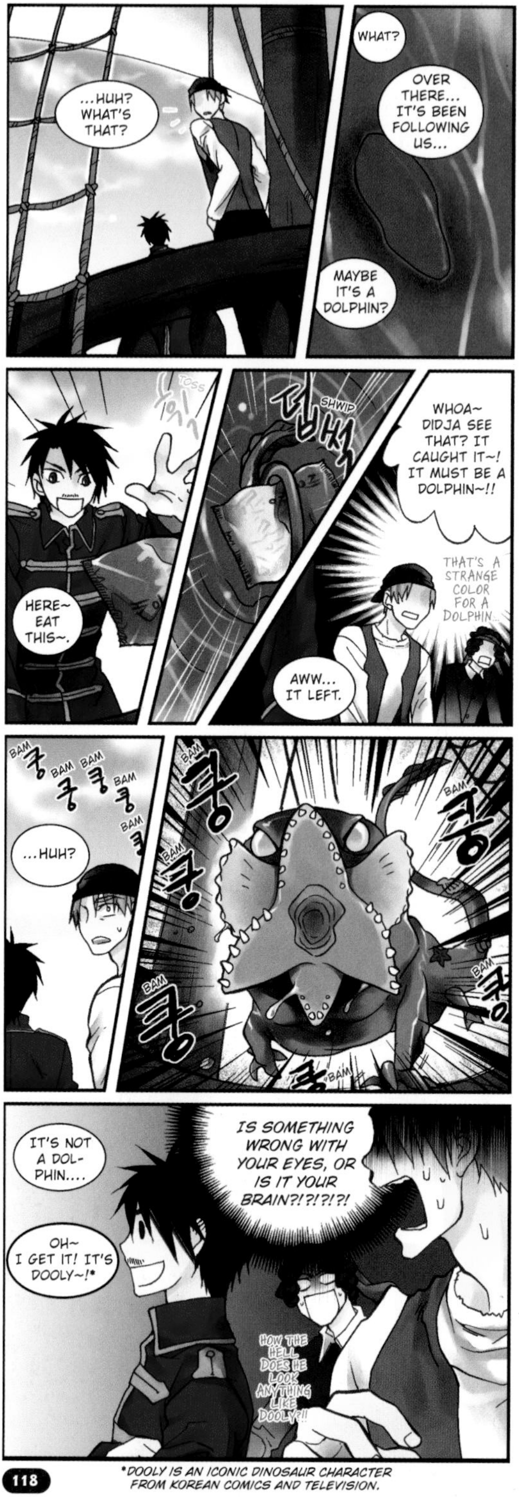
...HUH? WHAT'S THAT?
WHAT?
OVER THERE... IT'S BEEN FOLLOWING US...
MAYBE IT'S A DOLPHIN?
TOSS
HERE~ EAT THIS~.
SHWIP
WHOA~ DIDJA SEE THAT? IT CAUGHT IT~! IT MUST BE A DOLPHIN~!!
THAT'S A STRANGE COLOR FOR A DOLPHIN...
AWW... IT LEFT.
BAM BAM BAM BAM BAM
...HUH?
BAM
BAM
BAM
BAM
BAM
BAM
IT'S NOT A DOL-PHIN....
IS SOMETHING WRONG WITH YOUR EYES, OR IS IT YOUR BRAIN?!?!?!?!
OH~ I GET IT! IT'S DOOLY~!*
HOW THE HELL DOES HE LOOK ANYTHING LIKE DOOLY?!!

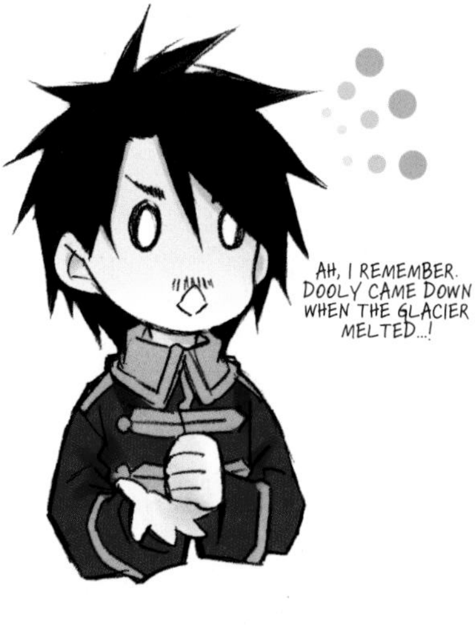
AH, I REMEMBER. DOOLY CAME DOWN WHEN THE GLACIER MELTED...!

*DOOLY IS AN ICONIC DINOSAUR CHARACTER FROM KOREAN COMICS AND TELEVISION.

#90. WHEN THE CREW IS IN DANGER

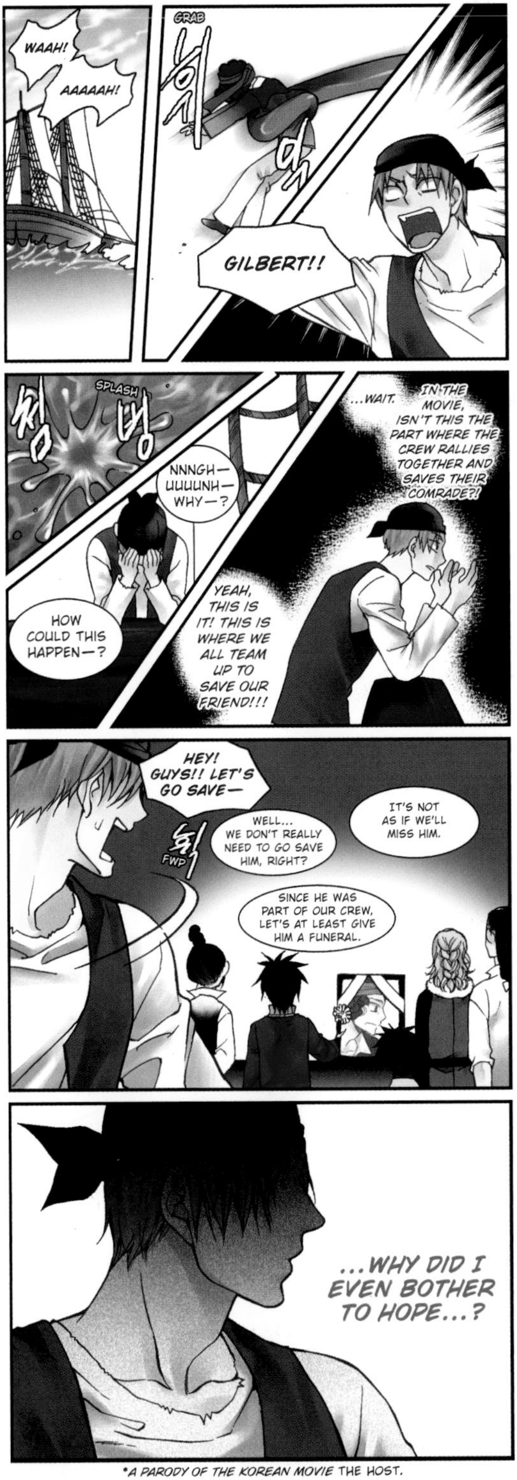
WAAH!
AAAAAH!
GRAB
GILBERT!!
첨벙
SPLASH
NNNGH— UUUUNH— WHY—?
HOW COULD THIS HAPPEN—?
...WAIT.
IN THE MOVIE, ISN'T THIS THE PART WHERE THE CREW RALLIES TOGETHER AND SAVES THEIR COMRADE?!
YEAH, THIS IS IT! THIS IS WHERE WE ALL TEAM UP TO SAVE OUR FRIEND!!!
HEY! GUYS!! LET'S GO SAVE—
휙
FWP
WELL... WE DON'T REALLY NEED TO GO SAVE HIM, RIGHT?
IT'S NOT AS IF WE'LL MISS HIM.
SINCE HE WAS PART OF OUR CREW, LET'S AT LEAST GIVE HIM A FUNERAL.
...WHY DID I EVEN BOTHER TO HOPE...?

*A PARODY OF THE KOREAN MOVIE THE HOST.

[fig. 1]
When a crew member's life is in danger:

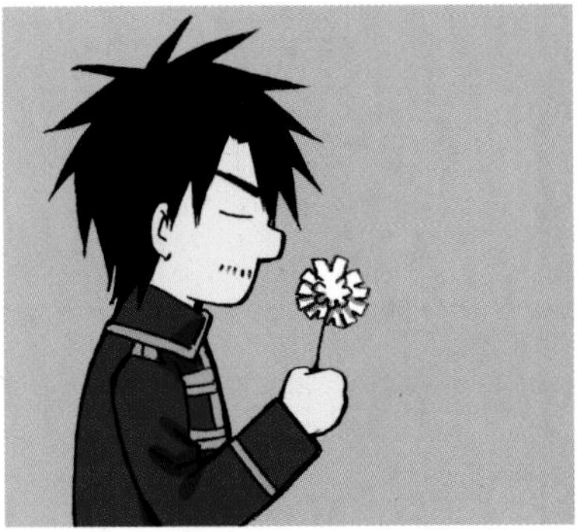

When a shipmate is about to meet his end, hold a proper funeral.

#91. EITHER WAY, THE CREW HELPS ONE BECOME STRONGER

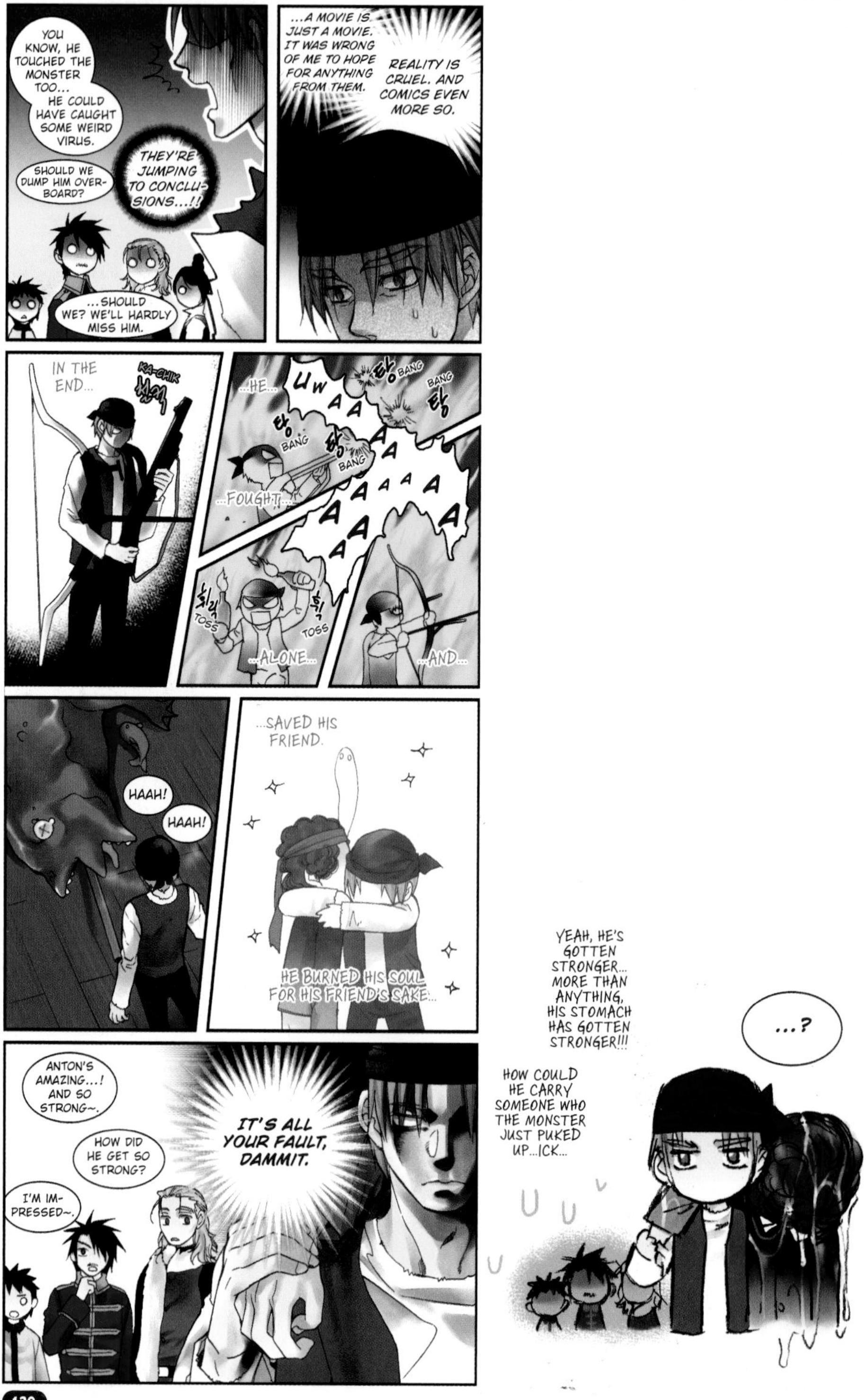

YOU KNOW, HE TOUCHED THE MONSTER TOO... HE COULD HAVE CAUGHT SOME WEIRD VIRUS.
SHOULD WE DUMP HIM OVERBOARD?
THEY'RE JUMPING TO CONCLUSIONS...!!
...SHOULD WE? WE'LL HARDLY MISS HIM.
...A MOVIE IS JUST A MOVIE. IT WAS WRONG OF ME TO HOPE FOR ANYTHING FROM THEM.
REALITY IS CRUEL. AND COMICS EVEN MORE SO.
IN THE END...
KA-CHIK
...HE...
UWAAAAAAAAAAAAAA
탕 BANG
탕 BANG
탕 BANG
탕 BANG
...FOUGHT...
TOSS
TOSS
...ALONE...
...AND...
HAAH!
HAAH!
...SAVED HIS FRIEND.
HE BURNED HIS SOUL FOR HIS FRIEND'S SAKE...
ANTON'S AMAZING...! AND SO STRONG~.
HOW DID HE GET SO STRONG?
I'M IMPRESSED~.
IT'S ALL YOUR FAULT, DAMMIT.
YEAH, HE'S GOTTEN STRONGER... MORE THAN ANYTHING, HIS STOMACH HAS GOTTEN STRONGER!!!
...?
HOW COULD HE CARRY SOMEONE WHO THE MONSTER JUST PUKED UP...ICK...

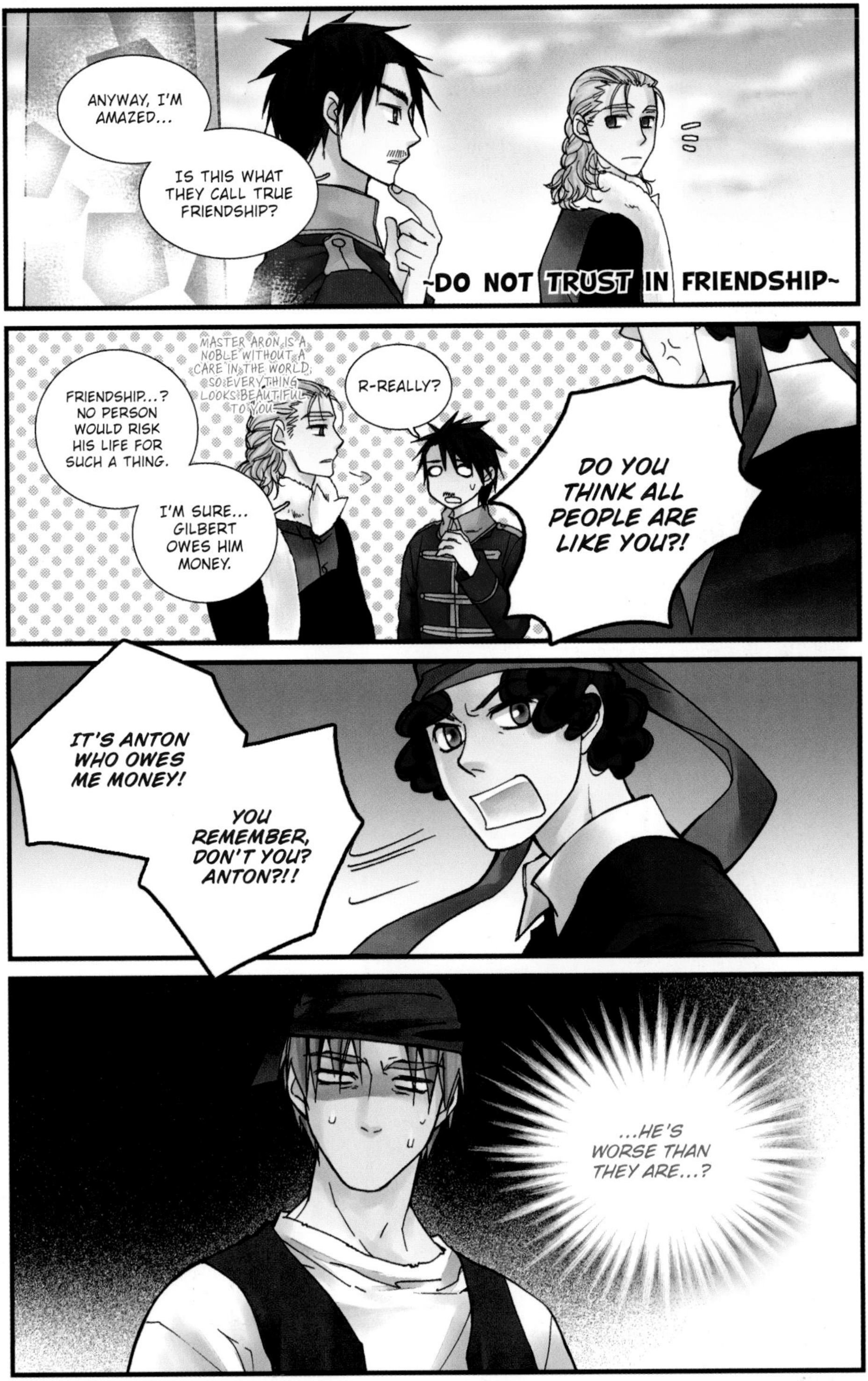
ANYWAY, I'M AMAZED...
IS THIS WHAT THEY CALL TRUE FRIENDSHIP?
~DO NOT TRUST IN FRIENDSHIP~
FRIENDSHIP...? NO PERSON WOULD RISK HIS LIFE FOR SUCH A THING.
I'M SURE... GILBERT OWES HIM MONEY.
MASTER ARON IS A NOBLE WITHOUT A CARE IN THE WORLD, SO EVERYTHING LOOKS BEAUTIFUL TO YOU...
R-REALLY?
DO YOU THINK ALL PEOPLE ARE LIKE YOU?!
IT'S ANTON WHO OWES ME MONEY!
YOU REMEMBER, DON'T YOU? ANTON?!!
...HE'S WORSE THAN THEY ARE...?

#92. OCEAN, PIRATES, AND...

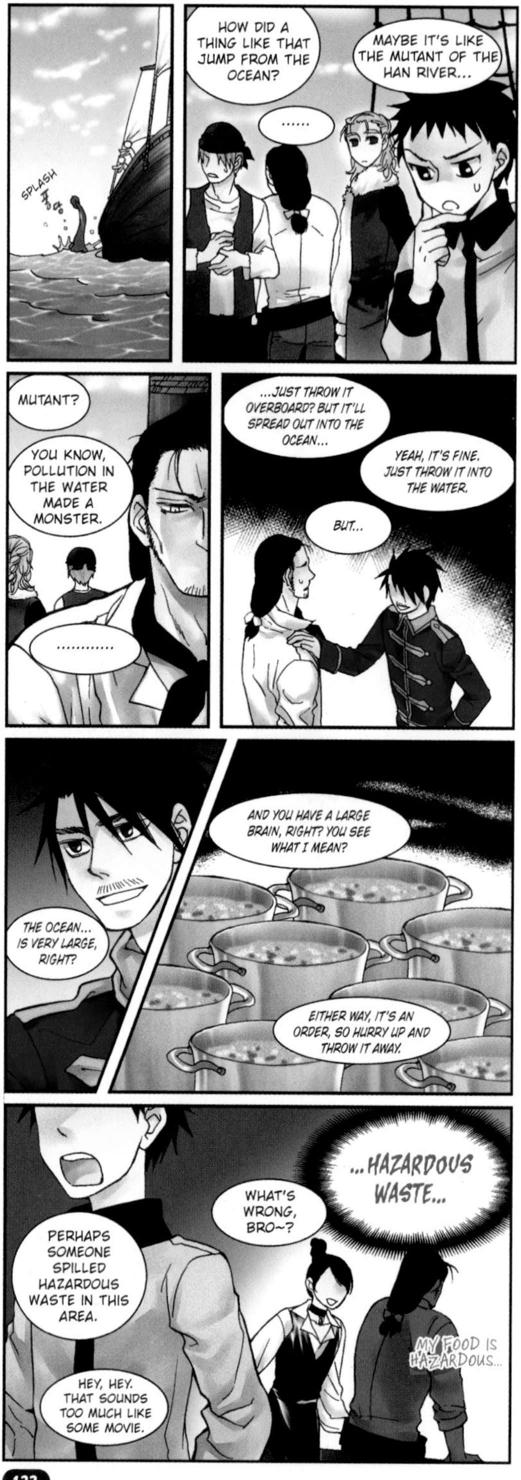
SPLASH
HOW DID A THING LIKE THAT JUMP FROM THE OCEAN?
MAYBE IT'S LIKE THE MUTANT OF THE HAN RIVER...
......
MUTANT?
YOU KNOW, POLLUTION IN THE WATER MADE A MONSTER.
....
...JUST THROW IT OVERBOARD? BUT IT'LL SPREAD OUT INTO THE OCEAN...
YEAH, IT'S FINE. JUST THROW IT INTO THE WATER.
BUT...
AND YOU HAVE A LARGE BRAIN, RIGHT? YOU SEE WHAT I MEAN?
THE OCEAN... IS VERY LARGE, RIGHT?
EITHER WAY, IT'S AN ORDER, SO HURRY UP AND THROW IT AWAY.
...HAZARDOUS WASTE...
WHAT'S WRONG, BRO~?
PERHAPS SOMEONE SPILLED HAZARDOUS WASTE IN THIS AREA.
HEY, HEY. THAT SOUNDS TOO MUCH LIKE SOME MOVIE.
MY FOOD IS HAZARDOUS...

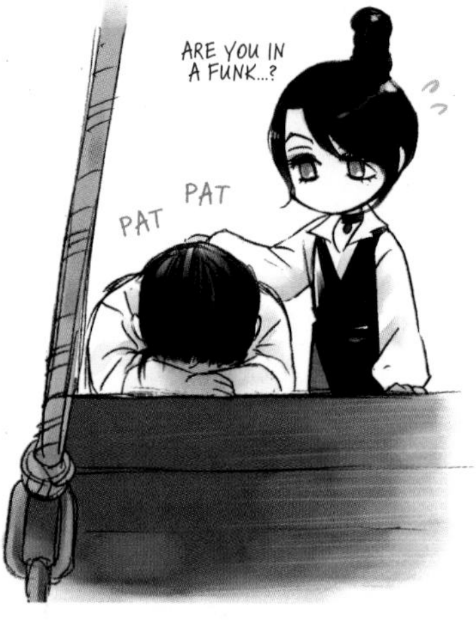
ARE YOU IN A FUNK...?
PAT
PAT

ROBIN & MONEY

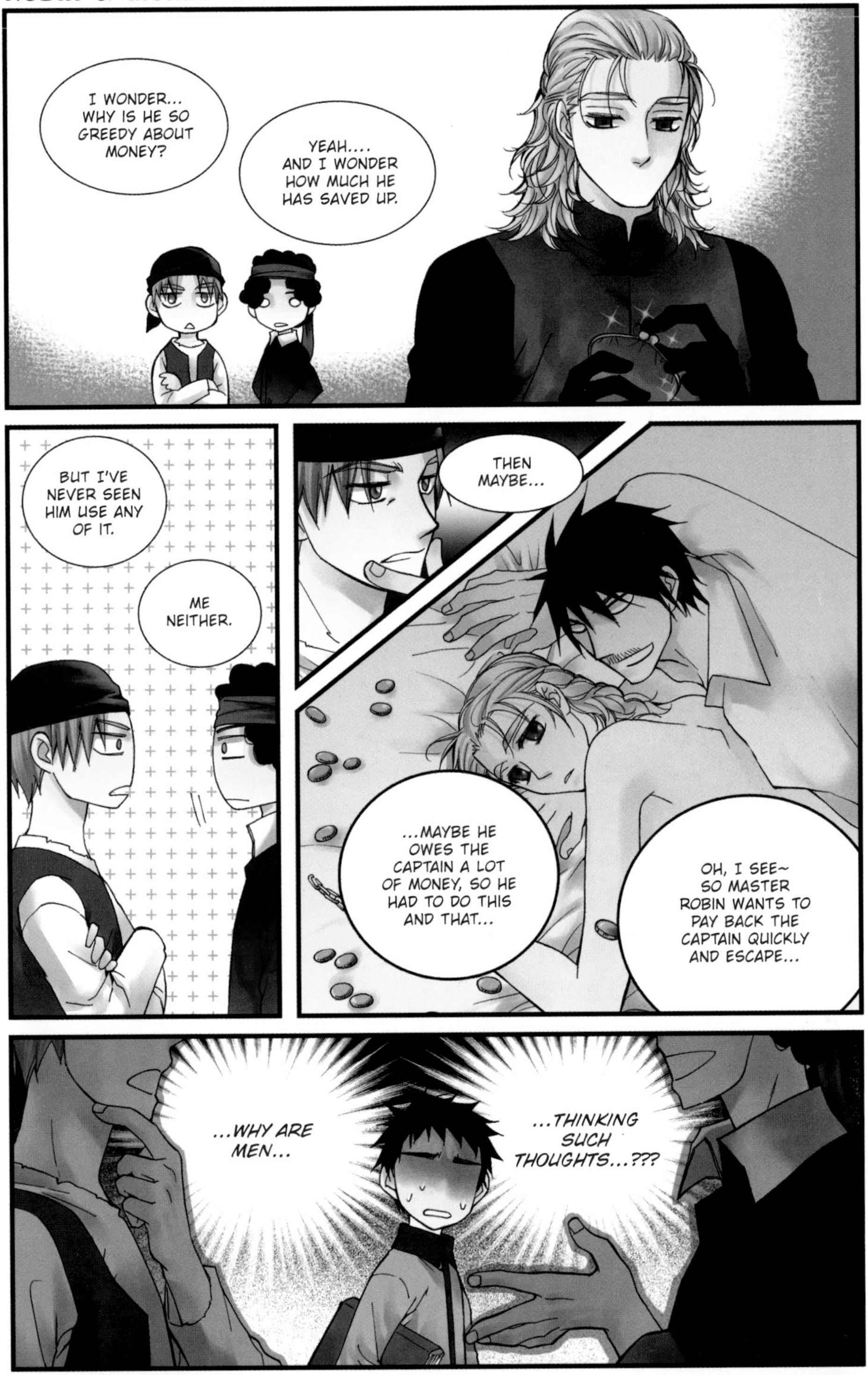
I WONDER... WHY IS HE SO GREEDY ABOUT MONEY?
YEAH.... AND I WONDER HOW MUCH HE HAS SAVED UP.
BUT I'VE NEVER SEEN HIM USE ANY OF IT.
ME NEITHER.
THEN MAYBE...
...MAYBE HE OWES THE CAPTAIN A LOT OF MONEY, SO HE HAD TO DO THIS AND THAT...
OH, I SEE~ SO MASTER ROBIN WANTS TO PAY BACK THE CAPTAIN QUICKLY AND ESCAPE...
...WHY ARE MEN...
...THINKING SUCH THOUGHTS...???

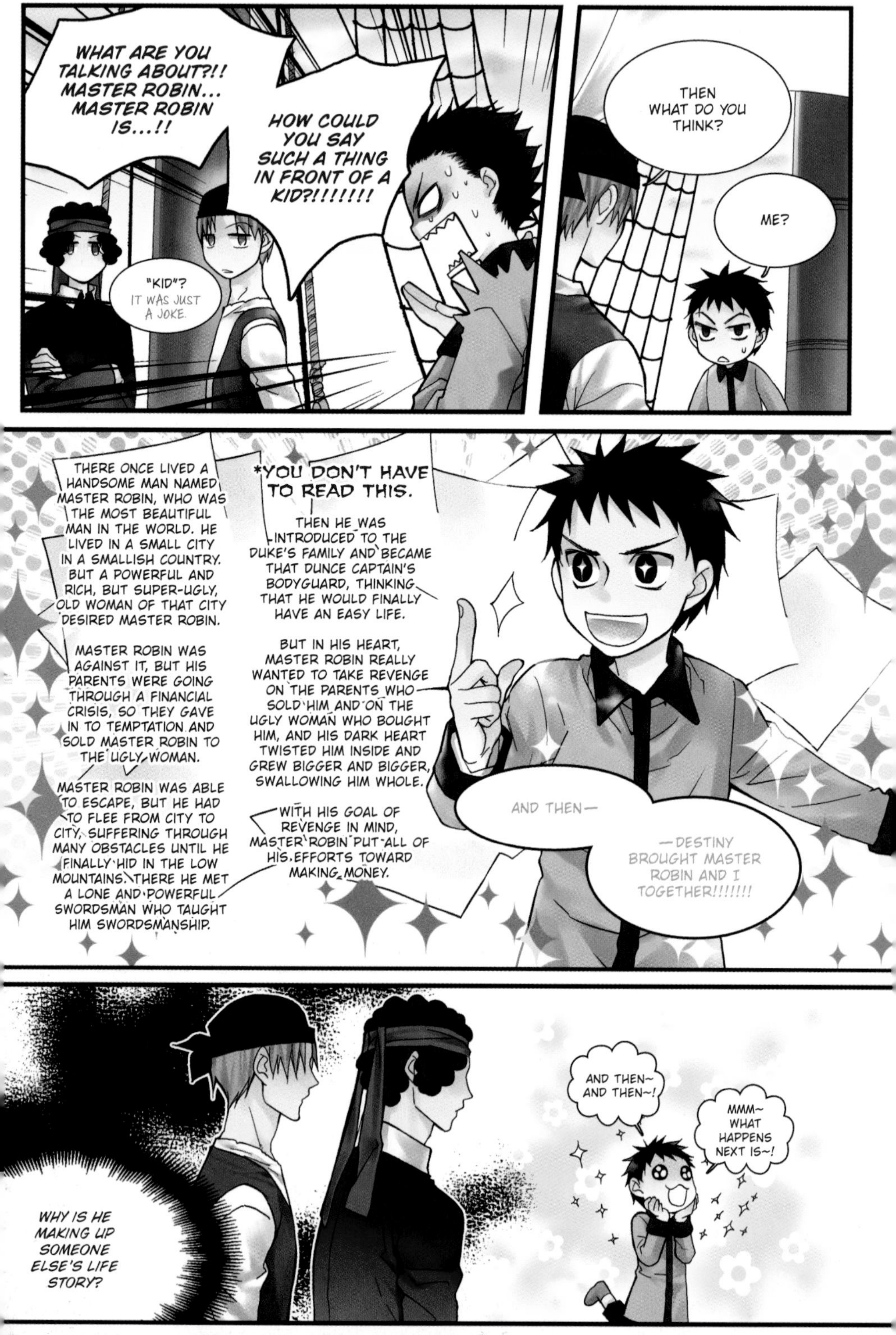
WHAT ARE YOU TALKING ABOUT?!! MASTER ROBIN... MASTER ROBIN IS...!!
HOW COULD YOU SAY SUCH A THING IN FRONT OF A KID?!!!!!!!
"KID"? IT WAS JUST A JOKE.
THEN WHAT DO YOU THINK?
ME?
*YOU DON'T HAVE TO READ THIS.
THERE ONCE LIVED A HANDSOME MAN NAMED MASTER ROBIN, WHO WAS THE MOST BEAUTIFUL MAN IN THE WORLD. HE LIVED IN A SMALL CITY IN A SMALLISH COUNTRY. BUT A POWERFUL AND RICH, BUT SUPER-UGLY, OLD WOMAN OF THAT CITY DESIRED MASTER ROBIN.
MASTER ROBIN WAS AGAINST IT, BUT HIS PARENTS WERE GOING THROUGH A FINANCIAL CRISIS, SO THEY GAVE IN TO TEMPTATION AND SOLD MASTER ROBIN TO THE UGLY WOMAN.
MASTER ROBIN WAS ABLE TO ESCAPE, BUT HE HAD TO FLEE FROM CITY TO CITY, SUFFERING THROUGH MANY OBSTACLES UNTIL HE FINALLY HID IN THE LOW MOUNTAINS. THERE HE MET A LONE AND POWERFUL SWORDSMAN WHO TAUGHT HIM SWORDSMANSHIP.
THEN HE WAS INTRODUCED TO THE DUKE'S FAMILY AND BECAME THAT DUNCE CAPTAIN'S BODYGUARD, THINKING THAT HE WOULD FINALLY HAVE AN EASY LIFE.
BUT IN HIS HEART, MASTER ROBIN REALLY WANTED TO TAKE REVENGE ON THE PARENTS WHO SOLD HIM AND ON THE UGLY WOMAN WHO BOUGHT HIM, AND HIS DARK HEART TWISTED HIM INSIDE AND GREW BIGGER AND BIGGER, SWALLOWING HIM WHOLE.
WITH HIS GOAL OF REVENGE IN MIND, MASTER ROBIN PUT ALL OF HIS EFFORTS TOWARD MAKING MONEY.
AND THEN—
—DESTINY BROUGHT MASTER ROBIN AND I TOGETHER!!!!!!!
AND THEN~ AND THEN~!
MMM~ WHAT HAPPENS NEXT IS~!
WHY IS HE MAKING UP SOMEONE ELSE'S LIFE STORY?

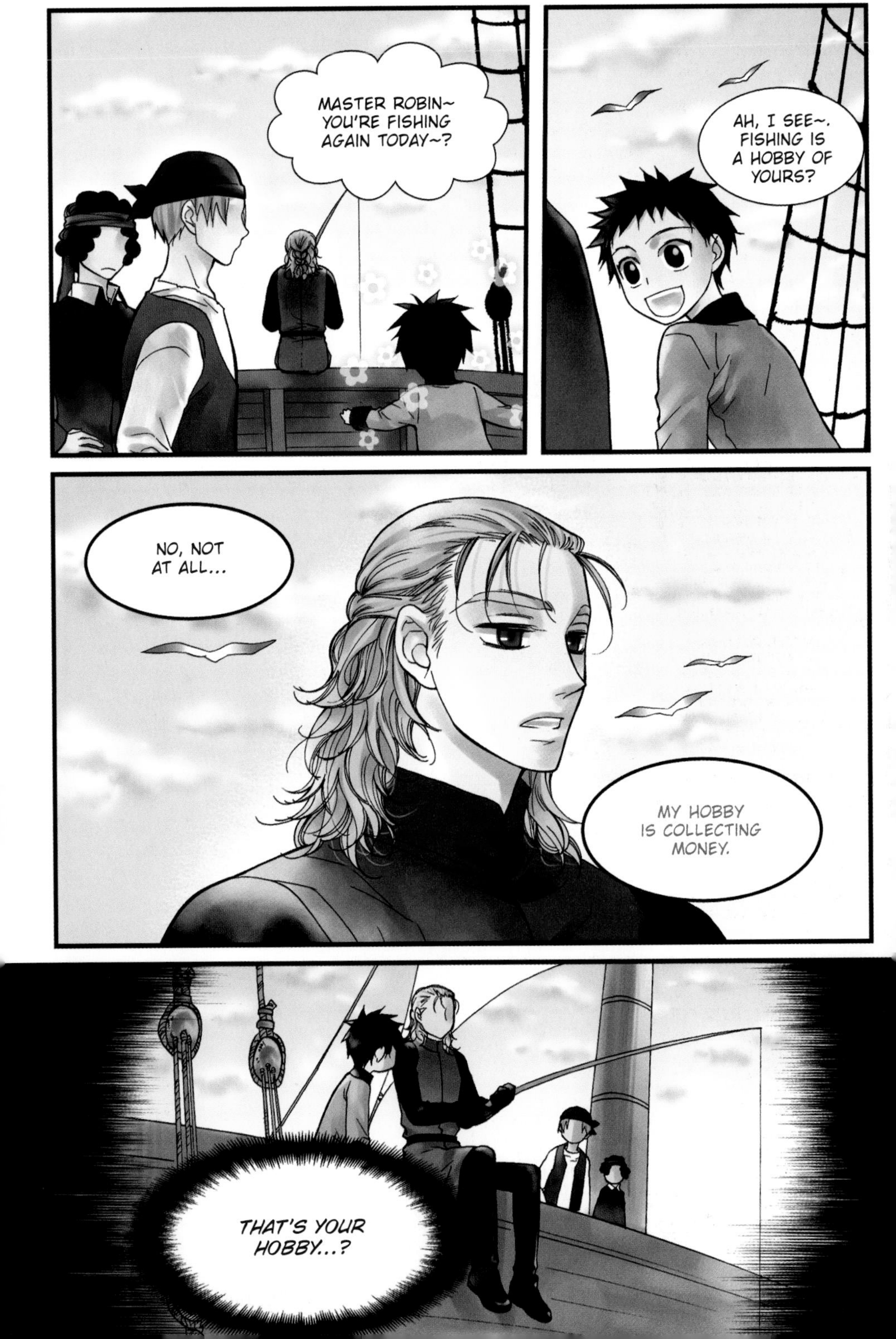
MASTER ROBIN~ YOU'RE FISHING AGAIN TODAY~?
AH, I SEE~. FISHING IS A HOBBY OF YOURS?
NO, NOT AT ALL...
MY HOBBY IS COLLECTING MONEY.
THAT'S YOUR HOBBY...?

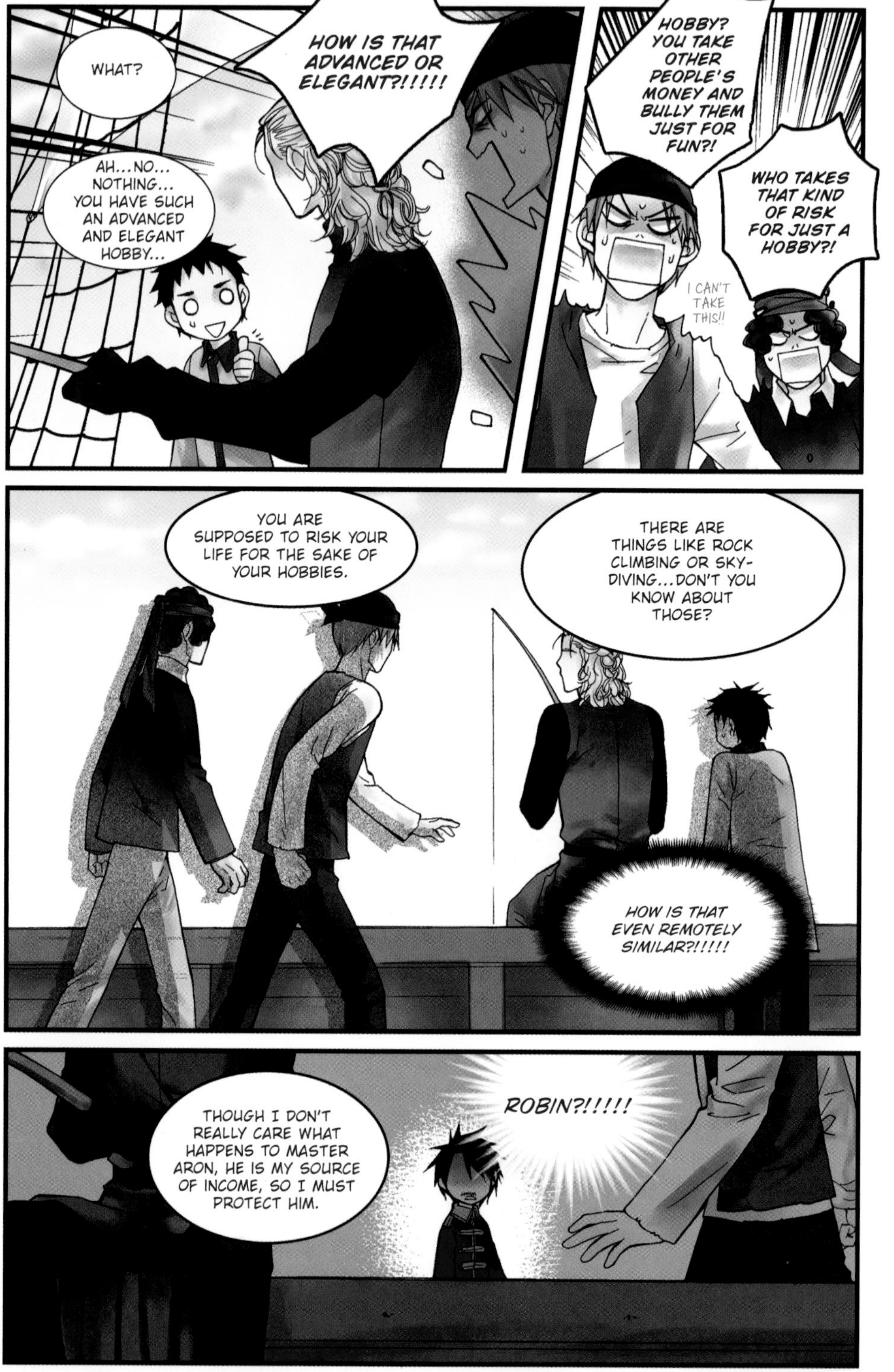
WHAT?
HOW IS THAT ADVANCED OR ELEGANT?!!!!!
AH...NO... NOTHING... YOU HAVE SUCH AN ADVANCED AND ELEGANT HOBBY...
HOBBY? YOU TAKE OTHER PEOPLE'S MONEY AND BULLY THEM JUST FOR FUN?!
WHO TAKES THAT KIND OF RISK FOR JUST A HOBBY?!
I CAN'T TAKE THIS!!
YOU ARE SUPPOSED TO RISK YOUR LIFE FOR THE SAKE OF YOUR HOBBIES.
THERE ARE THINGS LIKE ROCK CLIMBING OR SKY-DIVING...DON'T YOU KNOW ABOUT THOSE?
HOW IS THAT EVEN REMOTELY SIMILAR?!!!!!
THOUGH I DON'T REALLY CARE WHAT HAPPENS TO MASTER ARON, HE IS MY SOURCE OF INCOME, SO I MUST PROTECT HIM.
ROBIN?!!!!!

LET'S GO AGAIN~
LET'S GO AGAIN~

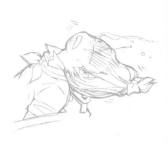

BEST OF
THE BEST

ARON'S
ABSURD
ARMADA

I see you~

CHARACTERS

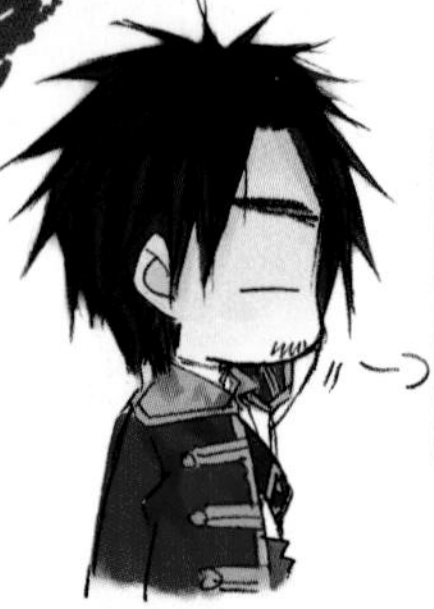

ARON

NOW EVERYONE'S ADJUSTED (TO HIM).
IF HE HIDES HIS MUSTACHE, HE'S NOT BAD LOOKING. (SOMETIMES.)
FROM TIME TO TIME, HE MIGHT EVEN BE CONSIDERED CUTE. (WHUT?)
ANYWAY, HE'S STILL THE CAPTAIN. SOMEHOW. (WHUUUA?!!)

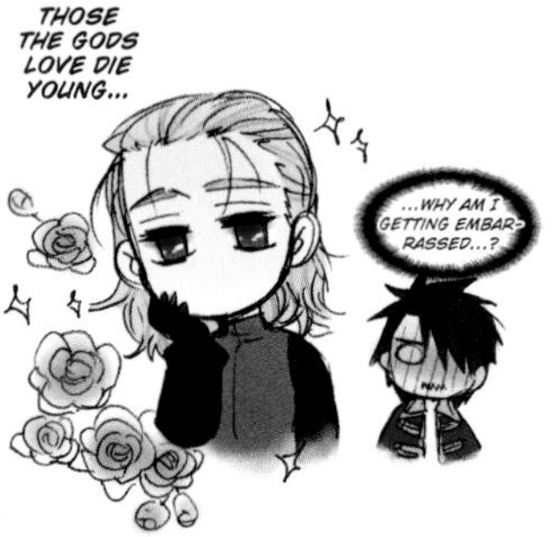
THOSE THE GODS LOVE DIE YOUNG...
...WHY AM I GETTING EMBAR-RASSED...?

ROBIN

ARON'S BODYGUARD FOR NOW.
HE'S PICKY AND OFTEN CONSUMED WITH SELF-IMPORTANCE.
HIS LIFE'S MOTTO IS THAT WORLD CENTERS AROUND GOLD AND MONEY.

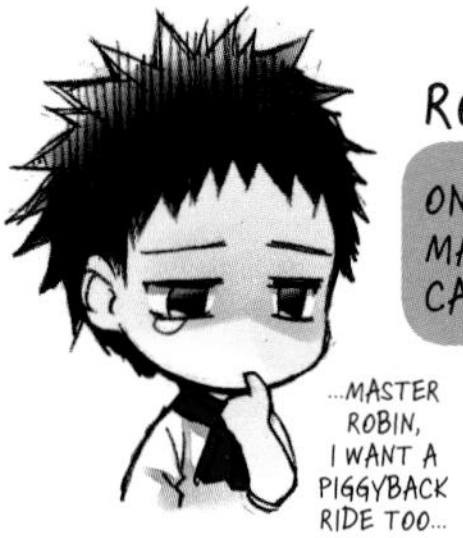
...MASTER ROBIN, I WANT A PIGGYBACK RIDE TOO...

RONNIE

ONLY FOLLOWS MASTER ROBIN. SHE LIKES TREASURE. SHE MANIPULATES ANTON AND GILBERT(?!!). NO ONE SEEMS TO CARE ABOUT HER TRUE GENDER ANYMORE.

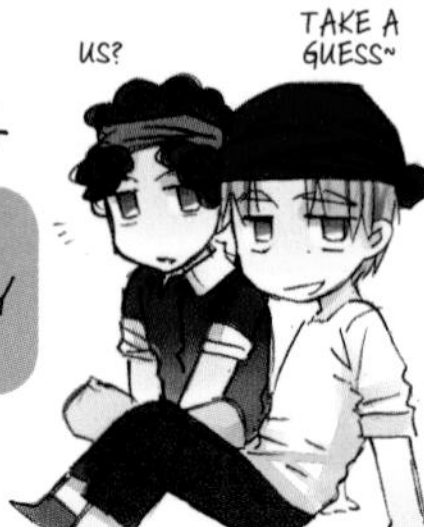
US?
TAKE A GUESS~

ANTON, GILBERT

THEY'VE APPEARED OFTEN ENOUGH TO BE REMEMBERED? AT LEAST THEY CAN BE DIFFERENTIATED NOW.

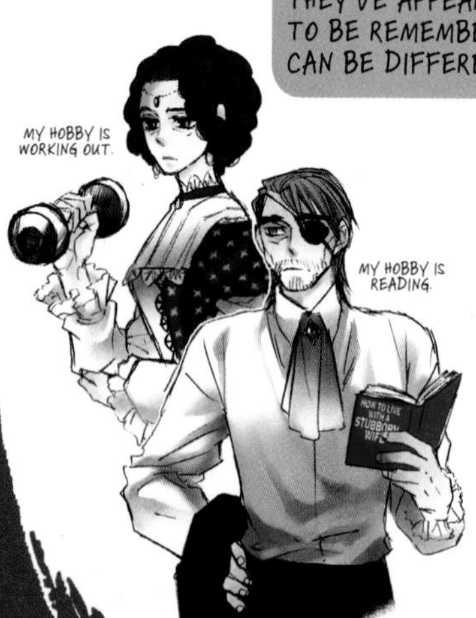
MY HOBBY IS WORKING OUT.
MY HOBBY IS READING.

ARON'S MOM, ARON'S DAD

A MOM WHO LOVES WEIGHT LIFTING AND A DAD WHO LOVES READING. THEY EACH SHOW DIFFERENT TYPES OF TOUGH LOVE TO ARON.

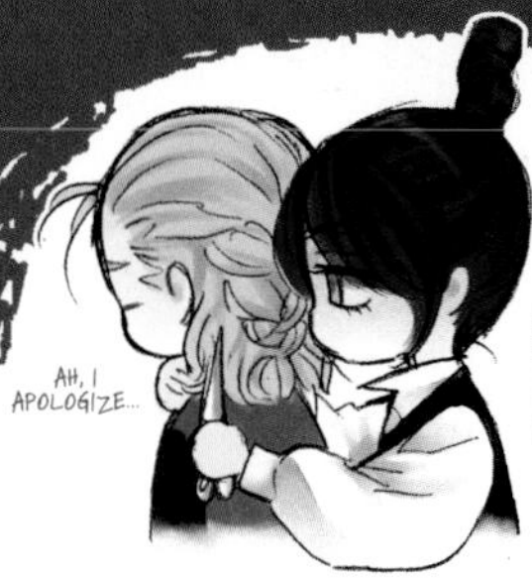
AH, I APOLOGIZE...

MERCEDES

A MAN WHO IS BOTH AN EXPERT IN MAGICAL MAKEOVERS AND A BLOODTHIRSTY ASSASSIN?!! HIS SALARY DREW ROBIN'S INTEREST.

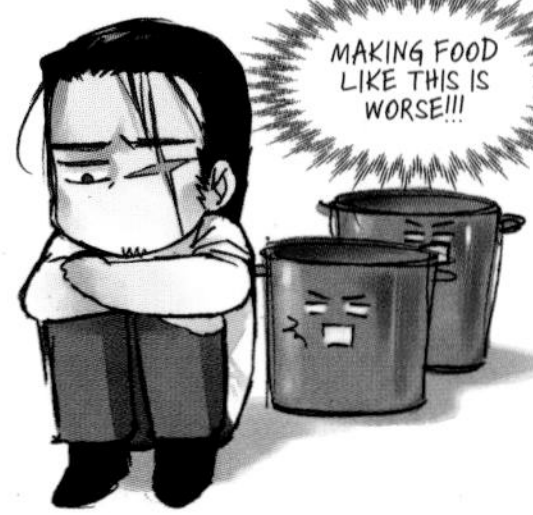
IT'S NOT GOOD TO PLAY WITH FOOD...
MAKING FOOD LIKE THIS IS WORSE!!!

VINCENT

A SOLIDLY BUILT CHEF, HE'S ALSO THE FIRST MAN IN THE WORLD TO MAKE FOOD(?) THAT CAN BE USED AS A WEAPON.

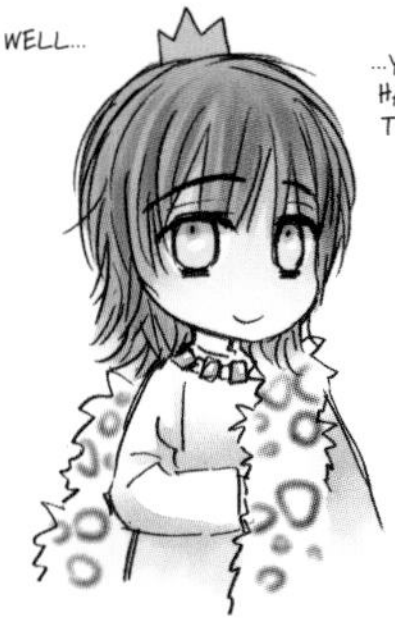
WELL...
...YOU DIDN'T HAVE TO GO THAT FAR...

KING

HE IS ARON'S MOTHER'S MOST HATED SUBJECT, EVEN THOUGH HE ADORES HER. HE HAS AN INCREDIBLY YOUTHFUL FACE, AND HIS KNIGHTS LOVE HIM. HE ALSO HAS STRANGE POWERS.

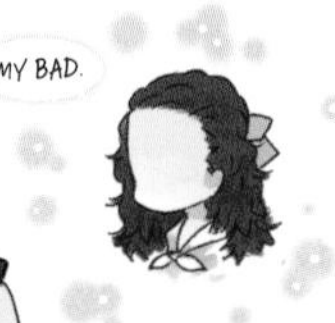
MY BAD.

LUTHER NELSON

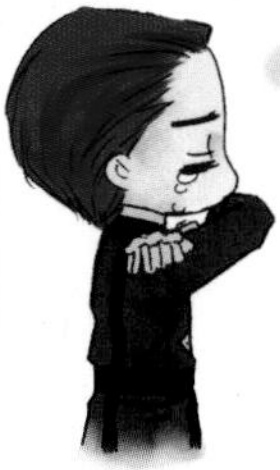

HIS LOVE IS UNREQUITED, BUT HE HIMSELF DOESN'T REALIZE IT. HE LIVES IN THE PALM OF DOROTHY'S HAND. UNFORTUNATELY HE HAS AN ANTAGONISTIC RELATIONSHIP WITH ARON, BUT IT DOESN'T SEEM TOO SERIOUS.

HOBBY IS READING ROMANCE NOVELS.

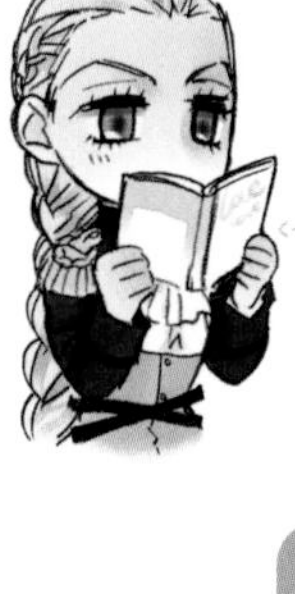
<-- SHE READS B.L. NOVELS FROM TIME TO TIME TOO.

DOROTHY NELSON

SHE IS UNABLE TO SEPARATE ASSUMPTIONS FROM FACTS. SHE FIRMLY BELIEVES THAT RONNIE IS AN HONEST AND BEAUTIFUL MAN. SHE IS ALSO VERY INTERESTED IN BOYS' LOVE.

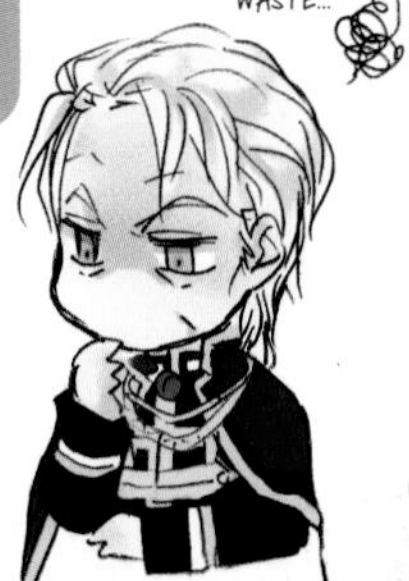
WHAT A WASTE...

ADMIRAL NELSON

HE AND ARON'S MOTHER ARE EVER AT ODDS. HE ABUSES LUTHER AND IS AN AMBITIOUS MAN. SOMETIMES HE'S A PRETTY COOL GUY. (WHUT?)

#93. THE BOY WHO CRIED WOLF

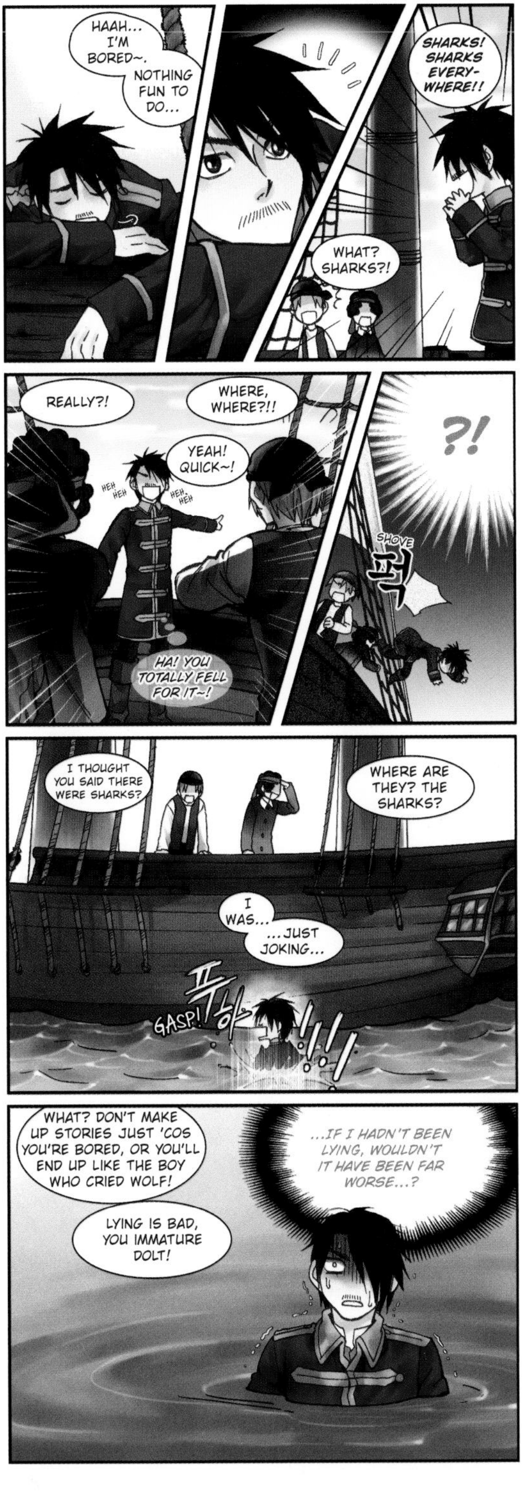
HAAH... I'M BORED~.
NOTHING FUN TO DO...
SHARKS! SHARKS EVERY-WHERE!!
WHAT? SHARKS?!
REALLY?!
WHERE, WHERE?!!
YEAH! QUICK~!
HEH HEH
HEH, HEH
HA! YOU TOTALLY FELL FOR IT~!
?!
SHOVE
퍽
I THOUGHT YOU SAID THERE WERE SHARKS?
WHERE ARE THEY? THE SHARKS?
I WAS...
...JUST JOKING...
푸하
GASP!
WHAT? DON'T MAKE UP STORIES JUST 'COS YOU'RE BORED, OR YOU'LL END UP LIKE THE BOY WHO CRIED WOLF!
LYING IS BAD, YOU IMMATURE DOLT!
...IF I HADN'T BEEN LYING, WOULDN'T IT HAVE BEEN FAR WORSE...?

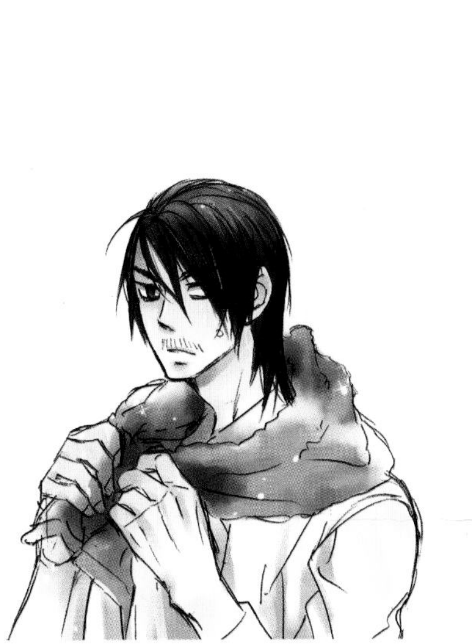

#94. ANXIETY AT HIS BACK

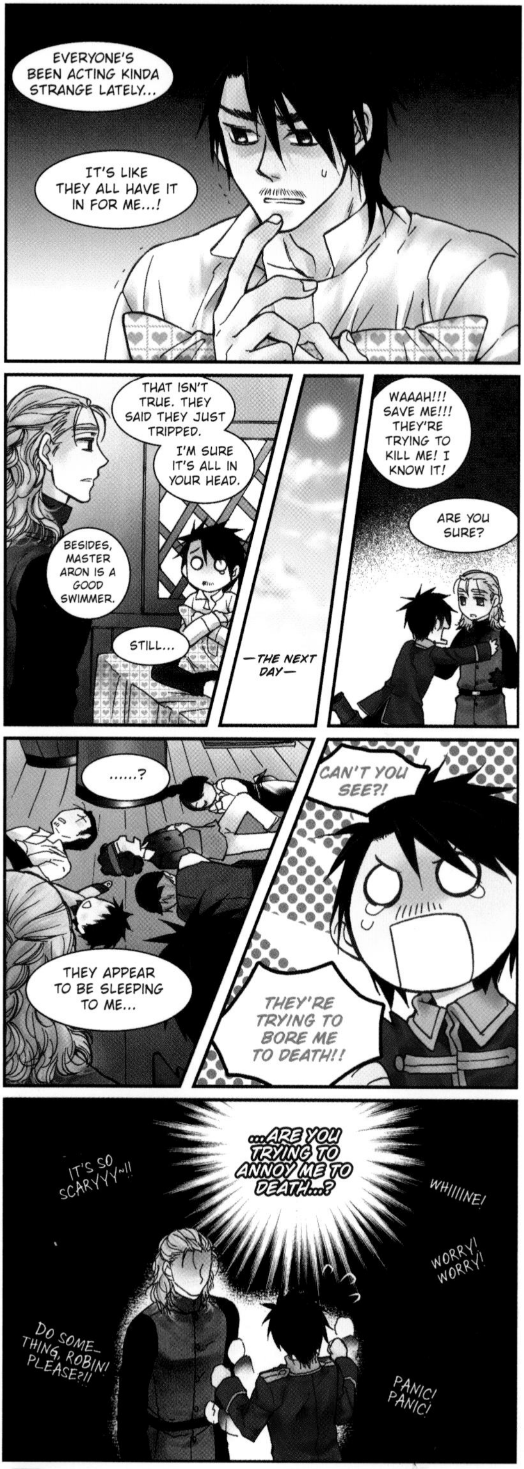
EVERYONE'S BEEN ACTING KINDA STRANGE LATELY...
IT'S LIKE THEY ALL HAVE IT IN FOR ME...!
THAT ISN'T TRUE. THEY SAID THEY JUST TRIPPED.
I'M SURE IT'S ALL IN YOUR HEAD.
BESIDES, MASTER ARON IS A GOOD SWIMMER.
STILL...
—THE NEXT DAY—
WAAAH!!! SAVE ME!!! THEY'RE TRYING TO KILL ME! I KNOW IT!
ARE YOU SURE?
......?
THEY APPEAR TO BE SLEEPING TO ME...
CAN'T YOU SEE?!
THEY'RE TRYING TO BORE ME TO DEATH!!
...ARE YOU TRYING TO ANNOY ME TO DEATH...?
IT'S SO SCARYYY~!!
WHIIIINE!
WORRY! WORRY!
DO SOME-THING, ROBIN! PLEASE?!!
PANIC! PANIC!

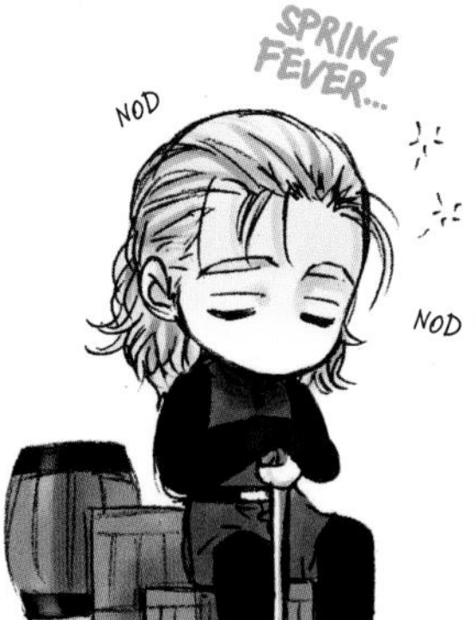
SPRING FEVER...
NOD
NOD

#95. LEGITIMATE SELF-DEFENSE

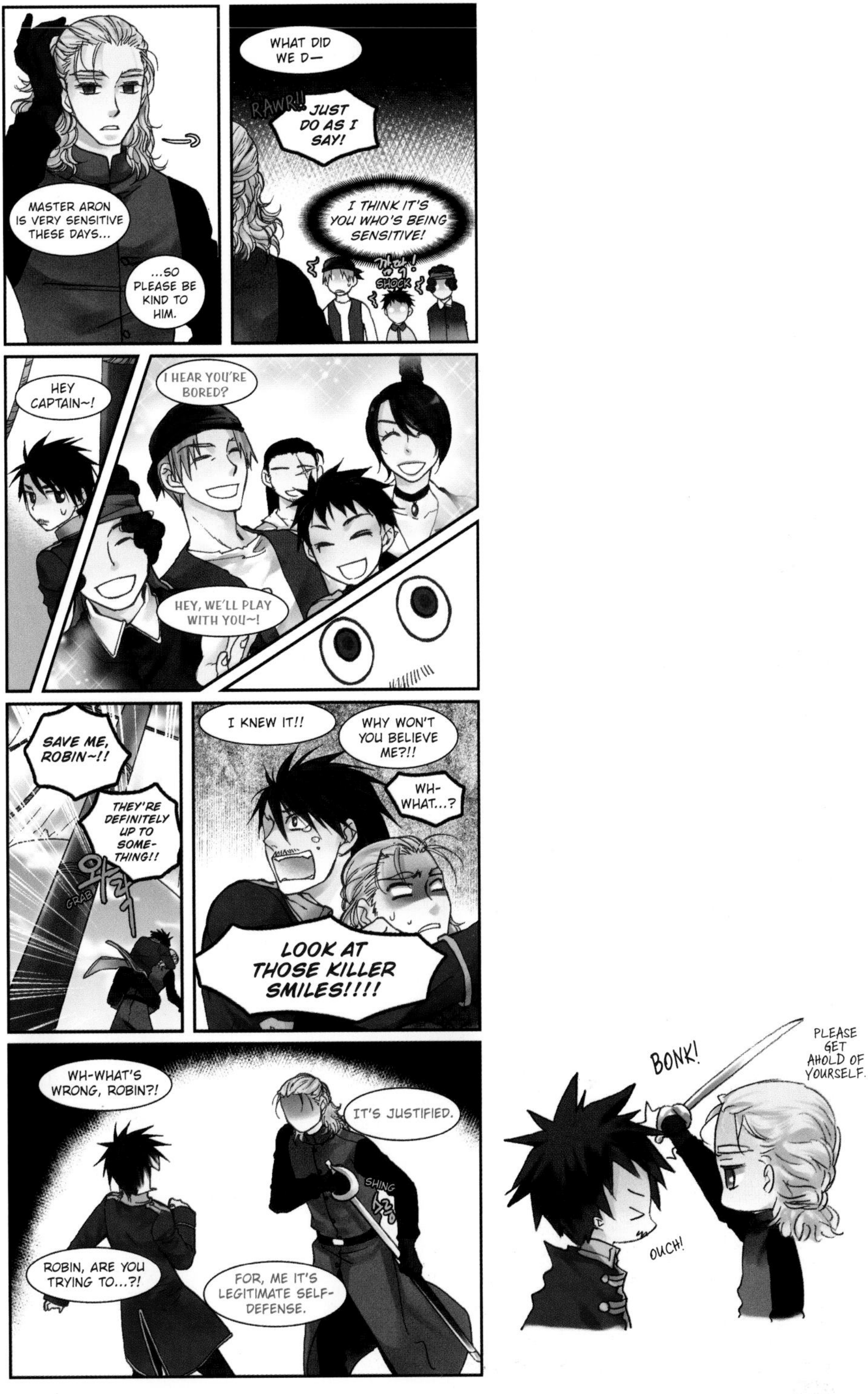

MASTER ARON IS VERY SENSITIVE THESE DAYS...
...SO PLEASE BE KIND TO HIM.
WHAT DID WE D—
RAWR!!
JUST DO AS I SAY!
I THINK IT'S YOU WHO'S BEING SENSITIVE!
SHOCK
HEY CAPTAIN~!
I HEAR YOU'RE BORED?
HEY, WE'LL PLAY WITH YOU~!
SAVE ME, ROBIN~!!
THEY'RE DEFINITELY UP TO SOME-THING!!
GRAB
I KNEW IT!!
WHY WON'T YOU BELIEVE ME?!!
WH-WHAT...?
LOOK AT THOSE KILLER SMILES!!!!
WH-WHAT'S WRONG, ROBIN?!
IT'S JUSTIFIED.
SHING
ROBIN, ARE YOU TRYING TO...?!
FOR, ME IT'S LEGITIMATE SELF-DEFENSE.
BONK!
PLEASE GET AHOLD OF YOURSELF.
OUCH!

#96. TRUST

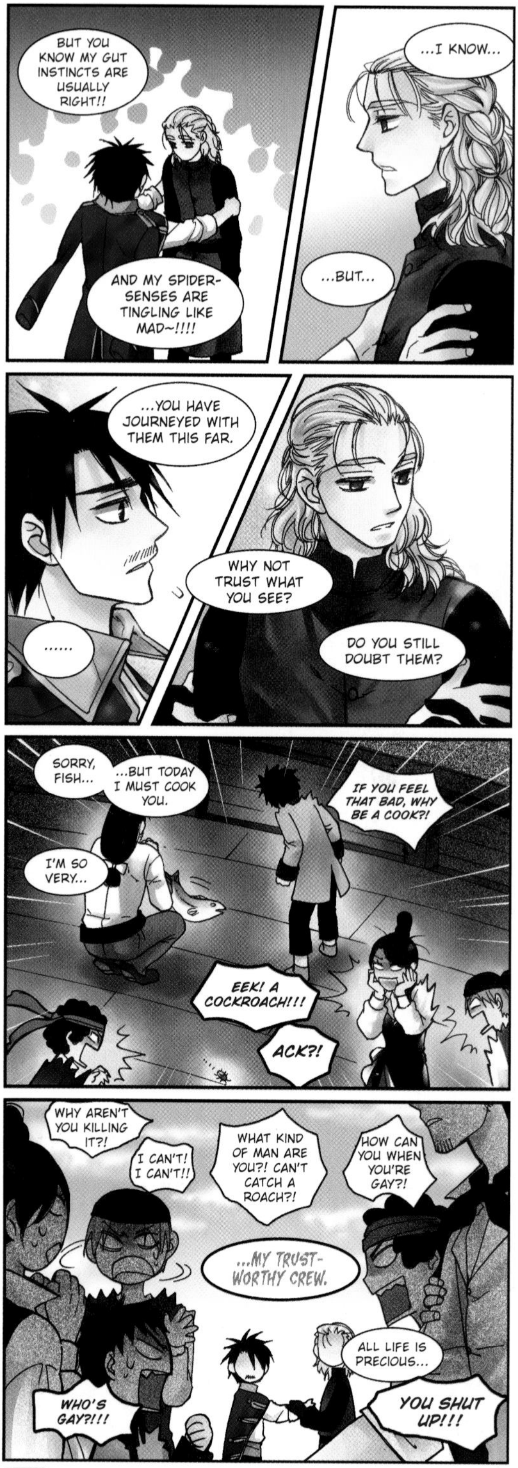
BUT YOU KNOW MY GUT INSTINCTS ARE USUALLY RIGHT!!
AND MY SPIDER-SENSES ARE TINGLING LIKE MAD~!!!!
...I KNOW...
...BUT...
...YOU HAVE JOURNEYED WITH THEM THIS FAR.
WHY NOT TRUST WHAT YOU SEE?
DO YOU STILL DOUBT THEM?
......
SORRY, FISH...
...BUT TODAY I MUST COOK YOU.
I'M SO VERY...
IF YOU FEEL THAT BAD, WHY BE A COOK?!
EEK! A COCKROACH!!!
ACK?!
WHY AREN'T YOU KILLING IT?!
I CAN'T! I CAN'T!!
WHAT KIND OF MAN ARE YOU?! CAN'T CATCH A ROACH?!
HOW CAN YOU WHEN YOU'RE GAY?!
...MY TRUST-WORTHY CREW.
ALL LIFE IS PRECIOUS...
WHO'S GAY?!!!
YOU SHUT UP!!!

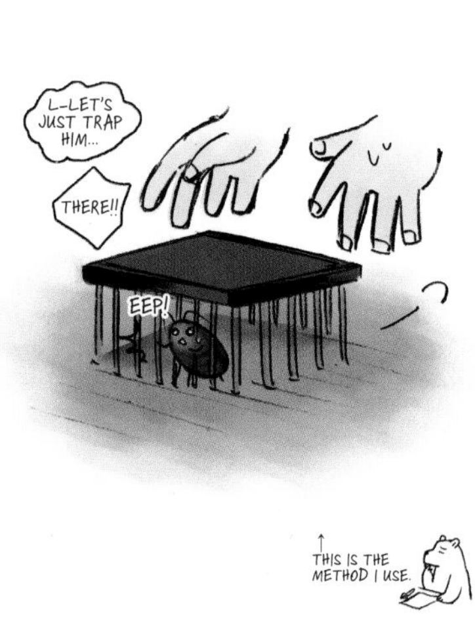
L-LET'S JUST TRAP HIM...
THERE!!
EEP!
THIS IS THE METHOD I USE.

#97. DANGER

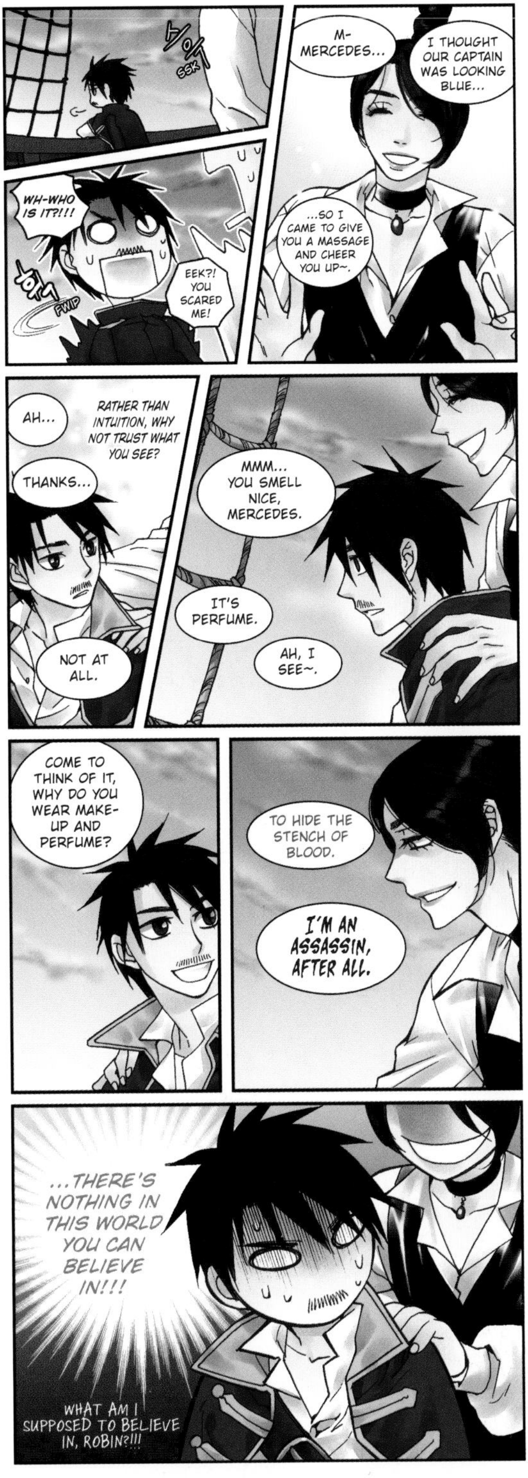
SSK
M-MERCEDES...
I THOUGHT OUR CAPTAIN WAS LOOKING BLUE...
WH-WHO IS IT?!!!
FWIP
EEK?! YOU SCARED ME!
...SO I CAME TO GIVE YOU A MASSAGE AND CHEER YOU UP~.
AH...
RATHER THAN INTUITION, WHY NOT TRUST WHAT YOU SEE?
THANKS...
NOT AT ALL.
MMM... YOU SMELL NICE, MERCEDES.
IT'S PERFUME.
AH, I SEE~.
COME TO THINK OF IT, WHY DO YOU WEAR MAKE-UP AND PERFUME?
TO HIDE THE STENCH OF BLOOD.
I'M AN ASSASSIN, AFTER ALL.
...THERE'S NOTHING IN THIS WORLD YOU CAN BELIEVE IN!!!
WHAT AM I SUPPOSED TO BELIEVE IN, ROBIN?!!!

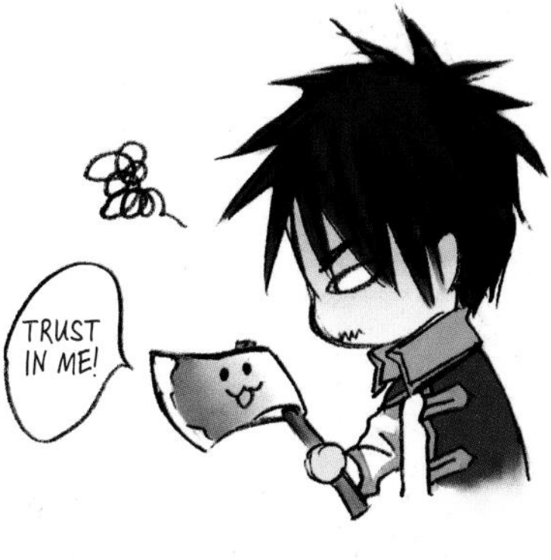
TRUST IN ME!

#98. HIS QUESTION

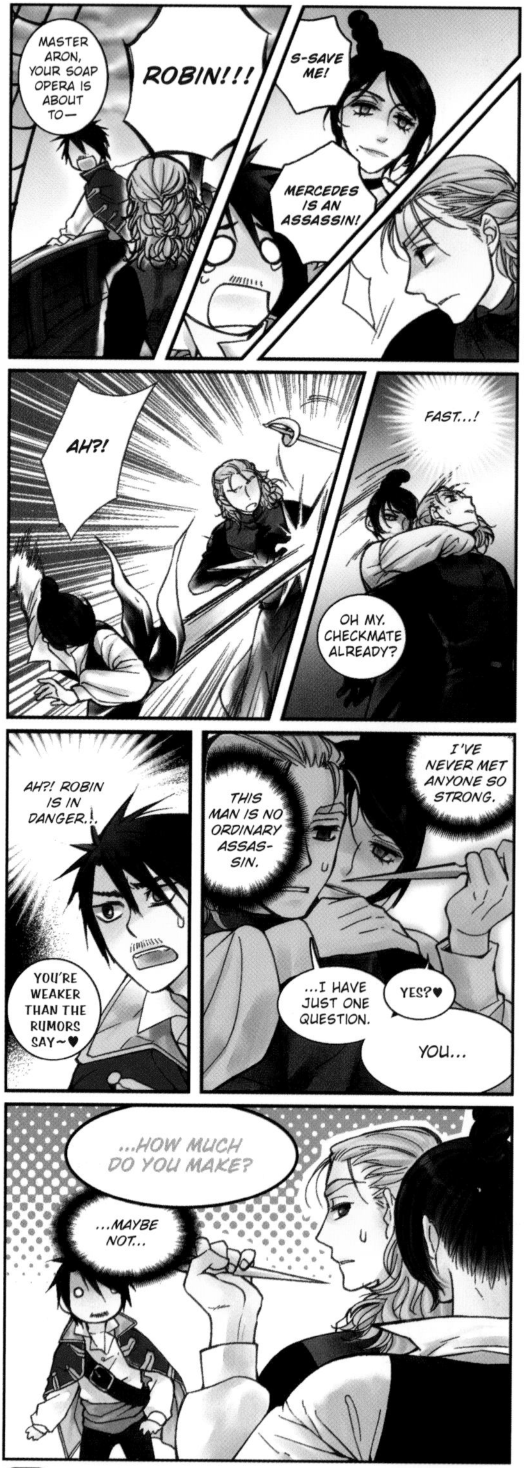
MASTER ARON, YOUR SOAP OPERA IS ABOUT TO—
ROBIN!!!
S-SAVE ME!
MERCEDES IS AN ASSASSIN!
AH?!
FAST...!
OH MY. CHECKMATE ALREADY?
AH?! ROBIN IS IN DANGER...
YOU'RE WEAKER THAN THE RUMORS SAY~♥
THIS MAN IS NO ORDINARY ASSAS-SIN.
I'VE NEVER MET ANYONE SO STRONG.
...I HAVE JUST ONE QUESTION.
YES?♥
YOU...
...HOW MUCH DO YOU MAKE?
...MAYBE NOT...

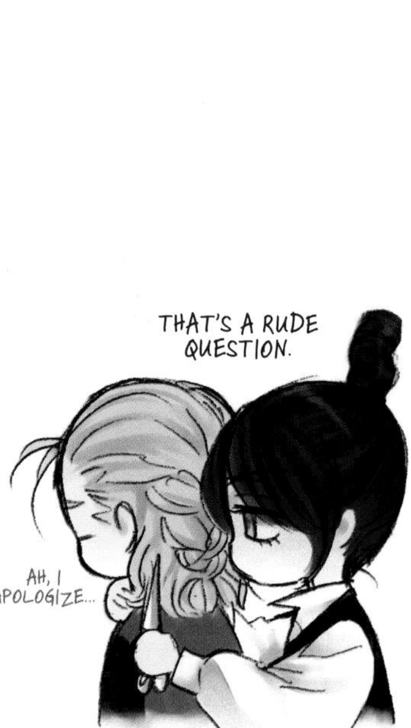
THAT'S A RUDE QUESTION.
AH, I APOLOGIZE...

#99. AH, I SEE

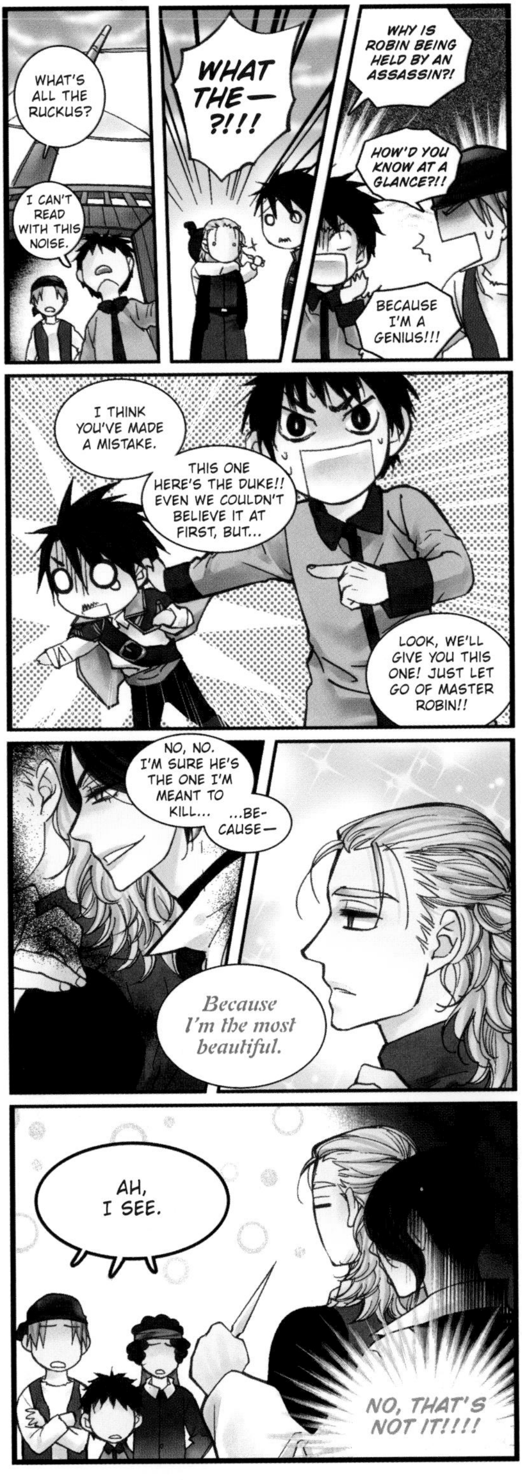

WHAT'S ALL THE RUCKUS?
I CAN'T READ WITH THIS NOISE.
WHAT THE— ?!!!
WHY IS ROBIN BEING HELD BY AN ASSASSIN?!
HOW'D YOU KNOW AT A GLANCE?!!
BECAUSE I'M A GENIUS!!!
I THINK YOU'VE MADE A MISTAKE.
THIS ONE HERE'S THE DUKE!! EVEN WE COULDN'T BELIEVE IT AT FIRST, BUT...
LOOK, WE'LL GIVE YOU THIS ONE! JUST LET GO OF MASTER ROBIN!!
NO, NO. I'M SURE HE'S THE ONE I'M MEANT TO KILL...
...BE-CAUSE—
Because I'm the most beautiful.
AH, I SEE.
NO, THAT'S NOT IT!!!!

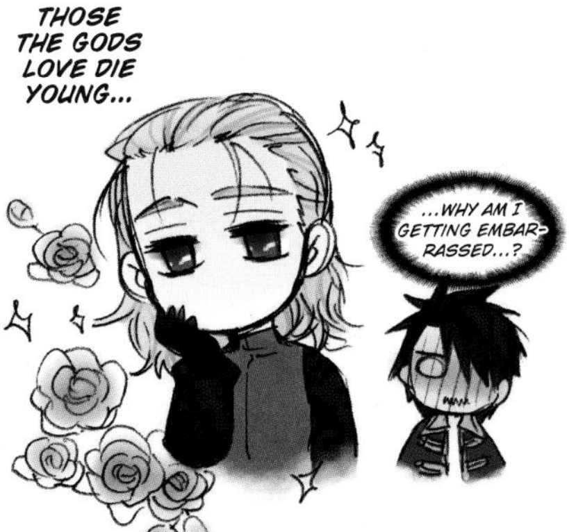

THOSE THE GODS LOVE DIE YOUNG...
...WHY AM I GETTING EMBAR-RASSED...?

#100. 100TH STRIP SPECIAL

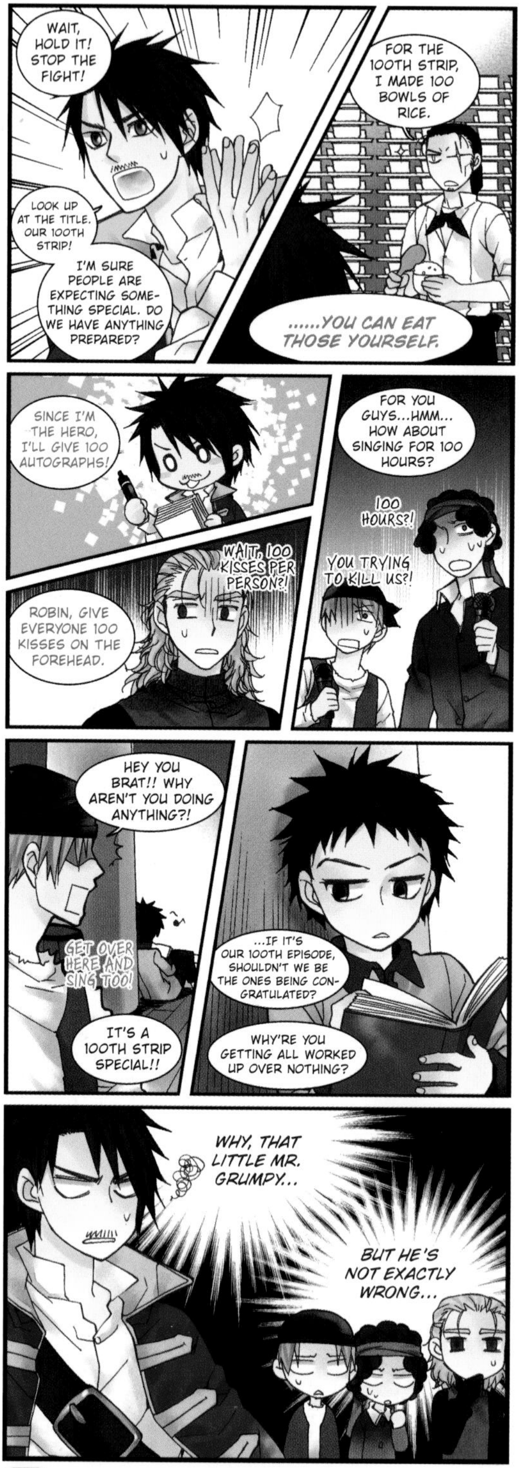
WAIT, HOLD IT! STOP THE FIGHT!
LOOK UP AT THE TITLE. OUR 100TH STRIP!
I'M SURE PEOPLE ARE EXPECTING SOMETHING SPECIAL. DO WE HAVE ANYTHING PREPARED?
FOR THE 100TH STRIP, I MADE 100 BOWLS OF RICE.
......YOU CAN EAT THOSE YOURSELF.
SINCE I'M THE HERO, I'LL GIVE 100 AUTOGRAPHS!
ROBIN, GIVE EVERYONE 100 KISSES ON THE FOREHEAD.
WAIT, 100 KISSES PER PERSON?!
FOR YOU GUYS...HMM... HOW ABOUT SINGING FOR 100 HOURS?
100 HOURS?!
YOU TRYING TO KILL US?!
HEY YOU BRAT!! WHY AREN'T YOU DOING ANYTHING?!
GET OVER HERE AND SING TOO!
IT'S A 100TH STRIP SPECIAL!!
...IF IT'S OUR 100TH EPISODE, SHOULDN'T WE BE THE ONES BEING CONGRATULATED?
WHY'RE YOU GETTING ALL WORKED UP OVER NOTHING?
WHY, THAT LITTLE MR. GRUMPY...
BUT HE'S NOT EXACTLY WRONG...

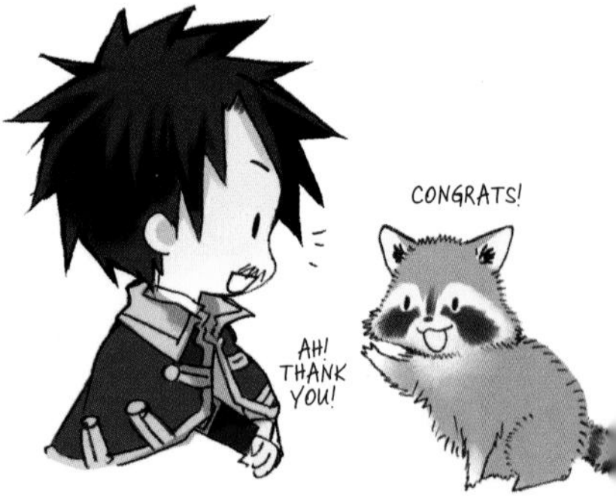
CONGRATS!
AH! THANK YOU!

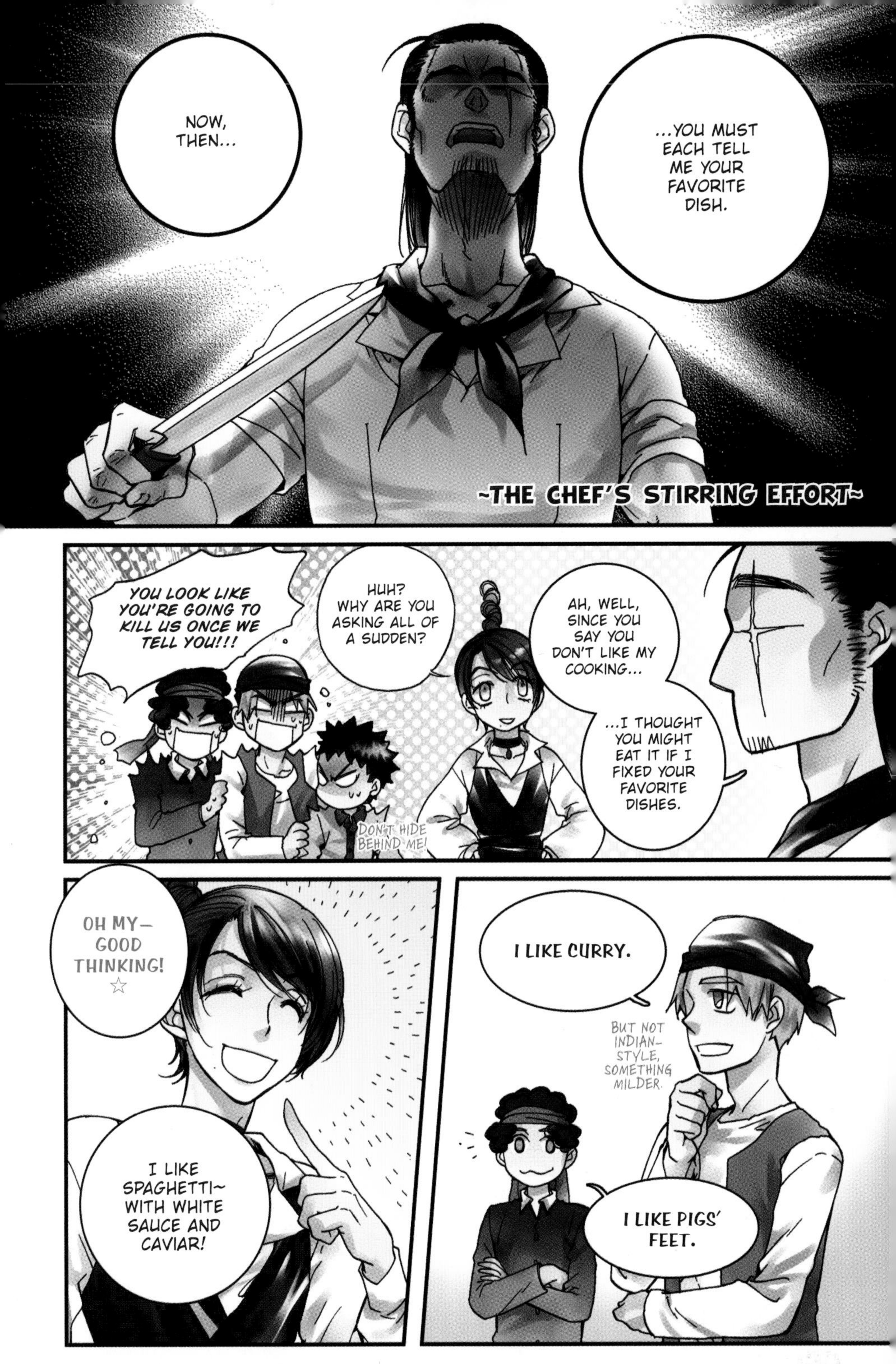
~THE CHEF'S STIRRING EFFORT~
NOW, THEN...
...YOU MUST EACH TELL ME YOUR FAVORITE DISH.
AH, WELL, SINCE YOU SAY YOU DON'T LIKE MY COOKING...
...I THOUGHT YOU MIGHT EAT IT IF I FIXED YOUR FAVORITE DISHES.
HUH? WHY ARE YOU ASKING ALL OF A SUDDEN?
YOU LOOK LIKE YOU'RE GOING TO KILL US ONCE WE TELL YOU!!!
DON'T HIDE BEHIND ME!
OH MY— GOOD THINKING! ☆
I LIKE SPAGHETTI~ WITH WHITE SAUCE AND CAVIAR!
I LIKE CURRY.
BUT NOT INDIAN-STYLE, SOMETHING MILDER.
I LIKE PIGS' FEET.

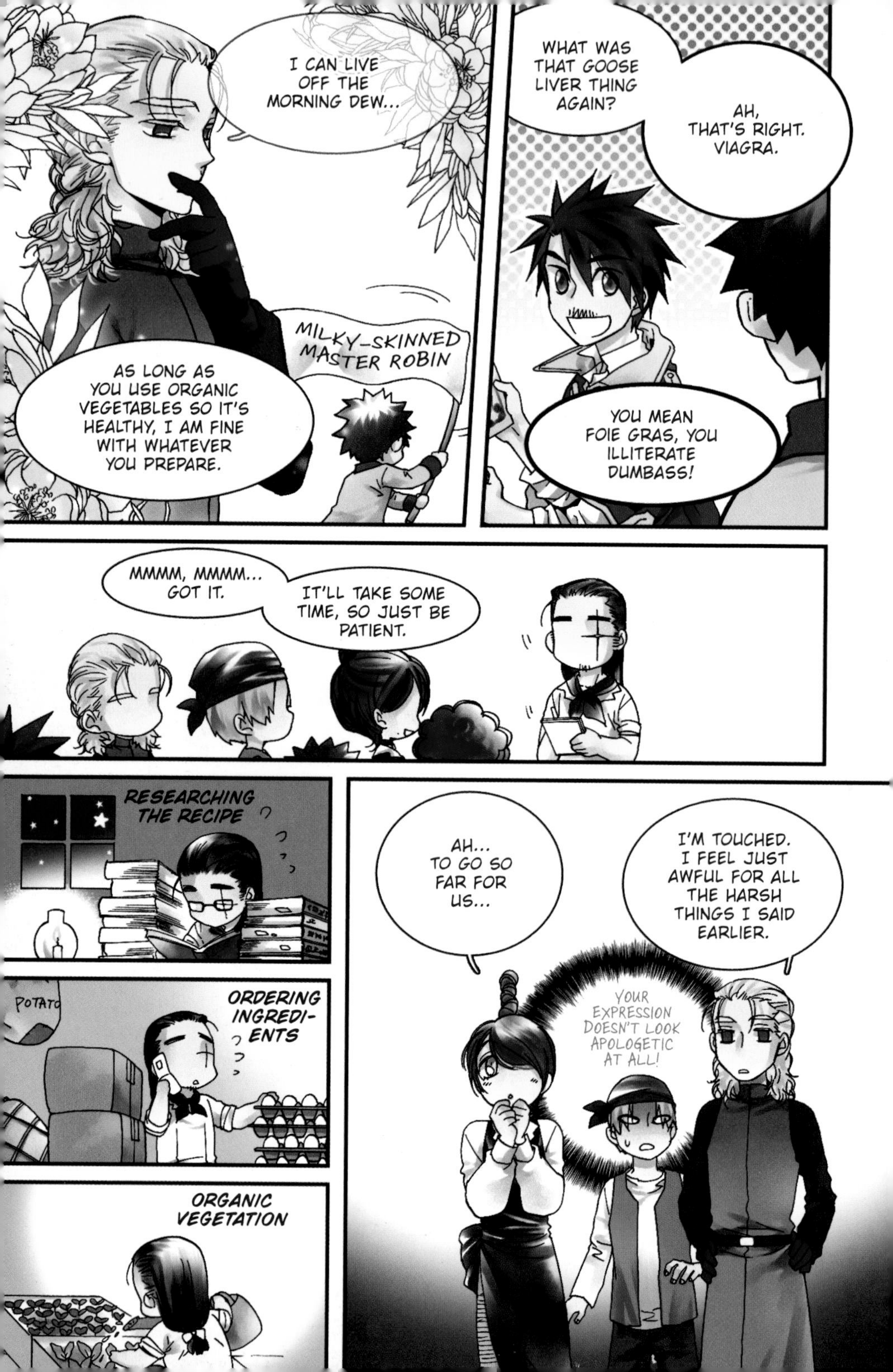
I CAN LIVE OFF THE MORNING DEW...
MILKY-SKINNED MASTER ROBIN
AS LONG AS YOU USE ORGANIC VEGETABLES SO IT'S HEALTHY, I AM FINE WITH WHATEVER YOU PREPARE.
WHAT WAS THAT GOOSE LIVER THING AGAIN?
AH, THAT'S RIGHT. VIAGRA.
YOU MEAN FOIE GRAS, YOU ILLITERATE DUMBASS!
MMMM, MMMM... GOT IT.
IT'LL TAKE SOME TIME, SO JUST BE PATIENT.
RESEARCHING THE RECIPE
POTATO
ORDERING INGREDI-ENTS
ORGANIC VEGETATION
AH... TO GO SO FAR FOR US...
I'M TOUCHED. I FEEL JUST AWFUL FOR ALL THE HARSH THINGS I SAID EARLIER.
YOUR EXPRESSION DOESN'T LOOK APOLOGETIC AT ALL!

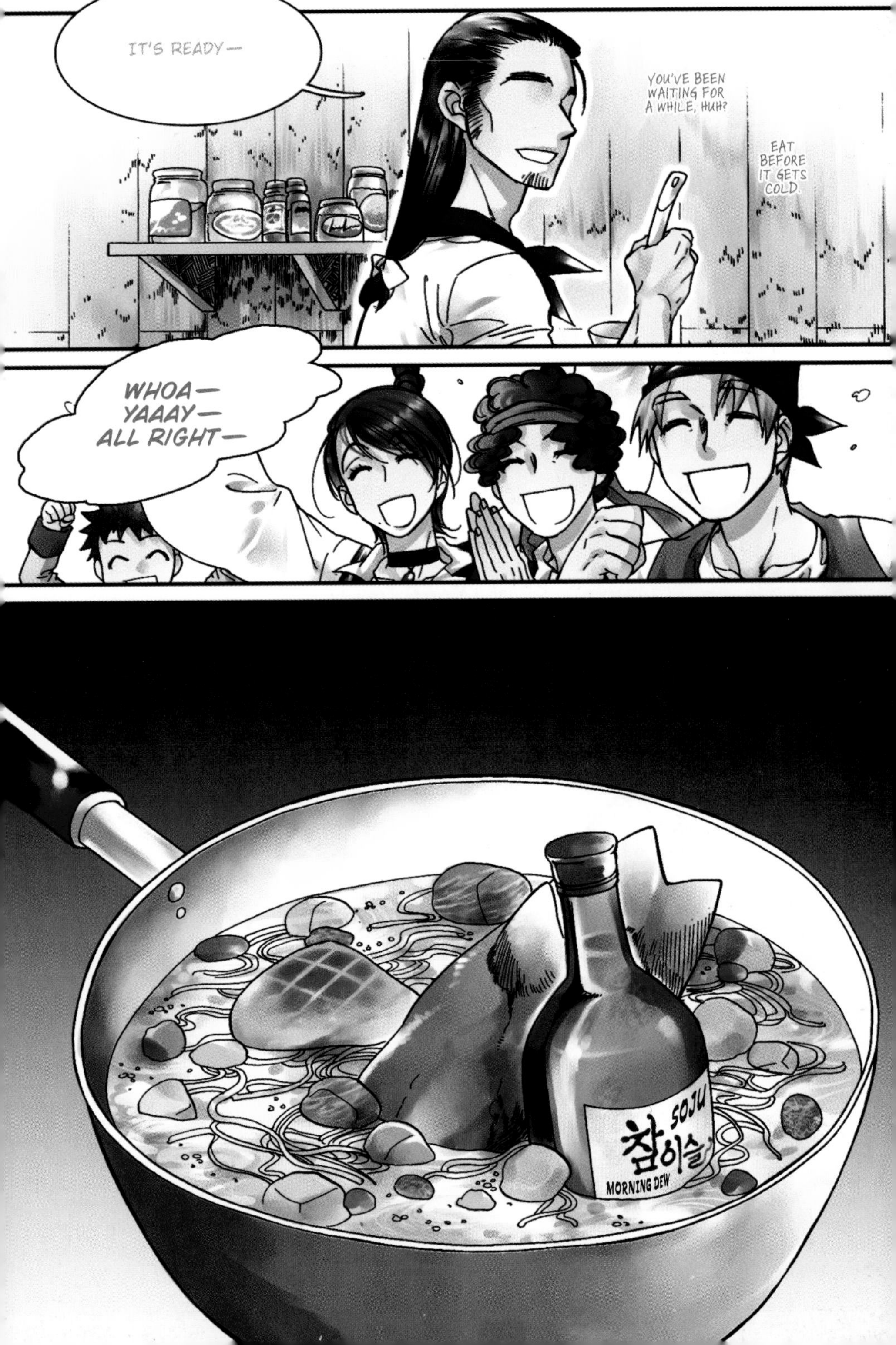
IT'S READY—
YOU'VE BEEN WAITING FOR A WHILE, HUH?
EAT BEFORE IT GETS COLD.
WHOA— YAAAY— ALL RIGHT—
SOJU
참이슬
MORNING DEW

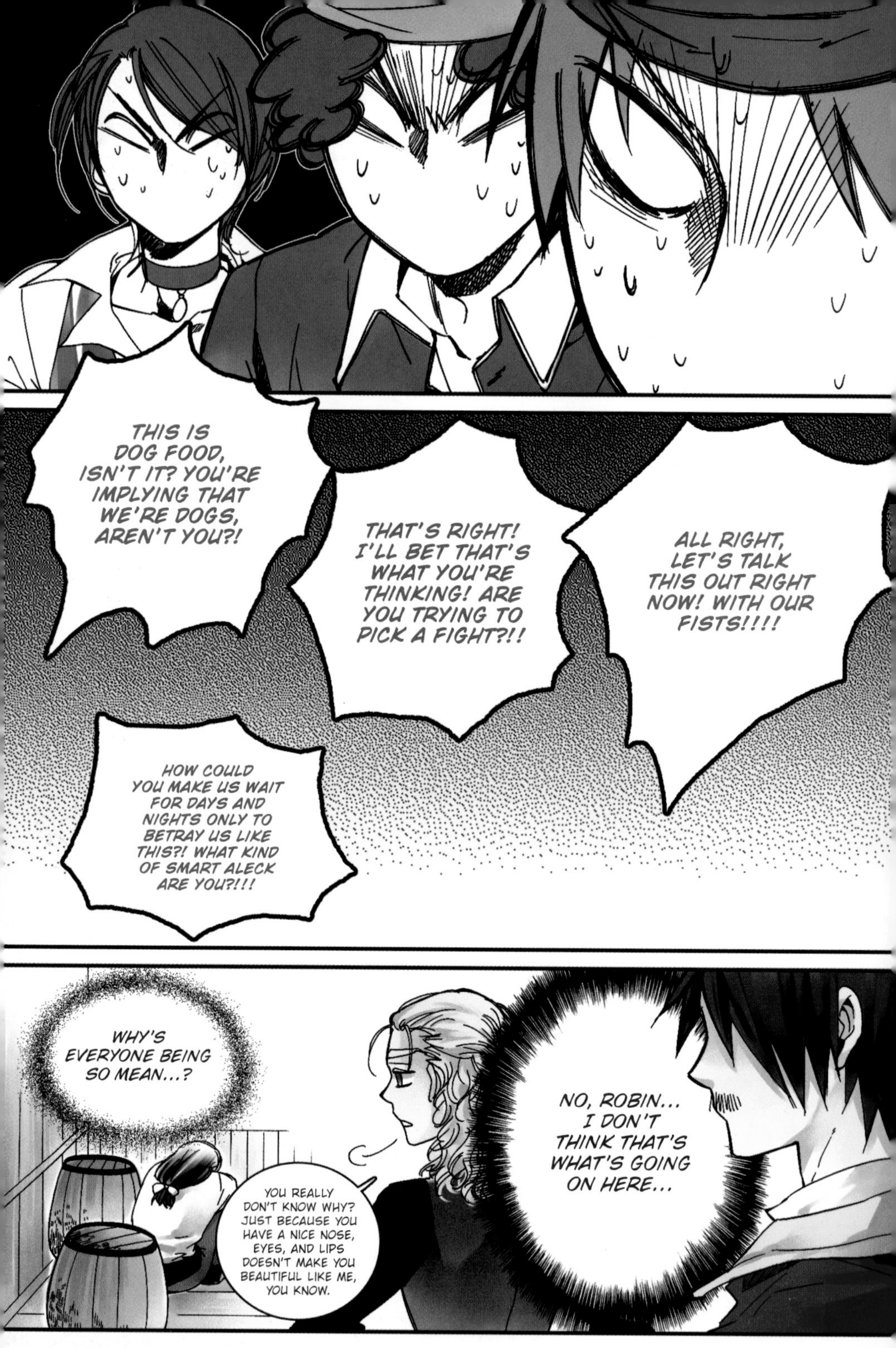
THIS IS DOG FOOD, ISN'T IT? YOU'RE IMPLYING THAT WE'RE DOGS, AREN'T YOU?!
THAT'S RIGHT! I'LL BET THAT'S WHAT YOU'RE THINKING! ARE YOU TRYING TO PICK A FIGHT?!!
ALL RIGHT, LET'S TALK THIS OUT RIGHT NOW! WITH OUR FISTS!!!!
HOW COULD YOU MAKE US WAIT FOR DAYS AND NIGHTS ONLY TO BETRAY US LIKE THIS?! WHAT KIND OF SMART ALECK ARE YOU?!!!
WHY'S EVERYONE BEING SO MEAN...?
NO, ROBIN... I DON'T THINK THAT'S WHAT'S GOING ON HERE...
YOU REALLY DON'T KNOW WHY? JUST BECAUSE YOU HAVE A NICE NOSE, EYES, AND LIPS DOESN'T MAKE YOU BEAUTIFUL LIKE ME, YOU KNOW.

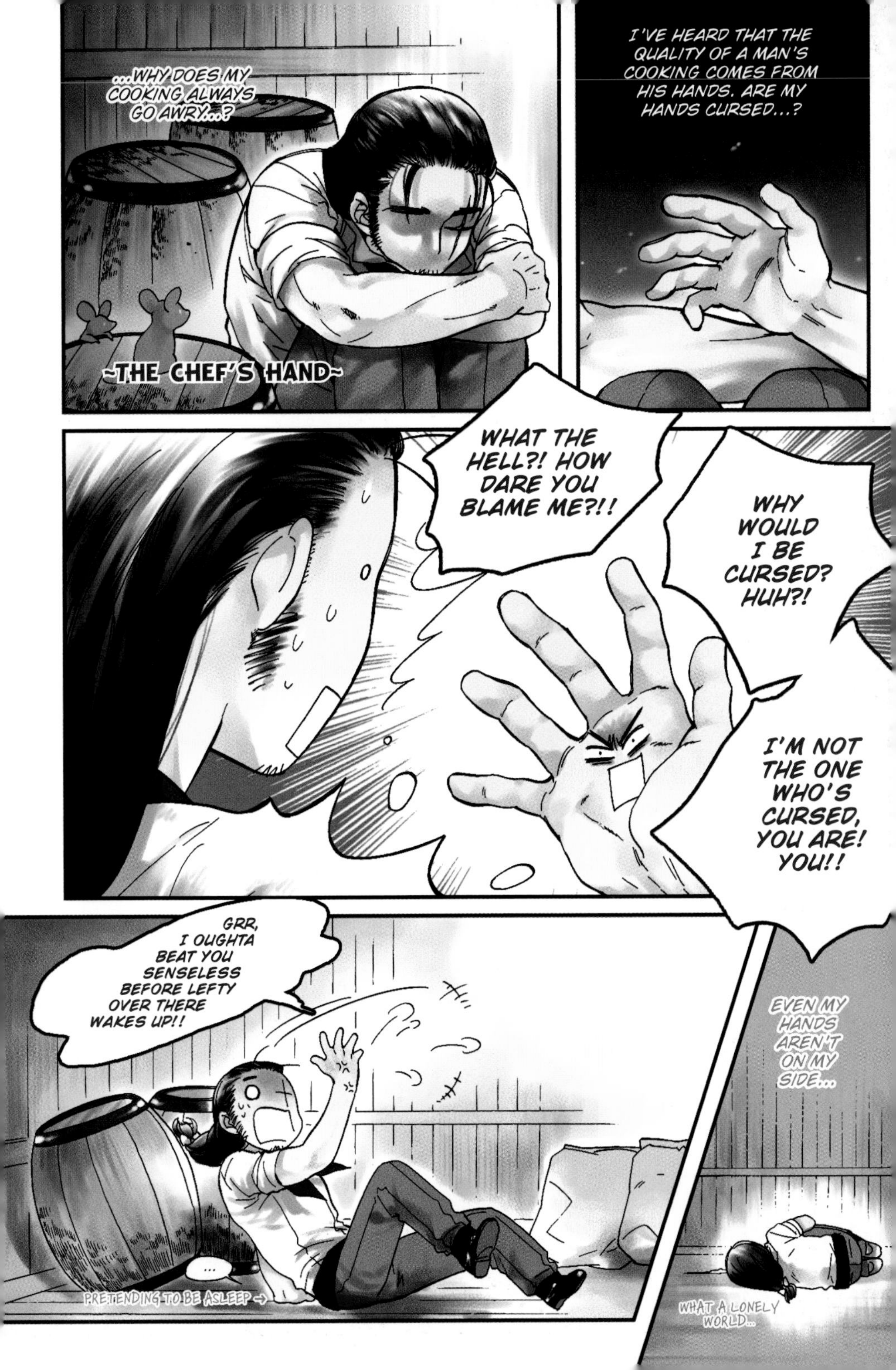

...WHY DOES MY COOKING ALWAYS GO AWRY...?
~THE CHEF'S HAND~
I'VE HEARD THAT THE QUALITY OF A MAN'S COOKING COMES FROM HIS HANDS. ARE MY HANDS CURSED...?
WHAT THE HELL?! HOW DARE YOU BLAME ME?!!
WHY WOULD I BE CURSED? HUH?!
I'M NOT THE ONE WHO'S CURSED, YOU ARE! YOU!!
GRR, I OUGHTA BEAT YOU SENSELESS BEFORE LEFTY OVER THERE WAKES UP!!
...
PRETENDING TO BE ASLEEP →
EVEN MY HANDS AREN'T ON MY SIDE...
WHAT A LONELY WORLD...

#101. THE FIRST TIME

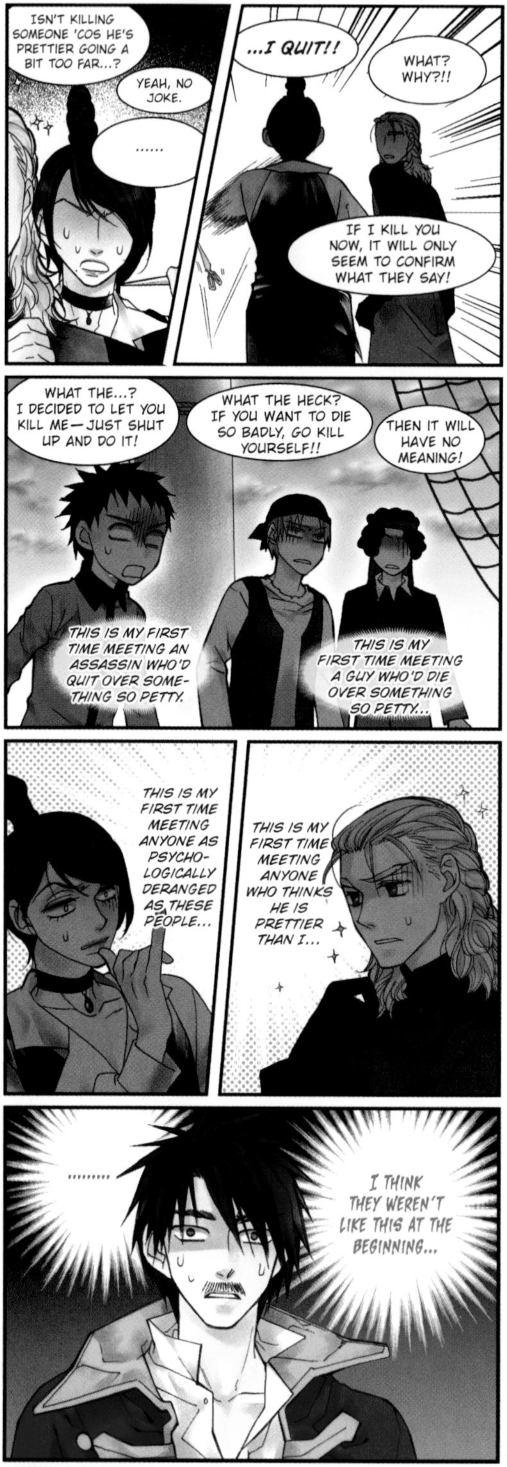

ISN'T KILLING SOMEONE 'COS HE'S PRETTIER GOING A BIT TOO FAR...?
YEAH, NO JOKE.
......
...I QUIT!!
WHAT? WHY?!!
IF I KILL YOU NOW, IT WILL ONLY SEEM TO CONFIRM WHAT THEY SAY!
WHAT THE...? I DECIDED TO LET YOU KILL ME—JUST SHUT UP AND DO IT!
WHAT THE HECK? IF YOU WANT TO DIE SO BADLY, GO KILL YOURSELF!!
THEN IT WILL HAVE NO MEANING!
THIS IS MY FIRST TIME MEETING AN ASSASSIN WHO'D QUIT OVER SOMETHING SO PETTY.
THIS IS MY FIRST TIME MEETING A GUY WHO'D DIE OVER SOMETHING SO PETTY...
THIS IS MY FIRST TIME MEETING ANYONE AS PSYCHOLOGICALLY DERANGED AS THESE PEOPLE...
THIS IS MY FIRST TIME MEETING ANYONE WHO THINKS HE IS PRETTIER THAN I...
....
I THINK THEY WEREN'T LIKE THIS AT THE BEGINNING...

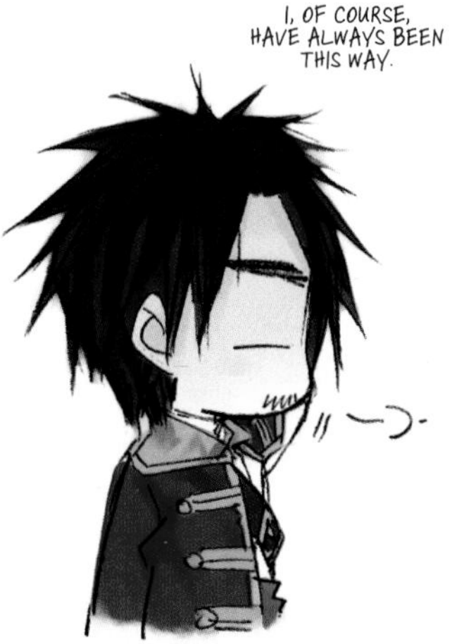

I, OF COURSE, HAVE ALWAYS BEEN THIS WAY.

#102. INTERROGATION 1

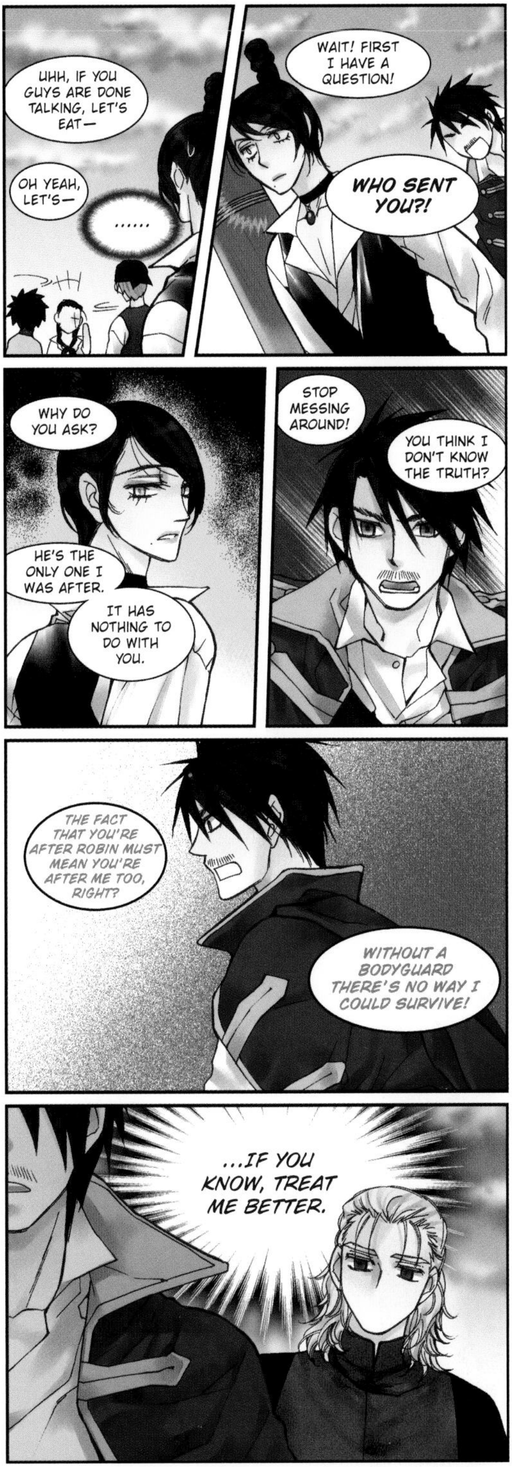
UHH, IF YOU GUYS ARE DONE TALKING, LET'S EAT—
OH YEAH, LET'S—
......
WAIT! FIRST I HAVE A QUESTION!
WHO SENT YOU?!
WHY DO YOU ASK?
HE'S THE ONLY ONE I WAS AFTER.
IT HAS NOTHING TO DO WITH YOU.
STOP MESSING AROUND!
YOU THINK I DON'T KNOW THE TRUTH?
THE FACT THAT YOU'RE AFTER ROBIN MUST MEAN YOU'RE AFTER ME TOO, RIGHT?
WITHOUT A BODYGUARD THERE'S NO WAY I COULD SURVIVE!
...IF YOU KNOW, TREAT ME BETTER.

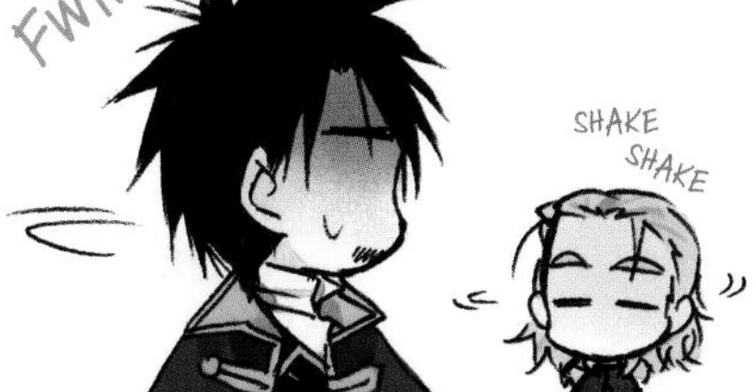
DID YOU JUST SAY SOMETHING?
FWIP
SHAKE SHAKE

#103. INTERROGATION 2

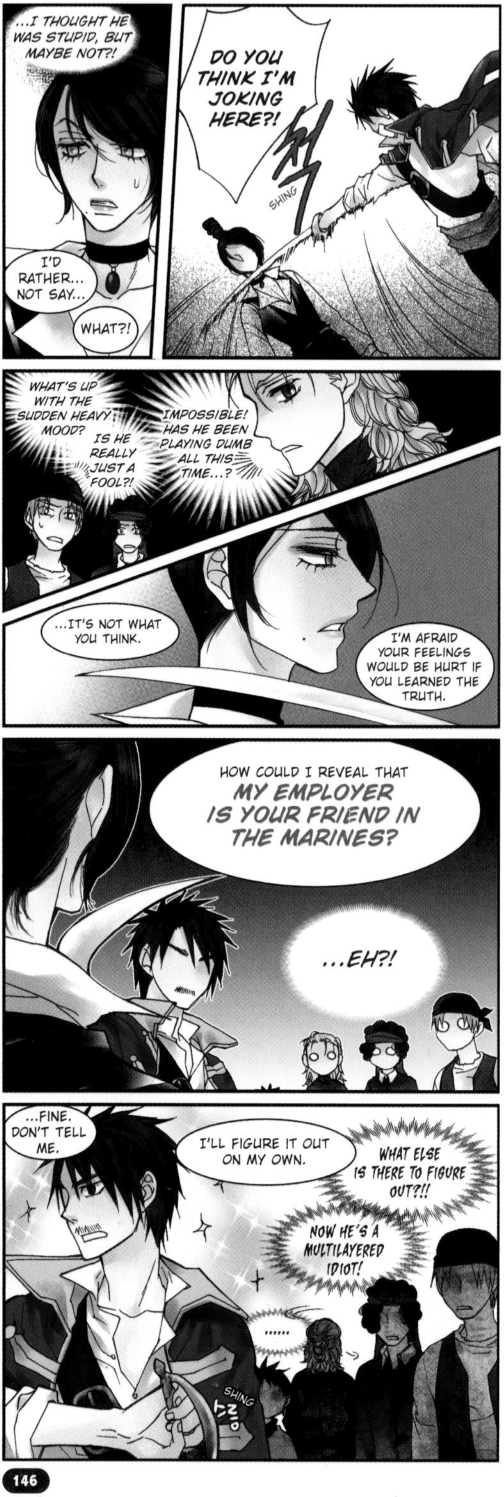

...I THOUGHT HE WAS STUPID, BUT MAYBE NOT?!
I'D RATHER... NOT SAY...
WHAT?!
DO YOU THINK I'M JOKING HERE?!
SHING
WHAT'S UP WITH THE SUDDEN HEAVY MOOD?
IS HE REALLY JUST A FOOL?!
IMPOSSIBLE! HAS HE BEEN PLAYING DUMB ALL THIS TIME...?
...IT'S NOT WHAT YOU THINK.
I'M AFRAID YOUR FEELINGS WOULD BE HURT IF YOU LEARNED THE TRUTH.
HOW COULD I REVEAL THAT MY EMPLOYER IS YOUR FRIEND IN THE MARINES?
...EH?!
...FINE. DON'T TELL ME.
I'LL FIGURE IT OUT ON MY OWN.
WHAT ELSE IS THERE TO FIGURE OUT?!!
NOW HE'S A MULTILAYERED IDIOT!
......
SHING

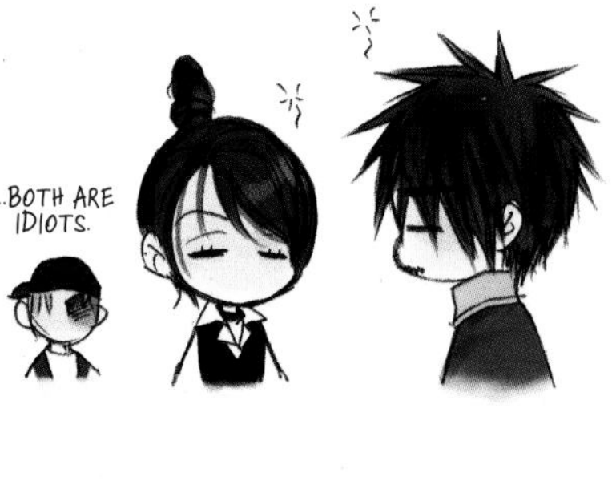

...BOTH ARE IDIOTS.

#104. THINKING

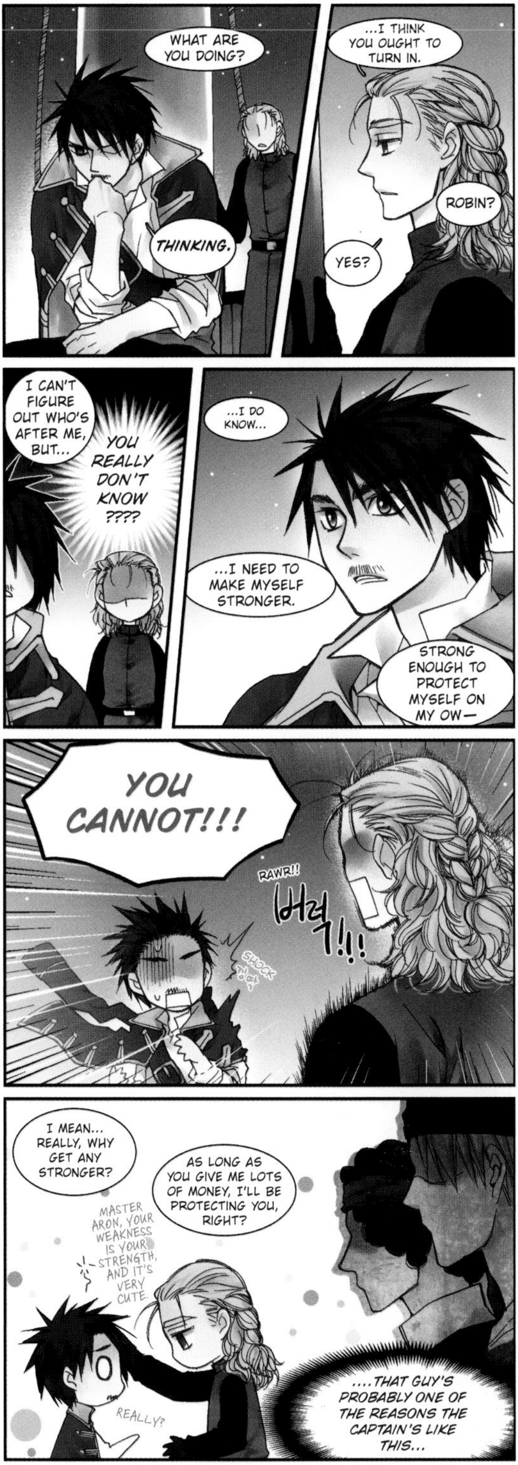

WHAT ARE YOU DOING?
THINKING.
...I THINK YOU OUGHT TO TURN IN.
ROBIN?
YES?
I CAN'T FIGURE OUT WHO'S AFTER ME, BUT...
YOU REALLY DON'T KNOW ????
...I DO KNOW...
...I NEED TO MAKE MYSELF STRONGER.
STRONG ENOUGH TO PROTECT MYSELF ON MY OW—
YOU CANNOT!!!
RAWR!!
버럭!!!
SHOCK
I MEAN... REALLY, WHY GET ANY STRONGER?
AS LONG AS YOU GIVE ME LOTS OF MONEY, I'LL BE PROTECTING YOU, RIGHT?
MASTER ARON, YOUR WEAKNESS IS YOUR STRENGTH, AND IT'S VERY CUTE.
REALLY?
....THAT GUY'S PROBABLY ONE OF THE REASONS THE CAPTAIN'S LIKE THIS...

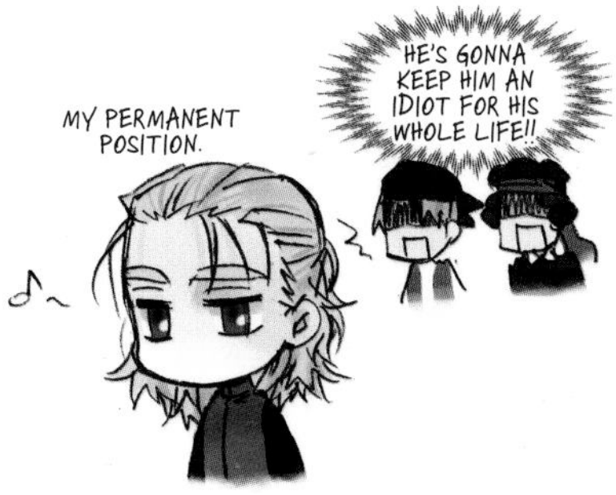

MY PERMANENT POSITION.
HE'S GONNA KEEP HIM AN IDIOT FOR HIS WHOLE LIFE!!

#105. LUTHER'S PREDICAMENT

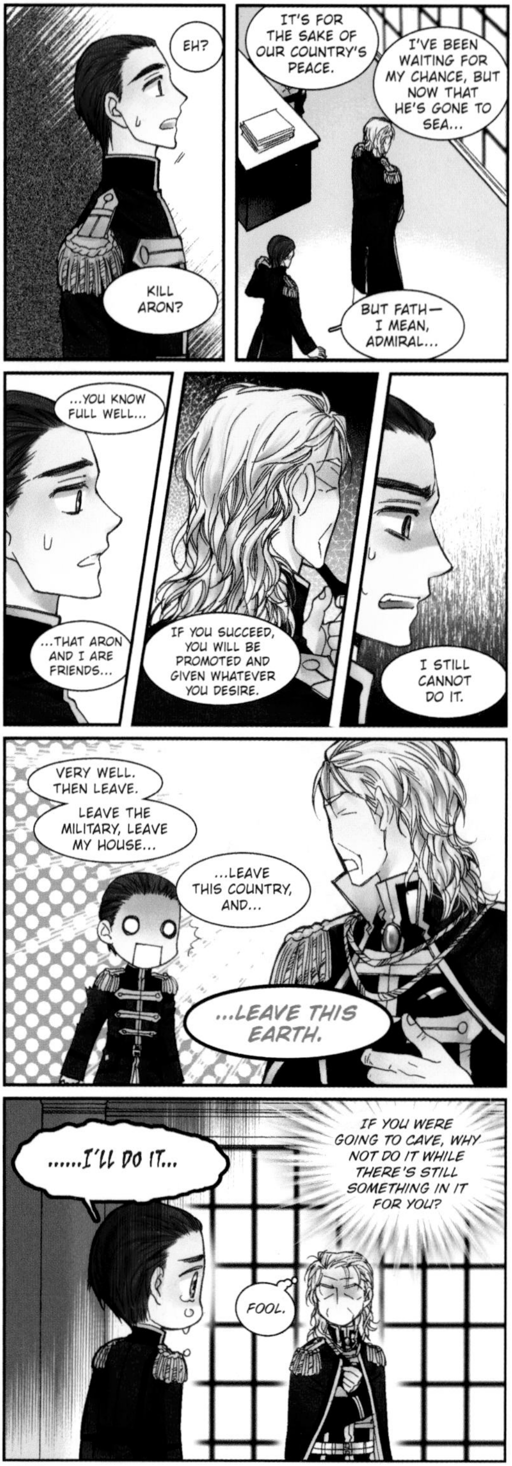
EH?
KILL ARON?
IT'S FOR THE SAKE OF OUR COUNTRY'S PEACE.
I'VE BEEN WAITING FOR MY CHANCE, BUT NOW THAT HE'S GONE TO SEA...
BUT FATH— I MEAN, ADMIRAL...
...YOU KNOW FULL WELL...
...THAT ARON AND I ARE FRIENDS...
IF YOU SUCCEED, YOU WILL BE PROMOTED AND GIVEN WHATEVER YOU DESIRE.
I STILL CANNOT DO IT.
VERY WELL. THEN LEAVE.
LEAVE THE MILITARY, LEAVE MY HOUSE...
...LEAVE THIS COUNTRY, AND...
...LEAVE THIS EARTH.
......I'LL DO IT...
IF YOU WERE GOING TO CAVE, WHY NOT DO IT WHILE THERE'S STILL SOMETHING IN IT FOR YOU?
FOOL.

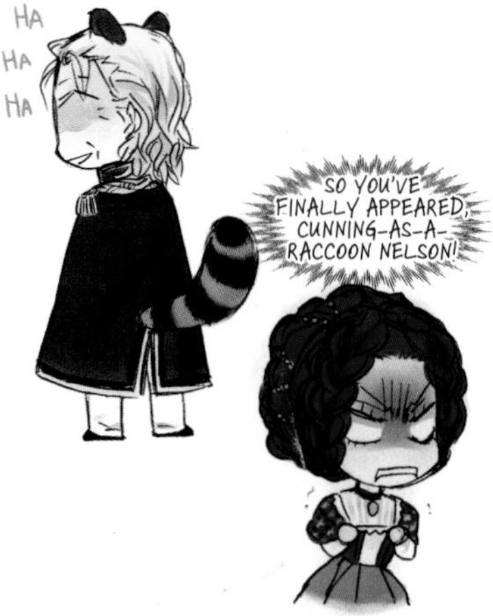
HA
HA
HA
SO YOU'VE FINALLY APPEARED, CUNNING-AS-A-RACCOON NELSON!

#106. DO YOUR OWN WORK

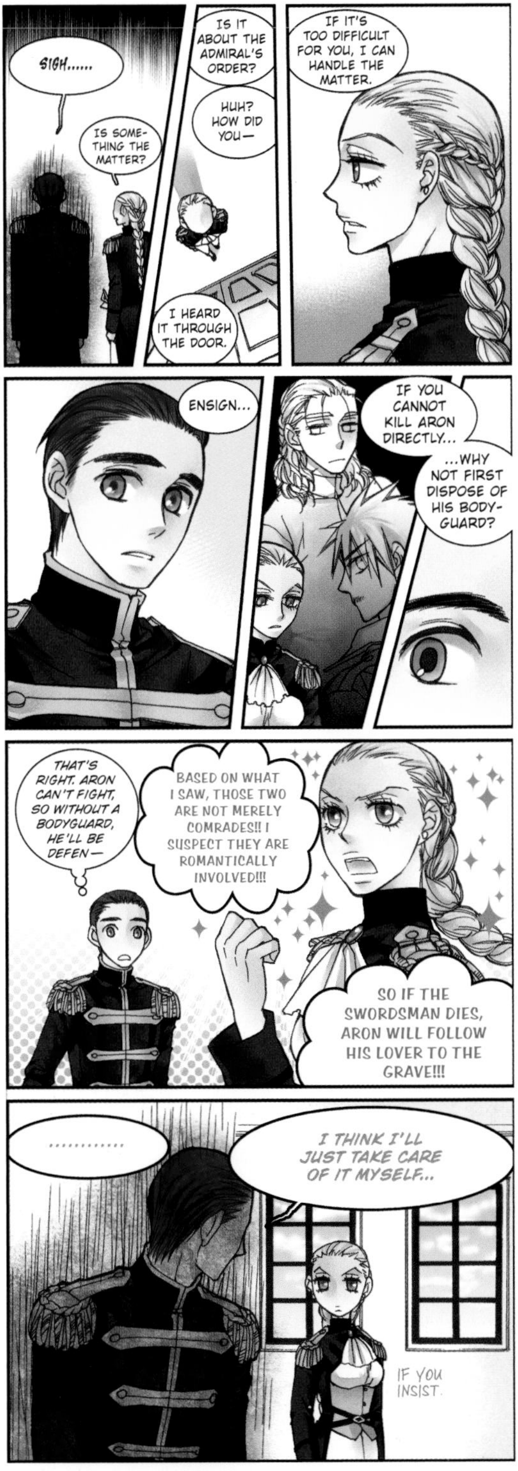
SIGH......
IS SOME-THING THE MATTER?
IS IT ABOUT THE ADMIRAL'S ORDER?
HUH? HOW DID YOU—
I HEARD IT THROUGH THE DOOR.
IF IT'S TOO DIFFICULT FOR YOU, I CAN HANDLE THE MATTER.
ENSIGN...
IF YOU CANNOT KILL ARON DIRECTLY...
...WHY NOT FIRST DISPOSE OF HIS BODY-GUARD?
THAT'S RIGHT. ARON CAN'T FIGHT, SO WITHOUT A BODYGUARD, HE'LL BE DEFEN—
BASED ON WHAT I SAW, THOSE TWO ARE NOT MERELY COMRADES!! I SUSPECT THEY ARE ROMANTICALLY INVOLVED!!!
SO IF THE SWORDSMAN DIES, ARON WILL FOLLOW HIS LOVER TO THE GRAVE!!!
....
I THINK I'LL JUST TAKE CARE OF IT MYSELF...
IF YOU INSIST.

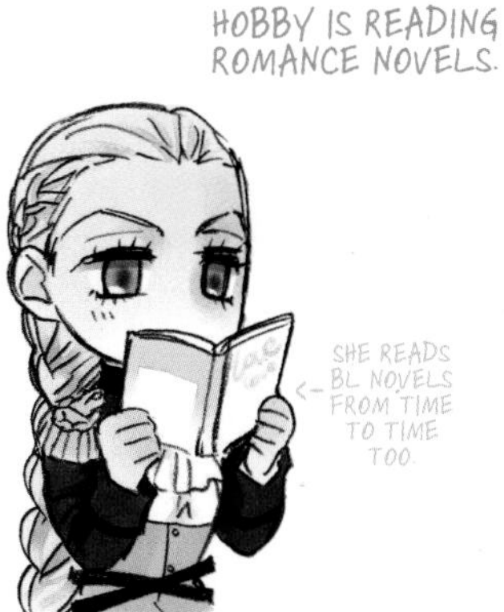
HOBBY IS READING ROMANCE NOVELS.
SHE READS BL NOVELS FROM TIME TO TIME TOO.

#107. DON'T TELL ME YOU WERE THINKING OF...

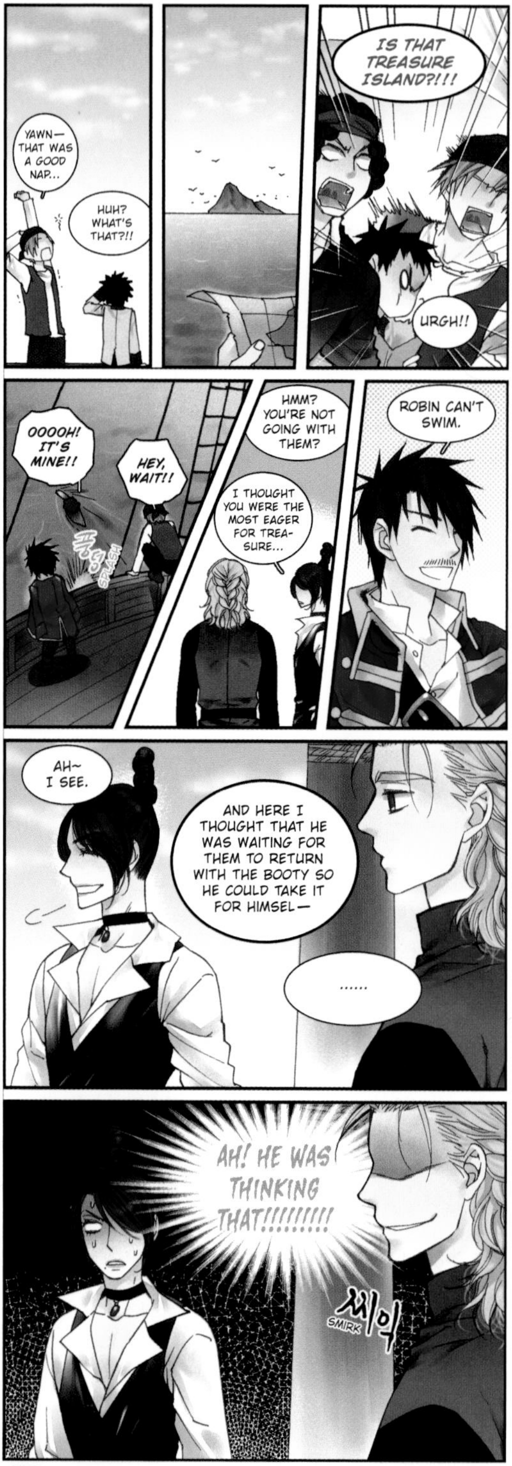
YAWN— THAT WAS A GOOD NAP...
HUH? WHAT'S THAT?!!
IS THAT TREASURE ISLAND?!!!
URGH!!
OOOOH! IT'S MINE!!
HEY, WAIT!!
SPLASH
HMM? YOU'RE NOT GOING WITH THEM?
I THOUGHT YOU WERE THE MOST EAGER FOR TREA- SURE...
ROBIN CAN'T SWIM.
AH~ I SEE.
AND HERE I THOUGHT THAT HE WAS WAITING FOR THEM TO RETURN WITH THE BOOTY SO HE COULD TAKE IT FOR HIMSEL—
......
AH! HE WAS THINKING THAT!!!!!!!!!!
SMIRK

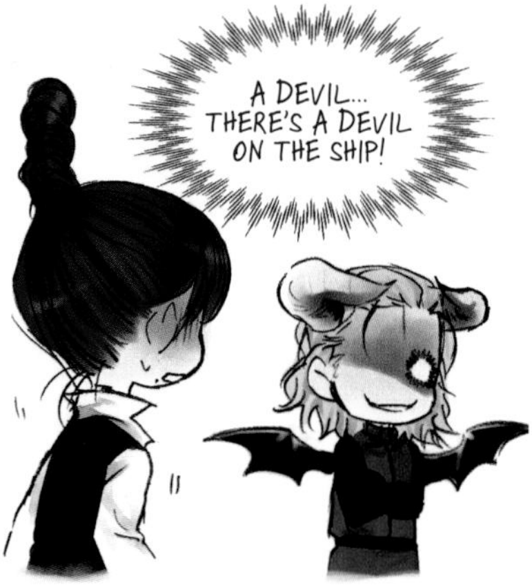
A DEVIL... THERE'S A DEVIL ON THE SHIP!

#108. I HATE SALT

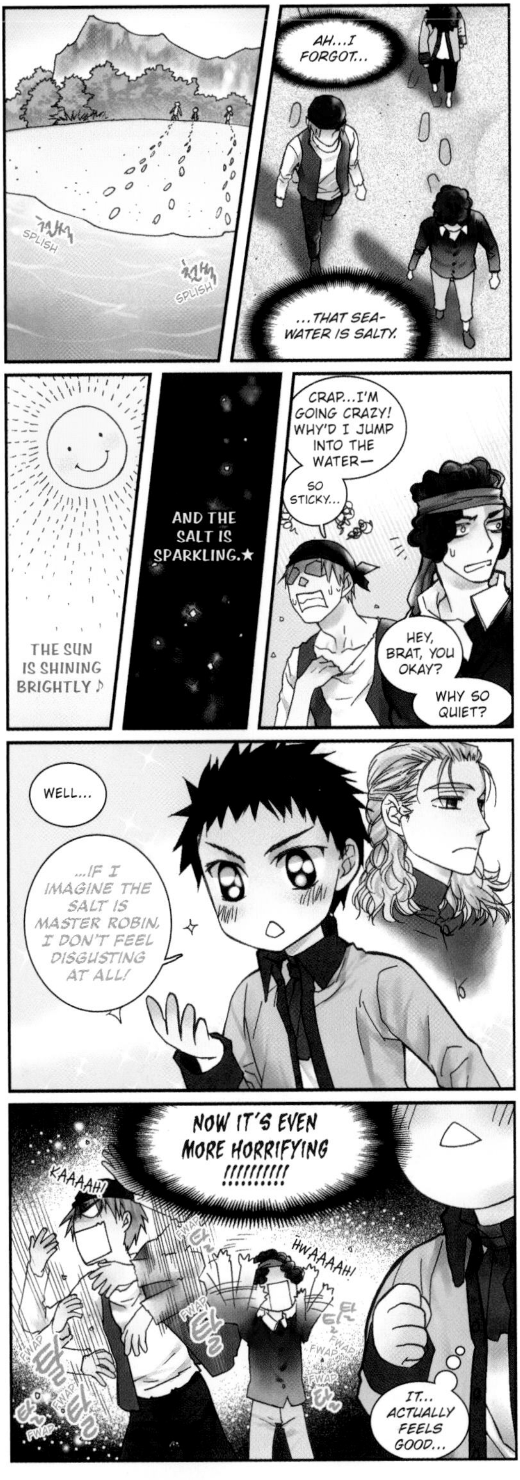
SPLISH
SPLISH
AH...I FORGOT...
...THAT SEA-WATER IS SALTY.
THE SUN IS SHINING BRIGHTLY ♪
AND THE SALT IS SPARKLING.★
CRAP...I'M GOING CRAZY! WHY'D I JUMP INTO THE WATER—
SO STICKY...
HEY, BRAT, YOU OKAY?
WHY SO QUIET?
WELL...
...IF I IMAGINE THE SALT IS MASTER ROBIN, I DON'T FEEL DISGUSTING AT ALL!
NOW IT'S EVEN MORE HORRIFYING !!!!!!!!!!
KAAAAAH!
HWAAAAAH!
FWAP
FWAP
FWAP
FWAP
FWAP
IT... ACTUALLY FEELS GOOD...

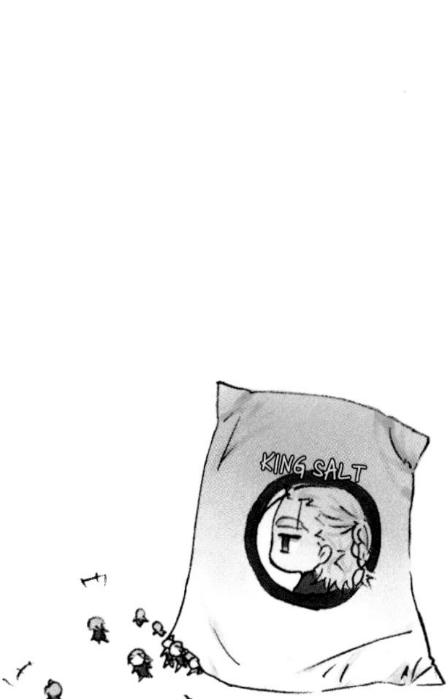
KING SALT

#109. WHEN YOU'RE YOUNG

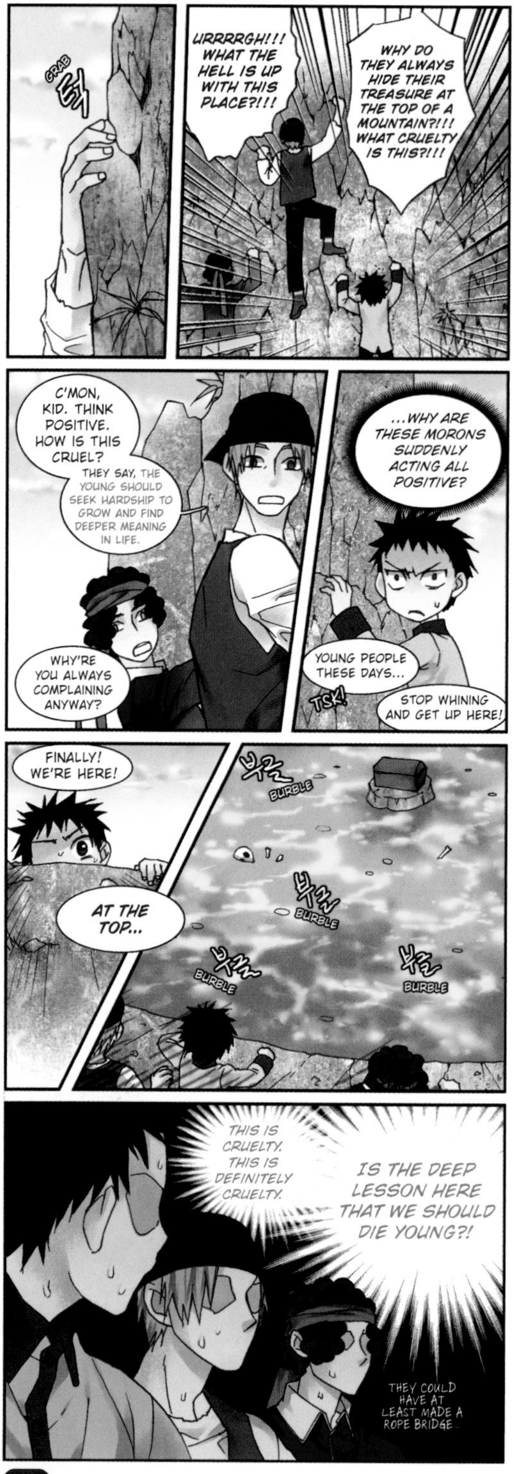
GRAB
URRRRGH!!! WHAT THE HELL IS UP WITH THIS PLACE?!!!
WHY DO THEY ALWAYS HIDE THEIR TREASURE AT THE TOP OF A MOUNTAIN?!!! WHAT CRUELTY IS THIS?!!!
C'MON, KID. THINK POSITIVE. HOW IS THIS CRUEL?
THEY SAY, THE YOUNG SHOULD SEEK HARDSHIP TO GROW AND FIND DEEPER MEANING IN LIFE.
WHY'RE YOU ALWAYS COMPLAINING ANYWAY?
...WHY ARE THESE MORONS SUDDENLY ACTING ALL POSITIVE?
YOUNG PEOPLE THESE DAYS...
TSK!
STOP WHINING AND GET UP HERE!
FINALLY! WE'RE HERE!
AT THE TOP...
BURBLE
BURBLE
BURBLE
BURBLE
THIS IS CRUELTY. THIS IS DEFINITELY CRUELTY.
IS THE DEEP LESSON HERE THAT WE SHOULD DIE YOUNG?!
THEY COULD HAVE AT LEAST MADE A ROPE BRIDGE...

MEANWHILE...

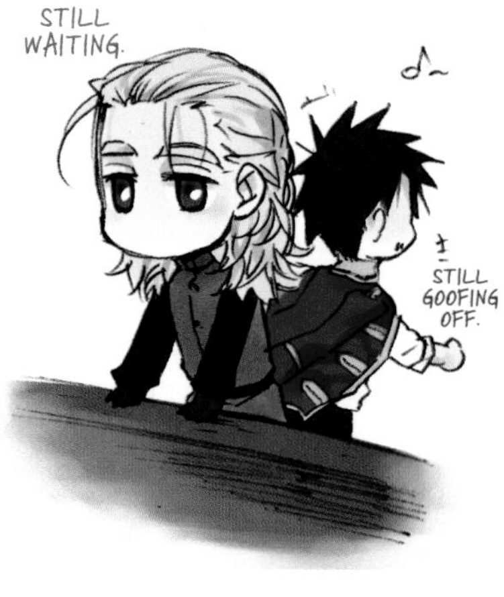
STILL WAITING.
STILL GOOFING OFF.

#110. THEORY VS. REALITY

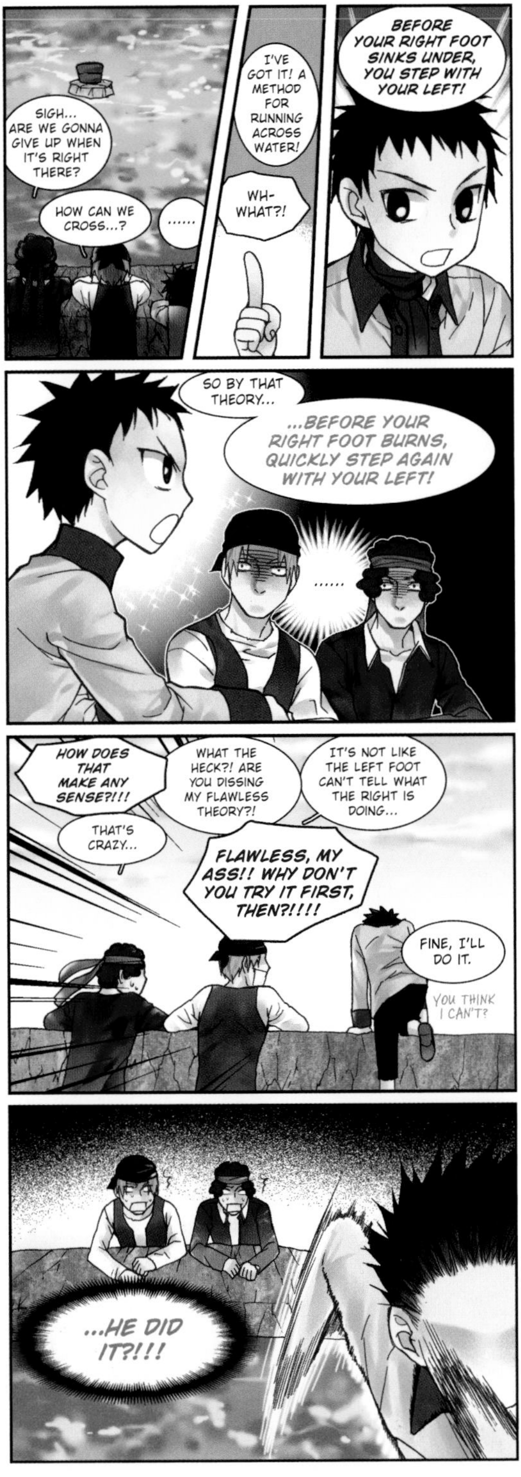
SIGH... ARE WE GONNA GIVE UP WHEN IT'S RIGHT THERE?
HOW CAN WE CROSS...?
......
I'VE GOT IT! A METHOD FOR RUNNING ACROSS WATER!
WH-WHAT?!
BEFORE YOUR RIGHT FOOT SINKS UNDER, YOU STEP WITH YOUR LEFT!
SO BY THAT THEORY...
...BEFORE YOUR RIGHT FOOT BURNS, QUICKLY STEP AGAIN WITH YOUR LEFT!
......
HOW DOES THAT MAKE ANY SENSE?!!!
THAT'S CRAZY...
WHAT THE HECK?! ARE YOU DISSING MY FLAWLESS THEORY?!
IT'S NOT LIKE THE LEFT FOOT CAN'T TELL WHAT THE RIGHT IS DOING...
FLAWLESS, MY ASS!! WHY DON'T YOU TRY IT FIRST, THEN?!!!!
FINE, I'LL DO IT.
YOU THINK I CAN'T?
...HE DID IT?!!!

Impossible is NOTHING

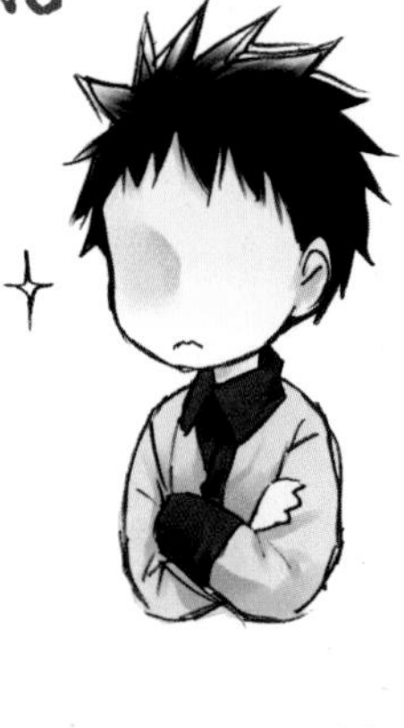

#111. YOU'RE NOT SO BAD, OR SO I THOUGHT

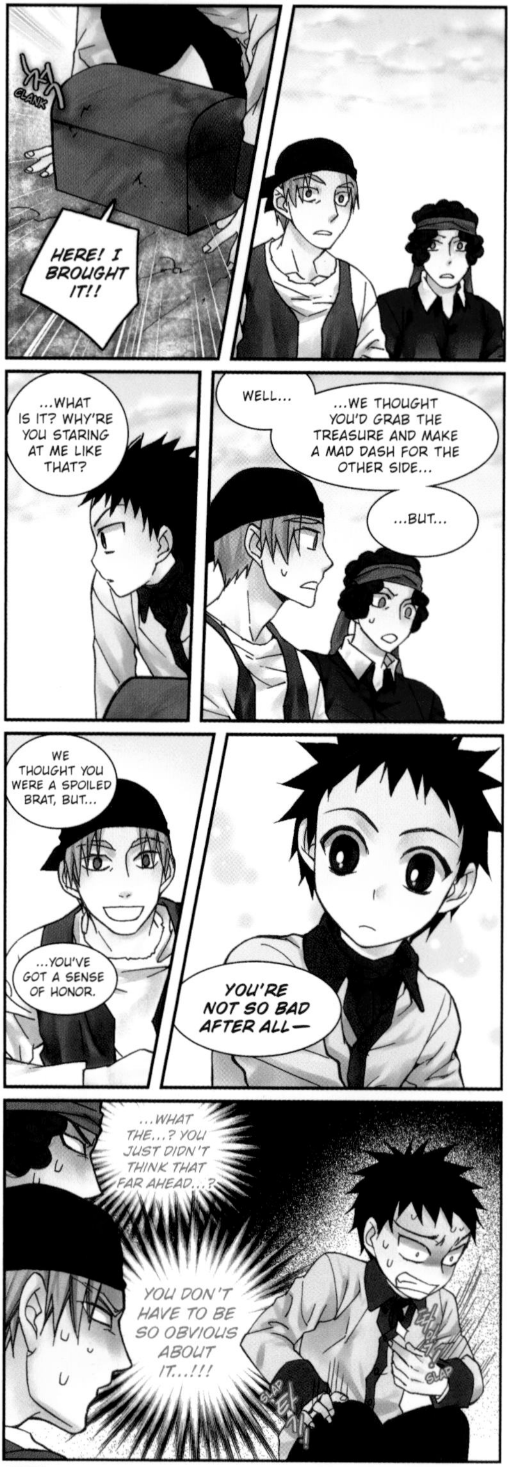
CLANK
HERE! I BROUGHT IT!!
...WHAT IS IT? WHY'RE YOU STARING AT ME LIKE THAT?
WELL...
...WE THOUGHT YOU'D GRAB THE TREASURE AND MAKE A MAD DASH FOR THE OTHER SIDE...
...BUT...
WE THOUGHT YOU WERE A SPOILED BRAT, BUT...
...YOU'VE GOT A SENSE OF HONOR.
YOU'RE NOT SO BAD AFTER ALL—
...WHAT THE...? YOU JUST DIDN'T THINK THAT FAR AHEAD...?
YOU DON'T HAVE TO BE SO OBVIOUS ABOUT IT...!!!
SLAP
SLAP

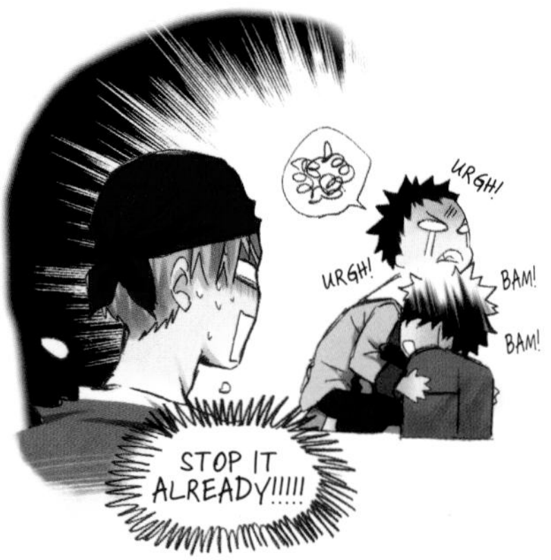
URGH!
URGH!
BAM!
BAM!
STOP IT ALREADY!!!!!

#112. PATIENCE IS BITTER

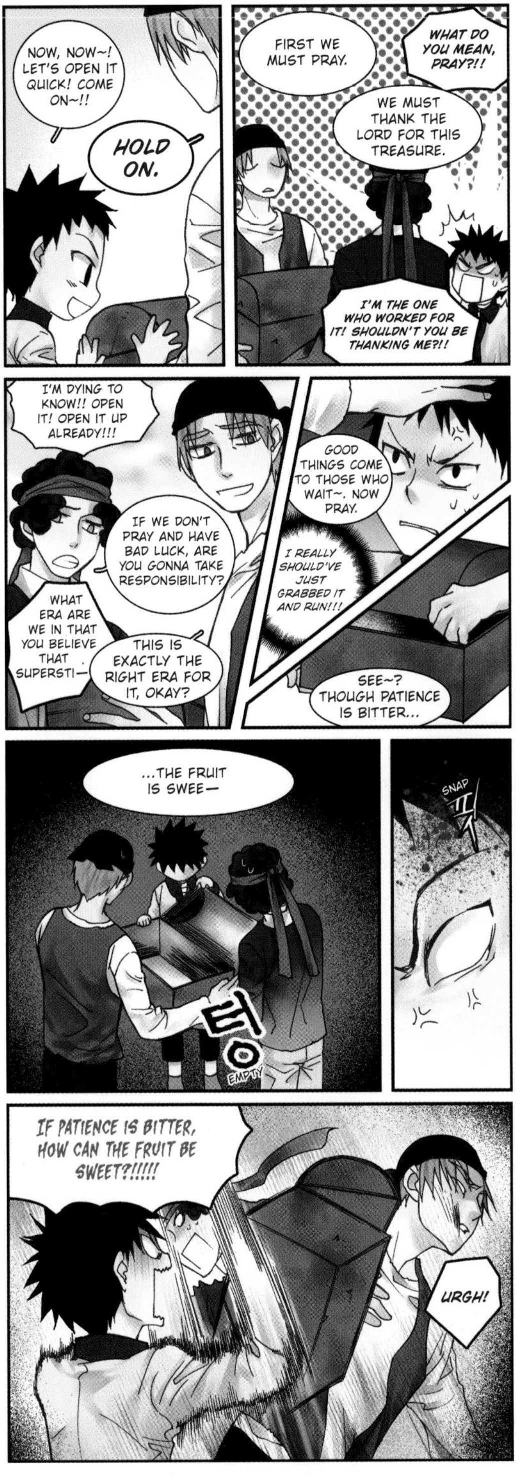
NOW, NOW~! LET'S OPEN IT QUICK! COME ON~!!
HOLD ON.
FIRST WE MUST PRAY.
WHAT DO YOU MEAN, PRAY?!!
WE MUST THANK THE LORD FOR THIS TREASURE.
I'M THE ONE WHO WORKED FOR IT! SHOULDN'T YOU BE THANKING ME?!!
I'M DYING TO KNOW!! OPEN IT! OPEN IT UP ALREADY!!!
IF WE DON'T PRAY AND HAVE BAD LUCK, ARE YOU GONNA TAKE RESPONSIBILITY?
WHAT ERA ARE WE IN THAT YOU BELIEVE THAT SUPERSTI—
THIS IS EXACTLY THE RIGHT ERA FOR IT, OKAY?
GOOD THINGS COME TO THOSE WHO WAIT~. NOW PRAY.
I REALLY SHOULD'VE JUST GRABBED IT AND RUN!!!
SEE~? THOUGH PATIENCE IS BITTER...
...THE FRUIT IS SWEE—
텅
EMPTY
SNAP
IF PATIENCE IS BITTER, HOW CAN THE FRUIT BE SWEET?!!!!!
URGH!

TODAY'S LESSON:

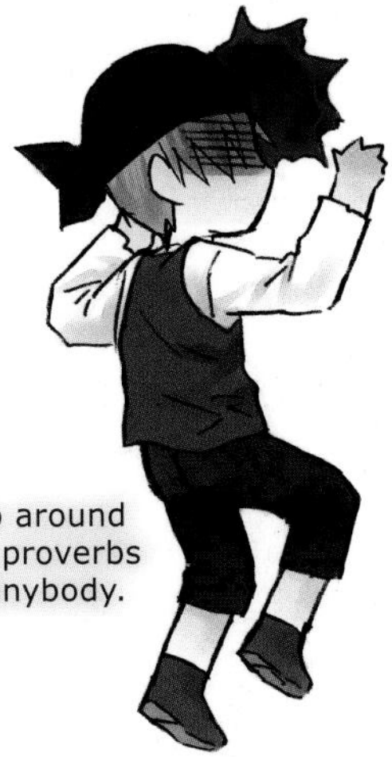

Don't go around spouting proverbs to just anybody.

#113. WORRIED

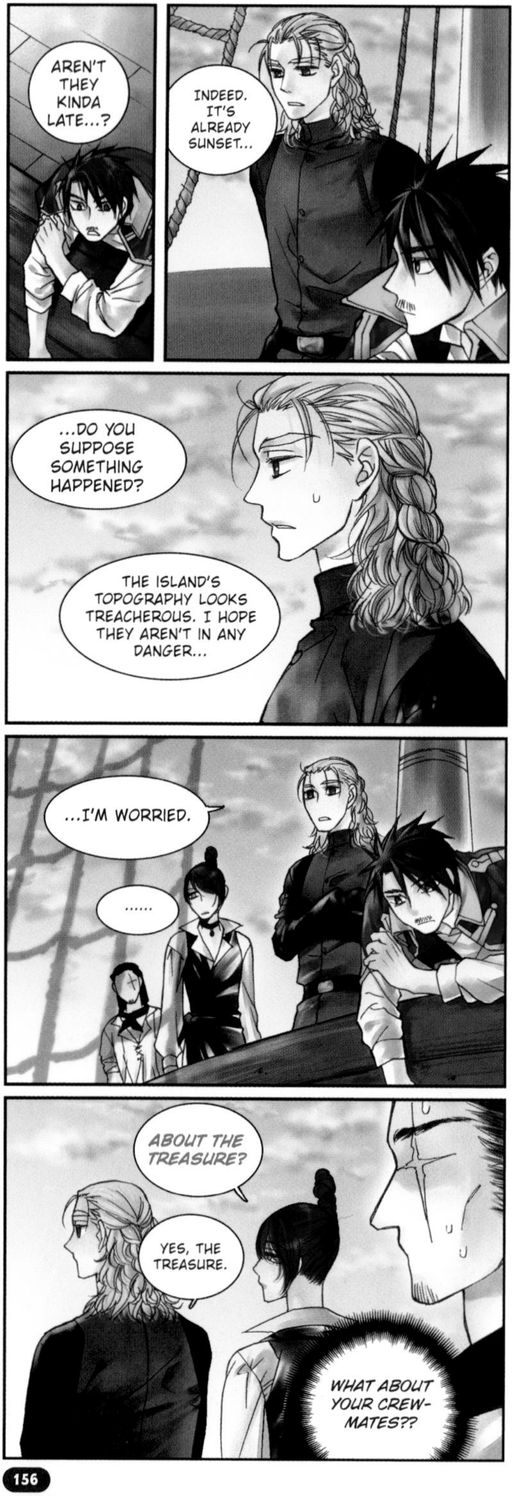
AREN'T THEY KINDA LATE...?
INDEED. IT'S ALREADY SUNSET...
...DO YOU SUPPOSE SOMETHING HAPPENED?
THE ISLAND'S TOPOGRAPHY LOOKS TREACHEROUS. I HOPE THEY AREN'T IN ANY DANGER...
...I'M WORRIED.
......
ABOUT THE TREASURE?
YES, THE TREASURE.
WHAT ABOUT YOUR CREW-MATES??

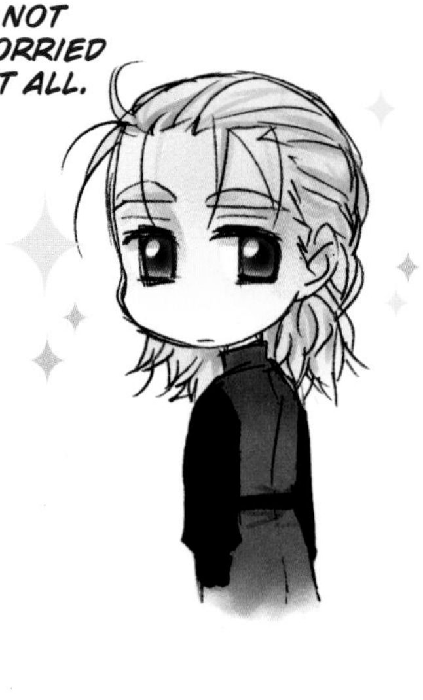
NOT WORRIED AT ALL.

#114. EVEN I WOULD

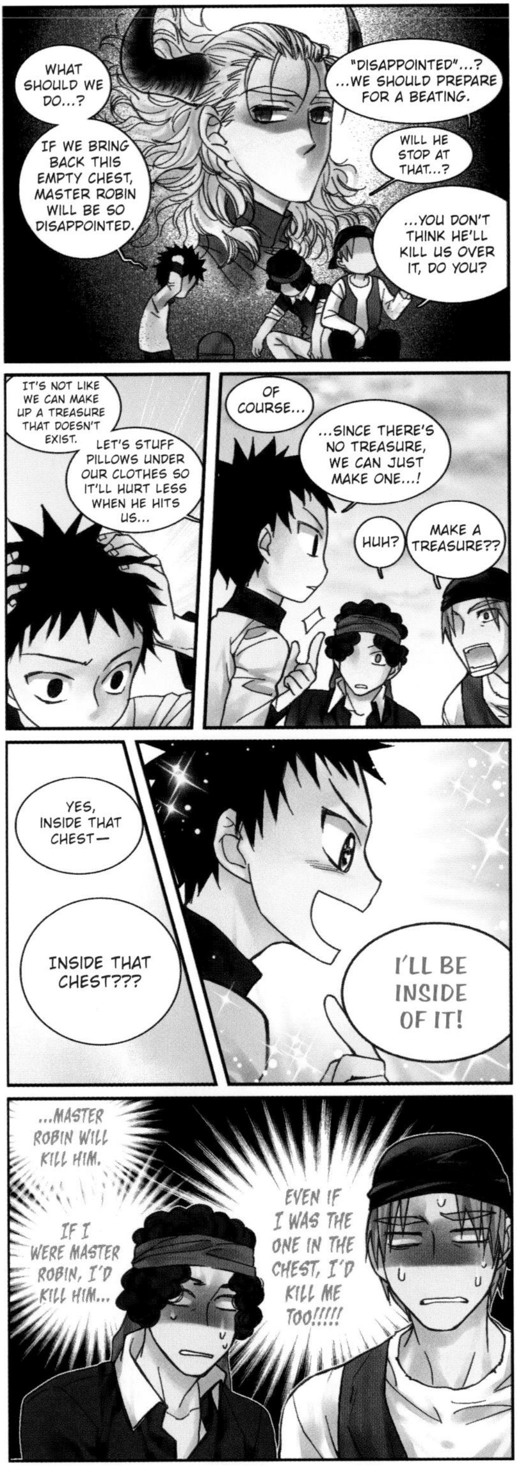
WHAT SHOULD WE DO...?
IF WE BRING BACK THIS EMPTY CHEST, MASTER ROBIN WILL BE SO DISAPPOINTED.
"DISAPPOINTED"...? ...WE SHOULD PREPARE FOR A BEATING.
WILL HE STOP AT THAT...?
...YOU DON'T THINK HE'LL KILL US OVER IT, DO YOU?
IT'S NOT LIKE WE CAN MAKE UP A TREASURE THAT DOESN'T EXIST.
LET'S STUFF PILLOWS UNDER OUR CLOTHES SO IT'LL HURT LESS WHEN HE HITS US...
OF COURSE...
...SINCE THERE'S NO TREASURE, WE CAN JUST MAKE ONE...!
HUH?
MAKE A TREASURE??
YES, INSIDE THAT CHEST—
INSIDE THAT CHEST???
I'LL BE INSIDE OF IT!
...MASTER ROBIN WILL KILL HIM.
IF I WERE MASTER ROBIN, I'D KILL HIM...
EVEN IF I WAS THE ONE IN THE CHEST, I'D KILL ME TOO!!!!!

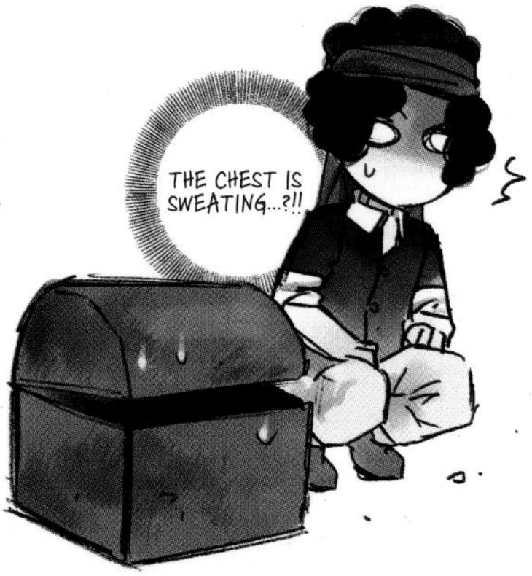
THE CHEST IS SWEATING...?!!

#115. PERSONAL ATTACK

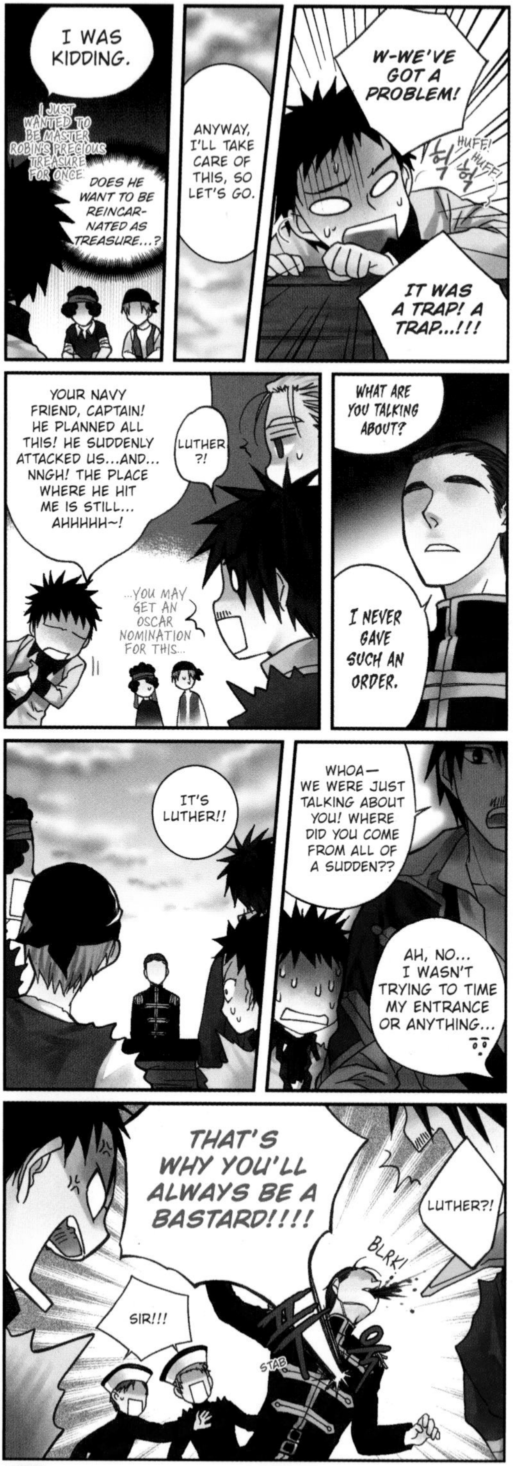
I WAS KIDDING.
I JUST WANTED TO BE MASTER ROBIN'S PRECIOUS TREASURE FOR ONCE.
DOES HE WANT TO BE REINCARNATED AS TREASURE...?
ANYWAY, I'LL TAKE CARE OF THIS, SO LET'S GO.
W-WE'VE GOT A PROBLEM!
헉 헉
HUFF! HUFF!
IT WAS A TRAP! A TRAP...!!!
YOUR NAVY FRIEND, CAPTAIN! HE PLANNED ALL THIS! HE SUDDENLY ATTACKED US...AND... NNGH! THE PLACE WHERE HE HIT ME IS STILL... AHHHHH~!
LUTHER?!
...YOU MAY GET AN OSCAR NOMINATION FOR THIS...
WHAT ARE YOU TALKING ABOUT?
I NEVER GAVE SUCH AN ORDER.
IT'S LUTHER!!
WHOA— WE WERE JUST TALKING ABOUT YOU! WHERE DID YOU COME FROM ALL OF A SUDDEN??
AH, NO... I WASN'T TRYING TO TIME MY ENTRANCE OR ANYTHING...
THAT'S WHY YOU'LL ALWAYS BE A BASTARD!!!!
LUTHER?!
BLRK!
SIR!!!
STAB

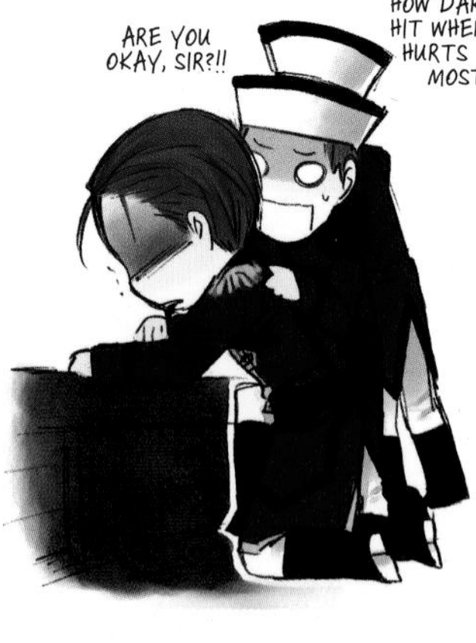
ARE YOU OKAY, SIR?!!
THAT JERK, HOW DARE HE HIT WHERE IT HURTS THE MOST!

#116. WORDS ARE MIGHTIER THAN THE SWORD

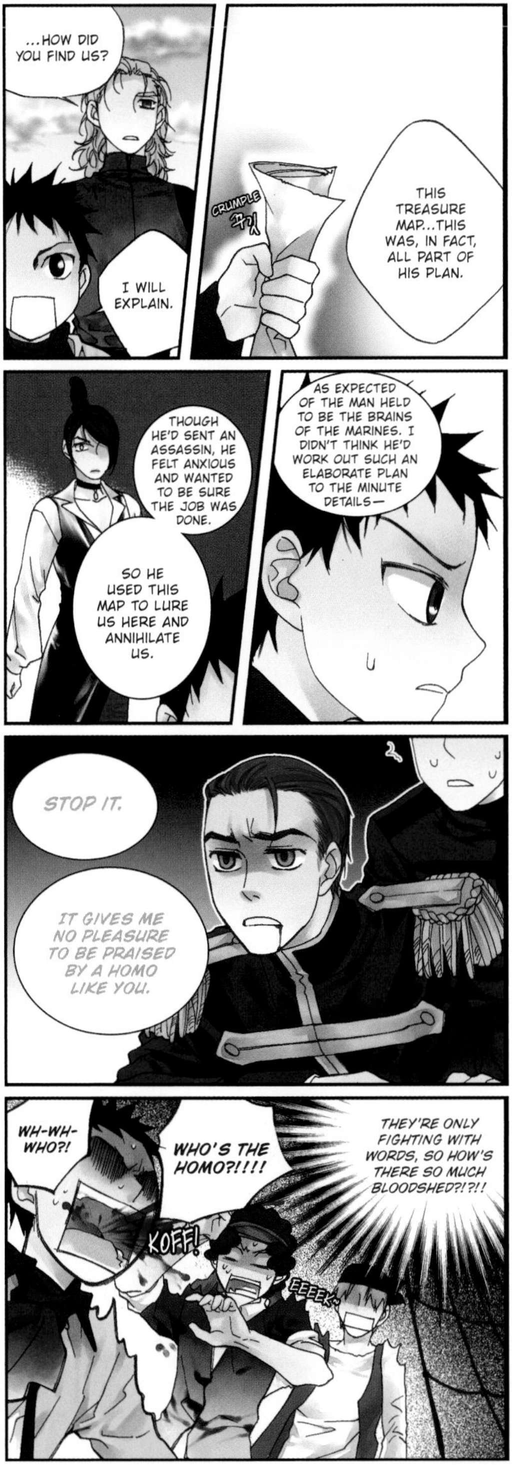

...HOW DID YOU FIND US?
I WILL EXPLAIN.
CRUMPLE
THIS TREASURE MAP...THIS WAS, IN FACT, ALL PART OF HIS PLAN.
THOUGH HE'D SENT AN ASSASSIN, HE FELT ANXIOUS AND WANTED TO BE SURE THE JOB WAS DONE.
SO HE USED THIS MAP TO LURE US HERE AND ANNIHILATE US.
AS EXPECTED OF THE MAN HELD TO BE THE BRAINS OF THE MARINES. I DIDN'T THINK HE'D WORK OUT SUCH AN ELABORATE PLAN TO THE MINUTE DETAILS—
STOP IT.
IT GIVES ME NO PLEASURE TO BE PRAISED BY A HOMO LIKE YOU.
WH-WH-WHO?!
WHO'S THE HOMO?!!!!
KOFF!
EEEEK~
THEY'RE ONLY FIGHTING WITH WORDS, SO HOW'S THERE SO MUCH BLOODSHED?!?!!

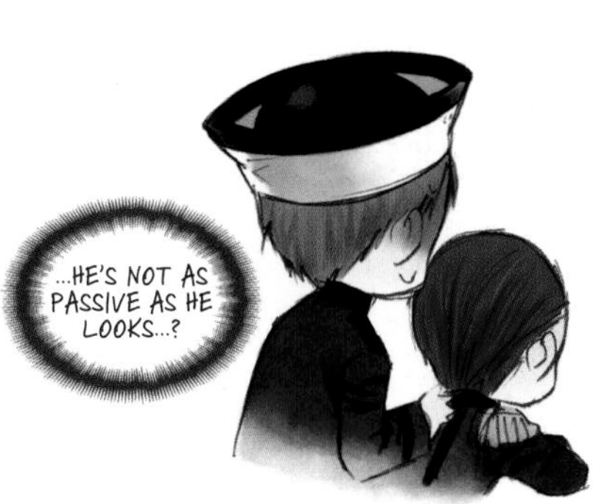

...HE'S NOT AS PASSIVE AS HE LOOKS...?

#117. EXCESSIVE PACKAGING

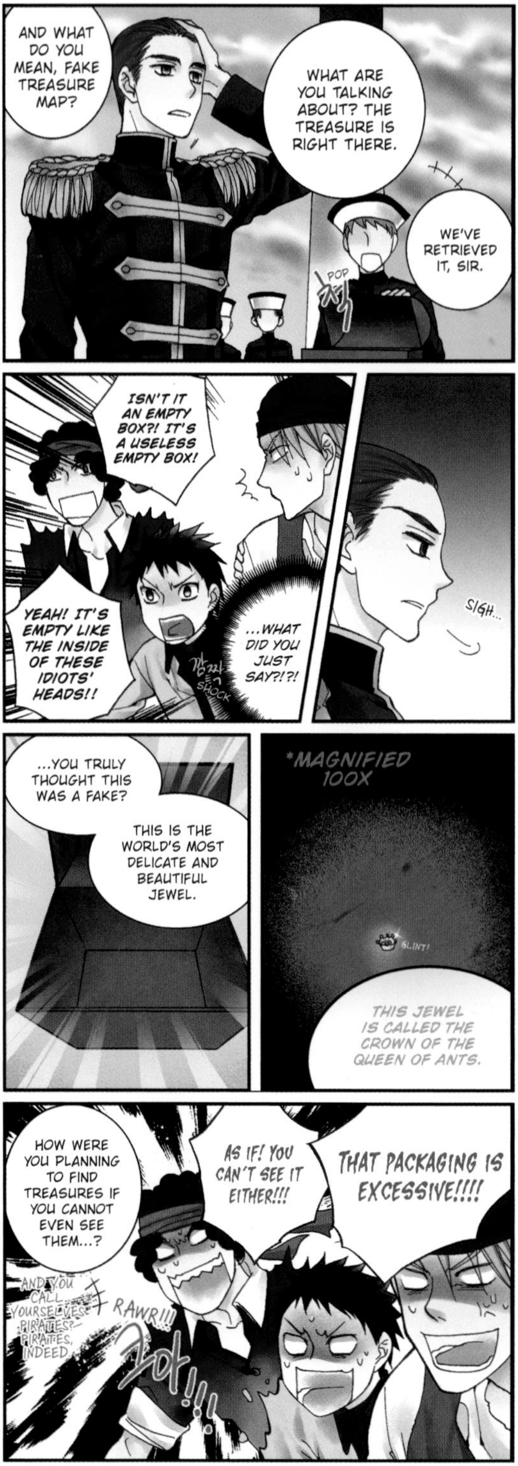
AND WHAT DO YOU MEAN, FAKE TREASURE MAP?
WHAT ARE YOU TALKING ABOUT? THE TREASURE IS RIGHT THERE.
WE'VE RETRIEVED IT, SIR.
POP
ISN'T IT AN EMPTY BOX?! IT'S A USELESS EMPTY BOX!
YEAH! IT'S EMPTY LIKE THE INSIDE OF THESE IDIOTS' HEADS!!
SHOCK
...WHAT DID YOU JUST SAY?!?!
SIGH...
...YOU TRULY THOUGHT THIS WAS A FAKE?
THIS IS THE WORLD'S MOST DELICATE AND BEAUTIFUL JEWEL.
*MAGNIFIED 100X
GLINT!
THIS JEWEL IS CALLED THE CROWN OF THE QUEEN OF ANTS.
HOW WERE YOU PLANNING TO FIND TREASURES IF YOU CANNOT EVEN SEE THEM...?
AND YOU CALL YOURSELVES PIRATES? PIRATES, INDEED.
AS IF! YOU CAN'T SEE IT EITHER!!!
THAT PACKAGING IS EXCESSIVE!!!!
RAWR!!!

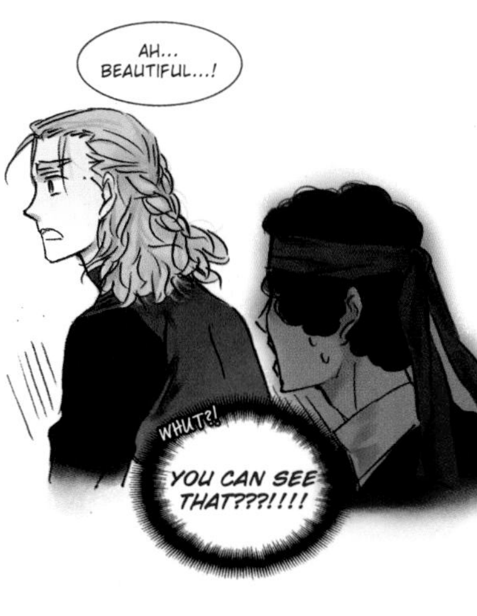
AH... BEAUTIFUL...!
WHUT?!
YOU CAN SEE THAT???!!!!

#118. BECAUSE WE'RE FRIENDS...

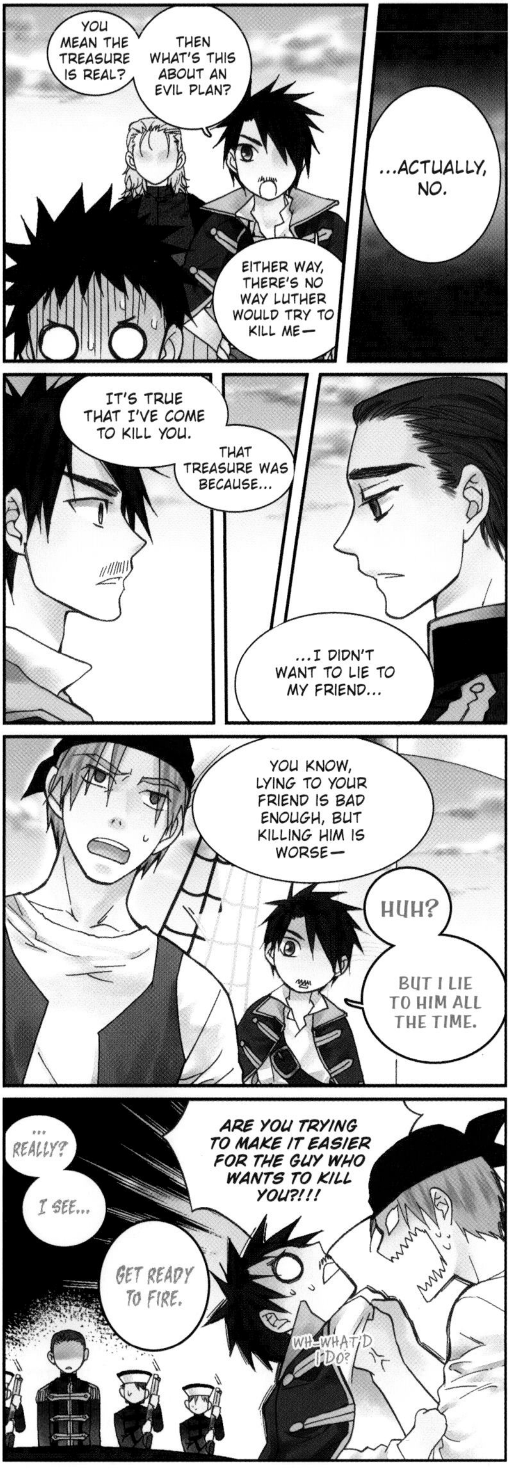
YOU MEAN THE TREASURE IS REAL?
THEN WHAT'S THIS ABOUT AN EVIL PLAN?
EITHER WAY, THERE'S NO WAY LUTHER WOULD TRY TO KILL ME—
...ACTUALLY, NO.
IT'S TRUE THAT I'VE COME TO KILL YOU.
THAT TREASURE WAS BECAUSE...
...I DIDN'T WANT TO LIE TO MY FRIEND...
YOU KNOW, LYING TO YOUR FRIEND IS BAD ENOUGH, BUT KILLING HIM IS WORSE—
HUH?
BUT I LIE TO HIM ALL THE TIME.
...REALLY?
I SEE...
GET READY TO FIRE.
ARE YOU TRYING TO MAKE IT EASIER FOR THE GUY WHO WANTS TO KILL YOU?!!!
WH-WHAT'D I DO?

*A MAN WHO HAS A LOT TO SAY ABOUT FRIENDSHIP.

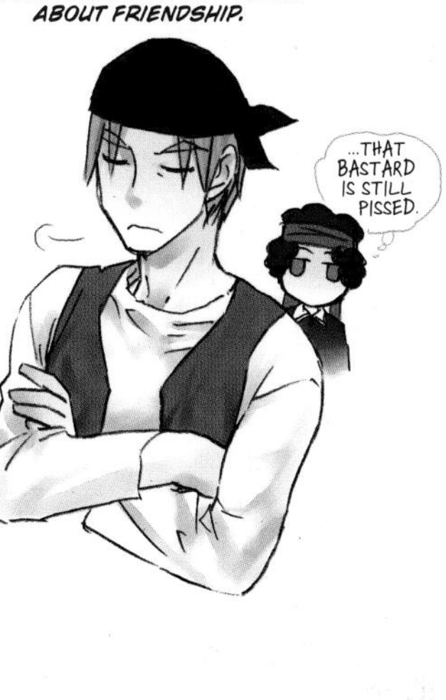
...THAT BASTARD IS STILL PISSED.

#119. DOESN'T EVERYONE?

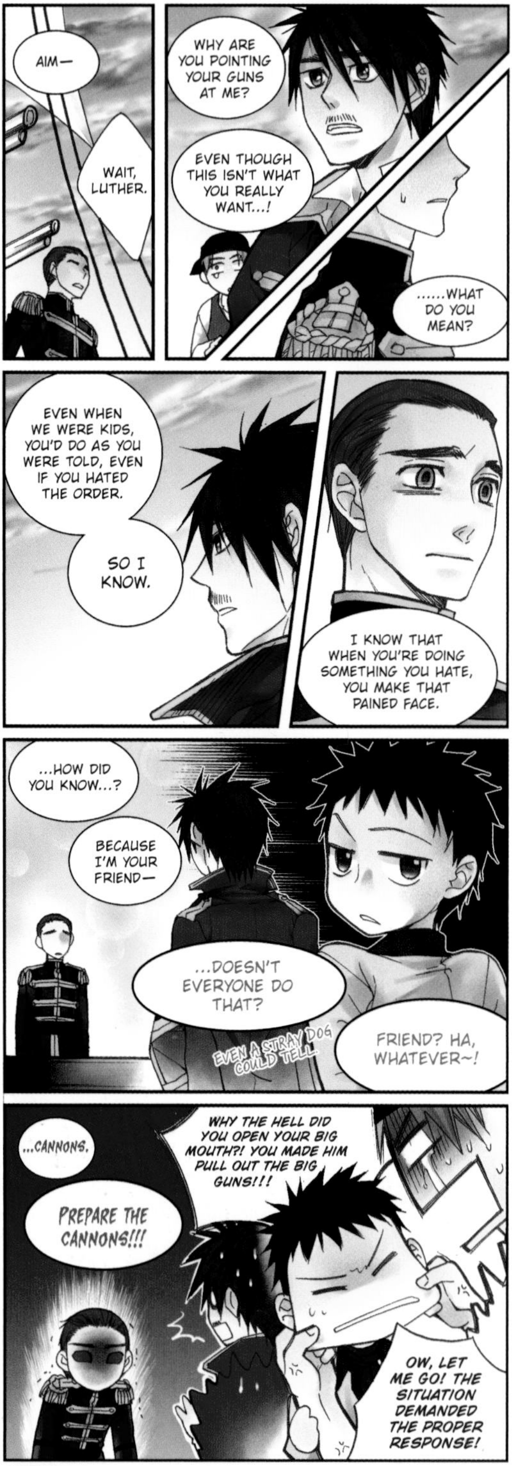
AIM—
WAIT, LUTHER.
WHY ARE YOU POINTING YOUR GUNS AT ME?
EVEN THOUGH THIS ISN'T WHAT YOU REALLY WANT...!
......WHAT DO YOU MEAN?
EVEN WHEN WE WERE KIDS, YOU'D DO AS YOU WERE TOLD, EVEN IF YOU HATED THE ORDER.
SO I KNOW.
I KNOW THAT WHEN YOU'RE DOING SOMETHING YOU HATE, YOU MAKE THAT PAINED FACE.
...HOW DID YOU KNOW...?
BECAUSE I'M YOUR FRIEND—
...DOESN'T EVERYONE DO THAT?
EVEN A STRAY DOG COULD TELL.
FRIEND? HA, WHATEVER~!
...CANNONS.
PREPARE THE CANNONS!!!
WHY THE HELL DID YOU OPEN YOUR BIG MOUTH?! YOU MADE HIM PULL OUT THE BIG GUNS!!!
OW, LET ME GO! THE SITUATION DEMANDED THE PROPER RESPONSE!

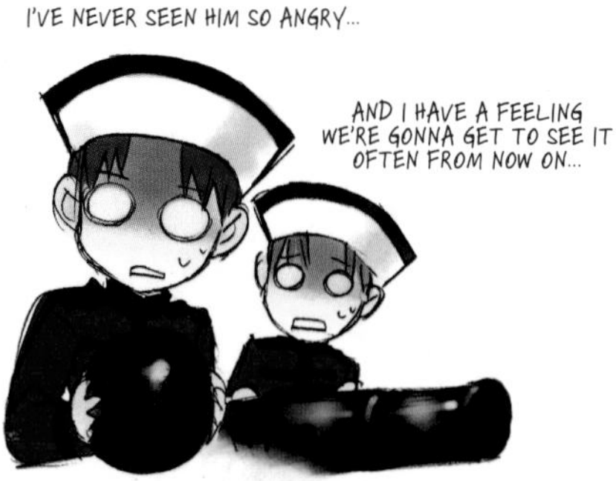
I'VE NEVER SEEN HIM SO ANGRY...
AND I HAVE A FEELING WE'RE GONNA GET TO SEE IT OFTEN FROM NOW ON...

#120. I WILL CONTINUE TO PROTECT WHAT I MUST PROTECT?

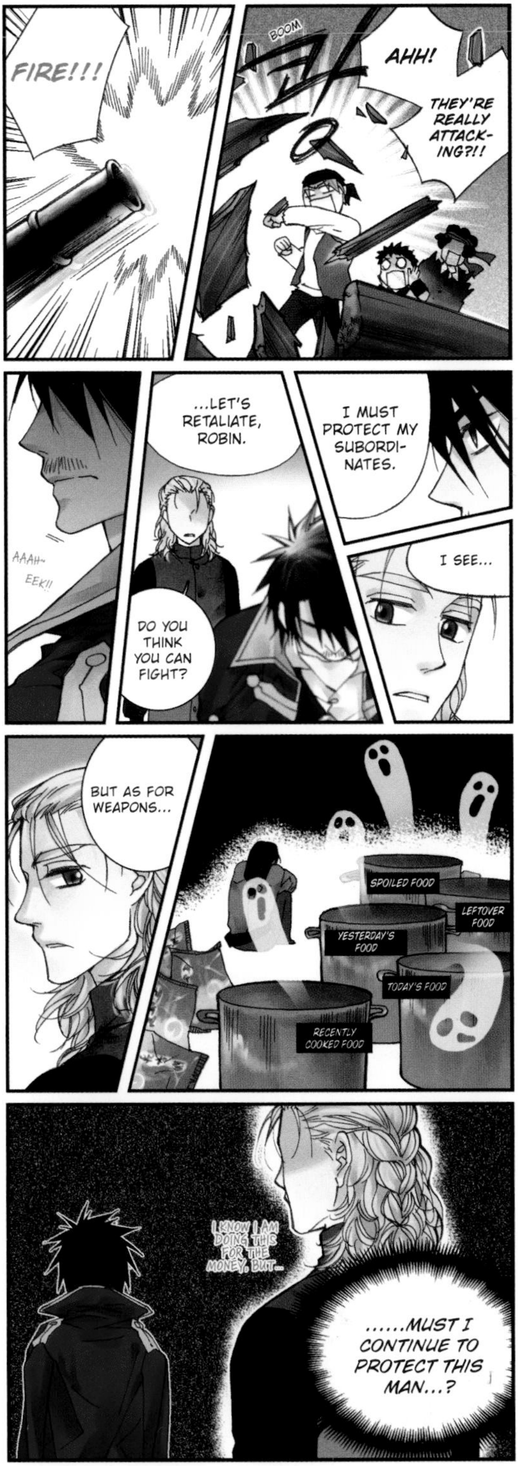

FIRE!!!
BOOM
AHH!
THEY'RE REALLY ATTACKING?!!
...LET'S RETALIATE, ROBIN.
I MUST PROTECT MY SUBORDINATES.
AAAH~ EEK!!
I SEE...
DO YOU THINK YOU CAN FIGHT?
BUT AS FOR WEAPONS...
SPOILED FOOD
LEFTOVER FOOD
YESTERDAY'S FOOD
TODAY'S FOOD
RECENTLY COOKED FOOD
I KNOW I AM DOING THIS FOR THE MONEY, BUT...
......MUST I CONTINUE TO PROTECT THIS MAN...?

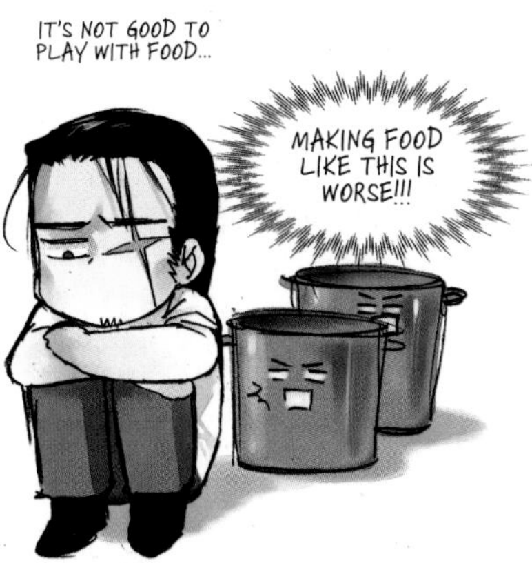

IT'S NOT GOOD TO PLAY WITH FOOD...
MAKING FOOD LIKE THIS IS WORSE!!!

#121. REACHING A CONSENSUS

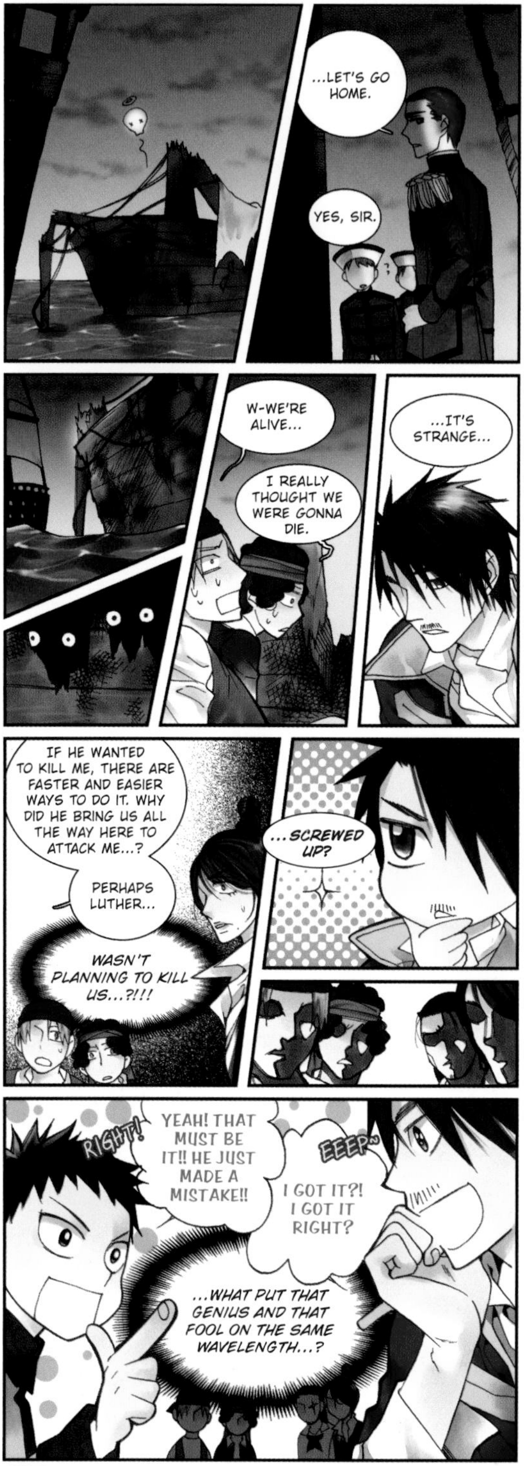
...LET'S GO HOME.
YES, SIR.
W-WE'RE ALIVE...
I REALLY THOUGHT WE WERE GONNA DIE.
...IT'S STRANGE...
IF HE WANTED TO KILL ME, THERE ARE FASTER AND EASIER WAYS TO DO IT. WHY DID HE BRING US ALL THE WAY HERE TO ATTACK ME...?
PERHAPS LUTHER...
...SCREWED UP?
WASN'T PLANNING TO KILL US...?!!!
RIGHT!
YEAH! THAT MUST BE IT!! HE JUST MADE A MISTAKE!!
EEEP~
I GOT IT?! I GOT IT RIGHT?
...WHAT PUT THAT GENIUS AND THAT FOOL ON THE SAME WAVELENGTH...?

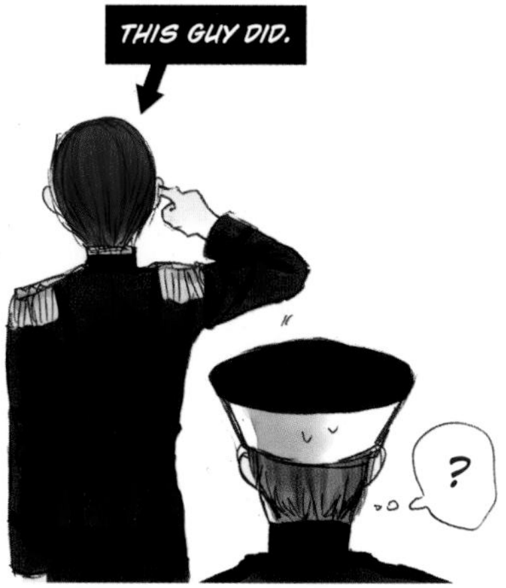
THIS GUY DID.
?

#122. ROBIN IS PISSED

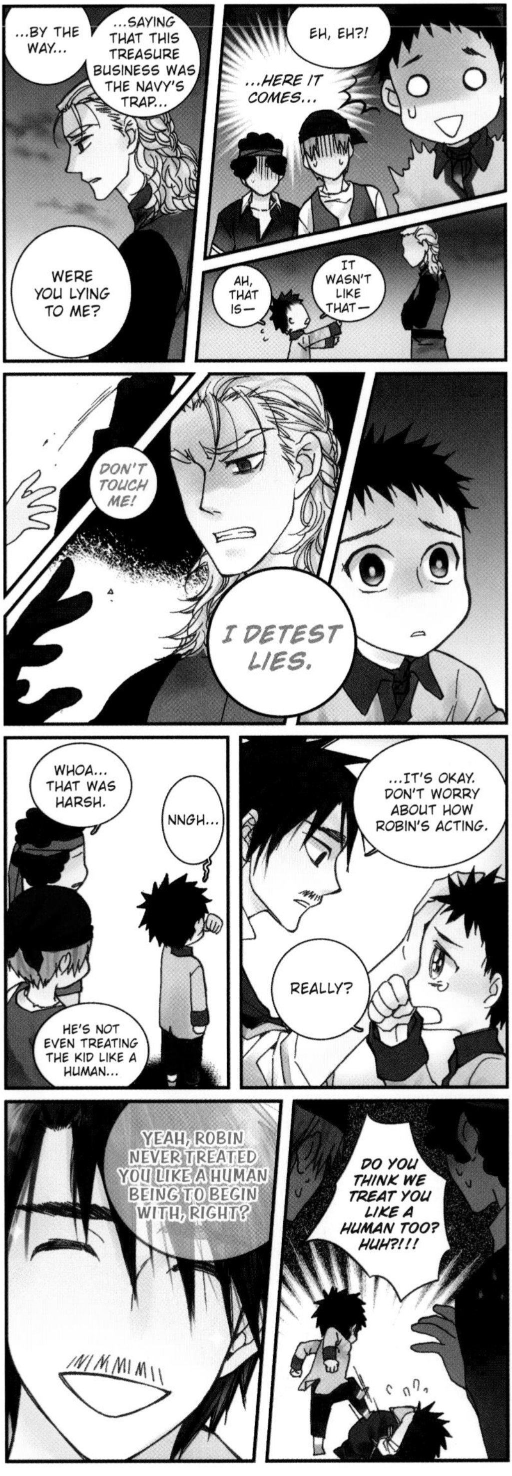
...BY THE WAY...
...SAYING THAT THIS TREASURE BUSINESS WAS THE NAVY'S TRAP...
EH, EH?!
...HERE IT COMES...
WERE YOU LYING TO ME?
AH, THAT IS—
IT WASN'T LIKE THAT—
DON'T TOUCH ME!
I DETEST LIES.
WHOA... THAT WAS HARSH.
NNGH...
HE'S NOT EVEN TREATING THE KID LIKE A HUMAN...
...IT'S OKAY. DON'T WORRY ABOUT HOW ROBIN'S ACTING.
REALLY?
YEAH, ROBIN NEVER TREATED YOU LIKE A HUMAN BEING TO BEGIN WITH, RIGHT?
DO YOU THINK WE TREAT YOU LIKE A HUMAN TOO? HUH?!!!

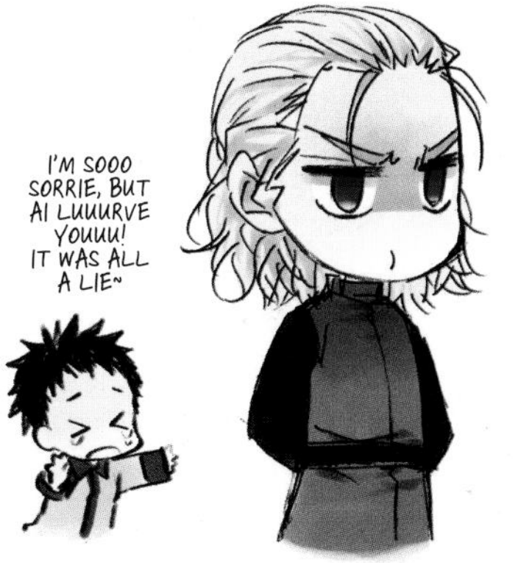
I'M SOOO SORRIE, BUT AI LUUURVE YOUUU! IT WAS ALL A LIE~

#123. WHAT DROVE HIM TO INSANITY

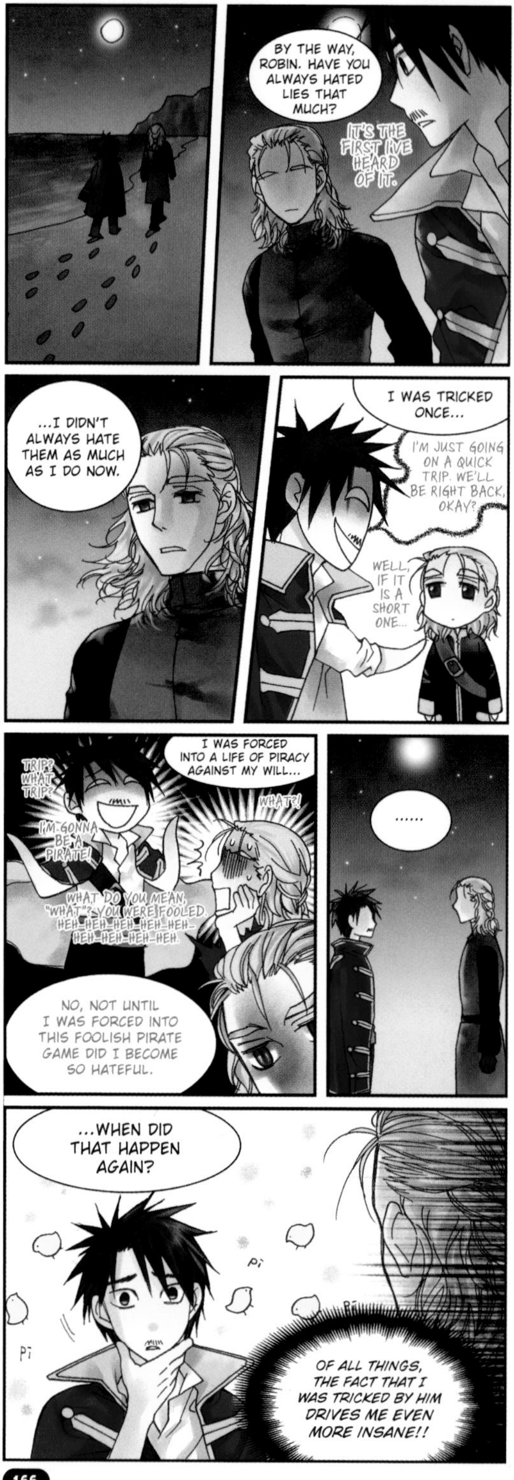

BY THE WAY, ROBIN. HAVE YOU ALWAYS HATED LIES THAT MUCH?
IT'S THE FIRST I'VE HEARD OF IT.
...I DIDN'T ALWAYS HATE THEM AS MUCH AS I DO NOW.
I WAS TRICKED ONCE...
I'M JUST GOING ON A QUICK TRIP. WE'LL BE RIGHT BACK, OKAY?
WELL, IF IT IS A SHORT ONE...
I WAS FORCED INTO A LIFE OF PIRACY AGAINST MY WILL...
TRIP? WHAT TRIP?
I'M GONNA BE A PIRATE!
WHAT?!
WHAT DO YOU MEAN, "WHAT"? YOU WERE FOOLED. HEH-HEH-HEH-HEH-HEH-HEH-HEH-HEH-HEH.
NO, NOT UNTIL I WAS FORCED INTO THIS FOOLISH PIRATE GAME DID I BECOME SO HATEFUL.
......
...WHEN DID THAT HAPPEN AGAIN?
Pi
Pi
Pi
OF ALL THINGS, THE FACT THAT I WAS TRICKED BY HIM DRIVES ME EVEN MORE INSANE!!

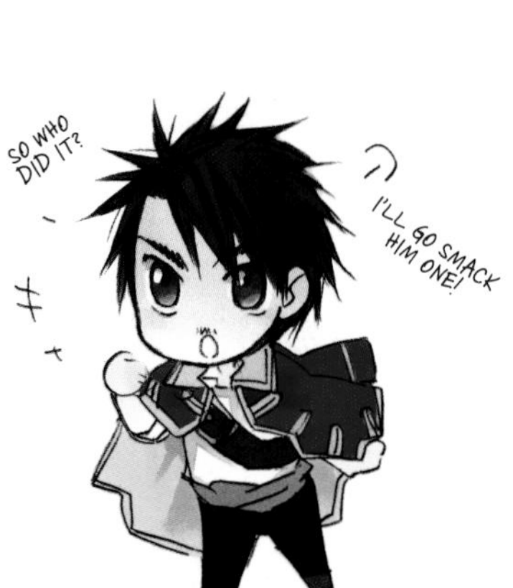

SO WHO DID IT?
I'LL GO SMACK HIM ONE!

#124. I HATE EVERYTHING

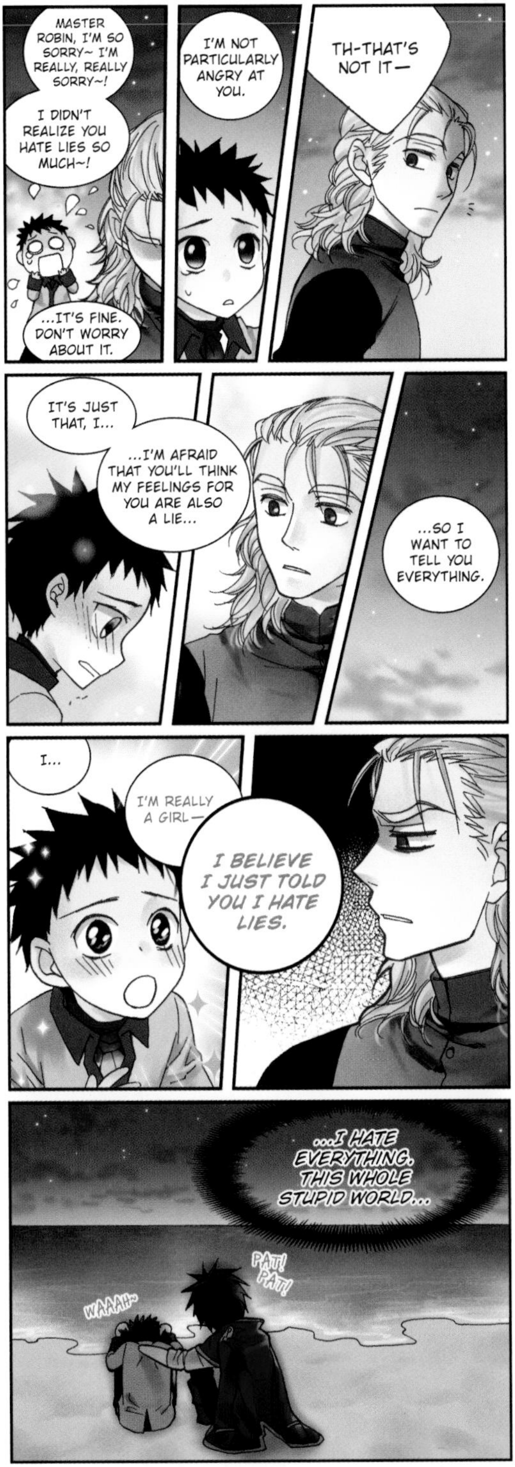
MASTER ROBIN, I'M SO SORRY~ I'M REALLY, REALLY SORRY~!
I DIDN'T REALIZE YOU HATE LIES SO MUCH~!
...IT'S FINE. DON'T WORRY ABOUT IT.
I'M NOT PARTICULARLY ANGRY AT YOU.
TH-THAT'S NOT IT—
IT'S JUST THAT, I...
...I'M AFRAID THAT YOU'LL THINK MY FEELINGS FOR YOU ARE ALSO A LIE...
...SO I WANT TO TELL YOU EVERYTHING.
I...
I'M REALLY A GIRL—
I BELIEVE I JUST TOLD YOU I HATE LIES.
...I HATE EVERYTHING. THIS WHOLE STUPID WORLD...
PAT! PAT!
WAAAH~

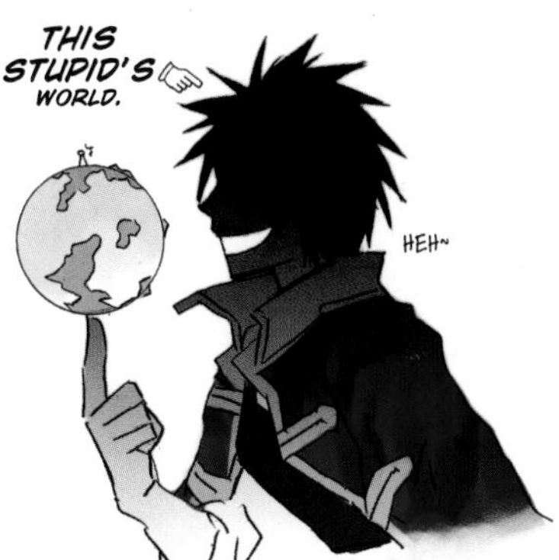
THIS STUPID'S WORLD.
HEH~

#125. WHEN MAROONED ON A DESERTED ISLAND

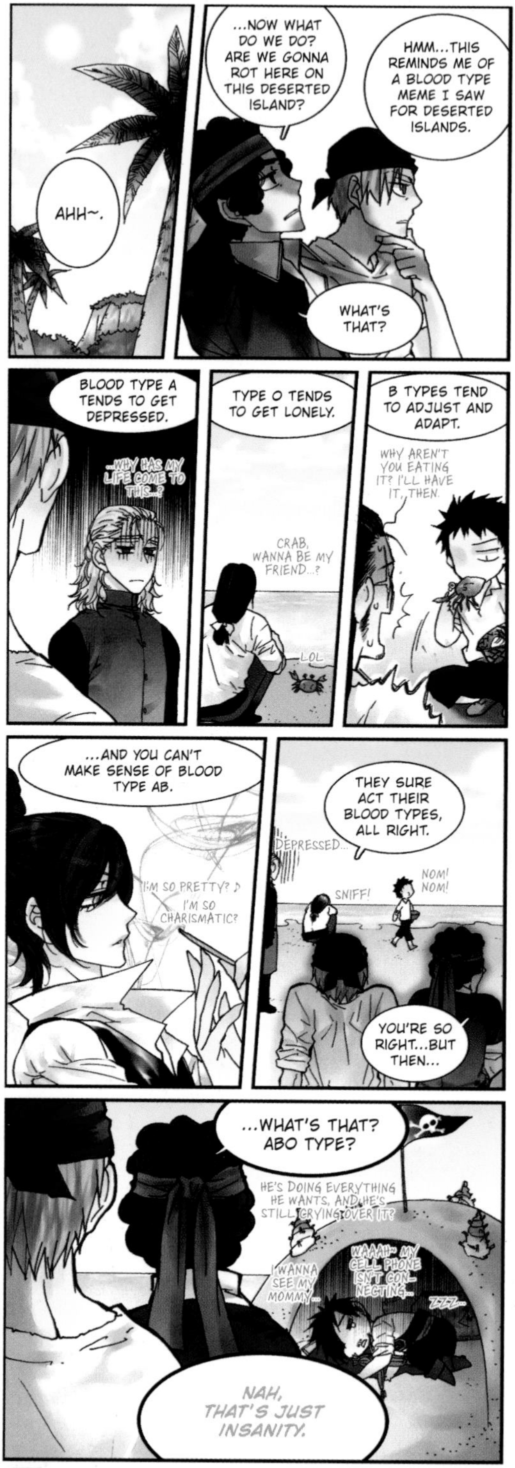

...NOW WHAT DO WE DO? ARE WE GONNA ROT HERE ON THIS DESERTED ISLAND?
HMM...THIS REMINDS ME OF A BLOOD TYPE MEME I SAW FOR DESERTED ISLANDS.
AHH~.
WHAT'S THAT?
BLOOD TYPE A TENDS TO GET DEPRESSED.
...WHY HAS MY LIFE COME TO THIS...?
TYPE O TENDS TO GET LONELY.
CRAB, WANNA BE MY FRIEND...?
LOL
B TYPES TEND TO ADJUST AND ADAPT.
WHY AREN'T YOU EATING IT? I'LL HAVE IT, THEN.
...AND YOU CAN'T MAKE SENSE OF BLOOD TYPE AB.
I'M SO PRETTY? ♪
I'M SO CHARISMATIC?
THEY SURE ACT THEIR BLOOD TYPES, ALL RIGHT.
DEPRESSED...
SNIFF!
NOM! NOM!
YOU'RE SO RIGHT...BUT THEN...
...WHAT'S THAT? ABO TYPE?
HE'S DOING EVERYTHING HE WANTS, AND HE'S STILL CRYING OVER IT?
I WANNA SEE MY MOMMY...
WAAAH~ MY CELL PHONE ISN'T CONNECTING...
ZZZ...
NAH, THAT'S JUST INSANITY.

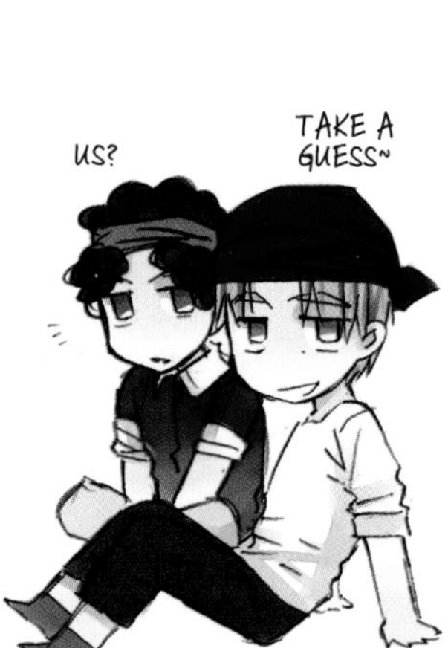

US?
TAKE A GUESS~

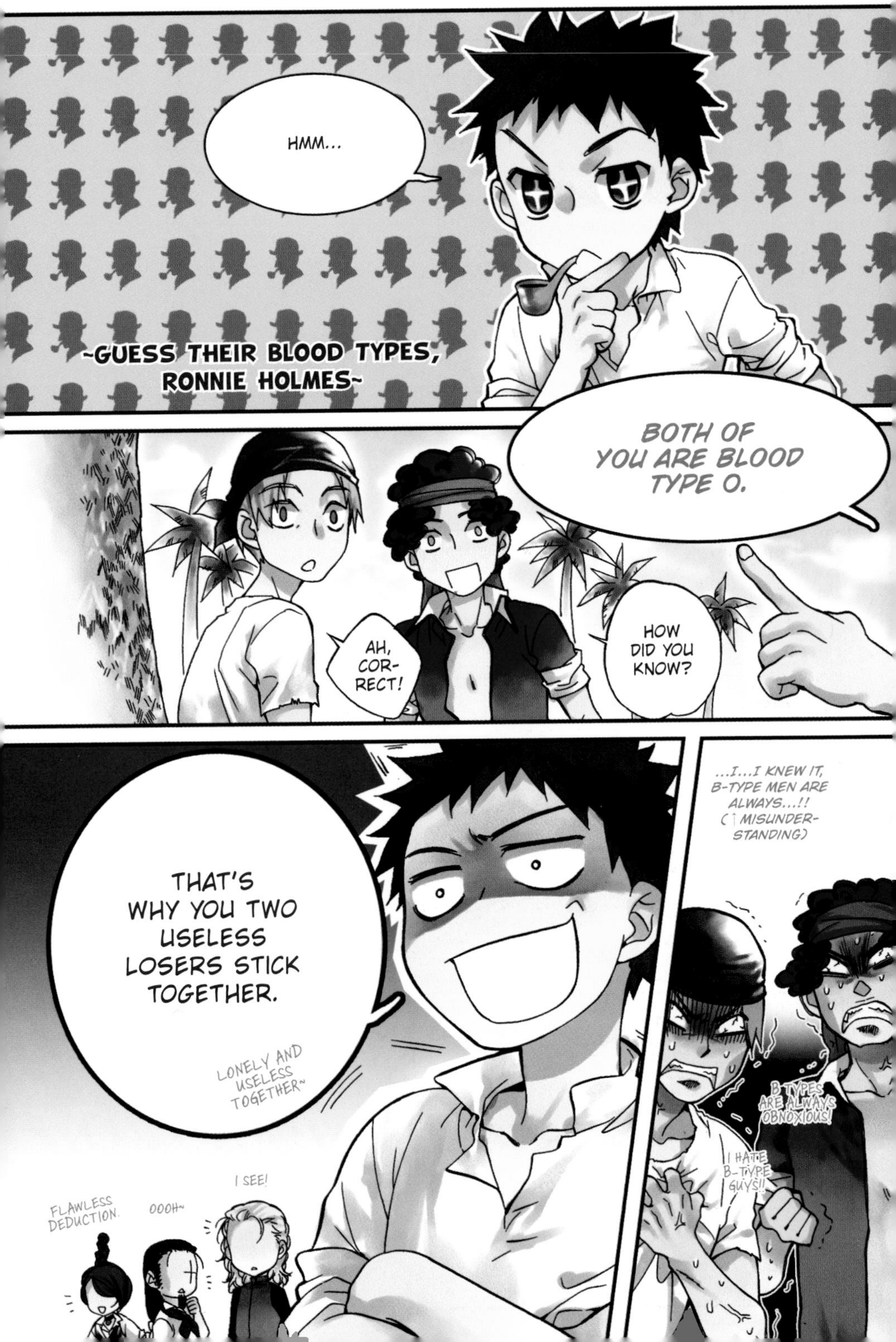
HMM...
~GUESS THEIR BLOOD TYPES, RONNIE HOLMES~
BOTH OF YOU ARE BLOOD TYPE O.
HOW DID YOU KNOW?
AH, COR-RECT!
...I...I KNEW IT, B-TYPE MEN ARE ALWAYS...!! (↑MISUNDER-STANDING)
THAT'S WHY YOU TWO USELESS LOSERS STICK TOGETHER.
LONELY AND USELESS TOGETHER~
B TYPES ARE ALWAYS OBNOXIOUS!
I HATE B-TYPE GUYS!!
I SEE!
OOOH~
FLAWLESS DEDUCTION.

#126. LIKE ON A VACATION

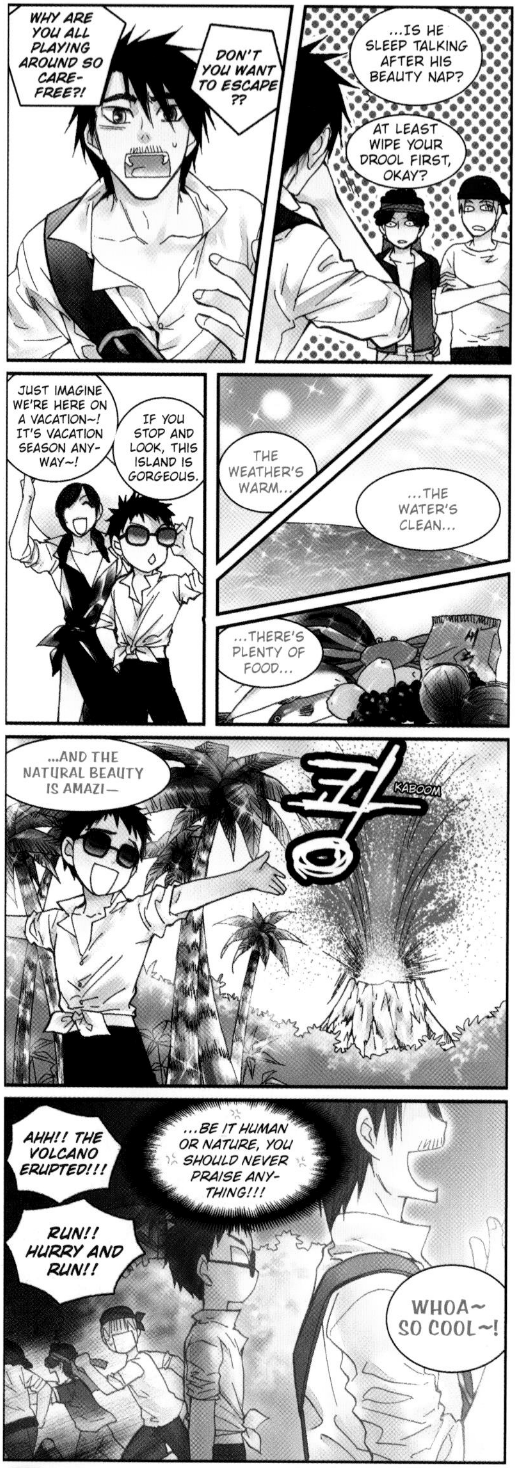
WHY ARE YOU ALL PLAYING AROUND SO CARE-FREE?!
DON'T YOU WANT TO ESCAPE ??
...IS HE SLEEP TALKING AFTER HIS BEAUTY NAP?
AT LEAST WIPE YOUR DROOL FIRST, OKAY?
JUST IMAGINE WE'RE HERE ON A VACATION~! IT'S VACATION SEASON ANY-WAY~!
IF YOU STOP AND LOOK, THIS ISLAND IS GORGEOUS.
THE WEATHER'S WARM...
...THE WATER'S CLEAN...
...THERE'S PLENTY OF FOOD...
...AND THE NATURAL BEAUTY IS AMAZI—
펑
KABOOM
AHH!! THE VOLCANO ERUPTED!!!
...BE IT HUMAN OR NATURE, YOU SHOULD NEVER PRAISE ANY-THING!!!
RUN!! HURRY AND RUN!!
WHOA~ SO COOL~!

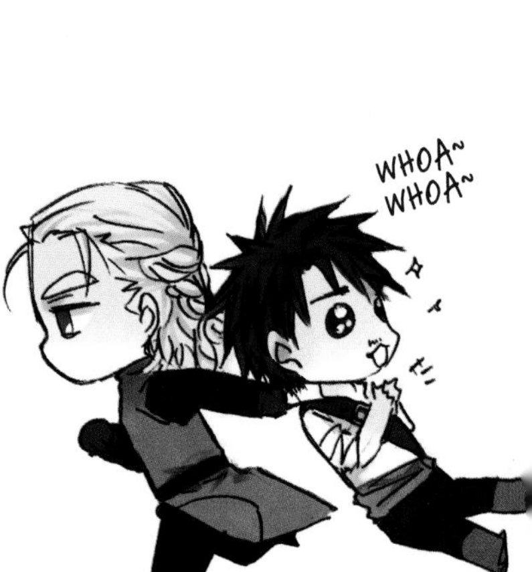
WHOA~ WHOA~

#127. HYPNOTISM

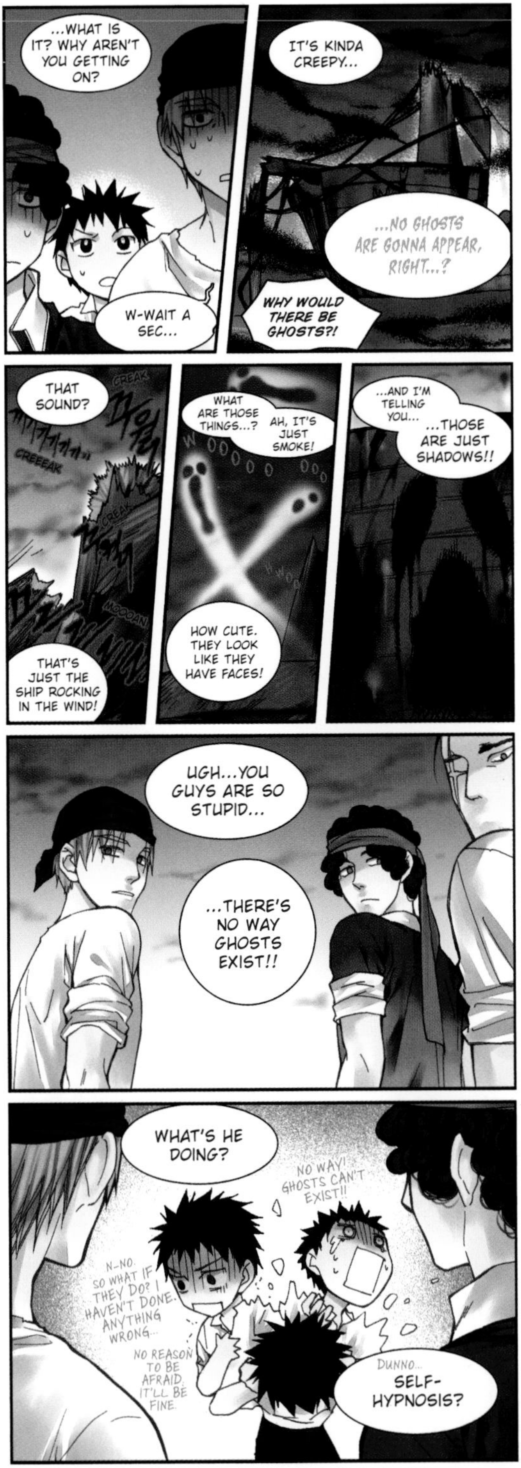
...WHAT IS IT? WHY AREN'T YOU GETTING ON?
W-WAIT A SEC...
IT'S KINDA CREEPY...
...NO GHOSTS ARE GONNA APPEAR, RIGHT...?
WHY WOULD THERE BE GHOSTS?!
THAT SOUND?
CREAK
CREEEAK
CREAK
MOODAN
THAT'S JUST THE SHIP ROCKING IN THE WIND!
WHAT ARE THOSE THINGS...?
AH, IT'S JUST SMOKE!
W OOOOO OOO
HOW CUTE. THEY LOOK LIKE THEY HAVE FACES!
...AND I'M TELLING YOU...
...THOSE ARE JUST SHADOWS!!
UGH...YOU GUYS ARE SO STUPID...
...THERE'S NO WAY GHOSTS EXIST!!
WHAT'S HE DOING?
NO WAY! GHOSTS CAN'T EXIST!!
N-NO. SO WHAT IF THEY DO? I HAVEN'T DONE ANYTHING WRONG...
NO REASON TO BE AFRAID. IT'LL BE FINE.
DUNNO... SELF-HYPNOSIS?

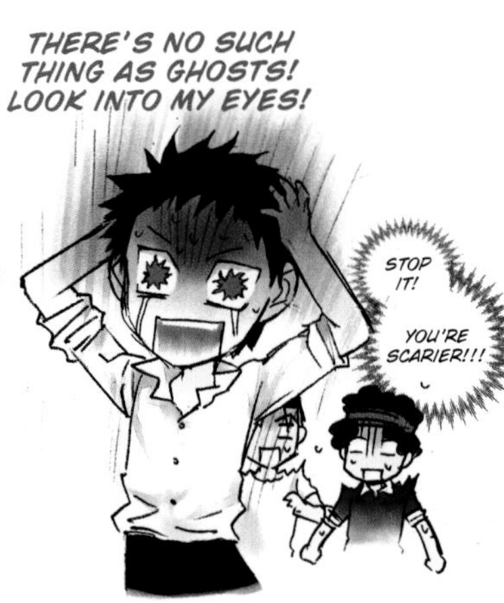
THERE'S NO SUCH THING AS GHOSTS! LOOK INTO MY EYES!
STOP IT!
YOU'RE SCARIER!!!

#128. MR. GHOST IS WATCHING YOU

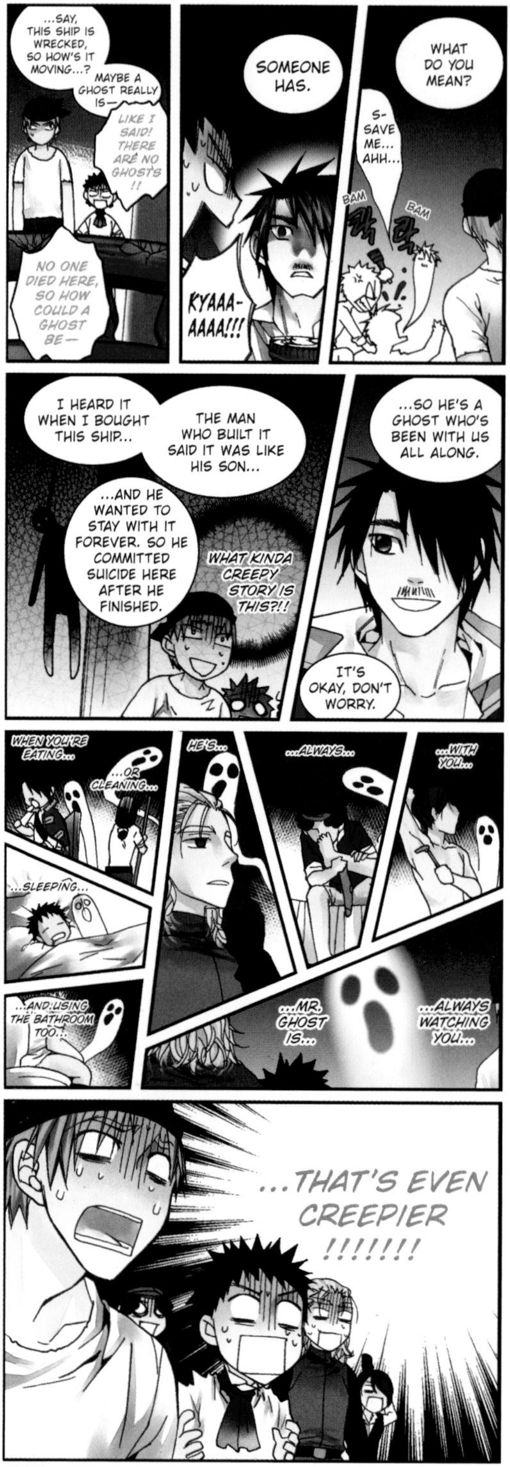
...SAY, THIS SHIP IS WRECKED, SO HOW'S IT MOVING...?
MAYBE A GHOST REALLY IS—
LIKE I SAID! THERE ARE NO GHOSTS !!
NO ONE DIED HERE, SO HOW COULD A GHOST BE—
SOMEONE HAS.
KYAAA-AAAA!!!
WHAT DO YOU MEAN?
S-SAVE ME... AHH...
BAM
BAM
I HEARD IT WHEN I BOUGHT THIS SHIP...
THE MAN WHO BUILT IT SAID IT WAS LIKE HIS SON...
...AND HE WANTED TO STAY WITH IT FOREVER. SO HE COMMITTED SUICIDE HERE AFTER HE FINISHED.
WHAT KINDA CREEPY STORY IS THIS?!!
...SO HE'S A GHOST WHO'S BEEN WITH US ALL ALONG.
IT'S OKAY, DON'T WORRY.
WHEN YOU'RE EATING...
...OR CLEANING...
...SLEEPING...
...AND USING THE BATHROOM TOO...
HE'S...
...ALWAYS...
...WITH YOU...
...MR. GHOST IS...
...ALWAYS WATCHING YOU...
...THAT'S EVEN CREEPIER !!!!!!!

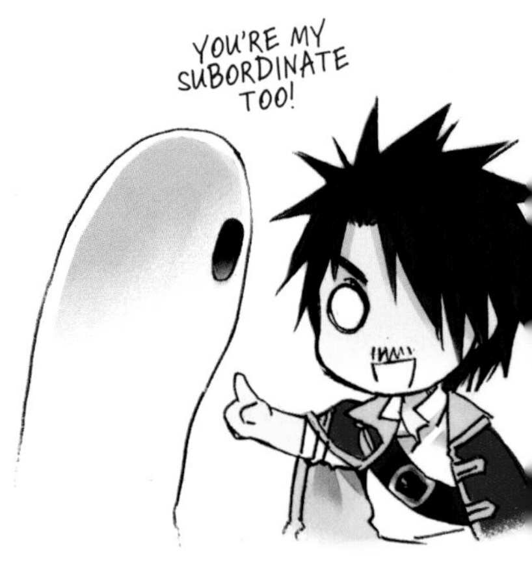
YOU'RE MY SUBORDINATE TOO!

#129. EVEN IN THE LION'S DEN

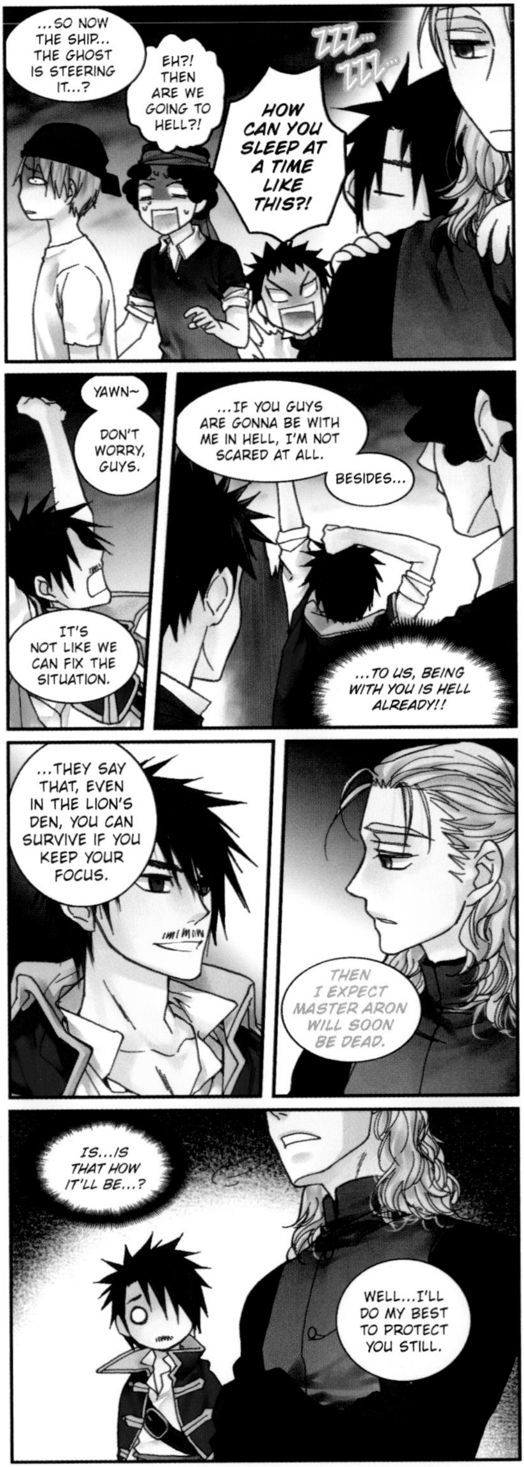
...SO NOW THE SHIP... THE GHOST IS STEERING IT...?
EH?! THEN ARE WE GOING TO HELL?!
ZZZ... ZZZ...
HOW CAN YOU SLEEP AT A TIME LIKE THIS?!
YAWN~
DON'T WORRY, GUYS.
IT'S NOT LIKE WE CAN FIX THE SITUATION.
...IF YOU GUYS ARE GONNA BE WITH ME IN HELL, I'M NOT SCARED AT ALL.
BESIDES...
...TO US, BEING WITH YOU IS HELL ALREADY!!
...THEY SAY THAT, EVEN IN THE LION'S DEN, YOU CAN SURVIVE IF YOU KEEP YOUR FOCUS.
THEN I EXPECT MASTER ARON WILL SOON BE DEAD.
IS...IS THAT HOW IT'LL BE...?
WELL...I'LL DO MY BEST TO PROTECT YOU STILL.

...MASTER ROBIN, I WANT A PIGGYBACK RIDE TOO...

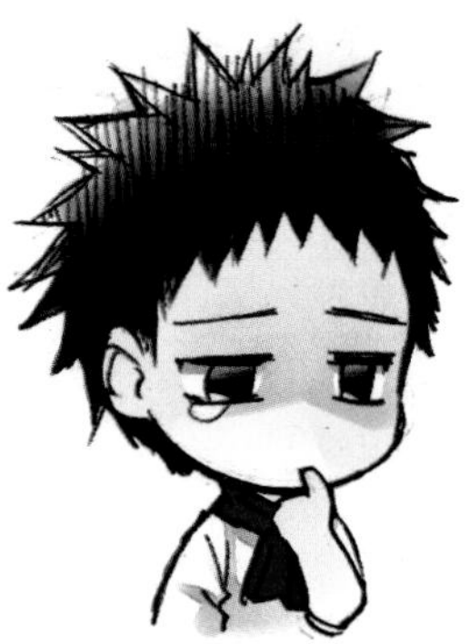

#130. BEST FRIEND

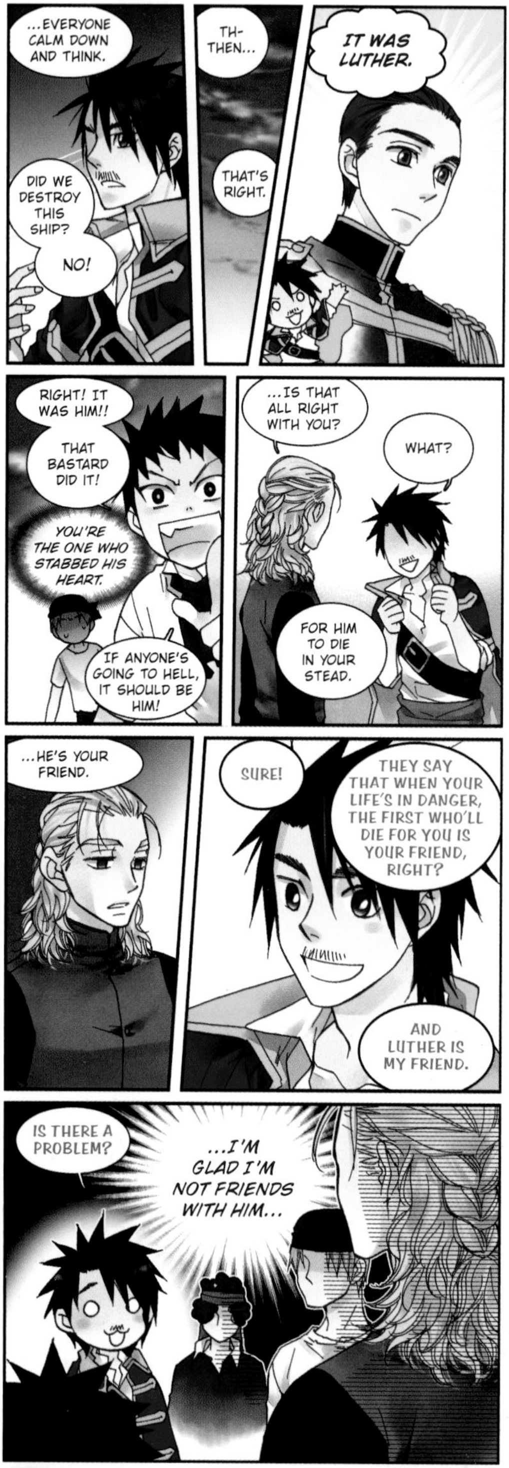
...EVERYONE CALM DOWN AND THINK.
DID WE DESTROY THIS SHIP?
NO!
TH- THEN...
THAT'S RIGHT.
IT WAS LUTHER.
RIGHT! IT WAS HIM!!
THAT BASTARD DID IT!
YOU'RE THE ONE WHO STABBED HIS HEART.
IF ANYONE'S GOING TO HELL, IT SHOULD BE HIM!
...IS THAT ALL RIGHT WITH YOU?
WHAT?
FOR HIM TO DIE IN YOUR STEAD.
...HE'S YOUR FRIEND.
SURE!
THEY SAY THAT WHEN YOUR LIFE'S IN DANGER, THE FIRST WHO'LL DIE FOR YOU IS YOUR FRIEND, RIGHT?
AND LUTHER IS MY FRIEND.
IS THERE A PROBLEM?
...I'M GLAD I'M NOT FRIENDS WITH HIM...

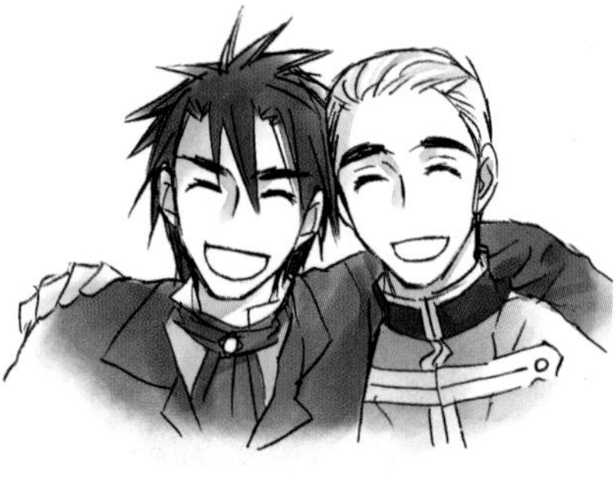

#131. BEST FRIEND 2

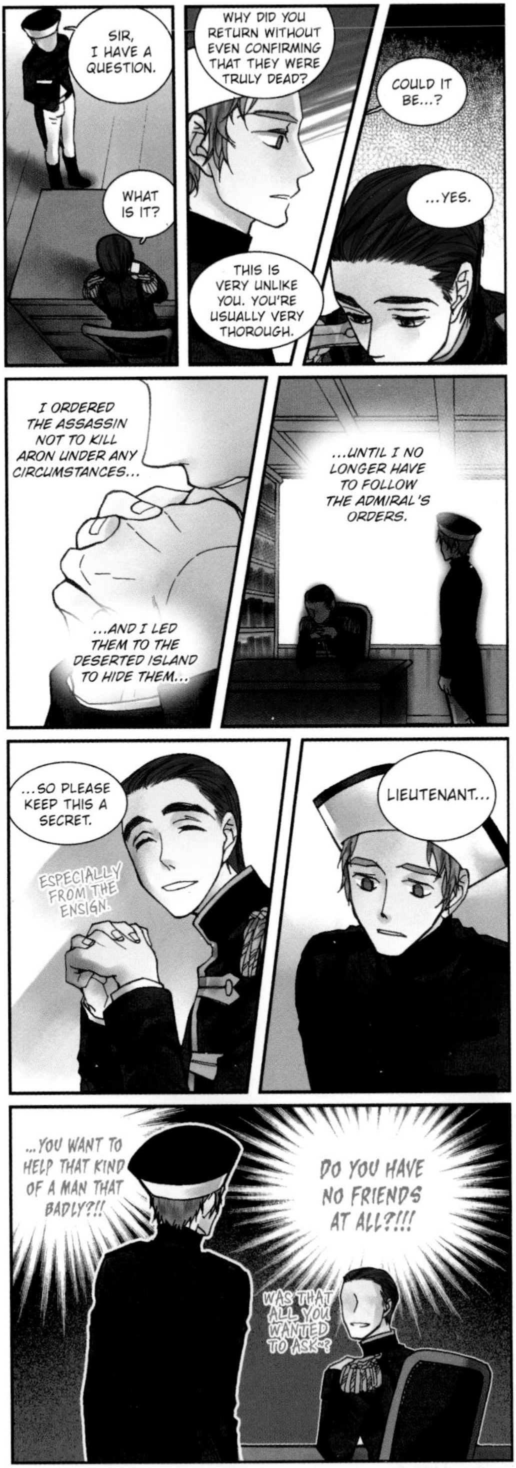
SIR, I HAVE A QUESTION.
WHAT IS IT?
WHY DID YOU RETURN WITHOUT EVEN CONFIRMING THAT THEY WERE TRULY DEAD?
THIS IS VERY UNLIKE YOU. YOU'RE USUALLY VERY THOROUGH.
COULD IT BE...?
...YES.
I ORDERED THE ASSASSIN NOT TO KILL ARON UNDER ANY CIRCUMSTANCES...
...AND I LED THEM TO THE DESERTED ISLAND TO HIDE THEM...
...UNTIL I NO LONGER HAVE TO FOLLOW THE ADMIRAL'S ORDERS.
...SO PLEASE KEEP THIS A SECRET.
ESPECIALLY FROM THE ENSIGN.
LIEUTENANT...
...YOU WANT TO HELP THAT KIND OF A MAN THAT BADLY?!!
DO YOU HAVE NO FRIENDS AT ALL?!!!
WAS THAT ALL YOU WANTED TO ASK~?

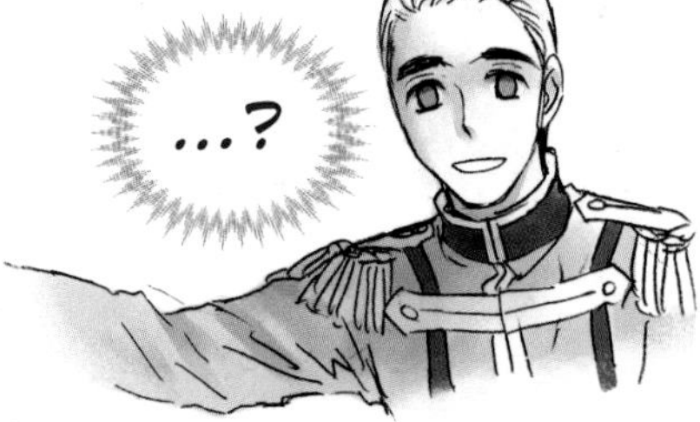
...?

*COMPARE WITH THE IMAGE ON #130.

#132. GOOD-BYE, MR. GHOST

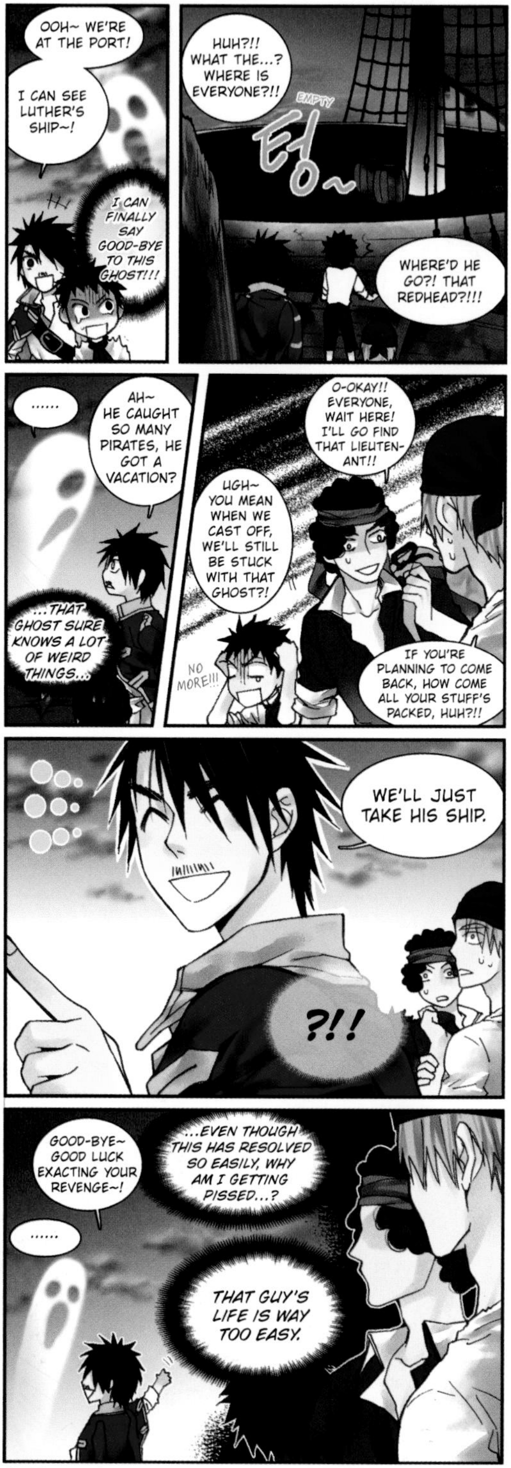

OOH~ WE'RE AT THE PORT!
I CAN SEE LUTHER'S SHIP~!
I CAN FINALLY SAY GOOD-BYE TO THIS GHOST!!!
HUH?!! WHAT THE...? WHERE IS EVERYONE?!!
EMPTY
텅~
WHERE'D HE GO?! THAT REDHEAD?!!!
......
AH~ HE CAUGHT SO MANY PIRATES, HE GOT A VACATION?
...THAT GHOST SURE KNOWS A LOT OF WEIRD THINGS...
O-OKAY!! EVERYONE, WAIT HERE! I'LL GO FIND THAT LIEUTEN-ANT!!
UGH~ YOU MEAN WHEN WE CAST OFF, WE'LL STILL BE STUCK WITH THAT GHOST?!
NO MORE!!!
IF YOU'RE PLANNING TO COME BACK, HOW COME ALL YOUR STUFF'S PACKED, HUH?!!
WE'LL JUST TAKE HIS SHIP.
?!!
GOOD-BYE~ GOOD LUCK EXACTING YOUR REVENGE~!
......
...EVEN THOUGH THIS HAS RESOLVED SO EASILY, WHY AM I GETTING PISSED...?
THAT GUY'S LIFE IS WAY TOO EASY.

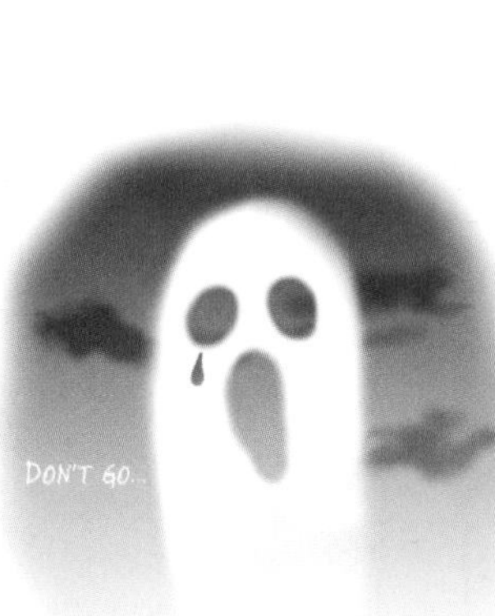

DON'T GO...

#133. OVERFLOWING ZEAL

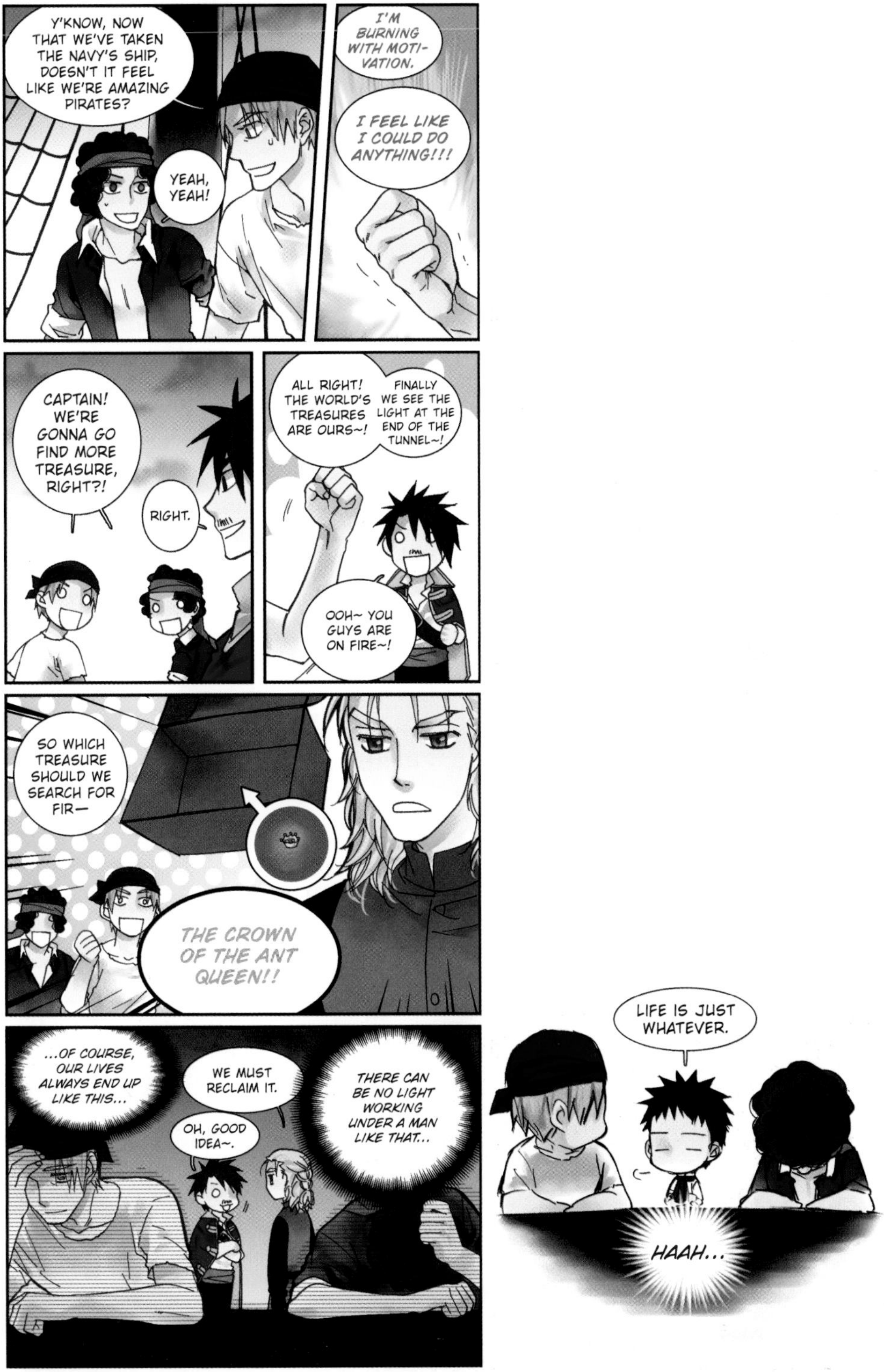

Y'KNOW, NOW THAT WE'VE TAKEN THE NAVY'S SHIP, DOESN'T IT FEEL LIKE WE'RE AMAZING PIRATES?
YEAH, YEAH!
I'M BURNING WITH MOTI-VATION.
I FEEL LIKE I COULD DO ANYTHING!!!
CAPTAIN! WE'RE GONNA GO FIND MORE TREASURE, RIGHT?!
RIGHT.
ALL RIGHT! THE WORLD'S TREASURES ARE OURS~!
FINALLY WE SEE THE LIGHT AT THE END OF THE TUNNEL~!
OOH~ YOU GUYS ARE ON FIRE~!
SO WHICH TREASURE SHOULD WE SEARCH FOR FIR—
THE CROWN OF THE ANT QUEEN!!
...OF COURSE, OUR LIVES ALWAYS END UP LIKE THIS...
WE MUST RECLAIM IT.
OH, GOOD IDEA~.
THERE CAN BE NO LIGHT WORKING UNDER A MAN LIKE THAT...
LIFE IS JUST WHATEVER.
HAAH...

#134. BIRTHDAY PRESENT

WHERE SHOULD WE GO?
CALENDAR
HMM... SOME-THING'S WRITTEN HERE...
THERE'S A BIRTHDAY PARTY BEING HELD FOR THE KING...
I THINK THEY TOOK THE CROWN AS A GIFT...
OHH~
ARE YOU READY?
YES.
...WHY MUST I GIVE MY REGARDS ON HIS BIRTHDAY...
IF YOU DON'T WISH TO GO, YOU NEEDN'T FORCE YOURSELF. I'LL GO ALONE.
BUT I MUST AT LEAST GIVE HIM HIS PRESENT.
...I CAN DELIVER IT FOR YOU. WHAT IS IT?
...BIRTHDAY PUNCHES.
NEVER MIND. I WILL GO.
I WILL DELIVER THEM PERSONALLY.
...DARLING, AT LEAST TAKE OFF THOSE RINGS...
SORRY, KING...

...I'LL SEND ALONG HIS PRESENT ANOTHER TIME.
IF I BRING IT NOW, IT COULD BE USED AS A MURDER WEAPON...
HARDCOVER.

#135. A WOMAN'S HEART

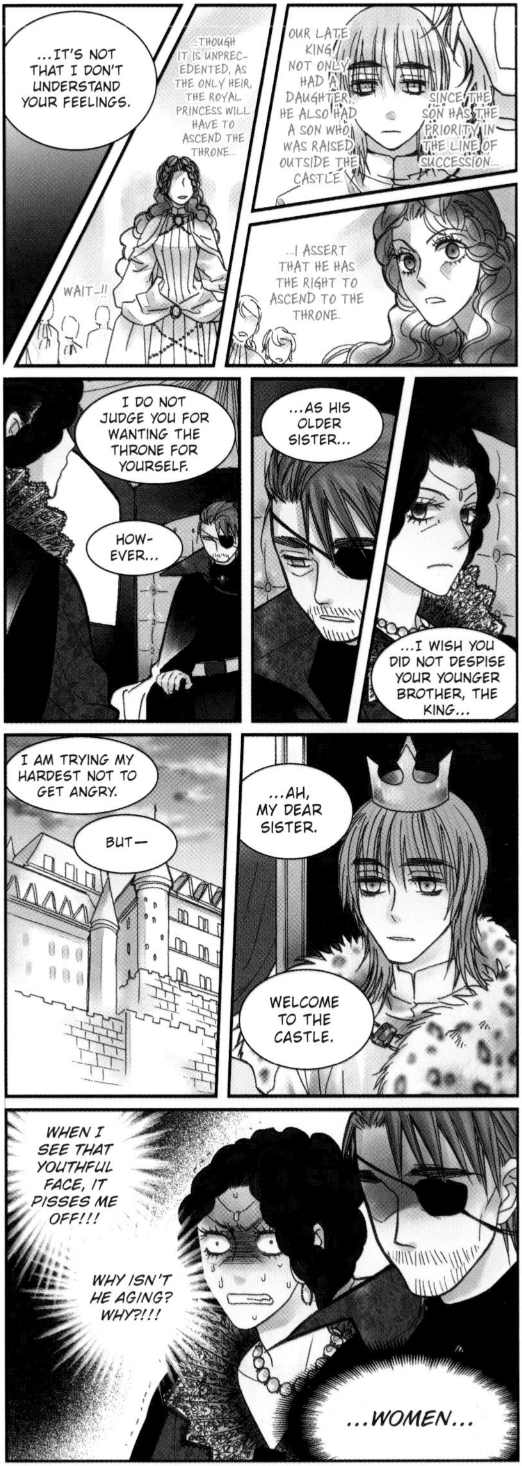

...IT'S NOT THAT I DON'T UNDERSTAND YOUR FEELINGS.
...THOUGH IT IS UNPRECEDENTED, AS THE ONLY HEIR, THE ROYAL PRINCESS WILL HAVE TO ASCEND THE THRONE...
WAIT...!!
OUR LATE KING NOT ONLY HAD A DAUGHTER, HE ALSO HAD A SON WHO WAS RAISED OUTSIDE THE CASTLE.
SINCE THE SON HAS THE PRIORITY IN THE LINE OF SUCCESSION...
...I ASSERT THAT HE HAS THE RIGHT TO ASCEND TO THE THRONE.
I DO NOT JUDGE YOU FOR WANTING THE THRONE FOR YOURSELF.
HOW-EVER...
...AS HIS OLDER SISTER...
...I WISH YOU DID NOT DESPISE YOUR YOUNGER BROTHER, THE KING...
I AM TRYING MY HARDEST NOT TO GET ANGRY.
BUT—
...AH, MY DEAR SISTER.
WELCOME TO THE CASTLE.
WHEN I SEE THAT YOUTHFUL FACE, IT PISSES ME OFF!!!
WHY ISN'T HE AGING? WHY?!!!
...WOMEN...

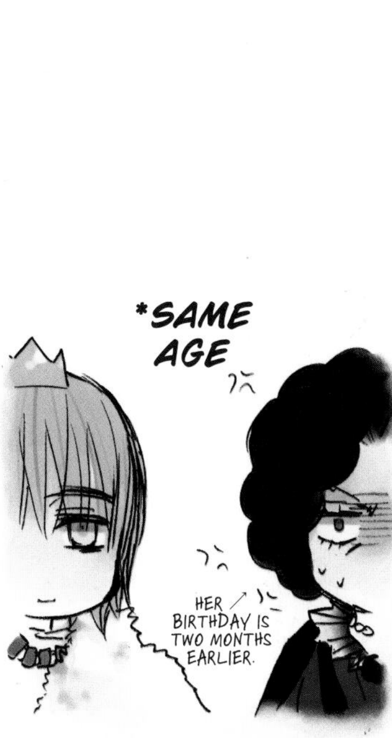

*SAME AGE
HER BIRTHDAY IS TWO MONTHS EARLIER.

#136. GETTING ALONG

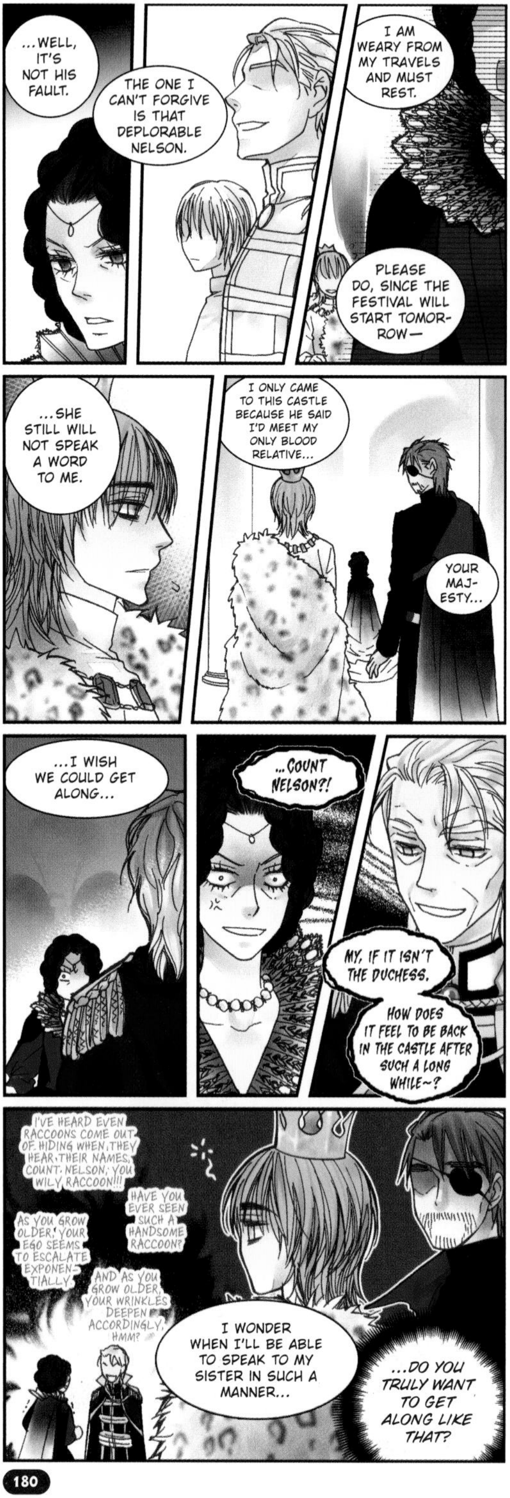

...WELL, IT'S NOT HIS FAULT.
THE ONE I CAN'T FORGIVE IS THAT DEPLORABLE NELSON.
I AM WEARY FROM MY TRAVELS AND MUST REST.
PLEASE DO, SINCE THE FESTIVAL WILL START TOMOR-ROW—
...SHE STILL WILL NOT SPEAK A WORD TO ME.
I ONLY CAME TO THIS CASTLE BECAUSE HE SAID I'D MEET MY ONLY BLOOD RELATIVE...
YOUR MAJ-ESTY...
...I WISH WE COULD GET ALONG...
...COUNT NELSON?!
MY, IF IT ISN'T THE DUCHESS.
HOW DOES IT FEEL TO BE BACK IN THE CASTLE AFTER SUCH A LONG WHILE~?
I'VE HEARD EVEN RACCOONS COME OUT OF HIDING WHEN THEY HEAR THEIR NAMES, COUNT NELSON, YOU WILY RACCOON!!!
HAVE YOU EVER SEEN SUCH A HANDSOME RACCOON?
AS YOU GROW OLDER, YOUR EGO SEEMS TO ESCALATE EXPONEN-TIALLY.
AND AS YOU GROW OLDER, YOUR WRINKLES DEEPEN ACCORDINGLY, HMM?
I WONDER WHEN I'LL BE ABLE TO SPEAK TO MY SISTER IN SUCH A MANNER...
...DO YOU TRULY WANT TO GET ALONG LIKE THAT?

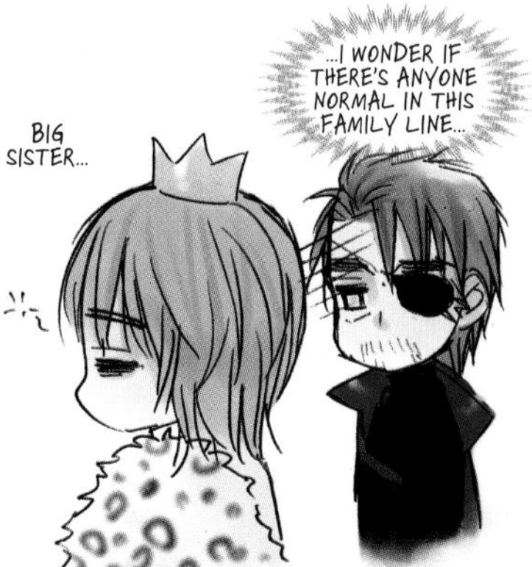

BIG SISTER...
...I WONDER IF THERE'S ANYONE NORMAL IN THIS FAMILY LINE...

#137. NO REGRETS

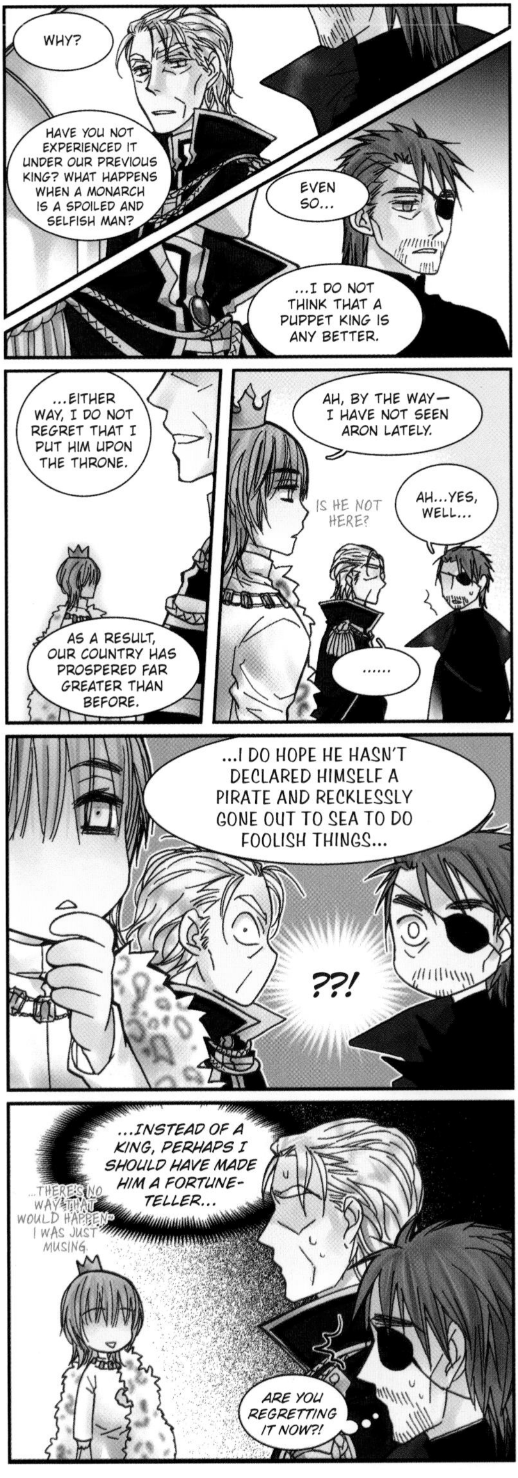

WHY?
HAVE YOU NOT EXPERIENCED IT UNDER OUR PREVIOUS KING? WHAT HAPPENS WHEN A MONARCH IS A SPOILED AND SELFISH MAN?
EVEN SO...
...I DO NOT THINK THAT A PUPPET KING IS ANY BETTER.
...EITHER WAY, I DO NOT REGRET THAT I PUT HIM UPON THE THRONE.
AS A RESULT, OUR COUNTRY HAS PROSPERED FAR GREATER THAN BEFORE.
AH, BY THE WAY— I HAVE NOT SEEN ARON LATELY.
IS HE NOT HERE?
AH...YES, WELL...
......
...I DO HOPE HE HASN'T DECLARED HIMSELF A PIRATE AND RECKLESSLY GONE OUT TO SEA TO DO FOOLISH THINGS...
??!
...INSTEAD OF A KING, PERHAPS I SHOULD HAVE MADE HIM A FORTUNE-TELLER...
...THERE'S NO WAY THAT WOULD HAPPEN~ I WAS JUST MUSING.
ARE YOU REGRETTING IT NOW?!

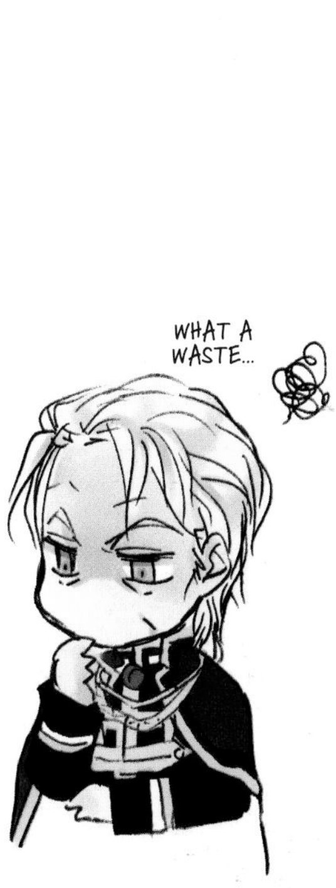

WHAT A WASTE...

#138. THERE'S NO SUCH THING AS IMPOSSIBLE

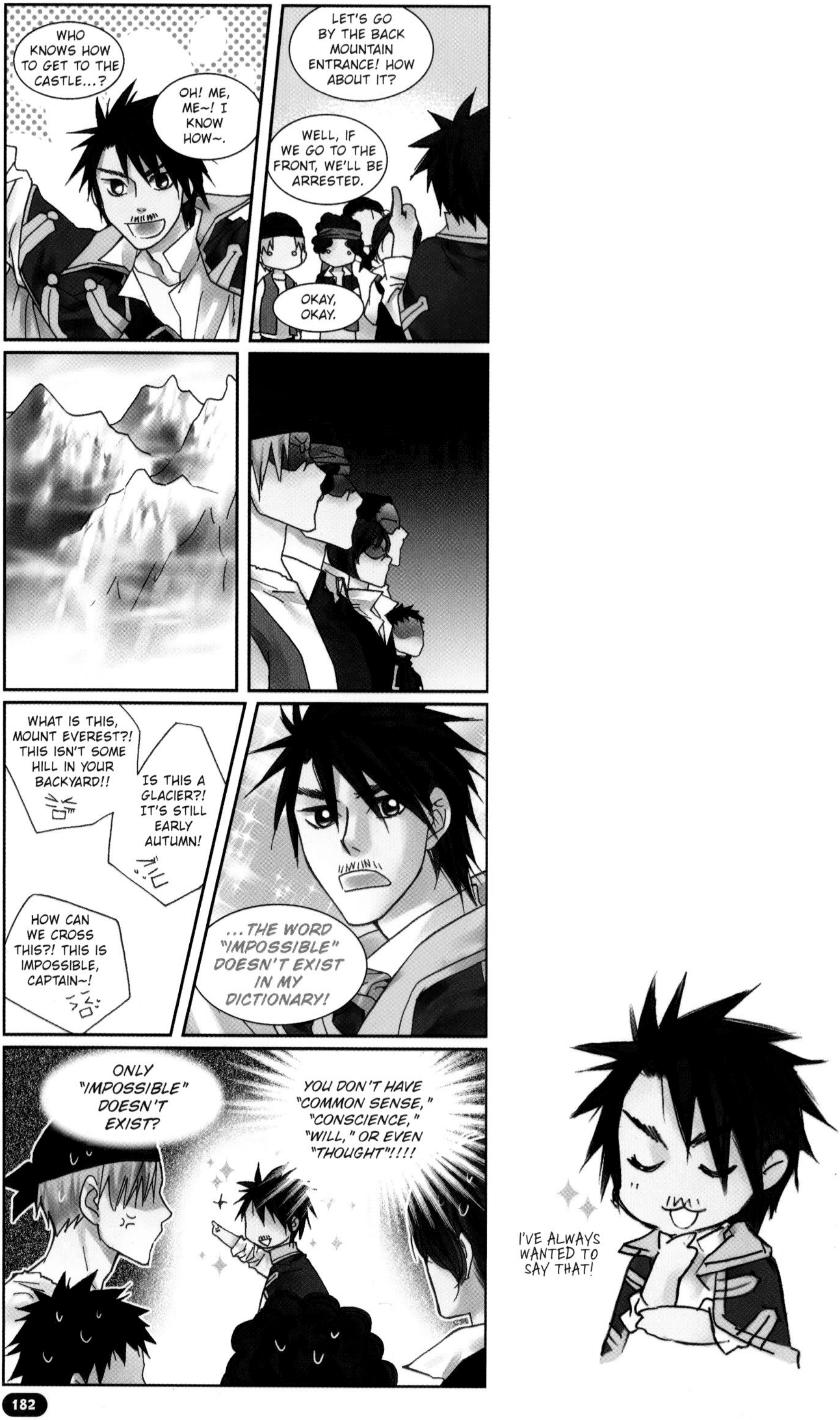

WHO KNOWS HOW TO GET TO THE CASTLE...?
OH! ME, ME~! I KNOW HOW~.
LET'S GO BY THE BACK MOUNTAIN ENTRANCE! HOW ABOUT IT?
WELL, IF WE GO TO THE FRONT, WE'LL BE ARRESTED.
OKAY, OKAY.
WHAT IS THIS, MOUNT EVEREST?! THIS ISN'T SOME HILL IN YOUR BACKYARD!!
IS THIS A GLACIER?! IT'S STILL EARLY AUTUMN!
HOW CAN WE CROSS THIS?! THIS IS IMPOSSIBLE, CAPTAIN~!
...THE WORD "IMPOSSIBLE" DOESN'T EXIST IN MY DICTIONARY!
ONLY "IMPOSSIBLE" DOESN'T EXIST?
YOU DON'T HAVE "COMMON SENSE," "CONSCIENCE," "WILL," OR EVEN "THOUGHT"!!!!
I'VE ALWAYS WANTED TO SAY THAT!

#139. NOTHING GOES RIGHT

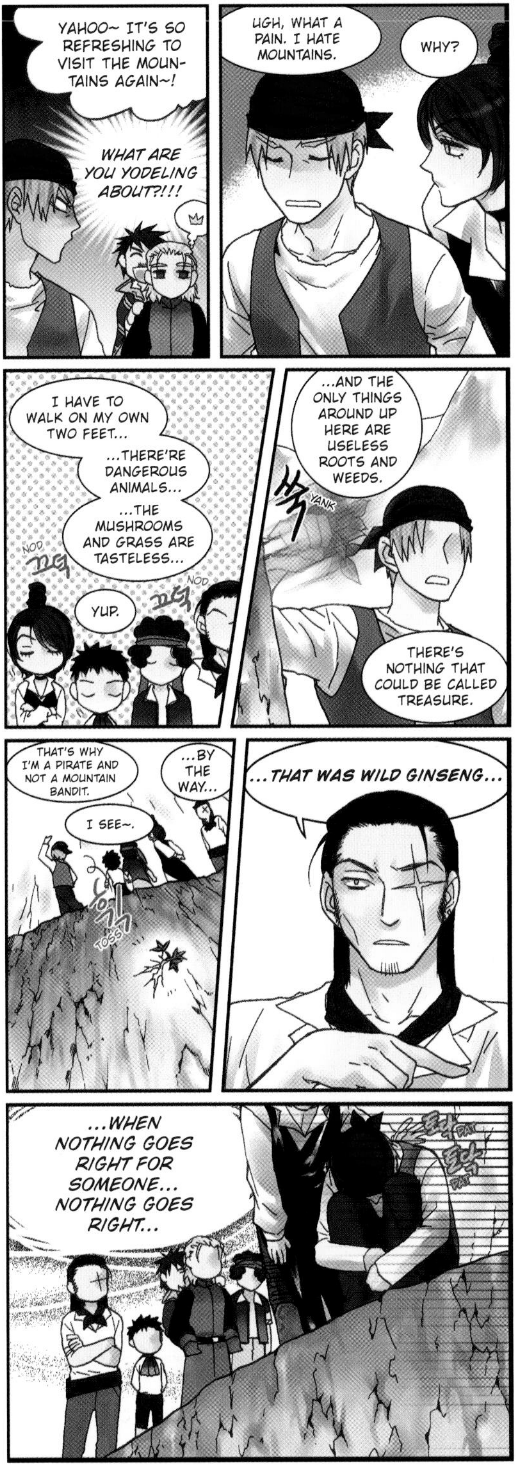

YAHOO~ IT'S SO REFRESHING TO VISIT THE MOUNTAINS AGAIN~!
WHAT ARE YOU YODELING ABOUT?!!!
UGH, WHAT A PAIN. I HATE MOUNTAINS.
WHY?
I HAVE TO WALK ON MY OWN TWO FEET...
...THERE'RE DANGEROUS ANIMALS...
...THE MUSHROOMS AND GRASS ARE TASTELESS...
끄덕 NOD
YUP.
끄덕 NOD
...AND THE ONLY THINGS AROUND UP HERE ARE USELESS ROOTS AND WEEDS.
쑥 YANK
THERE'S NOTHING THAT COULD BE CALLED TREASURE.
THAT'S WHY I'M A PIRATE AND NOT A MOUNTAIN BANDIT.
...BY THE WAY...
I SEE~.
휙 TOSS
...THAT WAS WILD GINSENG...
...WHEN NOTHING GOES RIGHT FOR SOMEONE... NOTHING GOES RIGHT...
토닥 PAT
토닥 PAT

THE REASON THE MOUNTAINS ARE SO BEAUTIFUL IS BECAUSE WILD GINSENG IS HIDDEN WITHIN.

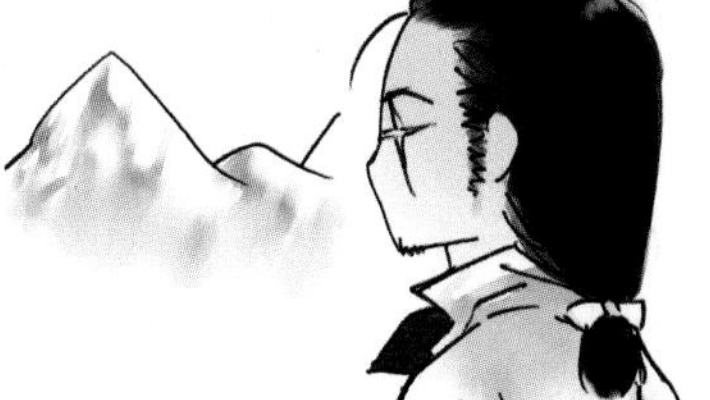

#140. IT'S ROUGH BEING BIG

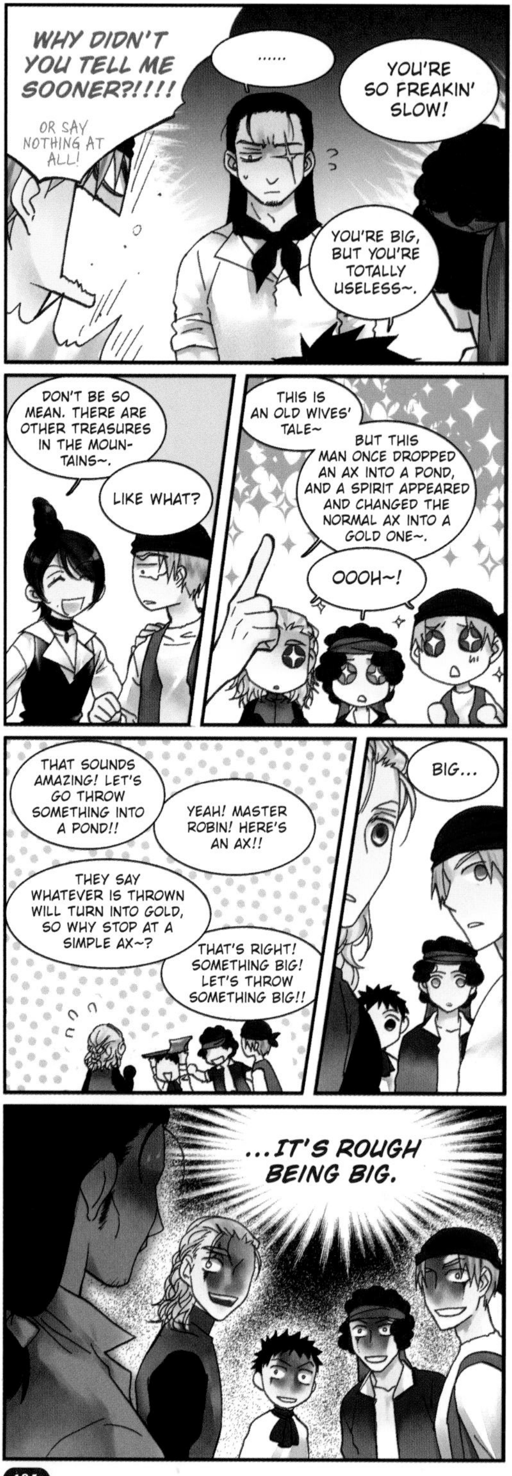
WHY DIDN'T YOU TELL ME SOONER?!!!!
OR SAY NOTHING AT ALL!
......
YOU'RE SO FREAKIN' SLOW!
YOU'RE BIG, BUT YOU'RE TOTALLY USELESS~.
DON'T BE SO MEAN. THERE ARE OTHER TREASURES IN THE MOUNTAINS~.
LIKE WHAT?
THIS IS AN OLD WIVES' TALE~
BUT THIS MAN ONCE DROPPED AN AX INTO A POND, AND A SPIRIT APPEARED AND CHANGED THE NORMAL AX INTO A GOLD ONE~.
OOOH~!
THAT SOUNDS AMAZING! LET'S GO THROW SOMETHING INTO A POND!!
YEAH! MASTER ROBIN! HERE'S AN AX!!
THEY SAY WHATEVER IS THROWN WILL TURN INTO GOLD, SO WHY STOP AT A SIMPLE AX~?
THAT'S RIGHT! SOMETHING BIG! LET'S THROW SOMETHING BIG!!
BIG...
...IT'S ROUGH BEING BIG.

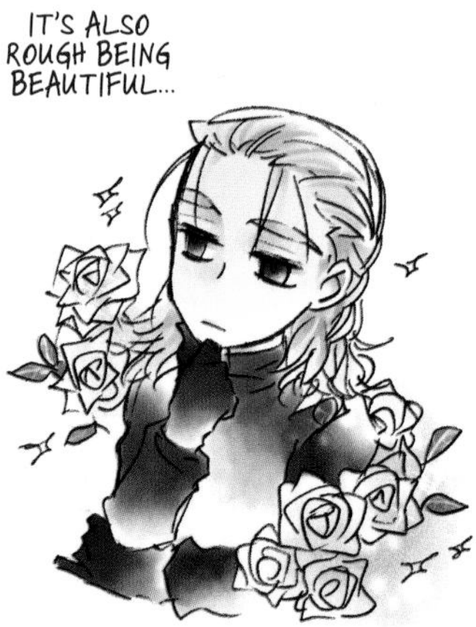
IT'S ALSO ROUGH BEING BEAUTIFUL...

#141. PROTECT NATURE

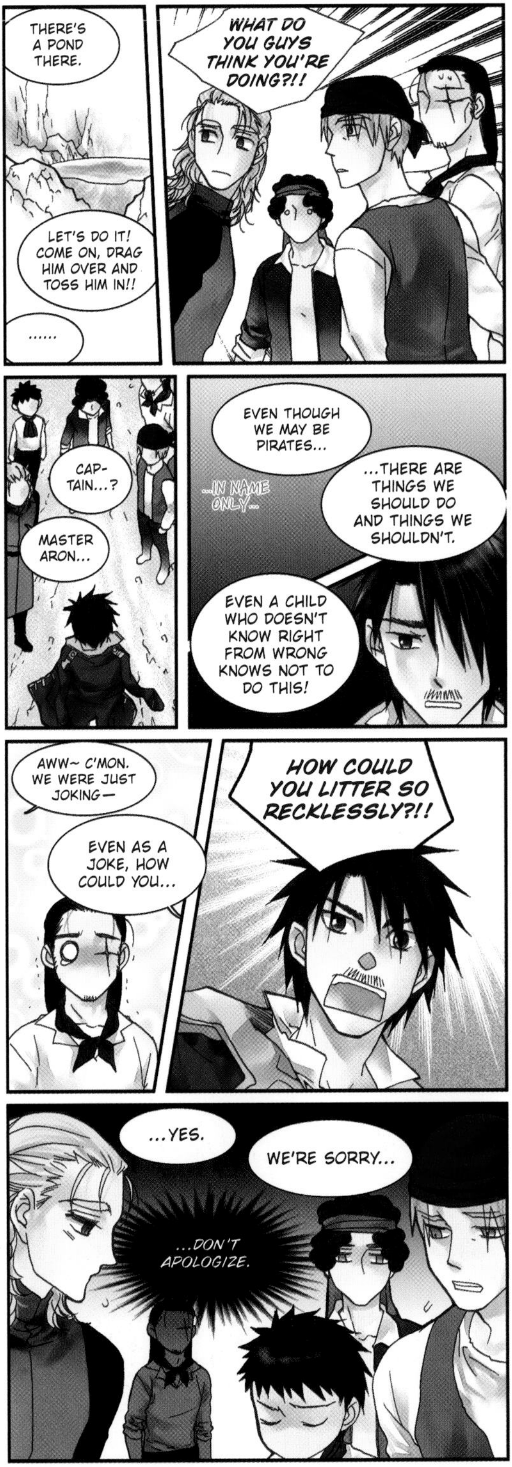

THERE'S A POND THERE.
WHAT DO YOU GUYS THINK YOU'RE DOING?!!
LET'S DO IT! COME ON, DRAG HIM OVER AND TOSS HIM IN!!
......
CAP-TAIN...?
MASTER ARON...
EVEN THOUGH WE MAY BE PIRATES...
...IN NAME ONLY...
...THERE ARE THINGS WE SHOULD DO AND THINGS WE SHOULDN'T.
EVEN A CHILD WHO DOESN'T KNOW RIGHT FROM WRONG KNOWS NOT TO DO THIS!
AWW~ C'MON. WE WERE JUST JOKING—
EVEN AS A JOKE, HOW COULD YOU...
HOW COULD YOU LITTER SO RECKLESSLY?!!
...YES.
WE'RE SORRY...
...DON'T APOLOGIZE.

ONLY YOU CAN PROTECT NATURE.

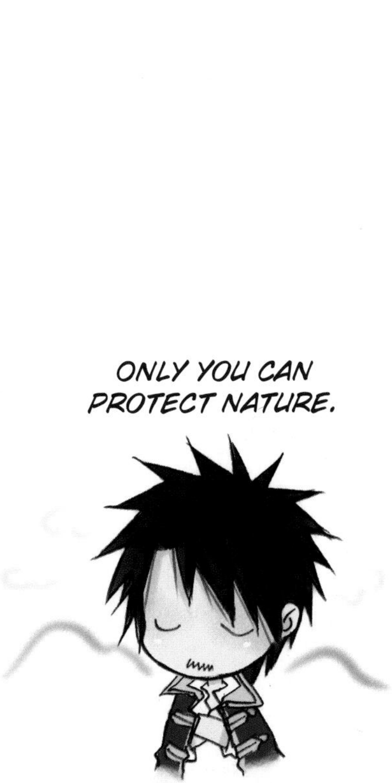

#142. THE CLOSER YOU GET

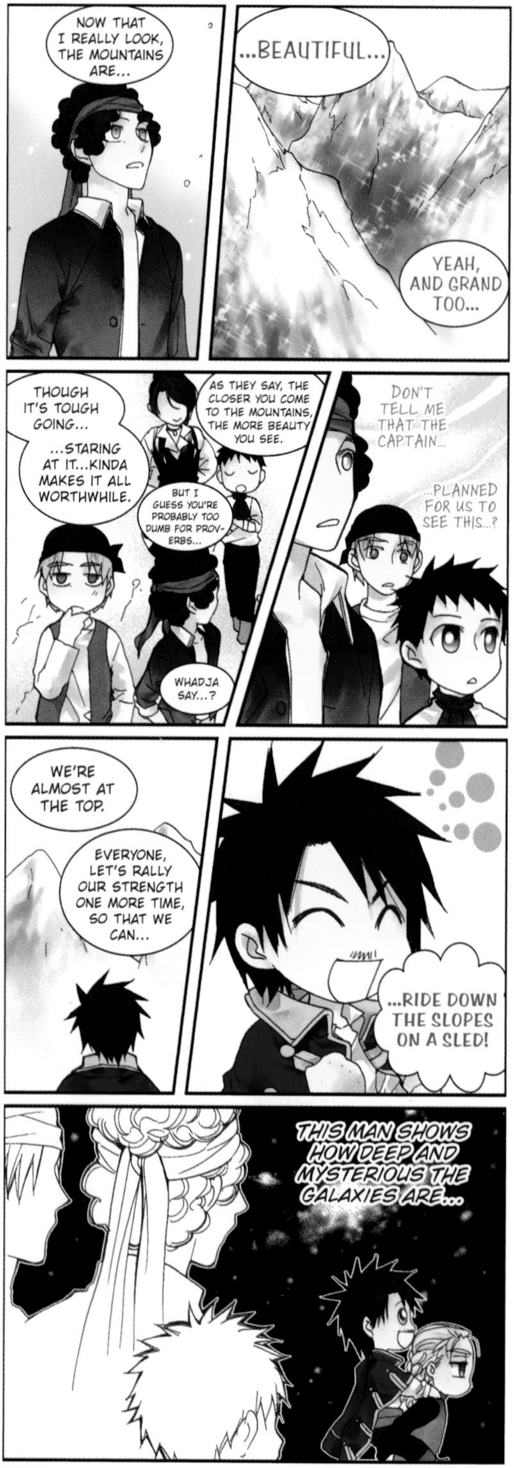
NOW THAT I REALLY LOOK, THE MOUNTAINS ARE...
...BEAUTIFUL...
YEAH, AND GRAND TOO...
THOUGH IT'S TOUGH GOING...
...STARING AT IT...KINDA MAKES IT ALL WORTHWHILE.
AS THEY SAY, THE CLOSER YOU COME TO THE MOUNTAINS, THE MORE BEAUTY YOU SEE.
BUT I GUESS YOU'RE PROBABLY TOO DUMB FOR PROVERBS...
WHADJA SAY...?
DON'T TELL ME THAT THE CAPTAIN...
...PLANNED FOR US TO SEE THIS...?
WE'RE ALMOST AT THE TOP.
EVERYONE, LET'S RALLY OUR STRENGTH ONE MORE TIME, SO THAT WE CAN...
...RIDE DOWN THE SLOPES ON A SLED!
THIS MAN SHOWS HOW DEEP AND MYSTERIOUS THE GALAXIES ARE...

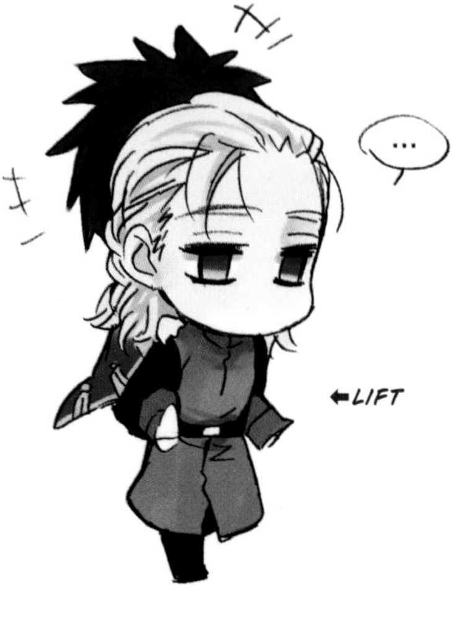
...
←LIFT

#143. MOUNTAIN BANDITS

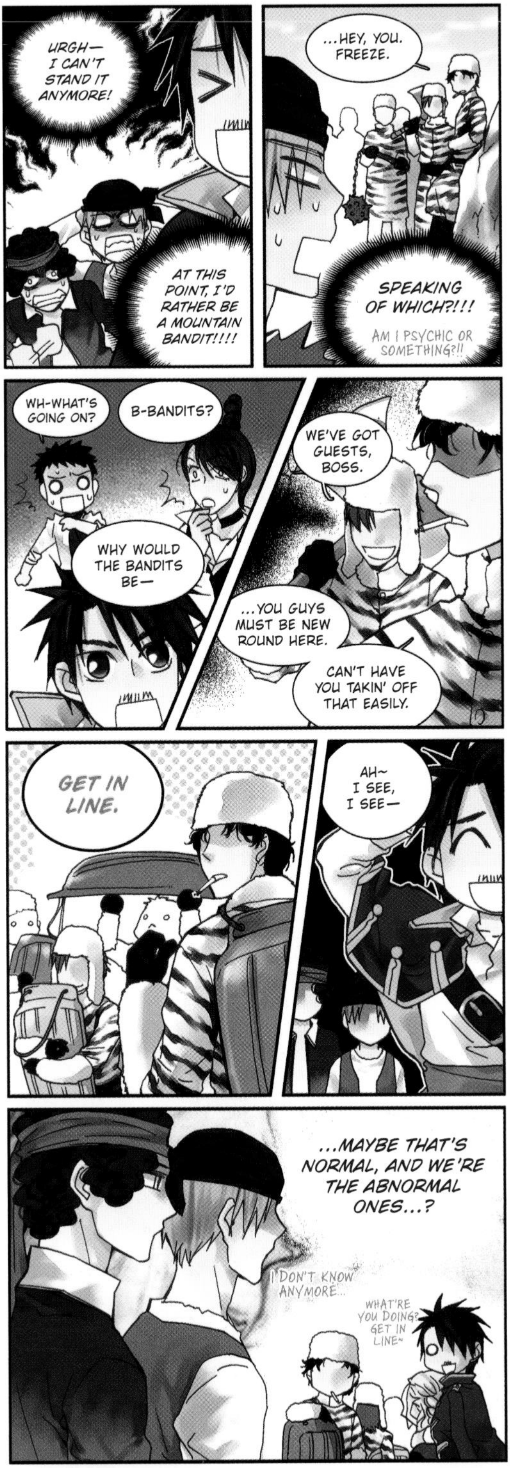
URGH— I CAN'T STAND IT ANYMORE!
AT THIS POINT, I'D RATHER BE A MOUNTAIN BANDIT!!!!
...HEY, YOU. FREEZE.
SPEAKING OF WHICH?!!!
AM I PSYCHIC OR SOMETHING?!!
WH-WHAT'S GOING ON?
B-BANDITS?
WHY WOULD THE BANDITS BE—
WE'VE GOT GUESTS, BOSS.
...YOU GUYS MUST BE NEW ROUND HERE.
CAN'T HAVE YOU TAKIN' OFF THAT EASILY.
GET IN LINE.
AH~ I SEE, I SEE—
...MAYBE THAT'S NORMAL, AND WE'RE THE ABNORMAL ONES...?
I DON'T KNOW ANYMORE...
WHAT'RE YOU DOING? GET IN LINE~

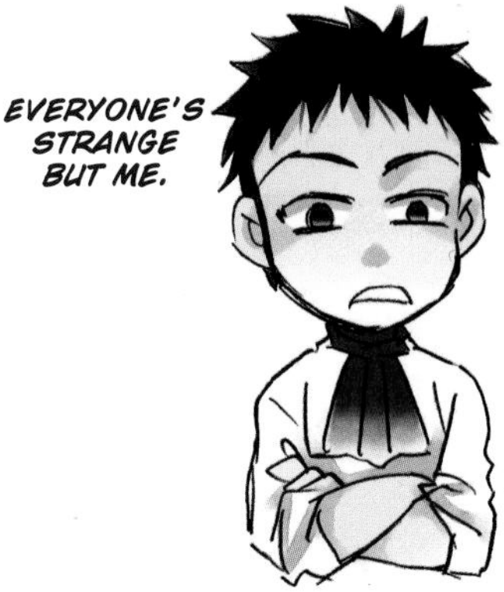
EVERYONE'S STRANGE BUT ME.

#144. THE BIRD

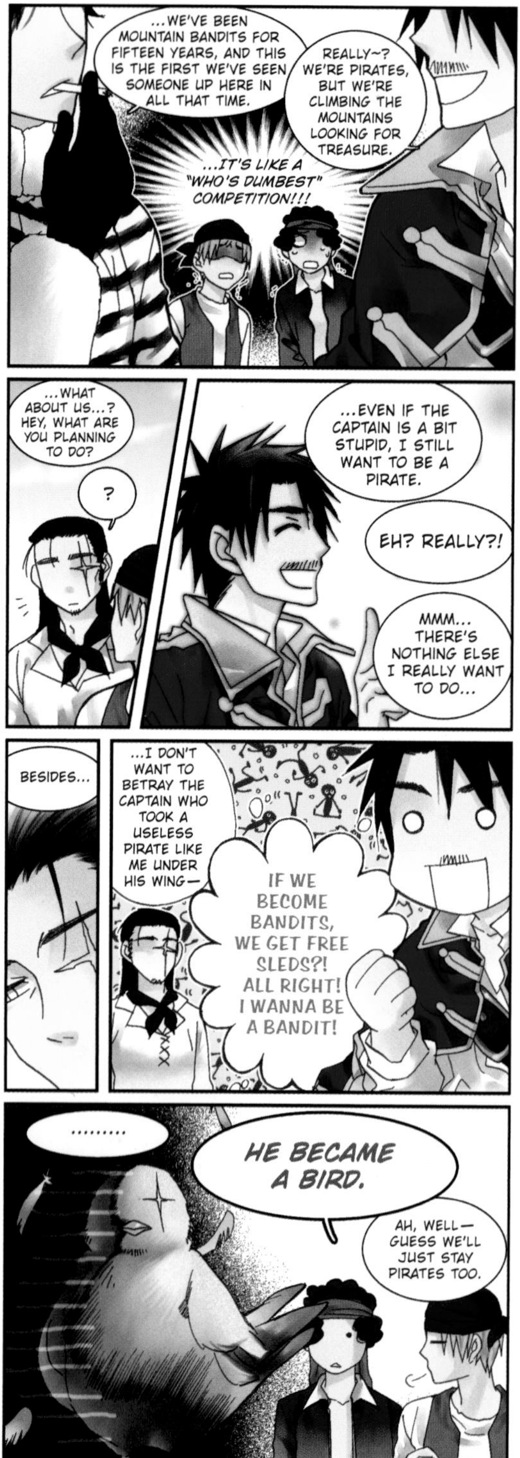

...WE'VE BEEN MOUNTAIN BANDITS FOR FIFTEEN YEARS, AND THIS IS THE FIRST WE'VE SEEN SOMEONE UP HERE IN ALL THAT TIME.
REALLY~? WE'RE PIRATES, BUT WE'RE CLIMBING THE MOUNTAINS LOOKING FOR TREASURE.
...IT'S LIKE A "WHO'S DUMBEST" COMPETITION!!!
...WHAT ABOUT US...? HEY, WHAT ARE YOU PLANNING TO DO?
?
...EVEN IF THE CAPTAIN IS A BIT STUPID, I STILL WANT TO BE A PIRATE.
EH? REALLY?!
MMM... THERE'S NOTHING ELSE I REALLY WANT TO DO...
BESIDES...
...I DON'T WANT TO BETRAY THE CAPTAIN WHO TOOK A USELESS PIRATE LIKE ME UNDER HIS WING—
IF WE BECOME BANDITS, WE GET FREE SLEDS?! ALL RIGHT! I WANNA BE A BANDIT!
....
HE BECAME A BIRD.
AH, WELL—GUESS WE'LL JUST STAY PIRATES TOO.

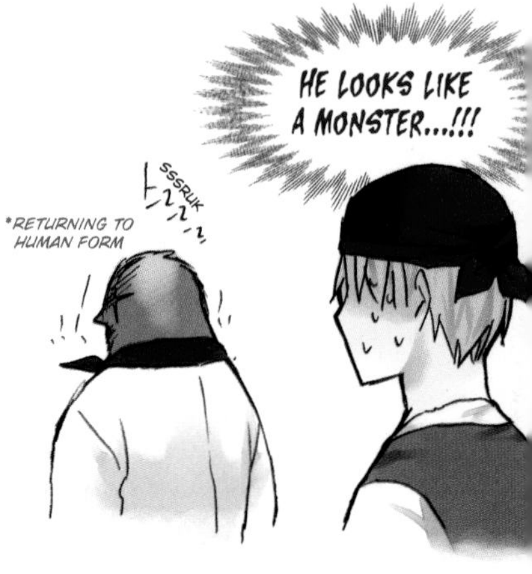

HE LOOKS LIKE A MONSTER...!!!
SSSRUK
*RETURNING TO HUMAN FORM

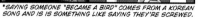

*SAYING SOMEONE "BECAME A BIRD" COMES FROM A KOREAN SONG AND IS IS SOMETHING LIKE SAYING THEY'RE SCREWED.

#145. STRANGE MEN

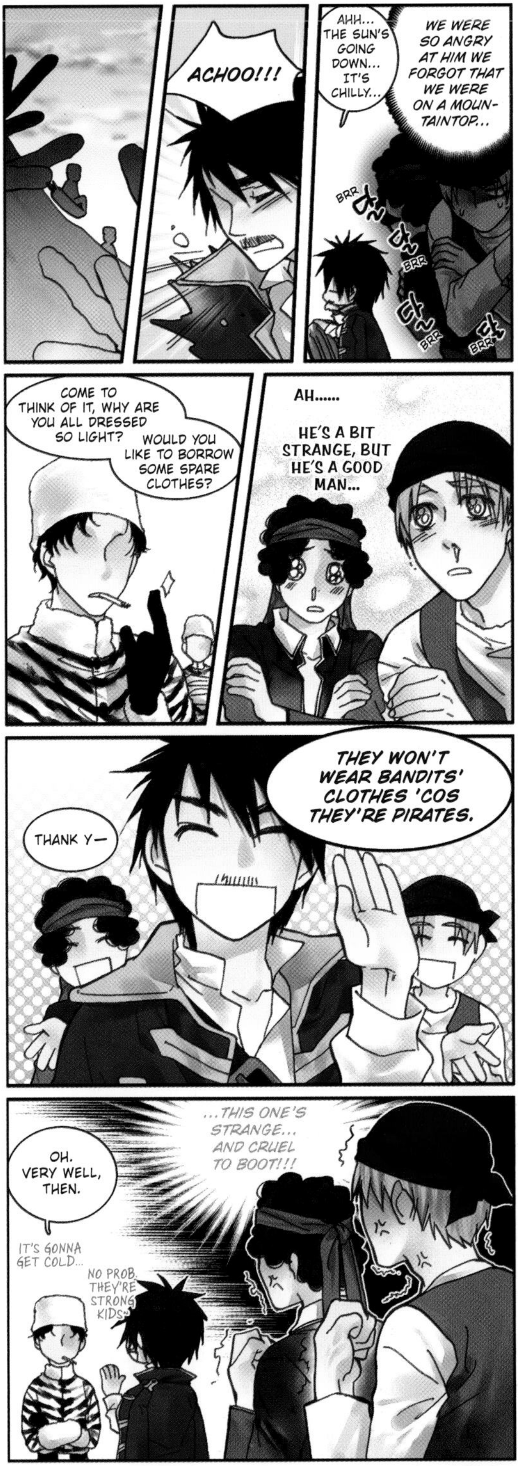
ACHOO!!!
AHH... THE SUN'S GOING DOWN... IT'S CHILLY...
WE WERE SO ANGRY AT HIM WE FORGOT THAT WE WERE ON A MOUNTAINTOP...
BRR
BRR
BRR
BRR
COME TO THINK OF IT, WHY ARE YOU ALL DRESSED SO LIGHT?
WOULD YOU LIKE TO BORROW SOME SPARE CLOTHES?
AH......
HE'S A BIT STRANGE, BUT HE'S A GOOD MAN...
THANK Y—
THEY WON'T WEAR BANDITS' CLOTHES 'COS THEY'RE PIRATES.
OH. VERY WELL, THEN.
...THIS ONE'S STRANGE... AND CRUEL TO BOOT!!!
IT'S GONNA GET COLD...
NO PROB. THEY'RE STRONG KIDS.

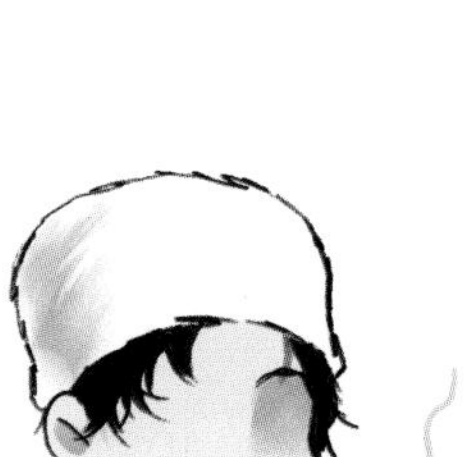

#146. SNOW WHITE

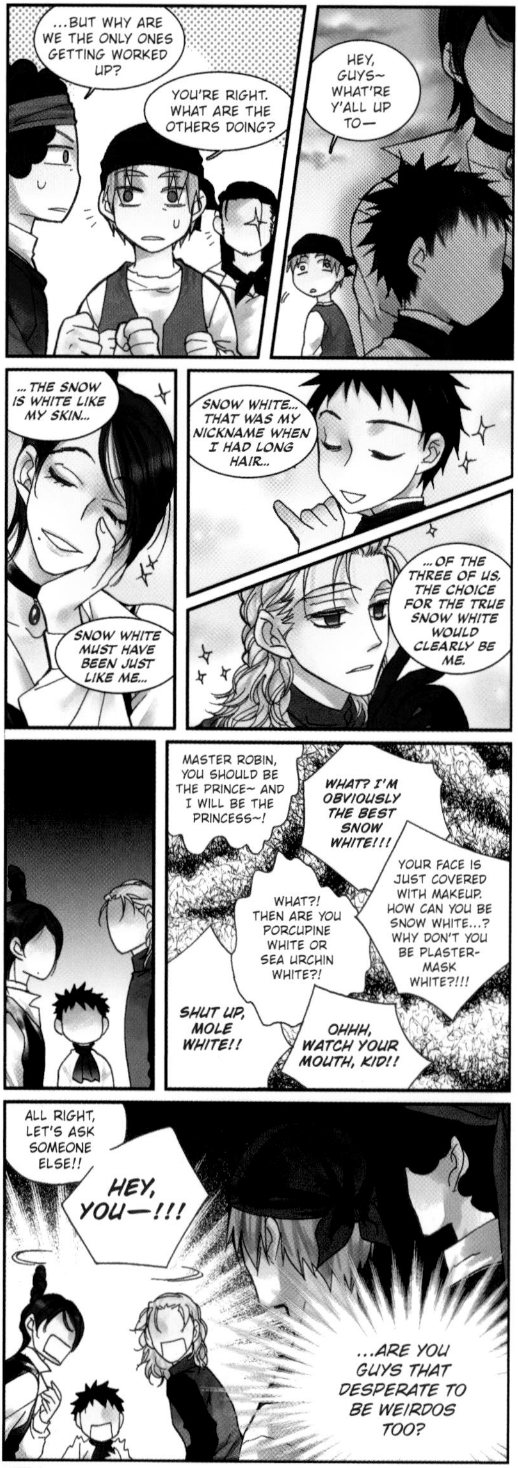
...BUT WHY ARE WE THE ONLY ONES GETTING WORKED UP?
YOU'RE RIGHT. WHAT ARE THE OTHERS DOING?
HEY, GUYS~ WHAT'RE Y'ALL UP TO—
...THE SNOW IS WHITE LIKE MY SKIN...
SNOW WHITE MUST HAVE BEEN JUST LIKE ME...
SNOW WHITE... THAT WAS MY NICKNAME WHEN I HAD LONG HAIR...
...OF THE THREE OF US, THE CHOICE FOR THE TRUE SNOW WHITE WOULD CLEARLY BE ME.
MASTER ROBIN, YOU SHOULD BE THE PRINCE~ AND I WILL BE THE PRINCESS~!
WHAT? I'M OBVIOUSLY THE BEST SNOW WHITE!!!
YOUR FACE IS JUST COVERED WITH MAKEUP. HOW CAN YOU BE SNOW WHITE...? WHY DON'T YOU BE PLASTER-MASK WHITE?!!!
WHAT?! THEN ARE YOU PORCUPINE WHITE OR SEA URCHIN WHITE?!
SHUT UP, MOLE WHITE!!
OHHH, WATCH YOUR MOUTH, KID!!
ALL RIGHT, LET'S ASK SOMEONE ELSE!!
HEY, YOU—!!!
...ARE YOU GUYS THAT DESPERATE TO BE WEIRDOS TOO?

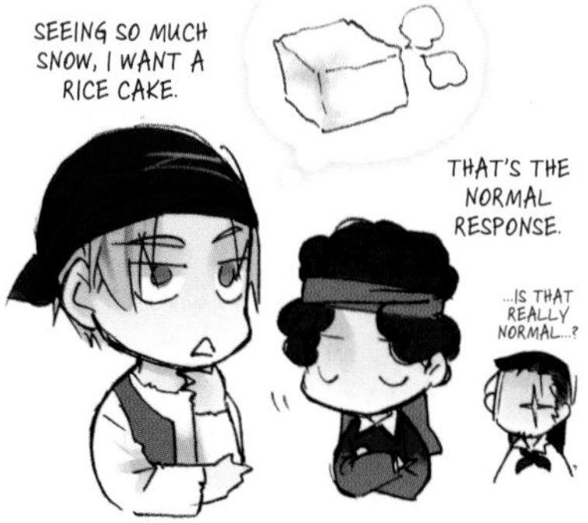
SEEING SO MUCH SNOW, I WANT A RICE CAKE.
THAT'S THE NORMAL RESPONSE.
...IS THAT REALLY NORMAL...?

#147. IT'S THAT BAD

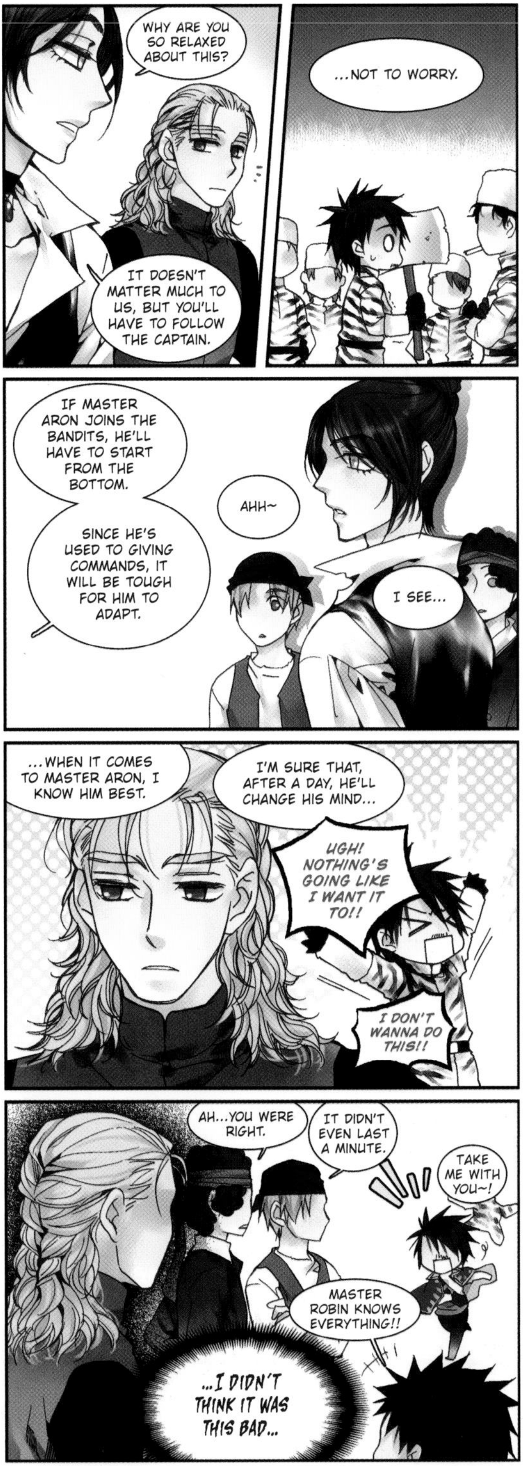
WHY ARE YOU SO RELAXED ABOUT THIS?
IT DOESN'T MATTER MUCH TO US, BUT YOU'LL HAVE TO FOLLOW THE CAPTAIN.
...NOT TO WORRY.
IF MASTER ARON JOINS THE BANDITS, HE'LL HAVE TO START FROM THE BOTTOM.
SINCE HE'S USED TO GIVING COMMANDS, IT WILL BE TOUGH FOR HIM TO ADAPT.
AHH~
I SEE...
...WHEN IT COMES TO MASTER ARON, I KNOW HIM BEST.
I'M SURE THAT, AFTER A DAY, HE'LL CHANGE HIS MIND...
UGH! NOTHING'S GOING LIKE I WANT IT TO!!
I DON'T WANNA DO THIS!!
AH...YOU WERE RIGHT.
IT DIDN'T EVEN LAST A MINUTE.
TAKE ME WITH YOU~!
MASTER ROBIN KNOWS EVERYTHING!!
...I DIDN'T THINK IT WAS THIS BAD...

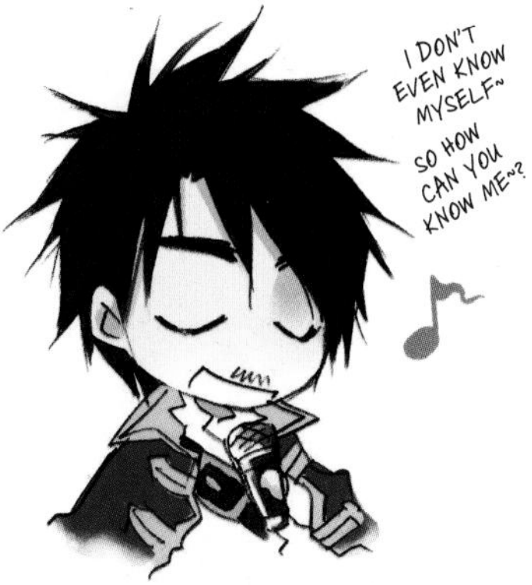
I DON'T EVEN KNOW MYSELF~
SO HOW CAN YOU KNOW ME~?

#148. LOSS OF MOTIVATION

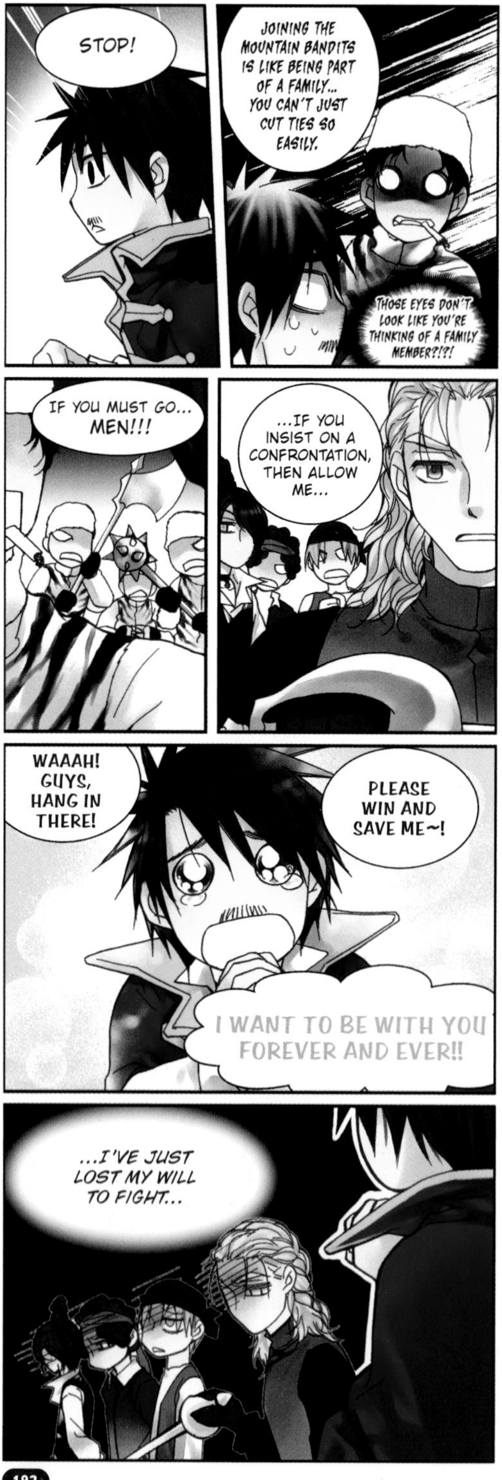
STOP!
JOINING THE MOUNTAIN BANDITS IS LIKE BEING PART OF A FAMILY... YOU CAN'T JUST CUT TIES SO EASILY.
THOSE EYES DON'T LOOK LIKE YOU'RE THINKING OF A FAMILY MEMBER?!?!
IF YOU MUST GO... MEN!!!
...IF YOU INSIST ON A CONFRONTATION, THEN ALLOW ME...
WAAAH! GUYS, HANG IN THERE!
PLEASE WIN AND SAVE ME~!
I WANT TO BE WITH YOU FOREVER AND EVER!!
...I'VE JUST LOST MY WILL TO FIGHT...

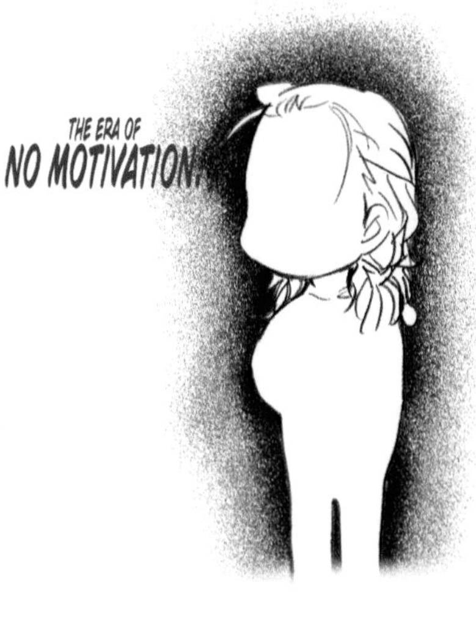
THE ERA OF
NO MOTIVATION!

#149. I'M SORRY, IT'S BECAUSE OF ME

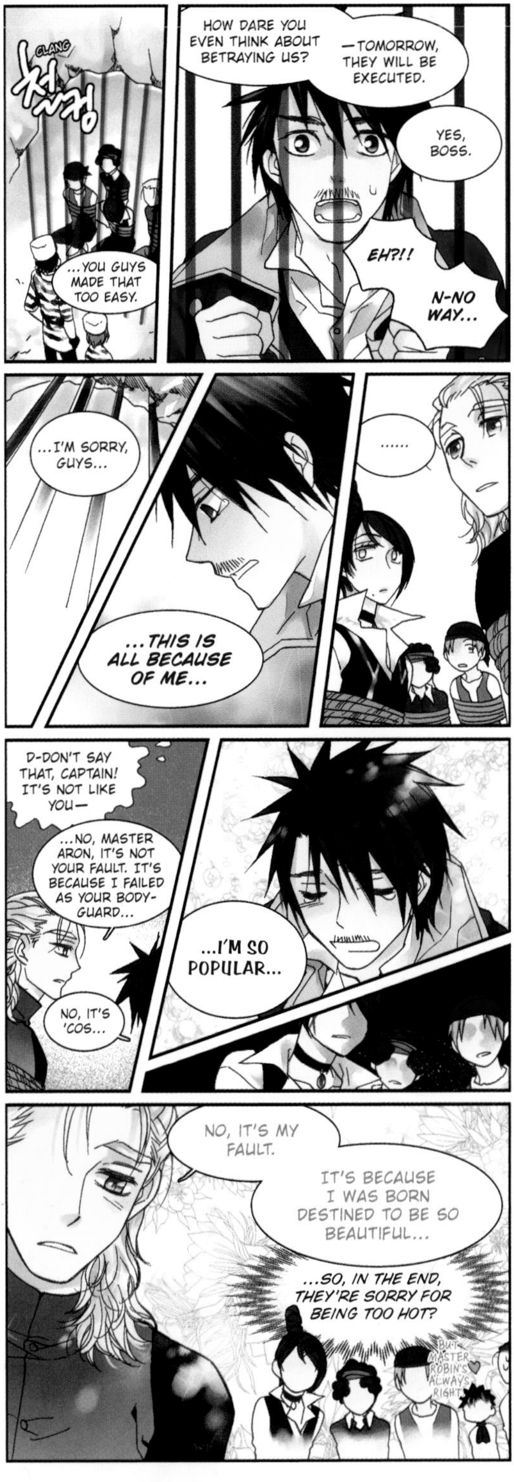
CLANG
...YOU GUYS MADE THAT TOO EASY.
HOW DARE YOU EVEN THINK ABOUT BETRAYING US?
—TOMORROW, THEY WILL BE EXECUTED.
YES, BOSS.
EH?!!
N-NO WAY...
...I'M SORRY, GUYS...
...THIS IS ALL BECAUSE OF ME...
......
D-DON'T SAY THAT, CAPTAIN! IT'S NOT LIKE YOU—
...NO, MASTER ARON, IT'S NOT YOUR FAULT. IT'S BECAUSE I FAILED AS YOUR BODY-GUARD...
...I'M SO POPULAR...
NO, IT'S 'COS...
NO, IT'S MY FAULT.
IT'S BECAUSE I WAS BORN DESTINED TO BE SO BEAUTIFUL...
...SO, IN THE END, THEY'RE SORRY FOR BEING TOO HOT?
BUT MASTER ROBIN'S ALWAYS RIGHT

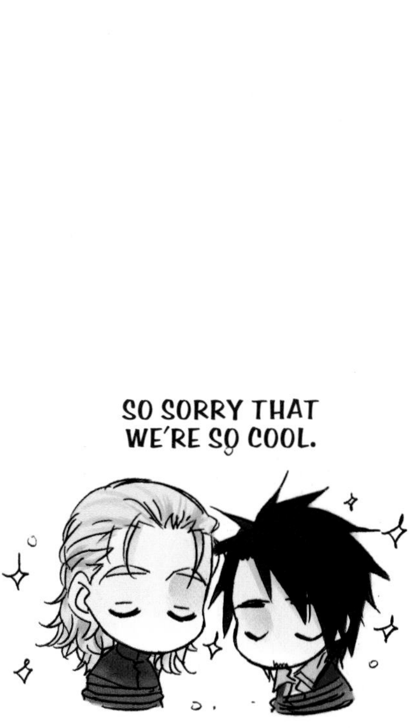
SO SORRY THAT WE'RE SO COOL.

#150. PROPHECY

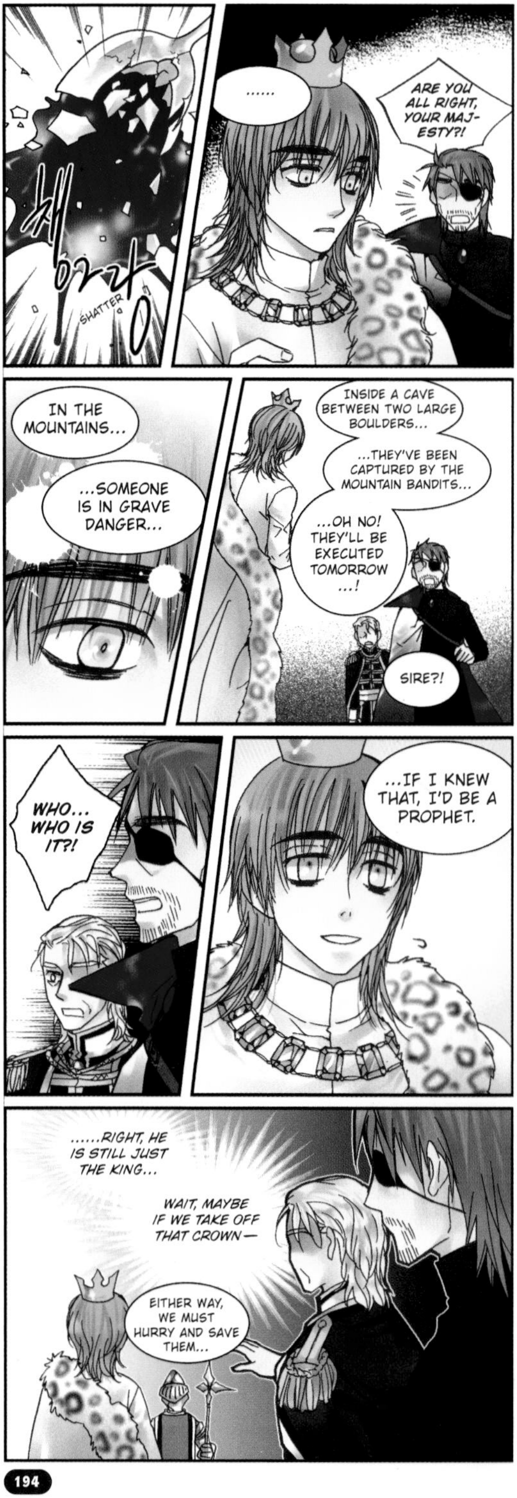
SHATTER
......
ARE YOU ALL RIGHT, YOUR MAJ-ESTY?!
IN THE MOUNTAINS...
...SOMEONE IS IN GRAVE DANGER...
INSIDE A CAVE BETWEEN TWO LARGE BOULDERS...
...THEY'VE BEEN CAPTURED BY THE MOUNTAIN BANDITS...
...OH NO! THEY'LL BE EXECUTED TOMORROW ...!
SIRE?!
WHO... WHO IS IT?!
...IF I KNEW THAT, I'D BE A PROPHET.
......RIGHT, HE IS STILL JUST THE KING...
WAIT, MAYBE IF WE TAKE OFF THAT CROWN—
EITHER WAY, WE MUST HURRY AND SAVE THEM...

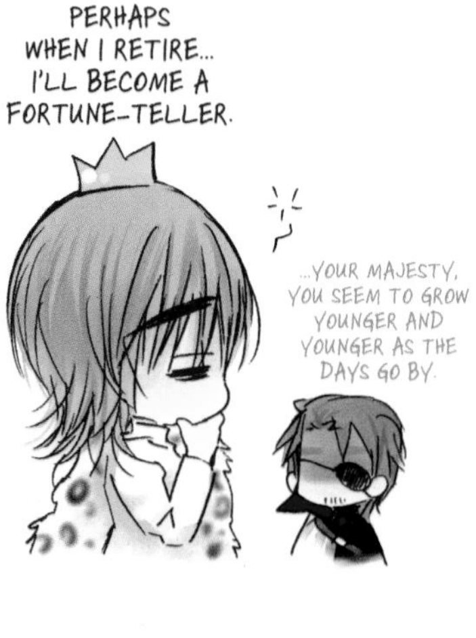
PERHAPS WHEN I RETIRE... I'LL BECOME A FORTUNE-TELLER.
...YOUR MAJESTY, YOU SEEM TO GROW YOUNGER AND YOUNGER AS THE DAYS GO BY.

#151. WE WILL SAVE YOU NOW

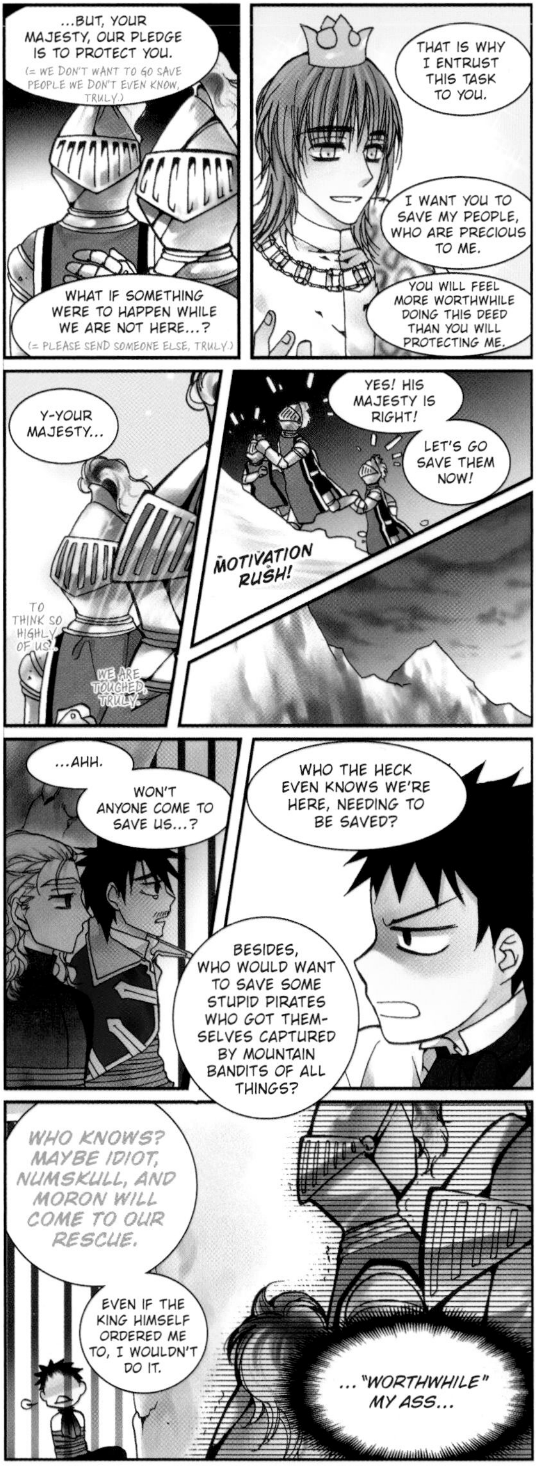
...BUT, YOUR MAJESTY, OUR PLEDGE IS TO PROTECT YOU.
(= WE DON'T WANT TO GO SAVE PEOPLE WE DON'T EVEN KNOW, TRULY.)
WHAT IF SOMETHING WERE TO HAPPEN WHILE WE ARE NOT HERE...?
(= PLEASE SEND SOMEONE ELSE, TRULY.)
THAT IS WHY I ENTRUST THIS TASK TO YOU.
I WANT YOU TO SAVE MY PEOPLE, WHO ARE PRECIOUS TO ME.
YOU WILL FEEL MORE WORTHWHILE DOING THIS DEED THAN YOU WILL PROTECTING ME.
Y-YOUR MAJESTY...
TO THINK SO HIGHLY OF US...
WE ARE TOUCHED, TRULY.
YES! HIS MAJESTY IS RIGHT!
LET'S GO SAVE THEM NOW!
MOTIVATION RUSH!
...AHH.
WON'T ANYONE COME TO SAVE US...?
WHO THE HECK EVEN KNOWS WE'RE HERE, NEEDING TO BE SAVED?
BESIDES, WHO WOULD WANT TO SAVE SOME STUPID PIRATES WHO GOT THEMSELVES CAPTURED BY MOUNTAIN BANDITS OF ALL THINGS?
WHO KNOWS? MAYBE IDIOT, NUMSKULL, AND MORON WILL COME TO OUR RESCUE.
EVEN IF THE KING HIMSELF ORDERED ME TO, I WOULDN'T DO IT.
... "WORTHWHILE" MY ASS...

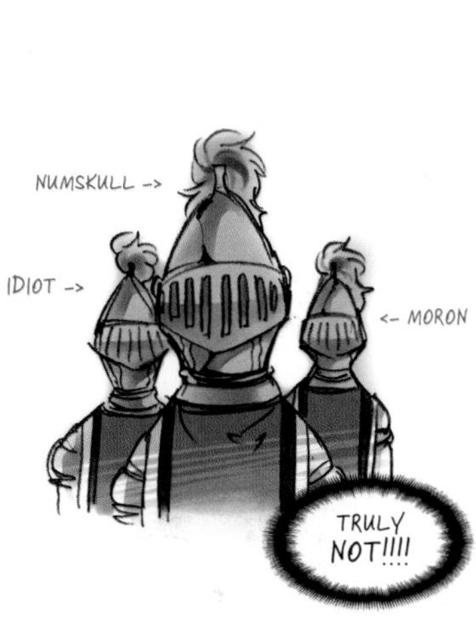
NUMSKULL ->
IDIOT ->
<- MORON
TRULY NOT!!!!

#152. I'LL PROTECT YOU

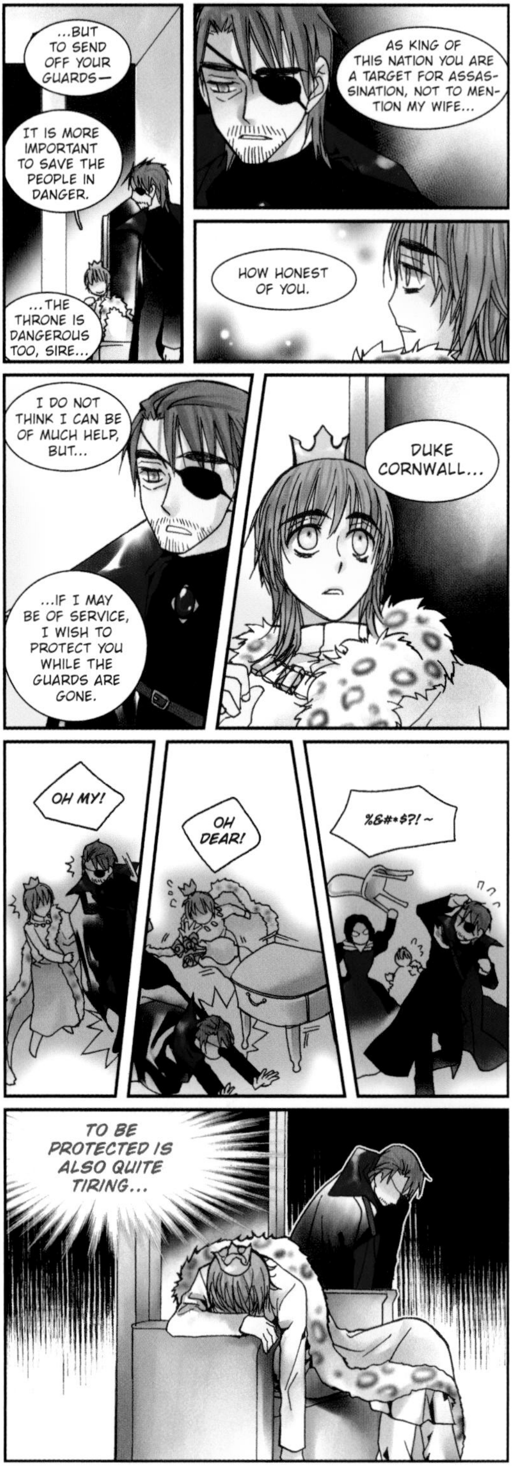

...BUT TO SEND OFF YOUR GUARDS—
AS KING OF THIS NATION YOU ARE A TARGET FOR ASSASSINATION, NOT TO MENTION MY WIFE...
IT IS MORE IMPORTANT TO SAVE THE PEOPLE IN DANGER.
...THE THRONE IS DANGEROUS TOO, SIRE...
HOW HONEST OF YOU.
I DO NOT THINK I CAN BE OF MUCH HELP, BUT...
...IF I MAY BE OF SERVICE, I WISH TO PROTECT YOU WHILE THE GUARDS ARE GONE.
DUKE CORNWALL...
OH MY!
OH DEAR!
%&#*$?! ~
TO BE PROTECTED IS ALSO QUITE TIRING...

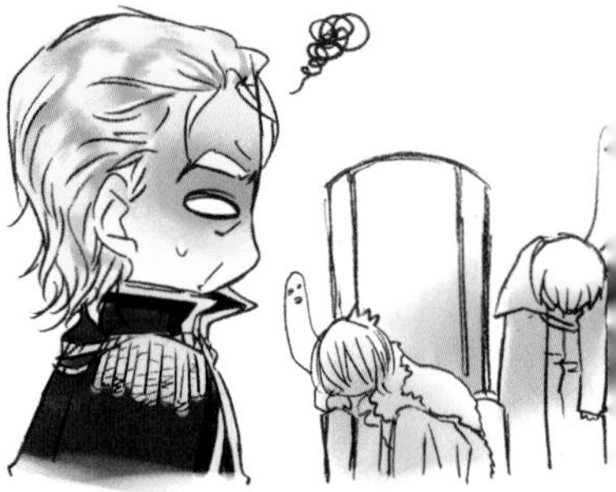

#153. SUPERPOWERS

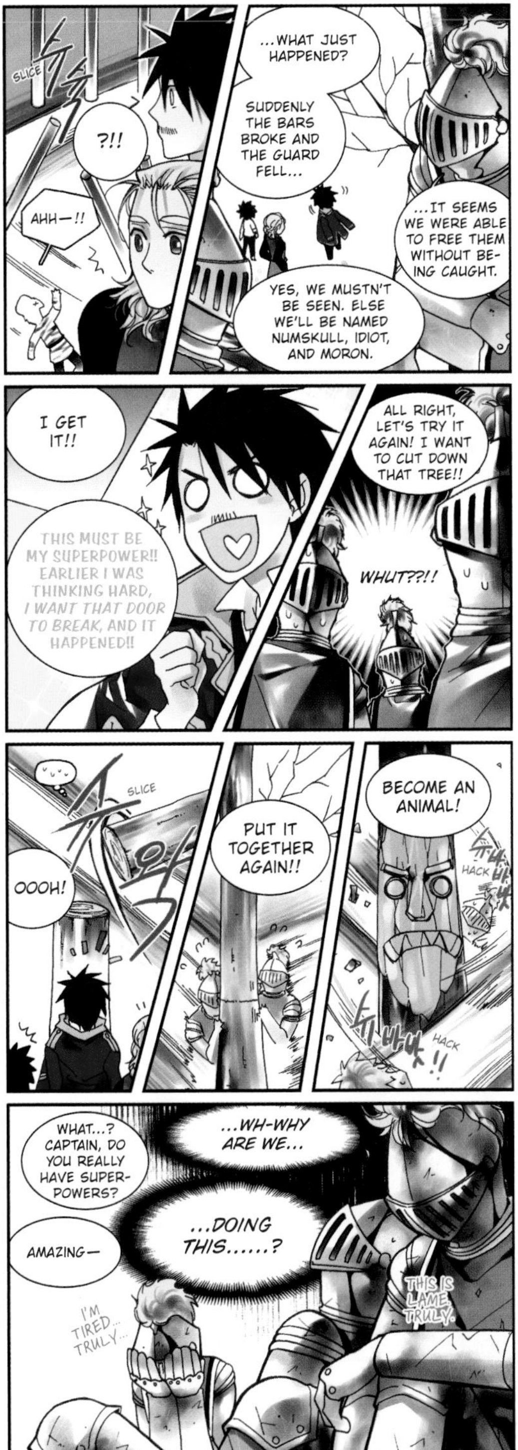
SLICE
?!!
AHH—!!
...WHAT JUST HAPPENED?
SUDDENLY THE BARS BROKE AND THE GUARD FELL...
...IT SEEMS WE WERE ABLE TO FREE THEM WITHOUT BEING CAUGHT.
YES, WE MUSTN'T BE SEEN. ELSE WE'LL BE NAMED NUMSKULL, IDIOT, AND MORON.
I GET IT!!
THIS MUST BE MY SUPERPOWER!! EARLIER I WAS THINKING HARD, I WANT THAT DOOR TO BREAK, AND IT HAPPENED!!
ALL RIGHT, LET'S TRY IT AGAIN! I WANT TO CUT DOWN THAT TREE!!
WHUT??!!
SLICE
OOOH!
PUT IT TOGETHER AGAIN!!
BECOME AN ANIMAL!
HACK
HACK
WHAT...? CAPTAIN, DO YOU REALLY HAVE SUPERPOWERS?
AMAZING—
...WH-WHY ARE WE...
...DOING THIS......?
THIS IS LAME. TRULY.
I'M TIRED... TRULY...

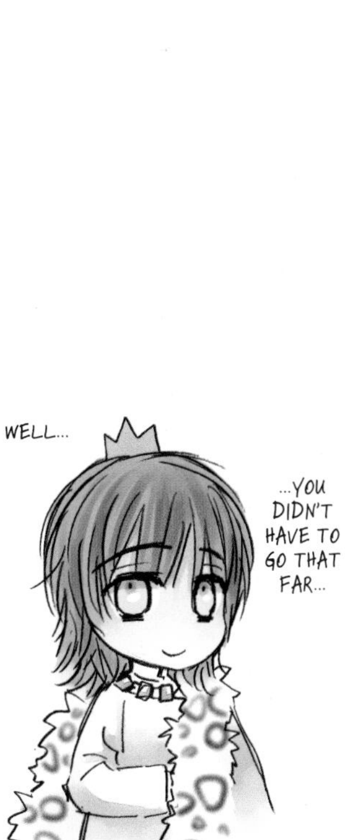
WELL...
...YOU DIDN'T HAVE TO GO THAT FAR...

#154. BREAD SOAKED IN TEARS

MAN, AND I THOUGHT I HAD SUPER-POWERS.

I BELIEVE I CAN FLY~!

NOW IT'S IMPOS-SIBLE!

BOO~

...PERHAPS IT WAS THE FAIRIES OF THE MOUNTAIN?

AH~ I SEE! THE FAIRIES OF THE MOUNTAIN!

THANK YOU, FAIRIES~!!

THEY CALLED US FAIRIES~.

AREN'T THEY KINDA CUTE?

AH— I'M HUNGRY. LET'S REST AND HAVE SOMETHING TO EAT!

NOW THAT HE MENTIONS IT, WE'RE HUN-GRY TOO...

IT'S BECAUSE HE MADE US DO ALL THAT EXTRA WORK...

SHOULD WE TAKE SOME OF THEIR FOOD?

YES, WE HAVE NO CHOICE.

LET'S EAT...

WE ARE THE FAIRIES WHO SAVED YOU. WE ARE TAKING JUST THREE PIECES OF BREAD BECAUSE WE ARE HUNGRY.

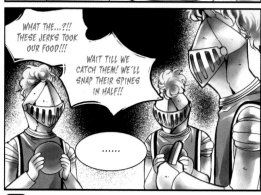

WHAT THE...?!! THESE JERKS TOOK OUR FOOD!!!

WAIT TILL WE CATCH THEM! WE'LL SNAP THEIR SPINES IN HALF!!

......

DON'T COMPLAIN ABOUT LIFE UNTIL YOU'VE HAD TO EAT TEAR-SOAKED BREAD.

#155. FOR HIS MAJESTY

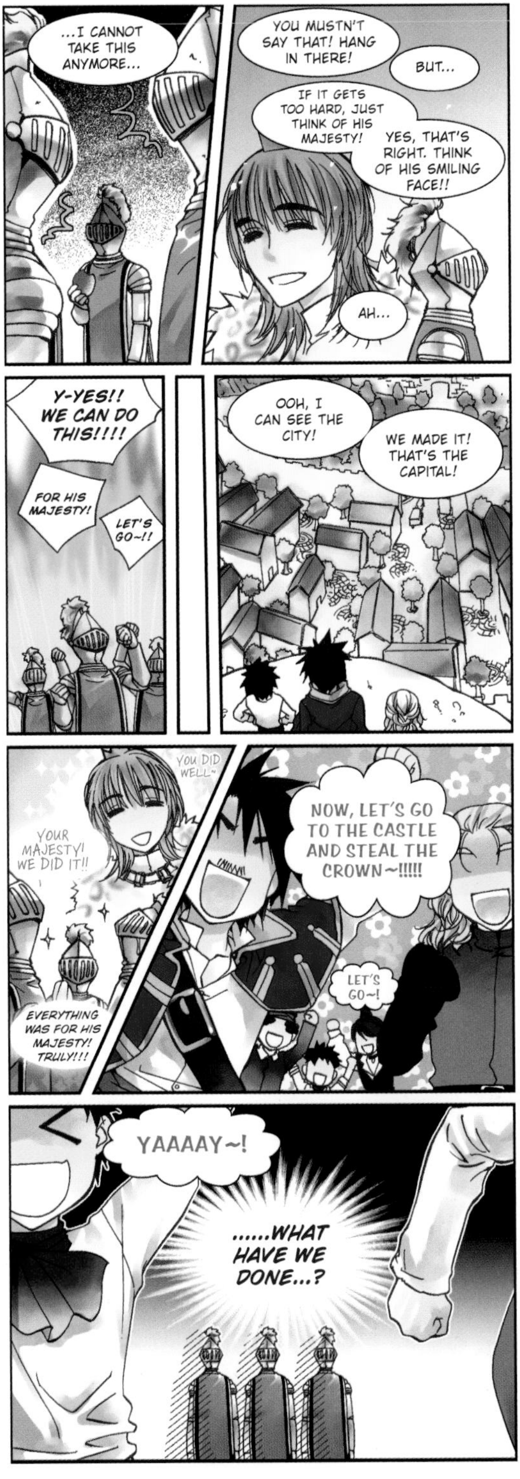
...I CANNOT TAKE THIS ANYMORE...
YOU MUSTN'T SAY THAT! HANG IN THERE!
BUT...
IF IT GETS TOO HARD, JUST THINK OF HIS MAJESTY!
YES, THAT'S RIGHT. THINK OF HIS SMILING FACE!!
AH...
Y-YES!! WE CAN DO THIS!!!!
FOR HIS MAJESTY!
LET'S GO~!!
OOH, I CAN SEE THE CITY!
WE MADE IT! THAT'S THE CAPITAL!
YOU DID WELL~
YOUR MAJESTY! WE DID IT!!
NOW, LET'S GO TO THE CASTLE AND STEAL THE CROWN~!!!!!
LET'S GO~!
EVERYTHING WAS FOR HIS MAJESTY! TRULY!!!
YAAAAY~!
......WHAT HAVE WE DONE...?

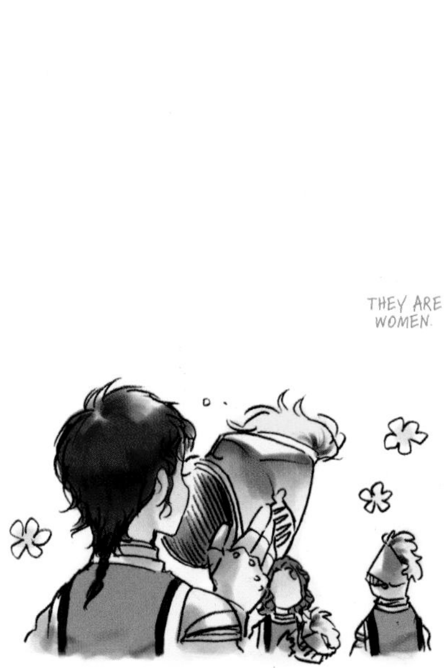
THEY ARE WOMEN.

#156. HIS MAJESTY HAS BEEN KIDNAPPED

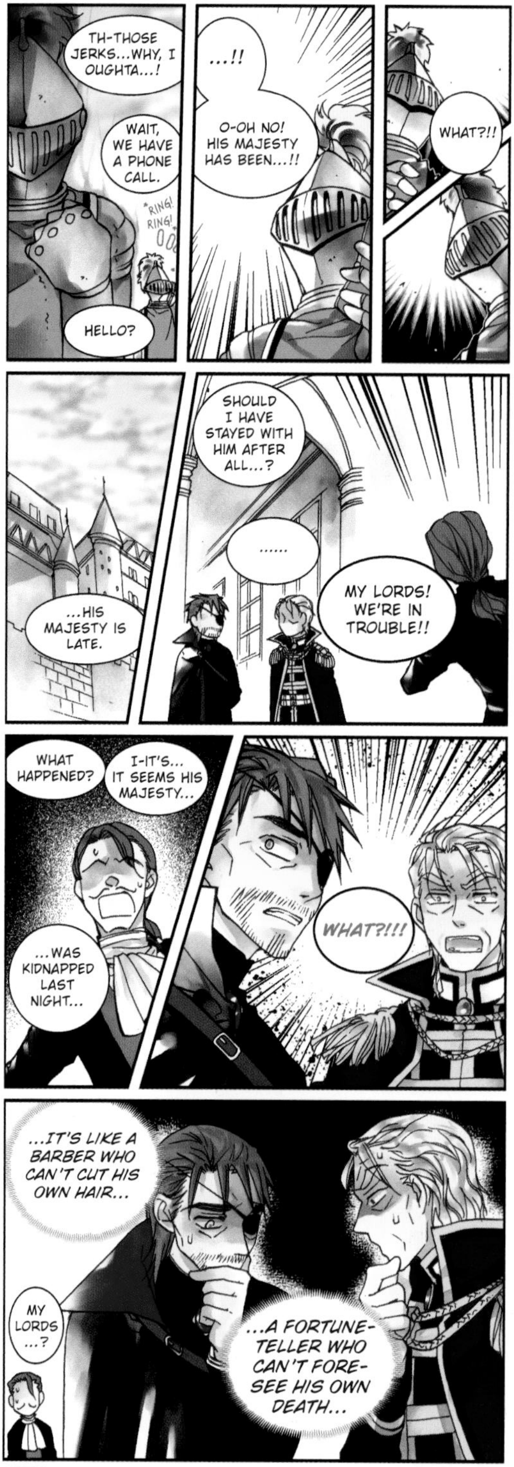
TH-THOSE JERKS...WHY, I OUGHTA...!
WAIT, WE HAVE A PHONE CALL.
RING! RING!
HELLO?
...!!
O-OH NO! HIS MAJESTY HAS BEEN...!!
WHAT?!!
SHOULD I HAVE STAYED WITH HIM AFTER ALL...?
...HIS MAJESTY IS LATE.
......
MY LORDS! WE'RE IN TROUBLE!!
WHAT HAPPENED?
I-IT'S... IT SEEMS HIS MAJESTY...
...WAS KIDNAPPED LAST NIGHT...
WHAT?!!!
...IT'S LIKE A BARBER WHO CAN'T CUT HIS OWN HAIR...
MY LORDS...?
...A FORTUNE-TELLER WHO CAN'T FORE-SEE HIS OWN DEATH...

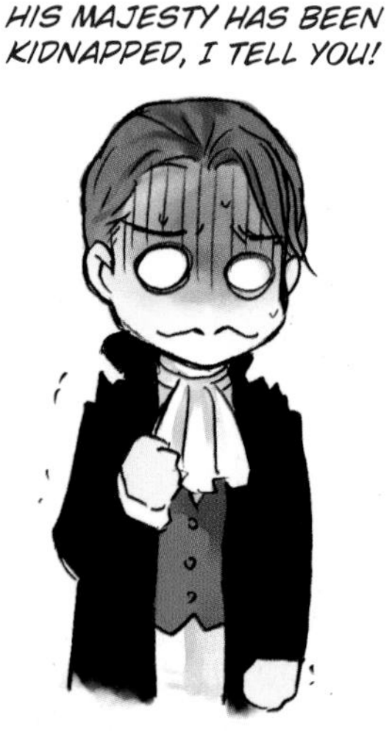
HIS MAJESTY HAS BEEN KIDNAPPED, I TELL YOU!

#157. YOU DESERVED THAT

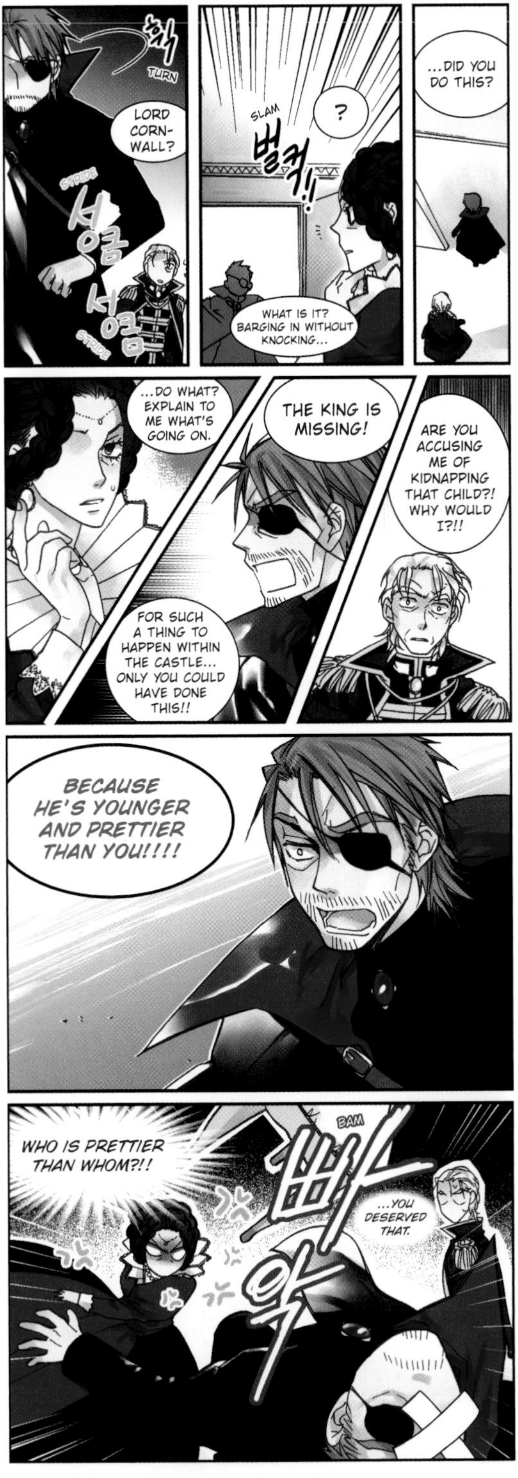

홱
TURN
LORD CORN-WALL?
STRIDE
성큼
성큼
STRIDE
SLAM
벌컥!!
?
WHAT IS IT? BARGING IN WITHOUT KNOCKING...
...DID YOU DO THIS?
...DO WHAT? EXPLAIN TO ME WHAT'S GOING ON.
THE KING IS MISSING!
FOR SUCH A THING TO HAPPEN WITHIN THE CASTLE... ONLY YOU COULD HAVE DONE THIS!!
ARE YOU ACCUSING ME OF KIDNAPPING THAT CHILD?! WHY WOULD I?!!
BECAUSE HE'S YOUNGER AND PRETTIER THAN YOU!!!!
WHO IS PRETTIER THAN WHOM?!!
BAM
빠악
...YOU DESERVED THAT.

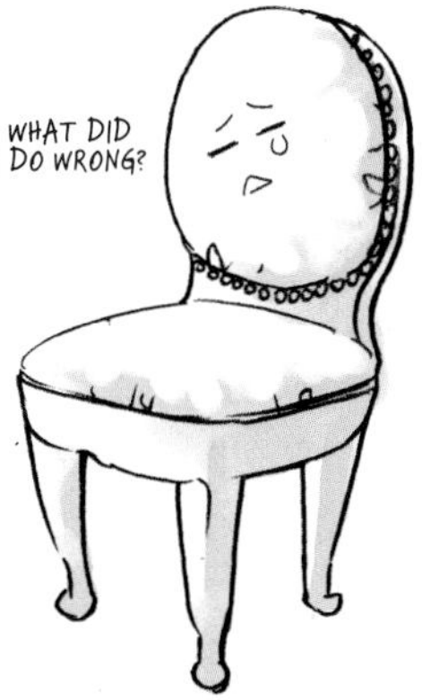

WHAT DID I DO WRONG?

#158. TEARS

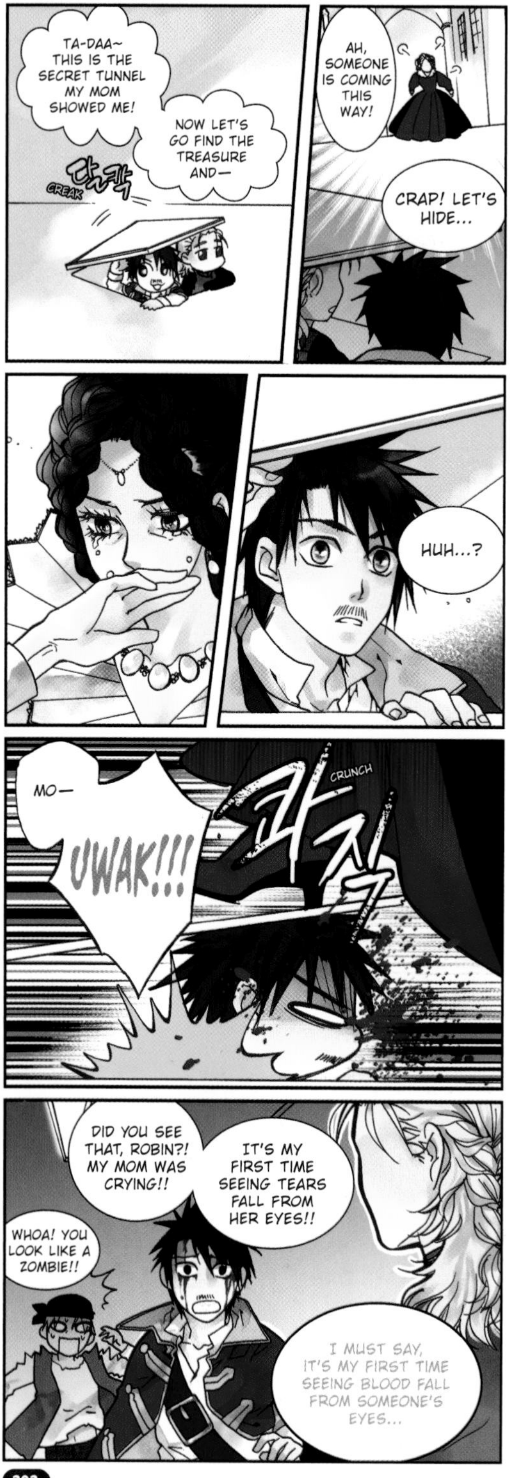

TA-DAA~ THIS IS THE SECRET TUNNEL MY MOM SHOWED ME!
NOW LET'S GO FIND THE TREASURE AND—
CREAK
AH, SOMEONE IS COMING THIS WAY!
CRAP! LET'S HIDE...
HUH...?
MO—
UWAK!!!
CRUNCH
DID YOU SEE THAT, ROBIN?! MY MOM WAS CRYING!!
IT'S MY FIRST TIME SEEING TEARS FALL FROM HER EYES!!
WHOA! YOU LOOK LIKE A ZOMBIE!!
I MUST SAY, IT'S MY FIRST TIME SEEING BLOOD FALL FROM SOMEONE'S EYES...

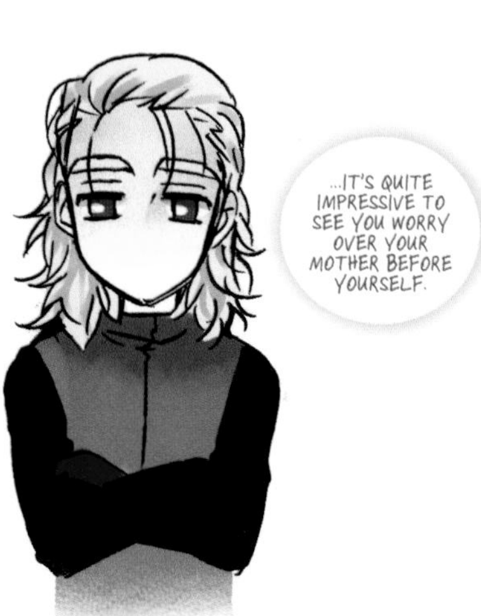

...IT'S QUITE IMPRESSIVE TO SEE YOU WORRY OVER YOUR MOTHER BEFORE YOURSELF.

#159. A WEAK MAN

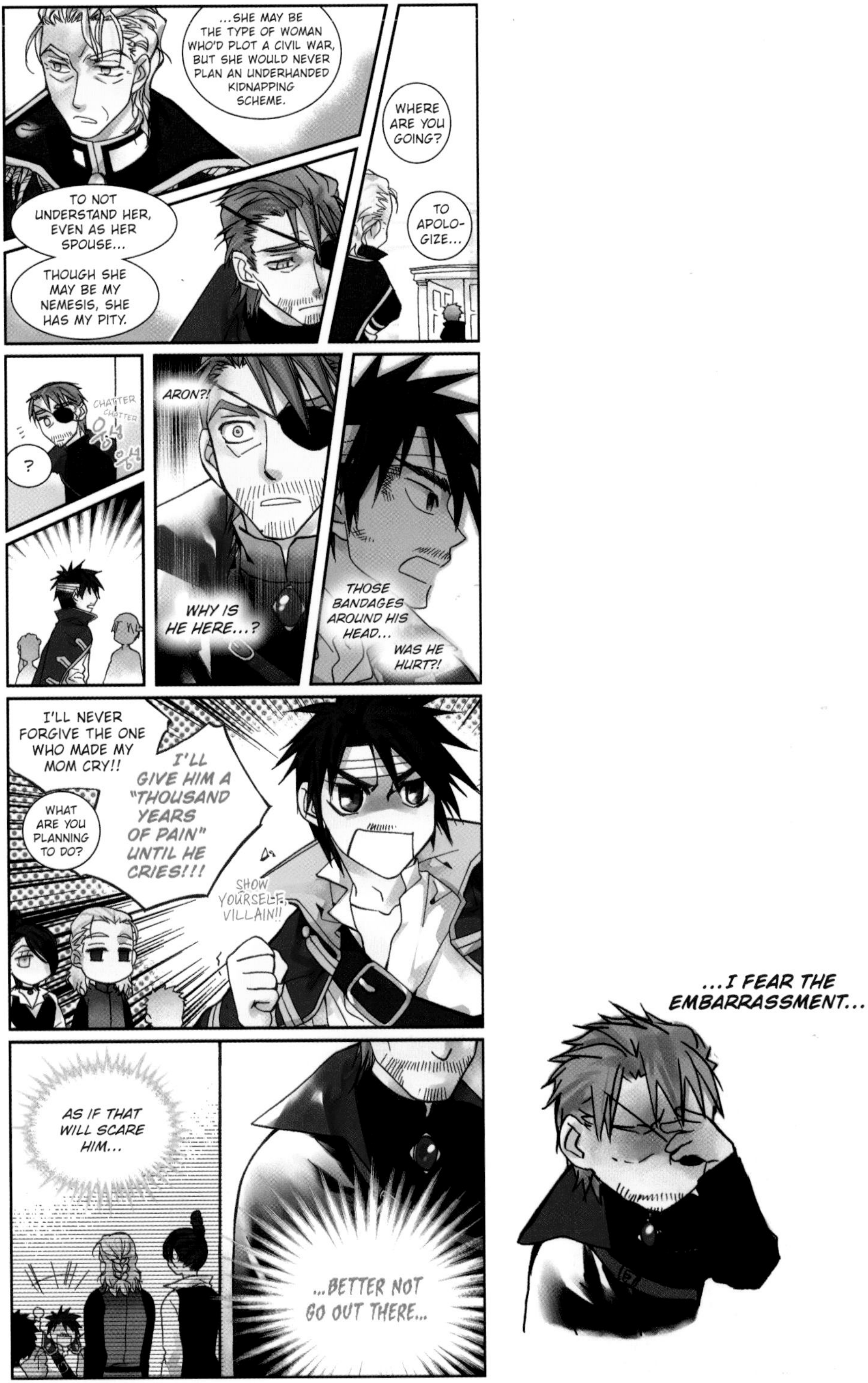

...SHE MAY BE THE TYPE OF WOMAN WHO'D PLOT A CIVIL WAR, BUT SHE WOULD NEVER PLAN AN UNDERHANDED KIDNAPPING SCHEME.
TO NOT UNDERSTAND HER, EVEN AS HER SPOUSE...
THOUGH SHE MAY BE MY NEMESIS, SHE HAS MY PITY.
WHERE ARE YOU GOING?
TO APOLO-GIZE...
CHATTER CHATTER
?
ARON?!
WHY IS HE HERE...?
THOSE BANDAGES AROUND HIS HEAD...
WAS HE HURT?!
I'LL NEVER FORGIVE THE ONE WHO MADE MY MOM CRY!!
I'LL GIVE HIM A "THOUSAND YEARS OF PAIN" UNTIL HE CRIES!!!
WHAT ARE YOU PLANNING TO DO?
SHOW YOURSELF, VILLAIN!!
AS IF THAT WILL SCARE HIM...
...BETTER NOT GO OUT THERE...
...I FEAR THE EMBARRASSMENT...

#160. WOMEN ARE FROM VENUS

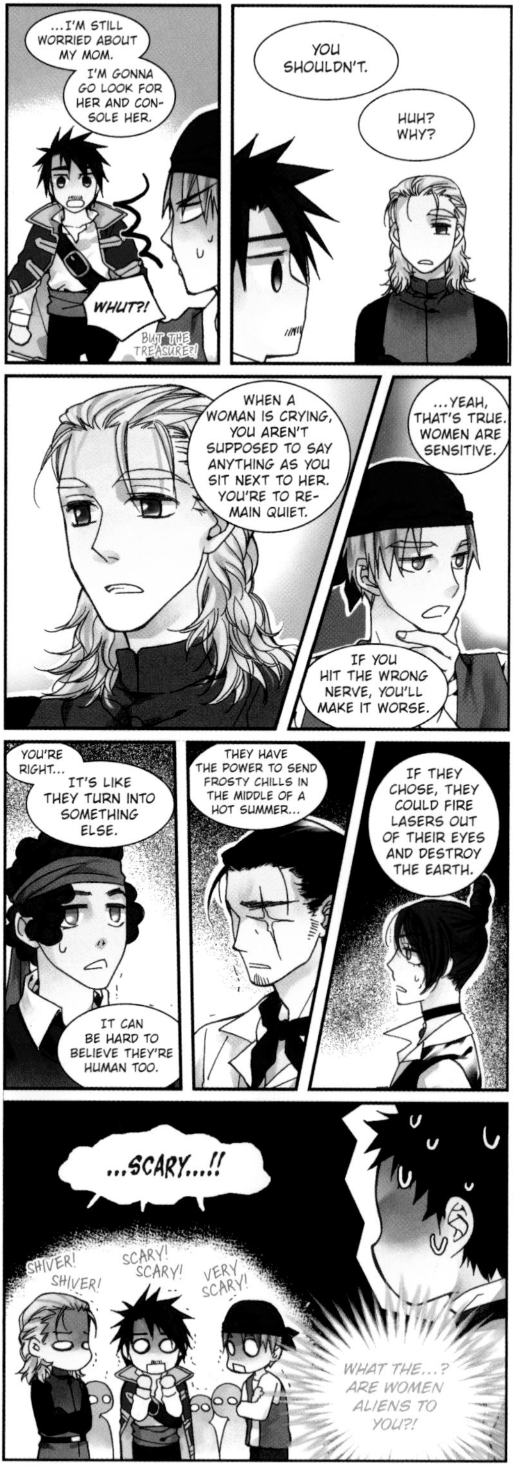
...I'M STILL WORRIED ABOUT MY MOM.
I'M GONNA GO LOOK FOR HER AND CON-SOLE HER.
WHUT?!
BUT THE TREASURE?!
YOU SHOULDN'T.
HUH? WHY?
WHEN A WOMAN IS CRYING, YOU AREN'T SUPPOSED TO SAY ANYTHING AS YOU SIT NEXT TO HER. YOU'RE TO RE-MAIN QUIET.
...YEAH, THAT'S TRUE. WOMEN ARE SENSITIVE.
IF YOU HIT THE WRONG NERVE, YOU'LL MAKE IT WORSE.
YOU'RE RIGHT...
IT'S LIKE THEY TURN INTO SOMETHING ELSE.
IT CAN BE HARD TO BELIEVE THEY'RE HUMAN TOO.
THEY HAVE THE POWER TO SEND FROSTY CHILLS IN THE MIDDLE OF A HOT SUMMER...
IF THEY CHOSE, THEY COULD FIRE LASERS OUT OF THEIR EYES AND DESTROY THE EARTH.
...SCARY...!!
SHIVER! SHIVER!
SCARY! SCARY!
VERY SCARY!
WHAT THE...? ARE WOMEN ALIENS TO YOU?!

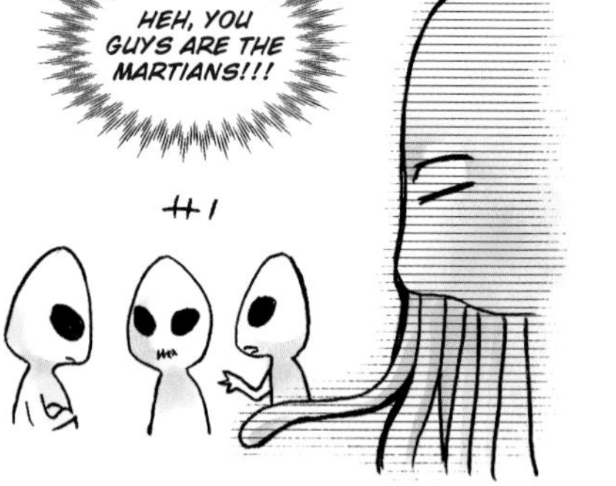
HEH, YOU GUYS ARE THE MARTIANS!!!

#161. UNUSUAL REACTION

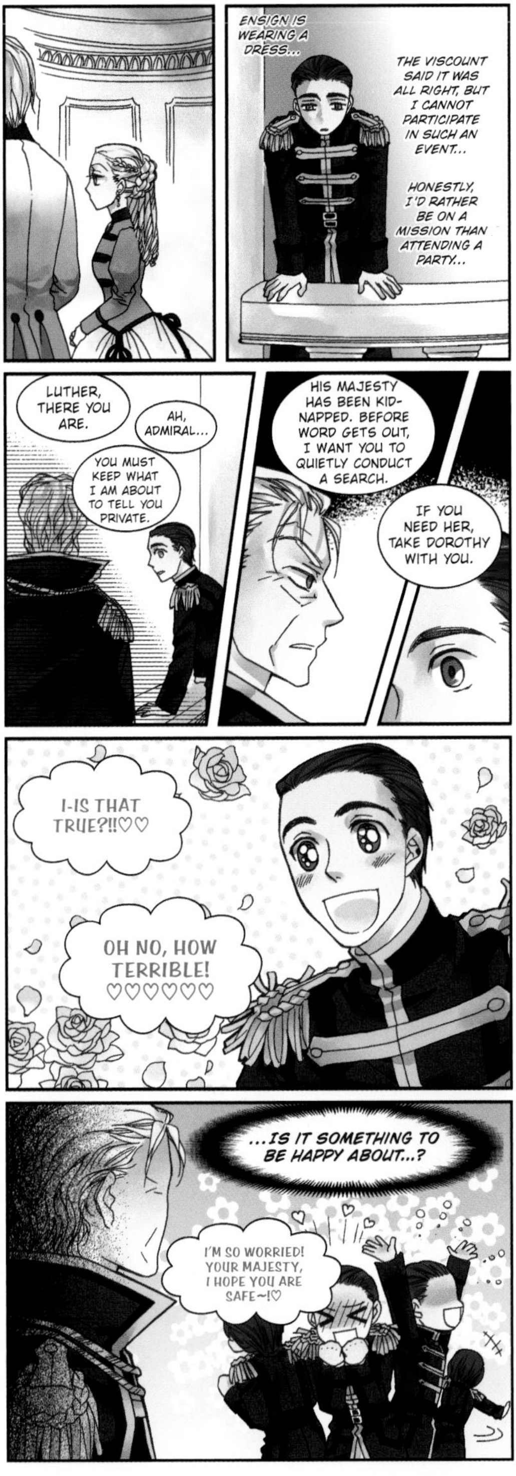
ENSIGN IS WEARING A DRESS...
THE VISCOUNT SAID IT WAS ALL RIGHT, BUT I CANNOT PARTICIPATE IN SUCH AN EVENT...
HONESTLY, I'D RATHER BE ON A MISSION THAN ATTENDING A PARTY...
LUTHER, THERE YOU ARE.
AH, ADMIRAL...
YOU MUST KEEP WHAT I AM ABOUT TO TELL YOU PRIVATE.
HIS MAJESTY HAS BEEN KID-NAPPED. BEFORE WORD GETS OUT, I WANT YOU TO QUIETLY CONDUCT A SEARCH.
IF YOU NEED HER, TAKE DOROTHY WITH YOU.
I-IS THAT TRUE?!!♡♡
OH NO, HOW TERRIBLE! ♡♡♡♡♡♡
...IS IT SOMETHING TO BE HAPPY ABOUT...?
I'M SO WORRIED! YOUR MAJESTY, I HOPE YOU ARE SAFE~!♡

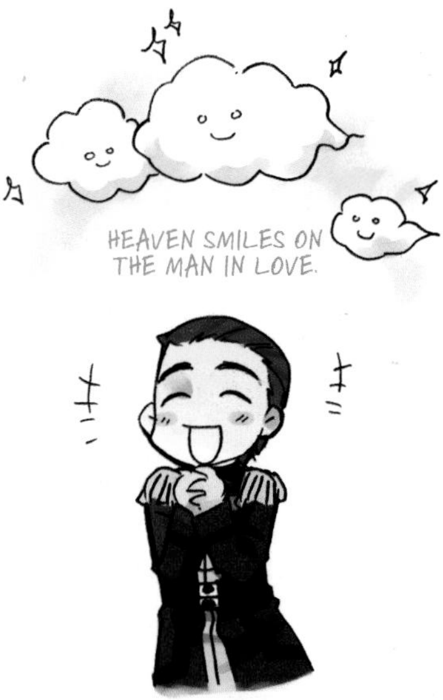
HEAVEN SMILES ON THE MAN IN LOVE.

#162. BLIND FOOL

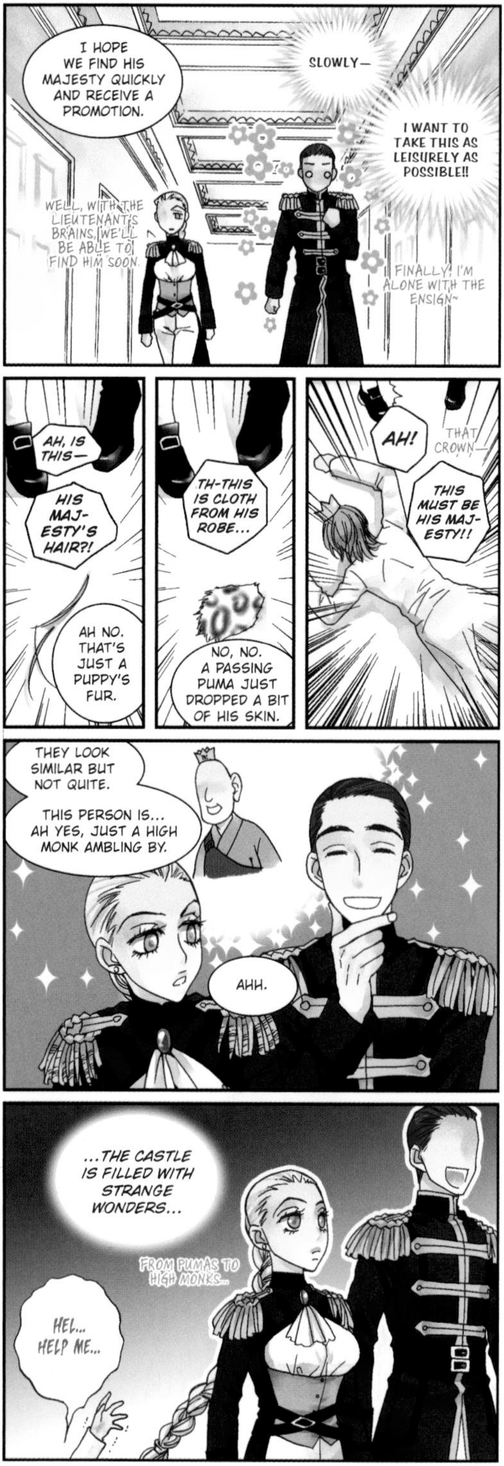
I HOPE WE FIND HIS MAJESTY QUICKLY AND RECEIVE A PROMOTION.
SLOWLY—
I WANT TO TAKE THIS AS LEISURELY AS POSSIBLE!!
WELL, WITH THE LIEUTENANT'S BRAINS, WE'LL BE ABLE TO FIND HIM SOON.
FINALLY! I'M ALONE WITH THE ENSIGN~
AH, IS THIS—
HIS MAJ-ESTY'S HAIR?!
AH NO. THAT'S JUST A PUPPY'S FUR.
TH-THIS IS CLOTH FROM HIS ROBE...
NO, NO. A PASSING PUMA JUST DROPPED A BIT OF HIS SKIN.
AH!
THAT CROWN—
THIS MUST BE HIS MAJ-ESTY!!
THEY LOOK SIMILAR BUT NOT QUITE.
THIS PERSON IS... AH YES, JUST A HIGH MONK AMBLING BY.
AHH.
...THE CASTLE IS FILLED WITH STRANGE WONDERS...
FROM PUMAS TO HIGH MONKS...
HEL... HELP ME...

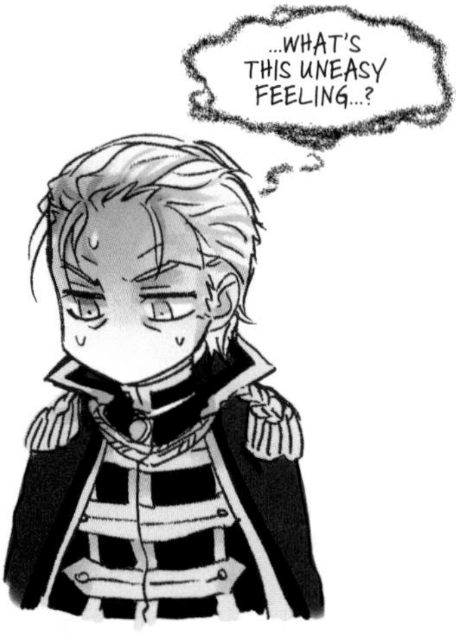
...WHAT'S THIS UNEASY FEELING...?

#163. GOLD AND STONE 1

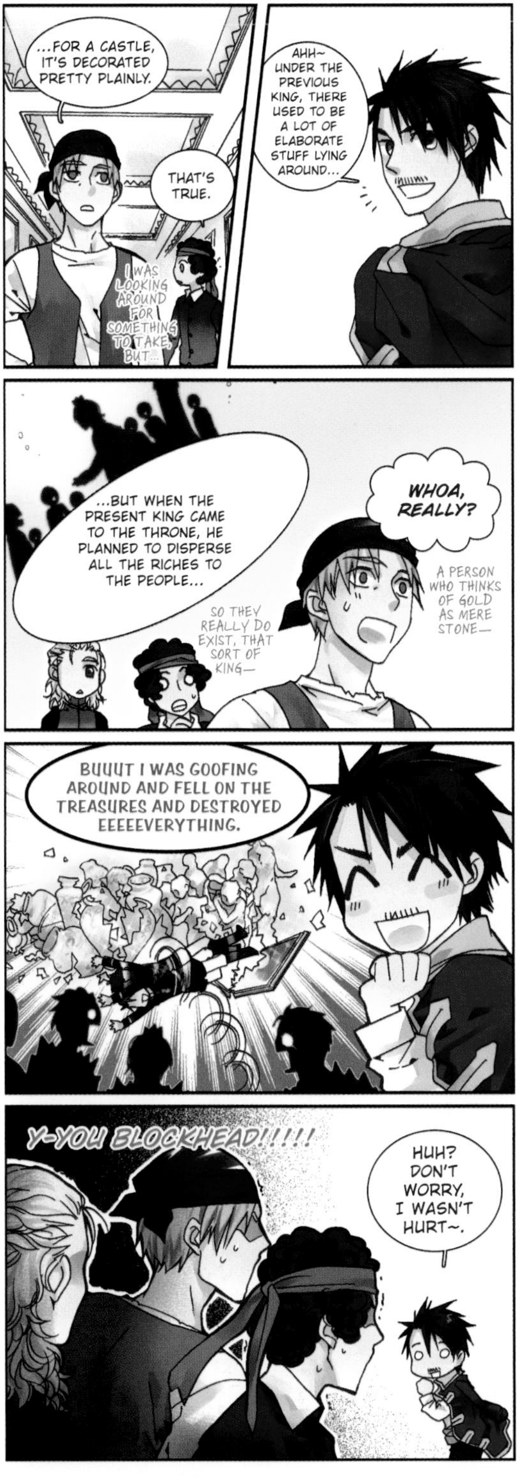
...FOR A CASTLE, IT'S DECORATED PRETTY PLAINLY.
THAT'S TRUE.
I WAS LOOKING AROUND FOR SOMETHING TO TAKE, BUT...
AHH~ UNDER THE PREVIOUS KING, THERE USED TO BE A LOT OF ELABORATE STUFF LYING AROUND...
...BUT WHEN THE PRESENT KING CAME TO THE THRONE, HE PLANNED TO DISPERSE ALL THE RICHES TO THE PEOPLE...
WHOA, REALLY?
A PERSON WHO THINKS OF GOLD AS MERE STONE—
SO THEY REALLY DO EXIST, THAT SORT OF KING—
BUUUT I WAS GOOFING AROUND AND FELL ON THE TREASURES AND DESTROYED EEEEEVERYTHING.
Y-YOU BLOCKHEAD!!!!!
HUH? DON'T WORRY, I WASN'T HURT~.

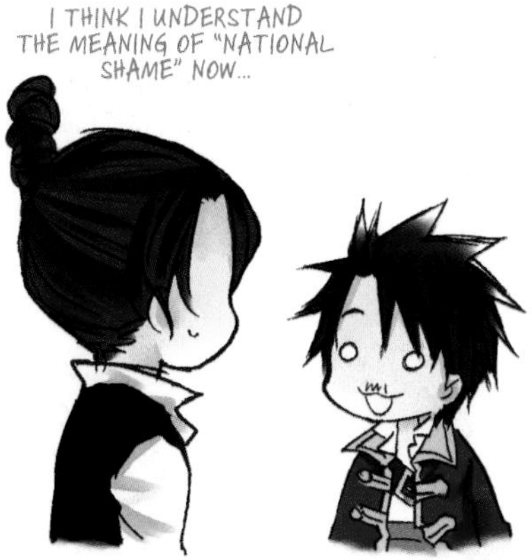
I THINK I UNDERSTAND THE MEANING OF "NATIONAL SHAME" NOW...

#164. GOLD AND STONE 2

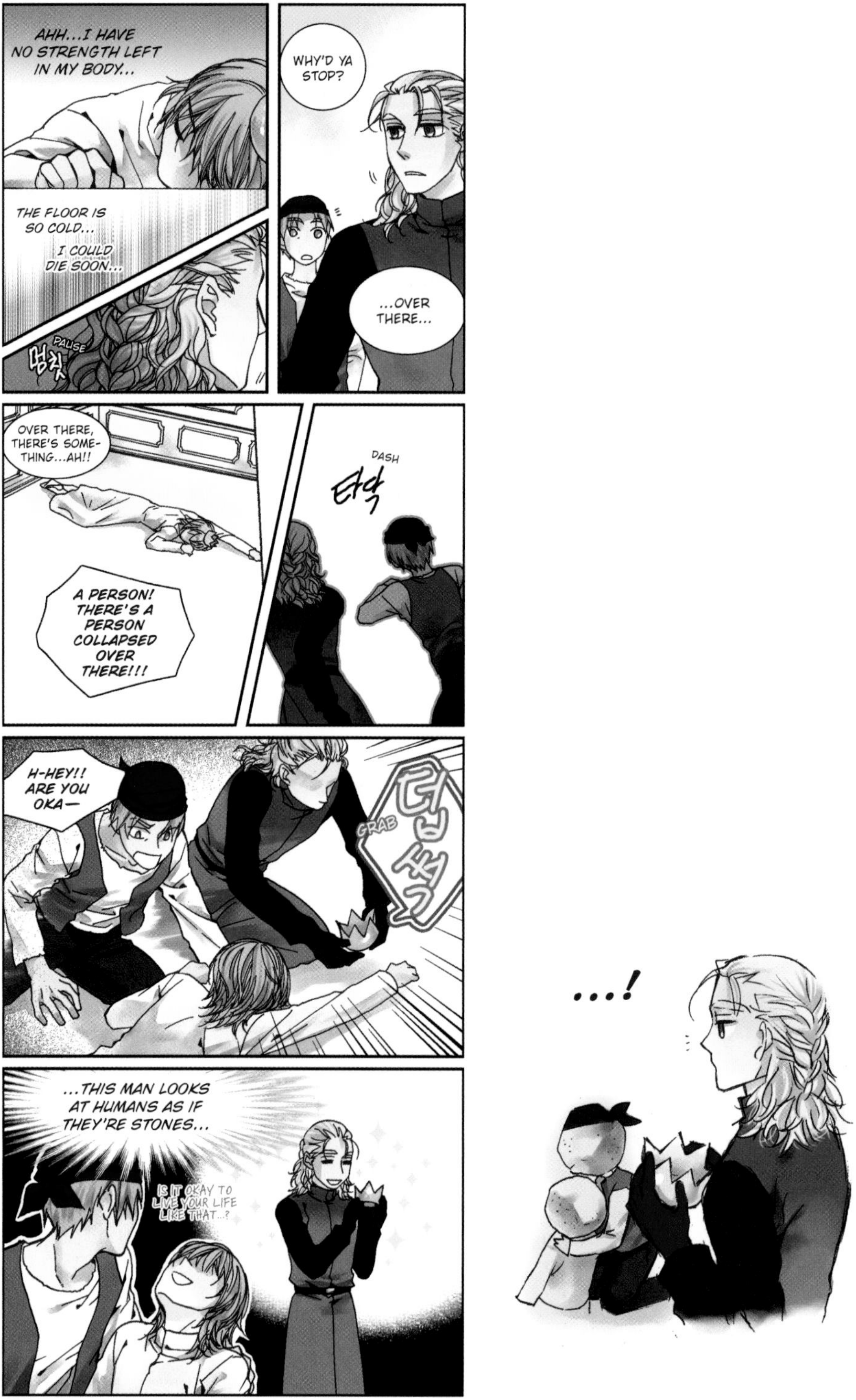
AHH...I HAVE NO STRENGTH LEFT IN MY BODY...
THE FLOOR IS SO COLD...
I COULD DIE SOON...
멈칫
PAUSE
WHY'D YA STOP?
...OVER THERE...
OVER THERE, THERE'S SOME-THING...AH!!
A PERSON! THERE'S A PERSON COLLAPSED OVER THERE!!!
타닥
DASH
H-HEY!! ARE YOU OKA—
덥석
GRAB
...THIS MAN LOOKS AT HUMANS AS IF THEY'RE STONES...
IS IT OKAY TO LIVE YOUR LIFE LIKE THAT...?
...!

#165. AN IRON HAND IN A VELVET GLOVE

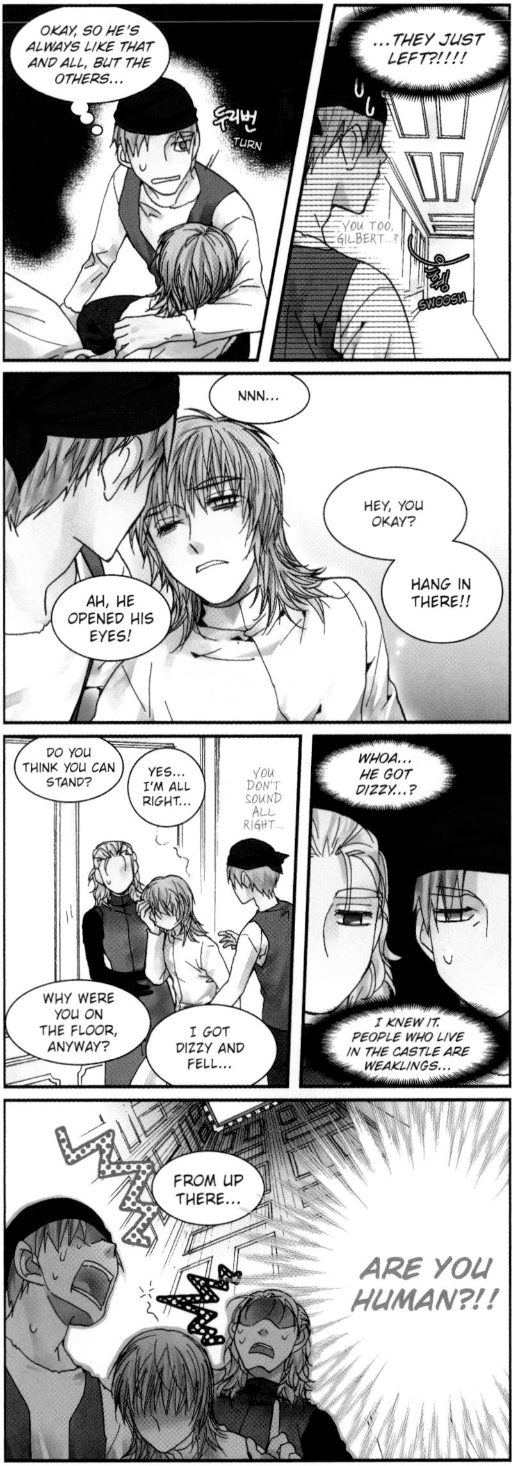
OKAY, SO HE'S ALWAYS LIKE THAT AND ALL, BUT THE OTHERS...
두리번
TURN
...THEY JUST LEFT?!!!!
YOU TOO, GILBERT...?
SWOOSH
NNN...
HEY, YOU OKAY?
HANG IN THERE!!
AH, HE OPENED HIS EYES!
DO YOU THINK YOU CAN STAND?
YES... I'M ALL RIGHT...
YOU DON'T SOUND ALL RIGHT...
WHY WERE YOU ON THE FLOOR, ANYWAY?
I GOT DIZZY AND FELL...
WHOA... HE GOT DIZZY...?
I KNEW IT. PEOPLE WHO LIVE IN THE CASTLE ARE WEAKLINGS...
FROM UP THERE...
ARE YOU HUMAN?!!

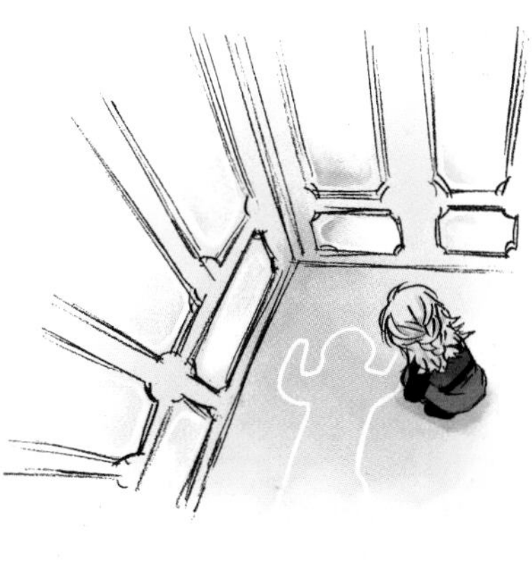

#166. RESPECT YOUR ELDERS

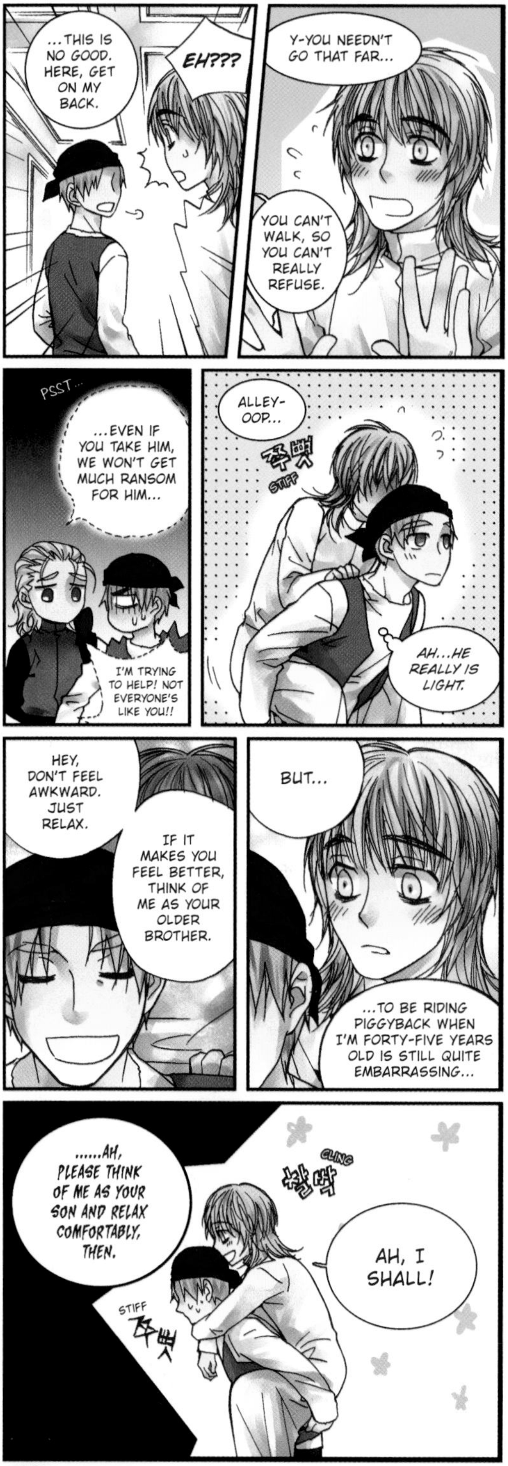
...THIS IS NO GOOD. HERE, GET ON MY BACK.
EH???
Y-YOU NEEDN'T GO THAT FAR...
YOU CAN'T WALK, SO YOU CAN'T REALLY REFUSE.
PSST...
...EVEN IF YOU TAKE HIM, WE WON'T GET MUCH RANSOM FOR HIM...
I'M TRYING TO HELP! NOT EVERYONE'S LIKE YOU!!
ALLEY-OOP...
주뼛
STIFF
AH...HE REALLY IS LIGHT.
HEY, DON'T FEEL AWKWARD. JUST RELAX.
IF IT MAKES YOU FEEL BETTER, THINK OF ME AS YOUR OLDER BROTHER.
BUT...
...TO BE RIDING PIGGYBACK WHEN I'M FORTY-FIVE YEARS OLD IS STILL QUITE EMBARRASSING...
......AH, PLEASE THINK OF ME AS YOUR SON AND RELAX COMFORTABLY, THEN.
CLING
AH, I SHALL!
STIFF
주뼛

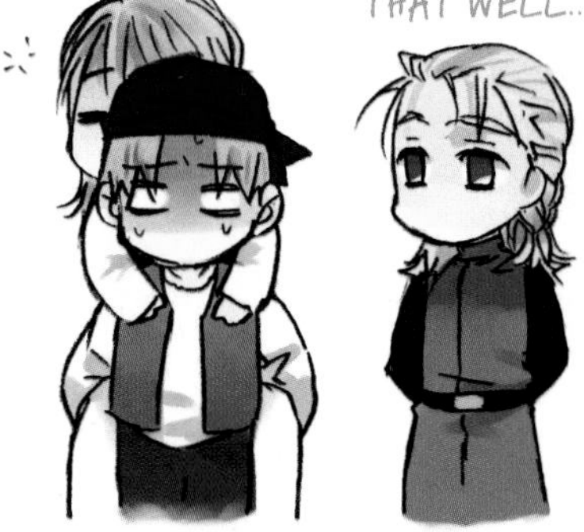
I HOPE I AGE THAT WELL...

#167. HANSEL AND GRETEL

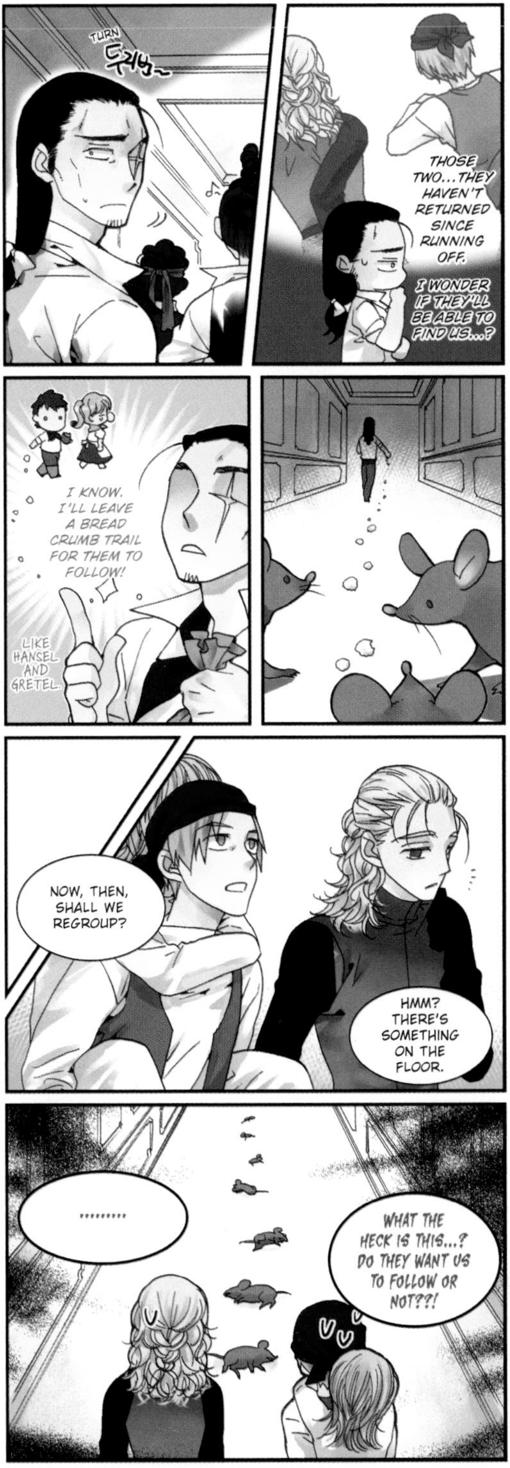

TURN
두리번~
THOSE TWO...THEY HAVEN'T RETURNED SINCE RUNNING OFF.
I WONDER IF THEY'LL BE ABLE TO FIND US...?
I KNOW. I'LL LEAVE A BREAD CRUMB TRAIL FOR THEM TO FOLLOW!
LIKE HANSEL AND GRETEL.
NOW, THEN, SHALL WE REGROUP?
HMM? THERE'S SOMETHING ON THE FLOOR.
....
WHAT THE HECK IS THIS...? DO THEY WANT US TO FOLLOW OR NOT??!

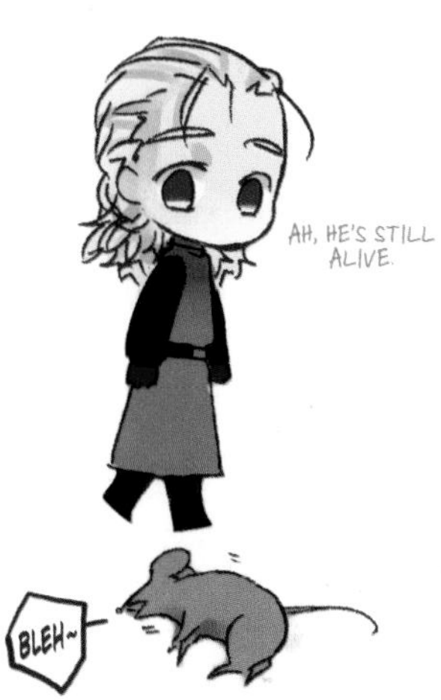

AH, HE'S STILL ALIVE.
BLEH~

#168. GETTING USED TO THIS

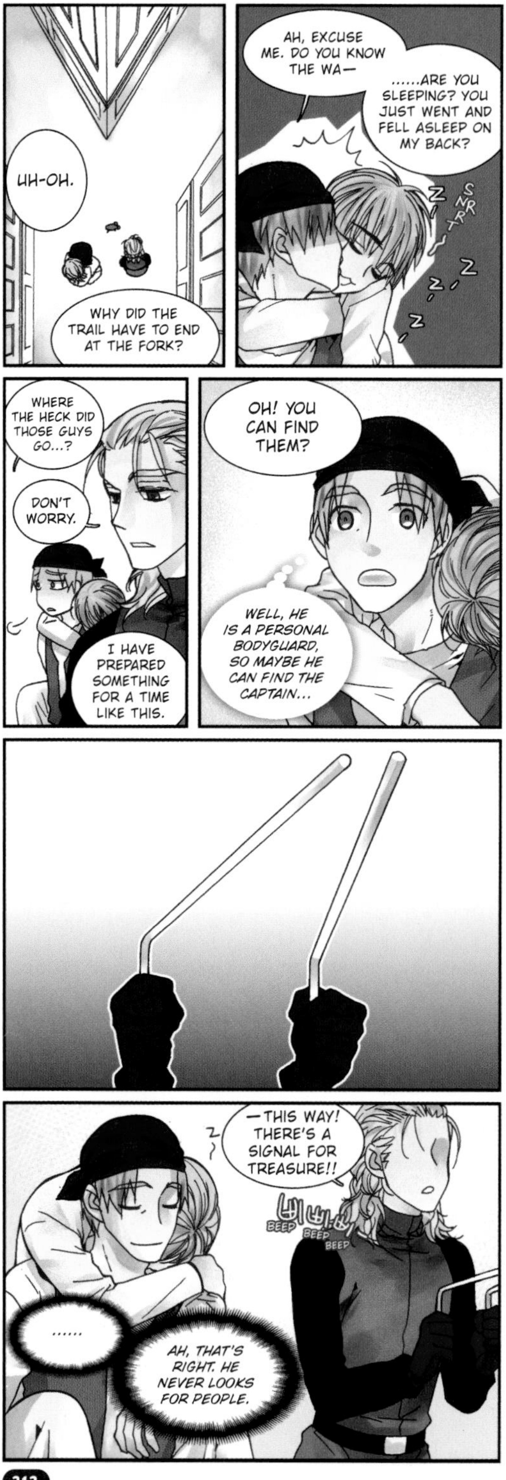
UH-OH.
WHY DID THE TRAIL HAVE TO END AT THE FORK?
AH, EXCUSE ME. DO YOU KNOW THE WA—
......ARE YOU SLEEPING? YOU JUST WENT AND FELL ASLEEP ON MY BACK?
Z Z Z Z
WHERE THE HECK DID THOSE GUYS GO...?
DON'T WORRY.
I HAVE PREPARED SOMETHING FOR A TIME LIKE THIS.
OH! YOU CAN FIND THEM?
WELL, HE IS A PERSONAL BODYGUARD, SO MAYBE HE CAN FIND THE CAPTAIN...
—THIS WAY! THERE'S A SIGNAL FOR TREASURE!!
BEEP BEEP BEEP
......
AH, THAT'S RIGHT. HE NEVER LOOKS FOR PEOPLE.

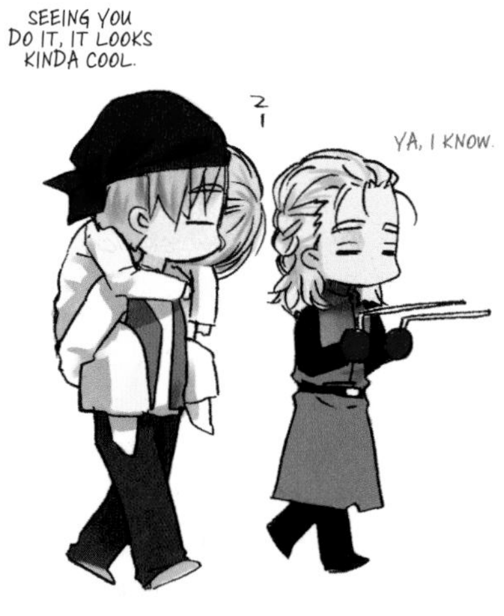
SEEING YOU DO IT, IT LOOKS KINDA COOL.
YA, I KNOW.

#169. PLAYING "THE EMPEROR'S NEW CLOTHES" GAME

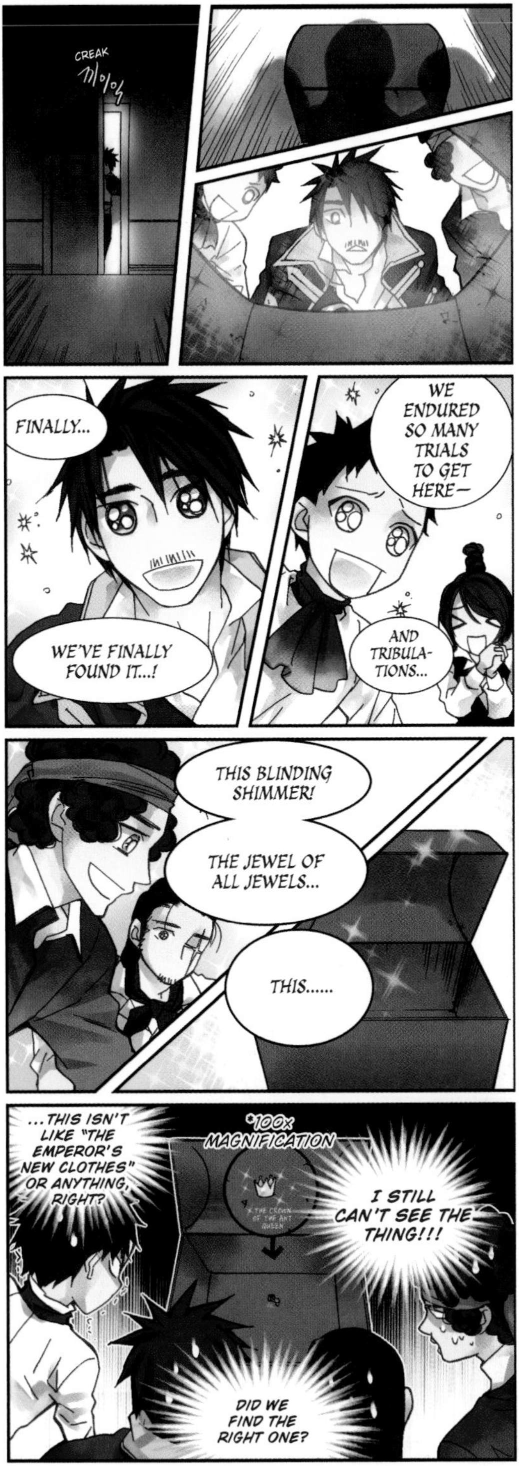
CREAK
끼이익
FINALLY...
WE'VE FINALLY FOUND IT...!
WE ENDURED SO MANY TRIALS TO GET HERE—
AND TRIBULATIONS...
THIS BLINDING SHIMMER!
THE JEWEL OF ALL JEWELS...
THIS......
...THIS ISN'T LIKE "THE EMPEROR'S NEW CLOTHES" OR ANYTHING, RIGHT?
*100x MAGNIFICATION
*THE CROWN OF THE ANT QUEEN
I STILL CAN'T SEE THE THING!!!
DID WE FIND THE RIGHT ONE?

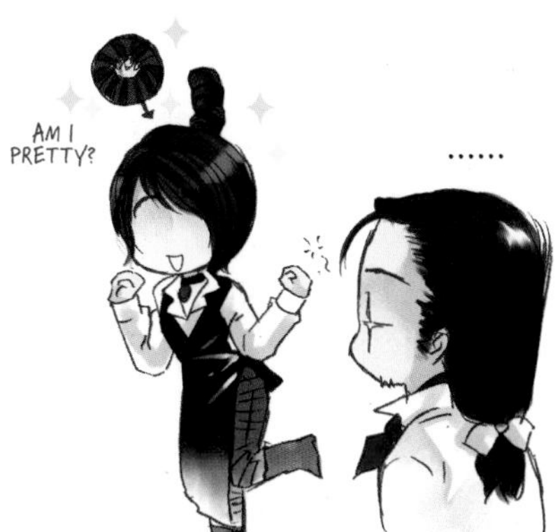
AM I PRETTY?
......

#170. MOTHER, WHY DID YOU HAVE TO...?

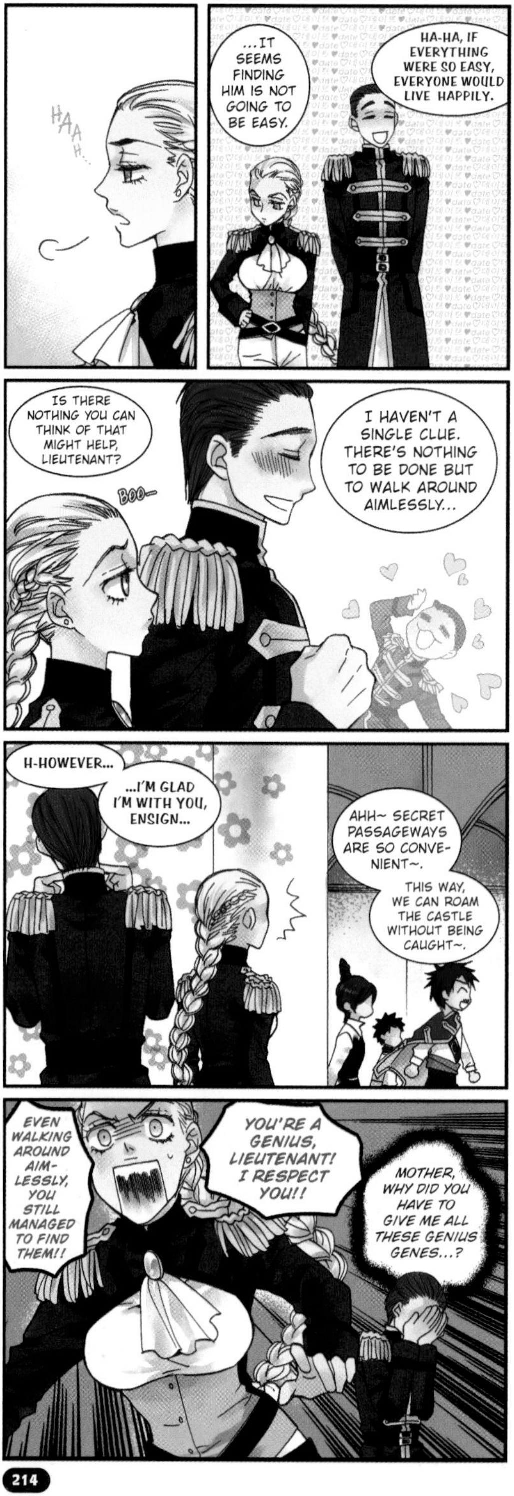

HAAH...
...IT SEEMS FINDING HIM IS NOT GOING TO BE EASY.
HA-HA, IF EVERYTHING WERE SO EASY, EVERYONE WOULD LIVE HAPPILY.
IS THERE NOTHING YOU CAN THINK OF THAT MIGHT HELP, LIEUTENANT?
I HAVEN'T A SINGLE CLUE. THERE'S NOTHING TO BE DONE BUT TO WALK AROUND AIMLESSLY...
BOO–
H-HOWEVER...
...I'M GLAD I'M WITH YOU, ENSIGN...
AHH~ SECRET PASSAGEWAYS ARE SO CONVE-NIENT~.
THIS WAY, WE CAN ROAM THE CASTLE WITHOUT BEING CAUGHT~.
EVEN WALKING AROUND AIM-LESSLY, YOU STILL MANAGED TO FIND THEM!!
YOU'RE A GENIUS, LIEUTENANT! I RESPECT YOU!!
MOTHER, WHY DID YOU HAVE TO GIVE ME ALL THESE GENIUS GENES...?

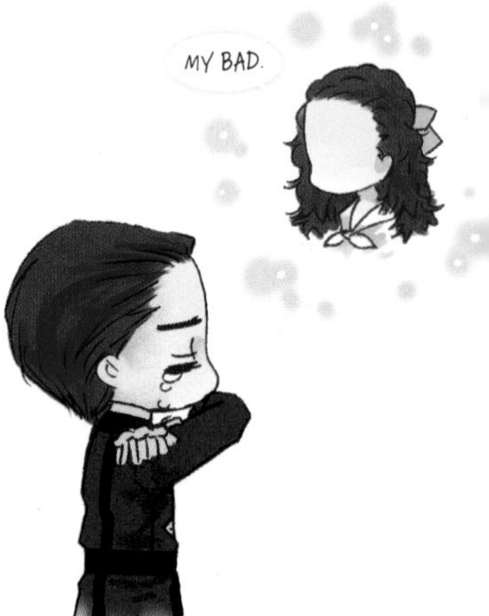

MY BAD.

#171. SO WHAT?

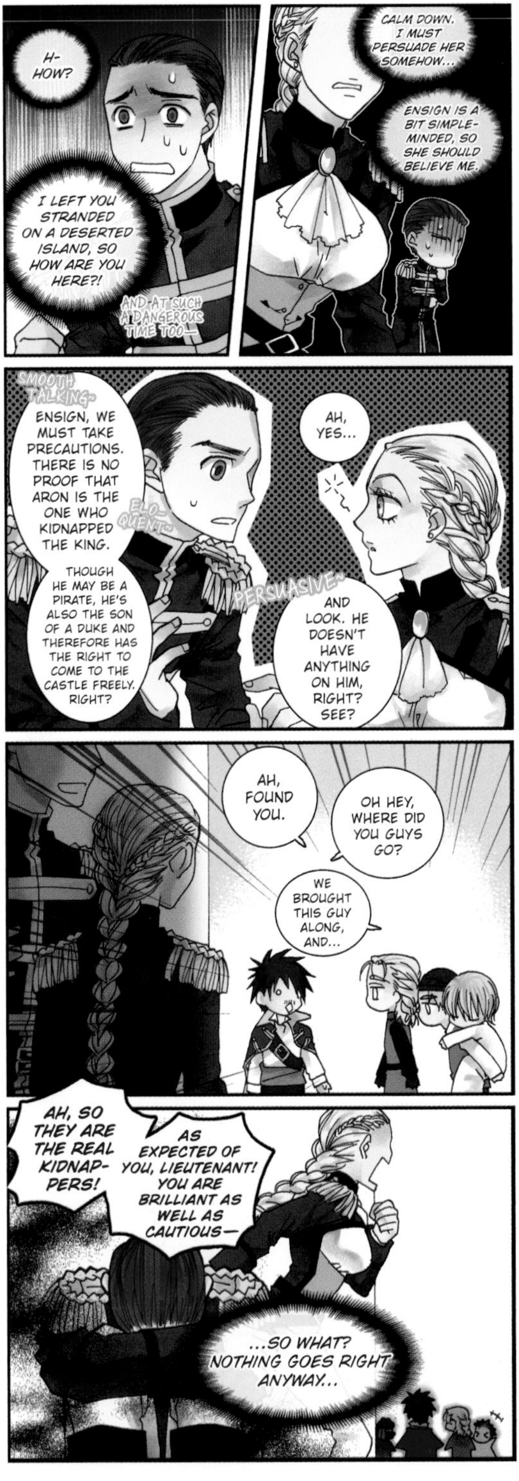
H-HOW?
I LEFT YOU STRANDED ON A DESERTED ISLAND, SO HOW ARE YOU HERE?!
AND AT SUCH A DANGEROUS TIME TOO—
CALM DOWN. I MUST PERSUADE HER SOMEHOW...
ENSIGN IS A BIT SIMPLE-MINDED, SO SHE SHOULD BELIEVE ME.
SMOOTH TALKING~
ENSIGN, WE MUST TAKE PRECAUTIONS. THERE IS NO PROOF THAT ARON IS THE ONE WHO KIDNAPPED THE KING.
ELO-QUENT~
THOUGH HE MAY BE A PIRATE, HE'S ALSO THE SON OF A DUKE AND THEREFORE HAS THE RIGHT TO COME TO THE CASTLE FREELY. RIGHT?
PERSUASIVE~
AH, YES...
AND LOOK. HE DOESN'T HAVE ANYTHING ON HIM, RIGHT? SEE?
AH, FOUND YOU.
OH HEY, WHERE DID YOU GUYS GO?
WE BROUGHT THIS GUY ALONG, AND...
AH, SO THEY ARE THE REAL KIDNAP-PERS!
AS EXPECTED OF YOU, LIEUTENANT! YOU ARE BRILLIANT AS WELL AS CAUTIOUS—
...SO WHAT? NOTHING GOES RIGHT ANYWAY...

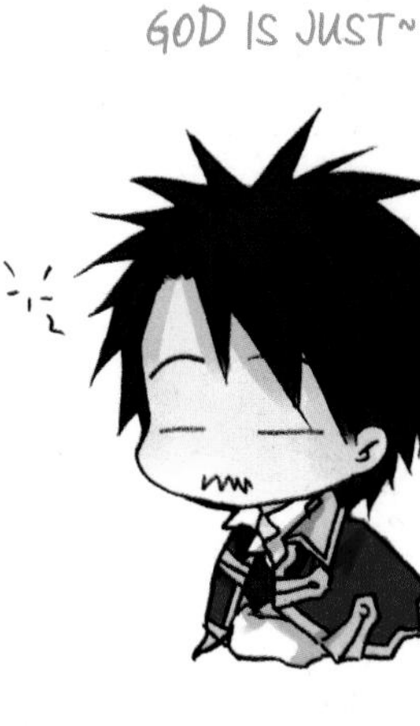
GOD IS JUST~

#172. SOMEONE YOU KNOW

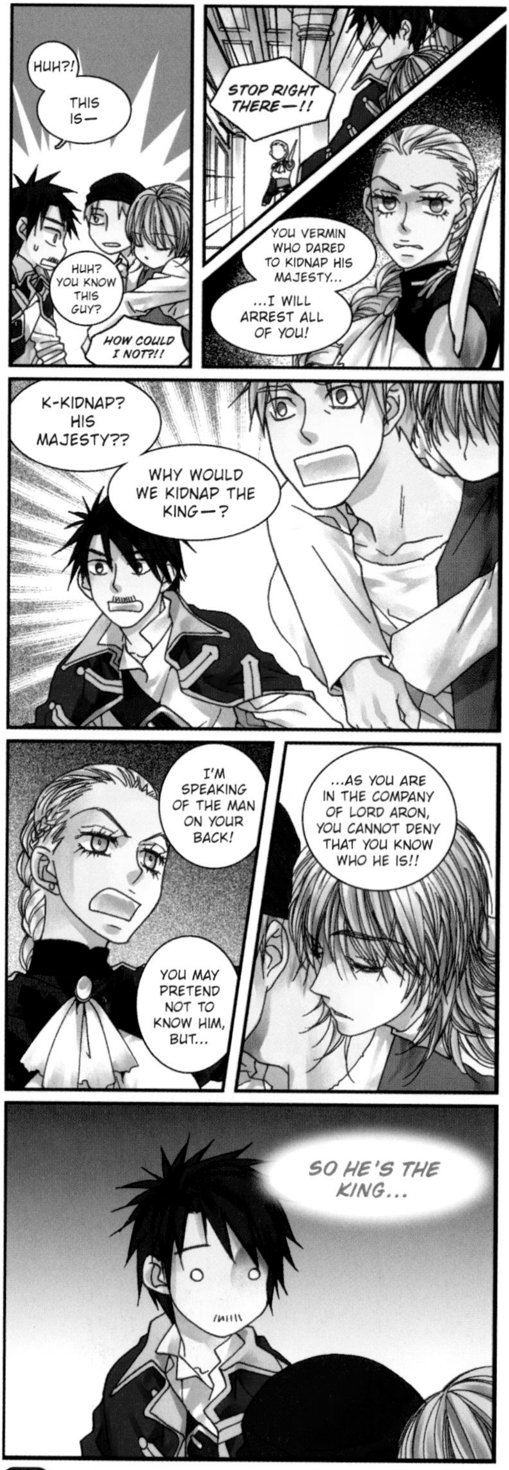
HUH?!
THIS IS—
HUH? YOU KNOW THIS GUY?
HOW COULD I NOT?!!
STOP RIGHT THERE—!!
YOU VERMIN WHO DARED TO KIDNAP HIS MAJESTY...
...I WILL ARREST ALL OF YOU!
K-KIDNAP? HIS MAJESTY??
WHY WOULD WE KIDNAP THE KING—?
I'M SPEAKING OF THE MAN ON YOUR BACK!
...AS YOU ARE IN THE COMPANY OF LORD ARON, YOU CANNOT DENY THAT YOU KNOW WHO HE IS!!
YOU MAY PRETEND NOT TO KNOW HIM, BUT...
SO HE'S THE KING...

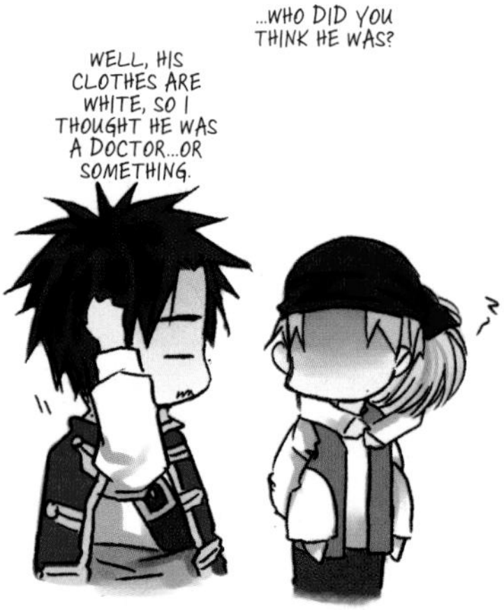
...WHO DID YOU THINK HE WAS?
WELL, HIS CLOTHES ARE WHITE, SO I THOUGHT HE WAS A DOCTOR...OR SOMETHING.

#173. ALONE

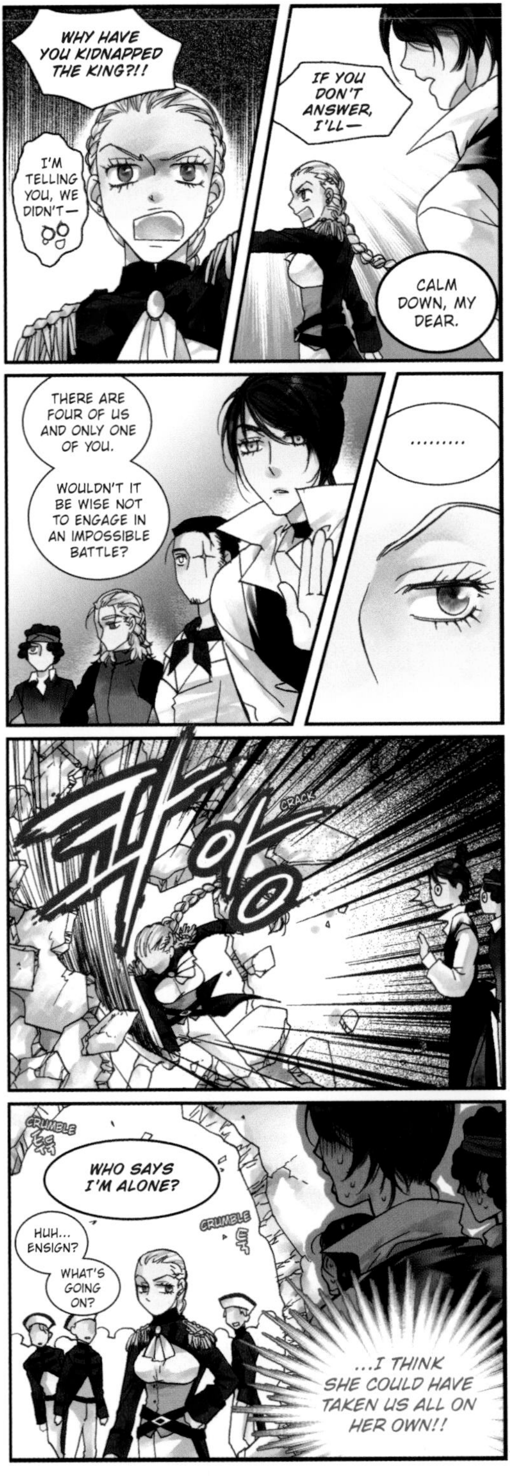
WHY HAVE YOU KIDNAPPED THE KING?!!
I'M TELLING YOU, WE DIDN'T—
IF YOU DON'T ANSWER, I'LL—
CALM DOWN, MY DEAR.
THERE ARE FOUR OF US AND ONLY ONE OF YOU.
WOULDN'T IT BE WISE NOT TO ENGAGE IN AN IMPOSSIBLE BATTLE?
....
CRACK
CRUMBLE
WHO SAYS I'M ALONE?
CRUMBLE
HUH... ENSIGN?
WHAT'S GOING ON?
...I THINK SHE COULD HAVE TAKEN US ALL ON HER OWN!!

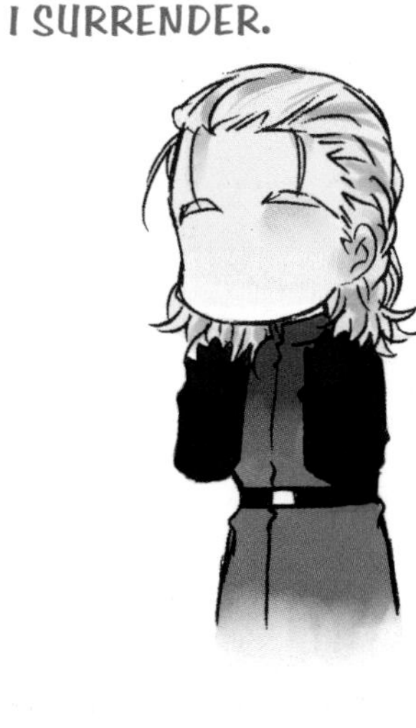
I SURRENDER.

#174. WORSE THAN TREASON

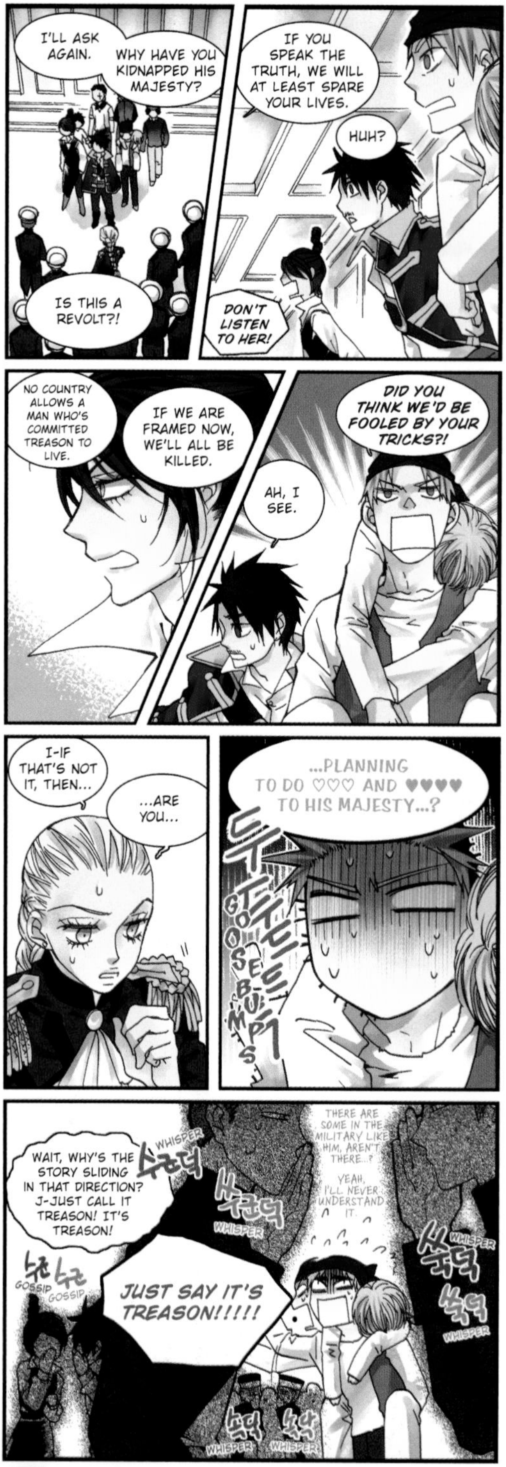

I'LL ASK AGAIN.
WHY HAVE YOU KIDNAPPED HIS MAJESTY?
IS THIS A REVOLT?!
IF YOU SPEAK THE TRUTH, WE WILL AT LEAST SPARE YOUR LIVES.
HUH?
DON'T LISTEN TO HER!
NO COUNTRY ALLOWS A MAN WHO'S COMMITTED TREASON TO LIVE.
IF WE ARE FRAMED NOW, WE'LL ALL BE KILLED.
DID YOU THINK WE'D BE FOOLED BY YOUR TRICKS?!
AH, I SEE.
I-IF THAT'S NOT IT, THEN...
...ARE YOU...
...PLANNING TO DO ♡♡♡ AND ♥♥♥♥ TO HIS MAJESTY...?
GOOSEBUMPS
WAIT, WHY'S THE STORY SLIDING IN THAT DIRECTION? J-JUST CALL IT TREASON! IT'S TREASON!
WHISPER
THERE ARE SOME IN THE MILITARY LIKE HIM, AREN'T THERE...?
YEAH, I'LL NEVER UNDERSTAND IT.
WHISPER
WHISPER
GOSSIP GOSSIP
JUST SAY IT'S TREASON!!!!!
WHISPER
WHISPER WHISPER

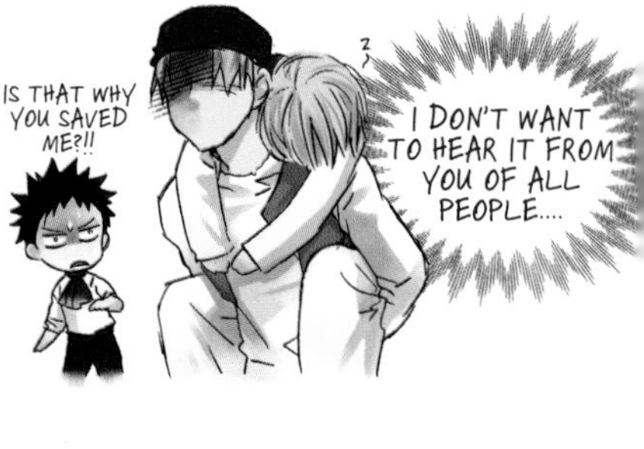

IS THAT WHY YOU SAVED ME?!!
I DON'T WANT TO HEAR IT FROM YOU OF ALL PEOPLE....

#175. MAY I HELP YOU?

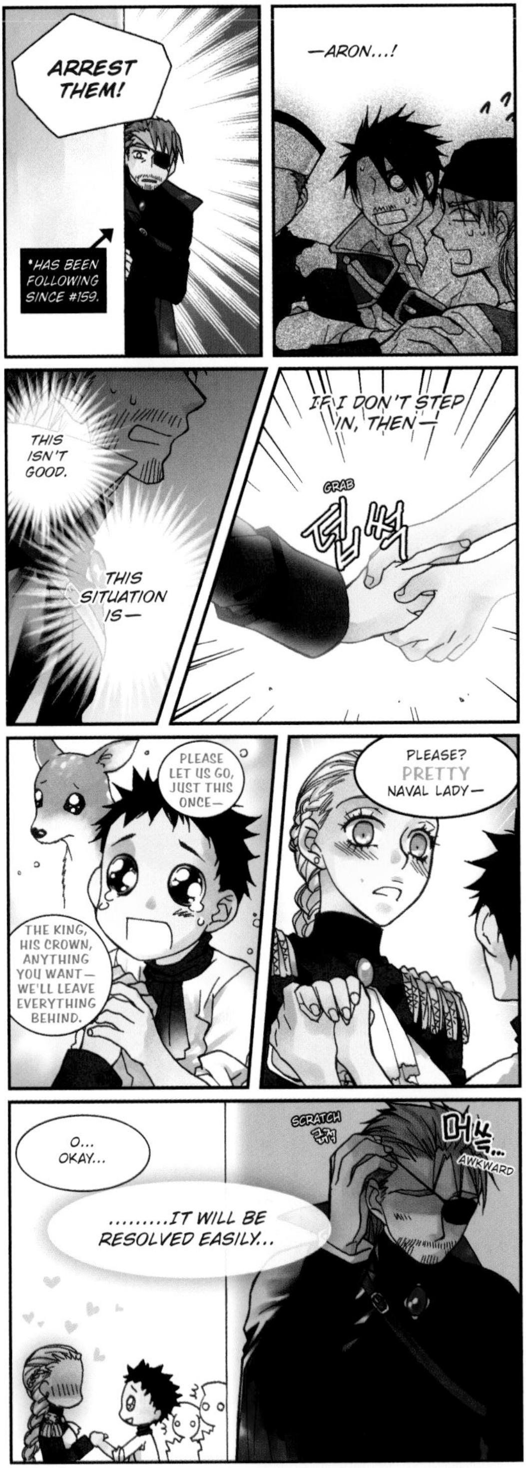

ARREST THEM!
*HAS BEEN FOLLOWING SINCE #159.
—ARON...!
THIS ISN'T GOOD.
THIS SITUATION IS—
IF I DON'T STEP IN, THEN—
GRAB
PLEASE LET US GO, JUST THIS ONCE—
THE KING, HIS CROWN, ANYTHING YOU WANT—WE'LL LEAVE EVERYTHING BEHIND.
PLEASE? PRETTY NAVAL LADY—
O... OKAY...
SCRATCH
AWKWARD
.........IT WILL BE RESOLVED EASILY...

*THE FIFTH PANEL'S TRUE IMAGE.

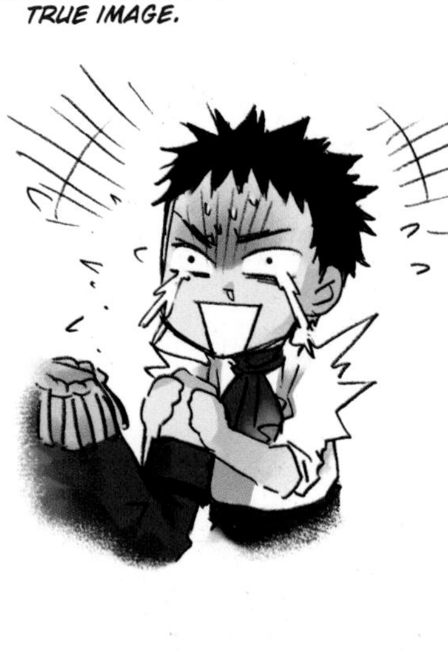

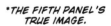

#176. BUT HE'S STILL SOMEONE ELSE'S SON

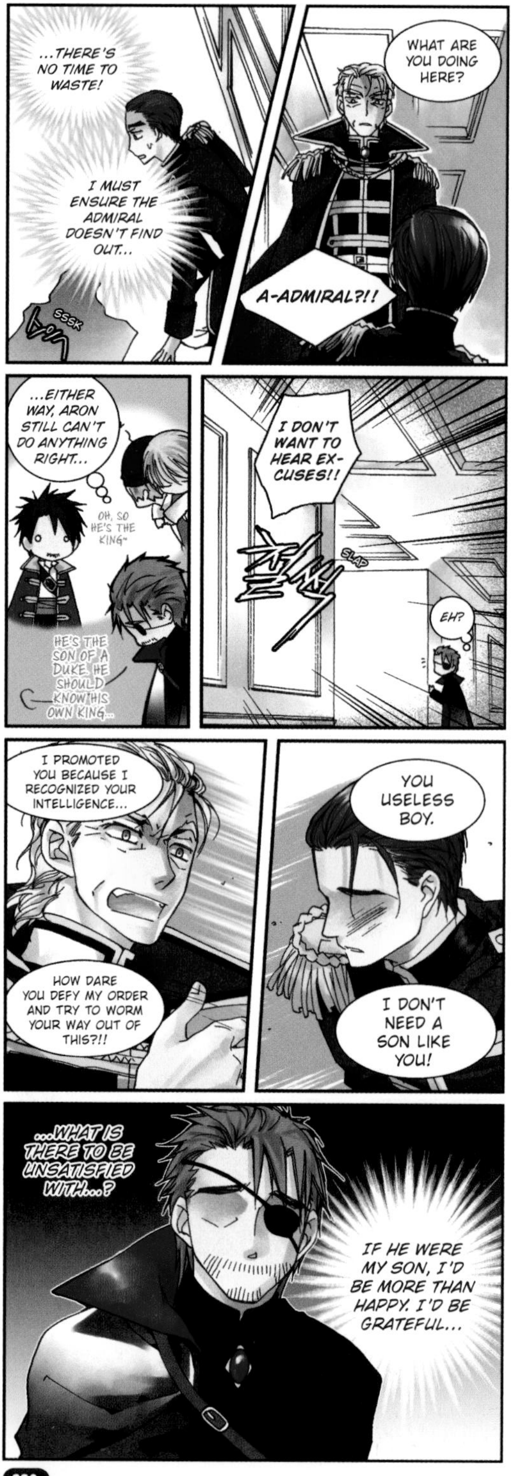

...THERE'S NO TIME TO WASTE!
I MUST ENSURE THE ADMIRAL DOESN'T FIND OUT...
SSSK
WHAT ARE YOU DOING HERE?
A-ADMIRAL?!!
...EITHER WAY, ARON STILL CAN'T DO ANYTHING RIGHT...
OH, SO HE'S THE KING~
HE'S THE SON OF A DUKE. HE SHOULD KNOW HIS OWN KING...
I DON'T WANT TO HEAR EXCUSES!!
SLAP
EH?
I PROMOTED YOU BECAUSE I RECOGNIZED YOUR INTELLIGENCE...
HOW DARE YOU DEFY MY ORDER AND TRY TO WORM YOUR WAY OUT OF THIS?!!
YOU USELESS BOY.
I DON'T NEED A SON LIKE YOU!
...WHAT IS THERE TO BE UNSATISFIED WITH...?
IF HE WERE MY SON, I'D BE MORE THAN HAPPY. I'D BE GRATEFUL...

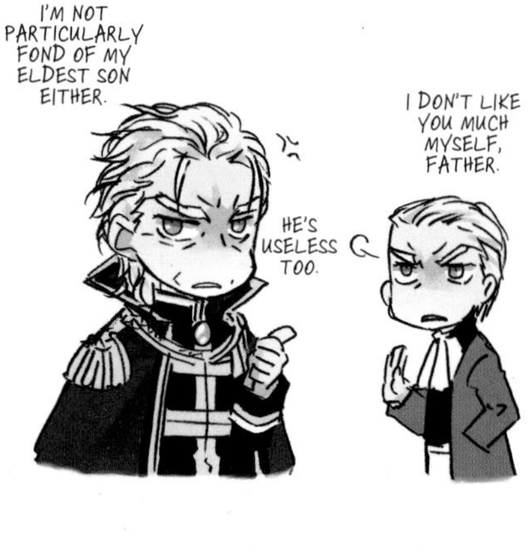

I'M NOT PARTICULARLY FOND OF MY ELDEST SON EITHER.
HE'S USELESS TOO.
I DON'T LIKE YOU MUCH MYSELF, FATHER.

#177. YEAH, YEAH. I KNOW, I KNOW.

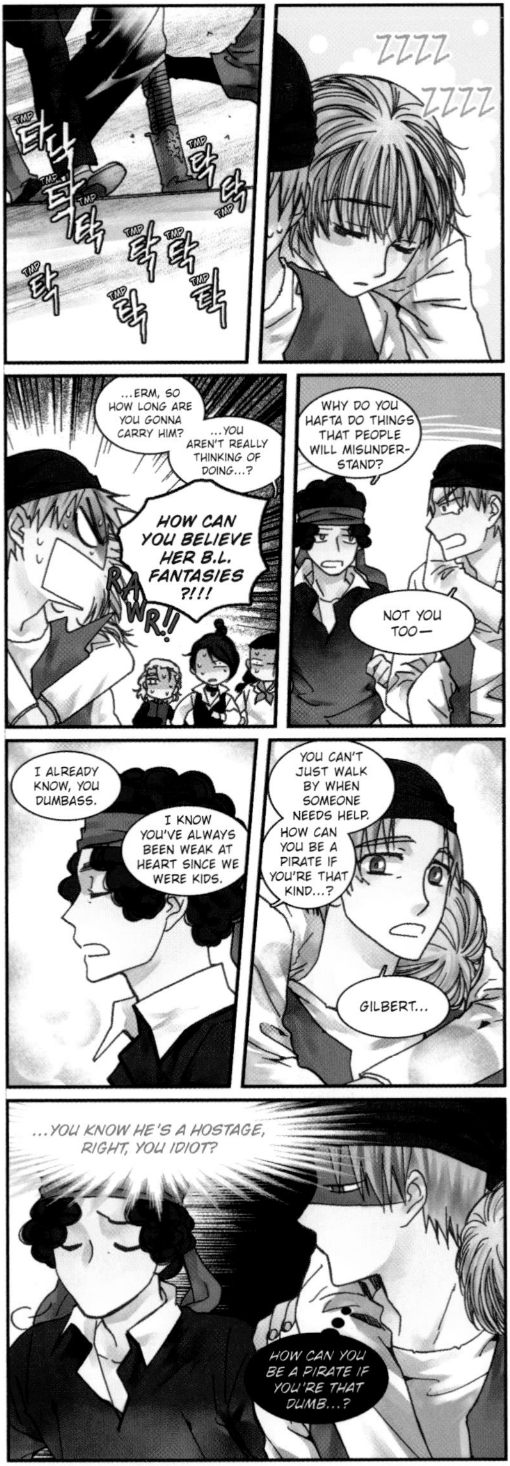

TMP 타닥
TMP 탁
TMP 탁
TMP 탁
TMP 탁
TMP 탁
TMP 탁
TMP 탁
TMP 탁
TMP 탁
ZZZZ
ZZZZ
...ERM, SO HOW LONG ARE YOU GONNA CARRY HIM?
...YOU AREN'T REALLY THINKING OF DOING...?
HOW CAN YOU BELIEVE HER B.L. FANTASIES ?!!!
RAWR!!
WHY DO YOU HAFTA DO THINGS THAT PEOPLE WILL MISUNDER-STAND?
NOT YOU TOO—
I ALREADY KNOW, YOU DUMBASS.
I KNOW YOU'VE ALWAYS BEEN WEAK AT HEART SINCE WE WERE KIDS.
YOU CAN'T JUST WALK BY WHEN SOMEONE NEEDS HELP.
HOW CAN YOU BE A PIRATE IF YOU'RE THAT KIND...?
GILBERT...
...YOU KNOW HE'S A HOSTAGE, RIGHT, YOU IDIOT?
HOW CAN YOU BE A PIRATE IF YOU'RE THAT DUMB...?

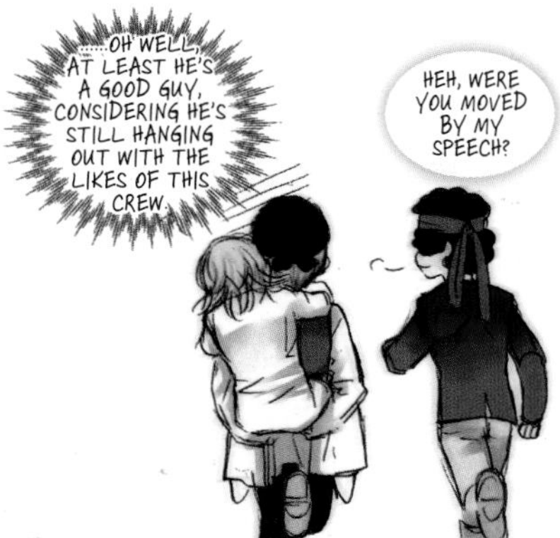

......OH WELL, AT LEAST HE'S A GOOD GUY, CONSIDERING HE'S STILL HANGING OUT WITH THE LIKES OF THIS CREW.
HEH, WERE YOU MOVED BY MY SPEECH?

#178. OCEAN STORY

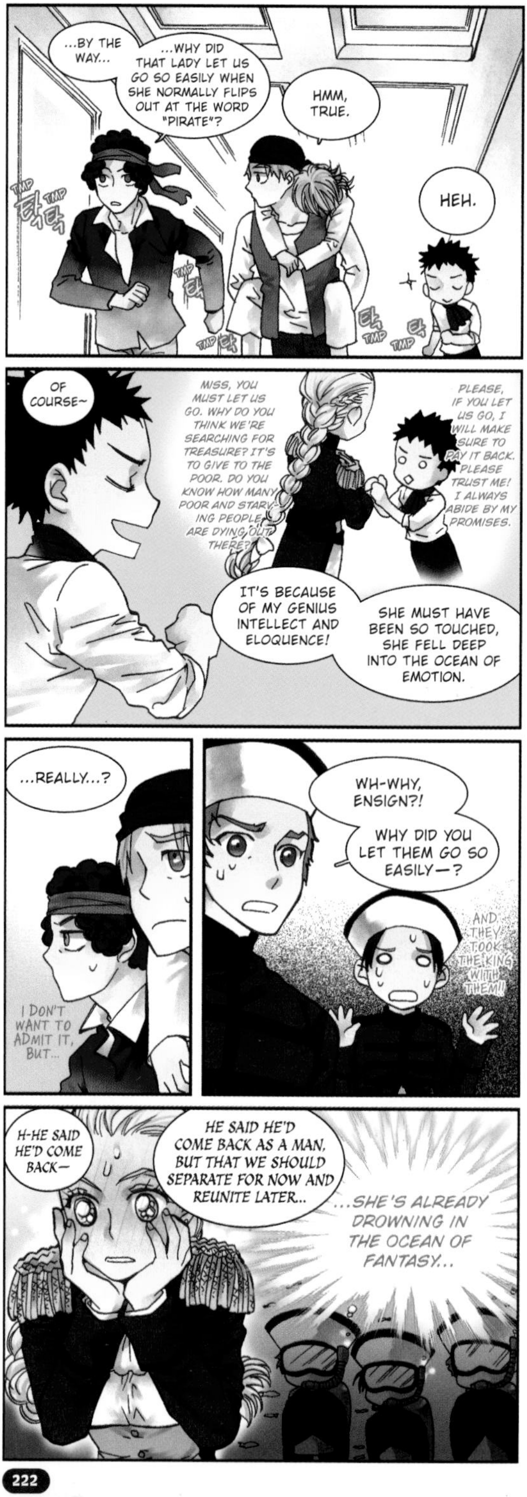

...BY THE WAY...
...WHY DID THAT LADY LET US GO SO EASILY WHEN SHE NORMALLY FLIPS OUT AT THE WORD "PIRATE"?
HMM, TRUE.
HEH.
TMP TMP TMP TMP TMP TMP
OF COURSE~
MISS, YOU MUST LET US GO. WHY DO YOU THINK WE'RE SEARCHING FOR TREASURE? IT'S TO GIVE TO THE POOR. DO YOU KNOW HOW MANY POOR AND STARVING PEOPLE ARE DYING OUT THERE?
PLEASE, IF YOU LET US GO, I WILL MAKE SURE TO PAY IT BACK. PLEASE TRUST ME! I ALWAYS ABIDE BY MY PROMISES.
IT'S BECAUSE OF MY GENIUS INTELLECT AND ELOQUENCE!
SHE MUST HAVE BEEN SO TOUCHED, SHE FELL DEEP INTO THE OCEAN OF EMOTION.
...REALLY...?
I DON'T WANT TO ADMIT IT, BUT...
WH-WHY, ENSIGN?!
WHY DID YOU LET THEM GO SO EASILY—?
AND THEY TOOK THE KING WITH THEM!!
H-HE SAID HE'D COME BACK—
HE SAID HE'D COME BACK AS A MAN, BUT THAT WE SHOULD SEPARATE FOR NOW AND REUNITE LATER...
...SHE'S ALREADY DROWNING IN THE OCEAN OF FANTASY...

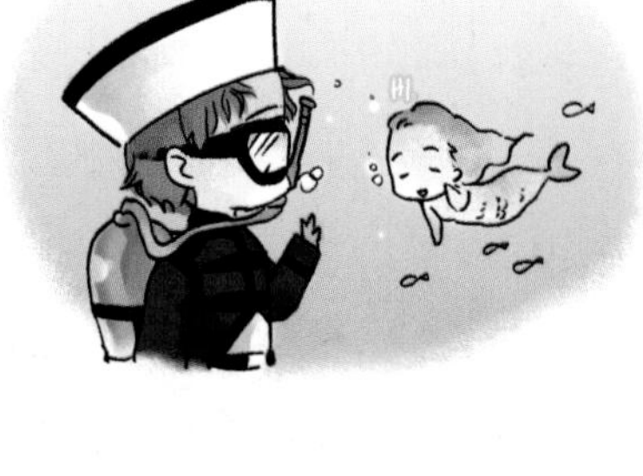

HI

#179. WHAT ARE YOU TALKING ABOUT?

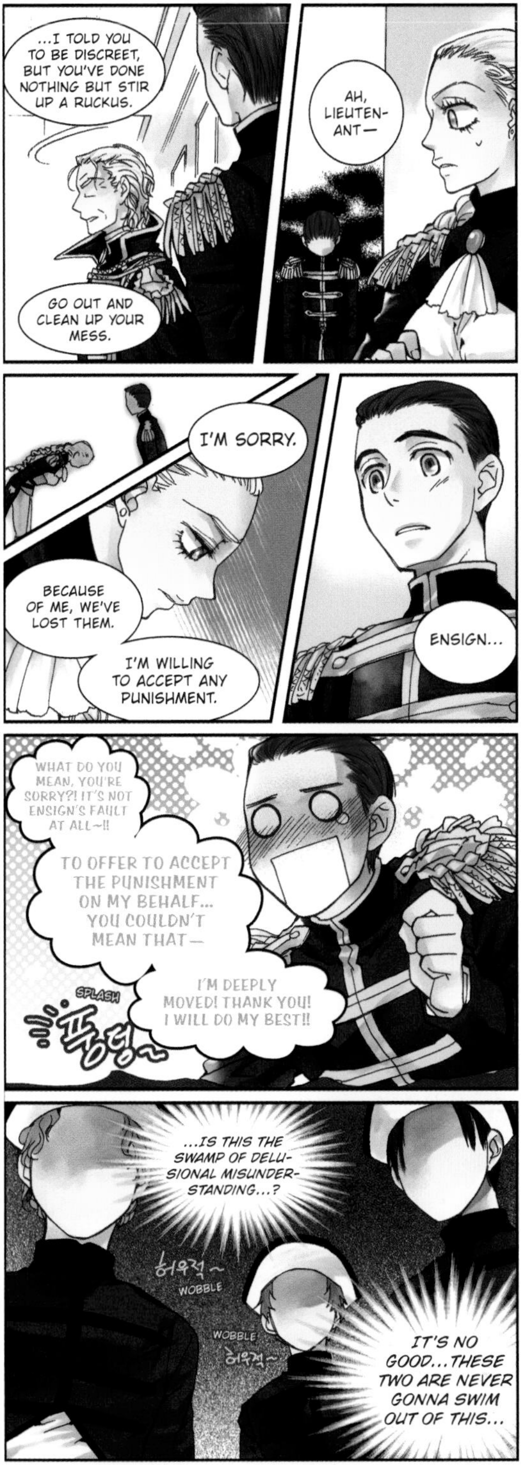
...I TOLD YOU TO BE DISCREET, BUT YOU'VE DONE NOTHING BUT STIR UP A RUCKUS.
GO OUT AND CLEAN UP YOUR MESS.
AH, LIEUTEN-ANT—
I'M SORRY.
BECAUSE OF ME, WE'VE LOST THEM.
I'M WILLING TO ACCEPT ANY PUNISHMENT.
ENSIGN...
WHAT DO YOU MEAN, YOU'RE SORRY?! IT'S NOT ENSIGN'S FAULT AT ALL~!!
TO OFFER TO ACCEPT THE PUNISHMENT ON MY BEHALF... YOU COULDN'T MEAN THAT—
I'M DEEPLY MOVED! THANK YOU! I WILL DO MY BEST!!
SPLASH
풍덩~
...IS THIS THE SWAMP OF DELU-SIONAL MISUNDER-STANDING...?
허우적~
WOBBLE
WOBBLE
허우적~
IT'S NO GOOD...THESE TWO ARE NEVER GONNA SWIM OUT OF THIS...

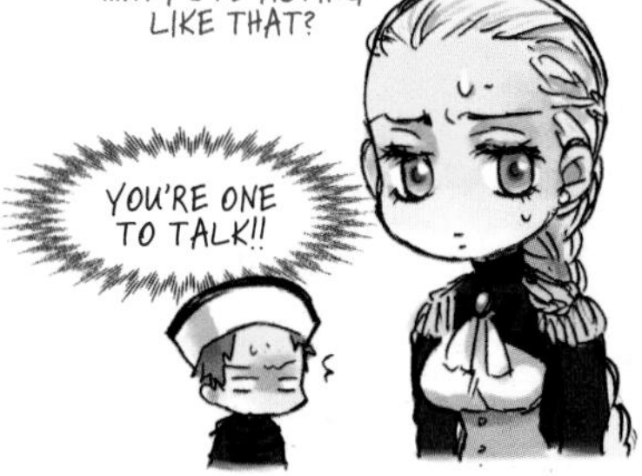
...WHY'S HE ACTING LIKE THAT?
YOU'RE ONE TO TALK!!

#180. MR. SOCRATES

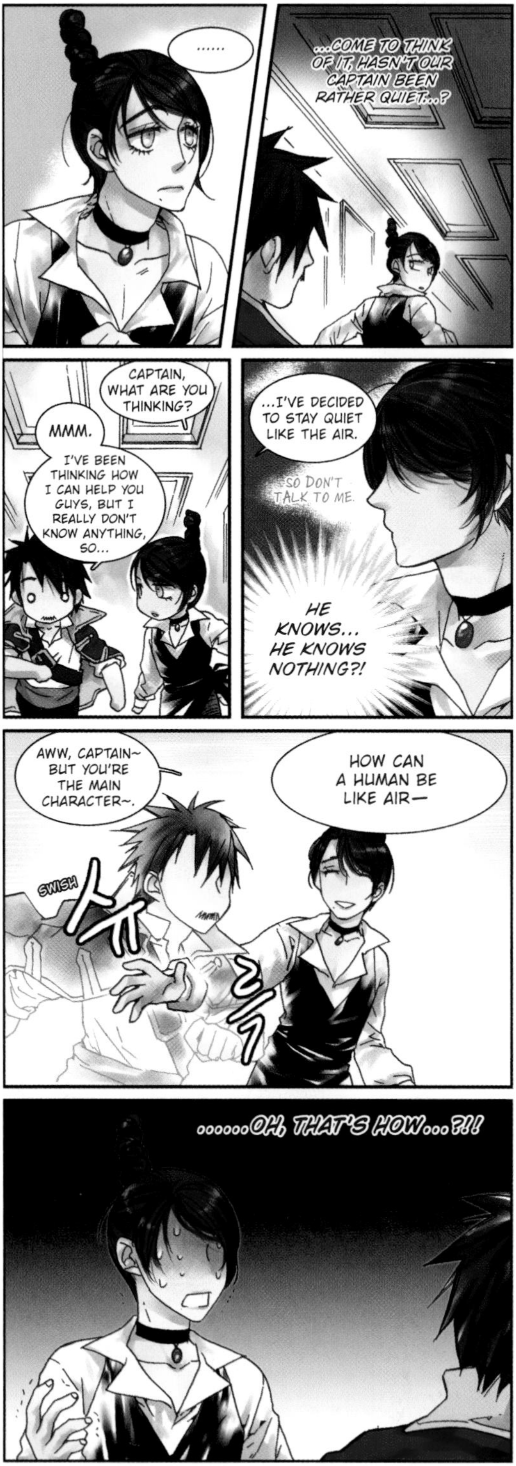
......
...COME TO THINK OF IT, HASN'T OUR CAPTAIN BEEN RATHER QUIET...?
CAPTAIN, WHAT ARE YOU THINKING?
MMM.
I'VE BEEN THINKING HOW I CAN HELP YOU GUYS, BUT I REALLY DON'T KNOW ANYTHING, SO...
...I'VE DECIDED TO STAY QUIET LIKE THE AIR.
SO DON'T TALK TO ME.
HE KNOWS... HE KNOWS NOTHING?!
AWW, CAPTAIN~ BUT YOU'RE THE MAIN CHARACTER~.
HOW CAN A HUMAN BE LIKE AIR—
SWISH
......OH, THAT'S HOW...?!!

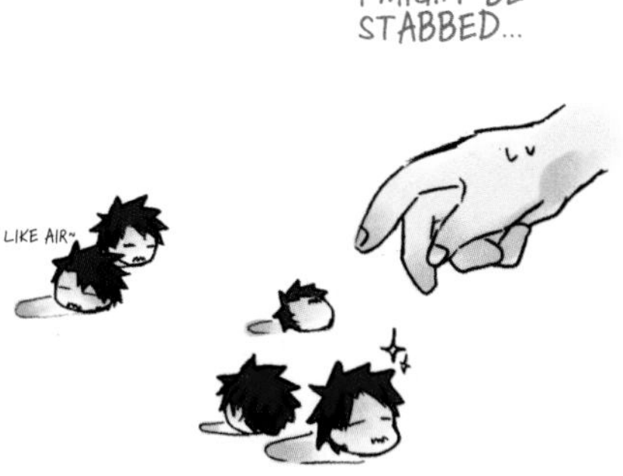
I MIGHT BE STABBED...
LIKE AIR~

#181. EVEN IF IT'S UNFORTUNATE, DON'T DO IT

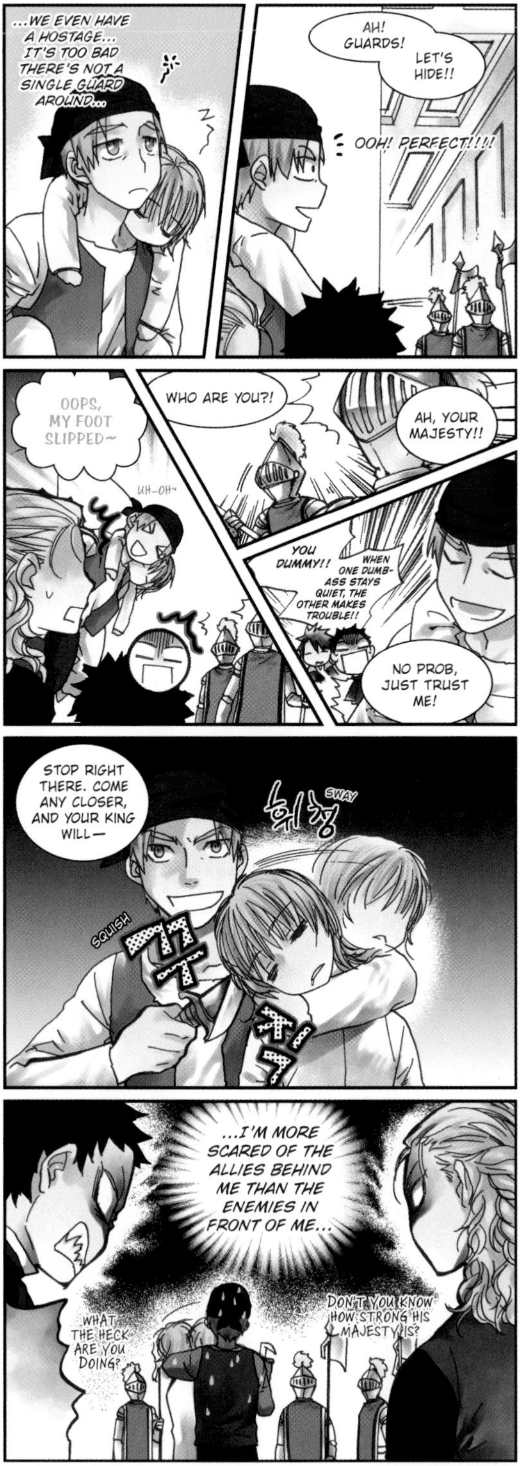
...WE EVEN HAVE A HOSTAGE... IT'S TOO BAD THERE'S NOT A SINGLE GUARD AROUND...
AH! GUARDS!
LET'S HIDE!!
OOH! PERFECT!!!!
OOPS, MY FOOT SLIPPED~
UH-OH~
WHO ARE YOU?!
AH, YOUR MAJESTY!!
YOU DUMMY!!
WHEN ONE DUMB-ASS STAYS QUIET, THE OTHER MAKES TROUBLE!!
NO PROB, JUST TRUST ME!
STOP RIGHT THERE. COME ANY CLOSER, AND YOUR KING WILL—
휘청
SWAY
SQUISH
...I'M MORE SCARED OF THE ALLIES BEHIND ME THAN THE ENEMIES IN FRONT OF ME...
WHAT THE HECK ARE YOU DOING?
DON'T YOU KNOW HOW STRONG HIS MAJESTY IS?

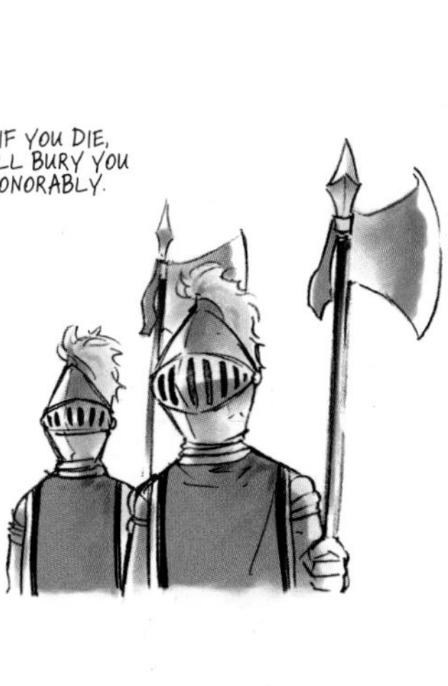
...IF YOU DIE, WE'LL BURY YOU HONORABLY.

#182. NOT EVERYONE KISSES

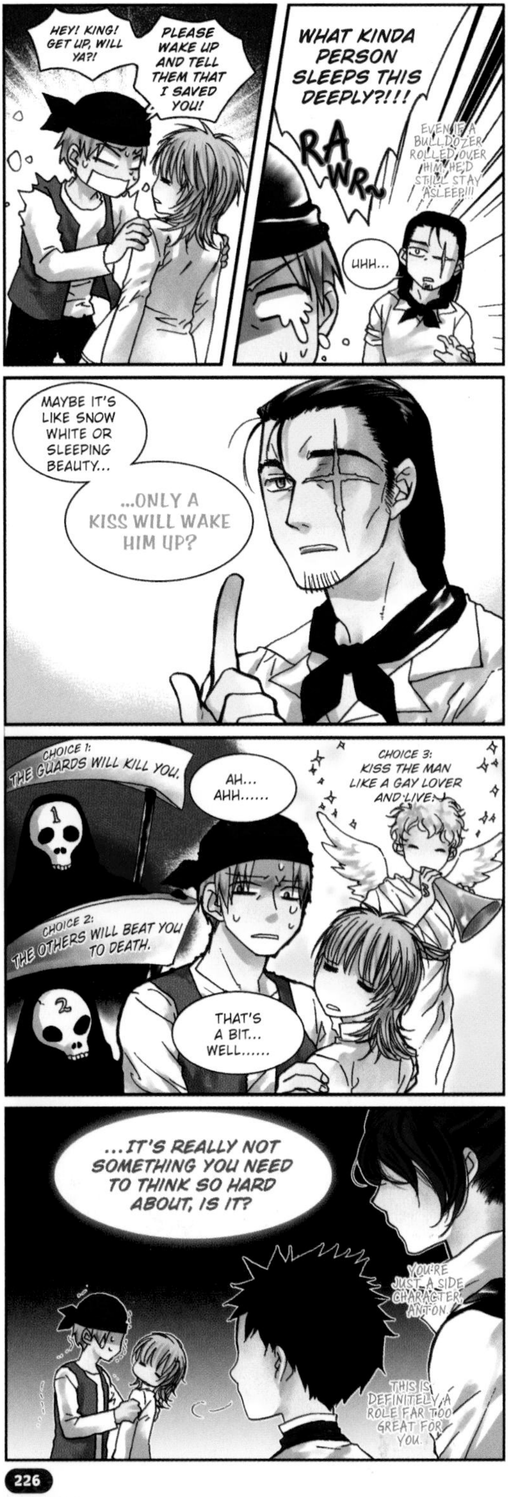

HEY! KING! GET UP, WILL YA?!
PLEASE WAKE UP AND TELL THEM THAT I SAVED YOU!
WHAT KINDA PERSON SLEEPS THIS DEEPLY?!!!
RAWR~
EVEN IF A BULLDOZER ROLLED OVER HIM HE'D STILL STAY ASLEEP!!!
UHH...
MAYBE IT'S LIKE SNOW WHITE OR SLEEPING BEAUTY...
...ONLY A KISS WILL WAKE HIM UP?
CHOICE 1: THE GUARDS WILL KILL YOU.
AH... AHH......
CHOICE 3: KISS THE MAN LIKE A GAY LOVER AND LIVE.
CHOICE 2: THE OTHERS WILL BEAT YOU TO DEATH.
THAT'S A BIT... WELL......
...IT'S REALLY NOT SOMETHING YOU NEED TO THINK SO HARD ABOUT, IS IT?
YOU'RE JUST A SIDE CHARACTER, ANTON.
THIS IS DEFINITELY A ROLE FAR TOO GREAT FOR YOU.

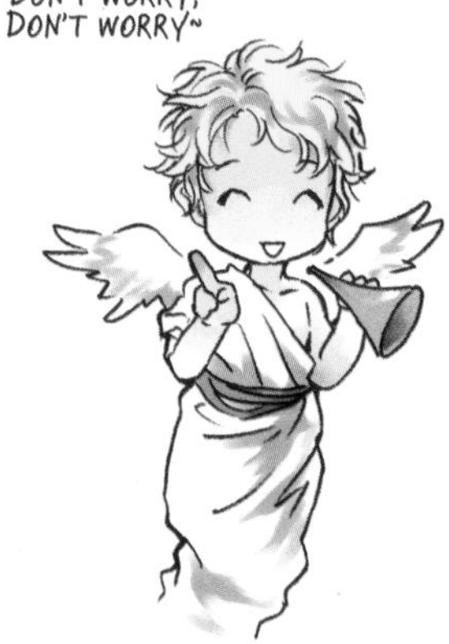

DON'T WORRY, DON'T WORRY~

#183. THE FOREST'S SLEEPING EVIL KING

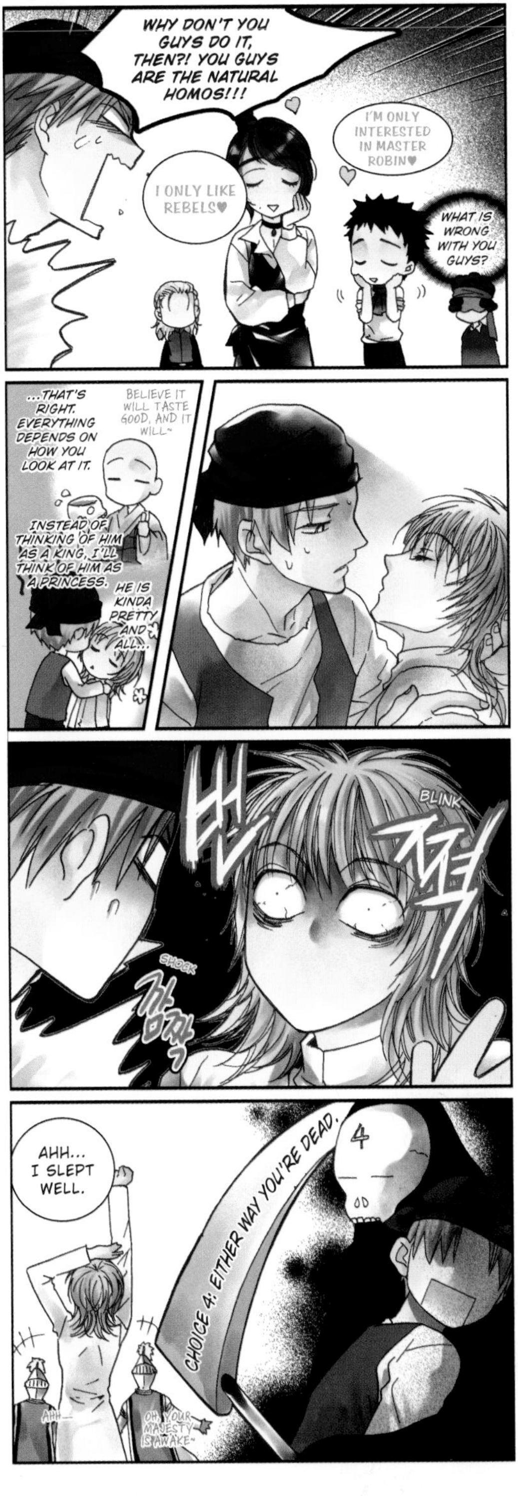
WHY DON'T YOU GUYS DO IT, THEN?! YOU GUYS ARE THE NATURAL HOMOS!!!
I ONLY LIKE REBELS♥
I'M ONLY INTERESTED IN MASTER ROBIN♥
WHAT IS WRONG WITH YOU GUYS?
...THAT'S RIGHT. EVERYTHING DEPENDS ON HOW YOU LOOK AT IT.
BELIEVE IT WILL TASTE GOOD, AND IT WILL~
INSTEAD OF THINKING OF HIM AS A KING, I'LL THINK OF HIM AS A PRINCESS.
HE IS KINDA PRETTY AND ALL...
번쩍
BLINK
깜짝
SHOCK
AHH... I SLEPT WELL.
CHOICE 4: EITHER WAY YOU'RE DEAD.
4
AHH...
OH, YOUR MAJESTY IS AWAKE~

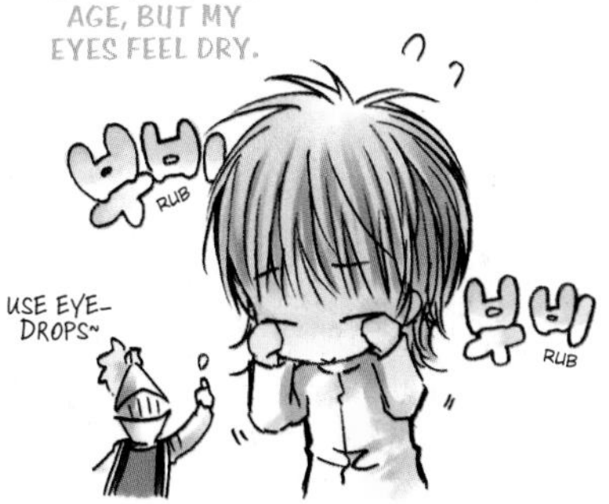
MUST BE BECAUSE OF MY AGE, BUT MY EYES FEEL DRY.
부비
RUB
부비
RUB
USE EYE-DROPS~

#184. LES MISERABLES

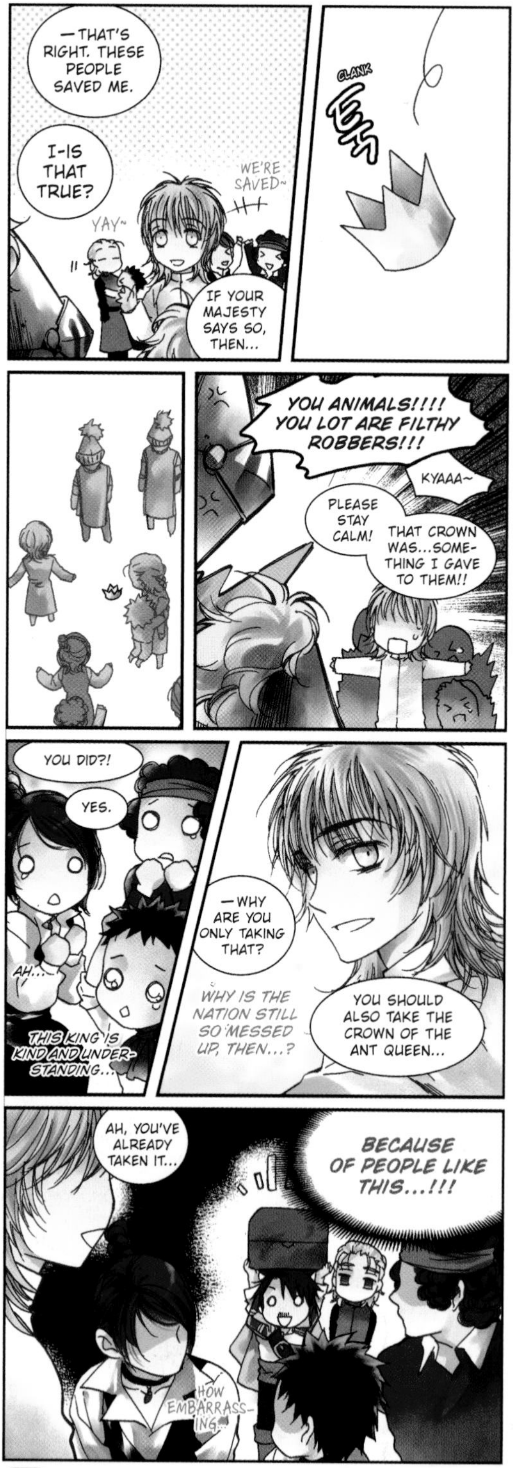

—THAT'S RIGHT. THESE PEOPLE SAVED ME.
I-IS THAT TRUE?
YAY~
WE'RE SAVED~
IF YOUR MAJESTY SAYS SO, THEN...
CLANK
YOU ANIMALS!!!! YOU LOT ARE FILTHY ROBBERS!!!
KYAAA~
PLEASE STAY CALM!
THAT CROWN WAS...SOMETHING I GAVE TO THEM!!
YOU DID?!
YES.
AH...
THIS KING IS KIND AND UNDERSTANDING...
—WHY ARE YOU ONLY TAKING THAT?
WHY IS THE NATION STILL SO MESSED UP, THEN...?
YOU SHOULD ALSO TAKE THE CROWN OF THE ANT QUEEN...
AH, YOU'VE ALREADY TAKEN IT...
BECAUSE OF PEOPLE LIKE THIS...!!!
HOW EMBARRASSING...

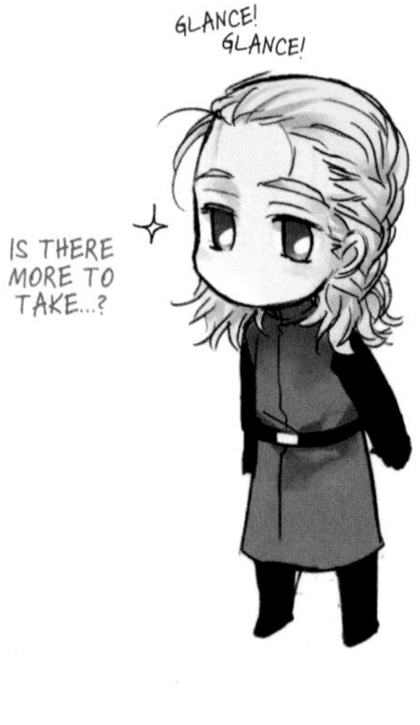

GLANCE! GLANCE!
IS THERE MORE TO TAKE...?

#185. THE MEANING OF A KISS

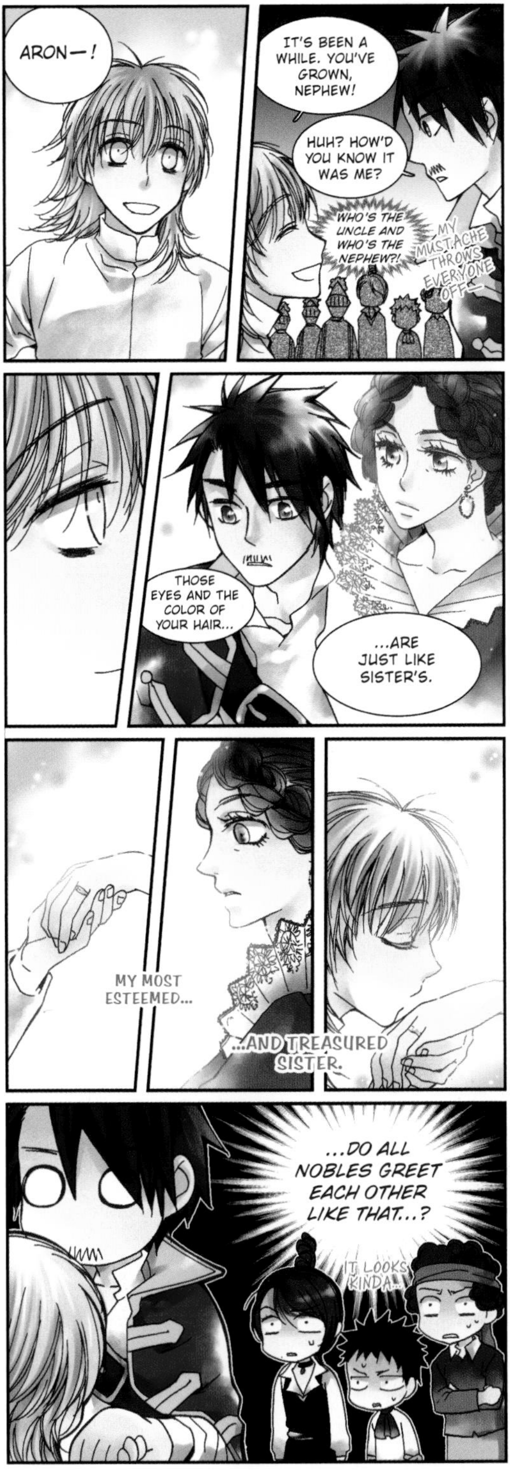
ARON—!
IT'S BEEN A WHILE. YOU'VE GROWN, NEPHEW!
HUH? HOW'D YOU KNOW IT WAS ME?
WHO'S THE UNCLE AND WHO'S THE NEPHEW?!
MY MUSTACHE THROWS EVERYONE OFF—
THOSE EYES AND THE COLOR OF YOUR HAIR...
...ARE JUST LIKE SISTER'S.
MY MOST ESTEEMED...
...AND TREASURED SISTER.
...DO ALL NOBLES GREET EACH OTHER LIKE THAT...?
IT LOOKS KINDA...

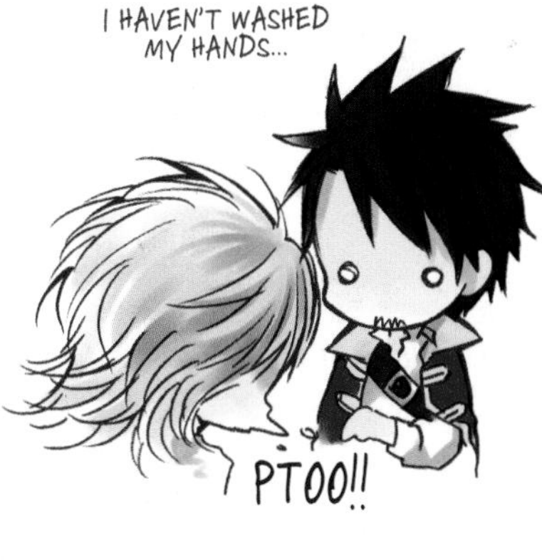
I HAVEN'T WASHED MY HANDS...
PTOO!!

#186. I'LL TAKE JESUS

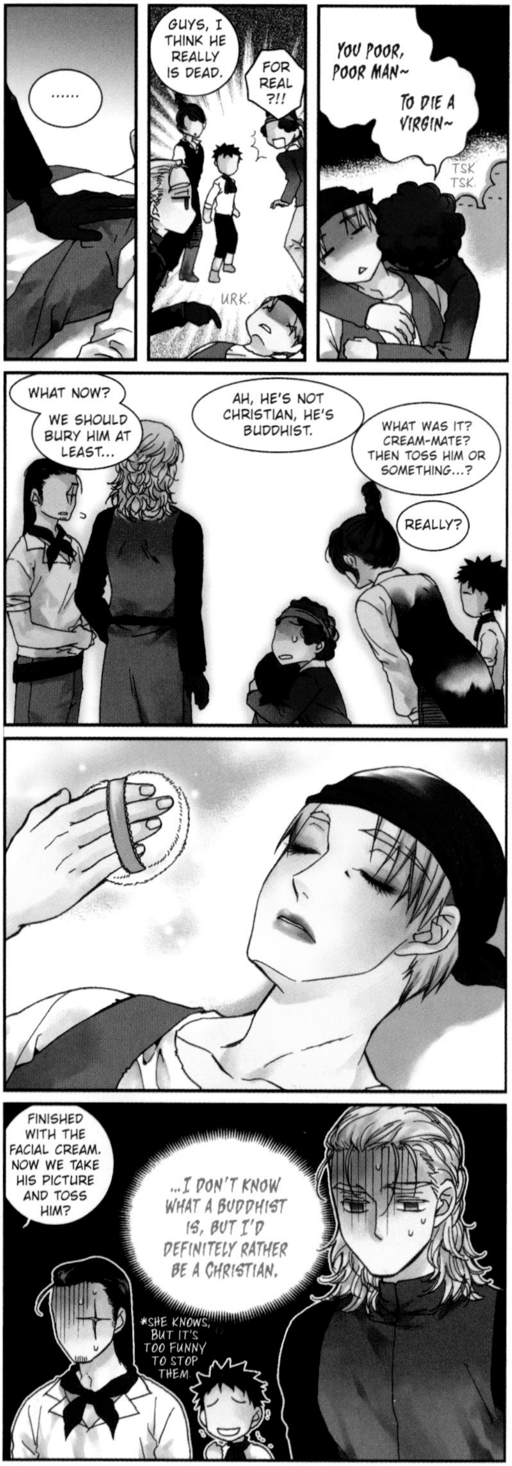

......
GUYS, I THINK HE REALLY IS DEAD.
FOR REAL ?!!
URK.
YOU POOR, POOR MAN~
TO DIE A VIRGIN~
TSK TSK.
WHAT NOW? WE SHOULD BURY HIM AT LEAST...
AH, HE'S NOT CHRISTIAN, HE'S BUDDHIST.
WHAT WAS IT? CREAM-MATE? THEN TOSS HIM OR SOMETHING...?
REALLY?
FINISHED WITH THE FACIAL CREAM. NOW WE TAKE HIS PICTURE AND TOSS HIM?
...I DON'T KNOW WHAT A BUDDHIST IS, BUT I'D DEFINITELY RATHER BE A CHRISTIAN.
*SHE KNOWS, BUT IT'S TOO FUNNY TO STOP THEM.

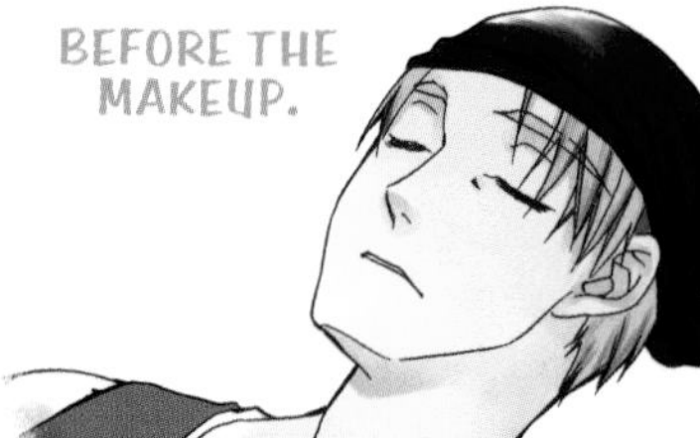

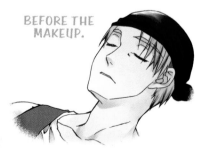

BEFORE THE MAKEUP.

#187. THE KING WHO REPAID HIS DEBT

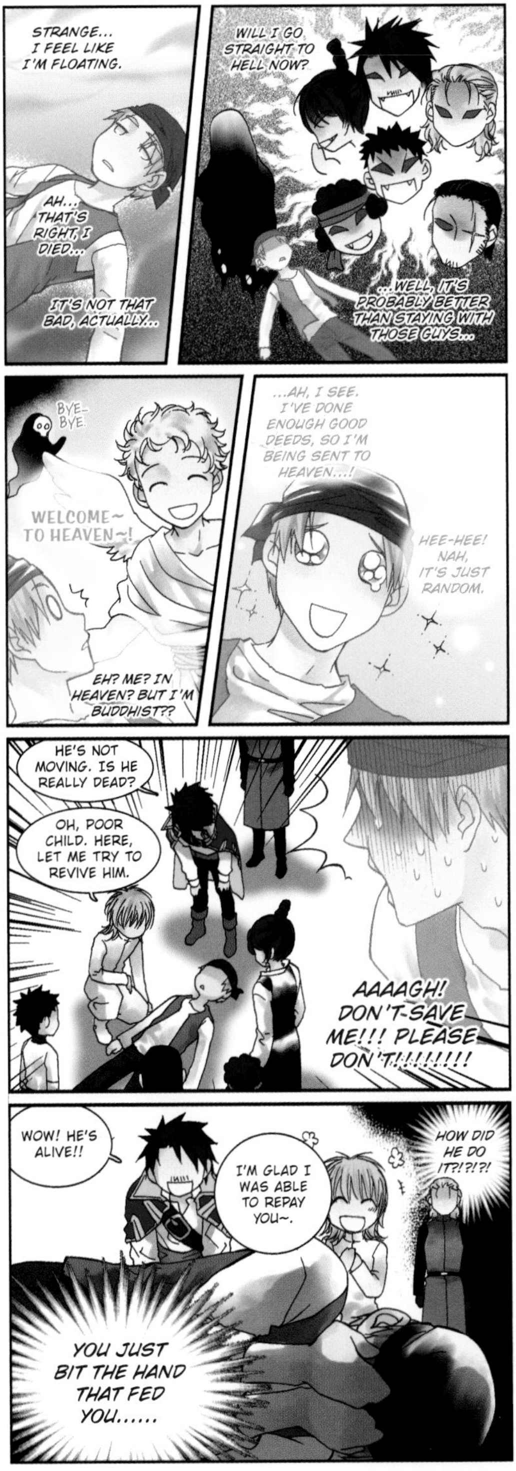

STRANGE... I FEEL LIKE I'M FLOATING.
AH... THAT'S RIGHT, I DIED...
IT'S NOT THAT BAD, ACTUALLY...
WILL I GO STRAIGHT TO HELL NOW?
...WELL, IT'S PROBABLY BETTER THAN STAYING WITH THOSE GUYS...
BYE-BYE.
WELCOME~ TO HEAVEN~!
EH? ME? IN HEAVEN? BUT I'M BUDDHIST??
...AH, I SEE. I'VE DONE ENOUGH GOOD DEEDS, SO I'M BEING SENT TO HEAVEN...!
HEE-HEE! NAH, IT'S JUST RANDOM.
HE'S NOT MOVING. IS HE REALLY DEAD?
OH, POOR CHILD. HERE, LET ME TRY TO REVIVE HIM.
AAAAGH! DON'T SAVE ME!!! PLEASE DON'T!!!!!!!!!
WOW! HE'S ALIVE!!
I'M GLAD I WAS ABLE TO REPAY YOU~.
HOW DID HE DO IT?!?!?!
YOU JUST BIT THE HAND THAT FED YOU......

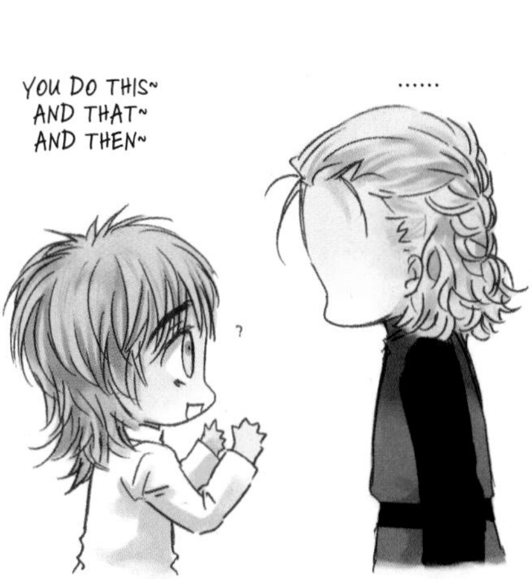

YOU DO THIS~ AND THAT~ AND THEN~
......

#188. ARREST IN THE NAME OF HOSPITALITY

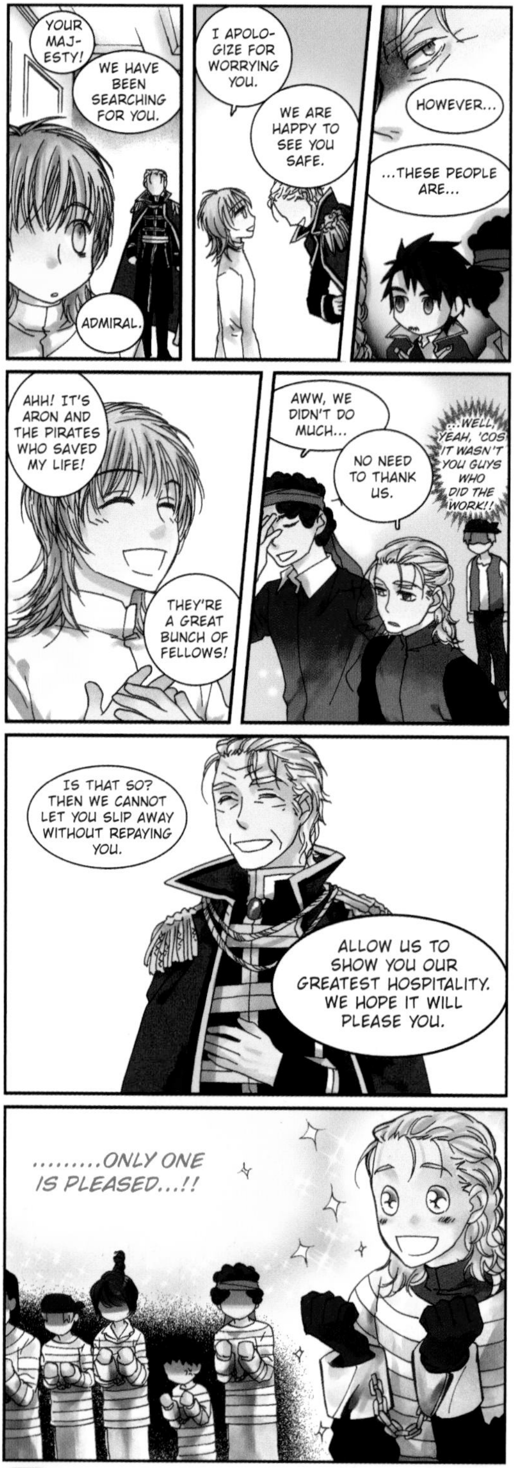
YOUR MAJ-ESTY!
WE HAVE BEEN SEARCHING FOR YOU.
ADMIRAL.
I APOLO-GIZE FOR WORRYING YOU.
WE ARE HAPPY TO SEE YOU SAFE.
HOWEVER...
...THESE PEOPLE ARE...
AHH! IT'S ARON AND THE PIRATES WHO SAVED MY LIFE!
THEY'RE A GREAT BUNCH OF FELLOWS!
AWW, WE DIDN'T DO MUCH...
NO NEED TO THANK US.
...WELL, YEAH, 'COS IT WASN'T YOU GUYS WHO DID THE WORK!!
IS THAT SO? THEN WE CANNOT LET YOU SLIP AWAY WITHOUT REPAYING YOU.
ALLOW US TO SHOW YOU OUR GREATEST HOSPITALITY. WE HOPE IT WILL PLEASE YOU.
.........ONLY ONE IS PLEASED...!!

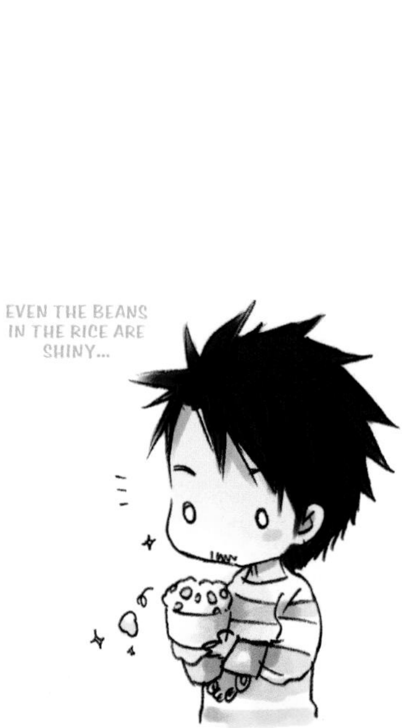
EVEN THE BEANS IN THE RICE ARE SHINY...

#189. RAGE INCARNATE

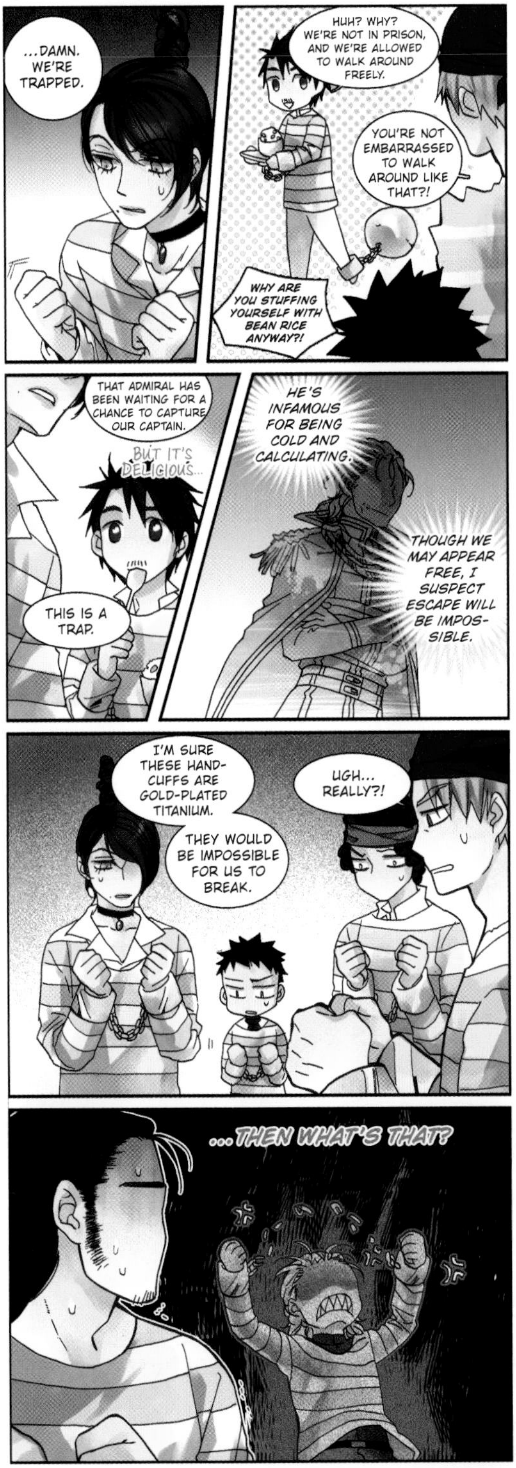

...DAMN. WE'RE TRAPPED.
HUH? WHY? WE'RE NOT IN PRISON, AND WE'RE ALLOWED TO WALK AROUND FREELY.
YOU'RE NOT EMBARRASSED TO WALK AROUND LIKE THAT?!
WHY ARE YOU STUFFING YOURSELF WITH BEAN RICE ANYWAY?!
THAT ADMIRAL HAS BEEN WAITING FOR A CHANCE TO CAPTURE OUR CAPTAIN.
BUT IT'S DELICIOUS...
THIS IS A TRAP.
HE'S INFAMOUS FOR BEING COLD AND CALCULATING.
THOUGH WE MAY APPEAR FREE, I SUSPECT ESCAPE WILL BE IMPOSSIBLE.
I'M SURE THESE HAND-CUFFS ARE GOLD-PLATED TITANIUM.
THEY WOULD BE IMPOSSIBLE FOR US TO BREAK.
UGH... REALLY?!
...THEN WHAT'S THAT?

RAGE INCARNATE

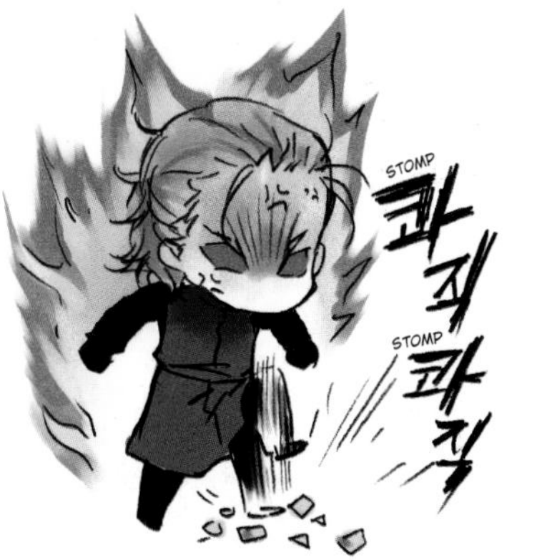

STOMP
콰직
STOMP
콰직

#190. SYMPATHY

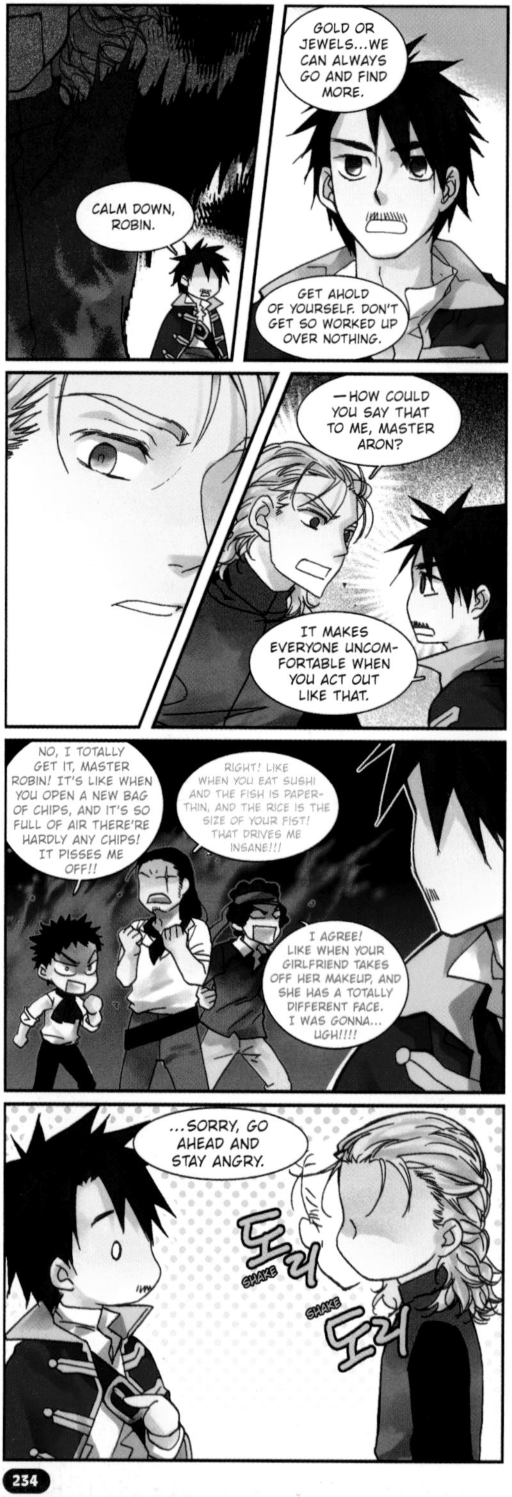
GOLD OR JEWELS...WE CAN ALWAYS GO AND FIND MORE.
CALM DOWN, ROBIN.
GET AHOLD OF YOURSELF. DON'T GET SO WORKED UP OVER NOTHING.
—HOW COULD YOU SAY THAT TO ME, MASTER ARON?
IT MAKES EVERYONE UNCOM-FORTABLE WHEN YOU ACT OUT LIKE THAT.
NO, I TOTALLY GET IT, MASTER ROBIN! IT'S LIKE WHEN YOU OPEN A NEW BAG OF CHIPS, AND IT'S SO FULL OF AIR THERE'RE HARDLY ANY CHIPS! IT PISSES ME OFF!!
RIGHT! LIKE WHEN YOU EAT SUSHI AND THE FISH IS PAPER-THIN, AND THE RICE IS THE SIZE OF YOUR FIST! THAT DRIVES ME INSANE!!!
I AGREE! LIKE WHEN YOUR GIRLFRIEND TAKES OFF HER MAKEUP, AND SHE HAS A TOTALLY DIFFERENT FACE. I WAS GONNA... UGH!!!!
...SORRY, GO AHEAD AND STAY ANGRY.
도리 SHAKE
도리 SHAKE

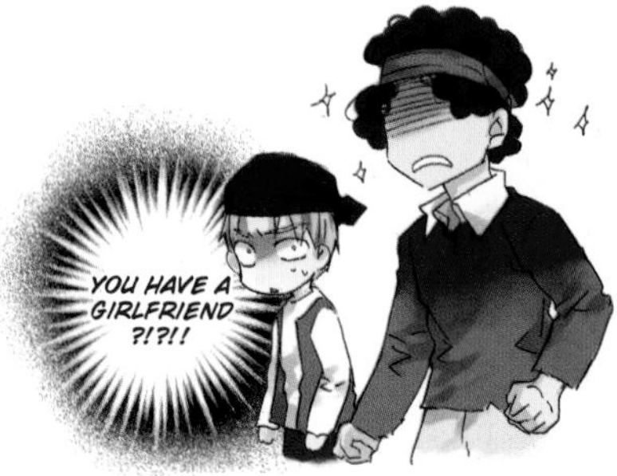
YOU HAVE A GIRLFRIEND ?!?!!

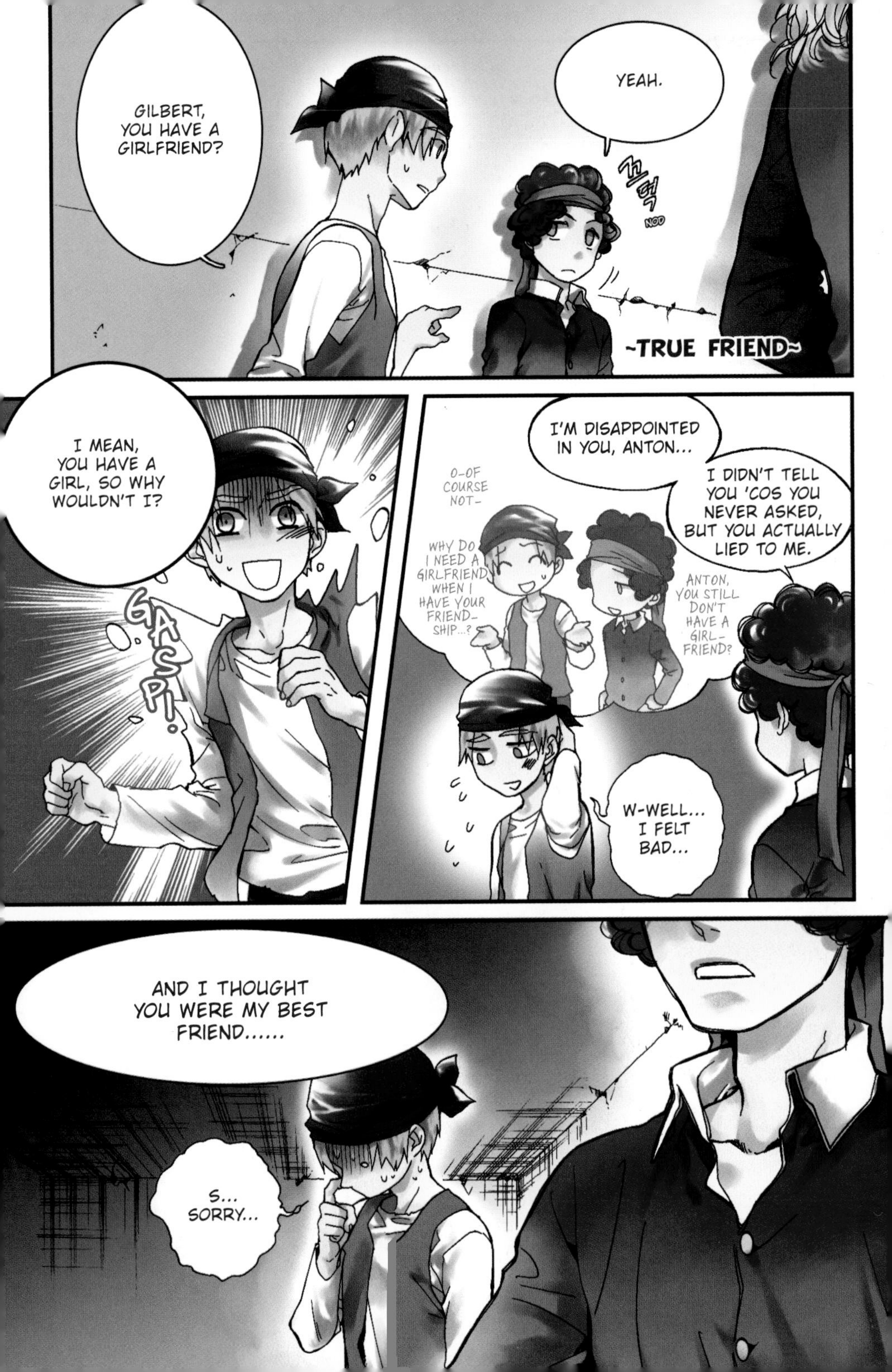
GILBERT, YOU HAVE A GIRLFRIEND?
YEAH.
끄덕
NOD
~TRUE FRIEND~
I MEAN, YOU HAVE A GIRL, SO WHY WOULDN'T I?
GASP!
I'M DISAPPOINTED IN YOU, ANTON...
O-OF COURSE NOT-
WHY DO I NEED A GIRLFRIEND WHEN I HAVE YOUR FRIENDSHIP...?
ANTON, YOU STILL DON'T HAVE A GIRLFRIEND?
I DIDN'T TELL YOU 'COS YOU NEVER ASKED, BUT YOU ACTUALLY LIED TO ME.
W-WELL... I FELT BAD...
AND I THOUGHT YOU WERE MY BEST FRIEND......
S... SORRY...

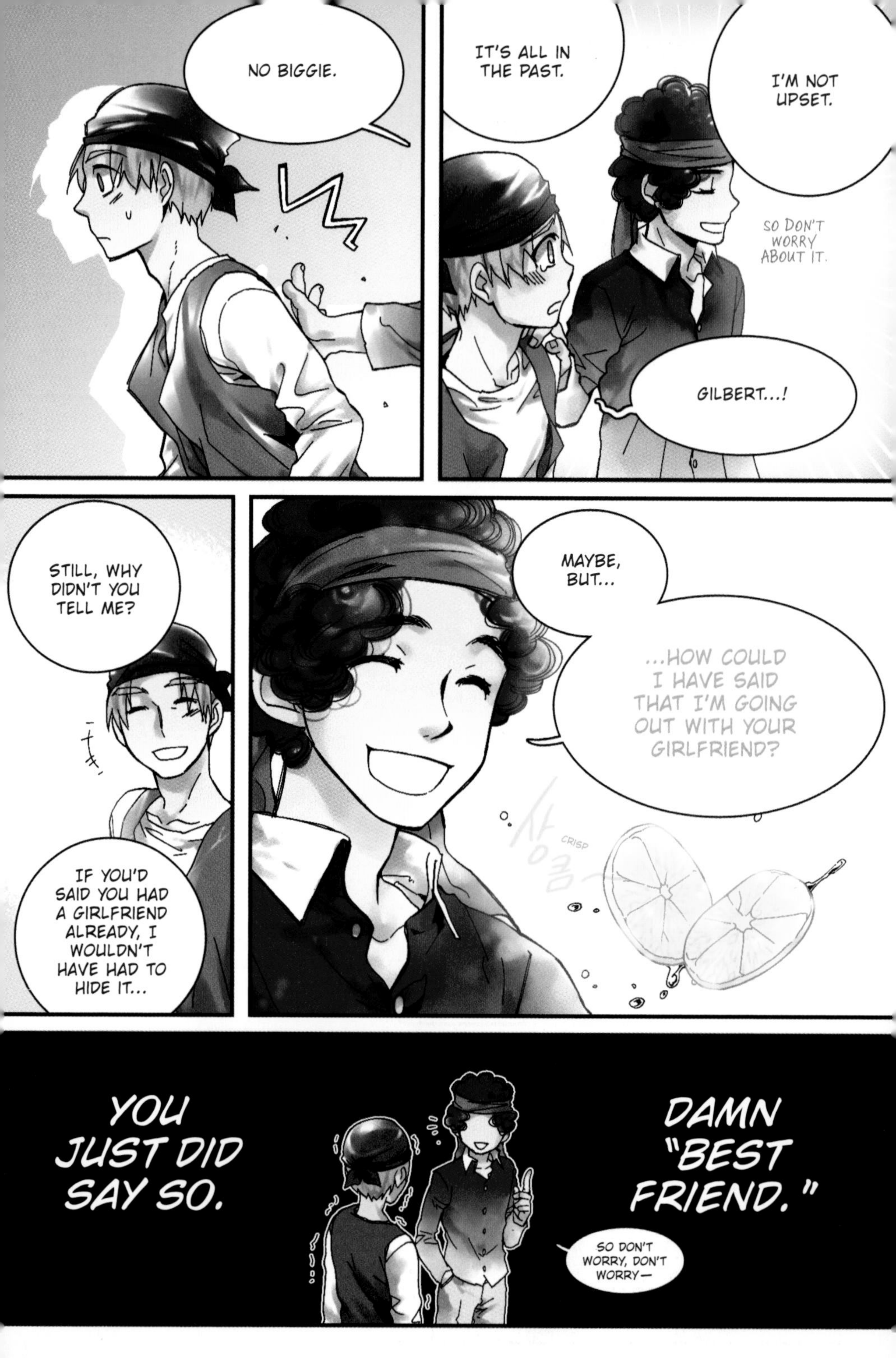
NO BIGGIE.
IT'S ALL IN THE PAST.
I'M NOT UPSET.
SO DON'T WORRY ABOUT IT.
GILBERT...!
STILL, WHY DIDN'T YOU TELL ME?
IF YOU'D SAID YOU HAD A GIRLFRIEND ALREADY, I WOULDN'T HAVE HAD TO HIDE IT...
MAYBE, BUT...
...HOW COULD I HAVE SAID THAT I'M GOING OUT WITH YOUR GIRLFRIEND?
CRISP
YOU JUST DID SAY SO.
DAMN "BEST FRIEND."
SO DON'T WORRY, DON'T WORRY—

#191. BECAUSE YOU'RE A MAN

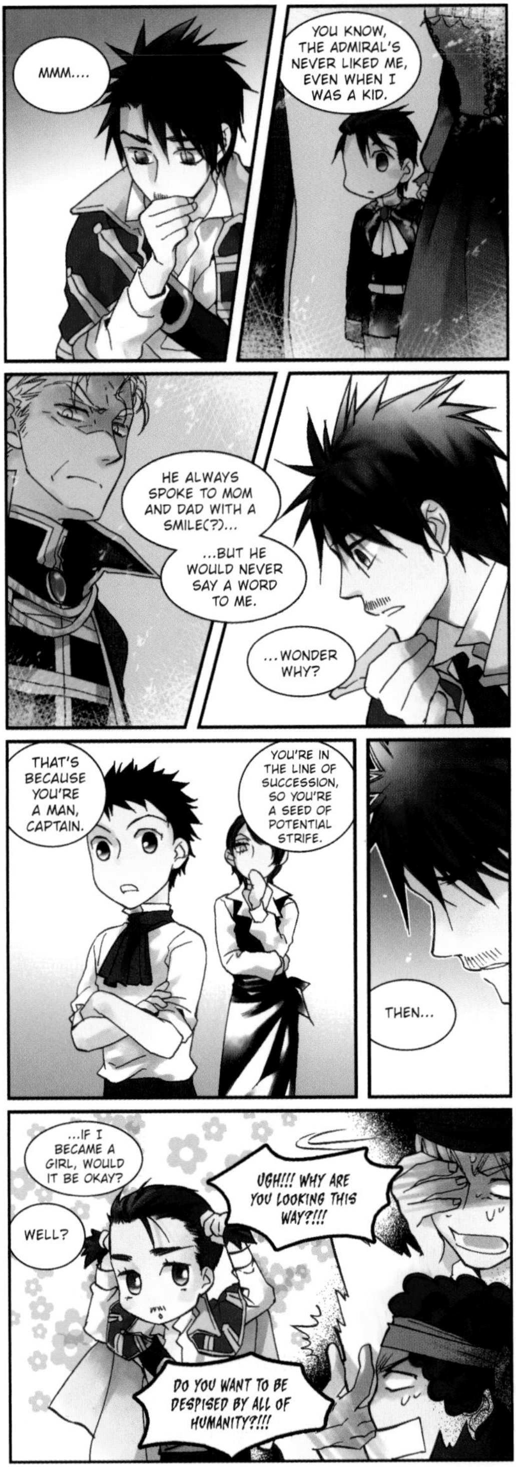
MMM....
YOU KNOW, THE ADMIRAL'S NEVER LIKED ME, EVEN WHEN I WAS A KID.
HE ALWAYS SPOKE TO MOM AND DAD WITH A SMILE(?)...
...BUT HE WOULD NEVER SAY A WORD TO ME.
...WONDER WHY?
THAT'S BECAUSE YOU'RE A MAN, CAPTAIN.
YOU'RE IN THE LINE OF SUCCESSION, SO YOU'RE A SEED OF POTENTIAL STRIFE.
THEN...
...IF I BECAME A GIRL, WOULD IT BE OKAY?
WELL?
UGH!!! WHY ARE YOU LOOKING THIS WAY?!!!
DO YOU WANT TO BE DESPISED BY ALL OF HUMANITY?!!!

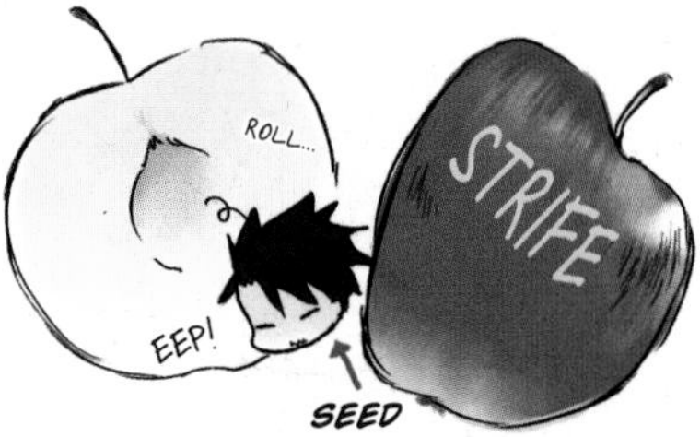
ROLL...
STRIFE
EEP!
SEED

#192. SEX ED FOR GROWN-UPS

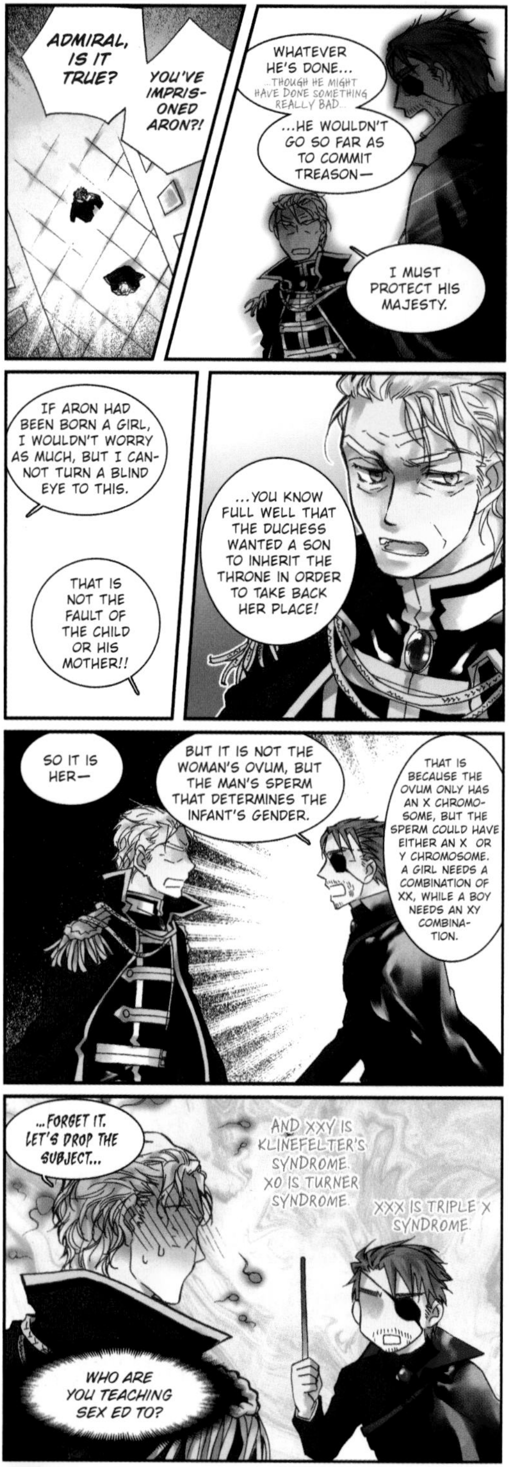
ADMIRAL, IS IT TRUE?
YOU'VE IMPRIS-ONED ARON?!
WHATEVER HE'S DONE...
...THOUGH HE MIGHT HAVE DONE SOMETHING REALLY BAD...
...HE WOULDN'T GO SO FAR AS TO COMMIT TREASON—
I MUST PROTECT HIS MAJESTY.
IF ARON HAD BEEN BORN A GIRL, I WOULDN'T WORRY AS MUCH, BUT I CAN-NOT TURN A BLIND EYE TO THIS.
...YOU KNOW FULL WELL THAT THE DUCHESS WANTED A SON TO INHERIT THE THRONE IN ORDER TO TAKE BACK HER PLACE!
THAT IS NOT THE FAULT OF THE CHILD OR HIS MOTHER!!
SO IT IS HER—
BUT IT IS NOT THE WOMAN'S OVUM, BUT THE MAN'S SPERM THAT DETERMINES THE INFANT'S GENDER.
THAT IS BECAUSE THE OVUM ONLY HAS AN X CHROMO-SOME, BUT THE SPERM COULD HAVE EITHER AN X OR Y CHROMOSOME. A GIRL NEEDS A COMBINATION OF XX, WHILE A BOY NEEDS AN XY COMBINA-TION.
...FORGET IT. LET'S DROP THE SUBJECT...
AND XXY IS KLINEFELTER'S SYNDROME. XO IS TURNER SYNDROME.
XXX IS TRIPLE X SYNDROME.
WHO ARE YOU TEACHING SEX ED TO?

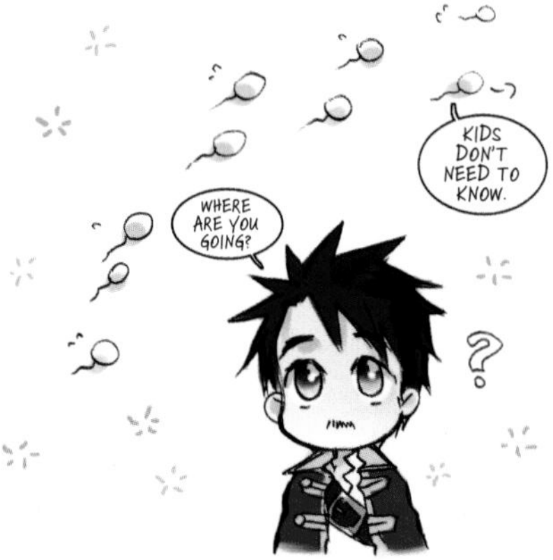
WHERE ARE YOU GOING?
KIDS DON'T NEED TO KNOW.

#193. ONLY ONE PERSON

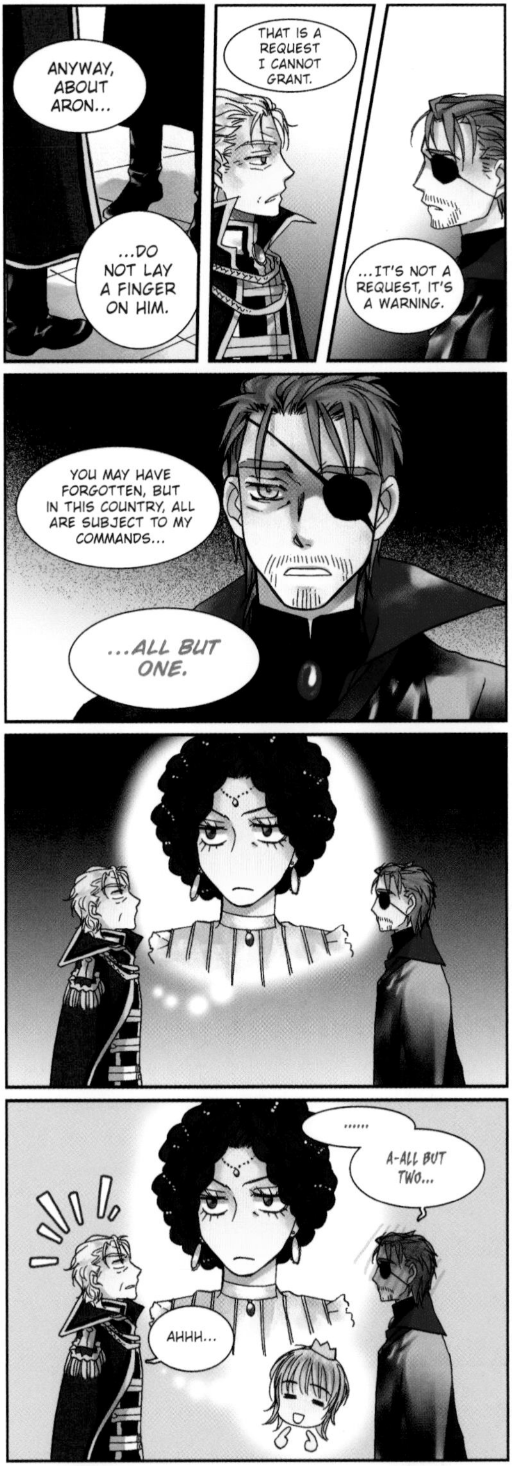

ANYWAY, ABOUT ARON...
...DO NOT LAY A FINGER ON HIM.
THAT IS A REQUEST I CANNOT GRANT.
...IT'S NOT A REQUEST, IT'S A WARNING.
YOU MAY HAVE FORGOTTEN, BUT IN THIS COUNTRY, ALL ARE SUBJECT TO MY COMMANDS...
...ALL BUT ONE.
......
A-ALL BUT TWO...
AHHH...

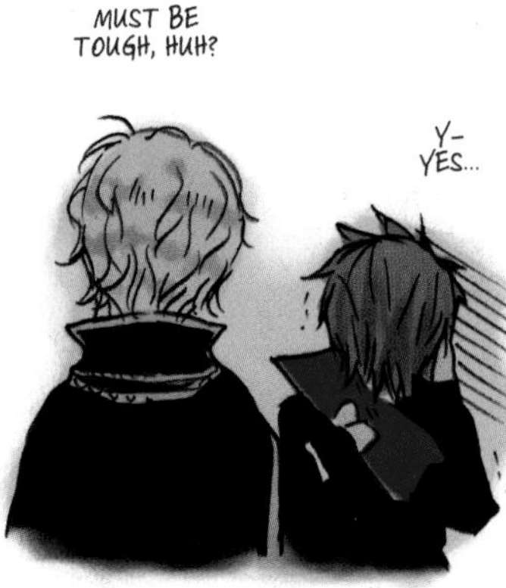

MUST BE TOUGH, HUH?
Y- YES...

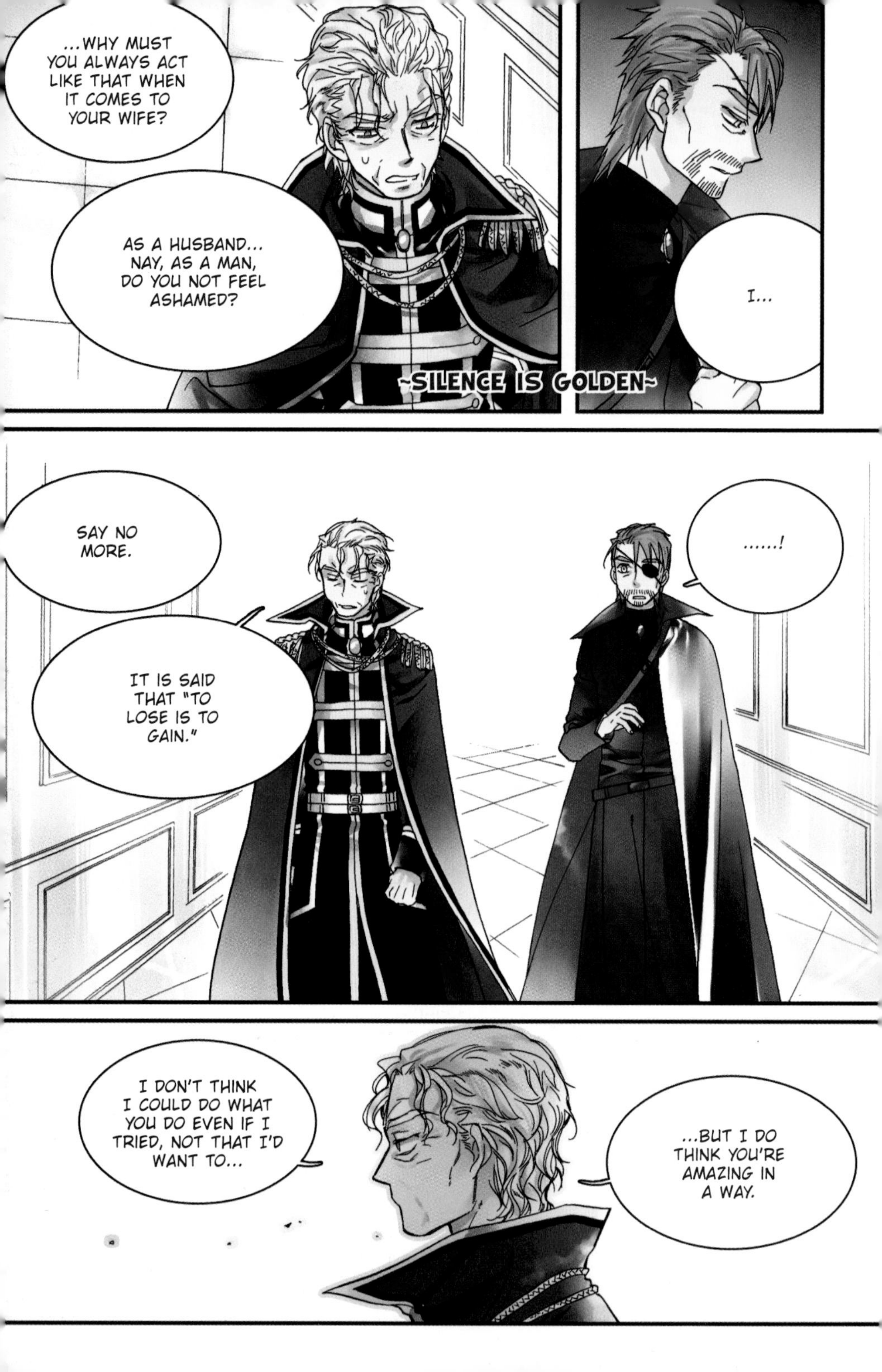
...WHY MUST YOU ALWAYS ACT LIKE THAT WHEN IT COMES TO YOUR WIFE?
AS A HUSBAND... NAY, AS A MAN, DO YOU NOT FEEL ASHAMED?
I...
~SILENCE IS GOLDEN~
SAY NO MORE.
IT IS SAID THAT "TO LOSE IS TO GAIN."
......!
I DON'T THINK I COULD DO WHAT YOU DO EVEN IF I TRIED, NOT THAT I'D WANT TO...
...BUT I DO THINK YOU'RE AMAZING IN A WAY.

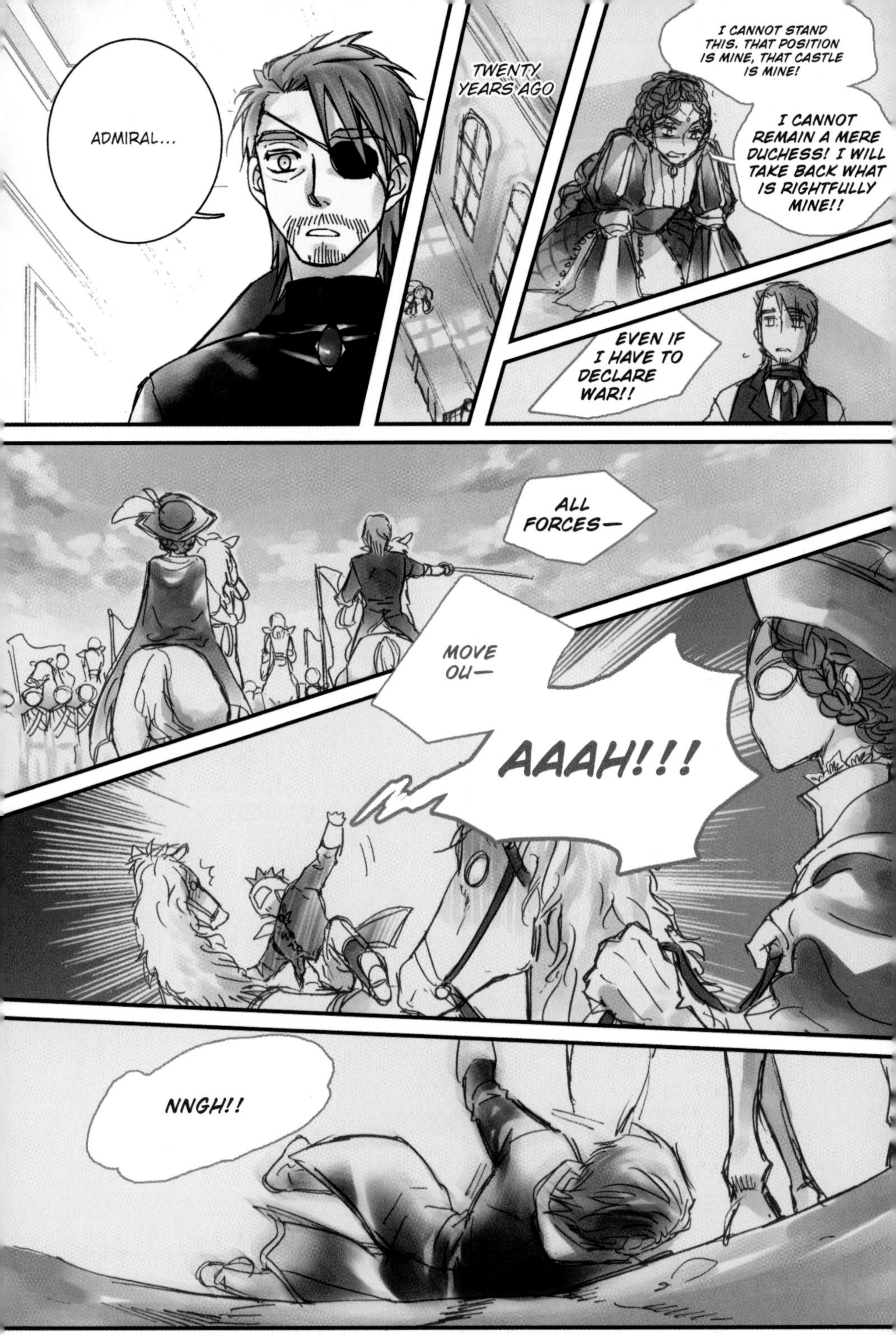
ADMIRAL...
TWENTY YEARS AGO
I CANNOT STAND THIS. THAT POSITION IS MINE, THAT CASTLE IS MINE!
I CANNOT REMAIN A MERE DUCHESS! I WILL TAKE BACK WHAT IS RIGHTFULLY MINE!!
EVEN IF I HAVE TO DECLARE WAR!!
ALL FORCES—
MOVE OU—
AAAH!!!
NNGH!!

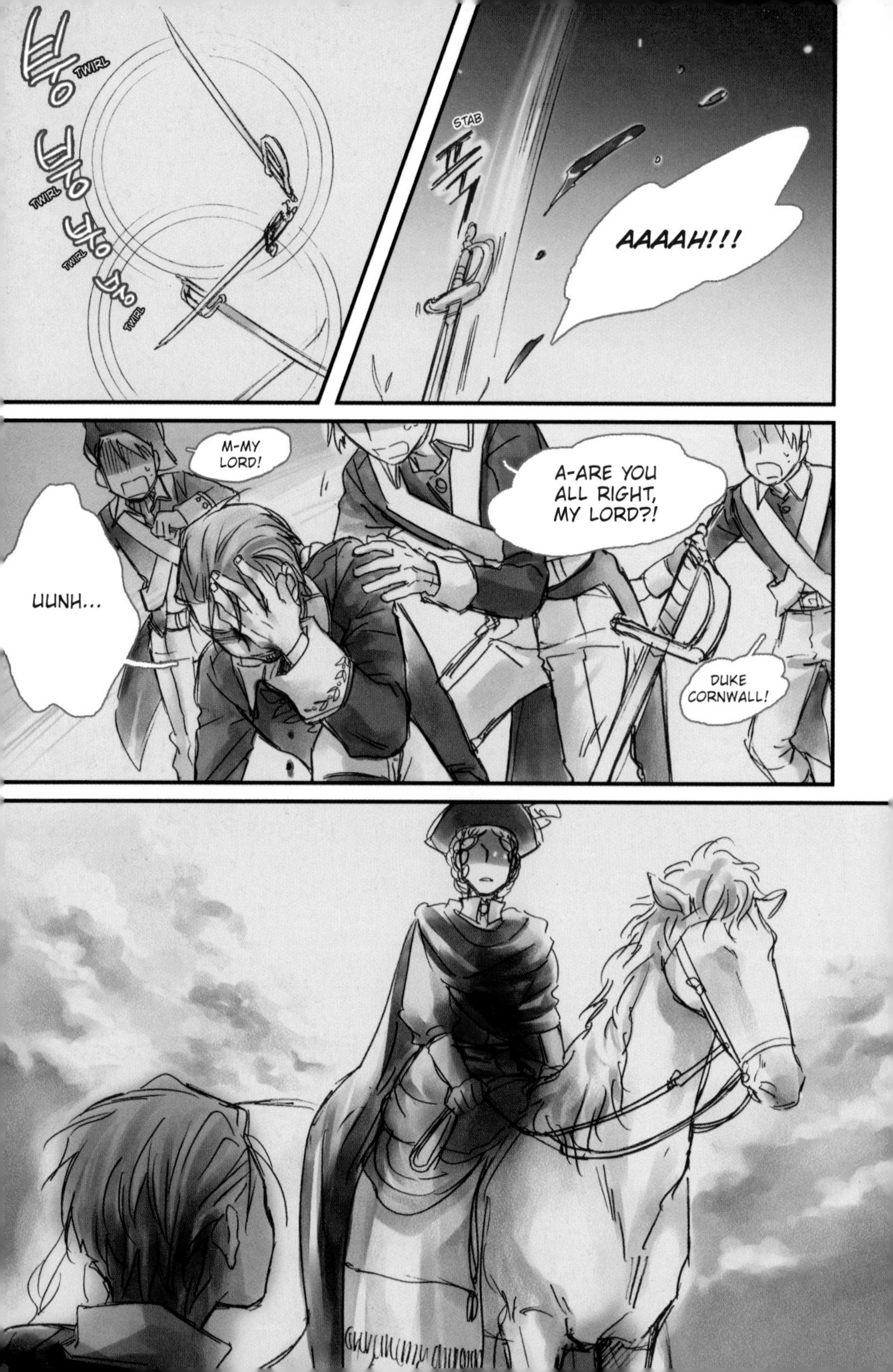
붕 TWIRL
붕 TWIRL
붕 TWIRL
붕 TWIRL
STAB
푹
AAAAH!!!
M-MY LORD!
A-ARE YOU ALL RIGHT, MY LORD?!
UUNH...
DUKE CORNWALL!

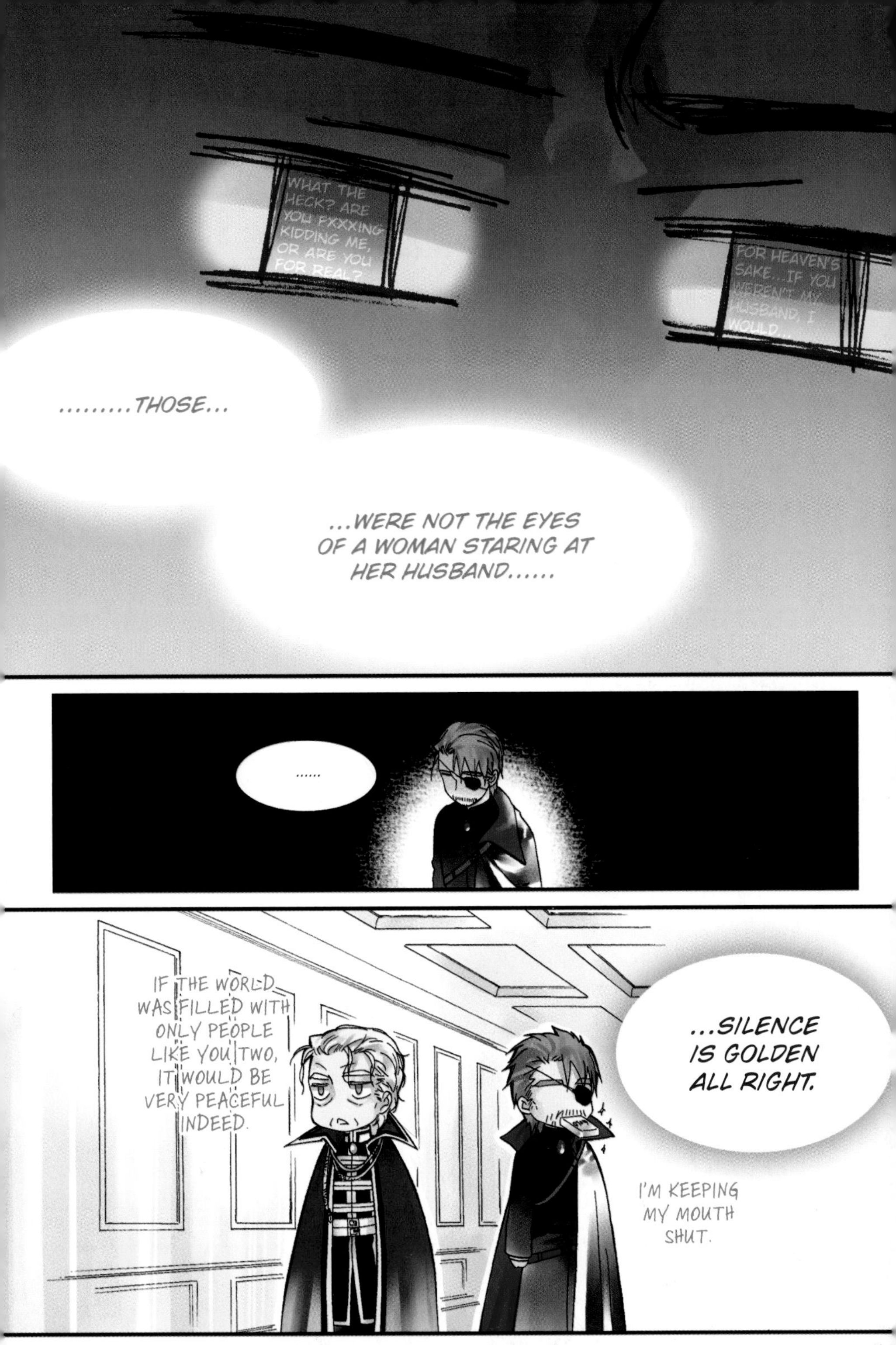

WHAT THE HECK? ARE YOU FXXXING KIDDING ME, OR ARE YOU FOR REAL?
FOR HEAVEN'S SAKE...IF YOU WEREN'T MY HUSBAND, I WOULD...
.........THOSE...
...WERE NOT THE EYES OF A WOMAN STARING AT HER HUSBAND......
......
IF THE WORLD WAS FILLED WITH ONLY PEOPLE LIKE YOU TWO, IT WOULD BE VERY PEACEFUL INDEED.
...SILENCE IS GOLDEN ALL RIGHT.
I'M KEEPING MY MOUTH SHUT.

#194. PROFESSIONAL TOUCH

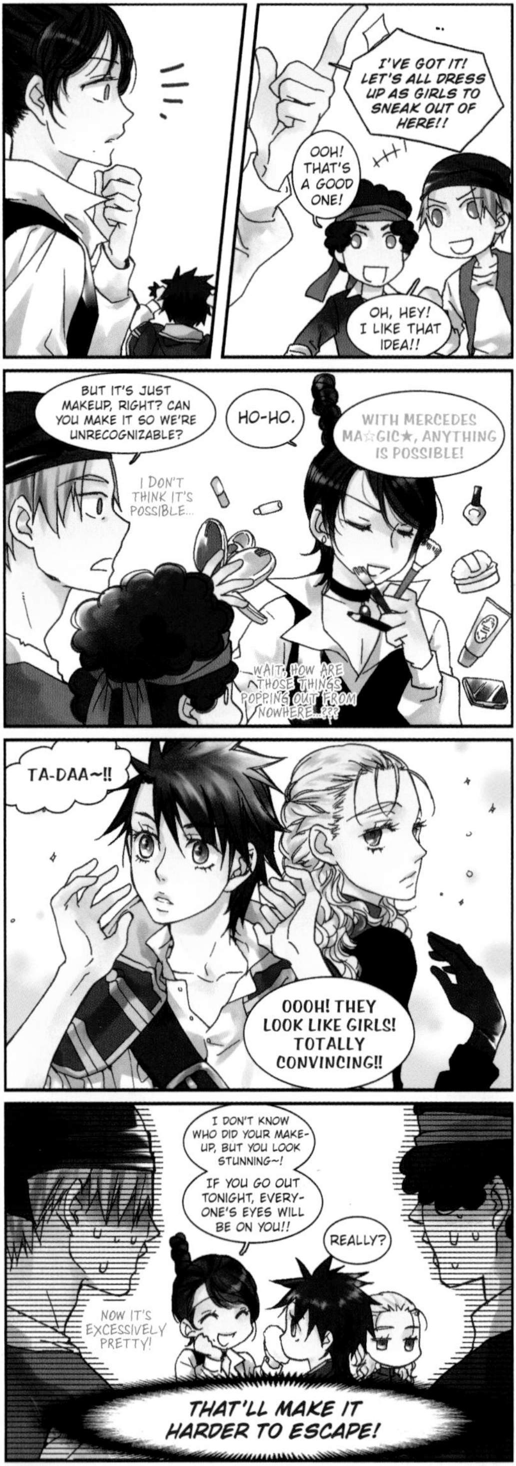
I'VE GOT IT! LET'S ALL DRESS UP AS GIRLS TO SNEAK OUT OF HERE!!
OOH! THAT'S A GOOD ONE!
OH, HEY! I LIKE THAT IDEA!!
BUT IT'S JUST MAKEUP, RIGHT? CAN YOU MAKE IT SO WE'RE UNRECOGNIZABLE?
I DON'T THINK IT'S POSSIBLE...
HO-HO.
WITH MERCEDES MA☆GIC★, ANYTHING IS POSSIBLE!
WAIT, HOW ARE THOSE THINGS POPPING OUT FROM NOWHERE...???
TA-DAA~!!
OOOH! THEY LOOK LIKE GIRLS! TOTALLY CONVINCING!!
I DON'T KNOW WHO DID YOUR MAKE-UP, BUT YOU LOOK STUNNING~!
IF YOU GO OUT TONIGHT, EVERYONE'S EYES WILL BE ON YOU!!
REALLY?
NOW IT'S EXCESSIVELY PRETTY!
THAT'LL MAKE IT HARDER TO ESCAPE!

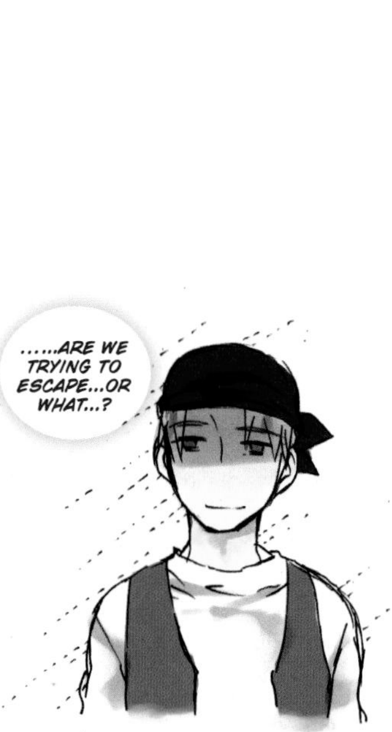
......ARE WE TRYING TO ESCAPE...OR WHAT...?

#195. THE FRIGHTENING TRUTH BEHIND THE FAIRY TALE

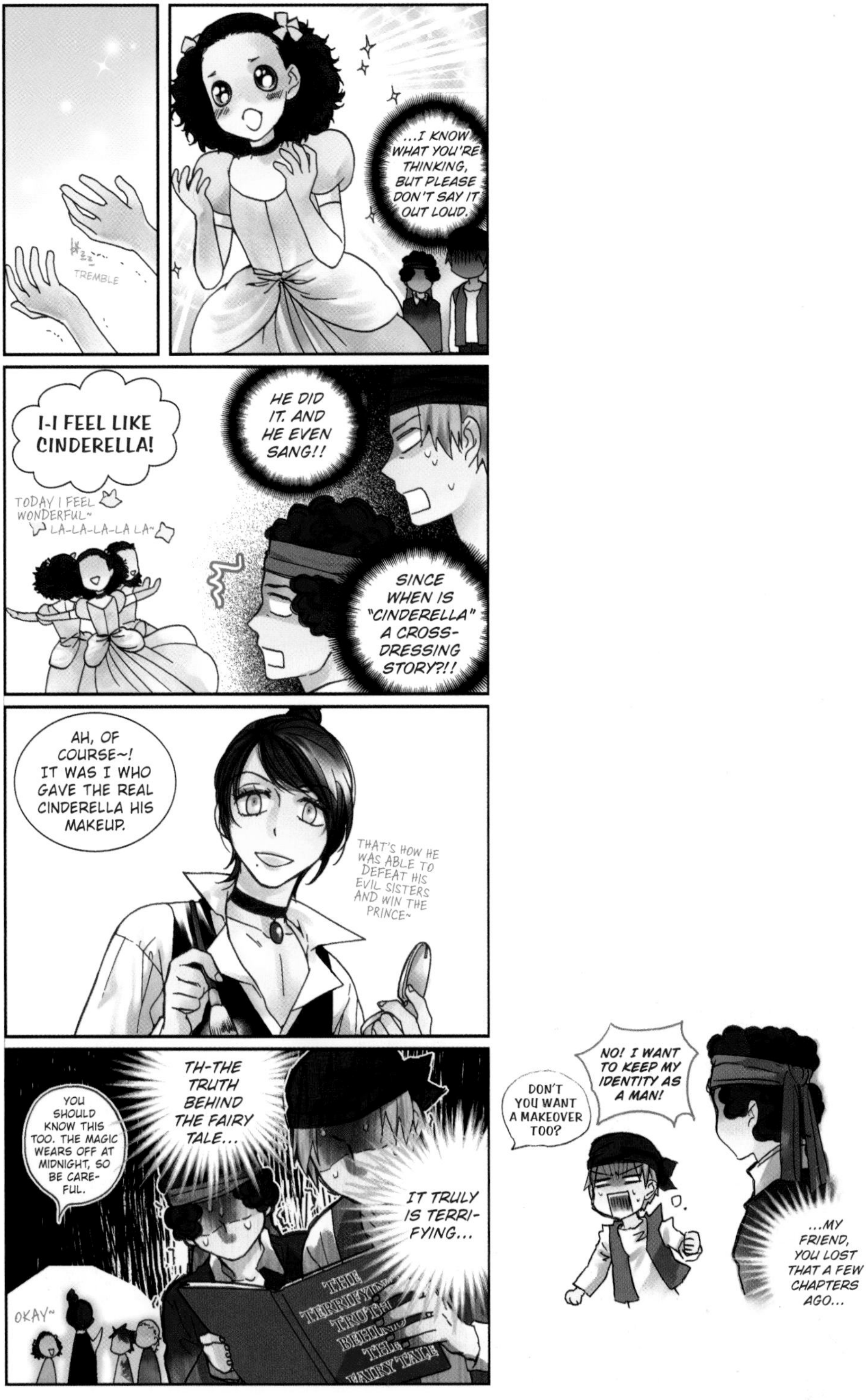
TREMBLE
...I KNOW WHAT YOU'RE THINKING, BUT PLEASE DON'T SAY IT OUT LOUD.
I-I FEEL LIKE CINDERELLA!
TODAY I FEEL WONDERFUL~ LA-LA-LA-LA LA~
HE DID IT. AND HE EVEN SANG!!
SINCE WHEN IS "CINDERELLA" A CROSS-DRESSING STORY?!!
AH, OF COURSE~! IT WAS I WHO GAVE THE REAL CINDERELLA HIS MAKEUP.
THAT'S HOW HE WAS ABLE TO DEFEAT HIS EVIL SISTERS AND WIN THE PRINCE~
YOU SHOULD KNOW THIS TOO. THE MAGIC WEARS OFF AT MIDNIGHT, SO BE CAREFUL.
OKAY~
TH-THE TRUTH BEHIND THE FAIRY TALE...
IT TRULY IS TERRIFYING...
THE TERRIFYING TRUTH BEHIND THE FAIRY TALE
DON'T YOU WANT A MAKEOVER TOO?
NO! I WANT TO KEEP MY IDENTITY AS A MAN!
...MY FRIEND, YOU LOST THAT A FEW CHAPTERS AGO...

#196. GHOST

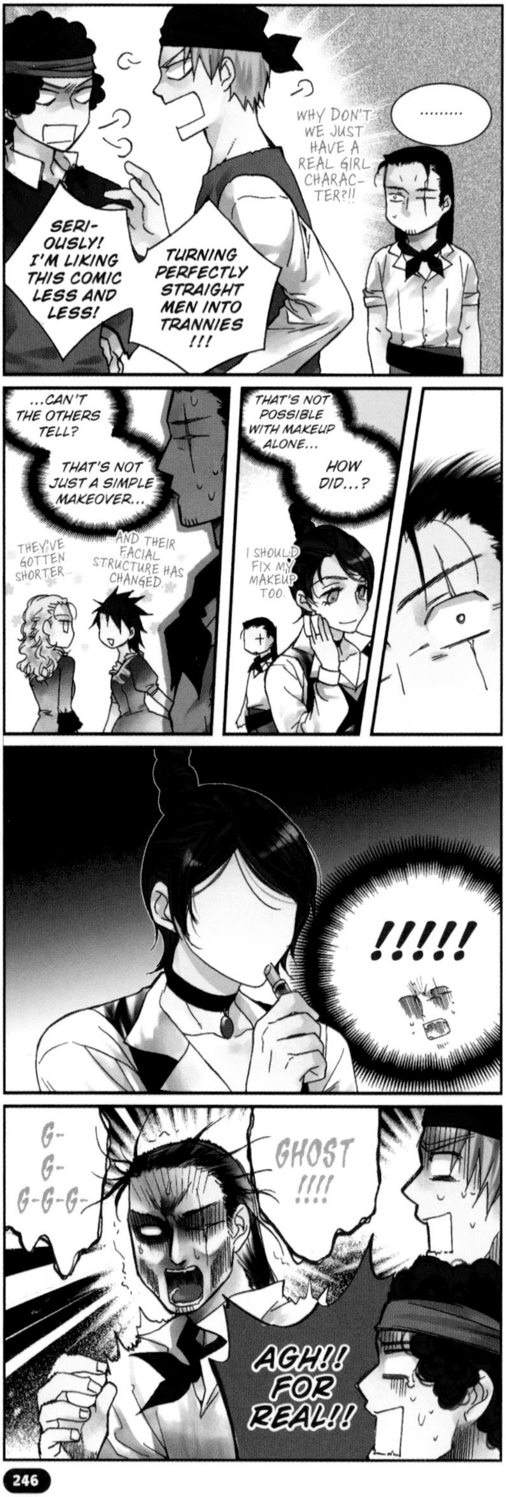

TURNING PERFECTLY STRAIGHT MEN INTO TRANNIES!!!
SERIOUSLY! I'M LIKING THIS COMIC LESS AND LESS!
WHY DON'T WE JUST HAVE A REAL GIRL CHARACTER?!!
....
...CAN'T THE OTHERS TELL?
THAT'S NOT JUST A SIMPLE MAKEOVER...
THEY'VE GOTTEN SHORTER...
AND THEIR FACIAL STRUCTURE HAS CHANGED.
THAT'S NOT POSSIBLE WITH MAKEUP ALONE...
HOW DID...?
I SHOULD FIX MY MAKEUP TOO.
!!!!!
G-G-G-G-G-
GHOST!!!!
AGH!! FOR REAL!!

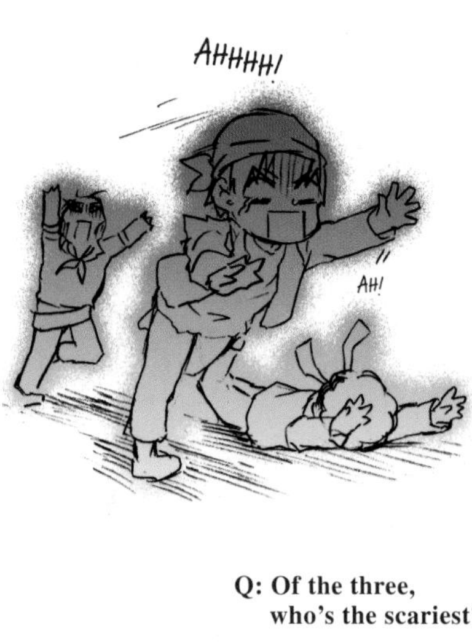

AHHHH!
AH!

Q: Of the three, who's the scariest?

#197. MAKEUP CAN MAKE A PERSON

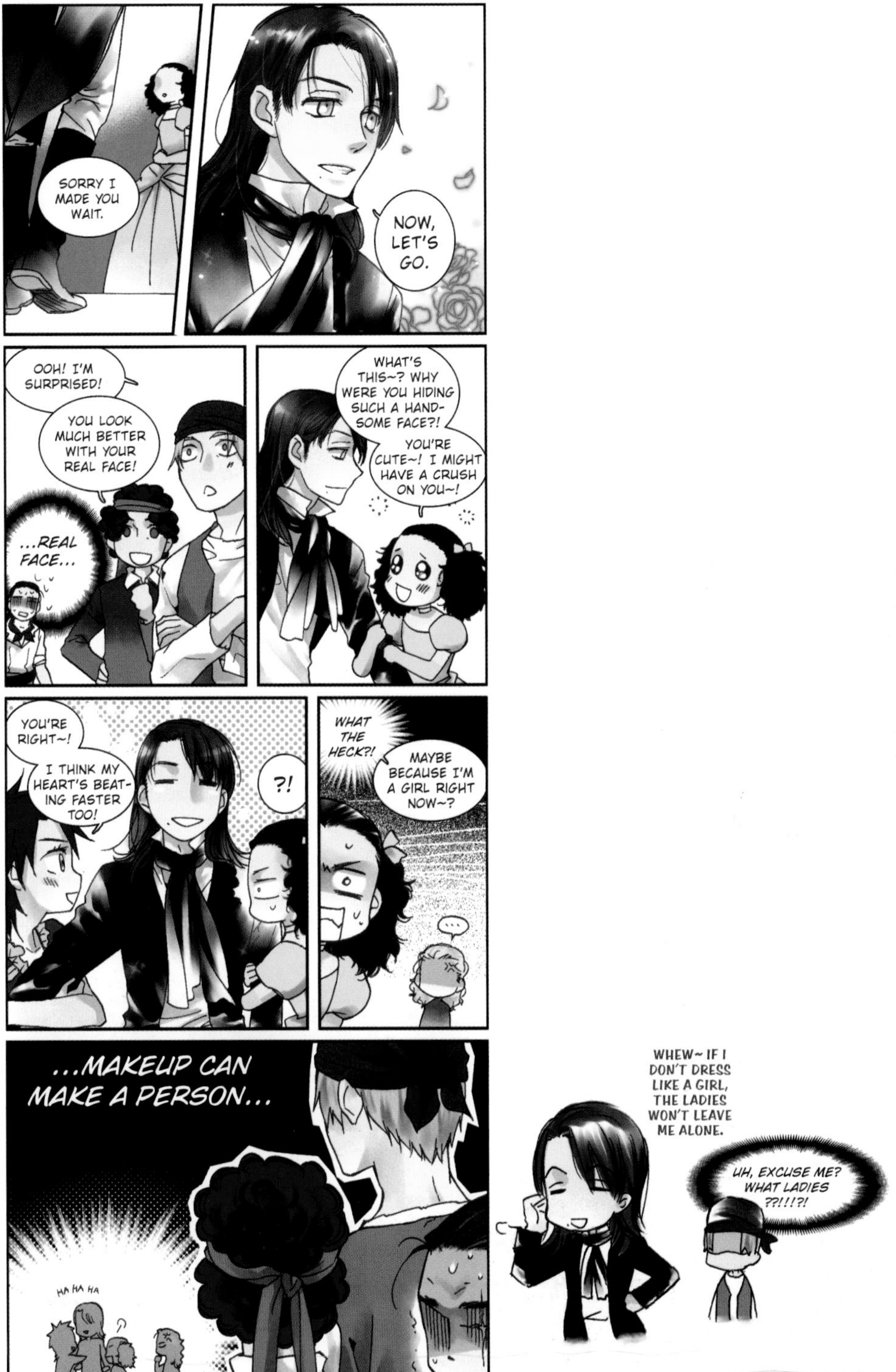

SORRY I MADE YOU WAIT.
NOW, LET'S GO.
OOH! I'M SURPRISED!
YOU LOOK MUCH BETTER WITH YOUR REAL FACE!
...REAL FACE...
WHAT'S THIS~? WHY WERE YOU HIDING SUCH A HAND-SOME FACE?!
YOU'RE CUTE~! I MIGHT HAVE A CRUSH ON YOU~!
YOU'RE RIGHT~!
I THINK MY HEART'S BEAT-ING FASTER TOO!
?!
WHAT THE HECK?!
MAYBE BECAUSE I'M A GIRL RIGHT NOW~?
...
...MAKEUP CAN MAKE A PERSON...
HA HA HA
WHEW~ IF I DON'T DRESS LIKE A GIRL, THE LADIES WON'T LEAVE ME ALONE.
UH, EXCUSE ME? WHAT LADIES ??!!!?!

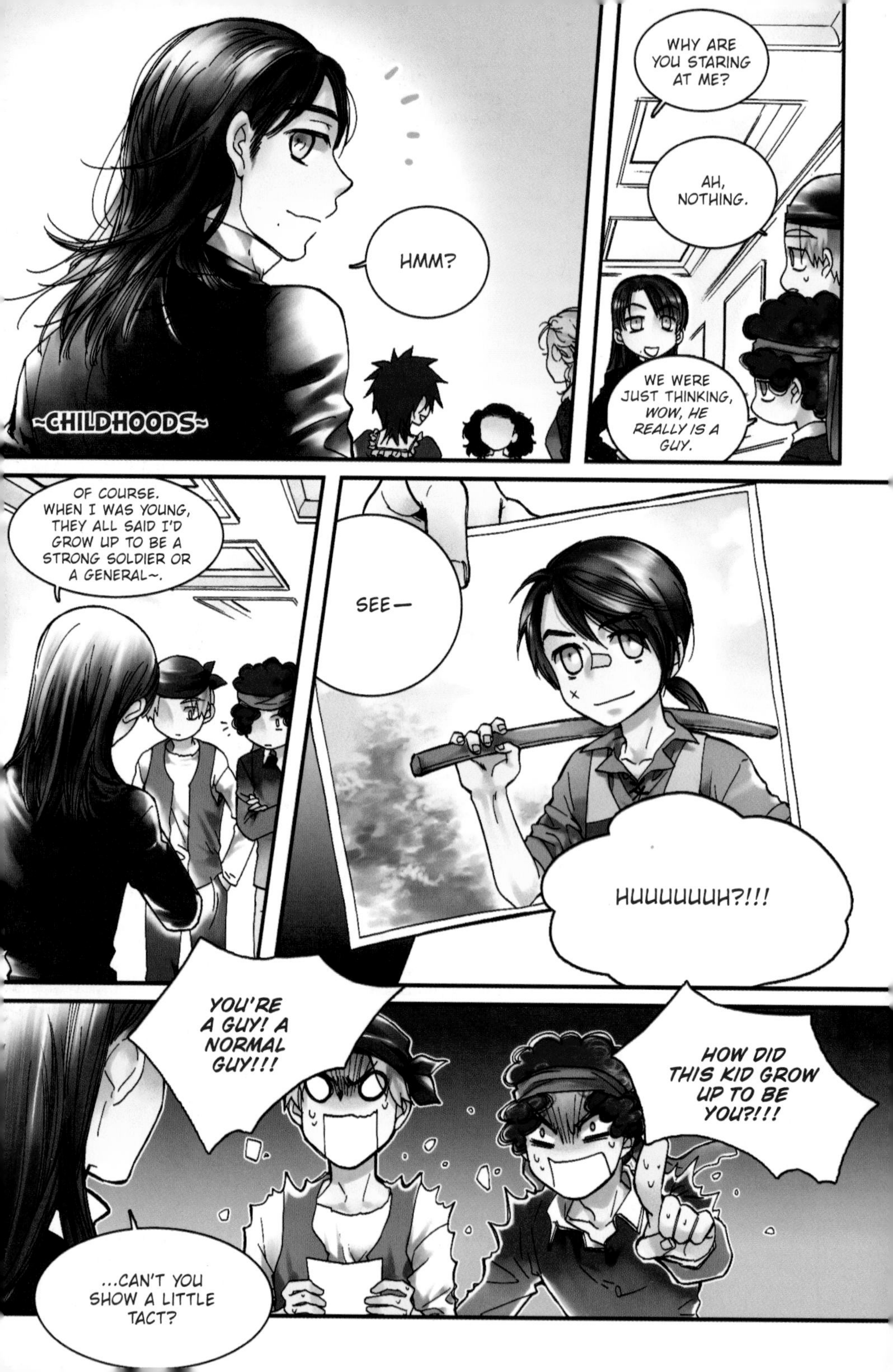
HMM?
~CHILDHOODS~
WHY ARE YOU STARING AT ME?
AH, NOTHING.
WE WERE JUST THINKING, WOW, HE REALLY IS A GUY.
OF COURSE. WHEN I WAS YOUNG, THEY ALL SAID I'D GROW UP TO BE A STRONG SOLDIER OR A GENERAL~.
SEE—
HUUUUUUH?!!!
YOU'RE A GUY! A NORMAL GUY!!!
HOW DID THIS KID GROW UP TO BE YOU?!!!
...CAN'T YOU SHOW A LITTLE TACT?

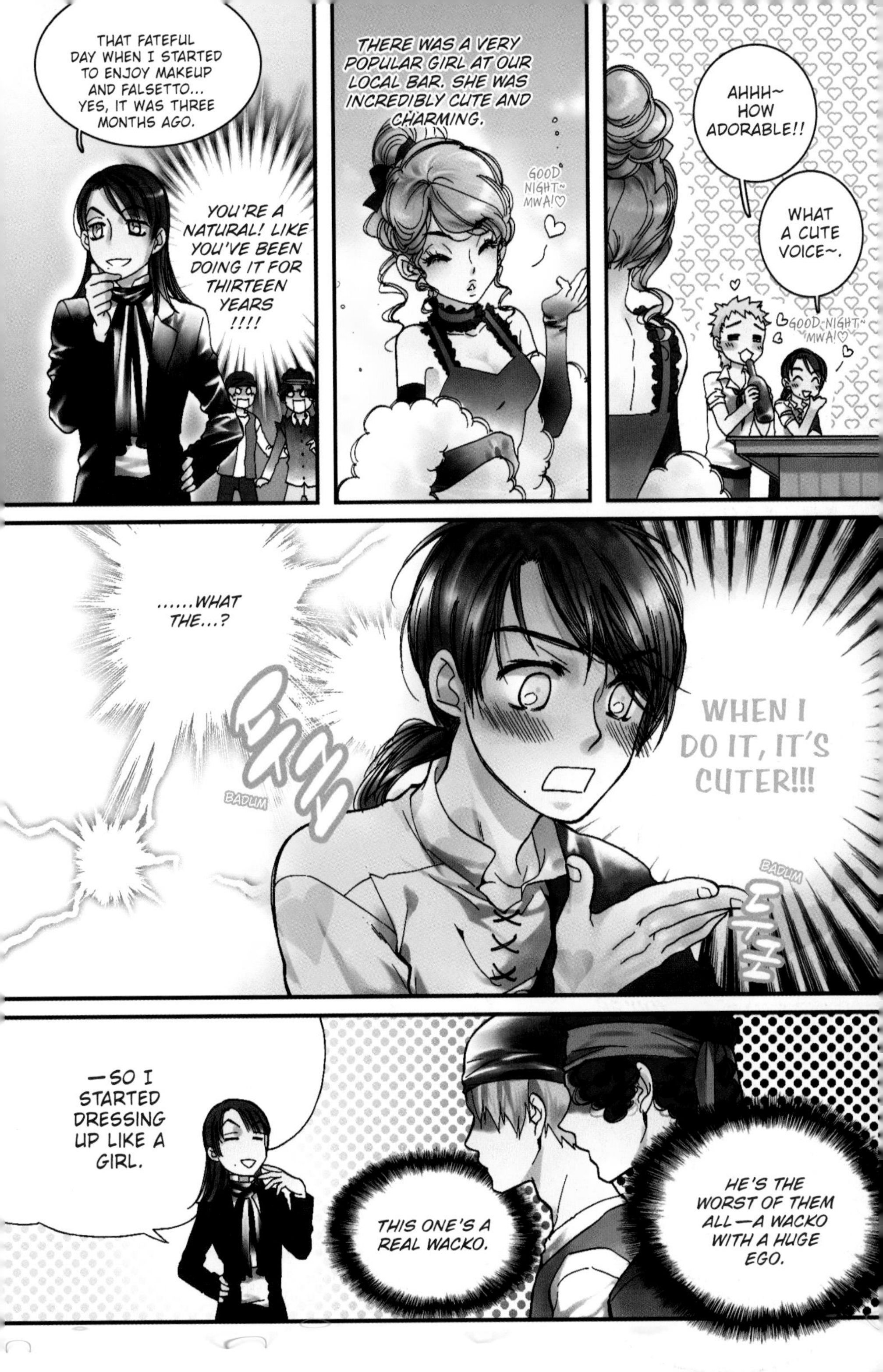
THAT FATEFUL DAY WHEN I STARTED TO ENJOY MAKEUP AND FALSETTO... YES, IT WAS THREE MONTHS AGO.
YOU'RE A NATURAL! LIKE YOU'VE BEEN DOING IT FOR THIRTEEN YEARS !!!!
THERE WAS A VERY POPULAR GIRL AT OUR LOCAL BAR. SHE WAS INCREDIBLY CUTE AND CHARMING.
GOOD NIGHT~ MWA!♡
AHHH~ HOW ADORABLE!!
WHAT A CUTE VOICE~.
GOOD NIGHT~ MWA!♡
......WHAT THE...?
BADUM
WHEN I DO IT, IT'S CUTER!!!
BADUM
—SO I STARTED DRESSING UP LIKE A GIRL.
THIS ONE'S A REAL WACKO.
HE'S THE WORST OF THEM ALL—A WACKO WITH A HUGE EGO.

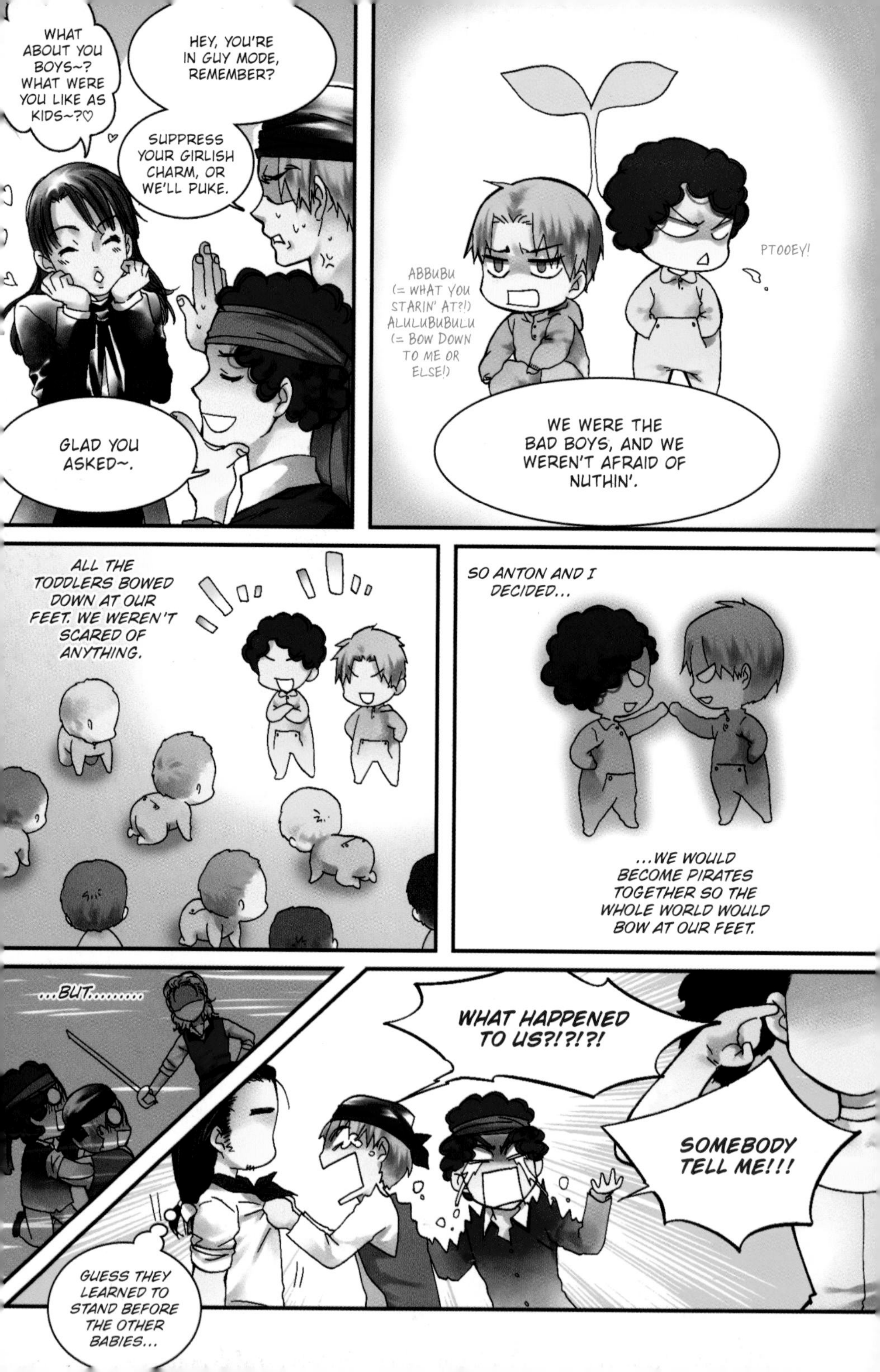
WHAT ABOUT YOU BOYS~? WHAT WERE YOU LIKE AS KIDS~?♡
HEY, YOU'RE IN GUY MODE, REMEMBER?
SUPPRESS YOUR GIRLISH CHARM, OR WE'LL PUKE.
GLAD YOU ASKED~.
ABBUBU (= WHAT YOU STARIN' AT?!) ALULUBUBULU (= BOW DOWN TO ME OR ELSE!)
PTOOEY!
WE WERE THE BAD BOYS, AND WE WEREN'T AFRAID OF NUTHIN'.
ALL THE TODDLERS BOWED DOWN AT OUR FEET. WE WEREN'T SCARED OF ANYTHING.
SO ANTON AND I DECIDED...
...WE WOULD BECOME PIRATES TOGETHER SO THE WHOLE WORLD WOULD BOW AT OUR FEET.
...BUT..........
WHAT HAPPENED TO US?!?!?!
SOMEBODY TELL ME!!!
GUESS THEY LEARNED TO STAND BEFORE THE OTHER BABIES...

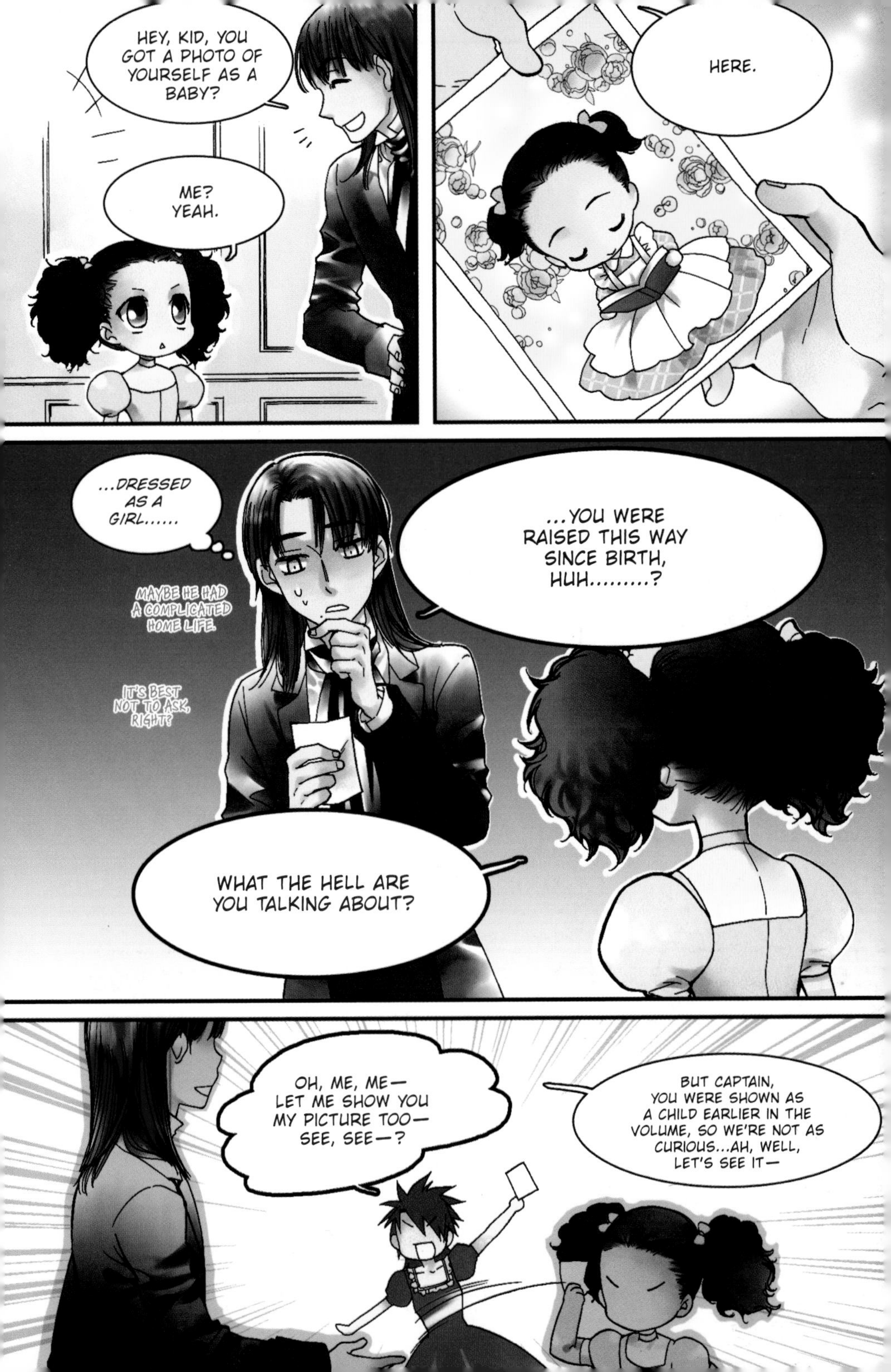
HEY, KID, YOU GOT A PHOTO OF YOURSELF AS A BABY?
ME? YEAH.
HERE.
...DRESSED AS A GIRL......
...YOU WERE RAISED THIS WAY SINCE BIRTH, HUH.........?
MAYBE HE HAD A COMPLICATED HOME LIFE.
IT'S BEST NOT TO ASK, RIGHT?
WHAT THE HELL ARE YOU TALKING ABOUT?
OH, ME, ME— LET ME SHOW YOU MY PICTURE TOO— SEE, SEE—?
BUT CAPTAIN, YOU WERE SHOWN AS A CHILD EARLIER IN THE VOLUME, SO WE'RE NOT AS CURIOUS...AH, WELL, LET'S SEE IT—

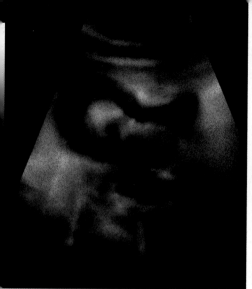

...WHAT IS THIS? IT'S KINDA DARK AND CREEPY???

MY SONOGRAM. THREE MONTHS OLD~.

THAT'S TOO YOUNG!!!!

WHAT ABOUT MASTER ROBIN?!

ACK!

I REALLY, REALLY, REEEEEALLY WANT TO SEE A PICTURE OF MASTER ROBIN WHEN HE WAS YOUNG!!

I'M SURE YOU WERE A SUPER-ULTRA-SPECIAL-CUTE PRETTY BOY!!

AHHH~

MYSELF WHEN I WAS YOUNG?

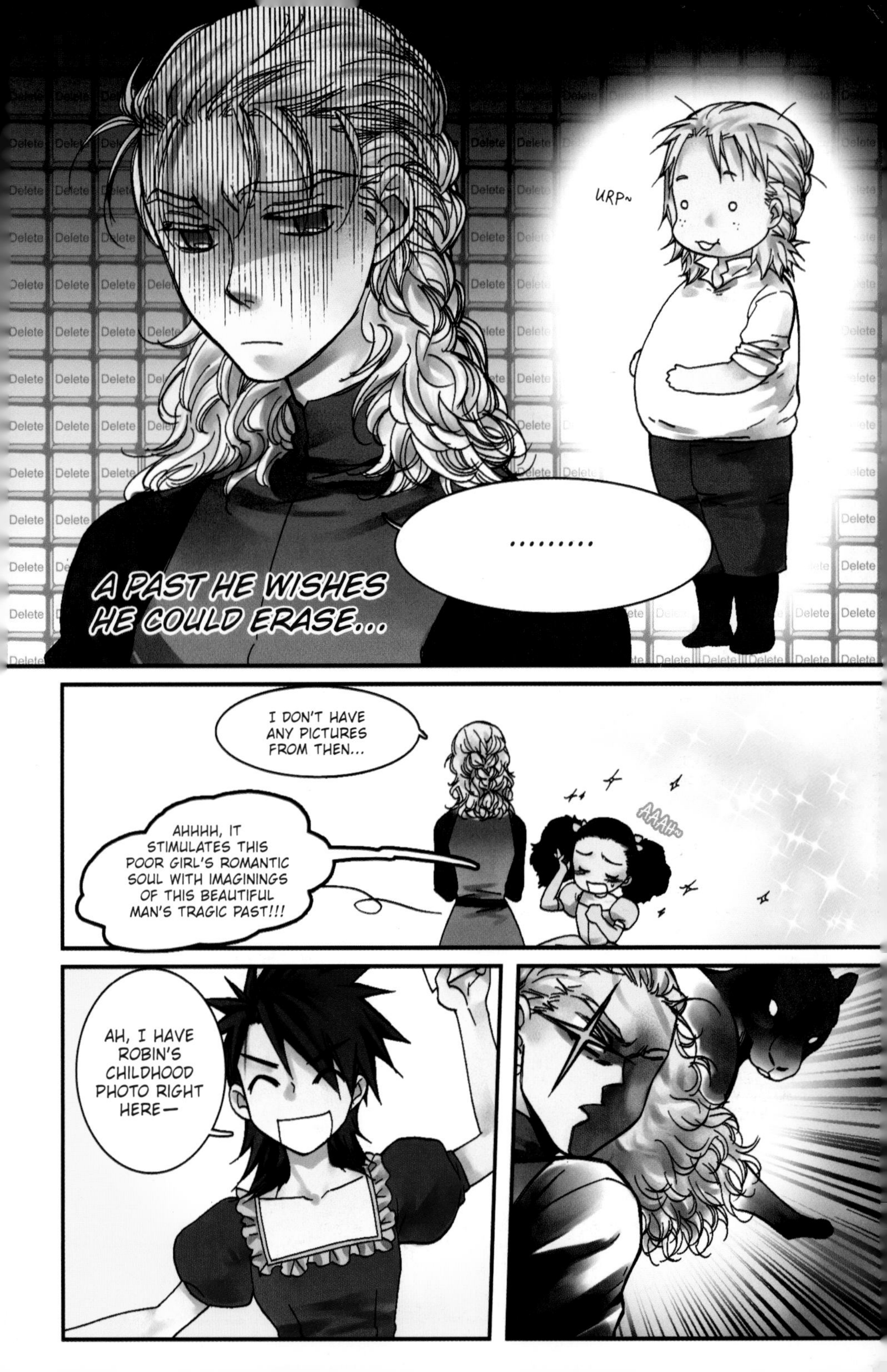
A PAST HE WISHES HE COULD ERASE...
URP~
....
I DON'T HAVE ANY PICTURES FROM THEN...
AHHHH, IT STIMULATES THIS POOR GIRL'S ROMANTIC SOUL WITH IMAGININGS OF THIS BEAUTIFUL MAN'S TRAGIC PAST!!!
AAAH~
AH, I HAVE ROBIN'S CHILDHOOD PHOTO RIGHT HERE—

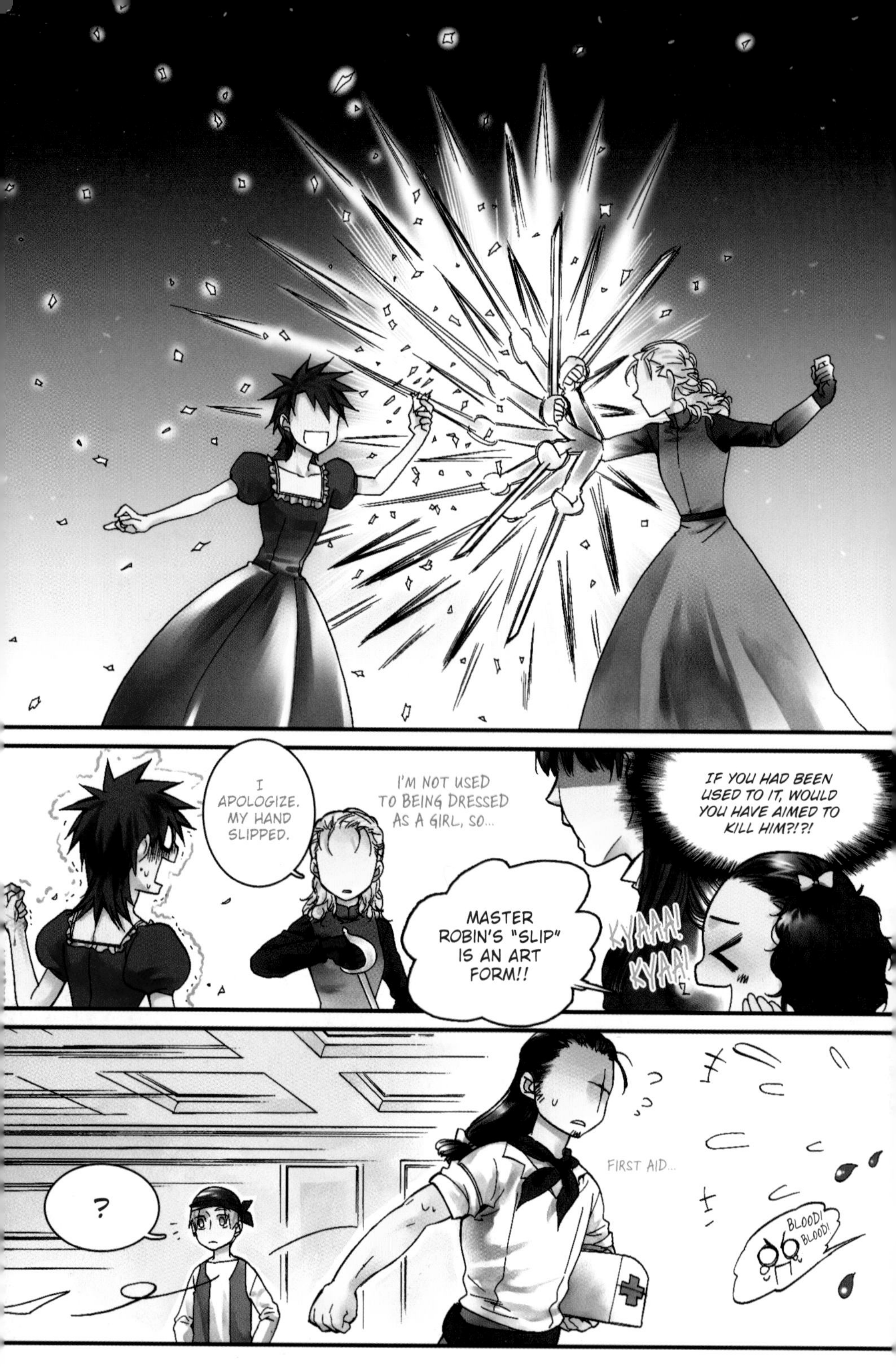

I APOLOGIZE. MY HAND SLIPPED.
I'M NOT USED TO BEING DRESSED AS A GIRL, SO...
IF YOU HAD BEEN USED TO IT, WOULD YOU HAVE AIMED TO KILL HIM?!?!
MASTER ROBIN'S "SLIP" IS AN ART FORM!!
KYAAA! KYAA!
?
FIRST AID...
BLOOD! BLOOD!

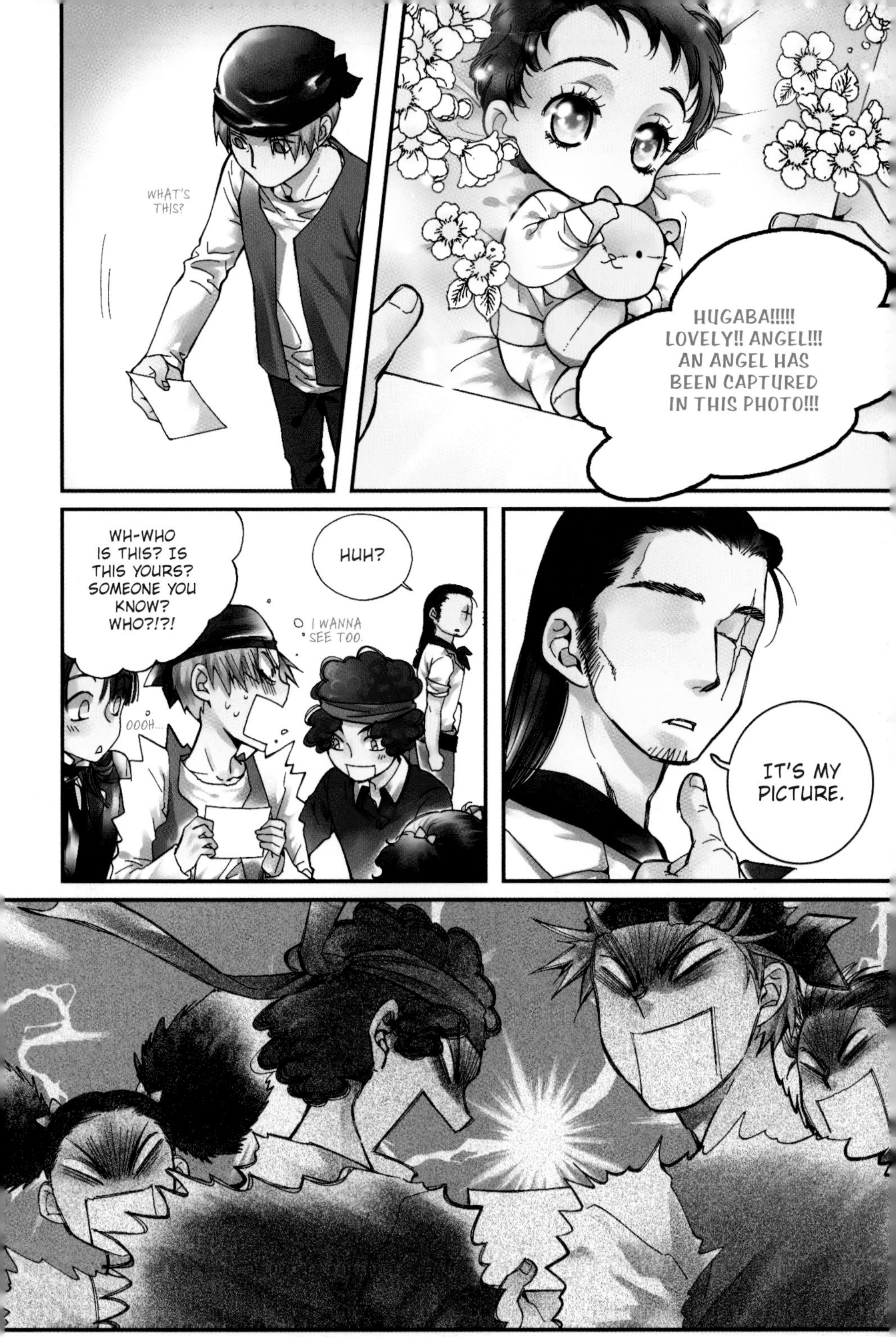
WHAT'S THIS?
HUGABA!!!!! LOVELY!! ANGEL!!! AN ANGEL HAS BEEN CAPTURED IN THIS PHOTO!!!
WH-WHO IS THIS? IS THIS YOURS? SOMEONE YOU KNOW? WHO?!?!
HUH?
I WANNA SEE TOO.
OOOH...
IT'S MY PICTURE.

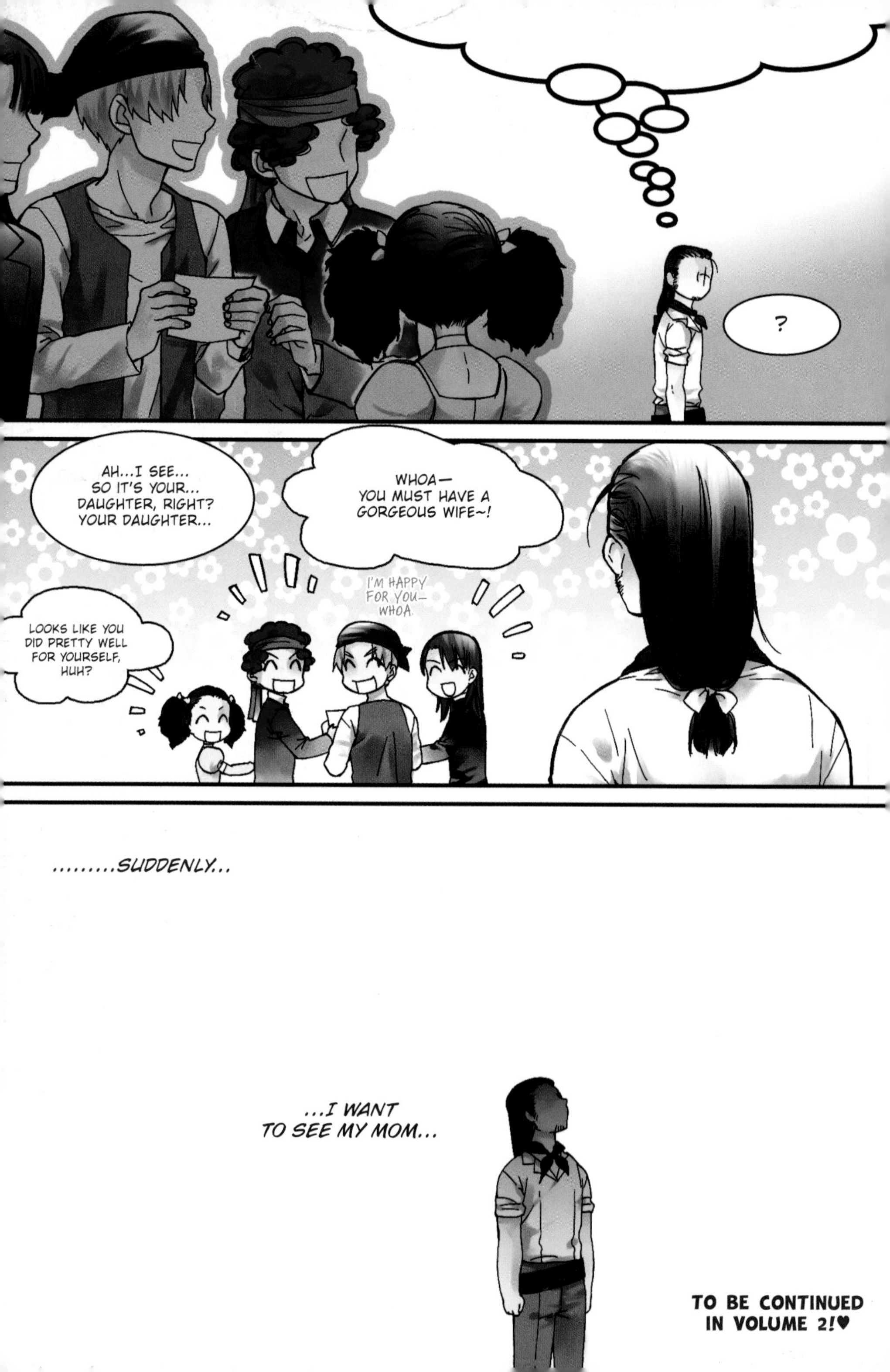
?
AH...I SEE... SO IT'S YOUR... DAUGHTER, RIGHT? YOUR DAUGHTER...
WHOA— YOU MUST HAVE A GORGEOUS WIFE~!
I'M HAPPY FOR YOU— WHOA.
LOOKS LIKE YOU DID PRETTY WELL FOR YOURSELF, HUH?
.........SUDDENLY...
...I WANT TO SEE MY MOM...
TO BE CONTINUED IN VOLUME 2!♥